THE Humanities

Cultural Roots and Continuities

Volume I—Three Cultural Roots
Third Edition

D. C. Heath and Company · Lexington, Massachusetts · Toronto

Acquisitions Editor: Paul Smith
Developmental Editor: Holt Johnson
Production Editor: Bryan Woodhouse
Designer: Mark Fowler
Production Coordinators: Kim Wallin and Lisa Arcese
Photo Researcher: Mary Stuart Lang
Text Permissions Editor: Margaret Roll

COVER: Giorgione, *Three Philosophers* (Kunsthistorisches Museum, Vienna)

Drawings by Eugene Wilson Brown, A.I.A.

International Standard Book Number: 0-669-15425-3

Library of Congress Catalog Card Number: 88-82179

10 9 8 7 6 5 4 3

Credits

American Folk Society Yoruba riddles reproduced by permission of the American Folklore Society from the *Journal of American Folklore*, Vol. 62, No. 243, 1949. Not for further reproduction.

Bantam Books, Inc. From *The Aeneid of Virgil*, a verse translation by Allen Mandelbaum. Copyright © 1973 by Allen Mandelbaum. Reprinted by permission of Bantam Books. All rights reserved.

Ulli Beier "Oriki Obatala," "Oriki Eshu," "Oriki Ogun," "Adiye," "Etu-Duiker," "New Yam," "Children," Yoruba funeral poems, Yoruba proverbs, and seven Yoruba riddles reprinted by permission of Ulli Beier. Translated by Bakare Gbadamosi and Ulli Beier.

Black Orpheus Two Yoruba Myths of Creation from *Black Orpheus*, VIII (June 1960). Courtesy of Lagos University Press, publishers of *Black Orpheus*.

Frank Cass & Co., Ltd. "The Kano Man" from *Hausa Tales and Traditions*, an English translation of Tatsuniyoyi na Hausa originally compiled by Frank Edgar. Reprinted by permission of Frank Cass & Co., Ltd.

Crown Publishers, Inc. "Forefathers," by Birago Diop, reprinted from *An African Treasury* by Langston Hughes. Copyright © 1960 by Langston Hughes. Used by permission of Crown Publishers, Inc.

David Higham Associates Two line drawings from Dante Alighieri, *The Divine Comedy, Hell*, translated by Dorothy L. Sayers. Reprinted by permission of David Higham Associates Limited.

Doubleday & Company, Inc. "Generation Gap" from *Christmas in Biafra and Other Poems* by Chinua Achebe. Copyright © 1971, 1973 by Chinua Achebe. Reprinted by permission of Doubleday & Company, Inc.

Henry John Drewal Efe ceremony poetry from "Efe: Voiced Power and Pageantry" by Henry John Drewal in *African Arts*, Volume III, No. 2 (Winter 1974). Recommended by *African Arts*.

Hakluyt Society "The Discovery of the Kingdom of Benin" from *Europeans in West Africa, 1450–1560*, Vol. I, J. W. Blake, translator and editor. Reprinted by permission of the Hakluyt Society, London.

Harcourt Brace Jovanovich, Inc. *Oedipus Rex of Sophocles: An English Version* by Dudley Fitts and Robert Fitzgerald, copyright, 1949, by Harcourt Brace Jovanovich, Inc.; renewed, 1977, by Cornelia Fitts and Robert Fitzgerald. Reprinted by permission of the publisher. CAUTION: All rights, including professional, amateur, motion picture, recitation, lecturing, public reading, radio broadcasting, and television are strictly reserved. Inquiries on all rights should be addressed to Harcourt Brace Jovanovich, Inc., Orlando, FL 32887.

Aristophanes' *Lysistrata: An English Version* by Dudley Fitts, copyright, 1954, by Harcourt Brace Jovanovich, Inc.; renewed 1982 by Cornelia Fitts, Daniel H. Fitts, and Deborah W. Fitts. Reprinted by permission of the publisher. CAUTION: All rights, including professional, amateur, motion picture, recitation, lecturing, public reading, radio broadcasting, and television are strictly reserved. Inquiries on all rights should be addressed to Harcourt Brace Jovanovich, Inc., Orlando, FL 32887.

Houghton Mifflin Company Shakespeare, *Othello*, from *The Complete Plays and Poems of William Shakespeare*, edited by William Allen Neilson and Charles Jarvis Hill. Copyright © 1942 by William Allen Neilson and Charles Jarvis Hill, renewed 1969 by Caroline Steiner and Margaret N. Helburn. Used by permission of Houghton Mifflin Company.

Humanities Press Inc. This condensed version of Niane's *Sundiata: An Epic of Old Mali*, translated by G.D. Pickett © 1965. Reprinted by permission of Humanities Press International Inc., Atlantic Highlands, NJ 07716.

Ibadan University Press Excerpts from Benin oral traditions reprinted from *A Short Story of Benin* by J.V. Egharevba. By permission of Ibadan University Press, Ibadan, Nigeria.

The Johns Hopkins University Press Music for "Quant'e bella giovinezza" transcribed and edited by Walter H. Rubsamen in "The Music for 'Quant'e bella giovinezza' and Other Carnival Songs by Lorenzo de' Medici" from *Art, Science and History in the Renaissance* edited by Charles S. Singleton. Copyright © 1968 by The Johns Hopkins University Press. Reprinted by permission of the publisher.

Macmillan Publishing Company Erasmus, *Ten Colloquies*, Translated by Craig R. Thompson. Copyright © 1986 by Macmillan Publishing Company. Copyright © 1957. Reprinted with permission of the publisher.

New American Library of New York From *The Inferno* by Dante Alighieri, translated by John Ciardi. Copyright © 1954, 1982 by John Ciardi. From *The Purgatorio* by Dante Alighieri, translated by John Ciardi. Copyright © 1957, 1959, 1960, 1961 by John Ciardi. From *The Paradiso* by Dante Alighieri, translated by John Ciardi. Reprinted by Arrangement with New American Library, New York, New York.

Northern Nigerian Publishing Company, Ltd. "Squirrel and Hedgehog," "The Blind Man with the Lamp," "Life Is Better than Wealth," "Hasara and Riba," and "The Rivals" from *Ka K'ara Karatu* (anonymous) translated by Roberta Ann Dunbar. Reprinted by permission of Northern Nigerian Publishing Company, Ltd., publishers of the Hausa version.

W.W. Norton & Company, Inc. Music and English version of "Be m'an perdut" are reprinted from *A Treasury of Early Music*, Compiled and Edited by Carl Parrish, by permission of W.W. Norton & Company, Inc. Copyright © 1958 by W.W. Norton & Company, Inc. Copyright © renewed 1986 by Mrs. Catherine C.

Preface

Changes in this Edition

This third edition of *The Humanities: Cultural Roots and Continuities* has benefited from the suggestions of readers, professors, and teachers from a wide variety of geographical locations and teaching situations, as well as from our own thinking about the problems of presenting the humanities in an integrated, interdisciplinary framework. Although the format and the spirit of the book remain basically the same, we have made some important changes. We have rewritten the introduction to reflect recent developments in thinking about the role of the humanities in education. In the Greco-Roman section of Volume I, we have added larger portions of *The Iliad* and *The Aeneid*; a discussion of and a passage from Aristotle's *Poetics*; and a more extensive treatment of Roman civilization. The Judeo-Christian section includes more chapters from the Old Testament (Psalms, Book of Amos) and more exploration of Jewish history, as well as more se-

lections from the New Testament (letters of the apostle Paul). We have adopted a verse translation of Chaucer's *The Miller's Tale* and we have included Erasmus's *The Shipwreck*. The chapter on the early Renaissance has been entirely reworked.

Readers of Volume II will note a more extended treatment of the scientific revolution, including excerpts from Bacon's *The New Organon* and from Hobbes's *Leviathan*, as well as a more in-depth study of seventeenth-century art. Although we continue to explore the Don Juan theme in various manifestations, we have eliminated Byron's *Don Juan* from the romantic section, and have added Tirso de Molina's *The Trickster of Seville* in the baroque section. In response to popular demand, we have eliminated Voltaire's *Micromegas* and substituted a somewhat abridged version of *Candide*. The romantic section now includes Wordsworth's "Tintern Abbey" and a section of Walt Whitman's "Song of Myself."

As in the second edition, we have retained the coverage of the contributions of women and the development of feminism in Western culture, but this time we have also included a chapter from a crucial, previously neglected text, Mary Wollstonecraft's *A Vindication of the Rights of Woman*. The influence of feminism in the visual arts also receives more attention, particularly with Judy Chicago's *The Dinner Party*. We have enlarged the treatment of the development of political theory with selections from Hobbes, Locke, and Rousseau, and we have written a section on the Great Awakening in the United States, with an extract from Jonathan Edwards. Our approach to the question of modernism is now more unified because of a focus on the theme of the city, illustrated by selections from Engels, Baudelaire, and T.S. Eliot. The arts of photography and cinema receive more attention here than in previous editions.

Our commitment to emphasizing the important contributions of Afro-Americans to our cultural heritage continues, but in this edition we have also given more recognition to the contributions of Hispanic cultures. Chapter 35, now entitled "New Americans on the World Cultural Scene: The Rise of Afro-American and Latin American Cultures" points out certain parallels in two "minority" cultures that began to assume worldwide importance around the same time, while subsequent chapters include literary and artistic works illustrating the impact of both cultures on modernism and postmodernism in the arts. New items include stories by Borges and Cabrera-Infante, poetry by Pablo Neruda and Ernesto Cardenal, examples of Latin American mural painting and architecture, poems by Sonia Sanchez and Gwendolyn Brooks, jazz of Ornette Coleman, and a story by Alice Walker.

Our new chapter on postmodernism reflects some of the latest thinking on the subject in what we believe is a lucid but not oversimplified approach to this complex issue. In addition to the new selections mentioned above, our treatment of postmodernism includes more poems and different prose by Adrienne Rich and a new short story by John Barth. The bibliography and information on audio-visual material in the Instructor's Guide has been updated and expanded.

Despite the several changes in and expanded coverage of this new edition, our overall view of the purpose of an interdisciplinary humanities text remains basically the same. We feel that in an introductory humanities course the student's personal growth should take place on three levels—historical, aesthetic, and philosophical. The overall purpose of the two volumes can best be described by breaking it down into these three categories.

The Historical Level

We stress the concept of "cultural roots" because one cannot understand the culture in which one lives without some notion of what went into its making. Therefore, we have made every effort here to link the "roots" discussed to aspects of the contemporary American cultural environment. This can be a knotty problem because such links can sometimes be too facile, and we would also like students to discover that cultures remote in time or space can be worth studying simply for themselves. Volume I treats three cultural roots: Greco-Roman, Judeo-Christian, and West African. This choice needs some justification, because many Americans have other cultural roots as well: oriental, Middle Eastern, North European, Hispanic, and Native American, to name a few. Still, the Greco-Roman and the Judeo-Christian traditions undoubtedly constitute the bases of the Western humanities. African culture, a long-neglected field of study, has contributed significantly to modern Afro-American art and thought and in many ways to Western culture in general. In addition, African culture offers the opportunity to study some fundamental aspects of the humanities in a truly interdisciplinary context.

In our examination of each of these "roots," we adopted the policy of focusing on one period and/or place. The focus for the Greco-Roman root is on fifth-century-B.C. Athens, that for the Judeo-Christian on medieval Europe, that for Africa on the Yoruba people. This means, for example, that some significant monuments of classical Greek drama, sculpture, and architecture can be examined rather extensively, while early Greece and Rome receive a briefer treatment. In our exploration of the Renaissance and Reformation periods we emphasize the fusion of the Greco-Roman and Judeo-Christian roots and focus on the development of humanism in fifteenth-century Italy and its diffusion in the north.

If we pursued the same metaphor, Volume II might

be called "stems, leaves, and flowers." Here, too, an attempt is made to focus and spread out, more than to survey and spread thin. The court of Louis XIV in the seventeenth century, the Enlightenment in France and America, the romantic movement, the Industrial Revolution, the modernist movement, and the controversial notion of postmodernism all provide centers around which the many interrelated facets of the humanities can be discussed.

The Aesthetic Level

On the whole, we follow the same "focal" principle in the aesthetic domain. In presenting music, we operate on the assumption that a student will retain more from listening to and analyzing an entire work than from reading music history and theory and hearing snippets. In dealing with art and literature, it is sometimes possible to make an important point with a photograph and a caption or with a close analysis of a brief literary passage. Likewise, in the presentation of major works in the focal periods, we assume that it is more useful for a student to look at the whole of Chartres cathedral than to skim the history of medieval art, and to read all of *Oedipus Rex* rather than bits and summaries from several Greek tragedies. With lengthy works, such as epics and novels, this is, of course, not possible. We have thus chosen portions of *The Iliad*, *The Aeneid*, and *The Divine Comedy* that are significant in themselves and representative of the whole.

Dance, an often-neglected art form, is given more extensive treatment here than in other humanities texts. Entire dance compositions can, of course, be appreciated only in live performance or film, and we suggest that instructors exploit those resources as much as possible. Although some art forms may seem unfamiliar to students at the beginning, it has been our experience that a long introductory chapter on how to look, listen, and read is largely wasted; therefore, we cover such matters in the introductions to individual works. Questions on the nature of genre are considered in the cultural context in which they originate, notably in ancient Greece. We place much importance on study questions that require the student to read, look, and listen carefully.

Although we try to avoid jargon, we feel that some knowledge of the technical vocabulary of criticism in the arts is essential for literate discussion. Difficult or unfamiliar terms appear in italics the first time they are used in any given chapter, indicating that they are defined in the Glossary.

The Philosophical Level

It may well be objected that we compromise the focal method in our presentation of philosophy, because no entire philosophical works appear in the book. This is largely due to considerations of space; but it is also true that, when dealing with a work in terms of certain fundamental ideas rather than in terms of aesthetic wholeness, the "snippet" method is not so objectionable. Beginning humanities students are probably not ready to read Aristotle's *Ethics* in its entirety, but they should be able to see how Aristotle's ideas are essential to the cultural roots of the modern world.

The student's personal growth in the philosophical area means, however, something much broader than his or her contact with formal philosophy. The (ideal) student—whose historical awareness is increased by an understanding of cultural roots and whose aesthetic sensitivity is heightened by personal confrontation with a variety of works of art—should also be able to grow intellectually through contact with diverse ideas. A humanities course should enable students to refine their thinking on the basic questions that affect all human beings, to formulate more clearly their personal values, and to discuss these with intellectual rigor rather than in vaporous "bull" sessions. Instructors should welcome debates that might arise from comparing Genesis and African mythology, the "woman" question in *Lysistrata* and in John Stuart Mill, or the relative merits of realistic and abstract art or tonal and atonal music. They and their students will find many more such issues for debate.

Individual instructors will decide which aspects of the humanities and which cultural roots they wish to emphasize. We believe that this book offers enough flexibility to be useful for a variety of approaches.

Mary Ann Frese Witt
Charlotte Vestal Brown
Roberta Ann Dunbar
Frank Tirro
Ronald G. Witt

Acknowledgments

Many people have contributed time, work, ideas, and encouragement to the creation of this book. Gratitude is due, first of all, to those who provided their own research and writing: In Volume II, Professor Ernest Mason of North Carolina Central University wrote the introduction to Freud as well as the material on Afro-American culture, and Professor John Kelly of North Carolina State University wrote the sections on Latin American culture. Professor Emeritus Alan Gonzalez, of North Carolina State University, wrote the material on the Spanish baroque. In Volume I, Professor Edmund Reiss wrote the sections on courtly love and on medieval English poetry.

The plan for the First (1980) Edition of *The Humanities* grew out of the four years I spent initiating and directing an interdisciplinary humanities program at North Carolina Central University in Durham. It would not have been possible without the stimulation and aid of my students and colleagues there. The late Professor Charles Ray and Dean Cecil Patterson provided me with the time, encouragement, and wherewithal to create the program. The professors who worked closely with me—Elizabeth Lee, Phyllis Lotchin, Ernest Mason, Norman Pendergraft, Earl Sanders, Winifred Stoelting, and Randolph Umberger—have all left their mark on this book. The generous support of the Kenan Foundation, which provided the humanities program with a four-year grant, enabled me to research and compile much of the material. The Kenan Foundation also provided me with the opportunity to attend numerous conferences on the humanities. The workshops given at North Carolina Central University by Clifford Johnson, of the Institute for Services to Education, also provided inspiration.

The authors wish to thank Bruce McNair for his painstaking assistance in updating the *Instructor's Guide*, as well as Roger Manley and Margaret S. Smith, who read portions of the third-edition manuscript and offered helpful advice and comments. We have all benefited greatly from the guidance, the wisdom, and the patience of Holt Johnson of D. C. Heath over the years of collaborative effort. Thanks are due as well to Bryan Woodhouse of D. C. Heath for his scrupulous attention to the details of the publishing process. We are also grateful to Henry C. Allan, Jr., Moraine Valley Community College; Mark Hawkins, Foothill College; Mary Kay Kramp, Alverno College; Cornelius A. Page, San Diego Mesa College; and Joan Sevick, Nassau Community College, for their helpful reviews, and to Betty Cowan and Dorothy Sapp of Duke University for assistance in preparing the manuscript.

I would like to express my continuing gratitude to, and friendship for, my collaborating authors.

Mary Ann Frese Witt

Contents

COLOR ILLUSTRATIONS

MAPS

Chronicle of Events

	AFRICA	MESOPOTAMIA-SYRIA-PALESTINE	GREECE
3000 B.C.			
	Lower and Upper Egypt unite First to Second Dynasty (3110–2615)	Sumerian city-states Successive waves of Semites occupy Palestine	
2900			
2800			
2700			
	Age of Pyramids (c. 2650–2150)		
2600			
2500			
2400			
2300			
2200			
2100			Minoan palace construction begins on island of Crete
2000		Phoenician (Canaanite) city culture	
1900			
1800		Babylonian Dynasty established	
1700			
	Hyksos invasions (1678–1570)		
1600			High point of Minoan civilization (1600–1400)
1500			
	Eighteenth Dynasty and Imperial Age (1525–1075)		
1400		Phoenicians develop alphabet	
	Akhenaten introduces monotheism (1370–1353)		Destruction of Minoan palace
1300			Mycenaean expansion
1200		Hebrews enter Palestine Phoenicians flourish (1200–900)	
1100			Traditional date for sack of Troy (c. 1184)
		Early Assyrian Empire Early Biblical books written Saul made King of Hebrews (c. 1025)	Greek cities on Aegean coast and Greek colonies in Asia Minor established

	AFRICA	MESOPOTAMIA-SYRIA-PALESTINE	ROME	GREEK POLITICAL EVENTS	GREEK CULTURAL EVENTS	
1000 B.C.		David King of Hebrews (1000–961)				
		Solomon (961–922)				
		Hebrew kingdom divides into Israel and Judah (922)				
900		Assyria conquers Phoenicians and Israel (876–605)				
	Phoenicians found Carthage (814)				Homer?	
800			Traditional date for founding of Rome (783)	Beginning of *polis*		
700	Iron age begins at Meroe	Nineveh falls (612) Neo-Babylonian Empire of Nebuchadnezzar				Archaic Age (750–480)
600		Jews taken captive to Babylon (586)			Sappho (c. 600) Beginning of Drama and Panathenian Festivals	
	Persia conquers Egypt (525)	Persians take Babylon (539) Jews return home (538) Darius of Persia (521–486)	Kings expelled and Republic created (509)		Aeschylus (525–456)	
500				Persian Wars (499–479) Pericles (498–427)	Euripides (480–406) Thucydides (470–400) Socrates (470–399) Building of Parthenon (447–432)	Classical Age (480–350)
				Peloponnesian War (431–404)	Plato (427–347) Aristophanes' *Lysistrata* (411) Sophocles' *Oedipus* (406)	The Golden Age. The Age of Pericles
400				Philip of Macedon (382–336) Alexander of Macedon (the Great) (356–323)	Aristotle (384–322) Epicurus (342–270)	
			Vigorous program of Roman conquest of Italy begins (343)		Zeno (336–264) and founding of Stoic school	Hellenistic Age (350–150)
	Alexander conquers Egypt (332) Greek dynasty rules (331–304)					
300			I Punic War (264–241)			
			Sardinia and Corsica annexed (238)			
			II Punic War (218–201)			
200						

AFRICA	MESOPOTAMIA-SYRIA-PALESTINE	ROME	GREEK POLITICAL EVENTS	GREEK CULTURAL EVENTS
200 — Nok civilization at its height (200 B.C.– 200 A.D.) Carthage sacked (146) Rome conquers North Africa		Terence (195–159) III Punic War (149–146)	Rome begins conquest of Greece	↓
100 —	Occupation of Israel by Romans (63) Reign of Herod the Great in Palestine (37 B.C.–4 A.D.)	Cicero (106–43) Caesar (100–44) Lucretius (99–55) Horace's *Satires* (35–29) Virgil's *Aeneid* (29–19) Augustus begins reign (27)		

AFRICA	ROME AND EUROPE	PAGAN AND CHRISTIAN CULTURE
A.D. —		Birth of Jesus Christ
	Death of Augustus (14) Conquest of Britain (43–51) Sack of Jerusalem (70)	Death of Paul (c. 62–64) Persecution of Christians by Nero (64)
100 —		Juvenal's *Satires* (c. 100) Roman Pantheon built (118–125)
200 —		
	Period of disorder (235–284)	Plotinus (205–270) and Neo-Platonism
300 —	Reforms of Diocletian (285–305)	
		Edict of Toleration by Constantine (313) Building of Old St. Peter's (330–340)
400 —		
	Alaric sacks Rome (410) Vandals sack Rome (455) Traditional date for end of Western Roman Empire (476)	
500 —		Justinian (483–565) extends Roman Empire in East and temporarily conquers parts of Italy, Africa, and Spain—Codifies Roman Law
600 — Moslem conquest of Africa		
700 — Empire of Ghana (700–1230)		
	Moslem conquest of Spain (711) Defeat of Moslems at Poitiers (732) Charlemagne (768–814)	
800 —		

AFRICA	ROME AND EUROPE	PAGAN AND CHRISTIAN CULTURE
	Second period of invasions (c. 800–950): Northmen, Hungarians, and Saracens	
Beginnings of Benin	Northmen establish Normandy (911) Otto I founds German Empire (962) Hugh Capet King of France (987)	First systematic teaching of Aristotle's Logic (975)

AFRICA	EUROPE	EUROPEAN CULTURE	
		Building of St. Sernin—Romanesque (11th and 12th centuries)	
	Norman invasion of England (1066) First Crusade (1095)	St. Bernard (1090–1153)	*Romanesque Style (11th and 12th centuries)*
		Play of Daniel (12th century) Rebuilding of St. Denis on new lines—early Gothic Bernart de Ventadorn (late 12th century) Marie de France (late 12th century) Chartres Cathedral begun (1194)	
Revolt of Mande peoples against Ghana (c. 1200) and rise of Mali Empire	Mongol invasion of Russia European embassy sent to China St. Louis (1214–1270)	Aquinas (1225–1274) Giotto (1276–1337) Dante's *Divine Comedy* (1300–1321)	
Mansa Musa pilgrimage to Mecca (1324) Exploration of Canaries (1330s and 1340s)	Hundred Years War begins (1337) First appearance of Black Death (1348–1350)	Petrarch (1304–1374) Boccaccio (1310–1375)	*Gothic Style (12th–15th centuries)*
		Bruni (1370–1444) Brunelleschi (1377–1446) Chaucer's *Canterbury Tales* (1390–1400)	
	Jeanne d'Arc burned (1431)	Masaccio (1401–1428) Henry the Navigator founds navigation school at Sagres (1419) Piero della Francesca (1420–1492) Medici dominate Florence (1434) Alberti's *On Painting* (1435) Leonardo da Vinci (1442–1519) Botticelli (1444–1510) Lorenzo il Magnifico (1449–1492)	*Renaissance Style (15th and 16th centuries)*
John Affonso d'Aveiro visits Benin (1485–1486)	Spanish Inquisition established (1478) Columbus discovers America (1492) DaGama sails for India (1497)	Pico della Mirandola (1463–1494) Isaac's *On the Death of Lorenzo* Erasmus (1466?–1536)	

	AFRICA	EUROPE	EUROPEAN CULTURE		NEW WORLD
1500	Duarte Pacheco Pereira's *Esmeraldo de situ orbis* (1507) Benin at the height of its power (16th and 17th centuries)		Michelangelo's *David* (1504) Raphael's *School of Athens* (1510–1511) Machiavelli's *Prince* (1513) First edition of Erasmus's *Colloquies* (1516) Luther publishes German *New Testament* (1521)	*Renaissance Style (15th and 16th centuries)*	First black slaves in New World (1505) Magellan circumnavigates the globe (1519) Cortez in Mexico (1519–1521) Verrazano establishes French claims in North America (1524)
1525		Peasants' Revolt in Germany (1525) Henry VIII declares himself head of Church of England (1534) Jesuit Order founded (1540) Council of Trent (1545–1563)	First edition of Calvin's *Institutes* (1536) Copernicus's *Revolution of Heavenly Bodies* (1543)		
1550		Peace of Augsburg legalizes Lutheranism in Germany (1555) Reign of Queen Elizabeth I of England (1558–1603) Wars of Religion begin in France (1561) Massacre of French Protestants (1572)	Titian (1477–1576) Bruegel (1520–1569)		Building of St. Augustine in Florida (1565)
1575		Defeat of Spanish Armada (1588) Edict of Nantes (1598)	First edition of Montaigne's *Essays* (1580–1588) Shakespeare (1564–1616) Kepler (1571–1630) Caravaggio's *Calling of St. Matthew* (1599–1600)		
1600		Thirty Years War begins (1618)	Rubens's *Raising of the Cross* (1609–1610) Giambattista Marino (1569–1625) John Donne (1572–1631) Descartes (1596–1650) Corneille (1606–1684) Bacon's *Novum Organum* (1620)		Settlement at Jamestown (1607) Founding of Quebec (1608) First slaves in Virginia (1619) Plymouth colony established (1620)
1625		Civil War in England begins (1643) Peace of Westphalia in Germany (1648)	Harvey demonstrates circulation of blood (1628) French Academy founded (1635) Tirsa de Molina's *The Trickster of Seville* 1635) Galileo's *Discourse on Two New Sciences* (1638) Richard Crashaw (1612–1649)		
1650					

	AFRICA	EUROPE	EUROPEAN CULTURE	NEW WORLD
1650		Restoration of English Monarchy (1660)	Hobbes' *Leviathan* (1651) Rome's Cornaro Chapel (1645–1652) Rembrandt (1606–1669) Milton (1609–1674) Lully (1632–1687) Royal Society of London created (1662) Construction of Versailles begins (1669)	New York City taken by English from Dutch (1664)
		Louis XIV (1638–1715)		
		Louis revokes Edict of Nantes (1685)	Molière's *Le Bourgeois Gentilhomme* (1670) Robert Boyle (1627–1691)	
			Newton publishes *Mathematical Principles* (1687) Locke's *An Essay Concerning Human Understanding* (1690)	Salem Witch Trials (1692)
1700	Foundation of Ashanti Confederacy (1701)	Union of Scotland and England (1707) War of Spanish Succession (1701–1713) Hanover (Windsor) dynasty begins in England (1714)	Darby cokes coal (1709) Johann Sebastian Bach (1685–1750)	
1725		War of Austrian Succession (1740–1748)	Building of Hôtel Soubise (1732) Kay's Flying Shuttle (1733) English repeal laws against witchcraft (1736) Great Awakening (1730s) Handel's *Messiah* (1742) Montesquieu's *Spirit of the Laws* (1748)	Georgia, last of original thirteen colonies, founded (1733)
1750		Death of George II (1760)	Volume I of the *Encyclopédie* (1751) Mozart (1756–1791) Rousseau's *On the Origins of Inequality* (1755) Voltaire's *Candide* (1759) First blast furnace (1761) Rousseau's *Social Contract* (1762) Watt patents steam engine (1769)	French and Indian War (1754–1763) English take Quebec (1759) English acquire Canada by Treaty of Paris (1763) Boston Massacre (1770)
		Accession of Louis XVI (1774)	Schiller (1759–1805)	
1775		Meeting of Estates General (May, 1789) Taking of Bastille (July, 1789) Fall of Robespierre (1794) Napoleon's coup d'état (1799)	Goethe's *Werther* (1787) Wollstonecraft's *Vindication of Rights of Women* (1792)	Revolutionary War begins (1775) Treaty of Paris ends war (1783) Constitution goes into effect (1789) Washington dies (1799)
1800	Rise of Fulani Empire (19th century) Britain abolishes slave trade (1807)	Napoleon Consul for life (1802) Napoleon crowned Emperor (1804) End of Holy Roman Empire (1806)	David (1748–1825) Madame de Staël (1766–1817) Wordsworth (1770–1850) Constable (1776–1837)	Jefferson elected President (1801)
1810	France abolishes slave trade (1815)	Defeat of Napoleon and Congress of Vienna (1815) Industrialization of England (1815–1850)	Stephenson's locomotive (1814) Byron (1788–1824) *Goya Executions of the 3rd of May* (1814) Blake (1757–1827)	War of 1812 (1812–1814) Founding of *North American Review* (1815)
1820				

	AFRICA	EUROPE	EUROPEAN CULTURE	NEW WORLD
1820				
	Liberia established (1832)	Greek War of Independence (1821–1829)	Beethoven's *Ninth Symphony* (1824)	
1830	France annexes Algeria (1830)	Revolutions in France, Germany, Italy, Belgium, and Poland (1830)	Heine (1797–1856)	
		Industrialization of France and Belgium (1830–1860)	Delacroix (1799–1863)	Emerson (1803–1882)
		Industrialization of Germany (1840–1870)		Poe (1809–1849)
1840			Dickens' *Old Curiosity Shop* (1840)	
			Giselle (1841)	
			Chopin (1810–1849)	
			Turner's *Rain, Steam, and Speed* (1845)	
		Revolutions in France, Italy, Germany, and Austria (1848)	Marx-Engels' *Communist Manifesto* (1848)	Mexican War (1846–1848)
				Gold discovered in California (1848)
1850				
	Livingstone at Victoria Falls (1853–1856)	Second Empire founded in France (1852)	Crystal Palace (1851)	Walt Whitman (1819–1892)
			Millet (1814–1875)	
			Courbet's *Manifesto* (1855)	
		Crimean War (1855)	Baudelaire (1821–1867)	
			Darwin's *Origin of Species* (1859)	
1860		Foundation of Kingdom of Italy (1860)		Civil War (1861–1865)
		Emancipation of serfs in Russia (1861)	Mill's *On Subjection of Women* (1861)	Emily Dickinson (1830–1886)
	Opening of Suez Canal (1869)	Creation of Dual Monarchy Austria-Hungary (1867)	Ford Maddox Brown's *Work* (1862–1863)	Period of Reconstruction (1867–1877)
			van Gogh (1853–1890)	
1870		Franco-Prussian War (1870–1871)	Nietzsche (1844–1900)	Stephen Crane (1871–1900)
		German Empire and Third French Republic created (1871)	Monet's *Impressions: Sunrise* (1873)	
	Brazza explores Lower Congo (1875)		Gauguin (1848–1903)	
		Dual Alliance: Germany and Austria-Hungary (1879)		
1880	France occupies Tunisia (1881)	Triple Alliance: Germany, Austria-Hungary, and Italy (1882)	Dostoevsky's *Brothers Karamazov* (1880)	William Dean Howells (1837–1920)
	Britain occupies Egypt (1882)			
	Germans in Togo and Cameroon (1886)			
	Gold found in South Africa (1886)	German-Russian Reinsurance Treaty (1887)	Mallarmé (1842–1898)	Henry James (1843–1916)
	Rhodes establishes Rhodesia (1889–1891)		Verlaine (1844–1896)	
1890			Rimbaud (1854–1891)	

	AFRICA	INTERNATIONAL POLITICS	EUROPEAN CULTURE	AMERICAN CULTURE
1890				
	French annex Guinea and Ivory Coast (1893)	Industrialization of Russia (1890–1914) Franco-Russian Alliance (1894)	Cézanne (1839–1906) Matisse (1869–1954)	Reliance Building (1891) Spanish-American War (1898) Chesnutt's *The Conjure Woman* (1899)
1900	British conquest of N. Nigeria (1900–1903)	Entente Cordiale: France and Great Britain (1902) First Russian Revolution (1905)	Apollinaire (1880–1918) Picasso's *Les demoiselles d'Avignon* (1907)	Louis H. Sullivan (1856–1924)
1910				
	Morocco becomes French protectorate (1912) Conquest of German colonies (1914–1915)	Balkan Wars (1912–1913) First World War (1914–1918) Russian Revolution (1917) Treaty of Versailles (1919) German Weimar Republic created (1919)	Duchamp's *Nude Descending a Staircase* (1912) Mondrian (1872–1944) Kandinsky's *On the Spiritual in Art* (1912) Stravinsky's *Rite of Spring* (1913) Kirchner's *Street* (1914) Bauhaus founded (1919)	Armory Show (1913) U.S. declares war on Germany and Austria-Hungary (1917) Harlem Renaissance (1919–1932)
1920		Irish Free State (1922) Mussolini establishes Fascism in Italy (1922) Great Depression begins (1929)	Kafka (1883–1924) Nijinsky (1890–1950) Hitler's *Mein Kampf* (1925–1926) Spengler's *Decline of the West* (1926–1928) Lipchitz' *Figure* (1926–1928) Brancusi's *Bird in Space* (1928)	W.E.B. Dubois (1868–1963) Mariano Azuela (1873–1952) Davis' *Egg Beater No. 1* (1927) Stock Market Crash (1929)
1930	Nigerian youth movement begins (early 1930s) Italy conquers Ethiopia (1936)	Hitler rises to power (1933) Official rearmament of Germany (1935) Spanish Civil War (1936–1939) Second World War begins (1939)	Freud's *Civilization and Its Discontents* (1930) Le Corbusier's *Villa Savoye* (1929–1930) Malraux's *la Condition humaine* (1933) James Joyce (1882–1941) Virginia Woolf (1882–1941) Picasso's *Guernica* (1937)	Shahn's *Passion of Sacco and Vanzetti* (1930) New Deal begins (1933) Louis Armstrong (1900–1971) Claude McKay (1890–1948) Jean Toomer (1894–1967) Georgia O'Keeffe (1887–1986)
1940				
	Ethiopia liberated (1941) Léopold Sédar Senghor (1903–) Léon Damas (1912–1987) Aimé Césaire (1913–)	Formation of United Nations (1945) Fourth French Republic established (1945) Communist takeover in E. Europe (1946–1948) China becomes communist (1949)	Giacometti (1901–1966) Sartre (1905–1980) Simone de Beauvoir (1908–1986)	Welles' *Citizen Kane* (1941) Japanese attack Pearl Harbor (1941) Albert Einstein (1879–1955) T.S. Eliot (1888–1965) E.E. Cummings (1894–1962) Richard Wright (1908–1960) Jackson Pollock (1912–1956) Charley Parker (1920–1955)
1950	Algerian War begins (1954) Morocco and Tunisia freed (1955) Ghana first colony to gain independence (1957) Guinea independent (1958) François Fanon (1925–1961) David Diop (1927–1960)	Korean War (1950–1953) Russian Sputnik (1957) Common Market (1957) de Gaulle's Fifth Republic (1958)	Camus (1913–1960) Charlie Chaplin (1889–1977) Arrabal's *Picnic on the Battlefield* (1952) Beckett's *Endgame* (1957) Levi's *If This Is a Man* (1958)	Frank Lloyd Wright (1869–1959) Ezra Pound (1885–1972) Langston Hughes (1902–1967) Duke Ellington (1899–1974) Martha Graham (1895–) Jorge Luis Borges (1899–1986)
1960				

	AFRICA	INTERNATIONAL POLITICS	EUROPEAN CULTURE	AMERICAN CULTURE
1960	Nigeria and most French colonies independent (1960) Algeria and Tanganyika freed (1962) Dennis Brutus (1924–)	Berlin Wall (1961) Beginning of Russia-China split (1962) Great Cultural Revolution in China (1966)	Jean Genet (1910–1985) Roland Barthes (1915–1980)	Ralph Ellison (1914–) Katherine Dunham (1919–) Kurt Vonnegut, Jr. (1922–) James Baldwin (1924–1987) Miles Davis (1926–) Ornette Coleman (1930–)
1970	Amin gains power in Uganda (1971) Breakdown of Portuguese African Empire (1974) Wathiong'O Ngugi (1938–) Soweto Uprising (1976)	Withdrawal of U.S. from Vietnam (1972) Oil price rise (1973) Shah leaves Iran and Khomeini takes power (1979) Russian troops sent to Afghanistan (1979)	Michel Foucault (1926–1984)	Adrienne Rich (1929–) Andy Warhol (1931–1987) Alvin Ailey (1931–) LeRoi Jones (1934–) Nikki Giovanni (1943–) Judy Chicago's *The Dinner Party* (1979)
1980	Rhodesia becomes Zimbabue (1980) Liberation struggles continue in Africa (1988)	Polish solidarity movement repressed (1981) Marcos ousted in Philippines (1986) Chernobyl nuclear explosion (1986) USA-USSR agreement on medium-range strategic force (1988)		Ernesto Cardenal (1925–) Guillermo Cabrera Infante (1929–) John Barth (1930–) Alice Walker (1944–)
1990				

The Humanities
VOLUME I

The Humanities and Education

The Return of the Humanities

Universities in the 1980s, in reaction to a tight job market and a changing economy, seem to have been characterized by student demand for career-oriented, pre-professional education rather than the traditional liberal arts education that many American colleges traditionally sought to provide. With the end of the decade, however, a reaction against this view of education has come about; educators, business and government leaders, and the students themselves have called for a return to, or perhaps a contemporary version of, the classical liberal education in both secondary schools and universities. Books such as Allan Bloom's *The Closing of the American Mind* and E. D. Hirsch, Jr.'s *Cultural Literacy*, along with proposals by Secretary of Education William Bennett, all advocating a return to the "great texts," have sparked debate, within and outside of the academy, on the nature and quality of secondary and higher education, and on the advisability of a core curriculum. The humanities stand at the center of the controversy.

Because the natural sciences and the social sciences are, on the whole, more oriented toward the latest discoveries in their fields, the humanities have become the repositories of the classical texts of our intellectual tradition. There seems to be widespread agreement that the process of educating human beings occurs in large part through the confrontation between a mind and a text. However, debate arises over the nature of the text the mind should confront and the nature of the questions the mind should ask. Is there a central, unchanging canon of "great books" that every educated North American should read, or can the list of "texts" include not only books excluded from the traditional canon but also other art forms, films, and all sorts of cultural phenomena? Do the great books have an unchanging core of truth that awaits discovery by each generation of students, or should they be reread in a radically new way or "deconstructed"? Finally, should the study of the humanities be limited to the Western tradition, or expanded to include great texts from other traditions?

We are not interested at this point in proposing solutions to the problems involved in re-evaluating the humanities, but rather in assuring that the study of them is approached with an awareness of the importance of the controversy. However, the very nature of a textbook such as this one does contain some assumptions that should be made explicit. One is that we are (whether we wish to be or not) heirs to an intellectual tradition that stems from Greco-Roman and Judeo-Christian roots, and that awareness of these roots and their continuities is essential to an understanding of ourselves, our culture, and our society. This does not imply that the canon received from this tradition must always be read in the same or in an uncritical fashion, nor that contributions previously neglected—particularly those written by women—should not now be included. A second assumption of this book is that the Greco-Roman and Judeo-Christian foundations are not our only cultural roots. There are others, including Native American, Germanic, Oriental, and African, to name a few. Because the task of including all of these in a single book would have been overwhelming, we were forced to make choices. The culture of West Af-

rica will be introduced here, partly because it has had such a profound effect on all of North America, and partly because it has both important connections and striking contrasts with the Western humanistic tradition. In order to understand the nature of this Western tradition in light of the present controversies over the humanities, it is necessary to examine the historical context in which the concept of "the humanities" arose.

Historical Development of the Humanities

The establishment of the humanities as a body of knowledge occurred in Italy some five hundred years ago. The Renaissance humanists, reacting against a curriculum dominated by theology in the Middle Ages, passionately devoted themselves to reading Latin and Greek pagan texts, because they believed that human-centered inquiry should be revived. The studies that they called the humanities—in Latin, *studia humanitatis*—thus centered around the literature of antiquity.

This focus on the human did not mean, however, that "man was the measure of all things." The human individual was the finest creature in God's creation and, like God, a maker, a doer, a creative force. Nonetheless, humans remained creatures, mortal and imperfect. The humanists' criticism of much medieval education was that it had concentrated on "man" as intellect outside a time frame. The human being was a product of history and a close study of the past, especially of the ancient Greek and Roman world, in which human achievement seemed to have been maximized, could guide people in the present and toward the future. Nor did the lessons of history contradict the truths found in the ultimate source of truth, the Holy Scriptures. For the humanists, moreover, the emotional component of human nature had to be recognized as a reality, and this recognition was the foundation for ethical development through the use of eloquence. Studying the writings of the ancients, models of eloquence, not only stimulated the mind but also aroused the passions to pursue the good. Having learned the lessons of effective presentation from the ancients, the humanists themselves not only helped others to lead a higher moral life but also, by conveying the message of Scripture, made their audience better Christians.

In spite of their affirmation of the basic dignity of all human beings, the Renaissance humanists definitely believed that some were more "human" than others. People who studied the humanities, according to them, actually acquired more "humanity," not only because they were able to think for themselves more creatively and to express themselves more fully but also because they acquired a deeper understanding of people. Ideally, this kind of humanistic growth should be available to all. In practice, however, it was available only to those with enough wealth, family support, or adequate patronage to have a certain amount of leisure. Moreover, the program of humanistic studies was, with a few notable exceptions, a male monopoly.

Although at times the study of the humanities in Europe and the United States has been associated with cultural snobbery, blind worship of tradition, and class privilege, it has also served to stimulate creative men and women to redefine the spirit of the humanities for their own time. Seventeenth-century humanists in Europe allied themselves with scientists to fight for the liberty of the questioning human mind against the dictates of established authority. Eighteenth-century humanists, speaking out for religious tolerance, for liberty, equality, and fraternity, helped to create revolutions. Nineteenth-century humanists struggled to save the human spirit from threatening industrial growth and technical progress. They also considerably broadened the areas encompassed by humanistic study through the creation of new fields such as folklore, comparative religion, art history, and music history. Pioneers in Oriental and African studies began the process of making us aware that the study of the humanities can include artistic and philosophical creations from traditions other than the Western one. Humanists such as the many intellectuals who fled Nazi Germany in the 1930s reaffirmed the humanistic demand for freedom of intellectual inquiry and artistic expression, as well as the opposition to oppression, intolerance, and fanaticism in all its forms. Humanists today (who, in contrast to the caricatured "secular humanists" defined by certain religious groups, may be deeply religious) continue to struggle against dogmatism and narrow definitions of truth. One constant,

humanistic value seems to be a commitment to the fullest possible development of the intellectual, moral, and aesthetic faculties of individual human beings, along with a belief that the study of the humanities may at least contribute to that endeavor.

The Humanities Today

We have come a long way from a study confined to Greek and Roman literature, but these are still relevant to our present concerns. A line from the Roman poet Terence, a slave of African origins, might in fact best define the ideal modern humanist.

Homo sum; humani nihil a me alienum puto.
(I am a man; I hold nothing human foreign to me.)

If being a humanist means having an interest in everything human, today's humanists must have broad interests indeed. The variety of human endeavors has extended the scope of the humanities to include such fields as film, radio and television, and computer productions, or, more generally, relations between values and technology. It has become difficult to define the scope of the humanities. The National Endowment gives us the following working definition:

The humanities are above all a way of thinking, a dimension of learning. The subjects of the humanities range from the study of great texts to the analysis of contemporary problems; the methods of the humanities are both those of particular disciplines and of broader interdisciplinary inquiry . . .

The humanities include, but are not limited to: history, philosophy, languages, linguistics, literature, archaeology, jurisprudence, history and criticism of the arts, ethics, comparative religion, and those aspects of the social sciences employing historical or philosophical approaches. This last category includes political theory, international relations, and other subjects primarily concerned with questions of quality and value rather than methodologies.

The Endowment distinguishes between the creative and performing arts and the humanities, which include the study and criticism of those arts. Yet this distinction, like others, is not hard and fast, because an artist, and for that matter a scientist, may also be a humanist. What is important, as we have seen in the previous section, is the respect for tradition coupled with the spirit of free inquiry, which has characterized the study of the humanities over the centuries.

Are traditional humanistic values adequate in a world that has seen Auschwitz and Hiroshima, in which massacre, torture, starvation, and oppression are constants in the evening news, in a world that lives under the threat of global nuclear war? Technological and economic events seem to shape the world in a way remote from individual minds. Some contemporary writers speak of our age as a kind of afterthought: postmodern, postindustrial, postChristian and even posthumanistic. It is thus certain that today's students of the humanities must, if they wish to carry on the tradition, find new ways of expressing its beliefs.

What, it may well be asked, can the study of the humanities do for a student in the final years of the twentieth century? We are no longer certain, as the Renaissance humanists were, that the study of the humanities will make one a better or "more human" person. Yet most of today's humanists do still believe that the study of the humanities involves a process of individual growth and self-knowledge that is as valid today as it was hundreds of years ago. True involvement with the humanities means stretching and expanding one's capacity for thought, sensitivity, and creativity. It means searching for the answers to fundamental questions, such as: What is good and evil? What is the nature of God? What constitutes the good life and the just society? What is beauty? What is love?

The study of the humanities will not provide ready-made answers to these or other questions, but it will provide contact with great minds and imaginations that have pondered them, and it should help students to prune away sloppiness and superficiality from their thinking. Understanding developed through work in the humanities may, it is hoped, change lives as well as ideas.

The Interdisciplinary Humanities

In this introductory text we cannot pretend to deal with all of the fields mentioned in the definition above. Our focus will be on literature, art history, cultural history, and music, with some attention to philosophy, dance and theater arts, and film. The interdisciplinary method of approaching the humanities stresses their

relationships but at the same time makes clear the limits and boundaries of each discipline.

What justifies studying a poem or story, a building, a statue, a dance, a musical composition, and a work of philosophy together? One reason often given is enriched understanding of a particular human culture: the study of the masks, dances, poetry, music, and religion of the Yoruba people will give more insight into their culture than will the study of their poetry alone. Another reason lies in the fact that the comparative method enables one art form to shed light on another. A third, more general, reason is that all of these enable us to understand more about the human spirit and its creative capacity.

The various disciplines in the humanities are all concerned with human values, beliefs, and emotions and with the way in which these are expressed through human creations. Philosophy and religion embody more or less systematically organized values and beliefs, whereas works of art (in literature, painting, music, or other) embody the creative expression of these values and beliefs. But these distinctions are not hard and fast. A philosophical tract may also be artistic, and a play or a statue may open up new dimensions in philosophy. The study of cultural history—of values and beliefs prevalent at certain times and places—helps to bind the humanities together, even if a work of genius may *oppose* prevailing values and systems.

What do the arts have in common? Let us suppose that for the creation of a work of art, basically two elements are needed: some kind of raw material and a creative mind. Some examples from the Western tradition come to mind: Michelangelo and a block of marble, Shakespeare and the English language, Beethoven and the tones of the scale and instruments of the orchestra. The artist works on the raw material, giving it shape and form. The finished product then bears the imprint of the artist's individual genius, but it also shows the influence of the cultural tradition and the era from which it comes. The combination of these will constitute its style. The work of art will also have a certain subject matter, structure, and theme that will be composed of the "fundamentals" of the art form used. All of these can be analyzed, step by step. A technical analysis of a work of art, though a necessary and useful step in the process of understanding, is still only a means to an end. The end can be called "aesthetic awareness"—the expansion of one's capacity to perceive meaning in art and react to it.

The artist gives shape, power, and expression to stone, words, or notes; and you, the humanities student, through some technical and historical knowledge and a willingness to expand your creative awareness, prepare yourself to receive a personal impact from the work of art. Of course, you can choose not to expand but rather to judge, through the limits and prejudices of your present experience, deciding immediately that you simply "like" or "dislike" or "agree with" or "don't agree with" certain works or ideas. In that case, you will not be receiving an education in the humanities. A humanistic education presupposes a willingness to open the mind and senses to the unfamiliar and to judge only after attempting to understand. And the interdisciplinary method invites speculation and comparisons that transcend traditional boundaries.

Culture, Cultural Roots, and the Humanities

Culture, a word that has acquired many meanings in recent years, is in need of some definition. We all feel that we belong to a group culture, whose values we may either defend or reject; and in the educational process (broadly speaking, not limited to schooling) we also acquire an individual culture. We may also classify certain works as belonging to "popular" or to "high" culture.

It may be useful to look at the root meaning of the word. In Latin, the verb *colere* means "to cultivate or till," and the noun *cultura*, "soil cultivation." Our word *agriculture* comes from this root and from the Latin word for *field*. Language often grows by metaphors, and here the word culture, applied to human beings, suggests that the human mind, especially the mind of a child, is like a field that must be tilled, fertilized, planted, and *cultivated* by parents, teachers, and other influential members of the society in which the child lives. Applied to an adult, it implies the acquisition of learning and knowledge not merely for their practical value but also for the growth of the mind in its intellectual, moral, and aesthetic capacities. It is in this sense that the black American poet Dudley Randall, describing the beliefs of the humanist W.E.B.

DuBois, speaks of "the right to cultivate the brain." [1] We are, of course, vitally concerned with culture in this sense of individual development in the humanities. The Renaissance humanists believed, as we have seen, that this sort of culture was best acquired through the study of Greek and Latin literature. For most humanists today, the study of any and all of the fields considered to be humanistic may further this goal.

If the humanities are concerned with culture in an individual sense, they are also concerned with it in a social or sociological sense. Let us return for a moment to the comparison between the child's mind and the farmer's field. As it is cultivated, that mind not only develops as an individual, but it also acquires certain habits, values, beliefs, ways of thinking, seeing, feeling, and expressing that attach the child to a certain culture. When we use the word in this sense, it might help to think of its meaning in the biological sciences. Certain types of bacteria growing in certain types of environments are called "cultures." When we extend this notion to human beings, we are aware of what it means to speak of a Western culture, an Oriental culture, an African culture. More specifically, we may speak of Slavic or Germanic or Latin culture, of Ibo or Bantu culture, of Japanese culture. We may speak of American culture, or we may break it down into Black culture, Italo-American culture, Midwestern culture, urban culture, rural culture, and so on. We may make other sorts of categories such as youth culture, female culture, male culture, and Baptist culture. There are, in other words, a variety of ways to slice the cultural pie.

Anthropologists looking at a culture are interested in its language, religion, social customs, food, and clothing; its moral and philosophical beliefs; its political, economic, and familial systems; and its plastic arts, poetry, tales, music, and dance. Humanists are interested in all of these things too, but particularly in a given culture's intellectual and artistic achievements. Ideally, in the study of the humanities, we should combine the two meanings of the word *culture* discussed here: we should both acquire individual culture and learn about a social culture. In reading a Greek tragedy or examin-

---

[1] In "Booker T. and W.E.B." The relevant lines are: "Some men rejoice in skill of hand, /And some in cultivating land, /But there are others who maintain /The right to cultivate the brain."

ing a piece of African sculpture, we learn something about the values, beliefs, and sense of beauty of a culture remote from us in time or space; but we also cultivate our own minds in the present through new aesthetic experience and contact with unfamiliar ideas. Human beings differ from bacteria in that they can flourish and develop through exposure to cultures different from their own.

Since the publication of Alex Haley's book on the search for his African origins in 1976, Americans have shown a growing interest in tracing their "roots." For black Americans, tracing family origins is perhaps doubly interesting because doubly difficult. Tracing one's *cultural* roots, however, can be an even more complex matter. On the American continent, particularly, where so many of us have so many different ethnic origins, we have all been influenced by a number of cultures. Thus an Afro-American may discover that he has some Irish cultural roots; an Anglo-American may find that certain aspects of his culture are native American or African. As we learn more about our world, through ever-faster communications, we also become

more acquainted with totally foreign cultures, which in turn become a part of our personal, individual culture. We begin to discover unexpected cultural roots when we ask questions like "what lies at the root of the ways in which I think, perceive, and express myself?" or "what are the origins of the books, films, TV programs, buildings, music, and visual stimuli of my culture?"

We stressed in the Preface that our treatment of cultural roots will concentrate on a few periods and a few works rather than attempt an exhaustive survey. In the study of modern culture in Volume II, which covers the period from the seventeenth century to the present, we will observe continuities from the three original cultural roots and add some new ones. There, too, rather than surveying, we will be examining a few works, places, and periods of significance to the formation of contemporary culture.

Not every one of you who reads this book will agree that all of the works presented here form part of your "cultural roots." Nevertheless, if you are willing to experience them openly and creatively, they will become part of your personal culture.

PART ONE

The Greco-Roman Root

1

Early Greece

The civilization of ancient Greece, which we can date roughly from about the eighth century to the first century B.C., and the civilization of ancient Rome, lasting from about the first century B.C. to the fifth century A.D., are often referred to collectively as *Greco-Roman* or as *classical*. This should not be interpreted to mean that their cultures were identical. There are many points of contrast, and, although the Romans assimilated a good deal of Greek culture, they added many unique features of their own. Still, they do share a common cluster of ways of thinking and creating that differ from those of other ancient cultures and that have clearly influenced the development of the Western humanistic tradition. Both Greeks and Romans gave human reason, in forms like rule by law and discussion through philosophy, more importance than mystical experience or reliance on tradition. In literature, art, and architecture, both cultures stressed balance, proportion, simplicity, and nobility as their criteria for beauty. Yet their view of human beings was not cold or merely rationalistic. The whole man was very much in view; and, if reason was to dominate the passions, the emotional, ecstatic side of human nature was also recognized as essential.

It is quite possible to argue that Western culture, particularly North American culture, has been more influenced by the Romans than by the Greeks. Yet we have chosen to focus attention here on Greek culture for three reasons: 1) the Greeks obviously came first and laid the basis for the later culture; 2) Greek culture was more concentrated and it is somewhat easier to get a coherent view of its lifestyle, art, and thought; and 3) in many instances the Greek cultural monuments, especially the tragedies, are more alive and significant for us today than are their Roman counterparts. We will devote most attention to the "classical" phase of Greek culture; but, to avoid confusion, it is necessary to remember that *all* of Greco-Roman culture is sometimes called classical, as when we speak of classical languages (Greek and Latin) or classical literature. The word was first adopted by Renaissance scholars, who used it in the sense of "first class" or "best" because they considered the artistic and literary style of the ancient Greeks and Romans as the model for all good art. That ideal model was generally accepted until the nineteenth century in the West. Now we also use the term *classical* to refer to the particular phase of Greek art and literature that, according to most historians of Greek culture, most perfectly expresses the ideals of the Greek aesthetic and the Greek view of life—Athens in the fifth century B.C., specifically 480–404. We will define the classical canons more specifically when examining the creations from this phase. First, however, it will be necessary to examine briefly the rise of Greek civilization and some important prior cultural developments.

Hellenism—The Rise of Greek Culture

What was so important about a small Mediterranean civilization that flourished over two thousand years ago in a country we now call Greece? History books and anthologies of literature often begin with the Greeks as if culture itself had begun there, but we know that is false. If we look at Greek civilization in the context of world history, we can see that it is a relative latecomer. The first human cultures arose in Africa; the first large-scale civilization was in the Middle East, in Mesopotamia. Great civilizations in Asia and Africa—notably those in the Indus valley in India, in China, and in Egypt—were highly developed while savage tribes still roamed in Greece. In fact, all of Western civilization can be seen as the child of Eastern civilization. The Greeks were not the first to create a written literature, painting, sculpture, music, or science. In many of these fields they borrowed heavily from Egypt. Yet the ways in which they developed the humanities and sciences were unique. Those developments are significant for our search for cultural roots because the Greeks were the first to express themselves in ways that can be designated as characteristically Western.

There is a more specific reason why the culture of the ancient Greeks is especially important to the study of the humanities. Theirs was the first culture that we can truly call humanistic. The Greeks were the first to be interested in, and indeed to glorify, human beings simply as human beings—for themselves and their own unique qualities rather than because of their place in a religious, familial, or social order. This stress on the value of the individual made Greek culture less conservative than its predecessors. In contrast to the stable, slowly changing, and long-lasting Egyptian culture, Greek culture was dynamic, rapidly changing, and short-lived.

Unfortunately, it used to be fairly commonplace for Western historians to assume that because the Greeks were different they were better, or because their culture changed more rapidly they contributed more to the development of the human spirit. We are now perhaps better able to see that the restless, dynamic character of Western culture has created its own problems, and also that we have much to learn from the older cultures of the rest of the world. At the risk of making too great a generalization, we might say that a religious sense of life, or the sense of being in touch with a supernatural, spiritual world, and the use of symbolism or suggestion to convey this in art, have characterized the African and Asiatic contributions to world culture. Philosophy, or the rational analysis of problems from a human point of view and a corresponding naturalism in art have been the legacies of the Greeks and their successors, the Romans.

Hellenism and Hebraism   The Greek view of life can also be effectively contrasted with that of the ancient Hebrews, whose culture gave rise to the other main root of Western culture. The adjective *Hellenic* and the noun *Hellenism* have come to stand for certain ways of thinking and feeling that can be traced back to the ancient Greeks. They derive from the Greek word for Greece, Ηελλας, *Hellas* in the Roman alphabet. In an influential essay, "Culture and Anarchy," written about a hundred years ago, the English poet and critic Matthew Arnold set down what he perceived to be the important contrasts between the two main sources of Western culture: Hellenism and Hebraism. The aim of Hellenism, in his opinion, is "to see things as they really are," while the aim of Hebraism is "conduct and obedience." The one stresses "right thinking," or reasoning for oneself; the other stresses "right acting," or obeying God's commandments. While scholars and thinkers have since attacked Arnold's oversimplified view, pointing out in particular that Greek culture was not all "sweetness and light" (as he put it), his basic categories still make sense.

"Man is the measure of all things," a statement by the Greek philosopher Protagoras, would have been inconceivable in an African or Far Eastern culture or in a Near Eastern one such as that of the ancient Hebrews. Contrast this with a question from the Bible, in Psalm 8, "What is man that Thou art mindful of him?" Although Greek thinkers were aware of the frailty of man, this question would not have occurred to them. Greek culture assumed that human beings were the primary interest of the gods, just as the gods themselves were glorified human beings. It was natural for men to be curious about, and attempt to interpret, the world around them.

Crete   How did the Hellenes (the Greeks) develop their particular form of culture? The first civilization to exist in the country now called Greece developed on the island of Crete in the Mediterranean Sea (see map) around 2000 B.C. The island's location between Egypt and mainland Greece is symbolic of its role in helping to transmit one culture to the other. The Minoans, as they were called after their legendary king, Minos, seem to have developed trade with Egypt (whose civilization had already been in existence for a thousand years) and to have led peaceful and creative lives. The form of government in Crete was apparently matriarchal; that is, it was ruled by a queen whose husband, the king, was ritually sacrificed each year. A mother-earth goddess was the principal deity in Minoan religion. A modern African scholar has interpreted the importance given to the female principle in Crete as evidence that Minoan civilization is basically African in its origins. Whether or not this theory is true, the matriarchal emphasis in Minoan culture certainly contrasts with the male-dominated later Greek culture.

Minoan artists used natural forms—plants, animals, fish, and fowl—to decorate walls, pottery, and gems. Their loosely structured, vividly colorful designs suggest a deep love for, and profound observation of, nature. The unfortified, elaborate, and labyrinthine palaces at Knossos (Fig. 1-1), Phaistos, and Mallia contrast sharply with the hierarchical, ceremonial, ritualistic tomb and temple complexes of Egypt. Built of wood, mudbrick, and stone, the multileveled palaces had light wells, folding doors, and winding stairs that connected apartments, ceremonial rooms, workshops, and storage areas. The beautiful *frescoes*, seal stones, jewelry, and other artifacts suggest a lifestyle in which satisfaction and pleasure were more important than ceremonial or military discipline.

1–1   Knossos, Crete: Palace, East Wing. (Eugene Brown)

EUXINE SEA

T H R A C E

MACEDON

Mt. Pangaeus +
Amphipolis •
Pella •
• Philippi

THASOS
SAMOTHRACE

CHALCIDICE

Byzantium •

Bosporus

PROPONTIS

BITHYNIA

Mt. Olympus +
• Potidaea
+ Mt. Athos
• Aegospotami

Hellespont

PHRYGIA

EPIRUS

+ Mt. Ossa

LEMNOS

TROAS

THESSALY

+ Mt. Pelion

MYSIA

CORCYRA

A
E
G
E
A
N

AEOLIS-IONIA

• Pergamum

Thermopylae
Pass)(

Artemisium
+

EUBOEA
SCYROS

LESBOS

LYDIA

Mt.
+ Sipylus
• Sardis

AETOLIA
Chaeronea
Delphi •
Coronea •
Thebes
Leuctra •
BOEOTIA
Plataea • Marathon
Eleusis • ATTICA
Megara • Athens • Carystus
SALAMIS

CHIOS

ITHACA

Gulf of Corinth

Meander R.

ACHAEA

Corinth •
ARCADIA
Mycenae •
Olympia • Argos •
ARGOLIS

Ephesus •

SAMOS

+ Mt. Mycale
• Miletus

S
E
A

CARIA

Mt.
+ Laurium
AEGINA

DELOS

Eurymedon R.

MESSENIA
• Sparta
LACONIA

MYRTOUM
SEA

NAXOS

• Cos
Cnidus •

LYCIA

MELOS

IONIAN

SEA

CRETAN SEA

RHODES

CLASSICAL GREECE

C R E T E
Mt. Ida +
• Knossos

M E D I T E R R A N E A N   S E A

In 1400 B.C. Crete was conquered by a more warlike people, the first we can truly call Greek. Wandering tribes from Europe, settling in mainland Greece, eventually developed a rich civilization centered in the city of Mycenae, which flourished between 1600 and 1200 B.C. This civilization is referred to either as Achaean, from the name of its principal tribe, or Mycenaean, from the name of the city. Within it a number of kings ruled over small, independent states. The most famous of these kings were Agamemnon, who ruled in My-

cenae with Queen Clytemnestra, and his brother Menelaus, who ruled in Sparta with Helen. Their names have become familiar to us because of the legend of the Trojan War. According to this legend Helen, the most beautiful woman in the world, ran away from her husband with Paris, the son of Priam, king of Troy. Troy was located in Asia Minor, and its ruins have been excavated in what is now Turkey. Determined to recapture Helen, the kings of Greece raised a huge fleet of ships commanded by Agamemnon. They sailed for

Troy and remained there for nine years, fighting and plundering but unable to take the city. In the tenth year Agamemnon quarreled with his most powerful fighter, Achilles. As Achilles and his followers withdrew from the fighting, the brother of Paris, Hektor, began to lead the Trojans toward victory. Achilles then returned to battle, succeeding in entering Troy; he killed Hektor but was soon killed himself. Although the Greeks were aided by powerful new allies such as Memnon, the black prince from Ethiopia, and Penthisilea, queen of the Amazons, with her female warriors, Troy still continued to hold out. It was finally overcome by a ruse devised by the "wily" Greek, Odysseus. The Greeks, pretending to acknowledge defeat, actually boarded their ships to prepare for departure, leaving behind them a huge wooden horse as an offering to the gods. The horse was, in fact, full of armed Greek soldiers. When the Trojans, overcome with curiosity, took it into their city, the Greeks came out and set fire to Troy. Thus the will of the gods was accomplished: Troy was subdued by the Achaeans, and Helen returned to Menelaus. Historians today believe that the Trojan war (ca. 1200 B.C.) was actually fought, but probably for economic reasons. More important for our cultural roots is the legendary material that has spawned a wealth of Western literature, beginning with the *Iliad* and the *Odyssey*.

Mycenae   The Mycenaean age of Greek culture, about which we have little factual information, is often called the heroic age because most of the heroic deeds such as the Trojan War that were later written and sung about took place then. In contrast to matriarchal Crete, it was a masculine-oriented and male-ruled society. The painting, sculpture, and architecture of Mycenae affirm this orientation. The citadel (Fig. 1-2) at Mycenae, overlooking the plain and visible from the sea, was heavily fortified. One entered it through the Lion Gate, so called for its monumental *relief sculpture* of two lions. The king's palace dominated the entire complex. A rectangular building with a deep porch on its narrow end, it contained a main room where the king received dignitaries, held court, and entertained. Frescoes of shields and warriors decorated the walls. The heraldic lions at the gate and the massive scale of the masonry create an image of power controlled by will, solemnity, and ritual.

Mycenae "rich in gold" was eventually destroyed by uncivilized invaders from the north, the Dorians. The next four hundred years are often called the "dark ages" of Greece. We know little about this period except that what would later become the classical city-states—Athens, Corinth, Argos, and finally Sparta—were beginning to emerge as centers of power.

Archaic Period   The next epoch of Greek culture is sometimes referred to as the Archaic period. *Archaic* refers to something in its initial stages. This period, which we can date from approximately 700–480 B.C., indeed saw the beginnings of several forms of Greek culture. In politics the unit of the city-state, or *polis*, was formed; and the form of government known as "democracy," which means in Greek "rule by the people," evolved. In architecture the Doric temple was created, and in sculpture the first free-standing human figures appeared. Greek vase painting was also developed during this time, and the first people who can properly be called philosophers began to speculate and

1–2   Mycenae, Lion Gate, c. 1250 B.C. (Eugene Brown)

reason about the nature of the universe. Early forms of drama evolved throughout this period; and Thespis, the founder of Greek drama as we know it, won the first dramatic contest in Athens in the sixth century B.C. We will discuss all of these forms in connection with their classical stages in the next chapter. Here we look at two elements of Greek culture that reached a kind of culmination in the Archaic period: religion and poetry—specifically the forms of the *epic* and the *lyric*.

Greek Religion and Mythology

The Greeks, in contrast to the ancient peoples of India and the Middle East, did not have what we might call a religious genius. They seem to have been too much oriented toward this world to have devised either a great theology or a literature of mystical experience. Unlike the early Hindu scriptures or the laws of the God of the Hebrews, the stories of the gods on Mount Olympus have given rise to no enduring religion. Why, then, have these stories been so appealing to people for so many generations, and why are names of gods and goddesses like Zeus, Apollo, and Aphrodite still familiar to us? Unlike the Hebrew and Christian God, who belongs to a realm inaccessible to humans except through faith, the Greek gods are comprehensible to human beings. They may be seen as a kind of wish fulfillment—they are like us but powerful, beautiful, and immortal; they live "at ease." Created through prescientific attempts to explain the universe, they embody deep, intuitive understandings of human psychology.

The terms *myth* and *mythology*, used in a variety of ways, need some clarification. In popular usage, a myth designates something that the person using the word believes to be untrue even though many people may accept it as true. Thus we speak of myths created by advertising or the myth of pure and honest government. Used by psychologists, anthropologists, or literary critics, however, the word has a much broader meaning, one that is nearly the opposite of its popular one. It comes from the Greek μυθος (mythos), which can mean "a word" or "a story." Every culture in the world has, or has had a set of stories passed down orally from one generation to the next that are called its myths; the body of a culture's myths is its mythology. Myths differ from legends (such as that of the Trojan War) in that they are not usually based on a historical event, situated in time. Myths take place outside of historical time, in what students of mythology call "sacred time" and the Australian aborigines call "dream time." They often attempt to explain the origins of some phenomenon of nature such as the creation of man or why the sun rises and sets. Their characters are gods, sacred beings, or semidivine heroes and heroines. Studies in comparative mythology show that many figures such as the sky god, the earth goddess, the vegetation god, the divine child, and the virgin mother are, with different names and in various forms, found in widely divergent cultures that apparently had no influence on each other. Calling such figures *archetypes*, the psychologist Carl Gustav Jung postulated a "collective unconscious" from which human beings drew their vital myths.

Far from being a pack of lies, as popular usage would have it, the myths of a particular culture represent for that culture the deepest form of truth—a reality which is lived and practiced through ritual. For those outside of the culture they may also portray profound human truths, whether in a psychological, sociological, or spiritual sense. Thus we may distinguish between mythological truth and factual truth. Because of the insights it offers on the human mind and emotions, Greek mythology has continuously inspired Western art, literature, and even science.

The notion of "mythological truth" also informs the way in which Western culture views its own religions. After the work of Charles Darwin and of Biblical criticism in the nineteenth century, many believing Jews and Christians found that they could no longer accept the account of the origin of the world and of man given in Genesis to be true in a literal sense; and yet most believers today accept it as true in a symbolical, religious, or mythological sense. Religion, of course, is much more than a particular set of myths, although these are part of it. The word means a "binding together" and implies a system of beliefs, rituals, and standards of conduct. Great world religions such as Judaism, Christianity, Islam, Hinduism, and Buddhism have given human beings a core of meaning to their lives outlasting political change, scientific discoveries, and other cultural developments. The religion of the ancient Greeks, despite the beauty of its mythology, was not one of these.

Gods and Goddesses It is not possible to mention all the Greek gods and goddesses and religious doctrines here, but we will look briefly at the Greek account of the origin of the world and at some of the major figures.

The Greeks believed that the creation of the universe came from Chaos, a great mass in which everything now existing was jumbled. The first beings to spring forth were a female divinity, earth (Gaea), and a male divinity, heaven (Uranus). It is worth noting here that nearly all myths of creation and religious systems except Judaism and Christianity have seen the need for a divine female role in creation. The children of Gaea and Uranus were the Titans, the first gods, whose leader was Cronos (Saturn, in Latin). (The Romans largely assimilated Greek religion, and all of the Greek gods and goddesses are probably more familiar under their Latin names, which will appear here in parentheses.) Cronos was deposed by his son Zeus (Jupiter). Zeus became lord of the heavens, his brother Poseidon (Neptune) lord of the sea, and their brother Dis (Pluto) lord of the underworld, or the realm of the dead. Hera (Juno), the wife of Zeus, was goddess of childbirth and protector of married women. Because the family of Zeus was said to live on Mount Olympus, its members were called the Olympian gods and goddesses. Some of the others are these:

Athena (Minerva), patron of the city of Athens and goddess of wisdom. She sprang full-grown from the head of Zeus.

Phoebus Apollo, god of the sun, reason, music, and medicine. He established the oracle at Delphi where the Greeks went to receive enigmatic prophecies about their future. He is associated with two Greek sayings: ''Know thyself'' and ''Nothing in excess.''

Dionysus (Bacchus), god of wine, ecstasy, fertility, and the theater.

Aphrodite (Venus), goddess of love and beauty. She caused amorous complications among gods and mortals as well as great happiness. Her son Eros (Cupid) was well known for shooting his arrows in the wrong place at the wrong time.

There were, of course, other gods and goddesses in the Olympian pantheon as well as demigods and semidivine heroes, but none of them, not even Zeus, was all-powerful in the way of the Jewish and Christian God. Above the gods was a concept of fate, or destiny. It was believed that every individual on earth had a *moira*, or pattern of life, to fulfill. Though the gods could predict what it would be, they did not directly intervene. Just how it would be fulfilled depended on the individual's character and the choices that he made in his life. We will see how this problem of the relations between man, gods, and fate is examined in the tragedy *Oedipus Rex*.

Greek religion was practiced throughout the ''heroic'' or Mycenaean age but was not systematically written down and explained until the Archaic period. Religious practices consisted of the sacrifice of animals and the pouring of libations (usually wine or oil) to the gods. Each god or goddess had a temple where his or her sacred image was kept and the gifts of the worshipers were stored. The rites usually took place before, not within, the temple. Thus the building and the area around it became a sanctuary. Here statues and *stele* (standing slabs of stone, painted or carved) were placed as offerings and commemoratives of events such as victories. Some of the important sanctuaries, like Delphi, belonged to all Greeks and had statues, stele, and small treasuries to hold offerings from each of the great city-states. Others, like the Athenian Acropolis, were the manifestation of the power and glory of a particular city.

The gods, for the Greeks, could take part in human affairs. This divine intervention is also reflected in the close association of a particular divinity with a city. Athens and Athena is the most famous example: Athena was said to be directly involved with the evolution of Athenian law and justice. Thus, religious observances became intermingled with political life in a complex way that enhanced the city's vitality and cohesiveness.

Long before Athens became the principal Greek city, the epic poems of Homer show to what extent the Greek gods were seen as involved with human activities.

Homer and the Epic

The poet Homer, who probably lived around 800 B.C., has been traditionally revered as the first writer of Western literature. Yet he was not a writer at all in the sense that we use the word today, and it is possible that he did not even know how to read and write. Homer belonged to an oral tradition, the nature of which we will study more fully in the chapter on African literature, and he was "a singer of tales." He composed, rather than wrote, his poems, probably basing them on a long tradition of singers who recited stories about the Trojan War, accompanied by the music of a stringed instrument, the lyre. The original purpose of this *epic* poetry was to "sing the famous deeds of men": to teach people in a pleasurable way about the great heroes of their culture. It should be stressed that Homer's poetry is not folk poetry—it is highly polished poetry, composed according to strict rules, but it was composed orally. Other cultures—African, Babylonian, Assyrian, Indian—have also produced great oral epics; and oral epics are still being created in the Balkan countries of Europe and other places (including Africa) that have retained an oral tradition. When we read Homer, we are reading an English text translated from an ancient Greek text that is a written version of the chanted oral epic. We do not know who decided to write down the Homeric poems or why and when this was done, but that act was in itself a momentous event for our cultural history. Homer's two great epics, the *Iliad* and the *Odyssey*, have been translated by generations of poets and scholars and are still widely read. They have also been instrumental in the creation of a long tradition of written epics.

The epic as a literary type was first defined by the first critic of Western literature, Aristotle (384–322 B.C.) in *The Poetics* (see pp. 119–21). Using Aristotle's definition, Thrall, Hibbard, and Holman in their *Handbook to Literature* define the epic for the modern reader thus: "A long narrative poem in elevated style presenting characters of high position in a series of adventures which form an organic whole through their relation to a central figure of heroic proportions and through their development of episodes important to the history of a nation of race."[1] There are four important elements to retain from this definition: style, hero, action, and culture. In spite of its folk origins, the epic uses a noble rhythmic pattern or *meter* (in Greek the six-foot line, dactylic hexameter) and intricate figures of speech. The epic hero, though he may have human faults, must be almost superhuman in courage, strength, and greatness of character. Epic actions often include great wars and range over an entire country or continent. Supernatural beings, in Homer's case the gods, are usually involved in these actions. The actions must be important ones in the history of a nation or race and the hero in some sense a savior of that nation or race. Thus the hero is not only a great individual but also a culture-hero. Achilles, the hero of the *Iliad*, exemplifies what Homer perceived to be the greatness of the Greeks, and he is instrumental in an event highly significant for their culture: the downfall of Troy.

The Homeric poems were written down and read years after they were composed. The epic became a written form in Western literature with the Latin poet Virgil's *Aeneid*. Important examples of the epic in English literature are *Beowulf* and Milton's *Paradise Lost*. The epic as a literary form began to die out in the nineteenth century when it was replaced by the novel. In American culture the film industry attempted to take over the form—think how many movies have been advertised as "epic." Even this form seems to be on its way out in the contemporary world. It could be argued that our culture no longer produces events and heroes of "epic" proportions.

Both of Homer's epics are concerned with the Trojan War. The *Iliad* (Greek for "Song of Troy") depicts the war itself, while the *Odyssey* depicts the long and adventurous return home of the hero of the Trojan horse episode, Odysseus. The *Iliad* has thus been called the epic of war and the *Odyssey* the epic of peace; yet both investigate the nature of these two fundamental states of human society. The *Iliad* presents war both in its terror and its glory. Through our own experience of these matters we can, as modern readers, relate to Homer's vivid portrayal of the human urge for violence and the human yearning for peace.

The *Iliad*   The opening lines of Homer's first epic tell the reader (or listener) exactly what the poet intends to do, and set the tone for the rest.

> Sing, goddess, the anger of Peleus' son Achilleus
> and its devastation, which put pains thousandfold
> upon the Achaians,

---

[1] William Flint Thrall, Addison Hibbard, and C. Hugh Holman, *A Handbook to Literature* (New York: The Odyssey Press, 1960), pp. 174–75.

hurled in their multitudes to the house of Hades
  strong souls
of heroes, but gave their bodies to be the delicate feasting
of dogs, of all birds, and the will of Zeus was accomplished
since that time when first there stood in division
  of conflict
Atreus' son the lord of men and brilliant Achilleus.

The translator of this passage, Richmond Lattimore, has attempted to render in English the stately rhythm of the Greek hexameter. You should be able to count six beats in each line. Even this short passage reveals Homer's attention to realistic detail—the line about the dead bodies—and his use of *epithets* or repeated modifiers that succinctly characterize a person or thing, such as "lord of men" for Atreus' son Agamemnon and "brilliant" for Achilles (Achilleus). One of the most famous of these (not in this passage) is "the rosy-fingered dawn."

The goddess invoked by Homer is the muse, who was supposed to inspire the poet to sing. The poem's subject as stated is not the general one of the war but the immediate one of the anger of Achilles. Yet the poet branches out from this internal theme of the individual character of his hero to the external one of the war and its destruction. He then extends his point of view to an even more universal one—this war and its outcome were the will of the supreme god Zeus. The introduction is rounded out by a return to the original subject. We now learn that Achilles was "angry" because of a conflict with Atreus' son (Agamemnon), and the poet is ready to begin his tale.

These three levels—which we might call the internal, the external, and the universal—remain in interplay throughout the *Iliad*. The story begins with an explanation of how Achilles came to be angry with Agamemnon. Briefly, Achilles feels that he has been dishonored because Agamemnon took from him his war prize and concubine, a girl named Briseis. We are

in the tenth year of the Trojan War, and Achilles withdraws himself from the fighting to prove to the Greeks how necessary he is to them. The gods become involved in this personal quarrel when Achilles prays to his mother Thetis, a sea divinity, to let the Greeks be defeated in his absence; she carries his prayer to Zeus. This is the situation at the end of the first book of the *Iliad*. Books 2–7 describe the fighting between the Greeks and Trojans and develop individual characters, human and divine. By the end of Book 8 the Greek leaders are discouraged, and Agamemnon offers to give Briseis back to Achilles, along with many other gifts, if he will rejoin the fighting. Achilles is too angry to accept. It is only when his best friend, Patroklos, has been killed by Hektor, son of King Priam of Troy, that he is moved to return to battle. He succeeds in driving the Trojans back, slays Hektor, and drags his body behind his chariot. The Greeks hold an elaborate funeral for Patroklos. The body of Hektor remains unburied, a sign of dishonor; but, when King Priam comes to Achilles to ask for his son's body, Achilles takes pity on the old man and the *Iliad* ends with the Trojans' funeral for Hektor.

Although no one selection can adequately represent the scope and power of the *Iliad*, Book 6 shows the contrast between its glorification of war and its portrayal of human tenderness and opposition to war. Although this book does not mention the principal hero, Achilles, it does develop the character of his opponent, the more mature and, to the modern reader, probably more sympathetic Hektor, the leader of the Trojans. The accounts of battle and of the various slayings of Greeks and Trojans, while an important aspect of the epic style, may not have much fascination for us. However, the drama of Hektor's encounter with Paris and Helen, the cause of the war that brought about so much suffering, and Hektor's subsequent farewell to his beloved wife Andromache and his small son have an undeniable and universal emotional impact.

HOMER

From the *Iliad*

BOOK 6

So the grim encounter of Achaians° and Trojans was left
to itself, and the battle veered greatly now one way, now in another,
over the plain as they guided their bronze spears at each other
in the space between the waters of Xanthos and Simoeis.

   First Telamonian Aias, that bastion of the Achaians,   5
broke the Trojan battalions and brought light to his own company,
striking down the man who was far the best of the Thracians,
Akamas, the huge and mighty, the son of Eussoros.
Throwing first, he struck the horn of the horse-haired helmet
and the bronze spear-point fixed in his forehead and drove inward   10
through the bone; and a mist of darkness clouded both eyes.

   Diomedes° of the great war cry cut down Axylos,
Teuthras' son, who had been a dweller in strong-founded Arisbe,
a man rich in substance and a friend to all humanity
since in his house by the wayside he entertained all comers.   15
Yet there was none of these now to stand before him and keep off
the sad destruction, and Diomedes stripped life from both of them,
Axylos and his henchman Kalesios, who was the driver
guiding his horses; so down to the underworld went both men.

   Now Euryalos° slaughtered Opheltios and Dresos,   20
and went in pursuit of Aisepos and Pedasos, those whom the naiad
nymph Abarbare had born to blameless Boukolion.
Boukolion himself was the son of haughty Laomedon,°
eldest born, but his mother conceived him in darkness and secrecy.
While shepherding his flocks he lay with the nymph and loved her,   25
and she conceiving bore him twin boys. But now Mekisteus'°
son unstrung the strength of these and the limbs in their glory,
Euryalos, and stripped the armour away from their shoulders.

   Polypoites the stubborn in battle cut down Astyalos,
while Odysseus° slaughtered one from Perkote, Pidytes,   30
with the bronze spear, and great Aretaon was killed by Teukros.
Nestor's° son Antilochos with the shining shaft killed

---

1. Achaians: Greeks.
12. Diomedes: Son of Tydeus, lord of Argos, one of the greatest of the Achaian fighters,
    prominent in battle until wounded by Paris.
20. Euryalos: Leader, with Diomedes and Sthenelos, of the men of Argos.
23. Laomedon: King of Troy, son of Ilos and father of Priam.
26. Mekisteus: (1) Father of Euryalos.
30. Odysseus: Son of Laertes, lord of Ithaka and the neighbouring islands, great fighter and
    counsellor, close friend of Agamemnon.
32. Nestor: Leader of the Pylians, once a great warrior and still active as a commander and
    counsellor, 1. 247-284, etc.; Father of Antilochos, 5.565; of Thrasymedes.

Ableros; the lord of men, Agamemnon,° brought death to Elatos,
whose home had been on the shores of Satnioeis' lovely waters,
sheer Pedasos. And Leitos the fighter caught Phylakos   35
as he ran away; and Eurypylos made an end of Melanthios.
   Now Menelaos° of the great war cry captured Adrestos
alive; for his two horses bolting over the level land
got entangled in a tamarisk growth, and shattered the curving
chariot at the tip of the pole; so they broken free went   40
on toward the city, where many beside stampeded in terror.
So Adrestos was whirled beside the wheel from the chariot
headlong into the dust on his face; and the son of Atreus,
Menelaos, with the far-shadowed spear in his hand, stood over him.
But Adrestos, catching him by the knees, supplicated: 45
"Take me alive, son of Atreus, and take appropriate ransom.
In my rich father's house the treasures lie piled in abundance;
bronze is there, and gold, and difficulty wrought iron,
and my father would make you glad with abundant repayment
were he to hear that I am alive by the ships of the Achaians."   50
   So he spoke, and moved the spirit inside Menelaos.
And now he was on the point of handing him to a henchman
to lead back to the fast Achaian ships; but Agamemnon
came on the run to join him and spoke his word of argument:
"Dear brother, o Menelaos, are you concerned so tenderly   55
with these people? Did you in your house get the best of treatment
from the Trojans? No, let not one of them go free of sudden
death and our hands; not the young man child that the mother carries
still in her body, not even he, but let all of Ilion's
people perish, utterly blotted out and unmourned for."   60
   The hero spoke like this, and bent the heart of his brother
since he urged justice. Menelaos shoved with his hand Adrestos
the warrior back from him, and powerful Agamemnon
stabbed him in the side and, as he writhed over, Atreides,
setting his heel upon the midriff, wrenched out the ash spear.   65
   Nestor in a great voice cried out to the men of Argos:
"O beloved Danaan fighters, henchmen of Ares,
let no man any more hand back with his eye on the plunder
designing to take all the spoil he can gather back to the vessels;
let us kill the men now, and afterwards at your leisure   70
all along the plain you can plunder the perished corpses."
   So he spoke, and stirred the spirit and strength in each man.
Then once more would the Trojans have climbed back into Ilion's°

----

33. Agamemnon: Son of Atreus (therefore sometimes called Atreides), brother of Menelaos,
    king of Mykenai and chief leader of the Achaians.
37. Menelaos: Son of Atreus, brother of Agamemnon, first husband of Helen, lord of
    Lakedaimon.
73. Ilion: Troy, the city of Ilos.

wall, subdued by terror before the warlike Achaians,
had not Priam's° son, Helenos, best by far of the augurs,   75
stood beside Aineias and Hektor° and spoken a word to them:
"Hektor and Aineias, on you beyond others is leaning
the battle-work of Trojans and Lykians, since you are our greatest
in every course we take, whether it be in thought or in fighting:
stand your ground here; visit your people everywhere; hold them   80
fast by the gates, before they tumble into their women's
arms, and become to our enemies a thing to take joy in.
Afterwards, when you have set all the battalions in motion,
the rest of us will stand fast here and fight with the Danaans
though we are very hard hit indeed; necessity forces us;   85
but you, Hektor, go back again to the city, and there tell
your mother and mine to assemble all the ladies of honour
at the temple of gray-eyed Athene high on the citadel;
there opening with a key the door to the sacred chamber
let her take a robe, which seems to her the largest and loveliest   90
in the great house, and that which is far her dearest possession,
and lay it along the knees of Athene the lovely haired. Let her
promise to dedicate within the shrine twelve heifers,
yearlings, never broken, if only she will have pity
on the town of Troy, and the Trojan wives, and their innocent children.   95
So she might hold back from sacred Ilion the son of Tydeus,°
that wild spear-fighter, the strong one who drives men to thoughts of
    terror,
who I say now is become the strongest of all the Achaians.
For never did we so fear Achilleus even, that leader
of men, who they say was born of a goddess. This man has gone clean   100
berserk, so that no one can match his warcraft against him."
    So he spoke, and Hektor did not disobey his brother,
but at once in all his armour leapt to the ground from his chariot
and shaking two sharp spears in his hands ranged over the whole host
stirring them up to fight and waking the ghastly warfare.   105
So they whirled about and stood their ground against the Achaians,
and the Argives° gave way backward and stopped their slaughtering,
and thought some one of the immortals must have descended
from the starry sky to stand by the Trojans, the way they rallied.
But Hektor lifted his voice and cried aloud to the Trojans:
"You high-hearted Trojans and far-renowned companions,
be men now, dear friends, and remember your furious valour

---

75. Priam: Son of Laomedon, king of Troy, father of Hektor, Paris and many other children.
76. Hektor: Son of Priam, field commander of the Trojans and their greatest fighter.
96. Tydeus: Father of Diomedes.
107. Argives: The same as Achaians.

until I can go back again to Ilion, and there tell
the elder men who sit as counsellors, and our own wives,
to make their prayer to the immortals and promise them hecatombs."   115
    So spoke Hektor of the shining helm, and departed;
and against his ankles as against his neck clashed the dark ox-hide,
the rim running round the edge of the great shield massive in the
    middle.
    Now Glaukos, sprung of Hippolochos, and the son of Tydeus
came together in the space between the two armies, battle-bent.   120
Now as these advancing came to one place and encountered,
first to speak was Diomedes of the great war cry:
"Who among mortal men are you, good friend? Since never
before have I seen you in the fighting where men win glory,
yet now you have come striding far out in front of all others   125
in your great heart, who have dared stand up to my spear far-
    shadowing.
Yet unhappy are those whose sons match warcraft against me.
But if you are some one of the immortals come down from the bright
    sky,
know that I will not fight against any god of the heaven,
since even the son of Dryas, Lykourgos the powerful, did not   130
live lone; he who tried to fight with the gods of the bright sky,
who once drove the fosterers of rapturous Dionysos
headlong down the sacred Nyseian hill, and all of them
shed and scattered their wands on the ground, stricken with an ox-
    goad
by murderous Lykourgos, while Dionysos in terror   135
dived into the salt surf, and Thetis took him to her bosom,
frightened, with the strong shivers upon him at the man's blustering.
But the gods who live at their ease were angered with Lykourgos,
and the son of Kronos° struck him to blindness, nor did he live long
afterwards, since he was hated by all the immortals.   140
Therefore neither would I be willing to fight with the blessed
gods; but if you are one of those mortals who eat what the soil yields,
come nearer, so that sooner you may reach your appointed
    destruction."
    Then in turn the shining son of Hippolochos answered:
"High-hearted son of Tydeus, why ask of my generation?   145
As is the generation of leaves, so is that of humanity.
The wind scatters the leaves on the ground, but the live timber
burgeons with leaves again in the season of spring returning.
So one generation of men will grow while another
dies. Yet if you wish to learn all this and be certain   150
of my genealogy: there are plenty of men who know it.

———

139. Son of Kronos: Zeus.

There is a city, Ephyre, in the corner of horse-pasturing
Argos; there lived Sisyphos, that sharpest of all men,
Sisyphos, Aiolos' son, and he had a son named Glaukos,
and Glaukos in turn sired Bellerophontes the blameless.   155
To Bellerophontes the gods granted beauty and desirable
manhood; but Proitos in anger devised evil things against him,
and drove him out of his own domain, since he was far greater,
from the Argive country Zeus had broken to the sway of his sceptre.
Beautiful Anteia the wife of Proitos was stricken   160
with passion to lie in love with him, and yet she could not
beguile valiant Bellerophontes, whose will was virtuous.
So she went to Proitos the king and uttered her falsehood:
'Would you be killed, o Proitos? Then murder Bellerophontes
who tried to lie with me in love, though I was unwilling.'   165
So she spoke, and anger took hold of the king at her story.
He shrank from killing him, since his heart was awed by such action,
but sent him away to Lykia, and handed him murderous symbols,
which he inscribed in a folding tablet, enough to destroy life,
and told him to show it to his wife's father, that he might perish.   170
Bellerophontes went to Lykia in the blameless convoy
of the gods; when he came to the running stream of Xanthos, and
  Lykia,
the lord of wide Lykia tendered him full-hearted honour.
Nine days he entertained him with sacrifice of nine oxen,
but afterwards when the rose fingers of the tenth dawn showed, then   175
he began to question him, and asked to be shown the symbols,
whatever he might be carrying from his son-in-law, Proitos.
Then after he had been given his son-in-law's wicked symbols
first he sent him away with orders to kill the Chimaira
none might approach; a thing of immortal make, not human,   180
lion-fronted and snake behind, a goat in the middle,
and snorting out the breath of the terrible flame of bright fire.
He killed the Chimaira, obeying the portents of the immortals.
Next after this he fought against the glorious Solymoi,°
and this he thought was the strongest battle with men that he entered;   185
but third he slaughtered the Amazons,° who fight men in battle.
Now as he came back the king spun another entangling
treachery; for choosing the bravest men in wide Lykia
he laid a trap, but these men never came home thereafter
since all of them were killed by blameless Bellerophontes.   190
Then when the king knew him for the powerful stock of the god,
he detained him there, and offered him the hand of his daughter,
and gave him half of all the kingly privilege. Thereto

---

184. Solymoi: Tribe in Asia Minor.
186. Amazons: A race of warrior women who invaded Asia Minor.

the men of Lykia cut out a piece of land, surpassing
all others, fine ploughland and orchard for him to administer.   195
His bride bore three children to valiant Bellerophontes,
Isandros and Hippolochos and Laodameia.
Laodameia lay in love beside Zeus of the counsels
and bore him godlike Sarpedon of the brazen helmet.
But after Bellerophontes was hated by all the immortals,   200
he wandered alone about the plain of Aleios, eating
his heart out, skulking aside from the trodden track of humanity.
As for Isandros his son, Ares the insatiate of fighting
killed him in close battle against the glorious Solymoi,
while Artemis° of the golden reins killed the daughter in anger.   205
But Hippolochos begot me, and I claim that he is my father;
he sent me to Troy, and urged upon me repeated injunctions,
to be always among the bravest, and hold my head above others,
not shaming the generation of my fathers, who were
the greatest men in Ephyre and again in wide Lykia.   210
Such is my generation and the blood I claim to be born from.''
   He spoke, and Diomedes of the great war cry was gladdened.
He drove his spear deep into the prospering earth, and in winning
words of friendliness he spoke to the shepherd of the people:
''See now, you are my guest friend from far in the time of our fathers.   215
Brilliant Oineus once was host to Bellerophontes
the blameless, in his halls, and twenty days he detained him,
and these two gave to each other fine gifts in token of friendship.
Oineus gave his guest a war belt bright with the red dye,
Bellerophontes a golden and double-handled drinking-cup,   220
a thing I left behind in my house when I came on my journey.
Tydeus, though, I cannot remember, since I was little
when he left me, that time the people of the Achaians perished
in Thebe. Therefore I am your friend and host in the heart of Argos;
you are mine in Lykia, when I come to your country.   225
Let us avoid each other's spears, even in the close fighting.
There are plenty of Trojans and famed companions in battle for me
to kill, whom the god sends me, or those I run down with my swift
   feet,
many Achaians for you to slaughter, if you can do it.
But let us exchange our armour, so that these others may know   230
how we claim to be guests and friends from the days of our fathers.''
   So they spoke, and both springing down from behind their horses
gripped each other's hands and exchanged the promise of friendship;
but Zeus the son of Kronos stole away the wits of Glaukos
who exchanged with Diomedes the son of Tydeus armour   235
of gold for bronze, for nine oxen's worth the worth of a hundred.

---

205. Artemis: Sister of Apollo.

Now as Hektor had come to the Skaian gates and the oak tree,
all the wives of the Trojans and their daughters came running about
  him
to ask after their sons, after their brothers and neighbours,
their husbands; and he told them to pray to the immortals,   240
all, in turn; but there were sorrows in store for many.
   Now he entered the wonderfully built palace of Priam.
This was fashioned with smooth-stone cloister walks, and within it
were embodied fifty sleeping chambers of smoothed stone
built so as to connect with each other; and within these slept   245
each beside his own wedded wife, the sons of Priam.
In the same inner court on the opposite side, to face these,
lay the twelve close smooth-stone sleeping chambers of his daughters
built so as to connect with each other; and within these slept,
each beside his own wedded wife, the sons of Priam.   250
There, there came to meet Hektor his bountiful mother
with Laodike, the loveliest looking of all her daughters.
She clung to his hand and called him by name and spoke to him:
  "Why then,
child, have you come here and left behind the bold battle?
Surely it is these accursed sons of the Achaians who wear you   255
out, as they fight close to the city, and the spirit stirred you
to return, and from the peak of the citadel lift your hands, praying
to Zeus. But stay while I bring you honey-sweet wine, to pour out
a libation to father Zeus and the other immortals,
first, and afterwards if you will drink yourself, be strengthened.   260
In a tired man, wine will bring back his strength to its bigness,
in a man tired as you are tired, defending your neighbours."
   Tall Hektor of the shining helm spoke to her answering:
"My honoured mother, lift not to me the kindly sweet wine,
for fear you stagger my strength and make me forget my courage;   265
and with hands unwashed I would take shame to pour the glittering
wine to Zeus; there is no means for a man to pray to the dark-misted
son of Kronos, with blood and muck all spattered upon him.
But go yourself to the temple of the spoiler Athene,
assembling the ladies of honour, and with things to be sacrificed,   270
and take a robe, which seems to you the largest and loveliest
in the great house, and that which is far your dearest possession.
Lay this along the knees of Athene the lovely haired. Also
promise to dedicate within the shrine twelve heifers,
yearlings never broken, if only she will have pity   275
on the town of Troy, and the Trojan wives, and their innocent
  children,
if she will hold back from sacred Ilion the sons of Tydeus,
that wild spear-fighter, the strong one who drives men to thoughts of
  terror.

So go yourself to the temple of the spoiler Athene,
while I go in search of Paris,° to call him, if he will listen   280
to anything I tell him. How I wish at this moment the earth might
open beneath him. The Olympian let him live, a great sorrow
to the Trojans, and high-hearted Priam and all of his children.
If only I could see him gone down to the house of the Death God,
then I could say my heart had forgotten its joyless affliction."   285
    So he spoke, and she going into the great house called out
to her handmaidens, who assembled throughout the city the highborn
women; while she descended into the fragrant store-chamber.
There lay the elaborately wrought robes, the work of Sidonian
women, whom Alexandros° himself, the godlike, had brought home   290
from the land of Sidon, crossing the wide sea, on that journey
when he brought back also gloriously descended Helen.°
Hekabe° lifted out one and took it as gift to Athene,
that which was the loveliest in design and the largest,
and shone like a star. It lay beneath the others. She went on   295
her way, and a throng of noble women hastened about her.
    When these had come to Athene's temple on the peak of the
        citadel,
Theano° of the fair cheeks opened the door for them, daughter
of Kisseus, and wife of Antenor, breaker of horses,
she whom the Trojans had established to be Athene's priestess.   300
With a wailing cry all lifted up their hands to Athene,
and Theano of the fair cheeks taking up the robe laid it
along the knees of Athene the lovely haired, and praying
she supplicated the daughter of powerful Zeus: "O lady,
Athene, our city's defender, shining among goddesses: 305
break the spear of Diomedes, and grant that the man be
hurled on his face in front of the Skaian gates; so may we
instantly dedicate within your shrine twelve heifers,
yearlings, never broken, if only you will have pity
on the town of Troy, and the Trojan wives, and their innocent
        children."   310
    She spoke in prayer, but Pallas Athene turned her head from her.
    So they made their prayer to the daughter of Zeus the powerful.
But Hektor went away to the house of Alexandros,
a splendid place he had built himself, with the men who at that time
were the best men for craftsmanship in the generous Troad,   315
who had made him a sleeping room and a hall and a courtyard
near the houses of Hektor and Priam, on the peak of the citadel.

---

280. Paris: Son of Priam and Hekabe, who carried Helen from Lakedaimon.
290. Alexandros: Another, and in the Iliad more usual, name for Paris.
292. Helen: Wife of Menelaos who ran away with Paris, the cause of the war.
293. Hekabe: Daughter of Dymas, Priam's queen.
298. Theano: Priestess of Athene.

There entered Hektor beloved of Zeus, in his hand holding
the eleven-cubit-long spear, whose shaft was tipped with a shining
bronze spearhead, and a ring of gold was hooped to hold it.   320
He found the man in his chamber busy with his splendid armour,
the corselet and the shield, and turning in his hands the curved bow,
while Helen of Argos was sitting among her attendant women
directing the magnificent work done by her handmaidens.

But Hektor saw him, and in words of shame he rebuked him: 325
"Strange man! It is not fair to keep in your heart this coldness.
The people are dying around the city and around the steep wall
as they fight hard; and it is for you that this war with its clamour
has flared up about our city. You yourself would fight with another
whom you saw anywhere hanging back from the hateful encounter.   330
Up then, to keep our town from burning at once in the hot fire."

Then in answer the godlike Alexandros spoke to him:
"Hektor, seeing you have scolded me rightly, not beyond measure,
therefore I will tell, and you in turn understand and listen.
It was not so much in coldness and bitter will toward the Trojans   335
that I sat in my room, but I wished to give myself over to sorrow.
But just now with soft words my wife was winning me over
and urging me into the fight, and that way seems to me also
the better one. Victory passes back and forth between men.
Come then, wait for me now while I put on my armour of battle,   340
or go, and I will follow, and I think I can overtake you."

He spoke, but Hektor of the shining helm gave him no answer,
but Helen spoke to him in words of endearment: "Brother
by marriage to me, who am a nasty bitch evil-intriguing,
how I wish that on that day when my mother first bore me   345
the foul whirlwind of the storm had caught me away and swept me
to the mountain, or into the wash of the sea deep-thundering
where the waves would have swept me away before all these things
    had happened.
Yet since the gods had brought it about that these vile things must be,
I wish I had been the wife of a better man than this is,   350
one who knew modesty and all things of shame that men say.
But this man's heart is no steadfast thing, nor yet will it be so
ever hereafter; for that I think he shall take the consequence.
But come now, come in and rest on this chair, my brother,
since it is on your heart beyond all that the hard work has fallen   355
for the sake of dishonoured me and the blind act of Alexandros,
us two, on whom Zeus set a vile destiny, so that hereafter
we shall be made into things of song for the men of the future."

Then tall Hektor of the shining helm answered her: "Do not, Helen,
make me sit with you, though you love me. You will not persuade
    me.   360

Already my heart within is hastening me to defend
the Trojans, who when I am away long greatly to have me.
Rather rouse this man, and let himself also be swift to action
so he may overtake me while I am still in the city.
For I am going first to my own house, so I can visit   365
my own people, my beloved wife and my son, who is little,
since I do not know if ever again I shall come back this way,
or whether the gods will strike me down at the hands of the
     Achaians.''
     So speaking Hektor of the shining helm departed
and in speed made his way to his own well-established dwelling,   370
but failed to find in the house Andromache of the white arms;
for she, with the child, and followed by one fair-robed attendant,
had taken her place on the tower in lamentation, and tearful.
When he saw no sign of his perfect wife within the house, Hektor
stopped in his way on the threshold and spoke among the
     handmaidens: 375
''Come then, tell me truthfully as you may, handmaidens:
where has Andromache of the white arms gone? Is she
with any of the sisters of her lord or the wives of his brothers?
Or has she gone to the house of Athene, where all the other
lovely-haired women of Troy propitiate the grim goddess?''   380
     Then in turn the hard-working housekeeper gave him an answer:
''Hektor, since you have urged me to tell you the truth, she is not
with any of the sisters of her lord or the wives of his brothers,
nor has she gone to the house of Athene, where all the other
lovely-haired women of Troy propitiate the grim goddess,   385
but she has gone to the great bastion of Ilion, because she heard that
the Trojans were losing, and great grew the strength of the Achaians.
Therefore she has gone in speed to the wall, like a woman
gone mad, and a nurse attending her carries the baby.''
     So the housekeeper spoke, and Hektor hastened from his home
backward by the way he had come through the well-laid streets. So   390
as he had come to the gates on his way through the great city,
the Skaian gates, whereby he would issue into the plain, there
at last his own generous wife came running to meet him,
Andromache, the daughter of high-hearted Eëtion;   395
Eëtion, who had dwelt underneath wooded Plakos,
in Thebe below Plakos, lord over the Kilikian people.
It was his daughter who was given to Hektor of the bronze helm.
She came to him there, and beside her went an attendant carrying
the boy in the fold of her bosom, a little child, only a baby,   400
Hektor's son, the admired, beautiful as a star shining,
whom Hektor called Skamandrios, but all of the others
Astyanax—lord of the city; since Hektor alone saved Ilion.

Hektor smiled in silence as he looked on his son, but she,
Andromache, stood close beside him, letting her tears fall,   405
and clung to his hand and called him by name and spoke to him:
      "Dearest,
your own great strength will be your death, and you have no pity
on your little son, nor on me, ill-starred, who soon must be your
      widow;
for presently the Achaians, gathering together,
will set upon you and kill you; and for me it would be far better   410
to sink into the earth when I have lost you, for there is no other
consolation for me after you have gone to your destiny—
only grief; since I have no father, no honoured mother.
It was brilliant Achilleus who slew my father, Eëtion,
when he stormed the strong-founded citadel of the Kilikians,   415
Thebe of the towering gates. He killed Eëtion
but did not strip his armour, for his heart respected the dead man,
but burned the body in all its elaborate war-gear
and piled a grave mound over it, and the nymphs of the mountains,
daughters of Zeus of the aegis, planted elm trees about it.   420
And they who were my seven brothers in the great house all went
upon a single day down into the house of the death god,
for swift-footed brilliant Achilleus slaughtered all of them
as they were tending their white sheep and their lumbering oxen;
and when he had led my mother, who was queen under wooded
      Plakos,   425
here, along with all his other possessions, Achilleus
released her again, accepting ransom beyond count, but Artemis
of the showering arrows struck her down in the halls of her father.
Hektor, thus you are father to me, and my honoured mother,
you are my brother, and you it is who are my young husband.   430
Please take pity upon me then, stay here on the rampart,
that you may not leave your child an orphan, your wife a widow,
but draw your people up by the fig tree, there where the city
is openest to attack, and where the wall may be mounted.
Three times their bravest came that way, and fought there to storm it   435
about the two Aiantes and renowned Idomeneus,
about the two Atreidai and the fighting son of Tydeus.
Either some man well skilled in prophetic arts had spoken,
or the very spirit within themselves had stirred them to the
      onslaught."
      Then tall Hektor of the shining helm answered her: "All these   440
things are in my mind also, lady; yet I would feel deep shame
before the Trojans, and the Trojan women with trailing garments,
if like a coward I were to shrink aside from the fighting;
and the spirit will not let me, since I have learned to be valiant
and to fight always among the foremost ranks of the Trojans,   445
winning for my own self great glory, and for my father.

For I know this thing well in my heart, and my mind knows it:
there will come a day when sacred Ilion shall perish,
and Priam, and the people of Priam of the strong ash spear.
But it is not so much the pain to come of the Trojans   450
that troubles me, not even of Priam the king nor Hekabe,
not the thought of my brothers who in their numbers and valour
shall drop in the dust under the hands of men who hate them,
as troubles me the thought of you, when some bronze-armoured
Achaian leads you off, taking away your day of liberty,   455
in tears; and in Argos you must work at the loom of another,
and carry water from the spring Messeis or Hypereia,
all unwilling, but strong will be the necessity upon you;
and some day seeing you shedding tears a man will say of you:
"This is the wife of Hektor, who was ever the bravest fighter   460
of the Trojans, breakers of horses, in the days when they fought about
    Ilion.
So will one speak of you; and for you it will be yet a fresh grief,
to be widowed of such a man who could fight off the day of your
    slavery.
But may I be dead and the piled earth hide me under before I
hear you crying and know by this that they drag you captive."   465
    So speaking glorious Hektor held out his arms to his baby,
who shrank back to his fair-girdled nurse's bosom
screaming, and frightened at the aspect of his own father,
terrified as he saw the bronze and the crest with its horse-hair,
nodding dreadfully, as he thought, from the peak of the helmet.   470
Then his beloved father laughed out, and his honoured mother,
and at once glorious Hektor lifted from his head the helmet
and laid it in all its shining upon the ground. Then taking
up his dear son he tossed him about in his arms, and kissed him,
and lifted his voice in prayer to Zeus and the other immortals: 475
"Zeus, and you other immortals, grant that this boy, who is my son,
may be as I am, pre-eminent among the Trojans,
great in strength, as am I, and rule strongly over Ilion;
and some day let them say of him: 'He is better by far than his
    father,'
as he comes in from the fighting; and let him kill his enemy   480
and bring home the blooded spoils, and delight the heart of his
    mother."
    So speaking he set his child again in the arms of his beloved
wife, who took him back again to her fragrant bosom
smiling in her tears; and her husband saw, and took pity upon her,
and stroked her with his hand, and called her by name and spoke to
    her: 485
"Poor Andromache! Why does your heart sorrow so much for me?
No man is going to hurl me to Hades, unless it is fated,
but as for fate, I think that no man yet has escaped it

once it has taken its first form, neither brave man nor coward.
Go therefore back to our house, and take up your own work,   490
the loom and the distaff, and see to it that your handmaidens
ply their work also; but the men must see to the fighting,
all men who are the people of Ilion, but I beyond others."

  So glorious Hektor spoke and again took up the helmet
with its crest of horse-hair, while his beloved wife went homeward,   495
turning to look back on the way, letting the live tears fall.
And as she came in speed into the well-settled household
of Hektor the slayer of men, she found numbers of handmaidens
within, and her coming stirred all of them into lamentation.
So they mourned in his house over Hektor while he was living   500
still, for they thought he would never again come back from the
  fighting
alive, escaping the Achaian hands and their violence.

  But Paris in turn did not linger long in his high house,
but when he had put on his glorious armour with bronze elaborate
he ran in the confidence of his quick feet through the city.   505
As when some stalled horse who has been corn-fed at the manger
breaking free of his rope gallops over the plain in thunder
to his accustomed bathing place in a sweet-running river
and in the pride of his strength holds high his head, and the mane
  floats
over his shoulders; sure of his glorious strength, the quick knees   510
carry him to the loved places and the pasture of horses;
so from uttermost Pergamos° came Paris, the son of
Priam, shining in all his armour of war as the sun shines,
laughing aloud, and his quick feet carried him; suddenly thereafter
he came on brilliant Hektor, his brother, where he yet lingered   515
before turning away from the place where he had talked with his lady.
It was Alexandros the godlike who first spoke to him:
"Brother, I fear that I have held back your haste, by being
slow on the way, not coming in time, as you commanded me."

  Then tall Hektor of the shining helm spoke to him in answer: 520
"Strange man! There is no way that one, giving judgment in fairness,
could dishonour your work in battle, since you are a strong man.
But of your own accord you hang back, unwilling. And my heart
is grieved in its thought, when I hear shameful things spoken about
  you
by the Trojans, who undergo hard fighting for your sake.   525
Let us go now; some day hereafter we will make all right
with the immortal gods in the sky, if Zeus ever grant it,
setting up to them in our houses the wine-bowl of liberty
after we have driven out of Troy the strong-greaved Achaians."

---

512. Pergamos or Pergamon: The citadel of Troy.

QUESTIONS

1. Point out the *epithets* used in this book. What is their effect?
2. What stories are told within the main story? What purpose do they serve?
3. How does the couple Paris/Helen contrast with the couple Hektor/Andromache?
4. The concept of fate will be an important one in our study of Greek tragedy. What notion of fate is elaborated here?
5. What role do the gods play in this book?

Sappho and the Lyric

With Homer, the individual poet begins to make his personal voice heard, even in the context of singing the deeds of heroes and great social events. But the trend toward individual expression of personal sentiment so characteristic of modern poetry came to perfection with the development of the *lyric* about two centuries after Homer. We use the word today for words set to music (song lyrics) or to describe a particular kind of poetry, characterized by a subjective presentation of an intense emotion, often (but not necessarily) love. Even if not set to music, lyric poetry usually has a musical effect on the listener or reader.

The lyric in Greece was inseparable from music; melody and rhythm were tied intimately to the words of the poem. The word meant simply "accompanied by the lyre," a stringed musical instrument (see Fig. 1-3) used in the cult of Apollo. The earliest lyric poets were primarily musicians who simultaneously composed both words and music. Their musical pieces (all of which have been lost) were probably simple tunes; at least they lacked any harmony in the modern sense. Lyric poetry developed along two lines: choric and monodic. The choral songs, sung by groups and usually performed at religious or festive occasions, were accompanied by dancing. The combined arts of the choral spoken word, music, and dance would develop into the choruses of classical Greek drama. The monodic (one voice, solo) lyric was performed at less formal occasions, sometimes at weddings, and used more personal and colloquial language.

The lyric spirit seems to have developed almost in

1-3 Vase representing imaginary portraits of Alcaeus and Sappho holding lyres, c. 470 B.C. (Courtesy, Staatliche Antikensammlungen und Glyptothek, Munich.)

opposition to the heroic, warlike ethos of earlier times. A fragment from the man who is generally considered the first lyric poet, Archilochos, makes this clear. Archilochos, who probably lived during the late eighth century B.C., fought as a mercenary soldier in the colonization of the Aegean island of Thasos. The Greek warrior was typically told to come home carrying his shield or *being* carried *on* it; loss of the shield meant loss of manly honor. But Archilochos presents a different view:

Well, what if some barbaric Thracian glories
   in the perfect shield I left under a bush?
I was sorry to leave it—but I saved my skin.
   Does it matter? O hell, I'll get a better one.

The lyric was to develop primarily in the islands of the Aegean sea and on the coast of Asia Minor where a peaceful, refined, graceful, and aristocratic life flourished. Most renowned for its lyric poetry was the island of Lesbos where the greatest poet of this period, Sappho, and her friend and fellow poet Alcaeus, flourished.

Sappho was something like the headmistress of a school of girls who were devoted to poetry and to the service of the goddess of love and beauty, Aphrodite. The term *lesbian* comes from the island and its customs, and it is true that Sappho formed passionate attachments to her pupils. A wife and mother, Sappho also wrote poems about love between men and women. Unfortunately, most of Sappho's poetry has come down to us only in fragments; in fact, only two poems, "Seizure" and "A Prayer to Aphrodite," both printed below, have remained intact. Sappho developed a metric stanza that became known as the "Sapphic" and was adopted by later lyric poets. Here is a rendering of a Sapphic stanza in English. The symbol (‾) stands for a long beat and (˘) for a short one.

The musical equivalent would be:

♩♪|♩♪|♩♫|♩♪|♩♪   for the first three lines
♩♫|♩♩   for the last line

Fadēd ĕvĕry vīolĕt, āll thĕ rōses
Gōne thĕ prŏmise glōriŏus, ănd thĕ vīctĭm,
Brōkĕn ĭn thĭs āngĕr ŏf Aphrŏdīte,
Yiēlds tŏ thĕ vīctŏr.

Even with this fixed meter, the poetry of Sappho seems straightforward, spontaneous, almost simple. She wrote without reservation about her personal world of emotions, and her apparently plain images have great evocative power. Perhaps most important for us is that in a world dominated by men she was an independent woman and sang proudly about the woman's sphere in which she lived. In keeping with the new lyric spirit,

she glorified her world of intimate emotions and friendships and her cult of Aphrodite as superior to politics or warfare. The translation of the fragments and poems below is by the contemporary American poet and scholar Willis Barnstone.

A PRAYER TO APHRODITE

On your dappled throne, Aphrodite,
sly eternal daughter of Zeus,
I beg you: do not crush me with grief,

but come to me now—as once
you heard my far cry, and yielded,
slipping from your father's house

to yoke the birds to your gold
chariot, and came. Handsome swallows
brought you swiftly to the dark earth,

their wings whipping the middle sky.
Happy, with deathless lips, you smiled:
"What is wrong, why have you called me?

What does your mad heart desire?
Whom shall I make love you, Sappho,
who is turning her back on you?

Let her run away, soon she'll chase you;
refuse your gifts, soon she'll give them.
She will love you, though unwillingly."

Then come to me now and free me
from fearful agony. Labor
for my mad heart, and be my ally.

SEIZURE

To me that man equals a god
as he sits before you and listens
closely to your sweet voice

and lovely laughter—which troubles
the heart in my ribs. For Brocheo,
when I look at you my voice fails,

my tongue is broken and thin fire
runs like a thief through my body.
My eyes are dead to light, my ears

pound, and sweat pours down over me.
I shudder, I am paler than grass,
and am intimate with dying—but

I must suffer everything, being poor.

TO APHRODITE OF THE FLOWERS, AT KNOSSOS

Come to the holy temple of the virgins
where the pleasant grove of apple trees
circles an altar smoking with frank-
    incense.

The roses leave shadow on the ground
and cool springs murmur through apple
    branches
where shuddering leaves pour down pro-
    found sleep.

In that meadow where horses have grown
glossy, and all spring flowers grow wild,
the anise shoots fill the air with a-
    roma.

And there our queen Aphrodite pours
celestial nectar in the gold cups,
which she fills gracefully with sud-
    den joy.

A LETTER TO ATTHIS   I

My Atthis, although our dear Anaktoria
lives in distant Sardis,
she thinks of us constantly, and

of the life we shared in days when for her
you were a splendid goddess,
and your singing gave her deep joy.

Now she shines among Lydian women as
when the red-fingered moon
rises after sunset, erasing

stars around her, and pouring light equally
across the salt sea
and over densely flowered fields;

and lucent dew spreads on the earth to
    quicken
roses and fragile thyme
and the sweet-blooming honey-lotus.

Now while our darling wanders she remem-
    bers lovely Atthis' love,
and longing sinks deep in her breast.

She cries loudly for us to come! We hear,
for the night's many tongues
carry her cry across the sea.

TO ANAKTORIA, NOW A SOLDIER'S WIFE IN LYDIA

Some say cavalry and some would claim
infantry or a fleet of long oars
is the supreme sight on the black earth.
    I say it is

the girl you love. And easily proved.
Did not Helen, who was queen of mortal
beauty, choose as first among mankind
    the very scourge

of Trojan honor? Haunted by Love
she forgot kinsmen, her own dear child,
and wandered off to a remote country.
    O weak and fitful

Woman bending before any man:
So Anaktoria, although you are
Far, do not forget your loving friends.
    And I for one

Would rather listen to your soft step
and see your radiant face—than watch
all the dazzling horsemen and armored
    Hoplites of Lydia.

FULL MOON

The glow and beauty of the stars
are nothing near the splendid moon
when in her roundness she burns silver
about the world.

THEN

In gold sandals
dawn like a thief
fell upon me.

SHRILL SONG

When sun sprays the earth
with straight-falling flames,
a cricket rubs his wings,
scraping up thin sweet song.

QUESTIONS

1. Contrast Sappho's view of the story of the origins of the Trojan War in "To Anaktoria" with Homer's.
2. What is the nature of love expressed in "Seizure" and "A Prayer to Aphrodite"?
3. What other emotions associated with love can you find in these poems?
4. What *images* does Sappho use? What effects do they have?
5. What themes besides love do you find in these poems?

2

Classical Greece:
Life and Art

The time between the world of Homer and Sappho and the world of "classical" Athens saw a growth in the population of Greece, greater material prosperity, and shifts in political power. The city-states in Mycenaean times had been governed by kings, but control had then passed to the nobles; now, in the seventh century B.C., a rising merchant class began to make its power felt. Through revolutions against the nobles, this class assumed control in several of the city-states through a strong man or *tyrant*. This word originally had no bad connotations; but, as these men began to depend more and more on force to impose their wills, the word took on its modern significance. Other governments soon replaced the tyrannies. The form of government that arose in the city-state of Athens was called *democracy*, which means in Greek "rule by the people." Athens' rival city-state, Sparta, did not go through the tyrant stage but retained an aristocratic government or *oligarchy,* which means in Greek "rule by the few." The relative advantages and disadvantages of these two opposing forms of government became an important theme in Greek thought during the period with which we are concerned here.

Athens and Sparta began as allies in a series of wars that were decisive for the political, economic, and cultural importance that Greece was to assume. Persia, the last great power of the Middle East, controlled an empire stretching from India and the Asiatic steppes to the Aegean and the Nile. Naturally, the Persians attempted to annex the tiny land of Greece to their empire. The surprise on all sides was great when the Greek allies, led by the Athenians, defeated the mighty Persian army, led by King Xerxes, at the naval battle of Salamis in 480 B.C. Prior to the battle, however, the Athenians themselves had had to evacuate their city before the advancing Persians. Xerxes took the city and burned the Acropolis but, defeated at Salamis, was forced to abandon Athens and return to Persia.

The Greeks saw this battle not only as a great military victory but, perhaps more importantly, as a cultural one. Persia represented to the Athenians in particular all the values that were anti-Greek. The Persian empire, with its political hierarchy and remote, powerful king at the top, was a far cry from the small state with its "rule by the people." Another negative value that the Persians represented is summed up by the Greek word *hubris.* This is best translated as arrogance, unbridled ambition, or stepping out of the boundaries that the gods have set for men. Xerxes' ambition to conquer the world and his manner of acting and treating himself more like a god than a man were seen to be examples of hubris. In the example of Xerxes' defeat, the Greeks could see a rhythm of tragedy: hubris leads man into folly, or actions which are contrary to reason; such acts bring on *nemesis.* Nemesis was the name of a Greek goddess, but the word is translated as retribution, punishment, or disaster. A tragedy written by Aeschylus in 472 B.C. entitled *The Persians* showed just this cycle. In opposition, the Greeks upheld an ideal they called *sophrosyne,* which means wisdom and moderation. It is perhaps best expressed by the famous motto of the oracle at Delphi: "Nothing in excess." We will see the importance of this concept to the art and thought that we call classical.

Politics and Life in Ancient Athens

Greek culture was concentrated in the *polis* (from which comes the word politics), a city-state. Territorially the polis included the city and the surrounding countryside; but, as it was customarily observed, no citizen should live more than a day's walk from the center. The contrast between the care lavished on public buildings and the humble construction of private houses demonstrates the important role of the polis in the lives of its citizens. The market, the courts, the temples were the focuses of activity, not private gardens and domiciles. It was generally believed that man could realize his humanity only through participation in its political processes. The polis provided the religious forms and the moral and cultural values that gave meaning and fullness to a citizen's existence. Citizenship was a privilege acquired by males through birth; normally both one's father and mother had to be natives of the state. Citizenship guaranteed membership in a political community and at least some share in the government of the polis. While in more aristocratic city-states participation was often limited to membership in an assembly with minimal powers, in fifth-century Athens every citizen over twenty-five was eligible for the whole range of state offices, which were filled for short terms either by election or by drawing lots.

All policy decisions and laws were made by the Assembly of the People, composed of the whole body of male citizens. Day-to-day matters and the responsibility of preparing an agenda for the frequent meetings of the Assembly were in the hands of a Council of Five Hundred. Chosen annually by lot, this council functioned by means of a rotating committee meeting daily. A variety of magistrates performed specialized tasks relating to finance and military matters, but the closely defined powers delegated them allowed almost no room for personal initiative. Ultimately all public officials were responsible to the Assembly, and anyone wishing to exert political authority in the state had to do so through his leadership within that body.

Despite its democratic constitution, Athens, like all Greek city-states, was a slaveholding society. Slaves numbered about 125,000, while citizens and their families made up about 100,000. A majority of the slaves were employed in domestic service, but about fifty thousand worked in industry and another ten thousand (surely the most unfortunate) toiled in the silver mines of Laurion. Apart from the mines, Athenian slavery was not oppressive. Citizens worked alongside slaves in industrial production, and it was usually difficult to distinguish slaves from free men by their dress. In a society where the productive capacity was low and consumption needs relatively simple, the use of slaves was not motivated by a desire for the luxurious life but rather for the creation of an amount of leisure so that citizens could carry out their duties as members of the polis.

The status of women in this society is a matter of debate. They were not citizens nor did they have rights in law. Marriage seems to have meant the passing from the protection of the father to that of the husband. Wives were expected to remain at home to supervise their household and the children. The women free to attend gatherings of men outside the home were either prostitutes or high-class courtesans—foreign women called *hetaerae*. On the other hand, tender scenes between husband and wife depicted on funeral vases suggest the existence of deep ties of affection between some married couples. Representations of strong, intelligent women in Greek tragedy and comedy indicate that such women, at least in the upper class, did exist; but, on the whole, we must think of Greek women as excluded from active roles in the community.

The great age of Athens fell between the end of the Persian Wars in 480 B.C. and the end of the Peloponnesian Wars in 404 B.C., when Athens was defeated by Sparta. The Peloponnesian Wars are so called because Sparta is located in that section of Greece called the Peloponnesus (see map). As rivals for commercial power and representatives of conflicting political ideologies, the two cites of Athens and Sparta came to an inevitable clash. The Athenian Thucydides, one of the first historians of Western culture, has given us both a chronicle of the war between the two city-states and a vision of the workings of history in his *History of the Peloponnesian War*, probably completed about 400 B.C. His history is conceived in terms related to classical tragedy. In particular, he sees the reckless Athenian attack on the city of Syracuse in Sicily as a manifestation of hubris, which led to the downfall of the Athenians. The most famous passage of this history, reprinted here, is a funeral oration for some young Athenian soldiers by the Athenian statesman Pericles. Pericles, who headed the Athenian democracy during its greatest (classical) period, speaks for the young men who died. He does so by praising the way of life for which they gave their own lives. The translation is by Benjamin Jowett.

THUCYDIDES

Pericles' Funeral Oration

I will speak first of our ancestors, for it is right and becoming that now, when we are lamenting the dead, a tribute should be paid to their memory. There has never been a time when they did not inhabit this land, which by their valor they have handed down from generation to generation, and we have received from them a free state. But if they were worthy of praise, still more were our fathers, who added to their inheritance, and after many a struggle transmitted to us their sons this great empire. And we ourselves assembled here to-day, who are still most of us in the vigor of life, have chiefly done the work of improvement, and have richly endowed our city with all things, so that she is sufficient for herself both in peace and war. Of the military exploits by which our various possessions were acquired, or of the energy with which we or our fathers drove back the tide of war, Hellenic or Barbarian, I will not speak; for the tale would be long and is familiar to you. But before I praise the dead, I should like to point out by what principles of action we rose to power, and under what institutions and through what manner of life our empire became great. For I conceive that such thoughts are not unsuited to the occasion, and that this numerous assembly of citizens and strangers may profitably listen to them.

Our form of government does not enter into rivalry with the institutions of others. We do not copy our neighbors, but are an example to them. It is true that we are called a democracy, for the administration is in the hands of the many and not of the few. But while the law secures equal justice to all alike in their private disputes, the claim of excellence is also recognized; and when a citizen is in any way distinguished, he is preferred to the public service, not as a matter of privilege, but as the reward of merit. Neither is poverty a bar, but a man may benefit his country whatever be the obscurity of his condition. There is no exclusiveness in our public life, and in our private intercourse we are not suspicious of one another, nor angry with our neighbor if he does what he likes; we do not put on sour looks at him which, though harmless, are not pleasant. While we are thus unconstrained in our private intercourse, a spirit of reverence pervades our public acts; we are prevented from doing wrong by respect for authority and for the laws, having an especial regard to those which are ordained for the protection of the injured as well as to those unwritten laws which bring upon the transgressor of them the reprobation of the general sentiment.

And we have not forgotten to provide for our weary spirits many relaxations from toil; we have regular games and sacrifices throughout the year; at home the style of our life is refined; and the delight which we daily feel in all these things helps to banish melancholy. Because of the greatness of our city the fruits of the whole earth flow in upon us; so that we enjoy the goods of other countries as freely as of our own.

Then, again, our military training is in many respects superior to that of our adversaries. Our city is thrown open to the world, and we never expel a foreigner or prevent him from seeing or learning anything of which the secret if revealed to an enemy might profit him. We rely not upon management or trickery, but upon our own hearts and hands. And in the matter of education, whereas they from early youth are always undergoing laborious exercises which are to make them brave, we live at ease, and yet are equally ready to face the perils which they face. And here is the proof. The Lacedaemonians come into Attica not by themselves, but with their whole confederacy following; we go alone into a neighbor's country; and although our opponents are fighting for their homes and we on a foreign soil, we have seldom any difficulty in overcoming them. Our enemies have never yet felt our united strength; the care of a navy divides our attention, and on land we are obliged to send our own citizens everywhere. But they, if they meet and defeat a part of our army, are as proud as if they had routed us all, and when defeated they pretend to have been vanquished by us all.

If then we prefer to meet danger with a light heart but without laborious training, and with a courage which is gained by habit and not enforced by law, are we not greatly the gainers? Since we do not anticipate the pain, although, when the hour comes, we can be as brave as those who never allow themselves to rest; and thus too our city is equally admirable in peace and in war. For we are lovers of the beautiful, yet simple in our tastes, and we cultivate the mind without loss of manliness. Wealth we employ, not for talk and ostentation, but when there is a real use for it. To avow poverty with us is no disgrace: the true disgrace is in doing nothing to avoid it. An Athenian citizen does not neglect the state because he takes care of his own household; and even those of us who are engaged in business have a very fair idea of politics. We alone regard a man who takes no interest in public affairs, not as a harmless, but as a useless character; and if few of us are originators, we are all sound judges of a policy. The great impediment to action is, in our opinion, not discussion, but the want of that knowledge which is gained by discussion preparatory to action. For we have a peculiar power of thinking before we act and of acting too, whereas other men are courageous from ignorance but hesitate upon reflection. And they are surely to be esteemed the bravest spirits who, having the clearest sense both of the pains and pleasures of life, do not on that account shrink from danger. In doing good, again, we are unlike others; we make our friends by conferring, not by receiving favors. Now he who confers a favor is the firmer friend, because he would fain by kindness keep alive the memory of an obligation; but the recipient is colder in his feelings, because he knows that in requiting another's generosity he will not be winning gratitude, but only paying a debt. We alone do good to our neighbors not upon a calculation of interest, but in the confidence of freedom and in a frank and fearless spirit. To sum up: I say that Athens is the school of Hellas, and that the individual Athenian in his own person seems to have the power of adapting himself to the most varied forms of action with the utmost versatility and grace. This is no passing and idle word, but truth and fact; and the assertion is verified by the position to which these qualities have raised the state. For in the hour of trial Athens alone among her contemporaries is superior to the report of her. No enemy who comes against her is indignant at the reverses which he sustains at the hands of such a city; no subject complains that his masters are unworthy of him. And we shall assuredly not be without witnesses; there are mighty monuments of our power which will make us the wonder of this and of succeeding ages; we shall not need the praises of Homer or of any other panegyrist whose poetry may please for the moment, although his representation of the facts will not bear the light of day. For we have compelled every land and every sea to open a path for our valor, and have everywhere planted eternal memorials of our friendship and of our enmity. Such is the city for whose sake these men nobly fought and died; they could not bear the thought that she might be taken from them; and every one of us who survive should gladly toil on her behalf.

COMMENTS AND QUESTIONS

1. Thucydides, through his spokesman Pericles, is defining a balanced system of government in a style that is also balanced. Define and point out the balances in style and content.
2. Where does Pericles describe the Athenian taste in art, and what is it?
3. What are the potential disadvantages of a democracy, and how does Athenian democracy avoid these disadvantages, according to Pericles?
4. How does Athenian democracy compare with modern democracies?

Thucydides' view of human history, like that of other Greek historians of his generation, was modeled on nature, which for them was a spectacle of incessant change. Indeed, human history changed more violently than anything else in their experience. While not deriving a historical law, they believed that in the general scheme of change certain causes normally produced specific effects. Particularly, excessive action in one direction produced a violent reaction in the other. Thus, examples of history could be used to teach individuals to control their emotional life so that they would resist excess and avoid disaster. In the case of political leaders, the consequences of lack of self-control could ruin not only themselves but their people. While stressing the use of reason to control man's

destiny, the Hellenic historians, however, saw in human history no general pattern, no direction, only ceaseless change.

Classical Greek Architecture and Sculpture

When the Athenians returned to Athens after their triumph over Xerxes at Salamis, they found a ravaged city. On the Acropolis, temples had been burned, statues toppled, and inscriptions destroyed or defaced. After the city rebuilt its fortifications, its leaders began the great rebuilding project on the Acropolis. This activity not only built morale, as Pericles said, but also provided jobs. The majestic buildings on the Acropolis, now ruined by time and subsequent wars, are the results of Pericles' building program. They and the sculpture adorning them constitute the best models for the ideals of the classical style (Fig. 2-1).

Like all cultural monuments, the buildings on the Acropolis have a history. To understand the accomplishments of the master builders and artisans who created the buildings, it is necessary to know something of the origins of architecture.

The Beginnings of Architecture Architecture surely began with the need for shelter, but people quickly sensed its potential for physical, visual representation of ideas like power, permanence, magic, and the sacred. People attended to houses and fortifications, but the greatest care was lavished on those buildings that served the king or god. The first sacred buildings may have been built of nothing more than walls of mud, mudbrick, or stones enclosing a small, irregular space without windows. The walls were probably thicker at the bottom and sloped inward toward the top. The first temples built by the Greeks were simple rectangular boxes, sometimes curved at one end. The *groundplan*—the term we use to designate a drawing of any building that shows in outline the walls, openings and supports—includes one room whose walls extend to flank the doorway. This room, called a *naos*, was for the cult statue, while the extended walls made an entrance porch, the *pronaos*; together they form the *cella*. Beams for the roof rested on the top edge of the cella walls and, when crossed to form a triangular shape, could carry a wooden *gable* or ridge pole that followed

2–1   Athens, Acropolis. General view. (Courtesy of TWA)

the long axis of the cella, leaving an open triangular space at each end called the *pediment*. The roof would slope down from the center to the sides, creating a deep overhang. Any opening or door in the wall weakened the wall structure, necessitating on either side of the opening a reinforcement in the form of wooden posts that supported a horizontal wooden beam, the *lintel*, spanning the posts. The combination of posts and lintels could carry the weight of the roof (Fig. 2-2).

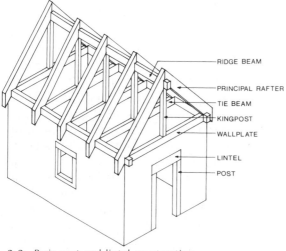

RIDGE BEAM

PRINCIPAL RAFTER

TIE BEAM

KINGPOST

WALLPLATE

LINTEL

POST

2–2   Basic post-and-lintel construction.

Combining walls with posts and lintels made possible a variety of spatial arrangements of rooms, doors, and windows. A comparison of Greek, Egyptian, Minoan, and Mycenaean architecture shows different uses of these simple elements. The Greeks, enclosing the cult statue in the cella, soon surrounded it with rows of columns or posts on all four sides to create a *colonnade*. Ceremonies took place outside at an altar placed on the long axis of the building that faced east.

Our description of these simple forms of architecture may enable us to define architecture. We use the word to describe the total process that begins with an idea or need, employs building systems (like post and lintel), applies local technology, and produces a structure. Architecture grows and changes with tradition and in response to need.

The creation of a building involves one set of events and actions. Our experience of the building becomes another series of events depending on a number of factors. One is our knowledge of what a building stands for—what it means to those who built it. Another is our knowledge of what a building is used for—its function. Yet another is our perception of how it stands up. Our bodies respond to the way in which weight and lift, support and balance occur in the built form. The Greeks used the smooth mass of the wall and the great downward pressing weight of the roof with its overhang to contrast with the dynamic power of the upward thrusting post or column. Similarly, the *rhythm* of light and dark created by the columns against the smooth cella wall also play a part in our perception of the temple.

The Greek Temple The architectural factor that became the most significant formal element of the Greek temple was the shape and scale of the column and its combination with other specific features—its capital (the cushion and flat block under the lintel) and the lintel, or *entablature*, above. The two most important combinations of *orders* are the *Doric* and the *Ionic*. Documents tell us that the Doric order evolved in the Dorian Peloponnesus. The Ionic order was first found in Asia Minor. Both were used by the Greeks of the fifth century (Fig. 2-3).

Observing the orders side by side, you can see that there is a difference in the height and thickness of the column, the presence or absence of a base for the column, the forms of the capital, and the lintel and *frieze* above the column. Vitruvius, a first-century B.C. Roman who wrote a treatise on architecture, tells us that the Doric was the most ancient order and was serious, grave, dignified, and masculine. The slender, lighter, more elegant Ionic was considered feminine. Femininity, in this case, was not associated with the gender of the gods but with the universal aspects of the female principle.

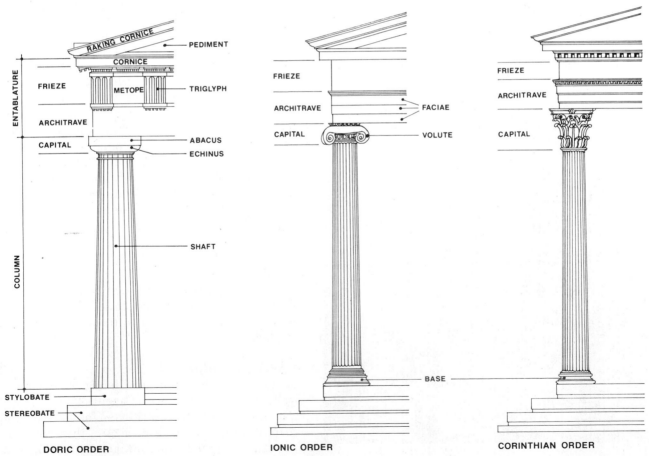

2–3 Classical Greek orders.

The Parthenon   The temple form, a cella with a colonnade on all four sides, became the rule for major temples; but its builders enriched and elaborated it, as we will see in the Parthenon. The Parthenon, built between 477 and 438 B.C., was designed and executed under the direction of Ictinus and Kallicrates, master builders (Figs. 2-4, 2-5). The sculptural program was directed by the sculptor, Phideas, who did some images himself and was solely responsible for the cult statue of Athena, placed in the cella. Tradition dictated that the temple be Doric; this one has six columns on its ends and seventeen down each flank. Located on the highest point of the Acropolis, the third temple to Athena Parthenos on that site, it was the crown of the complex. Forms originally built in mudbrick and wood, then in local stone, were now interpreted in gleaming white marble. The *pediment* on the west end, facing the sea, had its triangular space filled with sculptures depicting the story of Athena's rivalry with Poseidon for the homage of the city. The sculpture of the east pediment showed Athena's birth. The *metopes*, the spaces between the ends of the lateral beams of the roof, above the lintel, were sculpted in *low relief* with scenes from the Trojan War, the Battle of Gods and Giants, Lapiths and Centaurs, Greeks and Amazons, all historical allusions to the Greeks' struggle with the Persians—allegories for the struggle between light and darkness, civilization and barbarism. At the top of the cella walls was a sculpted frieze, showing the procession of the Panathenaea, the festival held every four years to honor Athena. Finally, the whole building was painted and polished. Capitals and moldings received color: blue, red, and gilding. Sculpture was given natural coloring; weapons, horse tack, shields, and other objects were bronze, brass, or gold. Within the cella, the gold and ivory cult statue was placed, at the far end from the door.

Surrounded by terraces, trees, statues, and stele, as well as the other buildings that soon rose around it, the Parthenon dominated the Acropolis. The entire complex was so moving that even the embittered Spartans did not destroy it when they finally defeated the Athenians in 404 B.C. Time and wars following the fall of the Roman empire ravaged the site, the worst destruction being the Venetian bombardment of 1678.

Even in the ruined state in which the Parthenon stands today, one senses an order of intractable stone formed into an ideal relationship between weight and support, repose and response, symmetry and rhythm. These characteristics recall the system of balances in Pericles' *Funeral Oration* or the search for a mean between passion and will, intuition and reason that we will observe in Greek philosophy. Perhaps we can better understand the Parthenon by looking now at Greek sculpture, whose origins lie in the same past and whose possibilities, like the temple form, seem completely realized by the late fifth century.

Greek Sculpture   Greek sculpture seems born of two almost contradictory desires: the desire to attain complete naturalism and the desire to make the figures ideal types. The gods and goddesses, votive figures, and even the more personalized portraits seem both human and divine.

Archaic Sculpture   The *Kouros* of Sounion (*Kouros* is Greek for youth, a standing male nude) was made in the *Archaic* period about 600 B.C. (Fig. 2-6). Over life size (ten feet) this free-standing male nude is characteristic of many such figures that exhibit some attempt to appear natural but are still confined to the stone block from which they were carved. One foot

2–4   Athens, Parthenon. (Greek National Tourist Organization)

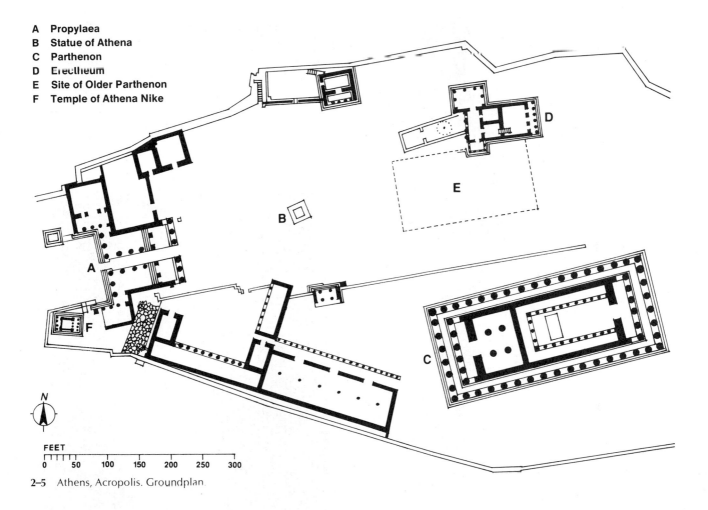

A Propylaea
B Statue of Athena
C Parthenon
D Erectheum
E Site of Older Parthenon
F Temple of Athena Nike

N

FEET
0   50   100   150   200   250   300

2–5   Athens, Acropolis. Groundplan.

steps forward, but the body weight does not shift. The body itself is really perceived as a columnar shape in which anatomical details are arranged in a symmetrical, stylized way.

Beginning with the head, the face, jawline, ears, and back of the head are seen as almost separate flat sections. The forehead, eyebrow ridge, and nose form one smooth plane, and the eyes are simplified into a wide open stare, the eyelids marked only by a groove. Similarly, the shoulders and chest flow into another smooth plane, where slight ridges, grooves, and swellings incorrectly delineate the body but are formally pleasing and symmetrical. The hip joint and the hips are reduced to one generalized swell into the thighs. Kneecaps are rigid designs, and the calves have some incised ridges for musculature. The spinal column is almost perfectly straight, and shoulder blades are incised grooves. The arms mask the sides of the body, and the clenched fists make the arms seem to press in toward the body.

The total impression is one of a compact, sculptural solid. It is a memorable and commanding form that deserves our attention because it is a familiar form—a human body—transformed into something timeless. The *Kouros* can be walked around and studied; touched and compared mentally with our own body's surface, texture, articulation, and movement. When we compare our flexible elbow, the soft flesh behind the knee, the loose, floating oval kneecap, and the soft ridges behind the neck and ears with those of this figure, we begin to realize that while the statue is *not* lifelike, its leg as the figure poses and balances. The body has become a flexible, smooth-muscled, and tactile form. One feels that a touch would reveal a yielding surface of skin and flesh. The body is perceived in the round; it reaches outside the imaginary lines of the block from which it was carved. Yet, because of its perfection, the sculpture remains separate from us. Not a blemish or scar, an undeveloped muscle, or unhappy emotion breaks the graceful forms of the body and face. Our

2–6 Kouros of Sounion, c. 600 B.C. (National Archaeological Museum, Athens)

own symmetry, the incised ridges, and the contrast between the way it is and what it seems to be—a human body—create a pleasing and enlightening experience. The *Kouros,* made to commemorate an event, inhabits a space different from our own, and we, like it, are confined to a different place and space. The columnar *Kore,* a female, is equally rigid and posed, yet the symmetry, balance, and harmony of the drapery of the figure, the hair, and the very stylized face are pleasing (Fig. 2-7).

Early Classical Sculpture The *Kritios Boy* found on the Acropolis was made about 480 B.C. (Fig. 2-8). How different he seems from the previous figures! The body now moves and turns—weight flows into one

2-7 Kore from Auxerre. Louvre, Paris. (© Arch Phot. Paris/ S.P.A.D.E.M., 1980)

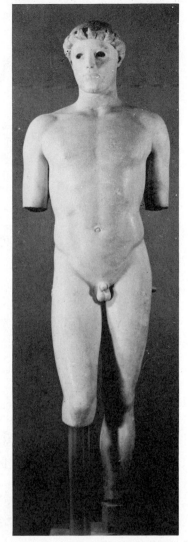

2–8   Kritios Boy, c. 480 B.C.
(Acropolis Museum, Athens)

own form would rarely compare favorably with this athletic perfection that seems to speak of self-restraint and control; perpetual youth and self-awareness. This is humanity idealized into what one *might* become.

Classical Sculpture   The development of free-standing figures toward this expressive perfection is paralleled in other kinds of sculpture. The frieze of the Panathenaic procession gives us more insight into the qualities of the ideal and the real that combine to make the expressive and dramatic scenes of classical art. The frieze has a rhythm that grows like that of an anthem.

On the southeast side, where the procession begins, figures stand or begin to walk slowly. Riders hold their horses, and the sacrificial beasts are readied. As the procession moves along the south flank and turns the western corner, the participants move more rapidly, clustering together. In the section illustrated here (Fig. 2-9), horses and riders, bodies mingling in the low sculpted relief, seem to push eagerly forward. Cloaks blow in the wind; manes and hair are breeze-tossed. As the procession reaches the east end, movement becomes quiet and figures halt in the presence of the gods and goddesses on Mount Olympus. The participants are almost anonymous, the ideally beautiful youths and maids of a procession still going on. The older priest-celebrants will always remain so, as will for all time the gods watching the ceremony.

In the blasted, broken fragments that remain from the Parthenon's pedimental sculptures, scholars and

2–9   Mounted Horses, followed by Men on Foot. Detail of Panathenaic procession from Parthenon frieze, 432 B.C. (British Museum, London)

2–10   Dionysus from east pediment of the Parthenon, c. 438–432 B.C. (Reproduced by Courtesy of the Trustees of the British Museum)

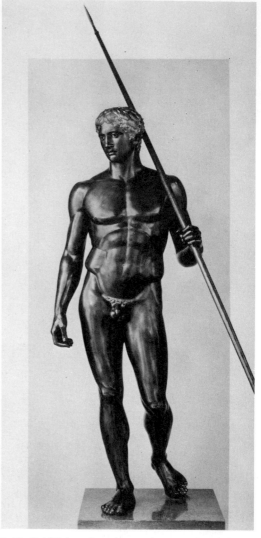

2–12   Polykleitos, Spearbearer, bronze. (Staatliche Antikensammlungen und Glyptothek, München)

2–11   Three Goddesses from east pediment of the Parthenon, c. 438–432 B.C. (Reproduced by Courtesy of the Trustees of the British Museum)

students of Greek sculpture see some of the most beautiful forms of the fifth century. Yet it is difficult for us, as novices, to penetrate the veil of destruction and time that lies over these forms. Only in the *Dionysus* (Fig. 2-10) or the now headless figures of the goddesses from the pediment can we begin to perceive the magnificent beauty of the body, perfectly harmonized with an expressive ideal (Fig. 2-11). The three ladies sit, lean, and recline to fit the space of the triangular pediment. Their bodies are substantial, weighty volumes. Their clothes do not conceal, but cling, turn, reveal, and emphasize the physical presence of these figures.

Let us now concentrate on a single classical sculpture, *The Spearbearer* by Polykleitos (Fig. 2-12). This figure is a bronze sculpture (the Greeks worked in bronze as much as stone), but the medium does not deny a comparison with the *Kritios Boy*. Of the two figures, which seems more confined in an imaginary blocklike space? How is movement suggested? Of the two bodies, which is more convincingly lifelike, which is more nearly perfect? Compare both works with a present-day athlete of the same general build. What does this tell you about the classical ideal? What is the mental or emotional state of each figure? Is it appealing? Does it enhance or contrast with the forms of the figures? What devices, like the material itself, help maintain the figures' physical and psychological distance?

Classical Architecture and Sculpture Compared Just as *The Spearbearer* harmonizes nature—the real with the ideal, of what one might be—the Parthenon harmonizes the forces of gravity and weight and the characteristics of the building system itself into a perfect balance of vertical and horizontal, compression and support (Fig. 2-4). The Parthenon's colonnade is not too tall or it would seem spindly; the columns are not too thick or they would be stumpy; the spaces between the columns are not too great or the rhythm they create would be broken; the lintels are not too long; neither are the capitals too large or small. The floor rises slightly to the center on both the long and short axis; the columns lean inward ever so slightly to counter visually the outward, downward pressure of the roof. The columns at the corner are slightly larger since they, as Vitruvius says, would seem too slender because they must be seen against light from both sides. The columns themselves swell slightly as though in vigorous, elastic response to the downward pressure of the roof. Greek architects grasped these fine points in the way that sculptors came to know the body. As head, neck, and chest become understood, as surface dissolves so that muscles swell and move rather than appear as ridges and grooves, as the body turns in space and becomes free of the solid compact mass of stone, so the Parthenon is lifted from the intractable marble to sit lightly in its landscape, its mass balanced between the reality of gravity and a thrust into bright light. To be seen from all sides, experienced during ceremonies, the building is like an ideal body, completely harmonious, self-aware and whole, mysterious and moving.

Other Classical Greek Buildings The temple form is a complete entity with its traditional, ritual, and formal demands; nevertheless, we should remember that it was not the only type of Greek building. There were theaters, meeting houses, and the colonnaded porticos of the market place. Moreover, the basic temple form itself was capable of elaborate variation, and it is in this context that we should see the Parthenon. Two buildings on the Acropolis help us to do so.

Built after the Parthenon, the Propylaea is a monumental gateway providing a secondary focus for processions, bridging the physical changes in the levels of entry and creating a place of passage from which one can focus on the sanctuary (Fig. 2-13). The master builders employed the Doric and Ionic orders; on the porticoes and exterior passages the Doric order gives substance to the idea of gateway and entrance. As the levels change, the interior Ionic columns stretch upward easily to carry the roof and visually lighten its weight. The complete gateway once acted also as entrance to the two wings, which were picture galleries containing scenes of Athenian victories.

The Erechtheum, on the north side of the Parthenon, is a very irregular but equally harmonious adjustment of building to the land and to the variety of functions it had to serve (Fig. 2-14). A number of shrines and ancient artifacts of the city had to be accommodated. To the east was a shallow Ionic portico; on the north side was a deeper, richer Ionic porch for entry to the rooms that contained ancient relics; on the south

2–13   Acropolis, Propylaea from the west. (Alinari/Editorial Photocolor Archives)

2–14   Acropolis, Erechtheum from the west side with porch of the Maidens. (Greek National Tourist Office)

side was the Porch of the Maidens, its flat roof supported by columns transformed into maidens, the *caryatid* order. Instead of a uniform building with a single *gable*, there are intersecting gables and two stories united with one. The Ionic order not only stretches but, along the west side, is also flattened into half-columns that unite the north and south porches, minimizing the change in location and in scale. Each porch has its own symmetry; but, in the balance of each against each, harmony is attained by the contrast of height and weight, openness and enclosure, shallowness and depth.

Greek architecture and sculpture were accompanied and enhanced by all the other arts: painting, music, dance, and drama. We know about painting only through written accounts, surviving vase painting, and later Roman copies of Greek work. But we do know that other arts shared in the conquest of space and movement and that, after the Parthenon, the builders' art continued to grow, flourish, and change. New needs inspired new ideas that provided a growing and changing art. After the Peloponnesian Wars new states acquired power and wealth; their ideals and beliefs were manifested in sculpture, painting, and building.

From Classical to Hellenistic Sculpture   The Cnidian *Aphrodite*, made in the fourth century B.C., was among the first nude female sculptures. The original statue was carved by the Greek Praxiteles for Aphrodite's important shrine on the island of Cnidos. The ideal female form had evolved at the same time as the ideal male form, and portraying the goddess nude had become widely accepted. The *Aphrodite* illustrated here (Fig. 2-15) is a Roman copy of the Greek original and lacks the sensual liveliness which writers ascribed to the original. But the artist's realization of the ideal female as a relaxed, elegant figure, unabashed by her nudity, which is so wonderfully revealed as she steps from the bath, fueled the imagination of artists for many centuries. This ideal was revived again by the Italian artists of the fifteenth century in their search for the classical female prototype. The later Roman Aphrodite from Cyrene, in North Africa (Fig. 2-16), relies on the same hipshot pose, general proportions, and support of the water jar and drapery as does the Aphrodite from Cnidos. Compare these figures with each other and with the *Spearbearer* (Fig. 2-12). How has the Greek ideal been extended to women? Is there any change from the previous centuries?

2-15 Praxiteles, Aphrodite of Cnidos, c. 350 B.C. (Vatican Museums, Rome—Alinari/Editorial Photocolor Archives)

2-16 Aphrodite of Cyrene, from North Africa, early first century B.C., marble. Museo Nazionale Romano, Rome (Alinari/Art Resource)

2-17 Altar of Zeus, Pergamon, c. 181–159 B.C. (Staatliche Museen zu Berlin, Antiken-Sammlung/ Photographische Abteilung)

2-18 Detail of Altar of Zeus, Zeus Fighting Three Giants. (Staatliche Museen zu Berlin, Antiken Sammlung Photographische Abteilung)

Another example of later Greek art is the great Altar of Zeus at Pergamon (Fig. 2-17). It was part of an architectural complex radically different from that of the Athenian Acropolis, and the form of the altar itself gives an idea of the many ways in which the Greek columnar orders and architectural details could be used to create new buildings and public spaces. The actual space of the altar is raised above the frieze, which has come down off the walls of the temple and out to the steps where the figures could be more easily seen and understood. The figures themselves are much more dramatic and graphically expressive than those of the *Panathenae.* Consider the striking differences of scale, depth of relief, and movement of figures (Fig. 2-18). In this detail of Zeus fighting three giants, the forms themselves seem almost trapped by the architectural framework, and as they struggle with each other they also seem to struggle to be free of the stones from which they are carved. The swirling drapery and heavy muscular bodies of these figures have an emotional power quite different from the calm mien imparted by sculptors of earlier generations.

For centuries, authorities in the field held that the diffusion of artists and builders, along with the evolution of new and more complex forms, represented a decline in the power and quality of Greek art and architecture, which reached its highest state in the classical period. Although modern scholarship questions this judgment against Hellenistic art (the term used to refer to the art of the third and second centuries B.C.), it is a tribute to the classical period that its goals and forms could provide sources and ideas for two millennia.

3

Classical Greece:
Drama

Along with its creativity in the visual arts, the age of Pericles saw a flourishing of drama. Drama, as we know it in the West, is in fact a creation of the Greeks. Theatergoing was more than a festive activity for Athenians; it was regarded as an important part of a citizen's education and was supported by the state. *Tragedies* and *comedies*, as well as other theatrical events, were performed annually at the festival of Dionysus, the god of wine, fertility, and ecstasy. The Athenian theatergoer, rather than going out for an evening's entertainment as we do, would devote a whole day to this activity. During the festival of Dionysus, which lasted for several days, business activities would cease, prisoners would be released from jail, and everyone—young, old, rich, poor, male, female, free, slave—would congregate at daybreak in a type of outdoor auditorium from which our football stadiums have been developed. There they would sit on stone benches, often to watch three tragedies, a *satyr play* (a grotesque skit in which the actors wore horses' tails and ears), and a comedy. The ruins of the theater of Dionysus on the Acropolis and the better-preserved theater at Epidaurus (Fig. 3-1) give us a clear idea of the circular orchestra, where the chorus sang and danced, and the *theatron*, the horseshoe-shaped area for the audience. A *skene*, or backdrop against which the actors performed, would have been set up in the back of the orchestra, facing the audience. Acoustics in this theater are still remarkable. A clear voice from the orchestra is deflected by the stone sides and can be heard without any form of artificial amplification.

Even though the Athenian theatergoer's experience was different from ours, it is recognizable to us because it is at the base of our own experience with the theater. We are all familiar with actors who act out a story and come into conflict with each other, but fifth-century B.C. Athens was, as far as we know, the first place in the world where this type of performance had been or was being staged. How did it come to be? Was the drama someone's invention or a long-standing development? It should be stated immediately that no one knows the definitive answer to this question. We can best examine it in relation to the two principal forms themselves, tragedy and comedy.

The Development of Tragedy

Tragedy developed into a full-fledged dramatic form sometime before the classical age and earlier than comedy. Τραγωιδια *(tragoidia)* in Greek comes from words meaning "goat" and "song." For this reason it has been assumed that tragedy developed from "goat songs" or choric performances similar to, or identical with, the grotesque satyr plays mentioned earlier. According to this theory, the serious play that we now know as tragedy would have begun as a kind of ecstatic comedy, perhaps far from Athens, in the Peloponnesus. Since tragedy was performed at the festival of Dionysus, many have also assumed that it grew out of some sort of religious ritual. According to one of these theories,

3–1 Epidaurus, theater from above. Polykleitos the Younger, c. 350 B.C. (Eugene Brown)

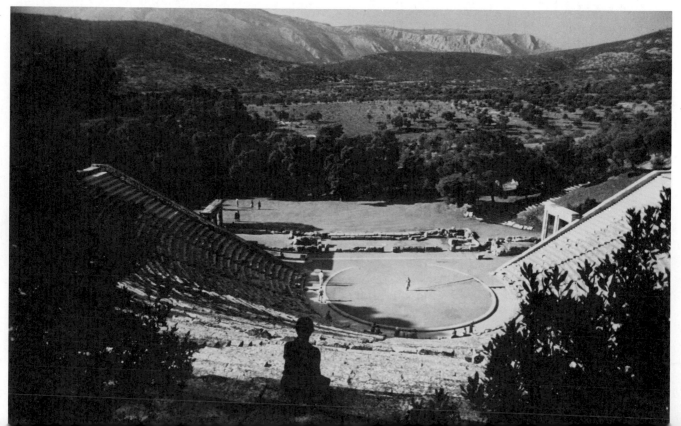

the chants of the priest and the response of the worshipers gave rise to the actors and chorus respectively. A recent theory holds that Greek tragedy had nothing to do with religious rituals but was essentially the creation of the first man of the theater, Thespis, who created drama out of poetic recitations of stories from Homer.

The tragedies written by Thespis probably had only one actor, along with a chorus. The actor, who probably represented an epic hero from Homer, would have to present his own story, which would be concentrated on his *pathos*, or suffering. The chorus would begin the play with a hymn to the gods and end with a lamentation over the hero. The *aulos*, a type of oboe and the characteristic instrument of the Dionysian cult, was employed in the performance of elegies, or songs of mourning; and it is likely that it was also used for instrumental preludes and interludes in the drama. In between the short scenes or *episodes* during which the hero spoke, the chorus would sing lyrics as a comment on his sufferings.

The Role of Music and Dance in Tragedy

From the beginning, tragedy was intimately associated with the arts of music and dance. The Greek word for *chorus*, which comes from the verb "to dance," indicates that the choruses were originally groups of dancers as well as singers (all men, as were the actors). It is probable that individual actors danced, too. Although there is little evidence on what the dances were like, we do know that they were mimetic; that is, they mimed or imitated the action of the play. The use of the hands was very important in expressing emotion, just as it is in oriental dancing today.

Music, instrumental as well as choral, also played an important role in creating emotional effects in tragedy. Just as the lyre was the instrument of lyric poetry, the aulos, a double-reeded wind instrument, was seen as most appropriate for tragedy. It had a shrill, piercing tone, perhaps associated with the ecstatic worship of Dionysus. The Greeks composed music in several *modes*, scales whose organization of notes differs from our modern major and minor system. Each mode was said to produce a special kind of feeling. In modern music, we distinguish between the forceful major mode and the wistful or melancholy minor mode. The Greek theory of modes was more complicated. The Dorian mode was considered manly and strong, appropriate for the training of young men, whereas the emotional Mixolydian mode was considered piercing and suitable for lamentations. Both, however, were appropriate for tragedy. The Greeks, as we will see in the section on philosophy, had great faith in the ability of music to influence and mold the characters of human beings. Unfortunately, very little Greek music remains—none from the classical period—so we can only conjecture what the total spectacle of an Athenian drama would have been like.

The Principal Greek Tragedians

Aeschylus The first tragedian whose plays are known to us is Aeschylus, who lived from 525 to 456 B.C. and thus participated in the growth and the glory of Athens. He was proud of having fought at the battle of Marathon. Aeschylus had the genius to add a second actor to the tragic form; thus, in his plays two actors appear at once on the stage. There is still a principal hero, whose sufferings are the main subject of the tragedy, but now he can be seen interacting with other human beings. The chorus, though, is still of major importance in the dramas of Aeschylus, who was himself a musician and was said to have been most attentive in fitting his choral songs to music. Aeschylus' most famous work is the trilogy, or series of three plays, entitled the *Oresteia* (Orestes plays). The first play in the trilogy is *Agamemnon*, the name of the king of Mycenae and leader of the Greeks in the Trojan War. In the play Agamemnon returns from the war, a glorious hero, only to be murdered by his wife Clytemnestra. In the second play, *The Libation Bearers*, Agamemnon's son Orestes avenges his father's death by killing his mother and her lover. In the final part of the trilogy Orestes is pursued by the Eumenides, horrible furies who torment him because of the slaying of his mother; but he is finally put on trial, judged, and acquitted by Athena, the patron goddess of Athens. The outcome of the trilogy shows the belief in law and the new system of justice developing in Athens.

Aeschylus wrote about ninety tragedies altogether. Besides the *Oresteia* those that survive are *The Persians*, *The Seven Against Thebes*, *Prometheus Bound*, and *The Suppliants*. The plots of all of Aeschylus' tragedies are extremely simple, and the characters are not what we would call "well rounded," but rather embodiments of a single passion. Everything is concentrated on the tragic event and the emotional and spiritual meaning of that event. This simplicity and concentration is, as we have seen in other art forms, part of what we mean by classical. Aeschylus' plays, in their spareness and grandeur, have been compared to early classical sculpture such as the *Kritios Boy*.

Sophocles   Sophocles (496–406 B.C.), a younger contemporary of Aeschylus, further developed the tragic form by adding a third actor. During his long life he wrote about 125 plays, of which only eight have come down to us. Of these, the best known are the plays of the Oedipus cycle: *Antigone*, *Oedipus Rex*, and *Oedipus at Colonus*. Unlike the *Oresteia*, these plays were not written as a trilogy but at different points of Sophocles' career. They are thus meant to be performed as individual plays. It is *Oedipus Rex*, the most renowned of all Greek tragedies, that we will study in detail here. Sophocles' characters, while maintaining a sense of classical balance and restraint, seem more human and alive than those of Aeschylus. They may be compared to "high" classical sculpture. The chorus has less importance relative to the actors than in Aeschylus' drama, but we should bear in mind that music and dance still played a vital role. Sophocles was himself a dancer.

Euripides   The next great tragedian, Euripides (480–406 B.C.), began to break out of the limits of classicism by creating more realistic characters and more complex plots. The traditional critical judgment on Euripides and his older contemporary holds that "Sophocles shows man as he ought to be and Euripides shows man as he is." Euripides' interest in individual psychology and in extreme real-life situations makes him in many ways closer to modern sensibilities. Although, like all ancient Greek playwrights, he uses old myths as the basis for his plots, Euripides appears to many readers as a religious skeptic or even an atheist. Euripides

also wrote an *Orestes*, which differs considerably from the trilogy by Aeschylus. Like all great psychological writers, he had a considerable interest in women, as shown in plays such as *Hippolytus*, which treats the myth of Phaedra driven mad by love, *The Trojan Women*, and *Medea*. The realism, emotionalism, and individuality of Euripides' characters make them comparable to postclassical or Hellenistic sculptures.

Oedipus: Legend and Tragedy

It is Sophocles, among these three tragedians, who now seems most representative of the cultural spirit of Athens in its classical, Periclean age. His *Oedipus Tyrannus*, here translated as the Latin word for king, *rex*, was probably first performed soon after a plague that swept over Athens in 429 B.C. Although the action is set in Greece's remote, legendary past in the city of Thebes, the Athenian audience would have identified immediately with the plague that has fallen like a curse on that city as the play opens. Through the writings of Aristotle, *Oedipus Rex* has come to stand for the most nearly perfect example of classical tragedy in the Western humanistic tradition.

One important notion to bear in mind while reading a Greek tragedy is that, unlike modern audiences, the Greeks who attended the festival of Dionysus did not attend a play for its plot suspense or to find out "what happens next." Today, when recommending a movie to a friend, we do not tell the plot for fear of spoiling it for him. Greek tragedies were all based on myths or legends that the theatergoers already knew. Thus, when they went to see *Oedipus*, they did not wonder what the play would be about, but rather what Sophocles had done with an old, familiar story. Since the tragedies at the festival of Dionysus were presented as a contest, the judges would also choose the best three tragedies on the basis of how well the already given material had been worked into dramatic form. It will therefore be useful to know something about the myth of Oedipus before approaching the tragedy.

The story takes place in a much earlier period of Greek history, when the city-states had been ruled by kings. The city of Thebes, it was told, was ruled by King Laius

(Laïos) and his queen, Jocasta (Iokastê). Thebes was founded by Laius' ancestor Cadmus, who was cursed by the gods and told that all of his descendants would receive some form of this curse. Thus Laius was told by a prophet of the god Apollo that he and Jocasta would bear a son who would kill his father and marry his mother. Hoping to avert this fate, the king and queen asked one of their shepherds to take their first-born son to Mount Cithaeron (Kithairon) near Thebes, to leave the baby to be exposed to die. The shepherd, out of pity for the child, gave him to a slave from the Greek city of Corinth, on the other side of the mountain, hoping that he would remain in that city and thus have no chance to fulfill the dreadful prophecy. The child is, of course, Oedipus, whose name means "swollen foot," a deformity he acquired from the pins put in his feet when he was left to die. He grows up believing that he is the natural son of King Polybus (Polybos) and Queen Meropê of Corinth, but one day he, too, receives a prophecy declaring that he will kill his father and marry his mother. He then flees Corinth and vows never to see his parents again.

During his travels Oedipus arrives at the outskirts of Thebes. There he gets into a quarrel with an old man whom he kills in a fit of anger—the man is Laius. He then finds that Thebes is under the control of a monster called the Sphinx, who has stationed herself outside the city and demands a yearly tribute from its citizens. Her power over Thebes can only be overcome if someone answers her riddle: "What walks on four legs in the morning, on two in the afternoon, and on three in the evening and is strongest when it uses the fewest number of legs?" Oedipus solves the riddle: the answer is *man*, who crawls on all fours as a baby, walks on two legs as an adult, and with a stick as an old man. Oedipus is hailed in Thebes as the savior of the city and given the hand of Laius' widow, Queen Jocasta, in marriage. Sophocles' play opens several years after this event, at a time when the city is again in peril and the people again look to Oedipus to help them. This time the trouble is a plague, a disease that is spreading among the people of Thebes, killing many of them.

The legend of Oedipus, no doubt originally an oral tale, contains many of the elements found in familiar folk or fairy tales—the curse, the prophecies, the riddle, and the hero-savior. There are numerous imaginable ways of treating this material. Sophocles' task was to mold it into the form of tragedy.

Unlike the oral folk tale that opens with "once upon a time," Sophocles does not begin the story at the beginning. Since Homer, it has been the rule in Western drama and fiction to begin "in the middle of things." *Oedipus* begins in the midst of a tense situation that demands a solution: a plague is raging; what will the king do? In fact, Sophocles begins his story after the important events have already occurred. The action of the play takes place in less than a day; yet the entire life of Oedipus, from his birth to his preparation for death, is brought into the development. Also, although we hear about Corinth and other parts of Thebes, the stage setting is in only one place—just outside the palace of the king and queen. There is only one plot or action in the play—no subplots or other distractions. There is certainly no comic relief, as found in Shakespeare. This simplicity of structure and unity of tone contribute to the play's classical quality. Just as in the Parthenon or the statue of *The Spearbearer*, everything nonessential is stripped away. What is left is a clear and balanced presentation of the essence of an aspect of life, rather than a realistic "slice of life." Part of the force and the impact of Greek tragedy lies in this classical simplicity.

If most of the story of Oedipus has taken place before the play begins, what *is* the plot or action of this tragedy? Most of it lies in the discovery of previous events. In this sense it resembles a detective story that opens after the crime has been committed. Oedipus begins by trying to find the answer to the question, "Who killed King Laius?" He ends by asking, and then answering, a much more profound question, "Who am I?" His tragedy, or his downfall, occurs when he finds the answer to his questions. As you read the play, notice how Sophocles builds up to the climactic point step by step. Try to determine, too, what emotional effect the tragic discovery of Oedipus has on you, the reader or spectator, and whether or not this changes by the end of the play. Notice how Sophocles has interpreted and portrayed the character of Oedipus. Finally, try to define for yourself what constitutes the personal tragedy of Oedipus and what makes the play a tragedy. This translation is by Dudley Fitts and Robert Fitzgerald.

SOPHOCLES

Oedipus Rex

CHARACTERS

OEDIPUS, *King of Thebes, supposed son of Polybos and Meropê, King and Queen of Corinth*
IOKASTÊ, *wife of Oedipus and widow of the late King Laïos*
KREON, *brother of Iokastê, a prince of Thebes*
TEIRESIAS, *a blind seer who serves Apollo*
PRIEST
MESSENGER, *from Corinth*
SHEPHERD, *former servant of Laïos*
SECOND MESSENGER, *from the palace*
CHORUS OF THEBAN ELDERS
CHORAGOS, *leader of the Chorus*
ANTIGONE *and* ISMENE, *young daughters of Oedipus and Iokastê. They appear in the Éxodos but do not speak.*
SUPPLIANTS, GUARDS, SERVANTS

THE SCENE.   *Before the palace of* OEDIPUS, *King of Thebes. A central door and two lateral doors open onto a platform which runs the length of the façade. On the platform, right and left, are altars; and three steps lead down into the orchêstra or chorus-ground. At the beginning of the action these steps are crowded by suppliants who have brought branches and chaplets of olive leaves and who sit in various attitudes of despair.* OEDIPUS *enters.*

PROLOGUE

OEDIPUS   My children, generations of the living
  In the line of Kadmos,[1] nursed at his ancient hearth:
  Why have you strewn yourselves before these altars
  In supplication, with your boughs and garlands?
  The breath of incense rises from the city
  With a sound of prayer and lamentation.
                                          Children,
  I would not have you speak through messengers,
  And therefore I have come myself to hear you—
  I, Oedipus, who bear the famous name.
  (*To a* PRIEST) You, there, since you are eldest in the
    company,
  Speak for them all, tell me what preys upon you,
  Whether you come in dread, or crave some blessing:
  Tell me, and never doubt that I will help you
  In every way I can; I should be heartless
  Were I not moved to find you suppliant here.

---

[1] Founder of Thebes.

PRIEST   Great Oedipus, O powerful king of Thebes!
  You see how all the ages of our people
  Cling to your altar steps: here are boys
  Who can barely stand alone, and here are priests
  By weight of age, as I am a priest of God,
  And young men chosen from those yet unmarried;
  As for the others, all that multitude,
  They wait with olive chaplets in the squares,
  At the two shrines of Pallas, and where Apollo
  Speaks in the glowing embers.
                              Your own eyes
  Must tell you: Thebes is tossed on a murdering sea
  And can not lift her head from the death surge.
  A rust consumes the buds and fruits of the earth;
  The herds are sick; children die unborn,
  And labor is vain. The god of plague and pyre
  Raids like detestable lightning through the city,
  And all the house of Kadmos is laid waste,
  All emptied, and all darkened: Death alone
  Battens upon the misery of Thebes.

  You are not one of the immortal gods, we know;
  Yet we have come to you to make our prayer
  As to the man surest in mortal ways
  And wisest in the ways of God. You saved us
  From the Sphinx, that flinty singer, and the tribute
  We paid to her so long; yet you were never
  Better informed than we, nor could we teach you:
  A god's touch, it seems, enabled you to help us.

  Therefore, O mighty power, we turn to you:
  Find us our safety, find us a remedy,
  Whether by counsel of the gods or of men.
  A king of wisdom tested in the past
  Can act in a time of troubles, and act well.
  Noblest of men, restore
  Life to your city! Think how all men call you
  Liberator for your boldness long ago;
  Ah, when your years of kingship are remembered,
  Let them not say *We rose, but later fell*—
  Keep the State from going down in the storm!
  Once, years ago, with happy augury,
  You brought us fortune; be the same again!
  No man questions your power to rule the land:
  But rule over men, not over a dead city!
  Ships are only hulls, high walls are nothing,
  When no life moves in the empty passageways.

OEDIPUS   Poor children! You may be sure I know
    All that you longed for in your coming here.
    I know that you are deathly sick; and yet,
    Sick as you are, not one is as sick as I.
    Each of you suffers in himself alone
    His anguish, not another's; but my spirit
    Groans for the city, for myself, for you.

    I was not sleeping, you are not waking me.
    No, I have been in tears for a long while
    And in my restless thought walked many ways.
    In all my search I found one remedy,
    And I have adopted it: I have sent Kreon,
    Son of Menoikeus, brother of the queen,
    To Delphi, Apollo's place of revelation,
    To learn there, if he can,
    What act or pledge of mine may save the city.
    I have counted the days, and now, this very day,
    I am troubled, for he has overstayed his time.
    What is he doing? He has been gone too long.
    Yet whenever he comes back, I should do ill
    Not to take any action the god orders.

PRIEST   It is a timely promise. At this instant
    They tell me Kreon is here.

OEDIPUS   O Lord Apollo!
    May his news be fair as his face is radiant!

PRIEST   Good news, I gather! he is crowned with bay,
    The chaplet is thick with berries.

OEDIPUS   We shall soon know;
    He is near enough to hear us now.

    (*Enter* KREON)

                      O prince:
Brother: son of Menoikeus:
    What answer do you bring us from the god?

KREON   A strong one. I can tell you, great afflictions
    Will turn out well, if they are taken well.

OEDIPUS   What was the oracle? These vague words
    Leave me still hanging between hope and fear.

KREON   Is it your pleasure to hear me with all these
    Gathered around us? I am prepared to speak,
    But should we not go in?

OEDIPUS   Speak to them all,
    It is for them I suffer, more than for myself.

KREON   Then I will tell you what I heard at Delphi.
    In plain words

The god commands us to expel from the land of
    Thebes
    An old defilement we are sheltering.
    It is a deathly thing, beyond cure;
    We must not let it feed upon us longer.

OEDIPUS   What defilement? How shall we rid ourselves
    of it?

KREON   By exile or death, blood for blood. It was
    Murder that brought the plague-wind on the city.

OEDIPUS   Murder of whom? Surely the god has named
    him?

KREON   My lord: Laïos once ruled this land,
    Before you came to govern us.

OEDIPUS   I know;
    I learned of him from others; I never saw him.

KREON   He was murdered; and Apollo commands us
    now
    To take revenge upon whoever killed him.

OEDIPUS   Upon whom? Where are they? Where shall
    we find a clue
    To solve that crime, after so many years?

KREON   Here in this land, he said. Search reveals
    Things that escape an inattentive man.

OEDIPUS   Tell me: Was Laïos murdered in his house,
    Or in the fields, or in some foreign country?

KREON   He said he planned to make a pilgrimage.
    He did not come home again.

OEDIPUS   And was there no one,
    No witness, no companion, to tell what happened?

KREON   They were all killed but one, and he got away
    So frightened that he could remember one thing
    only.

OEDIPUS   What was the one thing? One may be the
    key
    To everything, if we resolve to use it.

KREON   He said that a band of highwaymen attacked
    them,
    Outnumbered them, and overwhelmed the king.

OEDIPUS   Strange, that a highwayman should be so
    daring—
    Unless some faction here bribed him to do it.

KREON   We thought of that. But after Laïos' death
    New troubles arose and we had no avenger.

OEDIPUS   What troubles could prevent your hunting
    down the killers?

KREON   The riddling Sphinx's song

Made us deaf to all mysteries but her own.

OEDIPUS   Then once more I must bring what is dark to
    light.

It is most fitting that Apollo shows,
As you do, this compunction for the dead.
You shall see how I stand by you, as I should,
Avenging this country and the god as well,
And not as though it were for some distant friend,
But for my own sake, to be rid of evil.
Whoever killed King Laïos might—who knows?—
Lay violent hands even on me—and soon.
I act for the murdered king in my own interest.

Come, then, my children: leave the altar steps,
Lift up your olive boughs!
                        One of you go
And summon the people of Kadmos to gather here.
I will do all that I can; you may tell them that.

(*Exit a* PAGE)

So, with the help of God,
We shall be saved—or else indeed we are lost.

PRIEST   Let us rise, children. It was for this we came,
And now the king has promised it.
Phoibos[2] has sent us an oracle; may he descend
Himself to save us and drive out the plague.

(*Exeunt* OEDIPUS *and* KREON *into the palace by the central door. The* PRIEST *and the* SUPPLIANTS *disperse R and L. After a short pause the* CHORUS *enters the* orchêstra)

PARODOS [3]

Strophe 1

CHORUS   What is God singing in his profound
    Delphi of gold and shadow?

---

[2] Apollo.

[3] *Parodos* is the song or ode chanted by the chorus on their entry. It is accompanied by dancing and music played on an oboe. The chorus, in this play, represents elders of the city of Thebes. They remain on stage (on a level lower than the principal actors) for the remainder of the play. The choral odes and dances serve to separate one scene from another (there was no curtain in Greek theater) as well as to comment on the action, reinforce the emotion, and interpret the situation. The chorus also performs dance movements during certain portions of the scenes themselves. *Strophe* and *antistrophe* are terms denoting the movement and countermovement of the chorus from one side of their playing area to the other. When the chorus participates in dialogue with the other characters, their lines are spoken by the Choragos, their leader.

What oracle for Thebes, the sunwhipped city?
Fear unjoints me, the roots of my heart tremble.
Now I remember, O Healer, your power, and
    wonder:
Will you send doom like a sudden cloud, or weave it
Like nightfall of the past?
Speak to me, tell me, O
Child of golden Hope, immortal Voice.

Antistrophe 1

Let me pray to Athenê, the immortal daughter of
    Zeus,
And to Artemis her sister
Who keeps her famous throne in the market ring,
And to Apollo, archer from distant heaven—
O gods, descend! Like three streams leap against
The fires of our grief, the fires of darkness;
Be swift to bring us rest!
As in the old time from the brilliant house
Of air you stepped to save us, come again!

Strophe 2

Now our afflictions have no end,
Now all our stricken host lies down
And no man fights off death with his mind;
The noble plowland bears no grain,
And groaning mothers can not bear—
See, how our lives like birds take wing,
Like sparks that fly when a fire soars,
To the shore of the god of evening.

Antistrophe 2

The plague burns on, it is pitiless,
Though pallid children laden with death
Lie unwept in the stony ways,
And old gray women by every path
Flock to the strand about the altars
There to strike their breasts and cry
Worship of Phoibos in wailing prayers:
Be kind, God's golden child!

Strophe 3

There are no swords in this attack by fire,
No shields, but we are ringed with cries.
Send the besieger plunging from our homes
Into the vast sea-room of the Atlantic
Or into the waves that foam eastward of Thrace—
For the day ravages what the night spares—

Destroy our enemy, lord of the thunder!
Let him be riven by lightning from heaven!

Antistrophe 3

Phoibos Apollo, stretch the sun's bowstring,
That golden cord, until it sing for us,
Flashing arrows in heaven!
                              Artemis, Huntress,
Race with flaring lights upon our mountains!
O scarlet god, O golden-banded brow,
O Theban Bacchos in a storm of Maenads,

(*Enter* OEDIPUS, C)

Whirl upon Death, that all the Undying hate!
Come with blinding torches, come in joy!

SCENE I

OEDIPUS   Is this your prayer? It may be answered.
    Come,
    Listen to me, act as the crisis demands,
    And you shall have relief from all these evils.

    Until now I was a stranger to this tale,
    As I had been a stranger to the crime.
    Could I track down the murderer without a clue?
    But now, friends,
    As one who became a citizen after the murder,
    I make this proclamation to all Thebans:
    If any man knows by whose hand Laïos, son of
        Labdakos,
    Met his death, I direct that man to tell me
        everything,
    No matter what he fears for having so long withheld
        it.
    Let it stand as promised that no further trouble
    Will come to him, but he may leave the land in
        safety.

    Moreover: If anyone knows the murderer to be
        foreign,
    Let him not keep silent: he shall have his reward
        from me.
    However, if he does conceal it; if any man
    Fearing for his friend or for himself disobeys this
        edict,
    Hear what I propose to do:

    I solemnly forbid the people of this country,

Where power and throne are mine, ever to receive
    that man
Or speak to him, no matter who he is, or let him
Join in sacrifice, lustration, or in prayer.
I decree that he be driven from every house,
Being, as he is, corruption itself to us: the Delphic
Voice of Apollo has pronounced this revelation.
Thus I associate myself with the oracle
And take the side of the murdered king.

As for the criminal, I pray to God—
Whether it be a lurking thief, or one of a number—
I pray that that man's life be consumed in evil and
    wretchedness.
And as for me, this curse applies no less
If it should turn out that the culprit is my guest here,
Sharing my hearth.
                    You have heard the penalty.
I lay it on you now to attend to this
For my sake, for Apollo's, for the sick
Sterile city that heaven has abandoned.
Suppose the oracle had given you no command:
Should this defilement go uncleansed for ever?
You should have found the murderer: your king,
A noble king, had been destroyed!
                              Now I,
Having the power that he held before me,
Having his bed, begetting children there
Upon his wife, as he would have, had he lived—
Their son would have been my children's brother,
If Laïos had had luck in fatherhood!
(And now his bad fortune has struck him down)—
I say I take the son's part, just as though
I were his son, to press the fight for him
And see it won! I'll find the hand that brought
Death to Labdakos' and Polydoros' child,
Heir of Kadmos' and Agenor's line.[4]
And as for those who fail me,
May the gods deny them the fruit of the earth,
Fruit of the womb, and may they rot utterly!
Let them be wretched as we are wretched, and worse!

For you, for loyal Thebans, and for all
Who find my actions right, I pray the favor
Of justice, and of all the immortal gods.

---

[4] Father, grandfather, great-grandfather, and great-great-grandfather
of Laïos.

CHORAGOS   Since I am under oath, my lord, I swear
   I did not do the murder, I can not name
   The murderer. Phoibos ordained the search;
   Why did he not say who the culprit was?
OEDIPUS   An honest question. But no man in the
       world
   Can make the gods do more than the gods will.
CHORAGOS   There is an alternative, I think—
OEDIPUS   Tell me.
   Any or all, you must not fail to tell me.
CHORAGOS   A lord clairvoyant to the lord Apollo,
   As we all know, is the skilled Teiresias.
   One might learn much about this from him,
       Oedipus.
OEDIPUS   I am not wasting time:
   Kreon spoke of this, and I have sent for him—
   Twice, in fact; it is strange that he is not here.
CHORAGOS   The other matter—that old report—seems
       useless.
OEDIPUS   What was that? I am interested in all reports.
CHORAGOS   The king was said to have been killed by
       highwaymen.
OEDIPUS   I know. But we have no witnesses to that.
CHORAGOS   If the killer can feel a particle of dread,
   Your curse will bring him out of hiding!
OEDIPUS   No.
   The man who dared that act will fear no curse.

(*Enter the blind seer* TEIRESIAS, *led by a* PAGE)

CHORAGOS   But there is one man who may detect the
       criminal.
   This is Teiresias, this is the holy prophet
   In whom, alone of all men, truth was born.
OEDIPUS   Teiresias: seer: student of mysteries,
   Of all that's taught and all that no man tells,
   Secrets of Heaven and secrets of the earth:
   Blind though you are, you know the city lies
   Sick with plague; and from this plague, my lord,
   We find that you alone can guard or save us.

   Possibly you did not hear the messengers?
   Apollo, when we sent to him,
   Sent us back word that this great pestilence
   Would lift, but only if we established clearly
   The identity of those who murdered Laïos.
   They must be killed or exiled.

                              Can you use
   Birdflight[5] or any art of divination
   To purify yourself, and Thebes, and me
   From this contagion? We are in your hands.
   There is no fairer duty
   Than that of helping others in distress.
TEIRESIAS   How dreadful knowledge of the truth
       can be
   When there's no help in truth! I knew this well,
   But did not act on it: else I should not have come.
OEDIPUS   What is troubling you? Why are your eyes so
       cold?
TEIRESIAS   Let me go home. Bear your own fate, and
       I'll
   Bear mine. It is better so: trust what I say.
OEDIPUS   What you say is ungracious and unhelpful
   To your native country. Do not refuse to speak.
TEIRESIAS   When it comes to speech, your own is
       neither temperate
   Nor opportune. I wish to be more prudent.
OEDIPUS   In God's name, we all beg you—
TEIRESIAS   You are all ignorant.
   No; I will never tell you what I know.
   Now it is my misery; then, it would be yours.
OEDIPUS   What! You do know something, and will not
       tell us?
   You would betray us all and wreck the State?
TEIRESIAS   I do not intend to torture myself, or you.
   Why persist in asking? You will not persuade me.
OEDIPUS   What a wicked old man you are! You'd try a
       stone's
   Patience! Out with it! Have you no feeling at all?
TEIRESIAS   You call me unfeeling. If you could only
       see
   The nature of your own feelings . . .
OEDIPUS   Why,
   Who would not feel as I do? Who could endure
   Your arrogance toward the city?
TEIRESIAS   What does it matter?
   Whether I speak or not, it is bound to come.
OEDIPUS   Then, if "it" is bound to come, you are
       bound to tell me.
TEIRESIAS   No, I will not go on. Rage as you please.

————
[5] Prophets predicted the future or divined the unknown by observing
the flight of birds.

OEDIPUS   Rage? Why not!
       And I'll tell you what I think:
 You planned it, you had it done, you all but
 Killed him with your own hands: if you had eyes,
 I'd say the crime was yours, and yours alone.
TEIRESIAS   So? I charge you, then,
 Abide by the proclamation you have made:
 From this day forth
 Never speak again to these men or to me;
 You yourself are the pollution of this country.
OEDIPUS   You dare say that! Can you possibly think you have
 Some way of going free, after such insolence?
TEIRESIAS   I have gone free. It is the truth sustains me.
OEDIPUS   Who taught you shamelessness? It was not your craft.
TEIRESIAS   You did. You made me speak. I did not want to.
OEDIPUS   Speak what? Let me hear it again more clearly.
TEIRESIAS   Was it not clear before? Are you tempting me?
OEDIPUS   I did not understand it. Say it again.
TEIRESIAS   I say that you are the murderer whom you seek.
OEDIPUS   Now twice you have spat out infamy. You'll pay for it!
TEIRESIAS   Would you care for more? Do you wish to be really angry?
OEDIPUS   Say what you will. Whatever you say is worthless.
TEIRESIAS   I say you live in hideous shame with those
 Most dear to you. You can not see the evil.
OEDIPUS   Can you go on babbling like this for ever?
TEIRESIAS   I can, if there is power in truth.
OEDIPUS   There is:
 But not for you, not for you,
 You sightless, witless, senseless, mad old man!
TEIRESIAS   You are the madman. There is no one here
 Who will not curse you soon, as you curse me.
OEDIPUS   You child of total night! I would not touch you;
 Neither would any man who sees the sun.
TEIRESIAS   True: it is not from you my fate will come.
 That lies within Apollo's competence,
 As it is his concern.

OEDIPUS   Tell me, who made
 These fine discoveries? Kreon? or someone else?
TEIRESIAS   Kreon is no threat. You weave your own doom.
OEDIPUS   Wealth, power, craft of statesmanship!
 Kingly position, everywhere admired!
 What savage envy is stored up against these,
 If Kreon, whom I trusted, Kreon my friend,
 For this great office which the city once
 Put in my hands unsought—if for this power
 Kreon desires in secret to destroy me!

 He has bought this decrepit fortune-teller, this
 Collector of dirty pennies, this prophet fraud—
 Why, he is no more clairvoyant than I am!
          Tell us:
 Has your mystic mummery ever approached the truth?
 When that hellcat the Sphinx was performing here,
 What help were you to these people?
 Her magic was not for the first man who came along:
 It demanded a real exorcist. Your birds—
 What good were they? or the gods, for the matter of that?
 But I came by,
 Oedipus, the simple man, who knows nothing—
 I thought it out for myself, no birds helped me!
 And this is the man you think you can destroy,
 That you may be close to Kreon when he's king!
 Well, you and your friend Kreon, it seems to me,
 Will suffer most. If you were not an old man,
 You would have paid already for your plot.
CHORAGOS   We can not see that his words or yours
 Have been spoken except in anger, Oedipus,
 And of anger we have no need. How to accomplish
 The god's will best: that is what most concerns us.
TEIRESIAS   You are a king. But where argument's concerned
 I am your man, as much a king as you.
 I am not your servant, but Apollo's.
 I have no need of Kreon or Kreon's name.

 Listen to me. You mock my blindness, do you?
 But I say that you, with both your eyes, are blind:
 You can not see the wretchedness of your life,
 Nor in whose house you live, no, nor with whom.
 Who are your father and mother? Can you tell me?

You do not even know the blind wrongs
That you have done them, on earth and in the world
　　below.
But the double lash of your parents' curse will whip
　　you
Out of this land some day, with only night
Upon your precious eyes.
Your cries then—where will they not be heard?
What fastness of Kithairon[6] will not echo them?
And that bridal-descant of yours—you'll know it
　　then,
The song they sang when you came here to Thebes
And found your misguided berthing.
All this, and more, that you can not guess at now,
Will bring you to yourself among your children.

Be angry, then. Curse Kreon. Curse my words.
I tell you, no man that walks upon the earth
Shall be rooted out more horribly than you.

OEDIPUS   Am I to bear this from him?—Damnation
Take you! Out of this place! Out of my sight!

TEIRESIAS   I would not have come at all if you had not
　　asked me.

OEDIPUS   Could I have told that you'd talk nonsense,
　　that
You'd come here to make a fool of yourself, and of
　　me?

TEIRESIAS   A fool? Your parents thought me sane
　　enough.

OEDIPUS   My parents again!—Wait: who were my
　　parents?

TEIRESIAS   This day will give you a father, and break
　　your heart.

OEDIPUS   Your infantile riddles! Your damned
　　abracadabra!

TEIRESIAS   You were a great man once at solving
　　riddles.

OEDIPUS   Mock me with that if you like; you will find
　　it true.

TEIRESIAS   It was true enough. It brought about your
　　ruin.

OEDIPUS   But if it saved this town?

TEIRESIAS   (to the PAGE)   Boy, give me your hand.

OEDIPUS   Yes, boy; lead him away.

—While you are here
We can do nothing. Go; leave us in peace.

TEIRESIAS   I will go when I have said what I have to
　　say.
How can you hurt me? And I tell you again:
The man you have been looking for all this time,
The damned man, the murderer of Laïos,
That man is in Thebes. To your mind he is foreign-
　　born,
But it will soon be shown that he is a Theban,
A revelation that will fail to please.

A blind man,
Who has his eyes now; a penniless man, who is rich
　　now;
And he will go tapping the strange earth with his
　　staff.
To the children with whom he lives now he will be
Brother and father—the very same; to her
Who bore him, son and husband—the very same
Who came to his father's bed, wet with his father's
　　blood.

Enough. Go think that over.
If later you find error in what I have said,
You may say that I have no skill in prophecy.

(Exit TEIRESIAS, led by his PAGE. OEDIPUS goes into the
palace)

ODE I

Strophe 1

CHORUS   The Delphic stone of prophecies
Remembers ancient regicide
And a still bloody hand.
That killer's hour of flight has come.
He must be stronger than riderless
Coursers of untiring wind,
For the son[7] of Zeus armed with his father's thunder
Leaps in lightning after him;
And the Furies hold his track, the sad Furies.

Antistrophe 1

Holy Parnassos'[8] peak of snow
Flashes and blinds that secret man,

---

[6] The mountain where Oedipus was taken to be exposed as an infant.

[7] Apollo.
[8] Mountain sacred to Apollo.

That all shall hunt him down:
Though he may roam the forest shade
Like a bull gone wild from pasture
To rage through glooms of stone.
Doom comes down on him; flight will not avail him;
For the world's heart calls him desolate,
And the immortal voices follow, for ever follow.

Strophe 2

But now a wilder thing is heard
From the old man skilled at hearing Fate in the wing-
    beat of a bird.
Bewildered as a blown bird, my soul hovers and can
    not find
Foothold in this debate, or any reason or rest of
    mind.
But no man ever brought—none can bring
Proof of strife between Thebes' royal house,
Labdakos' line, and the son of Polybos;
And never until now has any man brought word
Of Laïos' dark death staining Oedipus the King.

Antistrophe 2

Divine Zeus and Apollo hold
Perfect intelligence alone of all tales ever told;
And well though this diviner works, he works in his
    own night;
No man can judge that rough unknown or trust in
    second sight,
For wisdom changes hands among the wise.
Shall I believe my great lord criminal
At a raging word that a blind old man let fall?
I saw him, when the carrion woman[9] faced him of
    old,
Prove his heroic mind. These evil words are lies.

SCENE II

KREON   Men of Thebes:
  I am told that heavy accusations
  Have been brought against me by King Oedipus.

  I am not the kind of man to bear this tamely.

  If in these present difficulties
  He holds me accountable for any harm to him

---

[9] The Sphinx.

Through anything I have said or done—why, then,
I do not value life in this dishonor.
It is not as though this rumor touched upon
Some private indiscretion. The matter is grave.
The fact is that I am being called disloyal
To the State, to my fellow citizens, to my friends.
CHORAGOS   He may have spoken in anger, not from
    his mind.
KREON   But did you not hear him say I was the one
  Who seduced the old prophet into lying?
CHORAGOS   The thing was said: I do not know how
    seriously.
KREON   But you were watching him! Were his eyes
    steady?
  Did he look like a man in his right mind?
CHORAGOS   I do not know.
  I can not judge the behavior of great men.
  But here is the king himself.

(*Enter* OEDIPUS)

OEDIPUS   So you dared come back.
  Why? How brazen of you to come to my house,
  You murderer!
                  Do you think I do not know
  That you plotted to kill me, plotted to steal my
    throne?
  Tell me, in God's name: am I coward, a fool,
  That you should dream you could accomplish this?
  A fool who could not see your slippery game?
  A coward, not to fight back when I saw it?
  You are the fool, Kreon, are you not? hoping
  Without support or friends to get a throne?
  Thrones may be won or bought: you could do
    neither.
KREON   Now listen to me. You have talked; let me
    talk, too.
  You can not judge unless you know the facts.
OEDIPUS   You speak well: there is one fact; but I find
    it hard
  To learn from the deadliest enemy I have.
KREON   That above all I must dispute with you.
OEDIPUS   That above all I will not hear you deny.
KREON   If you think there is anything good in being
    stubborn
  Against all reason, then I say you are wrong.

OEDIPUS   If you think a man can sin against his own
    kind
And not be punished for it, I say you are mad.
KREON   I agree. But tell me: What have I done to you?
OEDIPUS   You advised me to send for that wizard, did
    you not?
KREON   I did. I should do it again.
OEDIPUS   Very well. Now tell me:
    How long has it been since Laïos—
KREON   What of Laïos?
OEDIPUS   Since he vanished in that onset by the road?
KREON   It was long ago, a long time.
OEDIPUS   And this prophet,
    Was he practicing here then?
KREON   He was; and with honor, as now.
OEDIPUS   Did he speak of me at that time?
KREON   He never did,
    At least, not when I was present.
OEDIPUS   But . . . the enquiry?
    I suppose you held one?
KREON   We did, but we learned nothing.
OEDIPUS   Why did the prophet not speak against me
    then?
KREON   I do not know; and I am the kind of man
Who holds his tongue when he has no facts to go on.
OEDIPUS   There's one fact that you know, and you
    could tell it.
KREON   What fact is that? If I know it, you shall have
    it.
OEDIPUS   If he were not involved with you, he could
    not say
That it was I who murdered Laïos.
KREON   If he says that, you are the one that knows
    it!—
But now it is my turn to question you.
OEDIPUS   Put your questions. I am no murderer.
KREON   First, then: You married my sister?
OEDIPUS   I married your sister.
KREON   And you rule the kingdom equally with her?
OEDIPUS   Everything that she wants she has from me.
KREON   And I am the third, equal to both of you?
OEDIPUS   That is why I call you a bad friend.
KREON   No. Reason it out, as I have done.
    Think of this first: Would any sane man prefer
    Power, with all a king's anxieties,
    To that same power and the grace of sleep?

Certainly not I.
I have never longed for the king's power—only his
    rights.
Would any wise man differ from me in this?
As matters stand, I have my way in everything
With your consent, and no responsibilities.
If I were king, I should be a slave to policy.

How could I desire a scepter more
Than what is now mine—untroubled influence?
No, I have not gone mad; I need no honors,
Except those with the perquisites I have now.
I am welcome everywhere; every man salutes me,
And those who want your favor seek my ear,
Since I know how to manage what they ask.
Should I exchange this ease for that anxiety?
Besides, no sober mind is treasonable.
I hate anarchy
And never would deal with any man who likes it.
Test what I have said. Go to the priestess
At Delphi, ask if I quoted her correctly.
And as for this other thing: if I am found
Guilty of treason with Teiresias,
Then sentence me to death. You have my word
It is a sentence I should cast my vote for—
But not without evidence!
                You do wrong
When you take good men for bad, bad men for good.
A true friend thrown aside—why, life itself
Is not more precious!
              In time you will know this well:
For time, and time alone, will show the just man,
Though scoundrels are discovered in a day.

CHORAGOS   This is well said, and a prudent man
    would ponder it.
Judgments too quickly formed are dangerous.
OEDIPUS   But is he not quick in his duplicity?
    And shall I not be quick to parry him?
    Would you have me stand still, hold my peace, and
    let
    This man win everything, through my inaction?
KREON   And you want—what is it, then? To banish
    me?
OEDIPUS   No, not exile. It is your death I want,
    So that all the world may see what treason means.

KREON   You will persist, then? You will not believe
        me?
OEDIPUS   How can I believe you?
KREON   Then you are a fool.
OEDIPUS   To save myself?
KREON   In justice, think of me.
OEDIPUS   You are evil incarnate.
KREON   But suppose that you are wrong?
OEDIPUS   Still I must rule.
KREON   But not if you rule badly.
OEDIPUS   O city, city!
KREON   It is my city, too!
CHORAGOS   Now, my lords, be still. I see the queen,
        Iokastê, coming from her palace chambers;
        And it is time she came, for the sake of you both.
        This dreadful quarrel can be resolved through her.

        (*Enter* IOKASTÊ)

IOKASTÊ   Poor foolish men, what wicked din is this?
        With Thebes sick to death, is it not shameful
        That you should rake some private quarrel up?
        (*To* OEDIPUS) Come into the house.
                                —And you, Kreon, go now:
        Let us have no more of this tumult over nothing.
KREON   Nothing? No, sister: what your husband plans
        for me
        Is one of two great evils: exile or death.
OEDIPUS   He is right.
                        Why, woman I have caught him squarely
        Plotting against my life.
KREON   No! Let me die
        Accurst if ever I have wished you harm!
IOKASTÊ   Ah, believe it, Oedipus!
        In the name of the gods, respect this oath of his
        For my sake, for the sake of these people here!

Strophe 1

CHORAGOS   Open your mind to her, my lord. Be ruled
        by her, I beg you!
OEDIPUS   What would you have me do?
CHORAGOS   Respect Kreon's word. He has never
        spoken like a fool,
        And now he has sworn an oath.
OEDIPUS   You know what you ask?
CHORAGOS   I do.
OEDIPUS   Speak on, then.

CHORAGOS   A friend so sworn should not be baited so,
        In blind malice, and without final proof
OEDIPUS   You are aware, I hope, that what you say
        Means death for me, or exile at the least.

Strophe 2

CHORAGOS   No, I swear by Helios, first in Heaven!
        May I die friendless and accurst,
        The worst of deaths, if ever I meant that!
                It is the withering fields
                        That hurt my sick heart:
                Must we bear all these ills,
                        And now your bad blood as well?
OEDIPUS   Then let him go. And let me die, if I must,
        Or be driven by him in shame from the land of
                Thebes.
        It is your unhappiness, and not his talk,
        That touches me.
                                As for him—
        Wherever he goes, hatred will follow him.
KREON   Ugly in yielding, as you were ugly in rage!
        Natures like yours chiefly torment themselves.
OEDIPUS   Can you not go? Can you not leave me?
KREON   I can.
        You do not know me; but the city knows me,
        And in its eyes I am just, if not in yours.

        (*Exit* KREON)

Antistrophe 1

CHORAGOS   Lady Iokastê, did you not ask the King to
        go to his chambers?
IOKASTÊ   First tell me what has happened.
CHORAGOS   There was suspicion without evidence;
        yet it rankled
        As even false charges will.
IOKASTÊ   On both sides?
CHORAGOS   On both.
IOKASTÊ   But what was said?
CHORAGOS   Oh let it rest, let it be done with!
        Have we not suffered enough?
OEDIPUS   You see to what your decency has brought
        you:
        You have made difficulties where my heart saw
        none.

Antistrophe 2

CHORAGOS   Oedipus, it is not once only I have told
   you—
You must know I should count myself unwise
To the point of madness, should I now forsake you—
      You, under whose hand,
         In the storm of another time,
         Our dear land sailed out free.
         But now stand fast at the helm!
IOKASTÊ   In God's name, Oedipus, inform your wife
   as well:
Why are you so set in this hard anger?
OEDIPUS   I will tell you, for none of these men
   deserves
My confidence as you do. It is Kreon's work,
His treachery, his plotting against me.
IOKASTÊ   Go on, if you can make this clear to me.
OEDIPUS   He charges me with the murder of Laïos.
IOKASTÊ   Has he some knowledge? Or does he speak
   from hearsay?
OEDIPUS   He would not commit himself to such a
   charge,
But he has brought in that damnable soothsayer
To tell his story.
IOKASTÊ   Set your mind at rest.
If it is a question of soothsayers, I tell you
That you will find no man whose craft gives
   knowledge
Of the unknowable.
               Here is my proof:
An oracle was reported to Laïos once
(I will not say from Phoibos himself, but from
His appointed ministers, at any rate)
That his doom would be death at the hands of his
   own son—
His son, born of his flesh and of mine!

Now, you remember the story: Laïos was killed
By marauding strangers where three highways meet;
But his child had not been three days in this world
Before the king had pierced the baby's ankles
And left him to die on a lonely mountainside.

Thus, Apollo never caused that child
To kill his father, and it was not Laïos' fate
To die at the hands of his son, as he had feared.
This is what prophets and prophecies are worth!

Have no dread of them.
               It is God himself
Who can show us what he wills, in his own way.
OEDIPUS   How strange a shadowy memory crossed my
   mind,
Just now while you were speaking; it chilled my
   heart.
IOKASTÊ   What do you mean? What memory do you
   speak of?
OEDIPUS   If I understand you, Laïos was killed
At a place where three roads meet.
IOKASTÊ   So it was said;
We have no later story.
OEDIPUS   Where did it happen?
IOKASTÊ   Phokis, it is called: at a place where the
   Theban Way
Divides into the roads toward Delphi and Daulia.
OEDIPUS   When?
IOKASTÊ   We had the news not long before you came
And proved the right to your succession here.
OEDIPUS   Ah, what net has God been weaving for me?
IOKASTÊ   Oedipus! Why does this trouble you?
OEDIPUS   Do not ask me yet.
First, tell me how Laïos looked, and tell me
How old he was.
IOKASTÊ   He was tall, his hair just touched
With white; his form was not unlike your own.
OEDIPUS   I think that I myself may be accurst
By my own ignorant edict.
IOKASTÊ   You speak strangely.
It makes me tremble to look at you, my king.
OEDIPUS   I am not sure that the blind man can not see.
But I should know better if you were to tell me—
IOKASTÊ   Anything—though I dread to hear you ask
   it.
OEDIPUS   Was the king lightly escorted, or did he ride
With a large company, as a ruler should?
IOKASTÊ   There were five men with him in all: one
   was a herald.
And a single chariot, which he was driving.
OEDIPUS   Alas, that makes it plain enough!
                           But who—
Who told you how it happened?
IOKASTÊ   A household servant,
The only one to escape.
OEDIPUS   And is he still

A servant of ours?

IOKASTÊ   No; for when he came back at last
And found you enthroned in the place of the dead
    king,
He came to me, touched my hand with his, and
    begged
That I would send him away to the frontier district
Where only the shepherds go—
As far away from the city as I could send him.
I granted his prayer; for although the man was a
    slave,
He had earned more than this favor at my hands.

OEDIPUS   Can he be called back quickly?

IOKASTÊ   Easily.
But why?

OEDIPUS   I have taken too much upon myself
Without enquiry; therefore I wish to consult him.

IOKASTÊ   Then he shall come.
                        But am I not one also
To whom you might confide these fears of yours?

OEDIPUS   That is your right; it will not be denied you,
Now least of all; for I have reached a pitch
Of wild foreboding. Is there anyone
To whom I should sooner speak?

Polybos of Corinth is my father.
My mother is a Dorian: Meropê.
I grew up chief among the men of Corinth
Until a strange thing happened—
Not worth my passion, it may be, but strange.
At a feast, a drunken man maundering in his cups
Cries out that I am not my father's son! [10]

I contained myself that night, though I felt anger
And a sinking heart. The next day I visited
My father and mother, and questioned them. They
    stormed,
Calling it all the slanderous rant of a fool;
And this relieved me. Yet the suspicion
Remained always aching in my mind;
I knew there was talk; I could not rest;
And finally, saying nothing to my parents,
I went to the shrine at Delphi.

The god dismissed my question without reply;
He spoke of other things.
                        Some were clear,
Full of wretchedness, dreadful, unbearable:
As, that I should lie with my own mother, breed
Children from whom all men would turn their eyes;
And that I should be my father's murderer.

I heard all this, and fled. And from that day
Corinth to me was only in the stars
Descending in that quarter of the sky,
As I wandered farther and farther on my way
To a land where I should never see the evil
Sung by the oracle. And I came to this country
Where, so you say, King Laïos was killed.

I will tell you all that happened there, my lady.

There were three highways
Coming together at a place I passed;
And there a herald came towards me, and a chariot
Drawn by horses, with a man such as you describe
Seated in it. The groom leading the horses
Forced me off the road at his lord's command;
But as this charioteer lurched over towards me
I struck him in my rage. The old man saw me
And brought his double goad down upon my head
As I came abreast.
                        He was paid back, and more!
Swinging my club in this right hand I knocked him
Out of his car, and he rolled on the ground.
                                        I killed him.

I killed them all.
Now if that stranger and Laïos were—kin,
Where is a man more miserable than I?
More hated by the gods? Citizen and alien alike
Must never shelter me or speak to me—
I must be shunned by all.
                        And I myself
Pronounced this malediction upon myself!

Think of it: I have touched you with these hands,
These hands that killed your husband. What
    defilement!

Am I all evil, then? It must be so,
Since I must flee from Thebes, yet never again
See my own countrymen, my own country,

---

[10] Oedipus perhaps interprets this as an allegation that he is a bastard,
the son of Meropê but not of Polybos. The implication, at any rate,
is that he is not of royal birth, not the legitimate heir to the throne
of Corinth.

For fear of joining my mother in marriage
And killing Polybos, my father.
                                    Ah,
If I was created so, born to this fate,
Who could deny the savagery of God?

O holy majesty of heavenly powers!
May I never see that day! Never!
Rather let me vanish from the race of men
Than know the abomination destined me!

CHORAGOS   We too, my lord, have felt dismay at this.
    But there is hope: you have yet to hear the shepherd.

OEDIPUS   Indeed, I fear no other hope is left me.

IOKASTÊ   What do you hope from him when he
    comes?

OEDIPUS   This much:
    If his account of the murder tallies with yours,
    Then I am cleared.

IOKASTÊ   What was it that I said
    Of such importance?

OEDIPUS   Why, "marauders," you said,
    Killed the king, according to this man's story.
    If he maintains that still, if there were several,
    Clearly the guilt is not mine: I was alone.
    But if he says one man, singlehanded, did it,
    Then the evidence all points to me.

IOKASTÊ   You may be sure that he said there were
    several;
    And can he call back that story now? He can not.
    The whole city heard it as plainly as I.
    But suppose he alters some detail of it:
    He can not ever show that Laïos' death
    Fulfilled the oracle: for Apollo said
    My child was doomed to kill him; and my child—
    Poor baby!—it was my child that died first.
    No. From now on, where oracles are concerned,
    I would not waste a second thought on any.

OEDIPUS   You may be right.
                            But come: let someone go
    For the shepherd at once. This matter must be
    settled.

IOKASTÊ   I will send for him.
    I would not wish to cross you in anything,
    And surely not in this.—Let us go in.

(Exeunt into the palace)

ODE II

Strophe 1

CHORUS   Let me be reverent in the ways of right,
    Lowly the paths I journey on;
    Let all my words and actions keep
    The laws of the pure universe
    From highest Heaven handed down.
    For Heaven is their bright nurse,
    Those generations of the realms of light;
    Ah, never of mortal kind were they begot,
    Nor are they slaves of memory, lost in sleep:
    Their Father is greater than Time, and ages not.

Antistrophe 1

The tyrant is a child of Pride
Who drinks from his great sickening cup
Recklessness and vanity,
Until from his high crest headlong
He plummets to the dust of hope.
That strong man is not strong.
But let no fair ambition be denied;
May God protect the wrestler for the State
In government, in comely policy,
Who will fear God, and on His ordinance wait.

Strophe 2

Haughtiness and the high hand of disdain
Tempt and outrage God's holy law;
And any mortal who dares hold
No immortal Power in awe
Will be caught up in a net of pain:
The price for which his levity is sold.
Let each man take due earnings, then,
And keep his hands from holy things,
And from blasphemy stand apart—
Else the crackling blast of heaven
Blows on his head, and on his desperate heart.
Though fools will honor impious men,
In their cities no tragic poet sings.

Antistrophe 2

Shall we lose faith in Delphi's obscurities,
We who have heard the world's core
Discredited, and the sacred wood
Of Zeus at Elis praised no more?
The deeds and the strange prophecies
Must make a pattern yet to be understood.

Zeus, if indeed you are lord of all,
Throned in light over night and day,
Mirror this in your endless mind:
Our masters call the oracle
Words on the wind, and the Delphic vision blind!
Their hearts no longer know Apollo,
And reverence for the gods has died away.

SCENE III

(*Enter* IOKASTÊ)

IOKASTÊ   Princes of Thebes, it has occurred to me
To visit the altars of the gods, bearing
These branches as a suppliant, and this incense.
Our king is not himself: his noble soul
Is overwrought with fantasies of dread,
Else he would consider
The new prophecies in the light of the old.
He will listen to any voice that speaks disaster,
And my advice goes for nothing.

(*She approaches the altar, R*)

                                    To you, then, Apollo,
Lycéan lord, since you are nearest, I turn in prayer.
Receive these offerings, and grant us deliverance
From defilement. Our hearts are heavy with fear
When we see our leader distracted, as helpless sailors
Are terrified by the confusion of their helmsman.

(*Enter* MESSENGER)

MESSENGER   Friends, no doubt you can direct me:
Where shall I find the house of Oedipus,
Or, better still, where is the king himself?
CHORAGOS   It is this very place, stranger; he is inside.
This is his wife and mother of his children.
MESSENGER   I wish her happiness in a happy house,
Blest in all the fulfillment of her marriage.
IOKASTÊ   I wish as much for you: your courtesy
Deserves a like good fortune. But now, tell me:
Why have you come? What have you to say to us?
MESSENGER   Good news, my lady, for your house and
    your husband.
IOKASTÊ   What news? Who sent you here?
MESSENGER   I am from Corinth.
The news I bring ought to mean joy for you,
Though it may be you will find some grief in it.

IOKASTÊ   What is it? How can it touch us in both
    ways?
MESSENGER   The word is that the people of the
    Isthmus
Intend to call Oedipus to be their king.
IOKASTÊ   But old King Polybos—is he not reigning
    still?
MESSENGER   No. Death holds him in his sepulchre.
IOKASTÊ   What are you saying? Polybos is dead?
MESSENGER   If I am not telling the truth, may I die
    myself.
IOKASTÊ   (*to a* MAIDSERVANT)   Go in, go quickly;
    tell this to your master.

O riddlers of God's will, where are you now!
This was the man whom Oedipus, long ago,
Feared so, fled so, in dread of destroying him—
But it was another fate by which he died.

(*Enter* OEDIPUS, *C*)

OEDIPUS   Dearest Iokastê, why have you sent for me?
IOKASTÊ   Listen to what this man says, and then tell
    me
What has become of the solemn prophecies.
OEDIPUS   Who is this man? What is his news for me?
IOKASTÊ   He has come from Corinth to announce
    your father's death!
OEDIPUS   Is it true, stranger? Tell me in your own
    words.
MESSENGER   I can not say it more clearly: the king is
    dead.
OEDIPUS   Was it by treason? Or by an attack of illness?
MESSENGER   A little thing brings old men to their rest.
OEDIPUS   It was sickness, then?
MESSENGER   Yes, and his many years.
OEDIPUS   Ah!
Why should a man respect the Pythian hearth,[11] or
Give heed to the birds that jangle above his head?
They prophesied that I should kill Polybos,
Kill my own father; but he is dead and buried,
And I am here—I never touched him, never,
Unless he died of grief for my departure,
And thus, in a sense, through me. No. Polybos
Has packed the oracles off with him underground.

---

[11] Delphi.

They are empty words.

IOKASTÊ   Had I not told you so?

OEDIPUS   You had; it was my faint heart that betrayed
me.

IOKASTÊ   From now on never think of those things
again.

OEDIPUS   And yet—must I not fear my mother's bed?

IOKASTÊ   Why should anyone in this world be afraid,
Since Fate rules us and nothing can be foreseen?
A man should live only for the present day.

Have no more fear of sleeping with your mother:
How many men, in dreams, have lain with their
mothers!
No reasonable man is troubled by such things.

OEDIPUS   That is true; only—
If only my mother were not still alive!
But she is alive. I can not help my dread.

IOKASTÊ   Yet this news of your father's death is
wonderful.

OEDIPUS   Wonderful. But I fear the living woman.

MESSENGER   Tell me, who is this woman that you fear?

OEDIPUS   It is Meropê, man; the wife of King Polybos.

MESSENGER   Meropê? Why should you be afraid of her?

OEDIPUS   An oracle of the gods, a dreadful saying.

MESSENGER   Can you tell me about it or are you sworn
to silence?

OEDIPUS   I can tell you, and I will.
Apollo said through his prophet that I was the man
Who should marry his own mother, shed his father's
blood
With his own hands. And so, for all these years
I have kept clear of Corinth, and no harm has
come—
Though it would have been sweet to see my parents
again.

MESSENGER   And is this the fear that drove you out of
Corinth?

OEDIPUS   Would you have me kill my father?

MESSENGER   As for that
You must be reassured by the news I gave you.

OEDIPUS   If you could reassure me, I would reward
you.

MESSENGER   I had that in mind, I will confess: I
thought
I could count on you when you returned to Corinth.

OEDIPUS   No: I will never go near my parents again.

MESSENGER   Ah, son, you still do not know what you
are doing—

OEDIPUS   What do you mean? In the name of God tell
me!

MESSENGER   —if these are your reasons for not going
home.

OEDIPUS   I tell you, I fear the oracle may come true.

MESSENGER   And guilt may come upon you through
your parents?

OEDIPUS   That is the dread that is always in my heart.

MESSENGER   Can you not see that all your fears are
groundless?

OEDIPUS   Groundless? Am I not my parents' son?

MESSENGER   Polybos was not your father.

OEDIPUS   Not my father?

MESSENGER   No more your father than the man
speaking to you.

OEDIPUS   But you are nothing to me!

MESSENGER   Neither was he.

OEDIPUS   Then why did he call me son?

MESSENGER   I will tell you:
Long ago he had you from my hands, as a gift.

OEDIPUS   Then how could he love me so, if I was not
his?

MESSENGER   He had no children, and his heart turned
to you.

OEDIPUS   What of you? Did you buy me? Did you find
me by chance?

MESSENGER   I came upon you in the woody vales of
Kithairon.

OEDIPUS   And what were you doing there?

MESSENGER   Tending my flocks.

OEDIPUS   A wandering shepherd?

MESSENGER   But your savior, son, that day.

OEDIPUS   From what did you save me?

MESSENGER   Your ankles should tell you that.

OEDIPUS   Ah, stranger, why do you speak of that
childhood pain?

MESSENGER   I pulled the skewer that pinned your feet
together.

OEDIPUS   I have had the mark as long as I can
remember.

MESSENGER   That was why you were given the name
you bear.

OEDIPUS   God! Was it my father or my mother who
did it?
Tell me!

MESSENGER   I do not know. The man who gave you to
me
Can tell you better than I.

OEDIPUS   It was not you that found me, but another?

MESSENGER   It was another shepherd gave you to me.

OEDIPUS   Who was he? Can you tell me who he was?

MESSENGER   I think he was said to be one of Laïos'
people.

OEDIPUS   You mean the Laïos who was king here years
ago?

MESSENGER   Yes; King Laïos; and the man was one of
his herdsmen.

OEDIPUS   Is he still alive? Can I see him?

MESSENGER   These men here
Know best about such things.

OEDIPUS   Does anyone here
Know this shepherd that he is talking about?
Have you seen him in the fields, or in the town?
If you have, tell me. It is time things were made
plain.

CHORAGOS   I think the man he means is that same
shepherd
You have already asked to see. Iokastê perhaps
Could tell you something.

OEDIPUS   Do you know anything
About him, Lady? Is he the man we have summoned?
Is that the man this shepherd means?

IOKASTÊ   Why think of him?
Forget this herdsman. Forget it all.
This talk is a waste of time.

OEDIPUS   How can you say that,
When the clues to my true birth are in my hands?

IOKASTÊ   For God's love, let us have no more
questioning!
Is your life nothing to you?
My own is pain enough for me to bear.

OEDIPUS   You need not worry. Suppose my mother a
slave,
And born of slaves: no baseness can touch you.

IOKASTÊ   Listen to me, I beg you: do not do this thing!

OEDIPUS   I will not listen; the truth must be made
known.

IOKASTÊ   Everything that I say is for your own good!

OEDIPUS   My own good
Snaps my patience, then! I want none of it.

IOKASTÊ   You are fatally wrong! May you never learn
who you are!

OEDIPUS   Go, one of you, and bring the shepherd here.
Let us leave this woman to brag of her royal name.

IOKASTÊ   Ah, miserable!
That is the only word I have for you now.
That is the only word I can ever have.

(Exit into the palace)

CHORAGOS   Why has she left us, Oedipus? Why has
she gone
In such a passion of sorrow? I fear this silence:
Something dreadful may come of it.

OEDIPUS   Let it come!
However base my birth, I must know about it.
The Queen, like a woman, is perhaps ashamed
To think of my low origin. But I
Am a child of Luck; I can not be dishonored.
Luck is my mother; the passing months, my
brothers,
Have seen me rich and poor.
                        If this is so,
How could I wish that I were someone else?
How could I not be glad to know my birth?

ODE III

Strophe

CHORUS   If ever the coming time were known
To my heart's pondering,
Kithairon, now by Heaven I see the torches
At the festival of the next full moon,
And see the dance, and hear the choir sing
A grace to your gentle shade:
Mountain where Oedipus was found,
O mountain guard of a noble race!
May the god [12] who heals us lend his aid,
And let that glory come to pass
For our king's cradling-ground.

Antistrophe

Of the nymphs that flower beyond the years,
Who bore you,[13] royal child,
To Pan of the hills or the timberline Apollo,
Cold in delight where the upland clears,
Or Hermês for whom Kyllenê's heights are piled?

---

[12] Apollo.
[13] The chorus is suggesting that perhaps Oedipus is the son of one of
the immortal nymphs and of a god—Pan, Apollo, Hermes, or Dionysus. The "sweet god-ravisher" (below) is the presumed mother.

Or flushed as evening cloud,
Great Dionysos, roamer of mountains,
He—was it he who found you there,
And caught you up in his own proud
Arms from the sweet god-ravisher
Who laughed by the Muses' fountains?

SCENE IV

OEDIPUS   Sirs: though I do not know the man,
I think I see him coming, this shepherd we want:
He is old, like our friend here, and the men
Bringing him seem to be servants of my house.
But you can tell, if you have ever seen him.

(*Enter* SHEPHERD *escorted by* SERVANTS)

CHORAGOS   I know him, he was Laïos' man. You can
trust him.
OEDIPUS   Tell me first, you from Corinth: is this the
shepherd
We were discussing?
MESSENGER   This is the very man.
OEDIPUS   (*to* SHEPHERD)   Come here. No, look at me.
You must answer
Everything I ask.—You belonged to Laïos?
SHEPHERD   Yes: born his slave, brought up in his
house.
OEDIPUS   Tell me: what kind of work did you do for
him?
SHEPHERD   I was a shepherd of his, most of my life.
OEDIPUS   Where mainly did you go for pasturage?
SHEPHERD   Sometimes Kithairon, sometimes the hills
near-by.
OEDIPUS   Do you remember ever seeing this man out
there?
SHEPHERD   What would he be doing there? This man?
OEDIPUS   This man standing here. Have you ever seen
him before?
SHEPHERD   No. At least, not to my recollection.
MESSENGER   And that is not strange, my lord. But I'll
refresh
His memory: he must remember when we two
Spent three whole seasons together, March to
September,
On Kithairon or thereabouts. He had two flocks;
I had one. Each autumn I'd drive mine home
And he would go back with his to Laïos' sheepfold.—

Is this not true, just as I have described it?
SHEPHERD   True, yes; but it was all so long ago.
MESSENGER   Well, then: do you remember, back in
those days,
That you gave me a baby boy to bring up as my own?
SHEPHERD   What if I did? What are you trying to say?
MESSENGER   King Oedipus was once that little child.
SHEPHERD   Damn you, hold your tongue!
OEDIPUS   No more of that!
It is your tongue needs watching, not this man's.
SHEPHERD   My king, my master, what is it I have done
wrong?
OEDIPUS   You have not answered his question about
the boy.
SHEPHERD   He does not know . . . He is only making
trouble . . .
OEDIPUS   Come, speak plainly, or it will go hard with
you.
SHEPHERD   In God's name, do not torture an old man!
OEDIPUS   Come here, one of you; bind his arms
behind him.
SHEPHERD   Unhappy king! What more do you wish to
learn?
OEDIPUS   Did you give this man the child he speaks
of?
SHEPHERD   I did.
And I would to God I had died that very day.
OEDIPUS   You will die now unless you speak the truth.
SHEPHERD   Yet if I speak the truth, I am worse than
dead.
OEDIPUS   (*to* ATTENDANT)   He intends to draw it
out, apparently—
SHEPHERD   No! I have told you already that I gave him
the boy.
OEDIPUS   Where did you get him? From your house?
From somewhere else?
SHEPHERD   Not from mine, no. A man gave him to
me.
OEDIPUS   Is that man here? Whose house did he
belong to?
SHEPHERD   For God's love, my king, do not ask me any
more!
OEDIPUS   You are a dead man if I have to ask you
again.
SHEPHERD   Then . . . Then the child was from the
palace of Laïos.

OEDIPUS   A slave child? or a child of his own line?

SHEPHERD   Ah, I am on the brink of dreadful speech!

OEDIPUS   And I of dreadful hearing. Yet I must hear.

SHEPHERD   If you must be told, then . . .

They said it was Laïos' child;
But it is your wife who can tell you about that.

OEDIPUS   My wife!—Did she give it to you?

SHEPHERD   My lord, she did.

OEDIPUS   Do you know why?

SHEPHERD   I was told to get rid of it.

OEDIPUS   Oh heartless mother!

SHEPHERD   But in dread of prophecies . . .

OEDIPUS   Tell me.

SHEPHERD   It was said that the boy would kill
his own father.

OEDIPUS   Then why did you give him over to this old
man?

SHEPHERD   I pitied the baby, my king,
And I thought that this man would take him far
away
To his own country.

He saved him—but for what a fate!
For if you are what this man says you are,
No man living is more wretched than Oedipus.

OEDIPUS   Ah God!
It was true!
All the prophecies!
—Now,
O Light, may I look on you for the last time!
I, Oedipus,
Oedipus, damned in his birth, in his marriage
damned,
Damned in the blood he shed with his own hand!

(He rushes into the palace)

ODE IV

Strophe 1

CHORUS   Alas for the seed of men.
What measure shall I give these generations
That breathe on the void and are void
And exist and do not exist?
Who bears more weight of joy
Than mass of sunlight shifting in images,
Or who shall make his thought stay on
That down time drifts away?

Your splendor is all fallen.
O naked brow of wrath and tears,
O change of Oedipus!
I who saw your days call no man blest—
Your great days like ghosts gone.

Antistrophe 1

That mind was a strong bow.
Deep, how deep you drew it then, hard archer,
At a dim fearful range,
And brought dear glory down!
You overcame the stranger[14]—
The virgin with her hooking lion claws—
And though death sang, stood like a tower
To make pale Thebes take heart.
Fortress against our sorrow!
True king, giver of laws,
Majestic Oedipus!
No prince in Thebes had ever such renown,
No prince won such grace of power.

Strophe 2

And now of all men ever known
Most pitiful is this man's story:
His fortunes are most changed, his state
Fallen to a low slave's
Ground under bitter fate.
O Oedipus, most royal one!
The great door[15] that expelled you to the light
Gave at night—ah, gave night to your glory:
As to the father, to the fathering son.
All understood too late.
How could that queen whom Laïos won,
The garden that he harrowed at his height,
Be silent when that act was done?

Antistrophe 2

But all eyes fail before time's eye,
All actions come to justice there.
Though never willed, though far down the deep past,
Your bed, your dread sirings,
Are brought to book at last.
Child by Laïos doomed to die,
Then doomed to lose that fortunate little death,

---

14 The Sphinx.
15 Iokastê's womb.

Would God you never took breath in this air
That with my wailing lips I take to cry:
For I weep the world's outcast.
I was blind, and now I can tell why:
Asleep, for you had given ease of breath
To Thebes, while the false years went by.

EXODOS [16]

(*Enter, from the palace,* SECOND MESSENGER)

SECOND MESSENGER   Elders of Thebes, most honored
    in this land,
What horrors are yours to see and hear, what weight
Of sorrow to be endured, if, true to your birth,
You venerate the line of Labdakos!
I think neither Istros nor Phasis, those great rivers,
Could purify this place of all the evil
It shelters now, or soon must bring to light—
Evil not done unconsciously, but willed.

The greatest griefs are those we cause ourselves.
CHORAGOS   Surely, friend, we have grief enough
    already;
What new sorrow do you mean?
SECOND MESSENGER   The queen is dead.
CHORAGOS   O miserable queen! But at whose hand?
SECOND MESSENGER   Her own.
The full horror of what happened you can not know,
For you did not see it; but I, who did, will tell you
As clearly as I can how she met her death.

When she had left us,
In passionate silence, passing through the court,
She ran to her apartment in the house,
Her hair clutched by the fingers of both hands.
She closed the doors behind her; then, by that bed
Where long ago the fatal son was conceived—
That son who should bring about his father's
    death—
We heard her call upon Laïos, dead so many years,
And heard her wail for the double fruit of her
    marriage,
A husband by her husband, children by her child.

Exactly how she died I do not know:
For Oedipus burst in moaning and would not let us

Keep vigil to the end: it was by him
As he stormed about the room that our eyes were
    caught.
From one to another of us he went, begging a sword,
Hunting the wife who was not his wife, the mother
Whose womb had carried his own children and
    himself.
I do not know: it was none of us aided him,
But surely one of the gods was in control!
For with a dreadful cry
He hurled his weight, as though wrenched out of
    himself,
At the twin doors: the bolts gave, and he rushed in.
And there we saw her hanging, her body swaying
From the cruel cord she had noosed about her
    neck.
A great sob broke from him, heartbreaking to hear,
As he loosed the rope and lowered her to the ground.

I would blot out from my mind what happened next!
For the king ripped from her gown the golden
    brooches
That were her ornament, and raised them, and
    plunged them down
Straight into his own eyeballs, crying, "No more,
No more shall you look on the misery about me,
The horrors of my own doing! Too long you have
    known
The faces of those whom I should never have seen,
Too long been blind to those for whom I was
    searching!
From this hour, go in darkness!" And as he spoke,
He struck at his eyes—not once, but many times;
And the blood spattered his beard,
Bursting from his ruined sockets like red hail.

So from the unhappiness of two this evil has sprung,
A curse on the man and woman alike. The old
Happiness of the house of Labdakos
Was happiness enough: where is it today?
It is all wailing and ruin, disgrace, death—all
The misery of mankind that has a name—
And it is wholly and for ever theirs.
CHORAGOS   Is he in agony still? Is there no rest for
    him?
SECOND MESSENGER   He is calling for someone to open
    the doors wide

----

[16] Final scene.

So that all the children of Kadmos may look upon
His father's murderer, his mother's—no,
I can not say it!
                    And then he will leave Thebes,
Self-exiled, in order that the curse
Which he himself pronounced may depart from the
    house.
He is weak, and there is none to lead him,
So terrible is his suffering.
                    But you will see:
Look, the doors are opening; in a moment
You will see a thing that would crush a heart of
    stone.

(The central door is opened; OEDIPUS, *blinded, is led in)*

CHORAGOS   Dreadful indeed for men to see.
    Never have my own eyes
    Looked on a sight so full of fear.

    Oedipus!
    What madness came upon you, what daemon
    Leaped on your life with heavier
    Punishment than a mortal man can bear?
    No: I can not even
    Look at you, poor ruined one.
    And I would speak, question, ponder,
    If I were able. No.
    You make me shudder.
OEDIPUS   God. God.
    Is there a sorrow greater?
    Where shall I find harbor in this world?
    My voice is hurled far on a dark wind.
    What has God done to me?
CHORAGOS   Too terrible to think of, or to see.

Strophe 1

OEDIPUS   O cloud of night,
    Never to be turned away: night coming on,
    I can not tell how: night like a shroud!
    My fair winds brought me here.
                            O God. Again
    The pain of the spikes where I had sight,
    The flooding pain
    Of memory, never to be gouged out.
CHORAGOS   This is not strange.
    You suffer it all twice over, remorse in pain,
    Pain in remorse.

Antistrophe 1

OEDIPUS   Ah dear friend
    Are you faithful even yet, you alone?
    Are you still standing near me, will you stay here,
    Patient, to care for the blind?
                            The blind man!
    Yet even blind I know who it is attends me,
    By the voice's tone—
    Though my new darkness hide the comforter.
CHORAGOS   Oh fearful act!
    What god was it drove you to rake black
    Night across your eyes?

Strophe 2

OEDIPUS   Apollo. Apollo. Dear
    Children, the god was Apollo.
    He brought my sick, sick fate upon me.
    But the blinding hand was my own!
    How could I bear to see
    When all my sight was horror everywhere?
CHORAGOS   Everywhere; that is true.
OEDIPUS   And now what is left?
    Images? Love? A greeting even,
    Sweet to the senses? Is there anything?
    Ah, no, friends: lead me away.
    Lead me away from Thebes.
                            Lead the great wreck
    And hell of Oedipus, whom the gods hate.
CHORAGOS   Your misery, you are not blind to that.
    Would God you had never found it out!

Antistrophe 2

OEDIPUS   Death take the man who unbound
    My feet on that hillside
    And delivered me from death to life! What life?
    If only I had died,
    This weight of monstrous doom
    Could not have dragged me and my darlings down.
CHORAGOS   I would have wished the same.
OEDIPUS   Oh never to have come here
    With my father's blood upon me! Never
    To have been the man they call his mother's
        husband!
    Oh accurst! Oh child of evil,
    To have entered that wretched bed—
                            the selfsame one!
    More primal than sin itself, this fell to me.

CHORAGOS   I do not know what words to offer you.
   You were better dead than alive and blind.

OEDIPUS   Do not counsel me any more. This
      punishment
   That I have laid upon myself is just.
   If I had eyes,
   I do not know how I could bear the sight
   Of my father, when I came to the house of Death,
   Or my mother: for I have sinned against them both
   So vilely that I could not make my peace
   By strangling my own life.
                     Or do you think my children,
   Born as they were born, would be sweet to my eyes?
   Ah never, never! Nor this town with its high walls,
   Nor the holy images of the gods.
                     For I,
   Thrice miserable!—Oedipus, noblest of all the line
   Of Kadmos, have condemned myself to enjoy
   These things no more, by my own malediction
   Expelling that man whom the gods declared
   To be a defilement in the house of Laïos.
   After exposing the rankness of my own guilt,
   How could I look men frankly in the eyes?
   No, I swear it,
   If I could have stifled my hearing at its source,
   I would have done it and made all this body
   A tight cell of misery, blank to light and sound:
   So I should have been safe in my dark mind
   Beyond external evil.
                     Ah Kithairon!
   Why did you shelter me? When I was cast upon you,
   Why did I not die? Then I should never
   Have shown the world my execrable birth.

   Ah Polybos! Corinth, city that I believed
   The ancient seat of my ancestors: how fair
   I seemed, your child! And all the while this evil
   Was cancerous within me!
                     For I am sick
   In my own being, sick in my origin.

   O three roads, dark ravine, woodland and way
   Where three roads met: you, drinking my father's
      blood,
   My own blood, spilled by my own hand: can you
      remember

   The unspeakable things I did there, and the things
   I went on from there to do?
                     O marriage, marriage!
   That act that engendered me, and again the act
   Performed by the son in the same bed—
                     Ah, the net
   Of incest, mingling fathers, brothers, sons,
   With brides, wives, mothers: the last evil
   That can be known by men: no tongue can say
   How evil!
                No. For the love of God, conceal me
   Somewhere far from Thebes; or kill me; or hurl me
   Into the sea, away from men's eyes for ever.

   Come, lead me. You need not fear to touch me.
   Of all men, I alone can bear this guilt.

(Enter KREON)

CHORAGOS   Kreon is here now. As to what you ask,
   He may decide the course to take. He only
   Is left to protect the city in your place.
OEDIPUS   Alas, how can I speak to him? What right
      have I
   To beg his courtesy whom I have deeply wronged?
KREON   I have not come to mock you, Oedipus,
   Or to reproach you, either. (To ATTENDANTS)
                     —You, standing there:
   If you have lost all respect for man's dignity,
   At least respect the flame of Lord Helios:
   Do not allow this pollution to show itself
   Openly here, an affront to the earth
   And Heaven's rain and the light of day. No, take him
   Into the house as quickly as you can.
   For it is proper
   That only the close kindred see his grief.
OEDIPUS   I pray you in God's name, since your
      courtesy
   Ignores my dark expectation, visiting
   With mercy this man of all men most execrable:
   Give me what I ask—for your good, not for mine.
KREON   And what is it that you turn to me begging
      for?
OEDIPUS   Drive me out of this country as quickly as
      may be
   To a place where no human voice can ever greet me.
KREON   I should have done that before now—only,

God's will had not been wholly revealed to me.

OEDIPUS   But his command is plain: the parricide
Must be destroyed. I am that evil man.

KREON   That is the sense of it, yes; but as things are,
We had best discover clearly what is to be done.

OEDIPUS   You would learn more about a man like me?

KREON   You are ready now to listen to the god.

OEDIPUS   I will listen. But it is to you
That I must turn for help. I beg you, hear me.

The woman in there—
Give her whatever funeral you think proper:
She is your sister.
                    —But let me go, Kreon!
Let me purge my father's Thebes of the pollution
Of my living here, and go out to the wild hills,
To Kithairon, that has won such fame with me,
The tomb my mother and father appointed for me,
And let me die there, as they willed I should.

And yet I know
Death will not ever come to me through sickness
Or in any natural way: I have been preserved
For some unthinkable fate. But let that be.

As for my sons, you need not care for them.
They are men, they will find some way to live.
But my poor daughters, who have shared my table,
Who never before have been parted from their
        father—
Take care of them, Kreon; do this for me.

And will you let me touch them with my hands
A last time, and let us weep together?
Be kind, my lord,
Great prince, be kind!
                    Could I but touch them,
They would be mine again, as when I had my eyes.

(Enter ANTIGONE and ISMENE, attended)

Ah, God!
Is it my dearest children I hear weeping?
Has Kreon pitied me and sent my daughters?

KREON   Yes, Oedipus: I knew that they were dear to
        you
In the old days, and know you must love them still.

OEDIPUS   May God bless you for this—and be a
        friendlier

Guardian to you than he has been to me!

Children, where are you?
Come quickly to my hands: they are your
        brother's—
Hands that have brought your father's once clear
        eyes
To this way of seeing—
                    Ah dearest ones,
I had neither sight nor knowledge then, your father
By the woman who was the source of his own life!
And I weep for you—having no strength to see you—,
I weep for you when I think of the bitterness
That men will visit upon you all your lives.
What homes, what festivals can you attend
Without being forced to depart again in tears?
And when you come to marriageable age,
Where is the man, my daughters, who would dare
Risk the bane that lies on all my children?
Is there any evil wanting? Your father killed
His father; sowed the womb of her who bore him;
Engendered you at the fount of his own existence!
That is what they will say of you.
                            Then, whom
Can you ever marry? There are no bridegrooms for
        you,
And your lives must wither away in sterile
        dreaming.

O Kreon, son of Menoikeus!
You are the only father my daughters have,
Since we, their parents, are both of us gone for ever.
They are your own blood: you will not let them
Fall into beggary and loneliness;
You will keep them from the miseries that are mine!
Take pity on them; see, they are only children,
Friendless except for you. Promise me this,
Great prince, and give me your hand in token of it.

(KREON clasps his right hand)

Children:
I could say much, if you could understand me,
But as it is, I have only this prayer for you:
Live where you can, be as happy as you can—
Happier, please God, than God has made your father.

KREON   Enough. You have wept enough. Now go
        within.

OEDIPUS   I must; but it is hard.
KREON   Time eases all things.
OEDIPUS   You know my mind, then?
KREON   Say what you desire.
OEDIPUS   Send me from Thebes!
KREON   God grant that I may!
OEDIPUS   But since God hates me . . .
KREON   No, he will grant your wish.
OEDIPUS   You promise?
KREON   I can not speak beyond my knowledge.
OEDIPUS   Then lead me in.
KREON   Come now, and leave your children.
OEDIPUS   No! Do not take them from me!
KREON   Think no longer
That you are in command here, but rather think
How, when you were, you served your own
    destruction.

(Exeunt into the house all but the CHORUS; *the*
CHORAGOS *chants directly to the audience)*

CHORAGOS   Men of Thebes: look upon Oedipus.

This is the king who solved the famous riddle
And towered up, most powerful of men.
No mortal eyes but looked on him with envy,
Yet in the end ruin swept over him.

Let every man in mankind's frailty
Consider his last day; and let none
Presume on his good fortune until he find
Life, at his death, a memory without pain.

COMMENTS AND QUESTIONS

1. Describe Oedipus' character as fully as you can. To
   what extent is he a realistic human being and to
   what extent an ideal type?
2. What are Iokastê's religious beliefs? How does she
   serve as a foil to Oedipus?
3. What kinds of "blindness" are there in this play?
   Explain their significance.
4. Sophocles uses much tragic *irony* in this tragedy and
   in others. Irony, in this sense, means that the tragic
   figure says something "all too true," related to his

fate, that the audience understands but that he does
not. Find examples of tragic irony. What is their
effect?
5. To what extent is Oedipus a puppet of the gods and
   to what extent is he a free man?
6. *Oedipus Rex* has been interpreted both as a glorification of man and as a defense of religion that points
   out the limitations of man. Which view seems truer
   in your opinion?
7. What is Oedipus' attitude at the end of the play?
   What has he learned about himself and life? What is
   the difference between a tragic view of life and a
   merely pessimistic one?
8. Look up Freud's notion of the "Oedipus complex" if
   you are not familiar with it. To what extent is this
   useful for a modern interpretation of the tragedy?
9. If you were to take the legend of Oedipus and re-
   write it for the modern stage, film, or daytime television, what would you do with it? Is a modern tragedy
   possible?

Humanism and Tragedy

During the great classical age of Athens, intellectuals,
intrigued with new developments in science and philosophy, began to challenge the old, accepted religious
beliefs. In art, in politics, as in thought, man (rather
than the gods) was becoming, as the philosopher Protagoras said, "the measure of all things." Man's confidence in his own abilities and powers has perhaps
never been greater than at this time. We see this in
Oedipus in the hero's self-confidence at the beginning
of the play. The people of Thebes who look to him as
their savior treat him almost like a god. We see an extreme confidence in man's reason and a denial of the
power of the gods over man in Iokastê's scoffing at
prophecies. But here, as in other aspects, Sophocles portrays a balance between extremes. The outcome of the
tragedy shows that the gods, or fate, have the last word,
but it certainly does not show man to be a little puppet
whose destiny is simply to obey the divine will. Oedipus is "blind" in that he does not recognize the limits
set by divine power, but great in that he struggles to

find the truth through his own individual human reason. Sophocles wanted to warn his fellow Athenians not to neglect religion but he also wanted to demonstrate to them the greatness of human character and intelligence. Sophocles' faith in man, or his "humanism," is perhaps best exemplified in the famous choral ode in another of his tragedies, *Antigone* (translated by Elizabeth Wyckoff):

Many the wonders but nothing walks stranger than man.
This thing crosses the sea in the winter's storm,
making his path through the roaring waves.
And she, the greatest of gods, the earth—
ageless she is, and unwearied—he wears her away
as the ploughs go up and down from year to year
and his mules turn up the soil.

Gay nations of birds he snares and leads,
wild beast tribes and the salty brood of the sea,
with the twisted mesh of his nets, this clever man.
He controls with craft the beasts of the open air,
walkers on hills. The horse with his shaggy mane
he holds and harnesses, yoked about the neck,
and the strong bull of the mountain.

Language, and thought like the wind
and the feelings that make the town;
he has taught himself, and shelter against the cold,
refuge from rain. He can always help himself.
He faces no future helpless. There's only death
that he cannot find an escape from. He has contrived
refuge from illnesses once beyond all cure.

Clever beyond all dreams
the inventive craft that he has
which may drive him one time or another to well or ill.

Classical tragedy shows that a belief in the dignity and greatness of human beings is not incompatible with a full awareness of their limitations.

Greek Comedy

Tragedy, according to the philosopher Aristotle, provided a release for the emotions of pity and terror. Spectators would pity the unfortunate protagonist and would fear that they themselves might undergo a disaster, thus purging themselves of those emotions. What-

ever else went on at the festival of Dionysus, it must have offered an opportunity for the release of pent-up feelings. The people who attended it "let off steam" in all sorts of ways—first of all by feeling liberated from the everyday world of work and duty. There was drinking, feasting, carousing. At the plays themselves the idea was to participate emotionally as a spectator rather than merely to view passively. The Greeks, like most peoples of the world, recognized society's need for a true holiday, or festival—a time of collective celebration and liberation. The way that a culture celebrates, or organizes its festivals, says a great deal about its values. (Bear this in mind as we study festivals in medieval and Renaissance Europe and in Africa.) One might well ask if our contemporary society recognizes this need adequately. Do people who spend their days off at home watching television experience a release and liberation from the everyday world? Is there a basic difference between the theatrical and the media experience? Or do we provide other, communal ceremonies of celebration?

Comedy is one response to the human need to "let go" or to transcend the everyday world. Human beings, if they remain truly human, never lose the childlike need to play, and they certainly need to be able to laugh at their own and at others' shortcomings and to remember that life is not all earnestness and work. If we transcend the everyday world with tragedy through an almost religious sense of awe, we transcend it with comedy through our laughter. We laugh at a comic character either because he is quick, witty, and always able to outsmart the "bad guys" or, on the contrary, because he is always getting into trouble. Comedy is often worked out on the level of *action*, whereas tragedy is often worked out on the level of *thought*. While tragic writers tend to view man in the context of a universal human condition, comic writers often take a hard look at their immediate society, satirizing its customs and institutions. For this reason, it will be useful to look at the development of comedy in Greece and at the society in which Aristophanes was writing.

The word *comedy* comes from *komos*, which means a revel. It seems probable that fertility rituals and celebrations are at the origins of comedy. From the earliest days of Greece, groups of men, revelers, would go around from village to village, wearing huge artificial phalluses, telling jokes (often obscene ones), singing, and dancing. The community would participate in the revels. These were not only for fun but were also intended to increase fertility—in the land, in people, in animals. Worship of the phallus as a symbol of fertility is common among all "primitive" peoples, and Freud and Jung have shown that phallic symbols appear in the dreams of "civilized" people as well. Often, the *komos* would end with some sort of sexual union—a ritual orgy, a pairing off with mates, or a marriage. This was not meant to encourage free sex on all occasions but to ensure fertility.

We do not know exactly how comedy as an art form grew from these revels, but it was recognized as such at the festival of Dionysus in Athens around 486 B.C., thus later than tragedy. Aristophanes, the only Greek classical comic author whose works survive, composed "old comedies." In his comedies, many of the old ritual features of the *komos*—the big phalluses, padding, animal costumes, grotesque masks, colloquial speech, and obscene jokes—are retained. There are often two choruses in opposition to each other (in *Lysistrata*, the choruses of old men and old women). Certainly music and dance were of great importance. Of course, the purpose was no longer to promote fertility but to entertain people.

The situations in old comedy are often fantastic ones (in some, such as *The Birds* and *The Frogs*, the characters are dressed like animals), but the people or the institutions made fun of were real enough. About a hundred years after Aristophanes we find "new comedy," in the hands of its most famous practitioner, Menander, without phalluses, grotesque costumes, or indecent jokes. The new comedy was realistic rather than fantastic—it reflected everyday life and created stock, yet individualized characters. New comedy, such as that practiced by the Romans Plautus and Terence, is more similar to the comedies of manners with which we are familiar in modern theater, films, and television. The situations in new comedy often arise from misunderstandings, there is often a great deal of verbal play and wit, and the endings are happy. New comedy has lost touch with its origins in ritual fertility except that—even today—it often ends with a marriage or a happy love.

Lysistrata, first performed in 411 B.C., is essentially a comic fantasy about a real contemporary event. Athens and Sparta, as we saw in the section on politics, were the rival leaders in a series of battles, lasting from 431 to 404 B.C., called the Peloponnesian Wars. Aristophanes had long been a spokesman for peace—in one of his plays he even went so far as to suggest that in some instances the Athenians had treated the Spartans unfairly. Like many of his countrymen, he deplored the evolution of Athens from a democracy to a dictatorship, a seeming necessity in wartime. He was particularly opposed to the foolhardy naval expedition that the Athenians sent to Sicily in 415 B.C. This attack, which ended in defeat and brought the Athenians vast losses in ships and men, was really the turning point of the war. By the time of the writing of *Lysistrata*, it must have been apparent that the Spartans were winning the war and that a genuine negotiated peace treaty, which might have been possible earlier, was no longer possible. There are some sad underpinnings to this comedy: an idyllic dream of peace; a memory of the time when Athens and Sparta were allies and fought bravely together during the Persian Wars. Yet these serious concerns do not prevent *Lysistrata* from being a total comedy. Perhaps the human need to laugh at the world is even greater at times of disaster than in normal times. And perhaps Aristophanes is suggesting something that is of concern to us today: if men have been such failures at keeping peace in the world, might not women do better?

The play's title character (her name means "she who dissolves the armies") shows herself superior to the men in every way. She is the only one who keeps a cool head; she plans an effective strategy and negotiates the peace. Her plan for forcing peace negotiations—organizing the women of Athens and Sparta in a sex strike against their husbands—is highly comic but also effective. Because of its explicitness about sex, *Lysistrata* was forbidden reading in schools for a long time. Most modern readers, however, with less puritanical attitudes, find it extremely funny. Aristophanes' comedies, because of their use of Greek dialects and plays on words, are particularly difficult to translate. In this English version by Dudley Fitts, the woman from Sparta, Lampito, is given a Southern accent as the American equivalent of her Spartan dialect.

ARISTOPHANES

Lysistrata

CHARACTERS

LYSISTRATA
KALONIKE   *Athenian women*
MYRRHINE
LAMPITO, *a Spartan woman*
CHORUS
MAGISTRATE
KINESIAS, *husband of Myrrhine*
SPARTAN HERALD
SPARTAN AMBASSADOR
A SENTRY
ATHENIAN DRUNKARD

The supernumeraries include the BABY SON *of Kinesias;* STRATYLLIS, *a member of the hemichorus of Old Women; various individual speakers, both Spartan and Athenian.*
Until the exodos, the CHORUS *is divided into two hemichori: the first, of Old Men; the second, of Old Women. Each of these has its* CHORAGOS. *In the exodos, the hemichori return as Athenians and Spartans.*

THE SCENE.   *Athens. First, a public square; later, beneath the walls of the Acropolis; later, a courtyard within the Acropolis. Time: early in 411* B.C.

Athens; a public square; early morning; LYSISTRATA *sola.*

LYSISTRATA   If someone had invited them to a
    festival—
Bacchus's, say, or Pan's, or Aphrodite's, or
that Genetyllis business[1]—, you couldn't get through
    the streets,
what with the drums and the dancing. But now,
not a woman in sight!
               Except—oh, yes!

(*Enter* KALONIKE)

Here's one, at last. Good
morning, Kalonike.
KALONIKE   Good morning, Lysistrata.
                       Darling,
don't frown so! You'll ruin your face!
LYSISTRATA   Never mind my face.
Kalonike,

---

[1] References to cults of love and wine.

the way we women behave! Really, I don't blame the
    men
for what they say about us.
KALONIKE   No; I imagine they're right.
LYSISTRATA   For example: I call a meeting
to think out a most important matter—and what
    happens?
The women all stay in bed!
KALONIKE   Oh, they'll be along.
It's hard to get away, you know: a husband, a cook,
a child . . . Home life can be *so* demanding!
LYSISTRATA   What I have in mind is even more
    demanding.
KALONIKE   Tell me: what is it?
LYSISTRATA   Something big.
KALONIKE   Goodness! *How* big?
LYSISTRATA   Big enough for all of us.
KALONIKE   But we're not all here!
LYSISTRATA   We would be, if *that's* what was up!
               No, Kalonike,
this is something I've been turning over for nights;
and, I may say, sleepless nights.
KALONIKE   Can't be so hard, then,
if you've spent so much time on it.
LYSISTRATA   Hard or not,
it comes to this: Only we women can save Greece!
KALONIKE   Only we women? Poor Greece!
LYSISTRATA   Just the same,
it's up to us. First, we must liquidate
the Peloponnesians—
KALONIKE   Fun, fun!
LYSISTRATA   —and then the Boeotians.
KALONIKE   Oh! But not those heavenly eels![2]
LYSISTRATA   You needn't worry.
Athens shall have her sea food.—But here's the
    point:
If we can get the women from those places
to join us women here, why, we can save
all Greece!
KALONIKE   But dearest Lysistrata!
How can women do a thing so austere, so
political? We belong at home. Our only armor's
our transparent saffron dresses and
our pretty little shoes!

---

[2] Boeotia was famous for its sea food, especially its eels.

LYSISTRATA   That's it exactly.
Those transparent saffron dresses, those little shoes—
well, there we are!
KALONIKE   Oh?
LYSISTRATA   Not a single man would lift
his spear—
KALONIKE   I'll get my dress from the dyer's tomorrow!
LYSISTRATA   —or need a shield—
KALONIKE   The sweetest little negligée—
LYSISTRATA   —or bring out his sword.
KALONIKE   I know where I can buy
the dreamiest sandals!
LYSISTRATA   Well, so you see. Now, shouldn't
the women have come?
KALONIKE   Come? they should have *flown!*
LYSISTRATA   Athenians are always late.
                        But imagine!
There's no one here from the South Shore.
KALONIKE   They go to work early,
I can swear to that.
LYSISTRATA   And nobody from Acharnai.
They should have been here hours ago!
KALONIKE   Well, you'll get
that awful Theagenes woman: she's been having
her fortune told at Hecate's shrine.[3]
                        But look!
Someone at last! Can you see who they are?

(Enter MYRRHINE and other women)

LYSISTRATA   People from the suburbs.
KALONIKE   Yes! The entire
membership of the Suburban League!
MYRRHINE   Sorry to be late, Lysistrata.
                        Oh, come,
don't scowl so! Say something!
LYSISTRATA   My dear Myrrhine,
what is there to say? After all,
you've been pretty casual about the whole thing.
MYRRHINE   Couldn't find
my girdle in the dark, that's all.
                        But what *is*
"the whole thing"?
LYSISTRATA   Wait for the rest of them.

KALONIKE   I suppose so. But, look!
Here's Lampito!

(Enter LAMPITO with women from Sparta)

LYSISTRATA   Darling Lampito,
how pretty you are today! What a nice color!
Goodness, you look as though you could strangle a
    bull!
LAMPITO   Ah think Ah could! It's the work-out
in the gym every day; and, of co'se that dance of ahs
where y' kick yo' own tail.[4]
LYSISTRATA   What lovely breasts!
LAMPITO   Lawdy, when y' touch me lahk that,
Ah feel lahk a heifer at the altar!
LYSISTRATA   And this young lady?
Where is she from?
LAMPITO   Boeotia. Social-Register type.
LYSISTRATA   Good morning, Boeotian. You're as pretty
as green grass.
KALONIKE   And if you look,
you'll find that the lawn has just been cut.
LYSISTRATA   And this lady?
LAMPITO   From Corinth. But a good woman.
LYSISTRATA   Well, in Corinth
anything's possible.
LAMPITO   But let's get to work. Which one of you
called this meeting, and why?
LYSISTRATA   *I* did.
LAMPITO   Well, then:
what's up?
MYRRHINE   Yes, what *is* "the whole thing," after all?
LYSISTRATA   I'll tell you.—But first, one question.
MYRRHINE   Ask away!
LYSISTRATA   It's your husbands. Fathers of your
children. Doesn't it bother you
that they're always off with the Army? I'll stake my
life,
not one of you has a man in the house this minute!
KALONIKE   Mine's been in Thrace the last five
months, keeping an eye
on that General.[5]

---

[3] Theagenes was notoriously superstitious; his practice of never leaving home without consulting Hecate is here transferred to his wife.

---

[4] Among the physical exercises practiced by Greek girls was the strenuous *bibasis,* a dance in which the dancer kicked her buttocks with her heels.

[5] A certain Eukrates about whom nothing is known.

MYRRHINE   Mine's been in Pylos for seven.
LAMPITO   And mahn,
   whenever he gets a *dis*charge, he goes raht back
   with that li'l ole speah of his, and enlists again!
LYSISTRATA   And not the ghost of a lover to be found!
   From the very day the war began—
                                   those Milesians!
   I could skin them alive!
                      —I've not seen so much, even,
   as one of those devices they call Widow's Delight.
   But there! What's important is: I've found a way
   to end the war, are you with me?
MYRRHINE   I should *say* so!
   Even if I have to pawn my best dress and
   drink up the proceeds.[6]
KALONIKE   Me, too! Even if they split me
   right up the middle, like a flounder.
LAMPITO   Ah'm shorely with you.
   Ah'd crawl up Taygetos[7] on mah knees
   if that'd bring peace.
LYSISTRATA   Then here it is.
   Women! Sisters!
   If we really want our men to make an armistice,
   we must be ready to give up—
MYRRHINE   Give up what?
   Quick, tell us!
LYSISTRATA   But *will* you?
MYRRHINE   We will, even if it kills us.
LYSISTRATA   Then we must give up sleeping with our
      men. *(Long silence)*
   Oh? So now you're sorry? Won't look at me?
   Doubtful? Pale? All teary-eyed?
                         But come: be frank with me,
   as I've certainly been with you. Will you do it?
MYRRHINE   I couldn't. No.
   Let the war go on.
KALONIKE   Nor I. Let the war go on.
LYSISTRATA   You, you little flounder,
   ready to be split up the middle?
KALONIKE   Lysistrata, no!
   I'd walk through fire for you—you *know* I would!—,
      but don't
   ask us to give up *that!* Why, there's nothing like it!

LYSISTRATA   And you?
BOEOTIAN   No. I must say *I'd* rather walk through fire.
LYSISTRATA   You little salamanders!
   No wonder poets write tragedies about women.
   All we want's a quick tumble!
                              But you from Sparta:
   if you stand by me, we may win yet! Will you?
   It means so much!
LAMPITO   Ah sweah, it means *too* much!
   By the Two Goddesses,[8] it does! Asking a girl
   to sleep—Heaven knows how long!—in a great big
      bed
   with nobody there but herself! But Ah'll stay with
      you!
   Peace comes first!
LYSISTRATA   Spoken like a true Spartan!
KALONIKE   But, if—
               oh dear!
                  —if we give up what you tell us to,
   will there *be* any peace?
LYSISTRATA   Why, mercy, of course there will!
   We'll just sit snug in our very thinnest gowns,
   perfumed and powdered from top to bottom, and
      those men
   simply won't stand still! And when we say No,
   they'll go out of their minds! And there's your peace.
   You can take my word for it.
LAMPITO   Ah seem to remember
   that Colonel Menelaus threw his sword away
   when he saw Helen's breast all bare.
KALONIKE   But, goodness me!
   What if they just get up and leave us?
LYSISTRATA   Well,
   we'd have to fall back on ourselves, of course.
   But they won't.
KALONIKE   What if they drag us into the bedroom?
LYSISTRATA   Hang on to the door.
KALONIKE   What if they slap us?
LYSISTRATA   If they do, you'd better give in.
   But be sulky about it. Do I have to teach you how?
   You know there's no fun for men when they have to
      force you.
   There are millions of ways of getting them to see
      reason.

---

[6] Athenian women were frequently satirized for heavy drinking.
[7] A rugged mountain range in the Peloponnesus.

[8] Demeter and Persephone; a woman's oath.

Don't you worry: a man
doesn't like it unless the girl co-operates.

KALONIKE   I suppose so. Oh, all right! We'll go along!

LAMPITO   Ah imagine us Spahtans can arrange a
peace. But you
Athenians! Why, you're just war-mongerers!

LYSISTRATA   Leave that to me.
I know how to make them listen.

LAMPITO   Ah don't see how.
After all, they've got their boats; and there's lots of
money
piled up in the Acropolis.

LYSISTRATA   The Acropolis? Darling,
we're taking over the Acropolis today!
That's the older women's job. All the rest of us
are going to the Citadel to sacrifice—you understand
me?
And once there, we're in for good!

LAMPITO   Whee! Up the rebels!
Ah can see you're a good strateegist.

LYSISTRATA   Well, then, Lampito,
let's take the oath.

LAMPITO   Say it. We'll sweah.

LYSISTRATA   This is it.
—But Lord! Where's our Inner Guard? Never mind.
                                    —You see this
shield? Put it down there. Now bring me the victim's
entrails.

KALONIKE   But the oath?

LYSISTRATA   You remember how in Aeschylus' *Seven*⁹
they killed a sheep and swore on a shield? Well, then?

KALONIKE   But I don't see how you can swear for
peace on a shield.

LYSISTRATA   What else do you suggest?

KALONIKE   Why not a white horse?
We could swear by that.

LYSISTRATA   And where will you get a white horse?

KALONIKE   I never thought of that. *What* can we do?

MYRRHINE   I have it!
Let's set this big black wine-bowl on the ground
and pour in a gallon or so of Thasian,¹⁰ and swear
not to add one drop of water.

LAMPITO   Ah lahk *that* oath!

---

⁹ *Seven Against Thebes.*
¹⁰ A popular wine from Thasos.

LYSISTRATA   Bring the bowl and the wine-jug.

KALONIKE   Oh, what a simply *huge* one!

LYSISTRATA   Set it down; and, women, place your
hands on the gift-offering.

O Goddess of Persuasion! And thou, O Loving-cup!
Look upon this our sacrifice, and
be gracious!

KALONIKE   It spills out like blood. How red and pretty
it is!

LAMPITO   And Ah must say it smells good.

MYRRHINE   Let me swear first!

KALONIKE   No, by Aphrodite, let's toss for it!

LYSISTRATA   Lampito: all of you women: come, touch
the bowl, and repeat after me:
I WILL HAVE NOTHING TO DO WITH MY
HUSBAND OR MY LOVER

KALONIKE   *I will have nothing to do with my
husband or my lover*

LYSISTRATA   THOUGH HE COME TO ME IN
PITIABLE CONDITION

KALONIKE   *Though he come to me in pitiable
condition*
(Oh, Lysistrata! This is killing me!)

LYSISTRATA   I WILL STAY IN MY HOUSE
UNTOUCHABLE

KALONIKE   *I will stay in my house untouchable*

LYSISTRATA   IN MY THINNEST SAFFRON SILK

KALONIKE   *In my thinnest saffron silk*

LYSISTRATA   AND MAKE HIM LONG FOR ME.

KALONIKE   *And make him long for me.*

LYSISTRATA   I WILL NOT GIVE MYSELF

KALONIKE   *I will not give myself*

LYSISTRATA   AND IF HE CONSTRAINS ME

KALONIKE   *And if he constrains me*

LYSISTRATA   I WILL BE AS COLD AS ICE AND
NEVER MOVE

KALONIKE   *I will be as cold as ice and never move*

LYSISTRATA   I WILL NOT LIFT MY SLIPPERS
TOWARD THE CEILING

KALONIKE   *I will not lift my slippers toward the
ceiling*

LYSISTRATA   OR CROUCH ON ALL FOURS LIKE THE
LIONESS IN THE CARVING

KALONIKE   *Or crouch on all fours like the lioness in
the carving*

LYSISTRATA   AND IF I KEEP THIS OATH LET ME
DRINK FROM THIS BOWL

KALONIKE   *And if I keep this oath let me drink from
this bowl*

LYSISTRATA   IF NOT, LET MY OWN BOWL BE
FILLED WITH WATER.

KALONIKE   *If not, let my own bowl be filled with
water.*

LYSISTRATA   You have all sworn?

MYRRHINE   We have.

LYSISTRATA   Then thus
I sacrifice the victim. *(Drinks largely)*

KALONIKE   Save some for us!
Here's to you, darling, and to you, and to you! It's all
for us women. *(Loud cries off-stage)*

LAMPITO   What's all *that* whoozy-goozy?

LYSISTRATA   Just what I told you.
The older women have taken the Acropolis. Now
   you, Lampito,
rush back to Sparta. We'll take care of things here.
   And
be sure you get organized!
                              The rest of you girls,
up to the Citadel: and mind you push in the bolts.

KALONIKE   But the men? Won't they be after us?

LYSISTRATA   Just you leave
the men to me. There's not fire enough in the world
to make me open *my* door.

KALONIKE   I hope so, by Aphrodite!
At any rate,
let's remember the League's reputation for hanging
   on!

(Exeunt)

The hillside just under the Acropolis.

(Enter CHORUS OF OLD MEN *with burning torches and
braziers; much puffing and coughing)*

MALE CHORAGOS   Easy, Drakes, old friend! Don't skin
   your shoulders
with those damnable big olive-branches. What a job!

Strophe 1

OLD MEN   Forward, forward, comrades! Whew!
   The things that old age does to you!
   Neighbor Strymodoros, would you have thought it?

We've caught it—
                              And from women, too!
Women that used to board with us, bed with us—
Now, by the gods, they've got ahead of us,
Taken the Acropolis (Heaven knows why!),
Profaned the sacred statuar-y,
                              And barred the doors,
                                 The aggravating whores!

MALE CHORAGOS   Come, Philourgos, quick, pile your
   brushwood
next to the wall there.
                              These traitors to Athens and to us,
we'll fry each last one of them! And the very first
will be old Lykon's wife.[11]

Antistrophe 1

OLD MEN   By Demeter I swear it—(ouch!),
   I'll not perform the Kleomenes-crouch!
   How he looked—and a good soldier, too—
      When out he flew,
                              That filthy pouch
   Of a body of his all stinking and shaggy,
   Bare as an eel, except for the bag he
   Covered his rear with. Lord, what a mess!
   Never a bath in six years, I'd guess!
                              Unhappy Sparta,
                                 With such a martyr! [12]

MALE CHORAGOS   What a siege, friends! Seventeen
   ranks strong
we stood at the Gate, and never a chance for a nap.
And all because of women, whom the gods hate
(and so does Euripides).
                              It's enough to make a veteran
turn in his medals from Marathon!

Strophe 2

OLD MEN   Forward, men! Just up the hillside,
   And we're there!
   Keep to the path! A yoke of oxen
      Wouldn't care
         To haul this lumber. Mind the fire,
         Or it'll die before we're higher!
            Puff! Puff!
               This smoke will strangle me, sure enough!

---

[11] Rhodia, a famous belle of the day.

[12] Kleomenes, a king of Sparta, had captured the Acropolis but had
been forced to give it up.

Antistrophe 2

Holy Heracles, I'm blinded,
> Sure as fate!
> It's Lemnos-fire[13] we've been toting;
> And isn't it great
> To be singed by this infernal flame?
> (Laches, remember the Goddess: for shame!)
> Woof! Woof!
> A few steps more, and we're under the roof!

MALE CHORAGOS   It catches! It's blazing!

Down with your loads!
We'll sizzle 'em now,
By all the gods!
Vine-branches here, quick!
Light 'em up,
And in through the gate with 'em!
If that doesn't stop
Their nonsense—well,
We'll smoke 'em to Hell.
Ker*shoo!*
(What we really need
Is a grad-u-ate,
Top of his class,
From Samos Military State.[14]
Achoo!)
Come, do
Your duty, you!
Pour out your braziers,
Embers ablaze!
But first, Gentlemen, allow me to raise
The paean:

> *Lady*
> *Victory, now*
> *Assist thine adherents*
> *Here below!*
> Down with women!
> Up with men!
> *Io triumphe!* [15]

OLD MEN   Amen!

(*Enter* CHORUS OF OLD WOMEN *on the walls of the* Acropolis, *carrying jars of water to extinguish the fire set by the* CHORUS OF OLD MEN)

FEMALE CHORAGOS   Fire, fire!
Quickly, quickly, women, if we're to save ourselves!

Strophe

OLD WOMEN   Nikodike, run!
> Or Kalyke's done
> To a turn, and poor Kratylla's
> Smoked like a ham.
>   Damn
> These men and their wars,
> Their hateful ways!
> I nearly died before I got to the place
> Where we fill our jars:
>   Slaves pushing and jostling—
>   Such a hustling
> I never saw in all my days!

Antistrophe

> But here's water at last.
> Sisters, make haste
> And slosh it down on them,
> The silly old wrecks!
>   Sex
> Almighty! What they want's
> A hot bath? Send it down!
> And thou, Athena of Athens town,
> Assist us in drowning their wheezy taunts!
>   O Trito-born! [16] Helmet of Gold!
>   Help us to cripple their backs, the old
> Fools with their semi-incendiary brawn!

(*The* OLD MEN *capture a woman,* STRATYLLIS)

STRATYLLIS   Let me go! Let me go!
FEMALE CHORAGOS   You walking corpses,
  have you no shame?
MALE CHORAGOS   I wouldn't have believed it!
  An army of women in the Acropolis!
FEMALE CHORAGOS   So we scare you, do we? Grandpa,
  you've seen
  only our pickets yet!
MALE CHORAGOS   Hey, Phaidrias!
  Help me with the necks of these jabbering hens!

---

[13] Volcanic; Mount Moschylus on the island of Lemnos was the site of Vulcan's forge.

[14] At this time Samos was the headquarters of Athenian military activities.

[15] A ritual cry of triumph.

---

[16] Athena; according to some versions of her story, she was born at Lake Tritonis in Libya.

FEMALE CHORAGOS   Down with your pots, girls! We'll need both hands
if these antiques attack us.
MALE CHORAGOS   Want your face kicked in?
FEMALE CHORAGOS   Want to try my teeth?
MALE CHORAGOS   Look out! I've got a stick!
FEMALE CHORAGOS   You lay a half-inch of your stick
on Stratyllis,
And you'll never stick again!
MALE CHORAGOS   Fall apart!
FEMALE CHORAGOS   I'll chew your guts!
MALE CHORAGOS   Euripides! Master!
How well you knew women!
FEMALE CHORAGOS   Listen to him! Rhodippe,
up with the pots!
MALE CHORAGOS   Demolition of God,
what good are your pots?
FEMALE CHORAGOS   You refugee from the tomb,
What good is your fire?
MALE CHORAGOS   Good enough to make a pyre
to barbecue you!
FEMALE CHORAGOS   We'll squizzle your kindling!
MALE CHORAGOS   You think so?
FEMALE CHORAGOS   Yah! Just hang around a while!
MALE CHORAGOS   Want a touch of my torch?
FEMALE CHORAGOS   Your torch needs a bath.
MALE CHORAGOS   How about you?
FEMALE CHORAGOS   Soap for a senile bridegroom!
MALE CHORAGOS   Senile? Hold your trap!
FEMALE CHORAGOS   Just *you* try to hold it!
MALE CHORAGOS   The yammer of women!
FEMALE CHORAGOS   The yatter of men!
But you'll never sit in the jury-box again.
MALE CHORAGOS   Gentlemen, I beg you, burn off that
woman's hair!
FEMALE CHORAGOS   Let it come down! *(They empty
their pots on the men)*
MALE CHORAGOS   What a way to drown!
FEMALE CHORAGOS   Hot, hey?
MALE CHORAGOS   Say,
enough!
FEMALE CHORAGOS   Dandruff
needs watering. I'll make you
nice and fresh.
MALE CHORAGOS   For God's sake, you
sluts, hold off!

(Enter a MAGISTRATE *accompanied by four constables)*

MAGISTRATE   These degenerate women! What a
racket of little drums,
what a yapping for Adonis on every house-top!
It's like the time in the Assembly when I was
listening
to a speech—out of order, as usual—by that fool
Demostratos,[17] all about troops for Sicily,
that kind of nonsense—
                    and there was his wife
trotting around in circles howling
Alas for Adonis!—
                    and Demostratos insisting
we must draft every last Zakynthian that can walk—
and his wife up there on the roof,
drunk as an owl, yowling
Oh weep for Adonis!—
                    and that damned ox Demostratos
mooing away through the rumpus. That's what we
get
for putting up with this wretched woman-business!
MALE CHORAGOS   Sir, you haven't heard the half of it.
They laughed at us!
Insulted us! They took pitchers of water
and nearly drowned us! We're still wringing out our
clothes,
for all the world like unhousebroken brats.
MAGISTRATE   And a good thing, by Poseidon!
Whose fault is it if these women-folk of ours
get out of hand? We coddle them,
we teach them to be wasteful and loose. You'll see a
husband
go into a jeweler's. "Look," he'll say,
"jeweler," he'll say, "you remember that gold choker
"you made for my wife? Well, she went to a dance
last night
"and broke the clasp. Now, I've got to go to Salamis,
"and can't be bothered. Run over to my house
tonight,
"will you, and see if you can put it together for her."

---

[17] A well known demagogue; the speech alludes to the festival in honor of Adonis which four years earlier had coincided with the decision to undertake the disastrous Sicilian expedition. It was believed that the women's madness in lamenting Adonis had influenced the decision.

Or another one
goes to a cobbler—a good strong workman, too,
with an awl that was never meant for child's play.
  "Here,"
he'll tell him, "one of my wife's shoes is pinching
"her little toe. Could you come up about noon
"and stretch it out for her?"
                              Well, what do you expect?
Look at me, for example. I'm a Public Officer,
and it's one of my duties to pay off the sailors.
And where's the money? Up there in the Acropolis!
And those blasted women slam the door in my face!
But what are we waiting for?
                         —Look here, constable,
stop sniffing around for a tavern, and get us
some crowbars. We'll force their gates! As a matter of
  fact,
I'll do a little forcing myself.

(*Enter* LYSISTRATA, *above, with* MYRRHINE, KALONIKE,
and the BOEOTIAN)

LYSISTRATA   No need of forcing.
  Here I am, of my own accord. And all this talk
  about locked doors—! We don't need locked doors,
  but just the least bit of common sense.
MAGISTRATE   Is that so, ma'am!
                         —Where's my constable?
                              —Constable,
  arrest that woman, and tie her hands behind her.
LYSISTRATA   If he touches me, I swear by Artemis
  there'll be one scamp dropped from the public pay-
    roll tomorrow!
MAGISTRATE   Well, constable? You're not afraid, I
    suppose? Grab her,
  two of you, around the middle!
KALONIKE   No, by Pandrosos! [18]
  Lay a hand on her, and I'll jump on you so hard
  your guts will come out the back door!
MAGISTRATE   That's what *you* think!
  Where's the sergeant?—Here, you: tie up that trollop
    first,
  the one with the pretty talk!
MYRRHINE   By the Moon-Goddess! [19]

Just you try it, and you'd better call a surgeon!
MAGISTRATE   Another one!
                         Officer, seize that woman!
                                        I swear
  I'll put an end to this riot!
BOEOTIAN   By the Taurian, [20]
  one inch closer and you won't have a hair on your
    head!
MAGISTRATE   Lord, what a mess! And my constables
    seem to have left me.
  But—women get the best of us? By God, no!
                                        —Scythians! [21]
  Close ranks and forward march!
LYSISTRATA   "Forward," indeed!
  By the Two Goddesses, what's the sense in *that*?
  They're up against four companies of women
  armed from top to bottom.
MAGISTRATE   Forward, my Scythians!
LYSISTRATA   Forward, yourselves, dear comrades!
  You grainlettucebeanseedmarket girls!
  You garlicandonionbreadbakery girls!
  Give it to 'em! Knock 'em down! Scratch 'em!
  Tell 'em what you think of 'em! (*General mêlée; the
    Scythians yield*)
                         —Ah, that's enough!
  Sound a retreat; good soldiers don't rob the dead!
MAGISTRATE   A nice day *this* has been for the police!
LYSISTRATA   Well, there you are.—Did you really
    think we women
  would be driven like slaves? Maybe now you'll admit
  that a woman knows something about glory.
MAGISTRATE   Glory enough,
  especially glory in bottles! Dear Lord Apollo!
MALE CHORAGOS   Your Honor, there's no use talking
    to them. Words
  mean nothing whatever to wild animals like these.
  Think of the sousing they gave us! and the water
  was not, I believe, of the purest.
FEMALE CHORAGOS   You shouldn't have come after us.
    And if you try it again,
  you'll be one eye short!—Although, as a matter of
    fact,
  what I like best is just to stay at home and read,

---

[18] One of the daughters of the founder of Athens; a woman's oath.
[19] Artemis.

[20] Again Artemis, who was worshiped at Taurica Chersonesos.
[21] Athens' finest archers.

like a sweet little bride: never hurting a soul, no,
never going out. But if you *must* shake hornets'
   nests,
look out for the hornets!

Strophe

OLD MEN   Good God, what can we do?
      What are we coming to?
These women! Who could bear it? But, for that
   matter, who
         Will find
         What they had in mind
         When they seized Cranaos' city
         And held it (more's the pity!)
Against us men of Athens, and our police force, too?

MALE CHORAGOS   We might question them, I suppose.
   But I warn you, sir,
   don't believe anything you hear! It would be un-
   Athenian
   not to get to the bottom of this plot.
MAGISTRATE   Very well.
   My first question is this: Why, so help you God,
   did you bar the gates of the Acropolis?
LYSISTRATA   Why?
   To keep the money, of course. No money, no war.
MAGISTRATE   You think that money's the cause of
   war?
LYSISTRATA   I do.
   Money brought about the Peisandros business[22]
   and all the other attacks on the State. Well and good!
   They'll not get another cent here!
MAGISTRATE   And what will you do?
LYSISTRATA   What a question! From now on, we
   intend
   to control the Treasury.
MAGISTRATE   Control the Treasury!
LYSISTRATA   Why not? Does that seem strange? After
   all,
   we control our household budgets.
MAGISTRATE   But that's different!
LYSISTRATA   "Different"? What do you mean?
MAGISTRATE   I mean simply this:

it's the Treasury that pays for National Defense.
LYSISTRATA   Unnecessary. We propose to abolish war!
MAGISTRATE   Good God.—And National Security?
LYSISTRATA   Leave that to us.
MAGISTRATE   You?
LYSISTRATA   Us.
MAGISTRATE   We're done for, then!
LYSISTRATA   Never mind.
   We women will save you in spite of yourselves.
MAGISTRATE   What nonsense!
LYSISTRATA   If you like. But you must accept it, like it
   or not.
MAGISTRATE   Why, this is downright subversion!
LYSISTRATA   Maybe it is.
   But we're going to save you, Judge.
MAGISTRATE   I don't *want* to be saved!
LYSISTRATA   Tut. The death-wish. All the more
   reason.
MAGISTRATE   But the idea of women bothering
   themselves about peace and war!
LYSISTRATA   Will you listen to me?
MAGISTRATE   Yes. But be brief, or I'll—
LYSISTRATA   This is no time for stupid threats.
MAGISTRATE   By the gods,
   I'm losing my mind!
AN OLD WOMAN   That's nice. If you do, remember
   you've less to lose than *we* have.
MAGISTRATE   Quiet, you old buzzard!
   Now, Lysistrata: tell me what you're thinking.
LYSISTRATA   Glad to.
                  Ever since this war began
   we women have been watching you men, agreeing
      with you,
   keeping our thoughts to ourselves. That doesn't
      mean
   we were happy: we weren't, for we saw how things
      were going;
   but we'd listen to you at dinner
   arguing this way and that.
                         —Oh you, and your big
Top Secrets!—
                  And then we'd grin like little patriots
   (though goodness knows we didn't feel like
      grinning) and ask you:
   "Dear, did the Armistice come up in Assembly
      today?"

---

[22] A politician who, even as Aristophanes was completing this play, was bringing about the revolution of the Four Hundred, which overthrew Athenian democracy.

And you'd say, "None of your business! Pipe
      down!," you'd say.
And so we would.

AN OLD WOMAN   *I* wouldn't have, by God!

MAGISTRATE   You'd have taken a beating, then!
                                          —Please go on.

LYSISTRATA   Well, we'd be quiet. But then, you know,
      all at once
you men would think up something worse than ever.
Even *I* could see it was fatal. And, "Darling," I'd say,
"have you gone completely mad?" And my husband
      would look at me
and say, "Wife, you've got your weaving to attend to.
"Mind your tongue, if you don't want a slap. 'War's
" 'a man's affair!' " [23]

MAGISTRATE   Good words, and well pronounced!

LYSISTRATA   You're a fool if you think so.
                                  It was hard enough
to put up with all this banquet-hall strategy.
But then we'd hear you out in the public square:
"Nobody left for the draft-quota here in Athens?"
you'd say; and, "No," someone else would say, "not
      a man!"
And so we women decided to rescue Greece.
You might as well listen to us now: you'll have to,
      later.

MAGISTRATE   *You* rescue Greece? Absurd!

LYSISTRATA   You're the absurd one!

MAGISTRATE   You expect me to take orders from a
      woman?

LYSISTRATA   Heavens, if that's what's bothering you,
      take my veil,
here, and my girdle, and my market-basket. Go
      home
to your weaving and your cooking! I tell you, "War's
a woman's affair!"

FEMALE CHORAGOS   Down with your pitchers,
      comrades,
but keep them close at hand. It's time for a rally!

Antistrophe

OLD WOMEN   Dance, girls, dance for peace!
      Who cares if our knees

Wobble and creak? Shall we not dance for such allies
      as these?
            Their wit! their grace! their beauty!
            It's a municipal duty
To dance them luck and happiness who risk their all
      for Greece!

FEMALE CHORAGOS   Women, remember your
      grandmothers! Remember, you were born
among brambles and nettles! Dance for victory!

LYSISTRATA   O Eros, god of delight! O Aphrodite!
      Cyprian!
Drench us now with the savor of love!
Let these men, getting wind of us, dream such joy
that they'll tail us through all the provinces of
      Hellas!

MAGISTRATE   And if we do?

LYSISTRATA   Well, for one thing, we shan't have to
      watch you
going to market, a spear in one hand, and heavens
      knows
what in the other.

FEMALE CHORAGOS   Nicely said, by Aphrodite!

LYSISTRATA   As things stand now, you're neither men
      nor women.
Armor clanking with kitchen pans and pots—
you sound like a pack of Corybantes! [24]

MAGISTRATE   A man must do what a man must do.

LYSISTRATA   So I'm told.
But to see a General, complete with Gorgon-shield,
jingling along the dock to buy a couple of herrings!

FEMALE CHORAGOS   *I* saw a Captain the other day—
      lovely fellow he was,
nice curly hair—sitting on his horse; and—can you
      believe it?—
he'd just bought some soup, and was pouring it into
      his helmet!
And there was a soldier from Thrace
swishing his lance like something out of Euripides,
and the poor fruit-store woman got so scared
that she ran away and let him have his figs free!

MAGISTRATE   All this is beside the point.
                          Will you be so kind
as to tell me how you mean to save Greece?

---

[23] Quoted from Hektor's farewell to Andromache, *Iliad*, VI, 492.

[24] Wild and frenzied dancers; attendants of the goddess Cybele.

LYSISTRATA   Of course!
Nothing could be simpler.
MAGISTRATE   I assure you, I'm all ears.
LYSISTRATA   Do you know anything about weaving?
Say the yarn gets tangled: we thread it
this way and that through the skein, up and down,
until it's free. And it's like that with war.
We'll send our envoys
up and down, this way and that, all over Greece,
until it's finished.
MAGISTRATE   Yarn? Thread? Skein?
Are you out of your mind? I tell you,
war is a serious business.
LYSISTRATA   So serious
that I'd like to go on talking about weaving.
MAGISTRATE   All right. Go ahead.
LYSISTRATA   The first thing we have to do
is to wash our yarn, get the dirt out of it.
You see? Isn't there too much dirt here in Athens?
You must wash those men away.
                              Then our spoiled wool—
that's like your job-hunters, out for a life
of no work and big pay. Back to the basket,
citizens or not, allies or not,
or friendly immigrants!
                          And your colonies?
Hanks of wool lost in various places. Pull them
together, weave them into one great whole,
and our voters are clothed for ever.
MAGISTRATE   It would take a woman
to reduce state questions to a matter of carding and
    weaving!
LYSISTRATA   You fool! Who were the mothers whose
    sons sailed off
to fight for Athens in Sicily?
MAGISTRATE   Enough!
I beg you, do not call back those memories.
LYSISTRATA   And then,
instead of the love that every woman needs,
we have only our single beds, where we can dream
of our husbands off with the Army.
                              Bad enough for wives!
But what about our girls, getting older every day,
and older, and no kisses?
MAGISTRATE   Men get older, too.
LYSISTRATA   Not in the same sense.

                          A soldier's discharged,
and he may be bald and toothless, yet he'll find
a pretty young thing to go to bed with.
                              But a woman!
Her beauty is gone with the first grey hair.
She can spend her time
consulting the oracles and the fortune-tellers,
but they'll never send her a husband.
MAGISTRATE   Still, if a man can rise to the occasion—
LYSISTRATA (Furiously)   Rise? Rise, yourself!
Go invest in a coffin!
                    You've money enough.
                              I'll bake you
a cake for the Underworld.[25]
                          And here's your funeral
wreath! (She pours water upon him)
MYRRHINE   And here's another! (More water)
KALONIKE   And here's
my contribution! (More water)
LYSISTRATA   What are you waiting for?
All aboard Styx Ferry![26]
                        Charon's calling for you!
It's sailing-time: don't disrupt the schedule!
MAGISTRATE   The insolence of women! And to me!
No, by God, I'll go back to court and show
the rest of the Bench the things that might happen to
    them!

(Exit MAGISTRATE)

LYSISTRATA   Really, I suppose we should have laid out
    his corpse
on the doorstep, in the usual way.
                          But never mind!
We'll give him the rites of the dead tomorrow
    morning!

(Exit LYSISTRATA with MYRRHINE and KALONIKE)

Strophe 1

OLD MEN   Sons of Liberty, strip off your clothes for
    action! Men arise!

---

[25] A honey cake was usually placed in the hand of the dead to be
given to Cerberus, the three-headed dog guarding the gates of
Hades.
[26] The Styx was the river over which Charon ferried the souls of the
dead.

Shall we stand here limp and useless while old
  Cleisthenes'[27] allies
Prod a herd of furious grandmas to attempt to bring
  to pass
A female restoration of the Reign of Hippias?[28]
      Forbid it, gods misogynist!
      Return our Treasury, at least!
We must clothe ourselves and feed ourselves to face
  these civic rages,
And who can do a single thing if they cut off our
  wages?
MALE CHORAGOS   Gentlemen, we are disgraced
  forever if we allow
these madwomen to jabber about spears and shields
and make friends with the Spartans. What's a
  Spartan? a wild
wolf's a safer companion any day! No; their plan's
to bring back Dictatorship; and we won't stand for
  that!
From now on, let's go armed, each one of us
a new Aristogeiton!
          And to begin with,
I propose to poke a number of teeth
down the gullet of that harridan over there.

Antistrophe 1

OLD WOMEN   Hold your tongues, you senile bravoes,
  or I swear, when you get home
Your own mothers wouldn't know you! Strip for
  action, ladies, come!
I bore the holy vessels in my eighth year,[29] and at ten
I was pounding out the barley for Athena Goddess,[30]
  then
      They elected me Little Bear
      For Artemis at Brauron Fair,[31]
I'd been made a Basket-Carrier[32] by the time I came
  of age:

So trust me to advise you in this feminist rampage!
FEMALE CHORAGOS   As a woman, I pay my taxes to the
  State,
though I pay them in baby boys. What do you
  contribute,
you impotent horrors? Nothing but waste:
our treasury, the so-called Glory of the Persian Wars,
gone! rifled! parceled out for privilege! And you
have the insolence to control public policy,
leading us all to disaster!
              No, don't answer back
unless you want the heel of my slipper
slap against that ugly jaw of yours!

Strophe 2

OLD MEN   What impudence!
      What malevolence!
      Comrades, make haste,
All those of you who still are sensitive below the
  waist!
      Off with your clothes, men!
      Nobody knows when
        We'll put them back on.
          Remember Leipsydrion![33]
      We may be old,
      But let's be bold!
MALE CHORAGOS   Give them an inch, and we're done
  for! We'll have them
launching boats next and planning naval strategy.
Or perhaps they fancy themselves as cavalry!
That's fair enough: women know how to ride,
they're good in the saddle. Just think of Mikon's
  paintings,[34]
all those Amazons wrestling with men! No, it's time
to bridle these wild mares!

Antistrophe 2

OLD WOMEN   Hold on, or
      You *are* done for,
      By the Two Goddesses above!
Strip, strip, my women: we've got the veterans on the
  move!
      Tangle with me, Gramps,

---

[27] An Athenian of notorious bisexual tendencies.
[28] Last of the Athenian tyrants. He had ruled with his brother Hipparchos until the latter's death at the hands of the patriots Aristogeiton and Harmonius: Hippias was killed later at Marathon.
[29] Four girls of high birth between the ages of seven and eleven were
appointed to service in the Temple of Athena in the Acropolis.
[30] At ten a girl of aristocratic family was eligible to be Millmaid and
to grind the sacred grain of Athena.
[31] Brauron was a town on the coast of Attica where a ceremony to
Artemis was celebrated in which a little girl impersonated a bear.
[32] Girls carried baskets containing precious objects sacred to Athena.

---

[33] After the patriots had killed Hipparchos, they fled and fortified
themselves in Leipsydrion; after a heroic defense they were forced
to surrender.
[34] Mikon was one of the many painters who dealt with the invasion
of Attica by the Amazons, a fabulous race of warrior-women.

And you'll have cramps
   For the rest of your days!
     No more beans! No more cheese!
My two legs
Will scramble your eggs!

FEMALE CHORAGOS   If Lampito stands by me, and that elegant
   Theban girl, Ismenia—what good are *you?*
                      Pass your laws!
   Laws upon laws, you decrepit legislators!
   At the worst you're just a nuisance, rationing Boeotian eels
   on the Feast of Hecate, making our girls go without!
   That was statesmanship! And we'll have to put up with it
   until some patriot slits your silly old gizzards!

(Exeunt omnes)

The scene shifts to a court within the Acropolis.

(Re-enter LYSISTRATA*)*

FEMALE CHORAGOS   But Lysistrata! Leader! Why such a grim face?
LYSISTRATA   Oh the behavior of these idiotic women!
   There's something about the female temperament that I can't bear!
FEMALE CHORAGOS   What in the world do you mean?
LYSISTRATA   Exactly what I say.
FEMALE CHORAGOS   What dreadful thing has happened?
   Come, tell us: we're all your friends.
LYSISTRATA   It isn't easy
   to say it; yet, God knows, we can't hush it up.
FEMALE CHORAGOS   Well, then? Out with it!
LYSISTRATA   To put it bluntly,
   we're desperate for men.
FEMALE CHORAGOS   Almighty God!
LYSISTRATA   Why bring God into it?—No, it's just as I say.
   I can't manage them any longer: they've gone man-crazy,
   they're all trying to get out.
             Why, look:
   one of them was sneaking out the back door
   over there by Pan's cave,[35] another
   was sliding down the walls with rope and tackle;

another was climbing aboard a sparrow,[36] ready to take off
for the nearest brothel—I dragged *her* back by the hair!
They're all finding some reason to leave.
                    Look there!
There goes another one.
              —Just a minute, you!
Where are you off to so fast?
FIRST WOMAN   I've got to get home!
   I've a lot of Milesian wool, and the worms are spoiling it.
LYSISTRATA   Oh bother you and your worms! Get back inside!
FIRST WOMAN   I'll be back right away, I swear I will!
   I just want to get it stretched out on my bed.
LYSISTRATA   You'll do no such thing. You'll stay right here.
FIRST WOMAN   And my wool?
   You want it ruined?
LYSISTRATA   Yes, for all I care.
SECOND WOMAN   Oh dear! My lovely new flax from Amorgos—[37]
   I left it at home, all uncarded!
LYSISTRATA   Another one!
   And all she wants is someone to card her flax.
   Get back in there!
SECOND WOMAN   But I swear by the Moon-Goddess,
   the minute I get it done, I'll be back!
LYSISTRATA   I say No!
   If you, why not all the other women as well?
THIRD WOMAN   O Lady Eileithyia![38] Radiant goddess! Thou
   intercessor for women in childbirth! Stay, I pray thee,
   oh stay this parturition! Shall I pollute
   a sacred spot?
LYSISTRATA   And what's the matter with *you?*
THIRD WOMAN   I'm having a baby—any minute now!
LYSISTRATA   But you weren't pregnant yesterday.
THIRD WOMAN   Well, I am today!

---

[35] A grotto on the north side of the Acropolis.

[36] A bird sacred to Aphrodite; it had been harnessed to the chariot of the goddess.

[37] An island in the Aegean famed for its flax.

[38] The goddess invoked by women at childbirth; it was unlawful to bear children on the Acropolis because it was holy ground.

Let me go home for a midwife, Lysistrata:
there's not much time.
LYSISTRATA   I never heard such nonsense.
What's that bulging under your cloak?
THIRD WOMAN   A little baby boy.
LYSISTRATA   It certainly isn't. But it's something
    hollow,
    like a basin or— Why, it's the helmet of Athena!
    And you said you were having a baby!
THIRD WOMAN   Well, I am! So there!
LYSISTRATA   Then why the helmet?
THIRD WOMAN   I was afraid that my pains
    might begin here in the Acropolis; and I wanted
    to drop my chick into it, just as the dear doves do.
LYSISTRATA   Lies! Evasions!—But at least one thing's
    clear:
    you can't leave the place before your purification.
THIRD WOMAN   But I can't stay here in the Acropolis!
    Last night I dreamed
    of a snake.[39]
FIRST WOMAN   And those horrible owls,[40] the noise
    they make!
    I can't get a bit of sleep; I'm just about dead.
LYSISTRATA   You useless girls, that's enough: Let's
    have no more lying.
    Of course you want your men. But don't you
        imagine
    that they want you just as much? I'll give you my
        word,
    their nights must be pretty hard.
                          Just stick it out!
    A little patience, that's all, and our battle's won.
    I have heard an Oracle. Should you like to hear it?
FIRST WOMAN   An Oracle? Yes, tell us!
LYSISTRATA   Quiet, then.—Here
    is what it said:
    IF EVER THE SWALLOWS, ESCHEWING HOOPOE-
        BIRDS,
    SHALL CONSPIRE TOGETHER TO DENY THEM
        ALL ACCESS,
    THEIR GRIEF IS FOREVER OVER.
                          These are the words

from the Shrine itself.
                    AYE, AND ZEUS WILL REDRES
    THEIR WRONGS, AND SET THE LOWER ABOVE
    THE HIGHER.
FIRST WOMAN   Does that mean we'll be on top?
LYSISTRATA   BUT IF THEY RETIRE,
    EACH SWALLOW HER OWN WAY, FROM THIS
        HOLY PLACE,
    LET THE WORLD PROCLAIM NO BIRD OF
        SORRIER GRACE
    THAN THE SWALLOW.
FIRST WOMAN   I swear, *that* Oracle makes sense!
LYSISTRATA   Now, then, by all the gods,
    let's show that we're bigger than these annoyances.
    Back to your places! Let's not disgrace the Oracle.

(*Exeunt* LYSISTRATA *and the dissident women; the*
CHORUSES *renew their conflict*)

Strophe

OLD MEN   I know a little story that I learned way back
    in school
    Goes like this:
    Once upon a time there was a young man—and no
        fool—
    Named Melanion,[41] and his
    One aversi-on was marriage. He loathed the very
        thought!
    So he ran off to the hills, and in a special grot
    Raised a dog, and spent his days
    Hunting rabbits. And it says
    That he never never never did come home.
    It might be called a refuge *from* the womb.
    All right,
            all right,
                    all right!
    We're as pure as young Melanion, and we hate the
        very sight
    Of you sluts!
A MAN   How about a kiss, old woman?
A WOMAN   Here's an onion in your eye!
A MAN   A kick in the guts, then?
A WOMAN   Try, old bristle-tail, just try!

---

[39] The sacred snake of the Acropolis; it was never seen but was believed to guard the holy ground.
[40] Birds sacred to Athena.

[41] The suitor of Atalanta, who hated men. The Chorus of Old Men
have made him a hater of women.

A MAN   Yet they say Myronides[42]
On hands and knees
Looked just as shaggy fore and aft as I!

Antistrophe

OLD WOMEN   Well, *I* know a little story, and it's just as
good as yours.
Goes like this:
Once there was a man named Timon[43]—a rough
diamond, of course,
And that whiskery face of his
Looked like murder in the shrubbery. By God, he
was a son
Of the Furies, let me tell you! And what did he do
but run
From the world and all its ways,
Cursing mankind! And it says
That his choicest execrations as of then
Were leveled almost wholly at *old* men.
All right,
all right,
all right!
But there's one thing about Timon: he could always
stand the sight
Of us "sluts"!
A WOMAN   How about a crack in the jaw, Pop?
A MAN   I can take it, Ma—no fear!
A WOMAN   How about a kick in the face?
A MAN   You'd show your venerable rear.
A WOMAN   I may be old;
But I've been told
That I've nothing to worry about down there!

(*Re-enter* LYSISTRATA)

LYSISTRATA   Oh, quick, girls, quick! Come here!
FEMALE CHORAGOS   What is it?
LYSISTRATA   A man!
A man simply bulging with love!
O Cyprian Queen,
O Paphian, O Cythereian! Hear us and aid us!
FEMALE CHORAGOS   Where is this enemy?
LYSISTRATA   Over there, by Demeter's shrine.
FEMALE CHORAGOS   Damned if he isn't. But who *is* he?

----

[42] A famous Athenian general.
[43] A famous Athenian misanthrope.

MYRRHINE   My husband.
Kinesias.
LYSISTRATA   Oh then, get busy! Tease him!
Undermine him!
Wreck him! Give him everything—kissing, tickling,
nudging,
whatever you generally torture him with—: give him
everything
except what we swore on the wine we would not
give.
MYRRHINE   Trust me!
LYSISTRATA   I do. But I'll help you get him started.
The rest of you women, stay back.

(*Enter* KINESIAS)

KINESIAS   Oh God! Oh my God!
I'm stiff for lack of exercise. All I can do to stand up!
LYSISTRATA   Halt! Who are you, approaching our
lines?
KINESIAS   Me? I.
LYSISTRATA   A man?
KINESIAS   You have eyes, haven't you?
LYSISTRATA   Go away.
KINESIAS   Who says so?
LYSISTRATA   Officer of the Day.
KINESIAS   Officer, I beg you,
by all the gods at once, bring Myrrhine out!
LYSISTRATA   Myrrhine? And who, my good sir, are
you?
KINESIAS   Kinesias. Last name's Pennison. Her
husband.
LYSISTRATA   Oh, of course. I beg your pardon. We're
glad to see you.
We've heard so much about you. Dearest Myrrhine
is always talking about "Kinesias"—never nibbles an
egg
or an apple without saying
"Here's to Kinesias!"
KINESIAS   Do you really mean it?
LYSISTRATA   I do.
When we're discussing men, she always says,
"Well, after all, there's nobody like Kinesias!"
KINESIAS   Good God.—Well, then, please send her
down here.
LYSISTRATA   And what do *I* get out of it?
KINESIAS   A standing promise.

LYSISTRATA   I'll take it up with her.

(*Exit* LYSISTRATA)

KINESIAS   But be quick about it!
Lord, what's life without a wife? Can't eat. Can't
    sleep.
Every time I go home, the place is so empty, so
insufferably sad! Love's killing me! Oh,
hurry!

(*Enter* MANES, *a slave, with Kinesias' baby; the voice of*
MYRRHINE *is heard off-stage*)

MYRRHINE   But of course I love him! Adore him!—but
    no,
he hates love. No. I won't go down.

(*Enter* MYRRHINE, *above*)

KINESIAS   Myrrhine!
Darlingest little Myrrhine! Come down quick!
MYRRHINE   Certainly not.
KINESIAS   Not? But why, Myrrhine?
MYRRHINE   Why? You don't need me.
KINESIAS   Need you? My God, *look* at me!
MYRRHINE   So long! (*Turns to go*)
KINESIAS   Myrrhine, Myrrhine, Myrrhine!
If not for my sake, for our child! (*Pinches* BABY)
                —All right, you: pipe up!
BABY   Mummie! Mummie! Mummie!
KINESIAS   You hear that?
Pitiful, I call it. Six days now
with never a bath; no food; enough to break your
    heart!
MYRRHINE   My darlingest child! What a father *you*
    acquired!
KINESIAS   At least come down for his sake!
MYRRHINE   I suppose I must.
Oh, this mother business! [44]

(*Exit*)

KINESIAS   How pretty she is! And younger!
She's so much nicer when she's bothered!

(MYRRHINE *enters, below*)

MYRRHINE   Dearest child,

you're as sweet as your father's horrid. Give me a
    kiss.
KINESIAS   Now you see how wrong it was to get
    involved
in this scheming League of women. All this agony
for nothing!
MYRRHINE   Keep your hands to yourself!
KINESIAS   But our house
going to rack and ruin?
MYRRHINE   I don't care.
KINESIAS   And your knitting
all torn to pieces by the chickens? Don't you care?
MYRRHINE   Not at all.
KINESIAS   And our vows to Aphrodite?
Oh, *won't* you come back?
MYRRHINE   No.—At least, not until you men
make a treaty to end the war.
KINESIAS   Why, if that's all you want,
by God, we'll make your treaty!
MYRRHINE   Oh? Very well.
When you've done that, I'll come home. But
    meanwhile,
I've sworn an oath.
KINESIAS   Don't worry.—Now, let's have fun.
MYRRHINE   No! Stop it! I said no!
                —Although, of course,
I *do* love you.
KINESIAS   I know you do. Darling Myrrhine:
come, shall we?
MYRRHINE   Are you out of your mind? In front of the
    child?
KINESIAS   Take him home, Manes.

(*Exit* MANES *with baby*)

                          There. He's gone.
                          Come on!
There's nothing to stop us now.
MYRRHINE   You devil! But where?
KINESIAS   In Pan's cave. What could be snugger than
    that?
MYRRHINE   But my purification before I go back to the
    Citadel?
KINESIAS   There's always the Klepsydra.[45]
MYRRHINE   And my oath?

---

[44] A line that parodies Euripides' *Iphigenia at Aulis*, 917.

[45] A sacred spring near Pan's cave.

KINESIAS   Leave the oath to me.
After all, I'm the man.
MYRRHINE   Well . . . if you say so!
                              I'll go find a bed.
KINESIAS   Oh, bother a bed! The ground's good enough
    for me!
MYRRHINE   No. You're a bad man, but you deserve
    something better than dirt.

(*Exit* MYRRHINE)

KINESIAS   What a love she is! And how thoughtful!

(*Re-enter* MYRRHINE)

MYRRHINE   Here's your bed.
    Now let me get my clothes off.
                        But, good horrors!
    We haven't a mattress!
KINESIAS   Oh, forget the mattress!
MYRRHINE   No.
    Just lying on blankets? Too sordid!
KINESIAS   Give me a kiss.
MYRRHINE   Just a second.

(*Exit* MYRRHINE)

KINESIAS   I swear, I'll explode!

(*Re-enter* MYRRHINE)

MYRRHINE   Here's your mattress.
    Go to bed now. I'll just take my dress off.
                            But look—
    where's our pillow?
KINESIAS   I don't need a pillow!
MYRRHINE   Well, *I* do.

(*Exit* MYRRHINE)

KINESIAS   I don't suppose even Heracles
    would stand for this!

(*Re-enter* MYRRHINE)

MYRRHINE   There we are. Ups-a-daisy!
KINESIAS   So we are. Well, come to bed.
MYRRHINE   But I wonder:
    is everything ready now?
KINESIAS   I can swear to that. Come, darling!
MYRRHINE   Just getting out of my girdle.
                        But remember, now,

what you promised about the treaty!
KINESIAS   I'll remember.
MYRRHINE   But no coverlet!
KINESIAS   Damn it, I'll be
    your coverlet!
MYRRHINE   Be right back.

(*Exit* MYRRHINE)

KINESIAS   This girl and her coverlets
    will be the death of me.

(*Re-enter* MYRRHINE)

MYRRHINE   Here we are. Up you go!
KINESIAS   Up? I've been up for ages!
MYRRHINE   Some perfume?
KINESIAS   No, by Apollo!
MYRRHINE   Yes, by Aphrodite!
    I don't care whether you want it or not.

(*Exit* MYRRHINE)

KINESIAS   For love's sake, hurry!

(*Re-enter* MYRRHINE)

MYRRHINE   Here, in your hand. Rub it right in.
KINESIAS   Never cared for perfume.
    And this is particularly strong. Still, here goes!
MYRRHINE   What a nitwit I am! I brought you the
    Rhodian bottle! [46]
KINESIAS   Forget it.
MYRRHINE   No trouble at all. You just wait here.

(*Exit* MYRRHINE)

KINESIAS   God damn the man who invented perfume!

(*Re-enter* MYRRHINE)

MYRRHINE   At last! The right bottle!
KINESIAS   I've got the rightest
    bottle of all, and it's right here waiting for you.
    Darling, forget everything else. Do come to bed!
MYRRHINE   Just let me get my shoes off.
                        —And, by the way,
    you'll vote for the treaty?
KINESIAS   I'll think about it.

_____
[46] From Rhodes.

(MYRRHINE *runs away*)

There! That's done it! Off she runs,
with never a thought for the way I'm feeling. I must
have *some*one, or I'll go mad! Myrrhine
has just about ruined me.

                    And you, strutting little soldier:
what about you? There's nothing for it, I guess,
But an expedition to old Dog-fox's[47] bordello.

OLD MEN   She's left you in a sorry state:
            You have my sympathy.
        What upright citizen could bear
           Your pain? I swear, not I!
Just the look of you, with never a woman
To come to your aid! It isn't human!

KINESIAS   The agony!

MALE CHORAGOS   Well, why not?
        She has you on the spot!

FEMALE CHORAGOS   A lovelier girl never breathed, you
old sot!

KINESIAS   A lovelier girl? Zeus! Zeus!
        Produce a hurricane
        To hoist these lovely girls aloft
        And drop them down again
    Bump on our lances! Then they'd know
    What they do that makes men suffer so.

(*Exit* KINESIAS)

(*Enter a* SPARTAN HERALD)

HERALD   Gentlemen, Ah beg you will be so kind
as to direct me to the Central Committee.
Ah have a communication.

(*Re-enter* MAGISTRATE)

MAGISTRATE   Are you a man,
or a fertility symbol?

HERALD   Ah refuse to answer that question!
Ah'm a certified herald from Spahta, and Ah've
    come
to talk about an ahmistice.

MAGISTRATE   Then why
that spear under your cloak?

HERALD   Ah have no speah!

MAGISTRATE   You don't walk naturally, with your
    tunic
poked out so. You have a tumor, maybe,
or a hernia?

HERALD   No, by Castor![48]

MAGISTRATE   Well,
something's wrong, I can see that. And I don't like it.

HERALD   Colonel, Ah resent this.

MAGISTRATE   So I see. But what *is* it?

HERALD   A scroll
with a message from Spahta.

MAGISTRATE   Oh. I've heard about these scrolls.
    Well, then, man, speak out: How are things in
    Sparta?

HERALD   Hard, Colonel, hard! We're at a standstill.
Can't seem to think of anything but women.

MAGISTRATE   How curious! Tell me, do you Spartans
    think
that maybe Pan's to blame?

HERALD   Pan? No. Lampito and her little naked
    friends.
They won't let a man come near them.

MAGISTRATE   How are you handling it?

HERALD   Losing our minds,
    if you want to know, and walking around hunched
    over
like men carrying candles in a gale.
The women have sworn they'll have nothing to do
    with us
until we get a treaty.

MAGISTRATE   Yes, I know.
    It's a general uprising, sir, in all parts of Greece.
But as for the answer—
        Sir: go back to Sparta
and have them send us your Armistice Commission.
I'll arrange things in Athens.
        And I may say
that my standing is good enough to make them
    listen.

HERALD   A man after mah own heart! Sir, Ah thank
    you!

(*Exit* HERALD)

---

[47] Nickname for a famous procurer.

[48] One of Sparta's protective spirits.

Strophe

OLD MEN   Oh these women! Where will you find
                    A slavering beast that's more unkind?
                        Where a hotter fire?
                    Give me a panther, any day!
                    He's not so merciless as they,
                        And panthers don't conspire!

Antistrophe

OLD WOMEN   We may be hard, you silly old ass,
                        But who brought you to this stupid pass?
                            You're the ones to blame.
                        Fighting with us, your oldest friends,
                        Simply to serve your selfish ends—
                            Really, you have no shame!

MALE CHORAGOS   No, I'm through with women for
    ever! [49]

FEMALE CHORAGOS   If you say so.
    Still, you might put some clothes on. You look too
        absurd
    standing around naked. Come, get into this cloak.

MALE CHORAGOS   Thank you; you're right. I merely
    took it off
    because I was in such a temper.

FEMALE CHORAGOS   That's much better
    Now you resemble a man again.
                                Why have you been so horrid?
    And look: there's some sort of insect in your eye!
    Shall I take it out?

MALE CHORAGOS   An insect, is it? So that's
    what's been bothering me! Lord, yes: take it out!

FEMALE CHORAGOS   You might be more polite.
                                —But, heavens!
    What an enormous gnat!

MALE CHORAGOS   You've saved my life.
    That gnat was drilling an artesian well
    in my left eye.

FEMALE CHORAGOS   Let me wipe
    those tears away!—And now: one little kiss?

MALE CHORAGOS   Over my dead body!

FEMALE CHORAGOS   You're so difficult!

MALE CHORAGOS   These impossible women! How
    they do get around us!

---

[49] Parodies lines in Euripides' *Hippolytus*.

The poet was right: Can't live with them, or without
    them!
But let's be friends.
And to celebrate, you might lead off with an Ode.

Strophe

OLD WOMEN   Let it never be said
                        That my tongue is malicious:
                        Both by word and by deed
                    I would set an example that's noble and gracious.
                        We've had sorrow and care
                        Till we're sick of the tune.
                        Is there anyone here
                        Who would like a small loan?
                            My purse is crammed,
                            As you'll soon find;
                    And you needn't pay me back if the Peace gets
                        signed!
                            I've invited to lunch
                            Some Karystian rips—[50]
                            An esurient bunch,
                    But I've ordered a menu to water their lips!
                        I can still make soup
                        And slaughter a pig.
                        You're all coming, I hope?
                        But a bath first, I beg!
                            Walk right up
                            As though you owned the place,
                    And you'll get the front door slammed to in your
                        face!

(*Enter* SPARTAN AMBASSADOR, *with entourage*)

MALE CHORAGOS   The Commission has arrived from
    Sparta.
            How oddly
    they're walking!
                            Gentlemen, welcome to Athens!
    How is life in Laconia?

AMBASSADOR   Need we discuss that?
    Simply use your eyes.

OLD MEN   The poor man's right:
                                What a sight!

AMBASSADOR   Words fail me.

---

[50] The Karystians were allies of Athens at this time, but were disdained for their primitive manners and loose morals.

But come, gentlemen, call in your Commissioners,
and let's get down to a peace.

MALE CHORAGOS   The state we're in! Can't bear
a stitch below the waist. It's a kind of pelvic
paralysis.

AN ATHENIAN   Won't somebody call Lysistrata?
She has the answer.

A SPARTAN   Yes, there, look at him.
Same thing.
                    Seh, do y'all feel a certain strain
early in the morning?

ATHENIAN   I do, sir. It's worse than a strain.
A few more days, and there's nothing for us but
    Cleisthenes,
that broken blossom!

MALE CHORAGOS   But you'd better get dressed again.
You know these prudes who go around Athens with
    chisels,
looking for prominent statues.[51]

ATHENIAN   Sir, you are right.

SPARTAN   He certainly is! Ah'll put mah own clothes
back on.

(Enter ATHENIAN Commissioners)

AN ATHENIAN   They're no better off than we are!
                    —Greetings, Laconians!

SPARTAN (To one of his own group)   Colonel, we got
dressed just in time.
                    Ah sweah,
if they'd seen us the way we were, there'd have been
    a new war
between the states.

ATHENIAN   Call the meeting to order.
                    Now, Laconians,
what's your proposal?

AMBASSADOR   We'd lahk to consider peace.

ATHENIAN   Good. That's on our minds, too.
                    —Summon Lysistrata.
We'll never get anywhere without her.

AMBASSADOR   Lysistrata?
Summon Lysis-anybody![52] Only, summon!

MALE CHORAGOS   No need to summon:
here she is, herself.

(Enter LYSISTRATA)

                    Lysistrata! Lion of women!
This is your hour to be
hard and yielding, outspoken and sly, austere and
gentle. You see here
the best brains of Hellas (confused, I admit,
by your devious charming) met as one man
to turn the future over to you.

LYSISTRATA   That's fair enough,
unless you men take it into your heads
to turn to each other instead of to me. But I'd know
soon enough if you did!
                    —Where is that goddess of Peace?
Go, some of you: bring her here.

(Exeunt two SERVANTS)

                    And now,
summon the Spartan Commission. Treat them
    courteously:
our husbands have been lax in that respect.
Take them by the hand, women,
or by anything else, if they seem unwilling.
                    —Spartans:
you stand here. Athenians: on this side. Now listen
    to me.

(Re-enter SERVANTS, staggering under the weight of a
more than life-size statue of a naked woman: this is
PEACE)

I'm only a woman, I know; but I've a mind,
and I can distinguish between sense and foolishness.
I owe the first to my father; the rest
to the local politicians.[53] So much for that.
Now, then.
What I have to say concerns both sides in this war.
We are all Greeks.
Must I remind you of Thermopylae? of Olympia?
of Delphi? names deep in all our hearts?
And yet you men go raiding through the country,
Greek killing Greek, storming down Greek cities—
and all the time the Barbarian across the sea
is waiting for his chance.—That's my first point.

AN ATHENIAN   Lord! I can hardly contain myself!

---

[51] Statues with prominent male sexual organs, or phalloi.
[52] Lysistrata's name means "dissolver of armies."

[53] The preceding four lines are probably quoted from Euripides'
Melanippe the Wise.

LYSISTRATA   And you Spartans:
  Was it so long ago that Pericleides
  came here to beg our help?[54] I can see him still,
  his white face, his sombre gown. And what did he
        want?
  An army from Athens! Messenia
  was at your heels, and the sea-god splitting your
        shores.
  Well, Kimon and his men,
  four thousand infantry, marched out of here to save
        you.
  What thanks do we get? You come back to murder
        us.
ATHENIAN   Can't trust a Spartan, Lysistrata!
A SPARTAN   Ah admit it.
  When Ah look at those legs, Ah sweah Ah can't trust
        mahself!
LYSISTRATA   And you, men of Athens:
  you might remember that bad time when we were
        down,
  and an army came from Sparta
  and sent Hippias and the Thessalians
  whimpering back to the hills. That was Sparta,
  and only Sparta; without Sparta, we'd now be
  cringing helots, not walking about like free men!

(*From this point, the male responses are less to* LYSIS-
TRATA *than to the statue of* PEACE)

A SPARTAN   An eloquent speech!
AN ATHENIAN   An elegant construction!
LYSISTRATA   Why are we fighting each other? Why not
        make peace?
AMBASSADOR   Spahta is ready, ma'am,
  so long as we get that place back.
LYSISTRATA   Place? What place?
AMBASSADOR   Ah refer to Pylos.[55]
MAGISTRATE   Not while I'm alive, by God!
LYSISTRATA   You'd better give in.
MAGISTRATE   But—what were we fighting about?
LYSISTRATA   Lots of places left.
MAGISTRATE   All right. Well, then:

---

[54] In 464 B.C. during a revolt in Sparta, when an earthquake had just
   severely damaged the city.
[55] A lost Spartan possession; for the moment political and sexual desires become confused.

Hog Island first, and that gulf behind there, and the
        land between
  the Legs of Megara.
AMBASSADOR   Mah government objects.
LYSISTRATA   Over-ruled. Why fuss about a pair of legs?

(*General assent; the statue of* PEACE *is removed*)

AN ATHENIAN   Let's take off our clothes and plow our
        fields.
A SPARTAN   Ah'll fertilize mahn first, by the Heavenly
        Twins!
LYSISTRATA   And so you shall,
  once we have peace. If you are serious,
  go, both of you, and talk with your allies.
ATHENIAN   Too much talk already. We'll stand
        together!
  We've only one end in view. All that we want
  is our women: and I speak for our allies.
AMBASSADOR   Mah government concurs.
ATHENIAN   So does Karystos.
LYSISTRATA   Good.—But before you come inside
  to join your wives at supper, you must perform
  the usual lustration. Then we'll open
  our baskets for you, and all that we have is yours.
  But you must promise upright good behavior
  from this day on. Then each man home with his
        woman!
ATHENIAN   Let's get it over with!
SPARTAN   Lead on: Ah follow!
ATHENIAN   Quick as a cat can wink!

(*Exeunt all but the* CHORUSES)

Antistrophe

OLD WOMEN   Embroideries and
                    Twinkling ornaments and
                    Pretty dresses—I hand
  Them all over to you, and with never a qualm.
                    They'll be nice for your daughters
                    On festival days
                    When the girls bring the Goddess
                    The ritual prize.
                        Come in, one and all:
                        Take what you will.
  I've nothing here so tightly corked that you can't
        make it spill!

You may search my house,
But you'll not find
The least thing of use,
Unless your two eyes are keener than mine.
Your numberless brats
Are half starved? and your slaves?
Courage, grandpa! I've lots
Of grain left, and big loaves.
I'll fill your guts,
I'll go the whole hog;
But if you come too close to me, remember: 'ware
the dog!

(*Exeunt* CHORUSES)

(*An* ATHENIAN DRUNKARD *approaches the gate and is halted by a* SENTRY)

DRUNKARD   Open. The. Door.
SENTRY   Now, friend, just shove along!
So you want to sit down! If it weren't such an old
joke,
I'd tickle your tail with this torch. Just the sort of
thing
that this kind of audience appreciates.
DRUNKARD   I. Stay. Right. Here.
SENTRY   Oh, all right. But you'll see some funny
sights!
DRUNKARD   Bring. Them. On.
SENTRY   No, what am I thinking of?
The gentlemen from Sparta are just coming back
from supper.
Get out of here, or I'll scalp you!

(*Exit* DRUNKARD)

(*The general company re-enters; the two* CHORUSES *now represent* SPARTANS *and* ATHENIANS)

MAGISTRATE   I must say,
I've never tasted a better meal. And those Laconians!
They're gentlemen, by the Lord! Just goes to show:
a drink to the wise is sufficient. And why not?
A sober man's an ass.
Men of Athens, mark my words: the only efficient
Ambassador's a drunk Ambassador. Is that clear?
Look: we go to Sparta,
and when we get there we're dead sober. The result?
Everyone cackling at everyone else. They make
speeches;

and even if we understand, we get it all wrong
when we file our reports in Athens. But today—!
Everybody's happy. Couldn't tell the difference
between *Drink to Me Only* and
the *Star Spangled Athens.*
                What's a few lies,
washed down in good strong drink?

(*Re-enter* DRUNKARD)

SENTRY   God almighty,
he's back again!
DRUNKARD   I. Resume. My. Place.
A SPARTAN (*To an* ATHENIAN)   I beg you, seh,
take your instrument in your hand and play for us.
Ah'm told
you understand the intricacies of the floot?
Ah'd lahk to execute a song and dance
in honor of Athens,
                and, of course, of Spahta.

(*The following song is a solo—an aria—accompanied by the flute. The* CHORUS OF SPARTANS *begins a slow dance*)

DRUNKARD   Toot. On. Your. Flute.
SPARTAN CHORAGOS   Mnemosyne,[56]
Inspire once more the Grecian Muse
To sing of glory glory glory without end.
Sing Artemesion's shore,[57]
Where Athens fluttered the Persian fleet—
Alalai,[58] that great
Victory! Sing Leonidis and his men,
Those wild boars, sweat and blood
Down in a red drench. Then, then
The barbarians broke, though they had stood
A myriad strong before!
                O Artemis,
Virgin Goddess, whose darts
Flash in our forests: approve
This pact of peace, and join our hearts,
From this day on, in love.
Huntress, descend!
LYSISTRATA   All that will come in time.

---

[56] Goddess of memory and mother of the Muses.
[57] Where in 480 B.C. the Athenian fleet successfully engaged the Persians, while Leonidas and his Spartans were making their famous stand at Thermopylae.
[58] A war cry.

But now, Laconians,
take home your wives. Athenians, take yours.
Each man be kind to his woman; and you, women,
be equally kind. Never again, pray God,
shall we lose our way in such madness.
                                        —And now
let's dance our joy! (*From this point the dance
becomes general*)
CHORUS OF ATHENIANS   Dance!
                            Dance!
                                Dance, you Graces!
    Artemis, Dance!
                Dance, Phoebus, Lord of dancing!
    Dance, Dionysus, in a scurry of Maenads!
                    Dance, Zeus Thunderer!
    Dance, Lady Hera,
    Queen of the sky!
                Dance, dance, all you gods!
    Dance for the dearest, the bringer of peace,
    Deathless Aphrodite!
LYSISTRATA   Now let us have another song from
    Sparta.
CHORUS OF SPARTANS   From Taygetos' skyey summit,
            Laconian Muse, come down!
        Sing the glories of Apollo,
            Regent of Amyclae Town.
            Sing of Leda's Twins,
            Those gallant sons,
            On the banks of Eurotas—
            Alalai Evohe! [59]
        Here's to our girls
            With their tangling curls,
            Legs a-wriggle,
            Bellies a-jiggle,
                A riot of hair,
                A fury of feet,
    Evohe! Evohai! Evohe!
                        as they pass
        Dancing,
                dancing,
                    dancing,
                        to greet
        Athena of the House of Brass! [60]

---

[59] Now an orgiastic war cry.
[60] A famous temple on the acropolis of Sparta.

COMMENTS AND QUESTIONS

1. Like the tragedy *Oedipus Rex*, the comedy *Lysistrata* treats a selection of events taking place in a relatively short time. What, exactly, happens in *Lysistrata*? How has Aristophanes arranged the events? Where does the climax of the play fall, and how is it revealed?

2. Is the *tone* of *Lysistrata* entirely comic, or are there tragic or serious moments?

3. Do the characters in the play seem realistic to you? What makes them comic characters?

4. Which lines in the comedy seem especially funny to you? Why? Is the sexual explicitness in *Lysistrata* comic? Compare the treatment of sex here with the deadly seriousness of pornography. What is the difference?

5. *Lysistrata* is read more and more today as a play about women's liberation. Look for arguments both for and against this view in the play. What can you surmise about the actual social conditions of Greek women from this text? If the idea of the sex strike is not very realistic, the idea of women organizing themselves in order to achieve common goals is. What difficulties does Lysistrata encounter in the characters of the women themselves when she attempts to organize them? Can these be compared with the differences between "liberated" women and other women today? How are men viewed in this comedy?

4

Classical Greece: Philosophy and Ethical Thought

The ancient Greeks were, as far as we know, the first to attempt to understand their universe as an order governed by a rational principle. From the late sixth century B.C., a group of thinkers, usually called the Pre-Socratics because they flourished before Socrates, looked beyond the arbitrary, willful gods worshiped by the masses, in order to define a universal principle of rationality. Whereas the popular gods were like human beings, only more powerful, the philosophers were in search of a unitary principle giving order and intelligibility to the world. The most ancient philosophers can be considered physicists, in that they tried to locate the unitary principle in a material element. Thales (640–546? B.C.), the earliest of the group, believed the underlying element in all nature was water, whereas air and fire became the preferred choices of philosophers in later generations.

The first half of the fifth century B.C. in Greece saw the rapid breakdown of social order and government, which raised pressing questions about the individual's place in society. By mid-century, ethical questions became uppermost and Greek philosophy moved to focus on man rather than nature. The major intellectuals dominating Greece by this time were the Sophists. The Greek word *sophos* means wisdom, and the Sophists promised to teach wisdom for a price. In actual fact, their lessons were aimed at teaching students the art of eloquence to enable them to win influence in the new popular governments emerging all over the peninsula. They attacked the ideal of absolute right and wrong and taught that man was the measure of all things.

Socrates

Socrates (470?–399 B.C.) set himself to oppose the scepticism and self-interested orientation of the Sophists. He was convinced that there was an absolute set of moral laws and that most men in a confused way assumed this to be true. His general goal was to make men aware of their assumptions about what they thought they knew, not in order to make them skeptics, but so that they might begin the pursuit of knowledge in the proper way. He believed that knowledge begins with knowing what we do *not* know. So it was that the short, powerfully built, snub-nosed man, looking very much like a wrestler, spent most of his days in the streets of Athens, his native city, asking questions of his fellow citizens. Seemingly never satisfied with the first answer, he pushed his questions to the point where his companion in the dialogue had finally to admit that he did not know what he believed he knew at the outset. He became known as the gadfly of Athens—after the little gnat that pesters its object to desperation. Finally, he appeared so threatening to the traditions of his city that he was arrested and condemned to death for his detrimental influence on the youth of Athens.

Plato

Socrates never wrote a word, but his greatest disciple Plato (427?–347 B.C.) wrote volumes; in many of his writings, called *Dialogues*, he immortalized Socrates by making him the voice of the philosopher in the discussion. It is impossible to be certain how much of Plato's thought was borrowed from his master. At least the technique of seeking an immutable, eternal basis for our knowledge by interrogation certainly derived from

Socrates, but it was probably Plato who formulated the technique into a method. The typical dialogue begins with Socrates asking for the definition of justice, or of courage, or of virtue itself. The person questioned responds usually with confidence, giving a traditional commonsense definition. Further questioning shows the answer to be inadequate, and a second definition is proposed—only to be rejected in turn—then a third and even a fourth without any results. At length the discussant admits reluctantly that he is ignorant of what he believed himself to know. Perhaps the dialogue ends there, but frequently the interrogation continues until some positive conclusions are achieved.

It would appear that Socrates' main concern was ethical, but Plato extended Socrates' method to embrace a much wider variety of philosophical problems. Through the method of interrogation, or *dialectic*, Plato eventually established the existence of two levels of reality. From eternity there were three elements in the universe: a demiurge or creator God; a world of eternal unchanging Ideas or patterns, perfect exemplars of truth, beauty, and justice, and of all numbers, geometrical shapes, and natural things; and the receptacle, equivalent to pure space or matter. The work of the demiurge was to model the receptacle into shapes resembling the eternal patterns of the Ideas or forms. Because the matter he worked with was mobile, his creations could never remain fixed for long; but at least the world he fashioned represented or imitated imperfectly the immutable exemplars of the transcendent world. Before this life man had lived as a soul in the world of the Ideas and had beheld them in their splendor. Only like can know like: man could know the Ideas in this other world because he, like they, was divine.

Imprisoned at birth in a body, subject to the sensations of matter, the individual has forgotten that earlier life; nevertheless, enough remains to serve as the basis for judging experience. When we say that that thing is more beautiful than this thing, we are comparing both objects with a standard of beauty not found in our earthly experience but rather brought with us into this life from our contact in the upper world with the idea of pure beauty. The same is true with our judgment about other objects in our experience.

For Plato the soul is a divine entity, buried in a body from which at death it will escape. Because of our contact with the absolute beauty and good in a preexistence, we continue in this life to seek the experience we once had. Motivated by love of beauty and good, we strive to satisfy our needs through possession of material objects and other human beings. Only education can teach us the true end of our longing, directing our gaze away from the imperfect, transitory objects of this world to contemplation of the Ideas themselves of which these objects are but a dim reflection. Once in possession of the knowledge of mathematics, geometry, and other truths, we will come to look on our body and this world as a prison from which death will free us.

The psychology of the philosopher constituted the first attempt to define various aspects of the human personality. Plato believed that the human soul consists of three fundamental parts: the reason that governs, moral courage that pursues the honorable even against great obstacles, and the appetite. The third part of the soul must be kept in close confinement; otherwise it would topple reason from its seat and create chaos in the life of the soul. Moral courage, on the other hand, is the ally of reason. A loyal member of a Greek city-state, Plato was convinced that the individual could not attain moral perfection or reach the stage where his reason contemplated the eternal realities while living in a corrupt community. Plato's ideal state reflects in its organization the three divisions of the soul. Like the soul it has its rational principle in the guardians, those who were to govern the whole. The auxiliaries, the soldiers, correspond to moral courage; and the artisans, who do most of the hard work in the society, reflect the appetitive principle. Just as in the individual soul, the whole is in harmony when reason rules, so in the state ruled by philosophers everyone keeps his place, performs his function, and is content.

An important characteristic of Plato's method was to illustrate profound philosophical ideas through use of stories, in the manner of myths. The selection below is taken from Benjamin Jowett's translation of *The Republic*, Plato's great dialogue on justice, illustrated by the perfect state. Commonly known as "The *Allegory* of the Cave," this passage endeavors to dramatize the predicament of mankind, which takes the shifting, temporary things of this world for ultimate reality. It also describes the problem of the philosopher, who has looked on the realm of the Ideas through contemplation and who yet has to return to live in this world among the shadows with which his fellow men are content.

PLATO

The Allegory of the Cave

"And now," I said,[1] "let me show in a figure how far our nature is enlightened or unenlightened. Behold! Human beings living in an underground den, which has a mouth open towards the light and reaching all along the den; here they have been from their childhood, and have their legs and necks chained so that they cannot move, and can only see before them, being prevented by the chains from turning round their heads. Above and behind them a fire is blazing at a distance, and between the fire and the prisoners there is a raised way; and you will see, if you look, a low wall built along the way, like the screen which marionette players have in front of them, over which they show the puppets."

"I see."

"And do you see," I said, "men passing along the wall carrying all sorts of vessels, and statues and figures of animals made of wood and stone and various materials, which appear over the wall? Some of them are talking, others silent."

"You have shown me a strange image, and they are strange prisoners."

"Like ourselves," I replied; "and they see only their own shadows, or the shadows of one another, which the fire throws on the opposite wall of the cave?"

"True," he said; "how could they see anything but the shadows if they were never allowed to move their heads?"

"And of the objects which are being carried in like manner they would only see the shadows?"

"Yes," he said.

"And if they were able to converse with one another, would they not suppose that they were naming what was actually before them?"

"Very true."

"And suppose further that the prison had an echo which came from the other side, would they not be sure to fancy when one of the passers-by spoke that the voice which they heard came from the passing shadow?"

"No question," he replied.

---

[1] The speaker is Socrates.

"To them," I said, "the truth would be literally nothing but the shadows of the images."

"That is certain."

"And now look again, and see what will naturally follow if the prisoners are released and disabused of their error. At first, when any of them is liberated and compelled suddenly to stand up and turn his neck round and walk and look towards the light, he will suffer sharp pains; the glare will distress him, and he will be unable to see the realities of which in his former state he had seen the shadows; and then conceive someone saying to him that what he saw before was an illusion, but that now, when he is approaching nearer to being and his eye is turned towards more real existence, he has a clearer vision—what will be his reply? And you may further imagine that his instructor is pointing to the objects as they pass and requiring him to name them,—will he not be perplexed? Will he not fancy that the shadows which he formerly saw are truer than the objects which are now shown to him?"

"Far truer."

"And if he is compelled to look straight at the light, will he not have a pain in his eyes which will make him turn away to take refuge in the objects of vision which he can see, and which he will conceive to be in reality clearer than the things which are now being shown to him?" [2]

"True," he said.

"And suppose once more, that he is reluctantly dragged up a steep and rugged ascent, and held fast until he is forced into the presence of the sun himself, is he not likely to be pained and irritated? When he approaches the light his eyes will be dazzled, and he will not be able to see anything at all of what are now called realities."

"Not all in a moment," he said.

"He will require to grow accustomed to the sight of the upper world. And first he will see the shadows best, next the reflections of men and other objects in the water, and then the objects themselves; then he will gaze upon the light of the moon and the stars and the spangled heaven; and he will see the sky and the stars by night better than the sun or the light of the sun by day?"

"Certainly."

"Last of all he will be able to see the sun, and not mere reflections of him in the water, but he will see him in his own proper place, and not in another; and he will contemplate him as he is."

"Certainly."

"He will then proceed to argue that this is he who gives the season and the years, and is the guardian of all that is in the visible world, and in a certain way the cause of all things which he and his fellows have been accustomed to behold?"

"Clearly," he said, "he would first see the sun and then reason about him."

"And when he remembered his old habitation, and the wisdom of the den and his fellow prisoners, do you not suppose that he would felicitate himself on the change, and pity them?"

"Certainly, he would."

"And if they were in the habit of conferring honors among themselves on those who were quickest to observe the passing shadows and to remark which of them went before, and which followed after, and which were together; and who were therefore best able to draw conclusions as to the future, do you think that he would care for such honors and glories, or envy the possessors of them? Would he not say with Homer, 'Better to be the poor servant of a poor master' and to endure anything, rather than think as they do and live after their manner?"

"Yes," he said, "I think that he would rather suffer anything than entertain these false notions and live in this miserable manner."

"Imagine once more," I said, "such a one coming suddenly out of the sun to be replaced in his old situation;[3] would he not be certain to have his eyes full of darkness?"

"To be sure," he said.

"And if there were a contest, and he had to compete in measuring the shadows with the prisoners who had never moved out of the den, while his sight was still weak, and before his eyes had become steady (and the time which would be needed to acquire this new habit of sight might be very considerable), would he not be

---

[2] He will think the shadows to which he is accustomed more real than the puppets behind him that caused them. The puppets in turn he will find easier to look at than the living creatures in the world of sunlight outside, of which the puppets were but copies.

[3] Or "such a one going down again and taking his old position."

ridiculous? Men would say of him that up he went and down he came without his eyes; and that it was better not even to think of ascending; and if any one tried to loose another and lead him up to the light, let them only catch the offender, and they would put him to death."

"No question," he said.

"This entire allegory," I said, "you may now append, dear Glaucon, to the previous argument; the prison house is the world of sight, the light of the fire is the sun, and you will not misapprehend me if you interpret the journey upwards to be the ascent of the soul into the intellectual world according to my poor belief, which, at your desire, I have expressed—whether rightly or wrongly, God knows. But, whether true or false, my opinion is that in the world of knowledge the idea of good appears last of all, and is seen only with an effort; and, when seen, is also inferred to be the universal author of all things beautiful and right, parent of light and of the lord of light in this visible world, and the immediate source of reason and truth in the intellectual; and that this is the power upon which he who would act rationally either in public or private life must have his eye fixed."

"I agree," he said, "as far as I am able to understand you."

"Moreover," I said, "you must not wonder that those who attain to this beatific vision are unwilling to descend to human affairs; for their souls are ever hastening into the upper world where they desire to dwell; which desire of theirs is very natural, if our allegory may be trusted."

"Yes, very natural."

"And is there anything surprising in one who passes from divine contemplations to the evil state of man, misbehaving himself in a ridiculous manner; if, while his eyes are blinking and before he has become accustomed to the surrounding darkness, he is compelled to fight in courts of law, or in other places, about the images or the shadows of images of justice, and is endeavoring to meet the conceptions of those who have never yet seen absolute justice?"

"Anything but surprising," he replied.

"Anyone who has common sense will remember that the bewilderments of the eyes are of two kinds, and arise from two causes, either from coming out of the light or from going into the light, which is true of the mind's eye, quite as much as of the bodily eye; and he who remembers this when he sees anyone whose vision is perplexed and weak, will not be too ready to laugh; he will first ask whether that soul of man has come out of the brighter life, and is unable to see because unaccustomed to the dark, or having turned from darkness to the day is dazzled by excess of light. And he will count the one happy in his condition and state of being, and he will pity the other; or, if he have a mind to laugh at the soul which comes from below into the light, there will be more reason in this than in the laugh which greets him who returns from above out of the light into the den."

"That," he said, "is a very just distinction."

"But then, if I am right, certain professors of education must be wrong when they say that they can put a knowledge into the soul which was not there before, like sight into blind eyes."

"They undoubtedly say this," he replied.

"Whereas our argument shows that the power and capacity of learning exists in the soul already; and that just as the eye was unable to turn from darkness to light without the whole body, so too the instrument of knowledge can only by the movement of the whole soul be turned from the world of becoming into that of being, and learn by degrees to endure the sight of being, and of the brightest and best of being, or in other words, of the good."

COMMENTS AND QUESTIONS

1. If the manmade objects carried along the wall designate objects that we perceive in our experience with the world, what, then, do the shadows signify?
2. Why does Plato stress the difficulty that the prisoners have in looking at the light of the sun?
3. Why do prisoners receive their returning colleague as they do? What does this tell us of the position of the philosopher in society?
4. In what ways does this allegory attack contemporary Greek education?

The *Phaedo* depicts Socrates' last hours. Having been tried and found guilty for corrupting the youth of Athens, he has been sentenced to die by drinking a cup of poison. As the appointed time for the execution approaches, he spends his last hours in prison philosophizing with his friends, proving to the satisfaction of all that the soul is immortal. (Again Benjamin Jowett is the translator.)

PLATO

The Death of Socrates

"Tell me, then, what is that of which the inherence will render the body alive?"[1]

"The soul," he replied.

"And is this always the case?"

"Yes," he said, "of course."

"Then whatever the soul possesses, to that she comes bearing life?"

"Yes, certainly."

"And is there any opposite to life?"

"There is," he said.

"And what is that?"

"Death."

"Then the soul, as has been acknowledged, will never receive the opposite of what she brings."

"Impossible," replied Cebes.

"And now," he said, "what did we just now call that principle which repels the even?"

"The odd."

"And that principle which repels the musical or the just?"

"The unmusical," he said, "and the unjust."

"And what do we call that principle which does not admit of death?"

"The immortal," he said.

"And does the soul admit of death?"

"No."

"Then the soul is immortal?"

"Yes," he said.

"And may we say that this has been proven?"

"Yes, abundantly proven, Socrates," he replied.

"Supposing that the odd were imperishable, must not three be imperishable?"

"Of course."

"And if that which is cold were imperishable, when the warm principle came attacking the snow, must not

the snow have retired whole and unmelted—for it could never have perished, nor could it have remained and admitted the heat?"

"True," he said.

"Again, if the uncooling or warm principle were imperishable, the fire when assailed by cold would not have perished or have been extinguished, but would have gone away unaffected?"

"Certainly," he said. . . .

"And the same may be said of the immortal: if the immortal is also imperishable, then the soul will be imperishable as well as immortal; but if not, some other proof of her imperishableness will have to be given."

"No other proof is needed," he said; "for if the immortal, being eternal, is liable to perish, then nothing is imperishable."

"Yes," replied Socrates, "and yet all men will agree that God, and the essential form of life, and the immortal in general, will never perish."

"Yes, all men," he said; "that is true; and what is more, gods, if I am not mistaken, as well as men."

"Seeing then that the immortal is indestructible, must not the soul, if she is immortal, be also imperishable?"

"Most certainly."

"Then when death attacks a man, the mortal portion of him may be supposed to die, but the immortal retires at the approach of death and is preserved safe and sound?"

"True."

"Then, Cebes, beyond question, the soul is immortal and imperishable, and our souls will truly exist in another world!"

"I am convinced, Socrates," said Cebes, "and have nothing more to object; but if my friend Simmias, or anyone else, has any further objection to make, he had better speak out, and not keep silence, since I do not know to what other season he can defer the discussion, if there is anything which he wants to say or to have said."

"But I have nothing more to say," replied Simmias; "nor can I see any reason for doubt after what has been said. But I still feel and cannot help feeling uncertain in my own mind, when I think of the greatness of the subject and the feebleness of man."

---

[1]Or, "what is that which by its presence in the body makes it alive?"

"Yes, Simmias," replied Socrates, "that is well said: and I may add that first principles, even if they appear certain, should be carefully considered; and when they are satisfactorily ascertained, then, with a sort of hesitating confidence in human reason, you may, I think, follow the course of the argument; and if that be plain and clear, there will be no need for any further inquiry."

"Very true."

"But then, O my friends," he said, "if the soul is really immortal, what care should be taken of her, not only in respect of the portion of time which is called life, but of eternity! And the danger of neglecting her from this point of view does indeed appear to be awful. If death had only been the end of all, the wicked would have had a good bargain in dying, for they would have been happily quit not only of their body, but of their own evil together with their souls. But now, inasmuch as the soul is manifestly immortal, there is no release or salvation from evil except the attainment of the highest virtue and wisdom. For the soul, when on her progress to the world below, takes nothing with her but nurture and education; and these are said greatly to benefit or greatly to injure the departed, at the very beginning of his journey thither. . . .

"Wherefore, Simmias, seeing all these things, what ought not we to do that we may obtain virtue and wisdom in this life? Fair is the prize, and the hope great!

"A man of sense ought not to say, nor will I be very confident, that the description which I have given of the soul and her mansions is exactly true. But I do say that, inasmuch as the soul is shown to be immortal, he may venture to think, not improperly or unworthily, that something of the kind is true. The venture is a glorious one, and he ought to comfort himself with words like these, which is the reason why I lengthen out the tale. Wherefore, I say, let a man be of good cheer about his soul, who having cast away the pleasures and ornaments of the body as alien to him and working harm rather than good, has sought after the pleasures of knowledge; and has arrayed the soul, not in some foreign attire, but in her own proper jewels, temperance, and justice, and courage, and nobility, and truth—in these adorned she is ready to go on her journey to the world below, when her hour comes. You, Simmias and Cebes, and all other men will depart at some time or other. Me already, as a tragic poet would say, the voice of fate calls. Soon I must drink the poison; and I think that I had better repair to the bath first, in order that the women may not have the trouble of washing my body after I am dead."

When he had done speaking, Crito said: "And have you any commands for us, Socrates—anything to say about your children, or any other matter in which we can serve you?"

"Nothing particular, Crito," he replied; "only, as I have always told you, take care of yourselves; that is a service which you may be ever rendering to me and mine and to all of us, whether you promise to do so or not. But if you have no thought for yourselves, and care not to walk according to the rule which I have prescribed for you, not now for the first time, however much you may profess or promise at the moment, it will be of no avail."

"We will do our best," said Crito: "And in what way shall we bury you?"

"In any way that you like; but you must get hold of me, and take care that I do not run away from you." Then he turned to us, and added with a smile: "I cannot make Crito believe that I am the same Socrates who has been talking and conducting the argument; he fancies that I am the other Socrates whom he will soon see, a dead body—and he asks, How shall he bury me? And though I have spoken many words in the endeavor to show that when I have drunk the poison I shall leave you and go to the joys of the blessed—these words of mine, with which I was comforting you and myself, have had, as I perceive, no effect upon Crito. And therefore I want you to be surety for me to him now, as at the trial he was surety to the judges for me: but let the promise be of another sort; for he was surety for me to the judges that I would remain, and you must be my surety to him that I shall not remain, but go away and depart; and then he will suffer less at my death, and not be grieved when he sees my body being burned or buried. I would not have him sorrow at my hard lot, or say at the burial, Thus we lay out Socrates, or, Thus we follow him to the grave or bury him; for false words are not only evil in themselves, but they infect the soul with evil. Be of good cheer then, my dear Crito, and say that you are burying my body only, and do with that whatever is usual, and what you think best."

When he had spoken these words, he arose and went into a chamber to bathe; Crito followed him and told us to wait. So we remained behind, talking and thinking of the subject of discourse, and also of the greatness of our sorrow; he was like a father of whom we were being bereaved, and we were about to pass the rest of our lives as orphans. When he had taken the bath his children were brought to him (he had two young sons and an elder one); and the women of his family also came, and he talked to them and gave them a few directions in the presence of Crito; then he dismissed them and returned to us.

Now the hour of sunset was near, for a good deal of time had passed while he was within. When he came out, he sat down with us again after his bath, but not much was said. Soon the jailer, who was the servant of the Eleven, entered and stood by him, saying: "To you, Socrates, whom I know to be the noblest and gentlest and best of all who ever came to this place, I will not impute the angry feelings of other men, who rage and swear at me, when, in obedience to the authorities, I bid them drink the poison—indeed, I am sure that you will not be angry with me; for others, as you are aware, and not I, are to blame. And so fare you well, and try to bear lightly what must needs be—you know my errand." Then bursting into tears he turned away and went out.

Socrates looked at him and said: "I return your good wishes, and will do as you bid." Then turning to us, he said, "How charming the man is: since I have been in prison he has always been coming to see me, and at times he would talk to me, and was as good to me as could be, and now see how generously he sorrows on my account. We must do as he says, Crito; and therefore let the cup be brought, if the poison is prepared: if not, let the attendant prepare some."

"Yet," said Crito, "the sun is still upon the hill-tops, and I know that many a one has taken the draught late, and after the announcement has been made to him, he has eaten and drunk, and enjoyed the society of this beloved; do not hurry—there is time enough."

Socrates said: "Yes, Crito, and they of whom you speak are right in so acting, for they think that they will be gainers by the delay; but I am right in not following their example, for I do not think that I should gain anything by drinking the poison a little later; I should only be ridiculous in my own eyes for sparing and saving a life which is already forfeit. Please then to do as I say, and not to refuse me."

Crito made a sign to the servant, who was standing by; and he went out, and having been absent for some time, returned with the jailer carrying the cup of poison. Socrates said: "You, my good friend, who are experienced in these matters, shall give me directions how I am to proceed."

The man answered: "You have only to walk about until your legs are heavy, and then to lie down, and the poison will act."

At the same time he handed the cup to Socrates, who in the easiest and gentlest manner, without the least fear or change of colour or feature, looking at the man with all his eyes, Echecrates, as his manner was, took the cup and said: "What do you say about making a libation out of this cup to any god? May I, or not?"

The man answered: "We only prepare, Socrates, just so much as we deem enough."

"I understand," he said, "but I may and must ask the gods to prosper my journey from this to the other world—even so—and so be it according to my prayer." Then raising the cup to his lips, quite readily and cheerfully he drank off the poison. And hitherto most of us had been able to control our sorrow; but now when we saw him drinking, and saw too that he had finished the draught, we could no longer forbear, and in spite of myself my own tears were flowing fast; so that I covered my face and wept, not for him, but at the thought of my own calamity in having to part from such a friend. Nor was I the first; for Crito, when he found himself unable to restrain his tears, had got up, and I followed; and at that moment, Apollodorus, who had been weeping all the time, broke out in a loud and passionate cry which made cowards of us all.

Socrates alone retained his calmness: "What is this strange outcry?" he said. "I sent away the women mainly in order that they might not misbehave in this way, for I have been told that a man should die in peace. Be quiet then, and have patience." When we heard his words we were ashamed, and refrained our tears; and he walked about until, as he said, his legs began to fail, and then he lay on his back, according to the directions, and the man who gave him the poison now and then looked at his feet and legs; and after a while he pressed his foot hard, and asked him if he could feel; and he said, "No;" and then his leg, and so upwards and upwards, and showed us that he was cold and stiff. And he felt them himself, and said: "When the poison reaches the heart, that will be the end." He was beginning to grow cold about the groin, when he uncovered his face, for he had covered himself up, and said—they were his last words—he said: "Crito, I owe a cock to Asclepius; will you remember to pay the debt?"

"The debt shall be paid," said Crito, "is there anything else?" There was no answer to this question; but in a minute or two a movement was heard, and the attendants uncovered him; his eyes were set, and Crito closed his eyes and mouth.

Such was the end, Echecrates, of our friend; concerning whom I may truly say, that of all the men of his time whom I have known, he was the wisest and justest and best.

QUESTIONS

1. What is Socrates' proof for the immortality of the soul? Does it seem contrary to you?
2. The death of Socrates has served for 2,500 years as the humanistic example of how a man should die. Is it a relevant example for our age?
3. What moral values does Socrates uphold?

Aristotle

For Plato knowledge was essentially *deductive*, that is, it came from within the human mind and was applicable to the world. Man brought his categories of organization to experience. In his later years Plato came increasingly to conceive of the world of the ideas in terms of mathematical relationships. From Plato derives, therefore, the conception that mathematics is the key to understanding nature. By contrast, his student Aristotle (384–322 B.C.) approached the universe not as a mathematician but as a biologist. Knowledge of man and nature in Aristotle's judgment was *inductive*. It was derived by the human intellect from nature itself.

Like Plato, Aristotle requires that knowledge, to be knowledge, must be eternally and immutably true. Ac-

cordingly, there can only be knowledge of that which is eternal and unchanging. At the same time, however, Aristotle in his mature work considered Plato's belief in a world of the ideas as nonsense. There are not two levels of reality—the world we know and the world of perfect forms or ideas—there is only one reality. But how is knowledge possible in such a world where all seems in a state of constant change? What in our experience is immutable and eternal when all about us is moving from place to place, being born, dying, becoming bigger or less, changing colors and the like? Aristotle's reply is that there is no need to postulate a world of ideal forms because this needlessly duplicates the forms already in nature. There are in the universe of Aristotle a finite if immense number of different kinds of things, which he calls forms or species. The species are eternal and never change, but they never exist apart from individual members of that species. Each individual member of the species, say of man, carries within himself the form of man-ness that makes him "be" what he is. Individuals of a species differ one from the other (that is, they are individuals) because they differ in their matter. Each is composed of a different mass of bone and flesh. Individual men are born, grow old, and die, but the form or species lives on, passing from generation to generation of men to all eternity. Thus, Aristotle has found the eternal forms *in* the things of this world themselves. We experience them in our encounter with each of the individual representatives of the species. In sense experience my intellect has the power to grasp the eternal form in the individual. When, for example, I see a tree, I know it is a tree because my mind perceives the form of tree-ness in it. Gradually, through experience with different trees, I can develop a knowledge of the various operations of the species; this knowledge will be immutable and eternal because the species in itself never changes. What I learn generally about these trees will be true for all trees.

How does Aristotle explain the cause of change in the universe? Why do streams flow, flowers grow, and the heavenly spheres circle? Each individual thing in the universe for Aristotle moves and changes because it is attempting in this way to realize perfection in its form. Indirectly, however, God is the ultimate cause of all movement. Aristotle sets the earth at the center of the universe, ringing it round with ten revolving spheres. The innermost sphere takes the moon around the earth, the next the sun, and so on, moving outward for each of the planets until we reach the tenth sphere, which holds the fixed stars. Beyond that sphere lies God. Aristotle's God is perfect mind who exists eternally thinking only of Himself and absolutely motionless. He knows nothing of the universe below Him. Like Him, the universe with its species is eternal. He did not create them. His only relationship to the universe is that all objects on earth and in heaven are attracted to Him and attempt to imitate His perfection by being themselves perfect. In order to do so, they must undergo change. He is perfect and therefore unmoving. The individual members of the countless species of things must constantly strive to perfect their particular species in themselves; thus, they move. Aristotle's God, consequently, is not a creator god but the underlying cause of all universal motion through the attraction He exerts for them.

What is the nature of man and his destiny in such a universe? Whereas everything in the universe consists of matter and form, in living things the form is called a soul. Plants and animals have souls, but not as complex as those of human beings. Man, as opposed to all other living things, has the power to know truth. He is endowed with a mind that can grasp the forms of things and can develop a body of knowledge about nature through reasoning and observation. On the basis of the axiom "like alone can know like," does the fact that the human mind can know the eternal form found in individual members of a species mean that man's soul as opposed to the other living souls is immortal? Although we cannot be certain, Aristotle seems to reject personal immortality. The part of the human mind that grasps the forms in the things is specifically designated as immortal, but Aristotle describes it in such a way that is does not really belong to us individually and that, while the personal elements of our soul perish at death, it departs from us. Thus, men—like every other thing on earth—bear the species for their time; and, as this generation passes away, another rises to replace it.

If there is no afterlife for the human being, what is the nature of happiness? Aristotle replies: Man's happiness lies in the perfection of his form as man. Man's distinctive characteristic is that he is a rational animal; therefore, his highest good lies in perfecting his reason. Such perfection occurs in two areas. First of all, man must control his life through reason. Such a life is a virtuous life. Honesty, courage, temperance, and the like are virtues; they are different aspects of the behavior of a rational man. The second area in which reason must be perfected in order to obtain happiness is in the intellectual sphere. Since the human reason has a capacity to learn the truth, the rational man must study the sciences, mathematics, and divine things if he is to fulfill his nature. Aristotle himself, following his inductive method of investigation, produced an immense number of works devoted to the widest range of subjects, including botany, zoology, astronomy, physics, rhetoric, psychology, physiology, and political science.

But the attainment of moral and intellectual virtues is not sufficient to create happiness. Aristotle willingly acknowledged that even the virtuous man could not be happy if he was poor and sick. Accordingly, Aristotle maintained that while virtue was the highest good for happiness, man needed both health and a degree of wealth in order to reach his end. The demands placed on the individual by this kind of ethic were obviously not overly rigorous and could easily be met by the upper class of the Greek polis.

While differing from Plato on the place of the forms and on the immortality of the human soul among other things, Aristotle was in complete agreement with the older man who had once been his teacher on the close relationship between ethics and politics. For Aristotle, as for Plato, the state was man written large. Man was only an animal outside the state; only through the state could he attain moral and intellectual perfection. But whereas for Plato the best form of government was a monarchy ruled by a philosopher king, Aristotle, rejecting what he considered Plato's purely theoretical approach, opted for republican government as the best form of government in the world as it was. Through participation in the political life of his state, the citizen could maximize his power and talents, thereby finding happiness.

In the translation of Aristotle's *Politics* by Benjamin Jowett which follows, Aristotle describes the state as a self-sufficient community based on a union of villages, each one more or less composed of a large family. If the family is a natural institution, so, for Aristotle, is the state, because it is the culminating organization toward which political life tends. Only at the state level can the human community be self-sufficient and individuals live a truly virtuous life. Put another way, the state is prior to the family, not because it actually existed before the family, but because the desire to form a state is innate in man and constitutes the driving force in his political organization. Fathers rule over their families as kings rule over their subjects. Women and slaves are subordinate. Moreover, the passage reflects the low opinion the Hellenic Greeks had of the "barbarians"—i.e., male and female non-Greeks—whom they considered to be slaves by nature and unworthy of freedom. Although the passage does not say so explicitly, it prepares the way for Aristotle's assertion that, while the government of the family or village is royal, that of the state ought to be republican. Ideally, male family heads participate in a constitutional government and alternate between ruling and obeying.

ARISTOTLE

The Politics

He who thus considers things in their first growth and origin, whether a state or anything else, will obtain the clearest view of them. In the first place there must be a union of those who cannot exist without each other; namely, of male and female, that the race may continue (and this is a union which is formed, not of deliberate purpose, but because, in common with other animals and with plants, mankind have a natural desire to leave behind them an image of themselves), and of natural ruler and subject, that both may be preserved. For that which can foresee by the exercise of mind is by nature intended to be lord and master, and that which can with its body give effect to such foresight is a subject, and by nature a slave; hence master and slave have the same interest. Now nature has distinguished between the female and the slave. For she is not niggardly, like the smith who fashions the Delphian knife for many uses; she makes each thing for a single use, and every instrument is best made when intended for one and not for many uses. But among barbarians no distinction is made between women and slaves, because there is no natural ruler

among them: they are a community of slaves, male and female. Wherefore the poets say—

It is meet that Hellenes should rule over barbarians;

as if they thought that the barbarian and the slave were by nature one.

Out of these two relationships between man and woman, master and slave, the first thing to arise is the family, and Hesiod is right when he says—

First house and wife and an ox for the plough,

for the ox is the poor man's slave. The family is the association established by nature for the supply of men's everyday wants, and the members of it are called by Charondas 'companions of the cupboard', and by Epimenides the Cretan, 'companions of the manger.' But when several families are united, and the association aims at something more than the supply of daily needs, the first society to be formed is the village. And the most natural form of the village appears to be that of a colony from the family, composed of the children and grandchildren, who are said to be 'suckled with the same milk.' And this is the reason why Hellenic states were originally governed by kings; because the Hellenes were under royal rule before they came together, as the barbarians still are. Every family is ruled by the eldest, and therefore in the colonies of the family the kingly form of government prevailed because they were of the same blood. As Homer says:

Each one gives law to his children and to his wives.

For they lived dispersedly, as was the manner in ancient times. Wherefore men say that the Gods have a king, because they themselves either are or were in ancient times under the rule of a king. For they imagine, not only the forms of the Gods, but their ways of life to be like their own. . . .

Now, that man is more of a political animal than bees or any other gregarious animals is evident. Nature, as we often say, makes nothing in vain, and man is the only animal whom she has endowed with the gift of speech. And whereas mere voice is but an indication of pleasure or pain, and is therefore found in other animals (for their mature attains to the perception of pleasure and pain and the intimation of them to one another, and no further), the power of speech is intended to set forth the expedient and inexpedient, and therefore likewise the just and the unjust. And it is a characteristic of man that he alone has any sense of good and evil, of just and unjust, and the like, and the association of living beings who have this sense makes a family and a state.

Further, the state is by nature clearly prior to the family and to the individual, since the whole is of necessity prior to the part; for example, if the whole body be destroyed, there will be no foot or hand, except in an equivocal sense, as we might speak of a stone hand; for when destroyed the hand will be no better than that. But things are defined by their working and power; and we ought not to say that they are the same when they no longer have their proper quality, but only that they have the same name. The proof that the state is a creation of nature and prior to the individual is that the individual, when isolated, is not self-sufficing; and therefore he is like a part in relation to the whole. But he who is unable to live in society, or who has no need because he is sufficient for himself, must be either a beast or a god: he is no part of a state. A social instinct is implanted in all men by nature, and yet he who first founded the state was the greatest of benefactors. For man, when perfected, is the best of animals, but, when separated from law and justice, he is the worst of all; since armed injustice is the more dangerous, and he is equipped at birth with arms, meant to be used by intelligence and virtue, which he may use for the worst ends. Wherefore, if he have not virtue, he is the most unholy and the most savage of animals, and the most full of lust and gluttony. But justice is the bond of men in states for the administration of justice, which is the determination of what is just, is the principle of order in political society.

QUESTIONS

1. What, for Aristotle, makes certain men the masters of women and other men?
2. According to Aristotle, for what purpose did nature create woman?
3. What does Aristotle mean when he speaks of the state as the "final cause" of political life?
4. Why does Aristotle think that man within the state is the best of all animals and outside the state the worst?

Aristotle's discussion of the true gentleman presents the philosopher's ideal of the happy man in some detail. Virtue for Aristotle was fundamentally a mean between two extremes. Self-esteem was a mean between arrogance and humility. Generosity held the middle place between spendthriftiness and stinginess. The other virtues are similarly defined. Obviously again the classical ideal of balance, "nothing too much," is at work in Aristotle's ethics. The true gentleman must most of all cultivate the virtue of prudence: the ability to measure each situation and to determine the correct course of action. He must be able to establish the correct middle course for appropriate action. The resultant picture of the gentleman is very different from that of the later Christian ideal. We are clearly dealing with a member of the upper classes, affluent, confident, calculating, and disdainful of members of the lower classes, who have no hope of matching his standards of conduct. This selection from *Nicomachean Ethics* is translated by F. H. Peters.

ARISTOTLE

The High-Minded Man

High-mindedness would seem from its very name to have to do with great things; let us first ascertain what these are.

It will make no difference whether we consider the quality itself, or the man who exhibits the quality.

By a high-minded man we seem to mean one who claims much and deserves much: for he who claims much without deserving it is a fool; but the possessor of a virtue is never foolish or silly. The man we have described, then, is high-minded.

He who deserves little and claims little is temperate [or modest], but not high-minded: for high-mindedness [or greatness of soul] implies greatness, just as beauty implies stature; small men may be neat and well proportioned, but cannot be called beautiful.

He who claims much without deserving it is vain (though not every one who claims more than he deserves is vain).

He who claims less than he deserves is little-minded, whether his deserts be great or moderate, or whether they be small and he claims still less: but this little-mindedness is most conspicuous in him whose deserts are great; for what would he do if his deserts were less than they are?

The high-minded man, then, in respect of the greatness of his deserts occupies an extreme position, but in that he behaves as he ought, observes the mean; for he claims that which he deserves, while all the others claim too much or too little.

But now if he deserves much and claims much, and most of all deserves and claims the greatest things, there will be one thing with which he will be especially concerned. For desert has reference to external good things. Now, the greatest of external good things we may assume to be that which we render to the Gods as their due, and that which people in high stations most desire, and which is the prize appointed for the noblest deeds. But the thing that answers to this description is honour, which, we may safely say, is the greatest of all external goods. Honours and dishonours, therefore, are the field in which the high-minded man behaves as he ought.

And indeed we may see, without going about to prove it, that honour is what high-minded men are concerned with; for it is honour that great men claim and deserve.

The little-minded man falls short, whether we compare his claims with his own deserts or with what the high-minded man claims for himself.

The vain or conceited man exceeds what is due to himself, though he does not exceed the high-minded man in his claims.

But the high-minded man, as he deserves the greatest things, must be a perfectly good or excellent man; for the better man always deserves the greatest things, and the best possible man the greatest possible things. The really high-minded man, therefore, must be a good or excellent man. And indeed greatness in every virtue or excellence would seem to be necessarily implied in being a high-minded or great-souled man.

It would be equally inconsistent with the high-minded man's character to run along swinging his arms, and to commit an act of injustice; for what thing is there for love of which he would do anything unseemly, seeing that all things are of little account to him? . . .

. . . the gifts of fortune also are commonly thought to contribute to high-mindedness. For those who are well born are thought worthy of honour, and those who are powerful or wealthy; for they are in a position of superiority, and that which is superior in any good thing is always held in greater honour. And so these things do make people more high-minded in a sense; for such people find honour from some. But in strictness it is only the good man that is worthy of honour, though he that has both goodness and good fortune is commonly thought to be more worthy of honour. Those, however, who have these good things without virtue, neither have any just claim to great things, nor are properly to be called high-minded, for neither is possible without complete virtue.

The high-minded man is not quick to run into petty dangers, and indeed does not love danger, since there are few things that he much values; but he is ready to incur a great danger, and whenever he does so is unsparing of his life, as a thing that is not worth keeping at all costs.

It is his nature to confer benefits, but he is ashamed to receive them; for the former is the part of a superior, the latter of an inferior. And when he has received a benefit, he is apt to confer a greater in return; for thus his creditor will become his debtor and be in the position of a recipient of his favour.

It is thought, moreover, that such men remember those on whom they have conferred favours better than those from whom they have received them; for the recipient of a benefit is inferior to the benefactor, but such a man wishes to be in the position of a superior. So he likes to be reminded of the one, but dislikes to be reminded of the other. . . .

It is characteristic of the high-minded man, again never or reluctantly to ask favours, but to be ready to confer them, and to be lofty in his behaviour to those who are high in station and favoured by fortune, but affable to those of the middle ranks; for it is a difficult thing and a dignified thing to assert superiority over the former, but easy to assert it over the latter. A haughty demeanour in dealing with the great is quite consistent with good breeding, but in dealing with those of low estate is brutal, like showing off one's strength upon a cripple.

Another of his characteristics is not to rush in wherever honour is to be won, nor to go where others take the lead, but to hold aloof and to shun an enterprise, except when great honour is to be gained, or a great work to be done—not to do many things, but great things and notable.

Again, he must be open in his hate and in his love; for concealment shows fear.

He must care for truth more than for what men will think of him, and speak and act openly; he will not hesitate to say all that he thinks, as he looks down upon mankind. So he will speak the truth, except when he speaks ironically; and irony he will employ in speaking to the generality of men.

Another of his characteristics is that he cannot fashion his life to suit another, except he be a friend, for that is servile: and so all flatterers or hangers on of great men are of a slavish nature, and men of low natures become flatterers.

Nor is he easily moved to admiration; for nothing is great to him.

He readily forgets injuries; for it is not consistent with his character to brood on the past, especially on past injuries, but rather to overlook them.

He is no gossip; he will neither talk about himself nor about others; for he cares not that men should praise him, nor that others should be blamed (though, on the other hand, he is not very ready to bestow praise); and so he is not apt to speak evil of others, not even of his enemies, except with the express purpose of giving offence.

When an event happens that cannot be helped or is of slight importance, he is the last man in the world to cry out or to beg for help; for that is the conduct of a man who thinks these events very important.

He loves to possess beautiful things that bring no profit, rather than useful things that pay; for this is characteristic of the man whose resources are in himself.

Further, the character of the high-minded man seems to require that his gait should be slow, his voice deep, his speech measured; for a man is not likely to be in a hurry when there are few things in which he is deeply interested, nor excited when he holds nothing to be of very great importance: and these are the causes of a high voice and rapid movements.

This, then, is the character of the high-minded man.

But he that is deficient in this quality is called little-minded; he that exceeds, vain or conceited.

QUESTIONS

1. Would you like to have this man for a friend?
2. How would a Christian criticize this ideal?
3. What information about Greek social structure does this passage give us?

While Aristotle wrote extensively concerning the ideal man, he ignored the matter of the ideal woman. The selection from *The Politics* indicates that Aristotle shared the common prejudice of his society that woman was naturally inferior to man and not worthy of special analysis. In a treatise entitled "On the Generation of Animals," Aristotle writes that a female was simply a failed male. Nature in producing human beings aims at making a male offspring, but when the process is defective, a female is the result. Because the woman by nature is colder than the man, girls are usually born when the father is either young or old, that is, when he has not yet reached the heat of maturity or when past that point. This view of man as the most perfect creature in nature and of woman as a defective or second-rate man was to have long-range repercussions in Western culture. Yet one should not conclude that the ancient Greeks consistently viewed the female as inferior. The goddesses in Greek mythology, the ideal female form in sculpture, the admiration shown for Sappho, and characters such as Lysistrata in comedy and Antigone in tragedy attest to the contrary. Plato, as mentioned earlier, envisaged equality between superior men and women in *The Republic*.

The Poetics   In addition to having made enormous contributions to the fields of metaphysics, politics, and ethics, Aristotle was also the western world's first literary critic, and his views on poetic and dramatic form continue to be influential to this day. Having before him the major works of classical Greek literature, Aristotle in *The Poetics* sought not only to define the nature of the forms of the epic, tragedy, comedy, and the dithyramb, but also to produce a kind of manual for writers who wished to write in these forms. He was also, in a sense, answering his former master Plato, who thought that poetry, with its dangerous effects on emotions, ought to be banished from the ideal republic. For Aristotle, poetry was actually superior to history, because poetry deals with the general and the philosophical, whereas history treats the particular. All poetry, for Aristotle, is an imitation (*mimesis*) of life, but this imitation involves not merely the realistic copying of a "slice of life," but the condensation of life into a form, with a beginning, a middle, and an end, resulting in both pleasure and self-knowledge for the audience. For Aristotle, tragedy, because it portrays men as better than they actually are, and because its form is the most cohesive, is superior to both comedy and epic. Indeed, most of *The Poetics* concerns tragedy, and because Aristotle apparently never finished the section on comedy, we can only speculate as to what his views on that form might have been. The selections from *The Poetics* reprinted here deal primarily with tragedy, but also with the comparison of tragic to epic poetry. The translation is by Benjamin Jowett and Thomas Twining.

ARISTOTLE

The Poetics

FROM BOOK SECOND: OF TRAGEDY

I. Of the species of poetry which imitates in hexameters, and of comedy, we shall speak hereafter. Let us now consider Tragedy; collecting first, from what has been already said, its true and essential definition.

Tragedy, then, is an imitation of some action that is important, entire, and of a proper magnitude—by language, embellished and rendered pleasurable, but by different means in different parts—in the way, not of narration, but of action—effecting through pity and terror the correction and refinement of such passions.

By pleasurable language I mean a language that has the embellishments of rhythm, melody, and metre. And I add, by different means in different parts, because in some parts metre alone is employed, in others, melody. . . .

Again, tragedy being an imitation of an action, and the persons employed in that action being necessarily characterized by their manners and their sentiments, since it is from these that actions themselves derive their character, it follows that there must also be manners and sentiments as the two causes of actions, and,

consequently, of the happiness or unhappiness of all men. The imitation of the action is the fable: for by fable I now mean the contexture of incidents, or the plot. By manners, I mean whatever marks the characters of the persons; by sentiments, whatever they say, whether proving anything, or delivering a general sentiment, etc.

Hence all tragedy must necessarily contain six parts, which together constitute its peculiar character or quality: fable, manners, diction, sentiments, decoration, and music. Of these parts, two relate to the means, one to the manner, and three to the object of imitation. And these are all. These specific parts, if we may so call them, have been employed by most poets, and are all to be found in almost every tragedy. . . .

III. But of all these parts the most important is the combination of incidents or the fable. Because tragedy is an imitation, not of men, but of actions—of life, of happiness and unhappiness; for happiness consists in action, and the supreme good itself, the very end of life, is action of a certain kind—not quality. Now the manners of men constitute only their quality or characters; but it is by their actions that they are happy, or the contrary. Tragedy, therefore, does not imitate action for the sake of imitating manners, but in the imitation of action that of manners is of course involved. So that the action and the fable are the end of tragedy; and in everything the end is of principal importance. . . .

Add to this, that those parts of tragedy by means of which it becomes most interesting and affecting are parts of the fable; I mean revolutions and discoveries. . . .

IV. These things being thus adjusted, let us go on to examine in what manner the fable should be constructed; since this is the first and most important part of tragedy.

Now we have defined tragedy to be an imitation of an action that is complete and entire; and that has also a certain magnitude; for a thing may be entire and a whole, and yet not be of any magnitude.

(1) By entire I mean that which has a beginning, a middle, and an end. A beginning is that which does not necessarily suppose anything before it, but which requires something to follow it. An end, on the contrary, is that which supposes something to precede it, either

necessarily or probably, but which nothing is required to follow. A middle is that which both supposes something to precede and requires something to follow. The poet, therefore, who would construct his fable properly is not at liberty to begin or end where he pleases, but must conform to these definitions. . . .

In general, we may say that an action is sufficiently extended when it is long enough to admit of a change of fortune, from happy to unhappy, or the reverse, brought about by a succession, necessary or probable, of well-connected incidents. . . .

VII. Of simple fables or actions, the episodic are the worst. I call that an episodic fable, the episodes of which follow each other without any probable or necessary connection; a fault into which bad poets are betrayed by their want of skill, and good poets by the players: for in order to accommodate their pieces to the purposes of rival performers in the dramatic contests, they spin out the action beyond their powers, and are thus frequently forced to break the connection and continuity of its parts.

But tragedy is an imitation, not only of a complete action, but also of an action exciting terror and pity. Now that purpose is best answered by such events as are not only unexpected, but unexpected consequences of each other: for, by this means, they will have more of the wonderful than if they appeared to be the effects of chance; since we find that, among events merely casual, those are the most wonderful and striking which seem to imply design: as when, for instance, the statue of Mitys at Argos killed the very man who had murdered Mitys, by falling down upon him as he was surveying it; events of this kind not having the appearance of accident. It follows, then, that such fables as are formed on these principles must be the best. . . .

IX. A revolution is a change (such as has already been mentioned) into the reverse of what is expected from the circumstances of the action; and that produced, as we have said, by probable or necessary consequence.

Thus, in the *Oedipus*, the messenger, meaning to make Oedipus happy, and to relieve him from the dread he was under with respect to his mother, by making known to him his real birth, produces an effect directly contrary to his intention. . . .

A discovery—as, indeed, the word implies—is a change from unknown to known, happening between those characters whose happiness or unhappiness forms the catastrophe of the drama, and terminating in friendship or enmity.

The best sort of discovery is that which is accompanied by a revolution as in the *Oedipus*. . . .

XI. The order of the subject leads us to consider, in the next place, what the poet should aim at and what avoid in the construction of his fable; and by what means the purpose of tragedy may be best effected.

Now since it is requisite to the perfection of a tragedy that its plot should be of the complicated, not of the simple kind, and that it should imitate such actions as excite terror and pity (this being the peculiar property of the tragic imitation), it follows evidently, in the first place, that the change from prosperity to adversity should not be represented as happening to a virtuous character; for this raises disgust rather than terror or compassion. Neither should the contrary change, from adversity to prosperity, be exhibited in a vicious character: this, of all plans, is the most opposite to the genius of tragedy, having no one property that it ought to have; for it is neither gratifying in a moral view, nor affecting, nor terrible. Nor, again, should the fall of a very bad man from prosperous to adverse fortune by represented: because, though such a subject may be pleasing from its moral tendency, it will produce neither pity nor terror. For our pity is excited by misfortunes undeservedly suffered, and our terror by some resemblance between the sufferer and ourselves. Neither of these effects will, therefore, be produced by such an event.

There remains, then, for our choice, the character between these extremes: that of a person neither eminently virtuous or just, nor yet involved in misfortune by deliberate vice or villainy, but by some error of human frailty; and this person should also be someone of high fame and flourishing prosperity. For example, Oedipus, Thyestes, or other illustrious men of such families.

XII. Hence it appears that, to be well constructed, a fable, contrary to the opinion of some, should be single rather than double; that the change of fortune should not be from adverse to prosperous, but the reverse; and that it should be the consequence, not of vice, but of some great frailty, in a character such as has been described, or better rather than worse. . . .

XVIII. Every tragedy consists of two parts—the complication and the development. The complication is often formed by incidents supposed prior to the action, and by a part, also, of those that are within the action; the rest form the development. I call complication all that is between the beginning of the piece and the last part, where the change of fortune commences; development all between the beginning of that change and the conclusion. Thus, in the *Lynceus* of Theodectes, the events antecedent to the action and the seizure of the child constitute the complication; the development is from the accusation of murder to the end.

FROM BOOK THIRD: OF THE EPIC POEM

II. The epic poem differs from tragedy in the length of its plan and in its metre.

With respect to length a sufficient measure has already been assigned. It should be such as to admit of our comprehending at one view the beginning and the end, and this would be the case if the epic poem were reduced from its ancient length, so as not to exceed that of such a number of tragedies as are performed successively at one hearing. But there is a circumstance in the nature of epic poetry which affords it peculiar latitude in the extension of its plan. It is not in the power of tragedy to imitate several different actions performed at the same time; it can imitate only that one which occupies the stage, and in which the actors are employed. But the epic imitation, being narrative, admits of many such simultaneous incidents, properly related to the subject, which swell the poem to a considerable size.

FROM BOOK FIFTH: OF THE SUPERIORITY OF TRAGIC TO EPIC POETRY

III. Tragedy has the advantage in the following respects: It possesses all that is possessed by the epic; it might even adopt its metre: and to this it makes no inconsiderable addition, in the music and the decoration; by the latter of which the illusion is heightened,

and the pleasure arising from the action is rendered more sensible and striking.

It has the advantage of greater clearness and distinctness of impression, as well in reading as in representation.

It has also that of attaining the end of its imitation in a shorter compass: for the effect is more pleasurable when produced by a short and close series of impressions, than when weakened by diffusion through a long extent of time; as the *Oedipus* of Sophocles, for example, would be if it were drawn out to the length of the Iliad.

Further: there is less unity in all epic imitation, as appears from this—that any epic poem will furnish matter for several tragedies. For, supposing the poet to choose a fable strictly one, the consequence must be either that his poem, if proportionably contracted, will appear curtailed and defective, or, if extended to the usual length, will become weak and, as it were, diluted. If, on the other hand, we suppose him to employ several fables—that is, a fable composed of several actions—his imitation is no longer strictly one. The Iliad, for example, and the Odyssey contain many such subordinate parts, each of which has a certain magnitude and unity of its own; yet is the construction of those poems as perfect, and as nearly approaching to the imitation of a single action, as possible.

QUESTIONS

1. What does Aristotle consider to be the most important part of tragedy and why?
2. Note that Aristotle often uses Sophocles' *Oedipus* as his example of the ideal tragedy. Show how the concept "discovery" applies to the tragedy of Oedipus.
3. Aristotle contends that the ideal tragic figure becomes involved in misfortune not by deliberate villainy but "by some error of human frailty." Does this apply to Oedipus in your opinion? Why or why not? What other views of the tragic hero, besides those of Aristotle, are possible?
4. In Aristotle's view, what differentiates the epic from tragedy and why is tragedy superior?
5. Can you apply Aristotle's categories to modern forms (film, novel, television drama, etc.)?

5

The Culture
of Rome

❧

Hellenistic and Roman History and Thought

Hellenistic Empires Already before the deaths of Plato and Aristotle, their political philosophies, assuming as they did the existence of the independent city-state, were becoming out of date. Athens was conquered by Sparta in 404 B.C., and for about thirty years Sparta controlled the leadership of the Greek city-state system. Sparta, however, was neither intellectually suited nor powerful enough to carry such a burden, and in 371 B.C. the Spartans were defeated by the Thebans, who in turn became the leading military force in Greece. But the Greek city-states were so isolated and divided by rivalries that they fell easy prey to the armies of Philip II of Macedon, a kingdom in the northern part of the Aegean peninsula. By 338 B.C. almost all Greece was under Philip's control, and, when he died in 336 B.C., his place was taken by his son Alexander (356–323 B.C.). With

Alexander, the West took the offensive against the East. The armies of Macedon and Greece invaded and conquered the Persian empire, and Greek rule was established in the Near East and Egypt. Educated in the ideas of Greek culture partially instilled in him by Aristotle, who acted as his tutor for a time, Alexander diffused the civilization and language of Greece wherever his armies went (see map).

In the process, Greek culture became more cosmopolitan and sophisticated while remaining essentially Greek. Because of this modification in the character of Greek life, the age beginning with Alexander is referred to as Greek-like, or Hellenistic. The graceful nudity of the Cnidian Aphrodite and the dramatic power of the frieze for the Pergamon altar (Figs. 2-15 and 2-16) are examples of the expansion and transformation of Greek art. In philosophy, in contrast to the wide-ranging interest of earlier thinkers, there was a tendency toward specialization. Euclid produced his masterful geometrical treatise, *The Elements*; Archimedes did basic work in statistics and hydrostatics; great advances were also made in biology, astronomy, geography, and city planning.

The expansion of the frontiers of Greek culture, moreover, had a dissolving effect on the political and cultural shell around the individual created by the polis. Individuals came increasingly to live on their own. They found themselves in a larger, more international community than the one they had known. The sharp distinction drawn by Hellenic culture between the Greek, free by nature, and the barbarian, by nature a slave, broke down. However, freedom from the encompassing pressures of the integrated life of the polis made people uneasy. Eastern religions extending hope of personal immortality became popular. These cults often centered on a suffering god, who through his earthly death extended to his worshipers the hope of everlasting life. People in the Hellenistic empire also turned to philosophies focusing on the ethical conduct of the individual and providing a vision of political association more adapted to a period of world empire. These philosophies themselves gradually became more religious in nature.

Stoicism   Among the variety of new philosophical movements rising at the end of the fourth century, the one with the greatest future was Stoicism. First taught by Zeno (322–264 B.C.) at Athens, the Stoic doctrine taught that the principle of the world was reason. Reason was a divine essence that lay behind everything occurring in the universe and was the ultimate cause of all that happened. This rational principle was the Stoic God. Man was a rational creature whose soul, moreover, was a particle of that Divine Reason. Thus, all men were equal, one to the other, because each, whether slave or free, was a particle of the same divine substance. The Divine Reason operated according to certain laws. If man carefully examined his conscience, he would see in himself, as a particle of Divine Reason, the same laws. Every man, moreover, if he submitted himself to an honest examination, would produce the same conclusions: that it was wrong to kill, to steal, to hurt another human being. Thus, for the Stoic at the basis of every human mind lay the same principle of ethical action, a natural law, which was common to World Reason and the individual reason of man. What better kind of philosophy was there for a world state?

What of human happiness? Since the cause of the world was pure reason, everything had to happen for the best. Divine Reason was not a cold indifferent force but rather a providential goodness that aimed for the good of the whole. Man must learn to accept this external world as it is. The individual should not regret failures and lose control in times of success. Rather the individual must welcome everything calmly. To do so was to put oneself in accord with the World Reason and to follow one's own nature, which was essentially reason. Furthermore, because the principle of Divine Reason was beneficent, so the individual, truly following his own nature, would also be a force for good in the world and especially for other men. This doctrine gave a strong social direction to the followers of the school.

The early doctrine of the Stoics pictured the ethical ideal as apathy, indifference to all that was not concerned with virtue. The wise man was to do his duty regardless of the personal costs. Other "goods" of the soul, health and wealth (which for Aristotle were necessary for happiness), were irrelevant for the Stoic. Nor did the Stoic expect an eternal reward. At death the individual human soul of good and evil men alike would fall back into the reservoir of Divine Reason whence it came. With the centuries, however, Stoicism became less harsh, more reconciled to human weaknesses. By the first century B.C. adherents of the school rejected

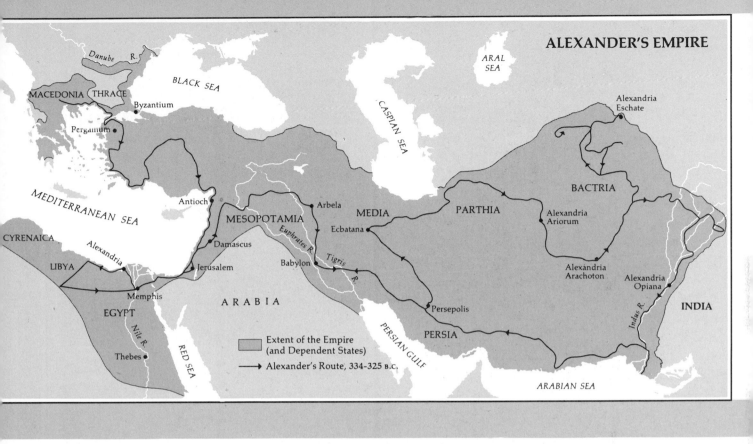

ALEXANDER'S EMPIRE

Extent of the Empire
(and Dependent States)
Alexander's Route, 334-325 B.C.

the ideal of apathy as inhuman and admitted that, if not "goods," health and wealth were nonetheless useful for happiness. Increasingly Stoics also came to believe in some kind of personal immortality of the human soul even though it was difficult to reconcile that belief with the general structure of their thought.

The Rise of Rome The great Macedonian empire of Alexander was unstable. When, after his death in 323, it was divided among his generals, disintegration set in. Throughout most of the third century B.C. a power vacuum existed in the Mediterranean area. By the beginning of the second century B.C. Rome gradually came to fill it. Founded sometime in the eighth century B.C. (the mythical date is 753 B.C.), Rome developed slowly. Only after five hundred years—after numerous wars and a series of annexation and treaty agreements—did Rome finally become mistress of Italy, around 260 B.C. But from there Roman frontiers expanded quickly. The Romans first expanded toward

the south and west to Sicily and Spain, bringing themselves into conflict with Carthage, the great maritime power on the northern coast of Africa. They then moved toward the east, where by the mid-second century they had destroyed the kingdom of Macedon and annexed Greece as the province of Achaia. By 100 B.C. Rome was for all practical purposes mistress of the Mediterranean.

In the following century and a half the major interest of the state was to push back the frontiers from the coasts of the inland sea. On the east Rome expanded into Arabia, the Levant, and Persian territory; on the south into the deserts of North Africa and Egypt; on the north into southern Germany and southern Russia; while Roman legions from Gaul invaded and conquered England. At the height of its empire in the century after Christ, Rome controlled most of Western Europe, the Middle East, and North Africa. To the north stretched the German forests, to the east the decaying Persian empire, to the south the deserts of Africa, and to the west Ireland and the ocean (see map, p. 126).

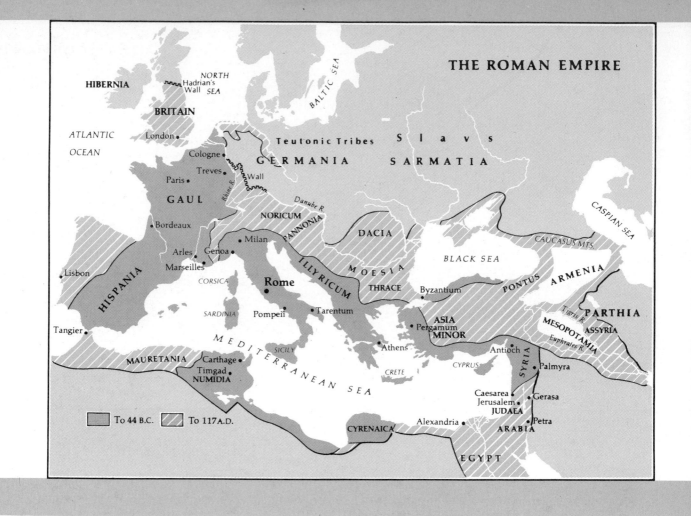

The Roman Empire

Italy, like Greece, had an area where political power was divided among numerous little city-states. Rome had been only one of a number in central Italy; and, as the city expanded its authority, Rome merely absorbed one city-state after another. In its subsequent expansion outside of Italy, Rome followed very much the same policy of preserving the city-states as the local center of government; where no such organization existed, Rome created the city-state afresh. By the first century B.C. the Roman empire consisted of a grouping of dependent city-states into provinces, the governors of which were officials sent out from the city council (called the Senate) of the supreme city-state, Rome.

The ancient Romans, unlike the Greeks, were not given to speculation and abstract thinking. They were a practical people, religiously tolerant, ferocious fighters, and devoutly patriotic. But they proved themselves very adaptable. If initially Romans conquered Greece, they in their turn were conquered by Greek culture. Especially attractive to the Romans, now moving to a position of ruling a good portion of the world, was the philosophy of Stoicism, with its stern insistence on duty. The Stoic conception of man as a particle of Divine Reason, moreover, provided the Romans with just the sort of theoretical background for a legal system designed to integrate the disparate territories of the world state.

Roman Law   The Roman world, consisting of myriads of city-states, big and little kingdoms, was a legal nightmare. Each of these areas had its own law code, and the task of the conqueror was to develop some kind of legal system that would provide justice for the whole. From at least the first century B.C. on, Roman jurists began transforming the Stoic conception of a natural law present in the consciousness of all men into practical forms. This task took centuries, and the final codification of Roman law was not finished until centuries after the Roman empire in the west had fallen to the barbarians. While allowing each of the city-states to keep its own peculiar set of laws, the Roman state in matters of basic law and procedure forced all parts of its territory from England to Asia to follow the principles of the law of nations, the *jus gentium*, those principles of justice derived by Roman jurists and statesmen from the abstract natural law found in man's consciousness. With time, following Rome's example, the individual city-states in other than basic principles of law tended as well to follow the law of Rome.

Cicero Perhaps the most eloquent testimony to the faith in the essential equality of all men is found in the writings of the great Roman statesman Marcus Tullius Cicero (106–43 B.C.). By Cicero's time, the old Roman Republic, centered on the Roman Senate, was creaking at the joints with aristocratic factions struggling for domination of the world state. The most gifted orator of his day, Cicero used his eloquence to defend the republican institutions from the twin threats of dictatorship and anarchy. He lived to realize that his political work was a failure and, dying, could only hope that the coming monarchy would be benevolent. Despite a busy political career, Cicero found time to translate the terminology and ideas of Greek philosophers into Latin and composed numerous philosophical works of his own. Although skeptical of the validity of vast systems of thought found in many philosophers like Plato and Aristotle, Cicero was vitally concerned with moral or ethical philosophy. He fervently believed that the eloquence of the orator, joined with moral philosophy, could have a tremendously positive effect on the hearts and minds of men. In a series of books primarily devoted to ethics and politics, *On Duties*, *On the Republic*, and *On the Laws*, he captured the Stoics' cosmopolitan vision of mankind, utilizing their conception of natural law as the background against which to judge the legal institutions and customs of his world. His God

was the Stoic Divine Reason, and man, being essentially rational, was a particle of God. God's reason is right reason and right reason applied to the world is God's law. Sharing reason with God, all men can know this law and thus distinguish the just from the unjust. The selection from *On the Laws*, translated by Clinton Walker Keyes, concerns the nature of justice. Cicero (M) is the major speaker of the dialogue. His friend Atticus (A) is the other. Against the argument that the law is a matter of convenience and custom, Cicero maintains that it is rooted in the consciences of all mankind.

CICERO

On the Laws

M. . . . that animal which we call man, endowed with foresight and quick intelligence, complex, keen, possessing memory, full of reason and prudence, has been given a certain distinguished status by the supreme God who created him; for he is the only one among so many different kinds and varieties of living beings who has a share in reason and thought, while all the rest are deprived of it. But what is more divine, I will not say in man only, but in all heaven and earth, than reason? And reason, when it is full grown and perfected, is rightly called wisdom. Therefore, since there is nothing better than reason, and since it exists both in man and God, the first common possession of man and God is reason. But those who have reason in common must also have right reason in common. And since right reason is Law, we must believe that men have Law also in common with the gods. Further, those who share Law must also share Justice; and those who share these are to be regarded as members of the same commonwealth. If indeed they obey the same authorities and powers, this is true in a far greater degree; but as a matter of fact they do obey this celestial system, the divine mind, and the God of transcendent power. Hence we must now conceive of this whole universe as one commonwealth of which both gods and men are members.

And just as in States distinctions in legal status are made on account of the blood relationships of families, according to a system which I shall take up in its proper place, so in the universe the same thing holds true, but on a scale much vaster and more splendid, so that men are grouped with Gods on the basis of blood relationship and descent. For when the nature of man is examined, the theory is usually advanced (and in all probability it is correct) that through constant changes and revolutions in the heavens, a time came which was suitable for sowing the seed of the human race. And when this seed was scattered and sown over the earth, it was granted the divine gift of the soul. For while the other elements of which man consists were derived from what is mortal, and are therefore fragile and perishable, the soul was generated in us by God. Hence we are justified in saying that there is a blood relationship between ourselves and the celestial beings; or we may call it a common ancestry or origin. Therefore among all the varieties of living beings, there is no creature except man which has any knowledge of God, and among men themselves there is no race either so highly civilized or so savage as not to know that it must believe in a god, even if it does not know in what sort of god it ought to believe. Thus it is clear that man recognizes God because, in a way, he remembers and recognizes the source from which he sprang.

Moreover, virtue exists in man and God alike, but in no other creature besides; virtue, however, is nothing else than Nature perfected and developed to its highest point; therefore there is a likeness between man and God. As this is true, what relationship could be closer or clearer than this one? For this reason, Nature has lavishly yielded such a wealth of things adapted to man's convenience and use that what she produces seems intended as a gift to us, and not brought forth by chance; and this is true, not only of what the fertile earth bountifully bestows in the form of grain and fruit, but also of the animals; for it is clear that some of them have been created to be man's slaves, some to supply him with their products, and others to serve as his food. Moreover innumerable arts have been discovered through the teachings of Nature; for it is by a skilful imitation of her that reason has acquired the necessities of life. Nature has likewise not only equipped man himself with nimbleness of thought, but has also given him the senses, to be, as it were, his attendants and messengers; she has laid bare the obscure and none too

[obvious] meanings of a great many things, to serve as the foundations of knowledge, as we may call them; and she has granted us a bodily form which is convenient and well suited to the human mind. For while she has bent the other creatures down toward their food, she has made man alone erect, and has challenged him to look up toward heaven, as being, so to speak, akin to him, and his first home. In addition, she has so formed his features as to portray therein the character that lies hidden deep within him; for not only do the eyes declare with exceeding clearness the innermost feelings of our hearts, but also the countenance, as we Romans call it, which can be found in no living thing save man, reveals the character. (The Greeks are familiar with the meaning which this word "countenance" conveys, though they have no name for it.) I will pass over the special faculties and aptitudes of the other parts of the body, such as the varying tones of the voice and the power of speech, which is the most effective promoter of human intercourse; for all these things are not in keeping with our present discussion or the time at our disposal; and besides, this topic has been adequately treated, as it seems to me, by Scipio in the books which you have read. But, whereas God has begotten and equipped man, desiring him to be the chief of all created things, it should now be evident, without going into all the details, that Nature, alone and unaided, goes a step farther; for, with no guide to point the way, she starts with those things whose character she has learned through the rudimentary beginnings of intelligence, and, alone and unaided, strengthens and perfects the faculty of reason.

A. Ye immortal gods, how far back you go to find the origins of Justice! And you discourse so eloquently that I not only have no desire to hasten on to the consideration of the civil law, concerning which I was expecting you to speak, but I should have no objection to your spending even the entire day on your present topic; for the matters which you have taken up, no doubt, merely as preparatory to another subject, are of greater import than the subject itself to which they form an introduction.

M. The points which are now being briefly touched upon are certainly important; but out of all the material of the philosophers' discussions, surely there comes nothing more valuable than the full realization that we are born for Justice, and that right is based, not upon men's opinions, but upon Nature. This fact will immediately be plain if you once get a clear conception of man's fellowship and union with his fellow-men. For no single thing is so like another, so exactly its counterpart, as all of us are to one another. Nay, if bad habits and false beliefs did not twist the weaker minds and turn them in whatever direction they are inclined, no one would be so like his own self as all men would be like all others. And so, however we may define man, a single definition will apply to all. This is a sufficient proof that there is no difference in kind between man and man; for if there were, one definition could not be applicable to all men; and indeed reason, which alone raises us above the level of the beasts and enables us to draw inferences, to prove and disprove, to discuss and solve problems, and to come to conclusions, is certainly common to us all, and, though varying in what it learns, at least in the capacity to learn it is invariable. For the same things are invariably perceived by the senses, and those things which stimulate the senses, stimulate them in the same way in all men; and those rudimentary beginnings of intelligence to which I have referred, which are imprinted on our minds, are imprinted on all minds alike; and speech, the mind's interpreter, though differing in the choice of words, agrees in the sentiments expressed. In fact, there is no human being of any race who, if he finds a guide, cannot attain to virtue.

The similarity of the human race is clearly marked in its evil tendencies as well as in its goodness. For pleasure also attracts all men; and even though it is an enticement to vice, yet it has some likeness to what is naturally good. For it delights us by its lightness and agreeableness; and for this reason, by an error of thought, it is embraced as something wholesome. It is through a similar misconception that we shun death as though it were a dissolution of nature, and cling to life because it keeps us in the sphere in which we were born; and that we look upon pain as one of the greatest of evils, not only because of its cruelty, but also because it seems to lead to the destruction of nature. In the same way, on account of the similarity between moral worth and renown, those who are publicly honoured are considered happy, while those who do not attain fame are thought miserable. Troubles, joys, desires, and

fears haunt the minds of all men without distinction, and even if different men have different beliefs, that does not prove, for example, that it is not the same quality of superstition that besets those races which worship dogs and cats as gods, as that which torments other races. But what nation does not love courtesy, kindliness, gratitude, and remembrance of favours bestowed? What people does not hate and despise the haughty, the wicked, the cruel, and the ungrateful? Inasmuch as these considerations prove to us that the whole human race is bound together in unity, it follows, finally, that knowledge of the principles of right living is what makes men better.

QUESTIONS

1. What does Cicero mean by Law?
2. What effect would this belief have on one's approach to law and custom?
3. What is the basis of the natural equality of man?

Intimately connected with the theme of justice in this passage is that of the dignity of man, who, in his possession of consciousness of the law, is akin to the gods. Cicero, like the ancient philosophers before him, looked on the human predicament as essentially one of ignorance. In Cicero's case, man was divine but had lowered himself by his commitment to the passions. The salvation of the individual lay in becoming aware of one's true nature and of training oneself to conform with the commandments of reason. Thus, as for Plato, Aristotle, and the Stoics, human happiness was within man's grasp. The task of the philosopher was to educate individuals in the truth; the rest was up to them.

The Question of Slavery   Despite what might appear as the revolutionary tendencies of these doctrines of the basic equality of men and their common human dignity, neither Cicero nor his Stoic predecessors intended them to be attacks on the institution of slavery in their society. As opposed to Plato and Aristotle—who generally considered the state to be natural to man and political life to be the means by which the individual realizes his humanity—these later thinkers maintained that the state was a creation brought into being to meet the needs of men who were already human beings. By the time of Cicero it was widely believed that mankind had originally existed in a state of nature without formal government. Without property and forced subjection men had led lives of peace and harmony. At some point when this tranquility was disrupted by passion, the state was instituted as a means for restoring peace. Both slavery and property were essential ingredients of the new order. Thus, while slavery was not natural, it was a necessary institution designed to fit a corrupted human nature and was consequently legitimate. The only practical corollary of the doctrines of equality and human dignity in regard to the institution of slavery itself was the admonition to masters to be humane with their chattels and to treat them more as hired workers than as possessions.

From Republic to Empire   Although Stoic beliefs continued to dominate the mentality of the Roman upper class in the centuries immediately after Cicero, the nature of Roman government was significantly altered at the center. The Roman Republic had been founded in 509 B.C. with the expulsion of the kings who had ruled the city-state since its founding in the eighth century B.C. Despite the expansion of Rome from a tiny power to the capital of a world government, the republican government had proven very durable. In the process, the original constitution, which had centered on a Senate composed of members of the upper or patrician class, had been modified to appease the demands of the lower classes, or plebeians, to have a share in political power. By the first century B.C., however, the republican institutions were breaking down under the pressure of groups of men competing for power in the state. Cicero struggled valiantly to preserve the old republican traditions, but in his lifetime he saw a number of individuals emerge briefly as de facto rulers of Rome. Had Julius Caesar (100–44 B.C.) not been assassinated, it seems likely that he eventually would have imposed himself on the state as its official master. As it was, after Caesar was murdered in 44 B.C., Rome had to suffer almost two decades of civil war before his nephew Octavius (whose title was Augustus Caesar) succeeded in establishing his authority.

Augustus Caesar   Although Augustus was designated as *imperator* among other titles, *imperator* merely meant that he was leader of the army. The title

princeps ("foremost") best describes his place in the state. He was the first citizen of Rome. He had no wish to become a despot and honestly endeavored to restore the old republican institutions, especially the Senate, to a position of power and honor. In his own hands were concentrated the direction of the army and control over most state finance. He also directly appointed governors to a number of provinces. On the other hand, all public business was debated by the Senate, the *princeps* frequently consulted the Senate on policy, and the senators ruled over a number of provinces and held high positions in both the army and imperial civil service. Although gradually over the next two hundred years, the *princeps* assumed more power at the expense of the Senate, he usually tried to maintain at least the trappings of the republican institutions.

With the establishment of the Principate, the empire remained, as before, organized around hundreds of cities with the territory attached to them; it stayed so to the end of the imperial period, but now for the first time there was a truly unified authority at the center. In the last century of the Republic the Roman Senators sent out as governors of the provinces had often treated their charges as a means for self-enrichment. With Augustus and his successors the provincials felt that there was an overseer in the capital to whom they could appeal for justice. While a number of the emperors like Caligula and Nero were probably madmen, on the whole the provinces saw their general condition improve with the Principate. The Roman world, moreover, was tired of years of civil war and longed for peace. With Augustus' assumption of power as *princeps* began a two-hundred-year period of peace, the *Pax Romana*, which Gibbon, the eighteenth-century author of *The Decline and Fall of the Roman Empire*, characterized as "perhaps the happiest period in the history of the human race."

Roman Art and Architecture

The practical, orderly aspects of Roman life are reflected in Roman art and architecture. Although they adopted Greek forms and techniques, the Romans used their statues and buildings not primarily in pursuit of ideal beauty but to proclaim the Roman system to the world.

Roman Sculpture   A bronze from the first century B.C., called the *Arringatore (The Orator),* presents a man who may have been a Roman official (Fig. 5-1). He stands before us as he might have stood in the forum any day of the week. His stance is simple and straightforward, as is the rendering of his features; here is a particular person, a physiognomy that could belong to no one but himself. He is not an ideal politician of any sort.

The realism that we see in *The Orator* is also evident in the many surviving portrait busts and heads. The Greeks did not accept the idea of portrait busts or heads, feeling that these detached objects were too reminiscent of a decapitated body. The Romans instituted the practice of taking portrait masks of the deceased, which were preserved at home and brought out for ceremonies. The patrician families sought to preserve their family's identity from generation to generation in this way.

By the time of Augustus the Romans had absorbed much from the Greek artists. Nevertheless, it is the combination of realism and the imperial ideal that makes distinctive portraits.

We know Augustus Caesar from statues, coins, and gems. As emperor he was priest-king, military leader, and ruler. It was important that he be represented in all the facets of his power not only to secure it for himself but also to make it legitimate. The statue of Augustus found at the imperial villa of Prima Porta is an excellent example of the military type of portrait (Fig. 5-2). Dressed in very decorative armor but without boots (therefore probably made after his death when he had been made a god and did not need boots), he stands alert but at ease, addressing his troops. The features are distinctively those of the emperor, virile and youthful. He has been ennobled and idealized by the absence of age, flaws, or any of the other makings of a fallible human. Compare the statue with *The Spearbearer* and *The Orator.* What has been taken from each, and what has been left behind in this effort to present Augustus, Imperator?

The *Ara Pacis Augustae,* (the Altar of the Peace of

5–1   Right: Arringatore (The Orator). (Archaeological Museum, Florence—Alinari/ Editorial Photocolor Archives)

5–2   Far right: Augustus of Prima Porta. (Vatican Museum, Rome—Alinari/ Editorial Photocolor Archives)

Augustus) probably begun in 13 B.C., was made to commemorate the peace brought about by the imperial might of Rome (Fig. 5-3). It is useful to compare it with the frieze of the Panathenaic festival (Fig. 2-9). At first sight it recalls the frieze, but there are subtle differences. First, the Greek procession is presented as an institutionalized event without regard to the particular individuals who participate. The *Ara Pacis* commemorates one specific historic moment—the moment when the altar was begun. Second, the figures of the *Ara Pacis* are more closely crowded together, as if they had indeed just gathered, giving them an air of immediacy and realism absent in the formal rhythms of the Parthenon frieze. Concentration is not directed toward the focal event but on the interaction between those who make up the event. This frieze has a false calm that seems comparable to the nobility and wisdom that overlay the ruthless Augustus. It was power and decisiveness that made the empire.

In the reliefs of *The Spoils from the Temple at Jerusalem* (Fig. 5-4) on the Arch of Titus, we confront an almost reportorial scene of victory. The conquering Romans return to the city with captives and treasure, including the great, sacred menorah (seven-branched candelabra) from the temple. The sculpture is carved in low relief, and the space is filled with people and objects. This somewhat crowded quality gives the relief an air of urgency and energy that seems to symbolize the power of Rome. This is not myth or allegory but the direct reality of success. To the Roman mind this record of victory will ensure an immortality of which no divinity is capable. No Athenian of the fifth century would have dared to so memorialize himself.

Roman Architecture As the Romans learned from the Greeks, so they also learned from other tribes and nations. Their system of building probably came from the Etruscans, a powerful tribe that lived in the peninsula until they were conquered by the Romans. To wall and post and lintel the Etruscans and then the Romans added the arch as a major building technique. It was not that arches were unknown before; it is simply that the Romans put them to multiple and innovating uses.

5–4 Arch of Titus, Rome. The Spoils from the Temple at Jerusalem. (Alinari/Editorial Photocolor Archives)

As a building system the true arch is a combination of *pier* (post) and a semicircle of material that replaces the *lintel* (Fig. 5-5). The arch itself is made of stones or bricks cut to fit so that they help hold each other in place. Erecting an arch requires a wooden scaffold with an arch-shaped top called a *centering*. This supports the arch while all the sections are being put into place. When the last top, center stone, the *keystone*, is inserted, the centering can be moved to the next arch. The diagram shows how an arch exerts pressure outward and downward, necessitating pressure at those points to keep it from falling apart.

A series of arches produces a *barrel vault*. The weight of the vault rests equally along the wall. When two barrel vaults intersect at right angles, a *groin vault* results (Fig. 5-5); the weight of the vault then rests on the corner piers instead of along the wall, which can then be opened up for doors and windows. An arch rotated in space 360 degrees produces a *dome*. Like a barrel vault, a dome's weight rests equally on the wall, which is its circumference.

To this potentially very rich collection of forms, the Romans added a much cheaper, faster means of building—brick and rubble masonry fill. To make this, a sticky liquid mass is poured into a form in which small rocks, gravel, and stones are introduced to give greater density and strength. When dried, the surface is covered with plaster or a thin layer of marble or granite called a *veneer*.

The types of building that assumed great importance in Rome are not the same as those which were important for fifth-century Athens. When we think of Athens, we see the great Acropolian complex of sacred buildings towering over the city. The Roman city seems more of a piece, less divided between sacred and secular. The Romans were among the first to develop city planning on an extensive basis, and their methods of planning are in themselves a significant guide to their values.

If we had a Roman town or city perfectly planned and preserved, we would see first that the city itself was a rectangle, bounded by walls and traversed by major

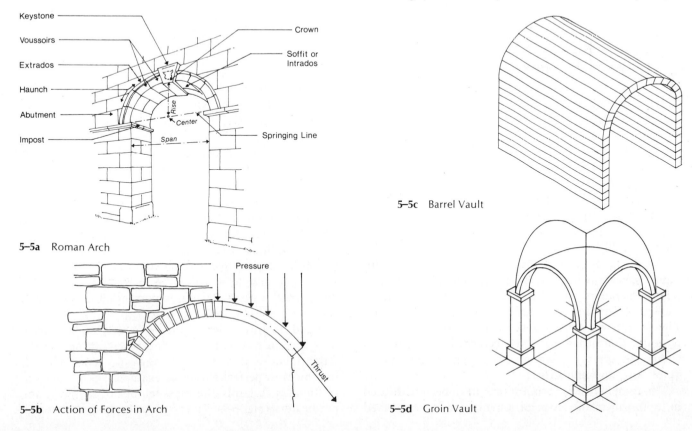

5–5a Roman Arch

5–5b Action of Forces in Arch

5–5c Barrel Vault

5–5d Groin Vault

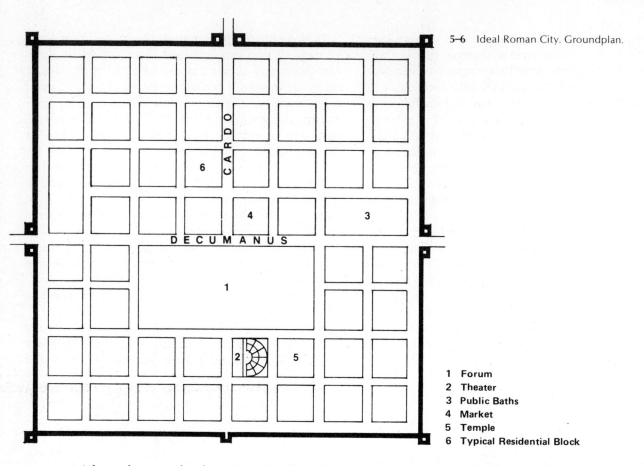

5–6   Ideal Roman City. Groundplan.

1   Forum
2   Theater
3   Public Baths
4   Market
5   Temple
6   Typical Residential Block

streets at right angles to each other (Fig. 5-6). These major streets were oriented to the cardinal points of the compass and traversed by other streets, also at exact right angles: this formed a grid pattern of city blocks, which were assigned different functions for living, markets, and areas of entertainment. The town would be reached by well-laid Roman roads and, if need be, fed water by aqueducts, like the Pont du Gard, still standing outside Nîmes in southern France (Fig. 5-7). At the center would be a *forum*.

The forum began as an open space with a rostrum for public speeches; but under Julius, then Augustus Caesar, it became a place for a temple with surrounding walkways. In time it included a law court *(basilica)*. The forum was for the reading of proclamations, the promulgation of laws, and the celebration of triumphs and religious rites. It was a visible sign of Roman conquest, law, and administration.

The temple in the forum might have been dedicated to Jupiter or to the emperor. One of the best preserved

Roman temples is the late republican *Maison Carrée* in southern France (Fig. 5-8). It is interesting to compare it with the Parthenon. The Roman temple has columns, a portico, and a gable roof; but what are the major visible differences? The raised basement or podium with its long flight of steps, the absence of a colonnade, the much deeper portico, and the attached half-round columns on its sides and back all contrast with the Parthenon. What does this suggest to you? Look at the plan of the forum illustrated above (Fig. 5-6). Where is the temple in the complex? What role does it play in the space? The temple was not the focus of the complex, but a part, among several important buildings, in a system.

In a different section of the perfectly planned imaginary Roman city, we would find the buildings for entertainment—baths, theaters, and an arena. Though not the most perfect surviving example, the Colosseum in Rome is certainly the most famous of the great amphitheaters (Fig. 5-9). Here spectacles and gladiatorial

Plate I Chartres, stained glass window,
Notre Dame de la Belle Verriere (detail).
(Giraudon/Art Resource)

Plate II Chartres, stained glass
window, *St. James Major* (detail).
(Giraudon/Art Resource)

Plate IV *Florence*, c. 1490. Carta della catena, Museo di Firenze com'era. (Scala/Art Resource)

Plate III Martini, *Annunciation*.
Panel painting, 10′ × 8′9″, 1333.
(Scala/Art Resource)

Plate V Giotto, *The Lamentation.*
Scrovegni Chapel, Padua.
(Scala/Art Resource)

Plate VI Masaccio, *The Tribute
Money.* Brancacci Chapel, Florence.
(Art Resource)

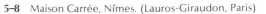

5–8   Maison Carrée, Nîmes. (Lauros-Giraudon, Paris)

5–7   Roman Aqueduct, Pont du Gard at Nîmes, France. (T. Lipscomb—Scala/Editorial Photocolor Archives)

5–9   Colosseum, Rome. (Alinari/Editorial Photocolor Archives)

5–10 Interior of Colosseum, Rome. (Alinari/Editorial Photocolor Archives)

5–11 Exterior Arches, Colosseum, Rome. (Alinari/Editorial Photocolor Archives)

combat took place. A view of the interior of the building shows that the Colosseum is essentially made up of a series of groin vaults and barrel vaults on massive walls that support tiers of seats and provide passageways (Fig. 5-10). But the arches that open to the outside are framed with half-round columns of Greek orders—the Doric, the Ionic, and another, the Corinthian (Fig. 5-11). These have been applied to the piers between the arches for articulation and decoration. No longer supporting a lintel, the columns are used to emphasize the scale and height of the exterior. It is appropriate that the most massive, the Doric, is on the bottom, while at the topmost tier we find a thin, flattened column, a *pilaster*, with a rich flat capital. This use of the column is radically different from that employed by the Greeks. The Colosseum is not sacred at all, but a setting for man and his sports.

The Romans, in short, transformed whatever seemed adequate to fulfill their needs. Another example is the Pantheon, a temple to all the planetary deities, dedi-

cated in Rome about 118–125 A.D. (Fig. 5-12). The plan (Fig. 5-13) shows us a great round, domed space contained within massive walls. Attached to the front is a deep portico that looks like one end of a Greek temple. The combination of circular and rectangular forms is among the first such combinations—a solution to give a sense of direction and ennobled entry to a round and therefore nondirectional space.

The interior presents us with the first important architectural space that is an interior (Fig. 5-14). The dome rises above the floor, and the only light spills in through the oculus, a round eye in the ceiling. This great hollow space creates a very different experience from the outdoor sanctuary of the Greeks or the Roman forum. It recalls the dome of heaven, the overarching sky; it seems to float or be suspended rather than to depend on the usual weight and support of the post and lintel system of building. The vital soaring quality of this majestic space and its accompanying technology will be influential for many centuries.

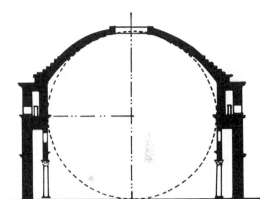

5–12   Pantheon, Rome.

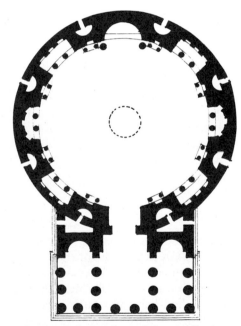

5–13   Pantheon, Rome. Groundplan and Section.

5–14   "The Interior of the Pantheon," Giovanni Paolo Panini. (National Gallery of Art, Washington, D.C. Samuel H. Kress Collection)

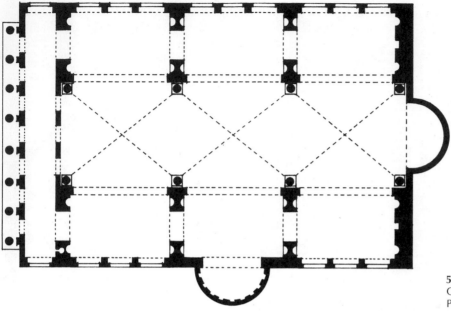

5–15 Basilica of Maxentius, Rome, with Groundplan. (Photo: Alinari/Editorial Photocolor Archives)

The creation of great interiors joins with the Greek forms to make a rich supply of ideas. The basilica, another element of the forum, was also a majestic interior space, with long interior colonnades. Half-domes rose above the curved ends where judges sat to dispense the law (Fig. 5-15). This vision of earthly power and administration of justice could be allied with the sacred architecture of Greece to form a complex series of symbols and ideas.

Roman Literature

As in other aspects of their culture, the Romans looked to Greek models for their literature. Greek literature began before the Greeks as a people had any political importance; with Rome it was the opposite. The Romans had been too busy organizing, building, and conquering to write; they began to do so only when, in the third century B.C., they dominated Greece and discovered Greek literature. The first real example of a literary work in Latin is a translation of Homer's *Odyssey*. Toward the end of the third century Plautus put some Greek "new comedies" into Latin, but his bawdy plays like *The Braggart Soldier* have something distinctively Roman about them. The plays of Terence

(195–159 B.C.), who was a slave of African origins, are more subdued and more subtle in their humor, closer to the Greek ideal of new comedy. At the time of Terence, more and more Roman men of letters were seriously studying Greek literature.

Roman oratory and rhetoric, of which we have already seen an example from Cicero, arose during the first century B.C. This was also the time of the great philosophical poet Lucretius, who explained the philosophy of Epicureanism (a philosophy opposed to Stoicism) in a long poem entitled *De rerum natura (On the Nature of Things)*. Catullus, a poet who admired and imitated Sappho, gave the Latin language a new lyric power.

Virgil and the *Aeneid* Rome's greatest poet was undoubtedly Virgil (70–19 B.C.), whose Latin name is Publius Vergilius Maro. During Virgil's lifetime Julius Caesar was murdered and Augustus Caesar became the first of Rome's emperors. The years of Augustus's reign (27 B.C.–A.D. 14), known as the "Augustan age," were viewed both by contemporaries and by later generations as Rome's golden years, comparable to Periclean Athens. These years indeed saw not only tremendous political and administrative achievements but also the finest Roman accomplishments in literature, as in other aspects of art and life. In the early years of this new era, Virgil wrote the great epic of Rome, named for its hero Aeneas, the *Aeneid*.

Highly conscious of living at a period of time when his native city was mistress of most of the known world and her glory was at its height, Virgil set out to write an epic poem in praise of Rome. Some even believe that Augustus might have commissioned him to write it. For an epic, there was only one model to which he could turn—Homer. Although Virgil's poem resembles both the *Iliad* and the *Odyssey* in that it is about a hero in battle and the wanderings of a hero and uses many similar literary devices, it differs in two basic ways. First, it is a literary, *written* work instead of an oral, *composed* one. Meant to be read instead of heard, it inaugurates the tradition of the written epic in Western literature. Second, Virgil's hero, Aeneas, is much less of an individual than is either Achilles or Odysseus. Homer's heroes represented the values of their culture in their own particular manner, but Virgil's hero seems to embody the values of his culture. Unlike Achilles or Odysseus, Aeneas is always sacrificing personal honor, glory, and happiness to something greater—and the "something greater" that seems to rule over the entire epic is the great destiny of Rome.

As in the case of the *Iliad*, the first lines of the *Aeneid* tell us a great deal about the poem as a whole. Here is the opening sentence in the original Latin:

Arma, virumque cano, Troiae qui primus ab oris
Italiam, fato profugus, Lavinaque venit
litora—

Here are the first seven lines put into twelve lines of English (Latin is a more concise language) by a modern translator, Allen Mandelbaum:

I sing of arms and of a man: his fate
had made him fugitive; he was the first
to journey from the coasts of Troy as far
as Italy and the Lavinian shores.
Across the lands and waters he was battered
beneath the violence of High Ones, for
the savage Juno's unforgetting anger;
and many sufferings were his in war—
until he brought a city into being
and carried in his gods to Latium;
from this have come the Latin race, the lords
of Alba, and the ramparts of high Rome.

The outline of the story of Aeneas and Aeneas' place as an instrument of Roman destiny is presented in these opening lines. First Virgil gives his subject, *"arms"* and *"a man,"* as Homer's subject was "the anger of Achilles." The *Aeneid* is about both war and the struggles of Aeneas. Aeneas was predestined by Fate, a concept that looms larger than the gods, to come from Troy to Italy. According to legend he was a Trojan who, after the Trojan War, escaped from his defeated city, piously carrying his old father on his shoulders. After long years of various hardships and delays, he at last arrived in Italy. There he married Lavinia, the daughter of King Latinus, thus uniting the Trojan people with the native Latin people to found the Roman race. Aeneas' enemy in his wanderings and struggles is Juno, queen of the gods and rival of Aeneas' mother, Venus. His protector is the king of the gods, Jupiter, who, allied with Fate, is assured victory in the end. Every act of Aeneas will be determined by the destiny marked out for him. He is not a mere puppet of Jupiter's; but, since he is conscious that he has a greater will to accomplish, he struggles against the traps laid for him by Juno and sacrifices personal happiness and comfort to the greater good. Virgil's prologue goes beyond the scope of the *Aeneid* itself, which ends with a duel between Aeneas and one of his Italian opponents. Aeneas founds the city of Lavinium with his bride *after* the close of the epic. Thirty years later his son establishes a new city, Alba Longa. Some three hundred years after that, Romulus and Remus, princes of Alba, found Rome, which will ultimately rule over not only all of Italy but most of the known world. This perspective puts Aeneas in his proper place. He is not a mere individual; he is an instrument of the great destiny of Rome.

For many readers the most interesting part of the *Aeneid* is Book 4, in which Aeneas falls in love with Dido, the queen of Carthage (Rome's great rival city in North Africa). Aeneas' decision to leave Dido after he has been with her for some time, and her consequent suicide, make him a heartless character for some readers; but Virgil intended to show in this episode the great personal tragedies that a public destiny like Aeneas' entails. (The translation is by Allen Mandelbaum.)

VIRGIL

From the *Aeneid*

BOOK 4

Too late. The queen is caught between love's pain
and press. She feeds the wound within her veins;
she is eaten by a secret flame. Aeneas'
high name, all he has done, again, again
come like a flood. His face, his words hold fast   5
her breast. Care strips her limbs of calm and rest.

A new dawn lights the earth with Phoebus'° lamp
and banishes damp shadows from the sky
when restless Dido turns to her heart's sharer:
"Anna, my sister, what dreams make me
          shudder?   10
Who is this stranger guest come to our house?
How confident he looks, how strong his chest
and arms! I think—and I have cause—that he
is born of gods. For in the face of fear

the mean must fall. What fates have driven him!   15
What trying wars he lived to tell! Were it not
my sure, immovable decision not
to marry anyone since my first love
turned traitor, when he cheated me by death,
were I not weary of the couch and torch,   20
I might perhaps give way to this one fault.
For I must tell you, Anna, since the time
Sychaeus, my poor husband, died and my
own brother° splashed our household gods with
          blood,
Aeneas is the only man to move   25
my feelings, to overturn my shifting heart.
I know too well the signs of the old flame.
But I should call upon the earth to gape
and close above me, or on the almighty
Father to take his thunderbolt, to hurl   30
me down into the shades, the pallid shadows
and deepest night of Erebus,° before
I'd violate you, Shame, or break your laws!
For he who first had joined me to himself
has carried off my love, and may he keep it   35
and be its guardian within the grave."
She spoke. Her breast became a well of tears.

And Anna answers: "Sister, you more dear
to me than light itself, are you to lose
all of your youth in dreary loneliness,   40
and never know sweet children or the soft
rewards of Venus? Do you think that ashes
or buried Shades will care about such matters?
Until Aeneas came, there was no suitor
who moved your sad heart—not in Libya nor,   45
before, in Tyre: you always scorned Iarbas
and all the other chiefs that Africa,
a region rich in triumphs, had to offer.
How can you struggle now against a love
that is so acceptable? Have you forgotten   50
the land you settled, those who hem you in?
On one side lie the towns of the Gaetulians,
a race invincible, and the unbridled
Numidians and then the barbarous Syrtis.°

---

7. Phoebus: Apollo, God of the Sun.

24. Pygmalion.
32. Erebus: The god of darkness.
54. The Gaetulians, Numidians, and Syrtians are neighboring African people. Iarbas is king of the Gaetylians.

And on the other lies a barren country,   55
stripped by the drought and by Barcaean raiders,
raging both far and near. And I need not
remind you of the wars that boil in Tyre°
and of your brother's menaces and plots.
For I am sure it was the work of gods   60
and Juno that has held the Trojan galleys
fast to their course and brought them here to
    Carthage.
If you marry Aeneas, what a city
and what a kingdom, sister, you will see!   65
With Trojan arms beside us, so much greatness
must lie in wait for Punic° glory! Only
pray to the gods for their good will, and having
presented them with proper sacrifices,
be lavish with your Trojan guests and weave
excuses for delay while frenzied winter   70
storms out across the sea and shatters ships,
while wet Orion° blows his tempest squalls
beneath a sky that is intractable.''

These words of Anna fed the fire in Dido.
Hope burned away her doubt, destroyed her
    shame.
First they move on from shrine to shrine,   75
    imploring
the favor of the gods at every altar.
They slaughter chosen sheep, as is the custom,
and offer them to Ceres° the lawgiver,
to Phoebus, Father Bacchus,° and—above all—   80
to Juno,° guardian of marriage. Lovely
Dido holds the cup in her right hand;
she pours the offering herself, midway
between a milk-white heifer's horns. She studies
slit breasts of beasts and reads their throbbing
    guts.   85
But oh the ignorance of augurs! How
can vows and altars help one wild with love?

Meanwhile the supple flame devours her marrow;
within her breast the silent wound lives on.
Unhappy Dido burns. Across the city   90
she wanders in her frenzy—even as
a heedless hind hit by an arrow when
a shepherd drives for game with darts among
the Cretan woods and, unawares, from far
leaves winging steel inside her flesh; she roams 95
the forests and the wooded slopes of Dicte,°
the shaft of death still clinging to her side.
So Dido leads Aeneas around the ramparts,
displays the wealth of Sidon° and the city
ready to hand; she starts to speak, then falters 100
and stops in midspeech. Now day glides away.
Again, insane, she seeks out that same banquet,
again she prays to her the trials of Troy,
again she hangs upon the teller's lips.

.   .   .   .

But now the guests are gone. The darkened moon, 105
in turn, conceals its light, the setting stars
invite to sleep; inside the vacant hall
she grieves alone and falls upon the couch
that he has left. Absent, she see, she hears
the absent one or draws Ascanius,°   110
his son and counterfeit, into her arms,
as if his shape might cheat her untellable love.

Her towers rise no more; the young of Carthage
no longer exercise at arms or build
their harbors or sure battlements for war;   115
the works are idle, broken off; the massive,
menacing rampart walls, even the crane,
defier of the sky, now lie neglected.

As soon as Jove's° dear wife sees that her Dido
is in the grip of such a scourge and that   120
no honor can withstand this madness, then

---

58. Tyre: A famous seaport of the Phoenicians, from which Dido
    fled with her supporters to found Carthage, a new city in Af-
    rica.
67. Punic: An equivalent of Phoenician.
72. Orion: A constellation of stars related to storms.
79. Ceres: Goddess of agriculture.
80. Bacchus: God of wine.
81. Juno: Queen of the gods and wife of Jupiter.

---

96. Dicte: A mountain in the eastern part of Crete.
99. Sidon: Ancient city of Phoenicians and mother-city of Tyre.
110. Ascanius: Young son of Aeneas and his dead Trojan wife
    Creusa.
119. Jove: Jupiter.

the daughter of Saturn° faces Venus:° "How
remarkable indeed: what splendid spoils
you carry off, you and your boy; how grand
and memorable is the glory if   125
one woman is beaten by the guile of two
gods. I have not been blind. I know you fear
our fortresses, you have been suspicious of
the houses of high Carthage. But what end
will come of all this hate? Let us be done   130
with wrangling. Let us make, instead of war,
an everlasting peace and plighted wedding.
You have what you were bent upon: she burns
with love; the frenzy now is in her bones.
Then let us rule this people—you and I—   135
with equal auspices; let Dido serve
a Phrygian° husband, let her give her Tyrians
and her pledged dowry into your right hand."

But Venus read behind the words of Juno
the motive she had hid: to shunt the kingdom   140
of Italy to Libyan° shores. And so
she answered Juno: "Who is mad enough
to shun the terms you offer? Who would prefer
to strive with you in war? If only fortune
favor the course you urge. For I am ruled   145
by fates and am unsure if Jupiter
would have the Trojans and the men of Tyre
become one city, if he like the mingling
of peoples and the writing of such treaties.
But you are his wife and it is right for you   150
to try his mind, to entreat him. Go. I'll follow."

Queen Juno answered her: "That task is mine.
But listen now while in few words I try
to tell you how I mean to bring about
this urgent matter. When tomorrow's Titan°   155
first shows his rays of light, reveals the world,
Aeneas and unhappy Dido plan
to hunt together in the forest. Then

while horsemen hurry to surround the glades
with nets, I shall pour down a black raincloud,   160
in which I have mixed hail, to awaken all
the heavens with my thundering. Their comrades
will scatter under cover of thick night.
Both Dido and the Trojan chief will reach
their shelter in the same cave. I shall be there.   165
And if I can rely on your goodwill,
I shall unite the two in certain marriage
and seal her as Aeneas' very own;
and this shall be their wedding." Cytherea°
said nothing to oppose the plan; she granted   170
what Juno wanted, smiling at its cunning.

Meanwhile Aurora rose; she left the Ocean.
And when her brightness fills the air, select
young men move from the gates with wide-
      meshed nets
and narrow snares and broad-blade hunting spears, 175
and then Massylian° horsemen hurry out
with strong, keen-scented hounds. But while the
      chieftains
of Carthage wait at Dido's threshold, she
still lingers in her room. Her splendid stallion,
in gold and purple, prances, proudly champing   180
his foaming bit. At last the queen appears
among the mighty crowd; upon her shoulders
she wears a robe of Sidon with embroidered
borders. Her quiver is of gold, her hair
has knots and ties of gold, a golden clasp   185
holds fast her purple cloak. Her Trojan comrades
and glad Ascanius advance behind her.
Aeneas, who is handsome past all others,
himself approaches now to join her, linking
his hunting band to hers. Just as Apollo,   190
when in the winter he abandons Lycia°
and Xanthus'° streams to visit his maternal
Delos,° where he renews the dances—Cretans,
Dryopians, and painted Agathyrsi,°

---

122. Saturn: Juno and enemy of the Trojans.
122. Venus: Goddess of love, true mother of Aeneas, and protec-
     tor of the Trojans.
137. Troy had been located on the coast of Phrygia.
141. Libyan: North African.
155. Titan: The sun.

169. Another name for Venus.
176. Massylian: Refers to a people of Africa.
191. Lycia: An area of Asia Minor where Apollo had an oracle.
192. Xanthus: A river of Lycia.
193. Delos: The island where Apollo was born.
194. Cretans, Dryopians, and Agathyrsi are peoples of the Medi-
     terranean basin.

mingling around the altars, shout—advances   195
upon the mountain ridges of high Cynthus°
and binds his flowing hair with gentle leaves
and braids its strands with intertwining gold;
his arrows clatter on his shoulder: no
less graceful is Aeneas as he goes;   200
an equal beauty fills his splendid face.
And when they reach the hills and pathless
        thickets,
the wild she-goats, dislodged from stony summits,
run down the ridges; from another slope
stags fling themselves across the open fields;   205
they mass their dusty bands in flight, forsaking
the hillsides. But the boy Ascanius
rides happy in the valleys on his fiery
stallion as he passes on his course
now stags, now goats; among the lazy herds   210
his prayer is for a foaming boar or that
a golden lion come down from the mountain.

Meanwhile confusion takes the sky, tremendous
turmoil, and on its heels, rain mixed with hail.
The scattered train of Tyre, the youth of Troy,   215
and Venus' Dardan° grandson in alarm
seek different shelters through the fields; the
        torrents
roar down the mountains. Dido and the Trojan
chieftain have reached the same cave. Primal
        Earth
and Juno, queen of marriages, together   220
now give the signal: lightning fires flash,
the upper air is witness to their mating,
and from the highest hilltops shout the nymphs.
That day was her first day of death and ruin.
For neither how things seem nor how they are
        deemed   225
moves Dido now, and she no longer thinks
of furtive love. For Dido calls it marriage,
and with this name she covers up her fault.

Then, swiftest of all evils, Rumor runs
straightway through Libya's mighty cities—
        Rumor,   230

whose life is speed, whose going gives her force.
Timid and small at first, she soon lifts up
her body in the air. She stalks the ground;
her head is hidden in the clouds. Provoked
to anger at the gods, her mother Earth   235
gave birth to her, last come—they say—as sister
to Coeus and Enceladus;° fast-footed
and lithe of wing, she is a terrifying
enormous monster with as many feathers
as she has sleepless eyes beneath each feather   240
(amazingly), as many sounding tongues
and mouths, and raises up as many ears.
Between the earth and skies she flies by night,
screeching across the darkness, and she never
closes her eyes in gentle sleep. By day   245
she sits as sentinel on some steep roof
or on high towers, frightening vast cities;
for she holds fast to falsehood and distortion
as often as to messages of truth.
Now she was glad. She filled the ears of all   250
with many tales. She sang of what was done
and what was fiction, chanting that Aeneas
one born of Trojan blood, had come, that lovely
Dido has deigned to join herself to him,
that now, in lust, forgetful of their kingdom,   255
they take long pleasure, fondling through the
        winter,
the slaves of squalid craving. Such reports
the filthy goddess scatters everywhere
upon the lips of men. At once she turns
her course to King Iarbas; and his spirit   260
is hot, his anger rages at her words.

Iarbas was the son of Hammon by
a ravished nymph of Garamantia.°
In his broad realm he had built a hundred
        temples,
a hundred handsome shrines for Jupiter.   265
There he had consecrated sleepless fire,
the everlasting watchman of the gods;
the soil was rich with blood of slaughtered herds,

---

196. Cynthus: A mountain on Delos.
216. Dardan: Dardanus was founder of the Trojan race.

237. Angered at the gods killing her children, the Titans, Earth
     bore the Giants, one of whom was Rumor.
263. King Iarbas had the Egyptian god Hammon for a father and a
     nymph from the interior of Africa for a mother.

and varied garlands flowered on the thresholds.
Insane, incited by that bitter rumor,   270
he prayed long—so they say—to Jupiter;
he stood before the altars in the presence
of gods, a suppliant with upraised hands:
"All-able Jove, to whom the Moorish nation,
feasting upon their figured couches, pour   275
Lenaean° sacrifices, do you see
these things? Or, Father, are we only trembling
for nothing when you cast your twisting thunder?
Those fires in the clouds that terrify
our souls—are they but blind and aimless
    lightning   280
that only stirs our empty mutterings?
A woman, wandering within our borders,
paid for the right to build a tiny city.
We gave her shore to till and terms of tenure.
She has refused to marry me, she has taken   285
Aeneas as a lord into her lands.
And now this second Paris, with his crew
of half-men, with his chin and greasy hair
bound up beneath a bonnet of Maeonia,°
enjoys his prey; while we bring offerings   290
to what we have believed to be your temples,
still cherishing your empty reputation."

And as he prayed and clutched the altar stone,
all-able Jupiter heard him and turned
his eyes upon the royal walls, upon   295
the lovers who had forgotten their good name.
He speaks to Mercury, commanding him:
"Be on your way, my son, call up the Zephyrs,
glide on your wings, speak to the Dardan
    chieftain
who lingers now at Tyrian Carthage, paying   300
not one jot of attention to the cities
the Fates have given him. Mercury, carry
across the speeding winds the words I urge:
his lovely mother did not promise such
a son to us; she did not save him twice   305
from Grecian arms for this—but to be master
of Italy, a land that teems with empire

and seethes with war; to father a race from
    Teucer's°
high blood, to place all earth beneath his laws.
But if the brightness of such deeds is not   310
enough to kindle him, if he cannot
attempt the task for his own fame, does he—
a father—grudge Ascanius the walls
of Rome? What is he pondering, what hope
can hold him here among his enemies,   315
not caring for his own Ausonian° sons
or for Lavinian° fields. He must set sail.
And this is all; my message lies in this."

His words were ended. Mercury made ready
to follow his great father's orders. First   320
he laces on his golden sandals: winged
to bear him, swift as whirlwinds, high across
the land and water. Then he takes his wand;
with this he calls pale spirits up from Orcus°
and down to dreary Tartarus° sends others;   325
he uses this to give sleep and recall it,
and to unseal the eyes of those who have died.
His trust in this, he spurs the winds and skims
the troubled clouds. And now in flight, he sights
the summit and high sides of hardy Atlas°   330
who props up heaven with his crest—Atlas,
whose head is crowned with pines and battered by
the wind and rain and always girdled by
black clouds; his shoulders' cloak is falling snow;
above the old man's chin the rivers rush;   335
his bristling beard is stiff with ice. Here first
Cyllene's° god poised on his even wings
and halted; then he hurled himself headlong
and seaward with his body, like a bird
that, over shores and reefs where fishes throng, 340
swoops low along the surface of the waters.
Not unlike this, Cyllene's god between
the earth and heaven as he flies, cleaving

---

276. Lenaean: Pertaining to Bacchus, god of wine.
289. Maeonia: An area of Asia Minor.

---

308. Teucer: An early king of Troy.
316. Ausonian: Pertaining to middle or lower Italy.
317. Lavinia: A city in Latium in Middle Italy near the sea coast.
324. Orcus: The underworld.
325. Tartarus: The infernal regions.
330. Atlas: A god who supports heaven on his shoulders.
337: Cyllene: A mountain in Greece, birth place of the winged
    god Mercury.

the sandy shore of Libya from the winds
that sweep from Atlas, father of his mother.   345

As soon as his winged feet have touched the
    outskirts,
he sees Aeneas founding fortresses
and fashioning new houses. And his sword
was starred with tawny jasper, and the cloak
that draped his shoulders blazed with Tyrian
    purple—   350
a gift that wealthy Dido wove for him;
she had run golden thread along the web.
And Mercury attacks at once. "Are you
now laying the foundation of high Carthage,
as servant to a woman, building her   355
a splendid city here? Are you forgetful
of what is your own kingdom, your own fate?
The very god of gods, whose power sways
both earth and heaven, sends me down to you
from bright Olympus. He himself has asked me   360
to carry these commands through the swift air:
what are you pondering or hoping for
while squandering your ease in Libyan lands?
For if the brightness of such deeds is not
enough to kindle you—if you cannot   365
attempt the task for your own fame—remember
Ascanius growing up, the hopes you hold
for Iülus,° your own heir, to whom are owed
the realm of Italy and land of Rome."
So did Cyllene's god speak out. He left   370
the sight of mortals even as he spoke
and vanished into the transparent air.

This vision stunned Aeneas, struck him dumb;
his terror held his hair erect; his voice
held fast within his jaws. He burns to flee   375
from Carthage; he would quit these pleasant
    lands,
astonished by such warnings, the command
of gods. What can he do? With what words dare
he face the frenzied queen? What openings
can he employ? His wits are split, they shift   380
here, there; they race to different places, turning

to everything. But as he hesitated,
this seemed the better plan: he calls Sergestus
and Mnestheus and the strong Serestus,° and
he asks them to equip the fleet in silence,   385
to muster their companions on the shore,
to ready all their arms, but to conceal
the reasons for this change; while he himself—
with gracious Dido still aware of nothing
and never dreaming such a love could ever   390
be broken—would try out approaches, seek
the tenderest, most tactful time for speech,
whatever dexterous way might suit his case.
And all are glad. They race to carry out
the orders of Aeneas, his commands.   395

But Dido—for who can deceive a lover?—
had caught his craftiness; she quickly sensed
what was to come; however safe they seemed,
she feared all things. That same unholy Rumor
brought her these hectic tidings: that the boats   400
were being armed, made fit for voyaging.
Her mind is helpless; raging frantically,
inflamed, she raves throughout the city—just
as a Bacchante when, each second year,
she is startled by the shaking of the sacred   405
emblems, the orgies urge her on, the cry
"o Bacchus" calls to her by night; Cithaeron°
incites her with its clamor. And at last
Dido attacks Aeneas with these words:

"Deceiver, did you even hope to hide   410
so harsh a crime, to leave this land of mine
without a word? Can nothing hold you back—
neither your love, the hand you pledged, nor even
the cruel death that lies in wait for Dido?
Beneath the winter sky are you preparing   415
a fleet to rush away across the deep
among the north winds, you who have no feeling?
What! Even if you were not seeking out
strange fields and unknown dwellings, even if
your ancient Troy were still erect, would you   420
return to Troy across such stormy seas?

---

368. Iülus: Another name for Ascanius.

384. Sergestus, Mnesthcus, and Serestus are Trojans.
407. Cithaeron: A mountain in Greece where the rites of Bacchus
    are celebrated.

Do you flee me? By tears, by your right hand—
this sorry self is left with nothing else—
by wedding, by the marriage we began,
if I did anything deserving of you   425
or anything of mine was sweet to you,
take pity on a fallen house, put off
your plan, I pray—if there is still place for
      prayers.
Because of you the tribes of Libya, all
the Nomad princes hate me, even my   430
own Tyrians are hostile; and for you
my honor is gone and that good name that once
was mine, my only claim to reach the stars.
My guest, to whom do you consign this dying
woman? I must say 'guest': this name is all   435
I have of one whom once I called my husband.
Then why do I live on? Until Pygmalion,
my brother, batters down my walls, until
Iarbas the Gaetulian takes me prisoner?
Had I at least before you left conceived   440
a son in me; if there were but a tiny
Aeneas playing by me in the hall,
whose face, in spite of everything, might yet
remind me of you, then indeed I should
not seem so totally abandoned, beaten."   445

Her words were ended. But Aeneas, warned
by Jove, held still his eyes; he struggled, pressed
care back within his breast. With halting words
he answers her at last: "I never shall
deny what you deserve, the kindnesses   450
that you could tell; I never shall regret
remembering Elissa° for as long
as I remember my own self, as long
as breath is king over these limbs. I'll speak
brief words that fit the case. I never hoped   455
to hide—do not imagine that—my flight;
I am not furtive. I have never held
the wedding torches as a husband; I
have never entered into such agreements.
If fate had granted me to guide my life   460
by my own auspices and to unravel
my troubles with unhampered will, then I

should cherish first the town of Troy, the sweet
remains of my own people and the tall
rooftops of Priam° would remain, my hand   465
would plant again a second Pergamus°
for my defeated men. But now Grynean°
Apollo's oracles would have me seize
great Italy, the Lycian prophecies
tell me of Italy: there is my love,   470
there is my homeland. If the fortresses
of Carthage and the vision of a city
in Libya can hold you, who are Phoenician,
why, then, begrudge the Trojans' settling on
Ausonian soil? There is no harm: it is   475
right that we, too, seek out a foreign kingdom.
For often as the night conceals the earth
with dew and shadows, often as the stars
ascend, afire, my father's anxious image
approaches me in dreams. Anchises° warns   480
and terrifies; I see the wrong I have done
to one so dear, my boy Ascanius,
whom I am cheating of Hesperia,°
the fields assigned by fate. And now the gods'
own messenger, sent down by Jove himself—   485
I call as witness both out lives—has brought
his orders through the swift air. My own eyes
have seen the god as he was entering
our walls—in broad daylight. My ears have drunk
his words. No longer set yourself and me   490
afire. Stop your quarrel. It is not
my own free will that leads to Italy."

But all the while Aeneas spoke, she stared
askance at him, her glance ran this way, that.
She scans his body with her silent eyes.   495
Then Dido thus, inflamed, denounces him:

"No goddess was your mother, false Aeneas,
And Dardanus no author of your race;
the bristling Caucasus was father to you

---

452. Elissa: Another name for Dido.

---

465. Priam: Late king of Troy.
466. Pergamus: Troy.
467. Grynean: Pertaining to an oracle of Apollo in Asia Minor.
480. Anchises: Aeneas' dead father.
483. Hesperia: A place of fabled orchards in the West; here it
      means Italy.

on his harsh crags; Hyrcanian tigresses   500
gave you their teats. And why must I dissemble?
Why hold myself in check? For greater wrongs?
For did Aeneas groan when I was weeping?
Did he once turn his eyes or, overcome,
shed tears or pity me, who was his loved one?   505
What shall I cry out first? And what shall follow?
No longer now does mighty Juno or
our Father, son of Saturn,° watch this earth
with righteous eyes. Nowhere is certain trust.
He was an outcast on the shore, in want.   510
I took him in and madly let him share
my kingdom; his lost fleet and his companions
I saved from death. Oh I am whirled along
in fire by the Furies! First the augur
Apollo, then the Lycian oracles,   515
and now, sent down by Jove himself, the gods'
own herald, carrying his horrid orders.
This seems indeed to be a work for High Ones,
a care that can disturb their calm. I do not
refute your words. I do not keep you back.   520
Go then, before the winds, to Italy.
Seek out your kingdom overseas; indeed,
if there be pious powers still, I hope
that you will drink your torments to the lees
among sea rocks and, drowning, often cry   525
the name of Dido. Then, though absent, I
shall hunt you down with blackened firebrands;
and when chill death divides my soul and body,
a Shade, I shall be present everywhere.
Depraved, you then will pay your penalties.   530
And I shall hear of it, and that report
will come to me below, among the Shadows."

Her speech is broken off; heartsick, she shuns
the light of day, deserts his eyes; she turns
away, leaves him in fear and hesitation,   535
Aeneas longing still to say so much.
As Dido faints, her servants lift her up;
they carry her into her marble chamber;
they lay her body down upon the couch.

But though he longs to soften, soothe her sorrow   540

---

508. Saturn was father of both Jupiter and his wife Juno.

and turn aside her troubles with sweet words,
though groaning long and shaken in his mind
because of his great love, nevertheless
pious Aeneas carries out the gods'
instructions. Now he turns back to his fleet.   545

At this the Teucrians indeed fall to.
They launch their tall ships all along the beach;
they set their keels, well-smeared with pitch,
      afloat.
The crewmen, keen for flight, haul from the
      forest
boughs not yet stripped of leaves to serve as oars   550
and timbers still untrimmed. And one could see
      them
as, streaming, they rushed down from all the city:
even as ants, remembering the winter,
when they attack a giant stack of spelt
to store it in their homes; the black file swarms   555
across the fields; they haul their plunder through
the grass on narrow tracks; some strain against
the great grains with their shoulders, heaving
      hard;
some keep the columns orderly and chide
the loiterers; the whole trail boils with work.   560

What were your feelings, Dido, then? What were
the sighs you uttered at that sight, when far
and wide, from your high citadel, you saw
the beaches boil and turmoil take the waters,
with such a vast uproar before your eyes?   565
Voracious Love, to what do you not drive
the hearts of men? Again, she must outcry,
again, a suppliant, must plead with him,
must bend her pride to love—and so not die
in vain, and with some way still left untried.   570

"Anna, you see them swarm across the beaches;
from every reach around they rush to sea:
the canvas calls the breezes, and already
the boisterous crewmen crown the sterns with
      garlands.
But I was able to foresee this sorrow;   575
therefore I can endure it, sister; yet
in wretchedness I must ask you for this
one service, Anna. Treacherous Aeneas

has honored you alone, confiding even
his secret feelings unto you; and you   580
alone know all his soft approaches, moods.
My sister, go—to plead with him, to carry
this message to my arrogant enemy.
I never trafficked with the Greeks at Aulis°
to root the Trojans out, I never sent   585
a fleet to Pergamus,° never disturbed
his father's ashes or Anchises' Shade,
that now Aeneas should ward off my words
from his hard ears. Where is he hurrying?
If he would only grant his wretched lover   590
this final gift: to wait for easy sailing
and favoring winds. I now no longer ask
for those old ties of marriage he betrayed,
nor that he lose his kingdom, be deprived
of lovely Latium;° I only ask   595
for empty time, a rest and truce for all
this frenzy, until fortune teaches me,
defeated, how to sorrow. I ask this—
pity your sister—as a final kindness.
When he has granted it, I shall repay   600
my debt, and with full interest, by my death."

So Dido pleads, and her poor sister carries
these lamentations, and she brings them back.
For lamentation cannot move Aeneas;
his graciousness toward any plea is gone.   605
Fate is opposed, the god makes deaf the hero's
kind ears. As when, among the Alps, north winds
will strain against each other to root out
with blasts—now on this side, now that—a stout
oak tree whose wood is full of years; the roar   610
is shattering, the trunk is shaken, and
high branches scatter on the ground; but it
still grips the rocks; as steeply as it thrusts
its crown into the upper air, so deep
the roots it reaches down to Tartarus: 615
no less than this, the hero; he is battered
on this side and on that by assiduous words;
he feels care in his mighty chest, and yet
his mind cannot be moved; the tears fall, useless.

---

584. Aulis: The town in Greece where the Greek fleet set sail to
  attack Troy.
586. Pergamus: Troy.
595. Latium: A town of central Italy noted above.

Then maddened by the fates, unhappy Dido   620
calls out at last for death; it tires her
to see the curve of heaven. That she may
not weaken in her plan to leave the light,
she sees, while placing offerings on the altars
with burning incense—terrible to tell—   625
the consecrated liquid turning black,
the outpoured wine becoming obscene blood.
But no one learns of this, not even Anna.
And more: inside her palace she had built
a marble temple to her former husband   630
that she held dear and honored wonderfully.
She wreathed that shrine with snow-white fleeces
    and
holy-day leaves. And when the world was seized
by night, she seemed to hear the voice and words
of her dead husband, calling out to Dido.   635
Alone above the housetops, death its song,
an owl often complains and draws its long
slow call into a wailing lamentation.
More, many prophecies of ancient seers
now terrify her with their awful warnings.   640
And in her dreams it is the fierce Aeneas
himself who drives her to insanity;
she always finds herself alone, abandoned,
and wandering without companions on
an endless journey, seeking out her people,   645
her Tyrians in a deserted land:
even as Pentheus,° when he is seized by frenzy,
sees files of Furies, and a double sun
and double Thebes appear to him; or when
Orestes, son of Agamemnon, driven   650
across the stage, flees from his mother armed
with torches and black serpents; on the threshold
the awful goddesses of vengeance squat.

When she had gripped this madness in her mind
and, beaten by her grief, resolved to die,   655
she plotted with herself the means, the moment.
Her face conceals her meaning; on her brow
she sets serenity, then speaks to Anna:
"My sister, wish me well, for I have found
a way that will restore Aeneas to me   660

---

647. Pentheus: A king of the Greek city of Thebes who was
  driven mad, seeing all things double.

or free me of my love for him. Near by
the bounds of Ocean and the setting sun
lies Ethiopia, the farthest land;
there Atlas, the incomparable, turns
the heavens, studded with their glowing stars,   665
upon his shoulders. And I have been shown
a priestess from that land—one of the tribe
of the Massylians°—who guards the shrine
of the Hesperides; for it was she
who fed the dragon and preserved the holy   670
branches upon the tree, sprinkling moist honey
and poppy, bringing sleep. She promises
to free, with chant and spell, the minds of those
she favors but sends anguish into others.
And she can stay the waters in the rivers   675
and turn the stars upon their ways; she moves
the nightly Shades; makes earth quake underfoot
and—you will see—sends ash trees down the
     mountains.
Dear sister, I can call the gods to witness,
and you and your dear life, that I resort   680
to magic arts against my will. In secret
build up a pyre within the inner courtyard
beneath the open air, and lay upon it
the weapons of the hero. He, the traitor,
has left them hanging in my wedding
     chamber.   685
Take all of his apparel and the bridal
bed where I was undone. You must destroy
all relics of the cursed man, for so
would I, and so the priestess has commanded."
This said, she is silent and her face is pale.   690
But Anna cannot dream her sister hides
a funeral behind these novel rites;
her mind is far from thinking of such frenzy;
and she fears nothing worse than happened when
Sychaeus died. And so, she does as told.   695

But when beneath the open sky, inside
the central court, the pyre rises high
and huge, with logs of pine and planks of ilex,
the queen, not ignorant of what is coming,
then wreathes the place with garlands, crowning
     it   700

with greenery of death; and on the couch
above she sets the clothes Aeneas wore,
the sword he left, and then his effigy.
Before the circling altars the enchantress,
her hair disheveled, stands as she invokes   705
aloud three hundred gods, especially
Chaos and Erebus and Hecate,°
the triple-shaped Diana,° three-faced virgin.
And she had also sprinkled waters that
would counterfeit the fountain of Avernus;°   710
she gathered herbs cut down by brazen sickles
beneath the moonlight, juicy with the venom
of black milk; she had also found a love charm
torn from the forehead of a newborn foal
before his mother snatched it. Did herself—   715
with salt cake in her holy hands, her girdle
unfastened, and one foot free of its sandal,
close by the altars and about to die—
now calls upon the gods and stars, who know
the fates, as witness; then she prays to any   720
power there may be, who is both just and
     watchful,
who cares for those who love without requital.

·   ·   ·   ·   ·   ·

Night. And across the earth the tired bodies
were tasting tranquil sleep; the woods and savage
waters were resting and the stars had reached   725
the midpoint of their gliding fall—when all
the fields are still, and animals and colored
birds, near and far, that find their home beside
the limpid lakes or haunt the countryside
in bristling thickets, sleep in silent night.   730
But not the sorrowing Phoenician; she
can not submit to sleep, can not admit
dark night into her eyes or breast; her cares
increase; again love rises, surges in her;
she wavers on the giant tide of anger.   735
She will not let things rest but carries on;
she still revolves these thoughts within her heart:
"What can I do? Shall I, whom he has mocked,

668. Massylians: African people who guard the sacred western
     orchards, here placed in North Africa.

707. Hecate: A goddess of the lower world.
708. Diana: Goddess of the chase and the moon, identified with
     Hecate.
710. Avernus: A lake of the lower world.

go back again to my old suitors, begging,
seeking a wedding with Numidians whom   740
I have already often scorned as bridegrooms?
Or should I sail away on Trojan ships,
to suffer there even their harshest orders?
Shall I do so because the Trojans once
received my help, and gratefulness for such   745
old service is remembered by the mindful?
But even if I wish it, would they welcome
someone so hated to their haughty ships?
For, lost one, do you not yet know, not feel
the treason of the breed of Laomedon?°   750
What then? Shall I accompany, alone,
the exultant sailors in their flight? Or call
on all my Tyrians, on all my troops
to rush upon them? How can I urge on
those I once dragged from Sidon, how can I   755
now force them back again upon the sea
and have them spread their canvas to the winds?
No; die as you deserve, and set aside
your sorrow by the sword. My sister, you,
won over by my tears—you were the first   760
to weigh me down with evils in my frenzy,
to drive me toward my enemy. And why
was it not given me to lead a guiltless
life, never knowing marriage, like a wild
beast, never to have touched such toils? I have
    not   765
held fast the faith I swore before the ashes
of my Sychaeus." This was her lament.

Aeneas on the high stern now was set
to leave; he tasted sleep; all things were ready.
And in his sleep a vision of the god   770
returned to him with that same countenance—
resembling Mercury in everything:
his voice and coloring and yellow hair
and all his handsome body, a young man's—
and seemed to bring a warning once again: 775
"You, goddess-born, how can you lie asleep
at such a crisis? Madman, can't you see
the threats around you, can't you hear the breath

of kind west winds? She conjures injuries
and awful crimes, she means to die, she stirs   780
the shifting surge of restless anger. Why
not flee this land headlong, while there is time?
You soon will see the waters churned by
    wreckage,
ferocious torches blaze, and beaches flame,
if morning finds you lingering on this coast.   785
Be on your way. Enough delays. An ever
uncertain and inconstant thing is woman."
This said, he was at one with the black night.

The sudden apparition terrifies
Aeneas. And he tears his body free   790
from sleep. He stirs his crewmen: "Quick!
    Awake!
Now man the benches, comrades, now unfurl
our sails with speed! Down from the upper air
a god was sent to urge us on again,
to rush our flight, to slice our twisted cables. 795
O holy one among the gods, we follow
your way, whoever you may be; again
rejoicing, we shall do as you command.
Be present, help us with your kindness, bring
your gracious constellations to the heavens."   800
He spoke; and from his scabbard snatches up
his glowing sword; with drawn blade, strikes the
    hawsers.
And all are just as eager, hurrying
to leave the shore; the ships conceal the sea.
They strain to churn the foam and sweep blue
    waters.   805

.   .   .   .   .   .

Now early Dawn had left Tithonus'° saffron
bed, scattering new light upon the earth.
As soon as from her lookout on the tower
the queen could see the morning whitening,
the fleet move on with level sails, the shores   810
and harbors now abandoned, without oarsmen,
she beat against her lovely breast three times,
then four, and tore her golden hair, and cried:

---

750. Laomedon: Legendary ancestor of the Trojans and a notorious perjurer.

---

806. Tithonus: Husband of Aurora, the dawn.

"O Jupiter, you let him go, a stranger
who mocked our kingdom! Will my men not
    ready   815
their weapons, hunt him down, pour from my
    city
and rip the galleys from their moorings? Quick!
Bring torches, spread your sails, and ply your oars!
What am I saying? Where am I? What madness
has turned awry what I had meant to do?   820
Poor Dido, does his foulness touch you now?
It should have then, when you gave him your
    scepter.
This is the right hand, this the pledge of one
who carries with him, so they say, the household
gods of his land, who bore upon his shoulders   825
his father weak with years. And could I not
have dragged his body off, and scattered him
piecemeal upon the waters, limb by limb?
Or butchered all his comrades, even served
Ascanius himself as banquet dish   830
upon his father's table? True enough—
the battle might have ended differently.
That does not matter. For, about to die,
need I fear anyone? I should have carried
my torches to his camp and filled his decks   835
with fire, destroyed the son, the father, that
whole race, and then have thrown myself upon
    them.
You, Sun, who with your flames see all that is
    done
on earth; and Juno, you, interpreter
and witness of my sorrows; Hecate,   840
invoked with shrieks, by night, at every city's
crossways; and you, the Furies; and the gods
that guard dying Elissa—hear these words
and turn your power toward my pain; as I
deserve, take up my prayers. If it must be   845
that he, a traitor, is to touch his harbor,
float to his coasts, and so the fates of Jove
demand and if this end is fixed; yet let
him suffer war and struggles with audacious
nations, and then—when banished from his
    borders   850
and torn from the embrace of Iülus—let him
beg aid and watch his people's shameful
    slaughter.

Not even when he has bent low before
an unjust peace may he enjoy his kingdom,
the light that he has wished for. Let him fall   855
before his time, unburied in the sand.
These things I plead; these final words I pour
out of my blood. Then, Tyrians, hunt down
with hatred all his sons and race to come;
send this as offering unto my ashes.   860
Do not let love or treaty tie our peoples.
May an avenger rise up from my bones,
one who will track with firebrand and sword
the Dardan settlers, now and in the future,
at any time that ways present themselves.   865
I call your shores to war against their shores,
your waves against their waves, arms with their
    arms.
Let them and their sons' sons learn what is war."

This said, she ran her mind to every side,
for she was seeking ways with which to
    slice—   870
as quickly as she can—the hated light;
and then, with these brief words, she turned to
    Barce,
Sychaeus' nurse—for Dido's own was now
black ashes in Phoenicia, her old homeland:
"Dear nurse, call here to me my sister Anna;   875
and tell her to be quick to bathe her body
with river water; see that she brings cattle
and all that is appointed for atonement.
So must my sister come; while you yourself
bind up your temples with a pious fillet.   880
I mean to offer unto Stygian Jove
the sacrifices that, as is ordained,
I have made ready and begun, to put
and end to my disquiet and commit
to flames the pyre of the Trojan chieftain."   885
So Dido spoke. And Barce hurried off;
she moved with an old woman's eagerness.

But Dido, desperate, beside herself
with awful undertakings, eyes bloodshot
and rolling, and her quivering cheeks flecked   890
with stains and pale with coming death, now
    bursts
across the inner courtyards of her palace.

She mounts in madness that high pyre,
    unsheathes
the Dardan sword, a gift not sought for such
an end. And when she saw the Trojan's clothes   895
and her familiar bed, she checked her thought
and tears a little, lay upon the couch
and spoke her final words: "O relics, dear
while fate and god allowed, receive my spirit
and free me from these cares; for I have lived   900
and journeyed through the course assigned by
    fortune.
And now my Shade will pass, illustrious,
beneath the earth; I have built a handsome city,
have seen my walls rise up, avenged a husband,
won satisfaction from a hostile brother: 905
o fortunate, too fortunate—if only
the ships of Troy had never touched our coasts."
She spoke and pressed her face into the couch.
"I shall die unavenged, but I shall die,"
she says. "Thus, thus, I gladly go below   910
to shadows. May the savage Dardan drink
with his own eyes this fire from the deep
and take with him the omen of my death."

Then Dido's words were done, and her
    companions
can see her fallen on the sword; the blade   915
is foaming with her blood, her hands are
    bloodstained.
Now clamor rises to the high rooftop.
Now rumor riots through the startled city.
The lamentations, keening, shrieks of women
sound through the houses; heavens echo mighty   920
wailings, even as if an enemy
were entering the gates, with all of Carthage
or ancient Tyre in ruins, and angry fires
rolling across the homes of men and gods.

And Anna heard. Appalled and breathless, she   925
runs, anxious, through the crowd, her nails
    wounding
her face; her fists, her breasts; she calls the dying
Dido by name: "And was it, then, for this,
my sister? Did you plan this fraud for me?
Was this the meaning waiting for me when   930
the pyre, the flames, the altar were prepared?

What shall I now, deserted, first lament?
You scorned your sister's company in death;
you should have called me to the fate you met;
the same sword pain, the same hour should have
    taken   935
the two of us away. Did my own hands
help build the pyre, and did my own voice call
upon our fathers' gods, only to find
me, heartless, far away when you lay dying?
You have destroyed yourself and me, my
    sister,   940
the people and the elders of your Sidon,
and all your city. Let me bathe your wounds
in water, and if any final breath
still lingers here, may my lips catch it up."
This said, she climbed the high steps, then she
    clasped   945
her half-dead sister to her breast, and moaning,
embraced her, dried the black blood with her
    dress.
Trying to lift her heavy eyes, the queen
falls back again. She breathes; the deep wound in
her chest is loud and hoarse. Three times she
    tried   950
to raise herself and strained, propped on her
    elbow;
and three times she fell back upon the couch.
Three times with wandering eyes she tried to find
high heaven's light and, when she found it,
    sighed.

But then all-able Juno pitied her   955
long sorrow and hard death and from Olympus°
sent Iris° down to free the struggling spirit
from her entwining limbs. For as she died
a death that was not merited or fated,
but miserable and before her time   960
and spurred by sudden frenzy, Proserpina°
had not yet cut a gold lock from her crown,

---

956. Olympus: Mountain home of the gods.
957. Iris: Goddess of the rainbow and Juno's messenger.
961. Proserpina: Goddess of the underworld and wife of Plato.
    She was supposed to cut a lock of hair from the head of the
    dying as an offering to the gods of the underworld.

not yet assigned her life to Stygian° Orcus.
On saffron wings dew-glittering Iris glides
along the sky, drawing a thousand shifting   965
colors across the facing sun. She halted
above the head of Dido: "So commanded,
I take this lock as offering to Dis;°
I free you from your body." So she speaks
and cuts the lock with her right hand; at
    once   970
the warmth was gone, the life passed to the
    winds.

QUESTIONS

1. How does Juno, an enemy of the Trojans, attempt to
   frustrate their mission to settle in Italy? Why does
   Venus, protectress of the Trojans, concede so easily
   to Juno? How are her plans foiled?
2. Is Dido's anger against Aeneas justified?
3. What tricks does Dido use in order to have her funeral pyre prepared?
4. Throughout the Middle Ages, Dido was used as a
   cautionary example for Christians. Why?
5. What purposes does Virgil's extensive use of similes
   throughout the work serve?

The poignancy of the love between Dido and Aeneas
is stressed in Book 6, where Aeneas, allowed to descend
into the underworld, visits the shades of illustrious
dead people. He glimpses the shade of Dido, tries to
embrace it, and calls out, "It was not of my own will,
Dido, I left your land." But Dido, still proud and angry
even as a ghost, turns away and disappears.

In the underworld Aeneas meets and converses with
the shade of his father, Anchises. Anchises reveals to
him the future of Rome, thus stressing the continuity
between past and future of which Aeneas is a pivotal
part. The passage printed below is Anchises' description of a parade of souls, witnessed by Aeneas, who will
be born on earth at future dates and who will all contribute to the glory of Rome. Augustus, he tells us, will
inaugurate Rome's "age of gold."

---

963. Stygian: Pertaining to one of the rivers of Orcus, the Underworld.
968. Dis: Pluto, god of the underworld.

BOOK 6

"More: Romulus, a son of Mars. He will
join Numitor, his grandfather, on earth
when Ilia, his mother, gives him birth
out of the bloodline of Assaracus.
You see the double plumes upon his crest: 1030
his parent Mars already marks him out
with his own emblem for the upper world.
My son, it is beneath his auspices
that famous Rome will make her boundaries
as broad as earth itself, will make her spirit   1035
the equal of Olympus, and enclose
her seven hills within a single wall,
rejoicing in her race of men: just as
the Berecynthian mother, tower-crowned,
when, through the Phrygian cities, she rides
    on   1040
her chariot, glad her sons are gods, embraces
a hundred sons of sons, and every one
a heaven-dweller with his home on high.

"Now turn your two eyes her, to look upon
your Romans, your own people. Here is
    Caesar   1045
and all the line of Iülus that will come
beneath the mighty curve of heaven. This,
this is the man you heard so often promised—
Augustus Caesar, son of a god, who will
renew a golden age in Latium,   1050
in fields where Saturn once was king, and stretch
his rule beyond the Garamantes and
the Indians—a land beyond the paths
of year and sun, beyond the constellations,
where on his shoulders heaven-holding Atlas   1055
revolves the axis set with blazing stars.
And even now, at his approach, the kingdom
of Caspia and land of Lake Maeotis
shudder before the oracles of gods;
the seven mouths of Nile, in terror, tremble.   1060
For even Hercules himself had never
crossed so much of the earth, not even when
he shot the brazen-footed stage and brought
peace to the groves of Erymanthus and
made Lerna's monster quake before his
    arrows;   1065

nor he who guides his chariot with reins
of vine leaves, victor Bacchus, as he drives
his tigers down from Nysa's steepest summits.
And do we, then, still hesitate to extend
our force in acts of courage? Can it be   1070
that fear forbids our settling in Ausonia?
From this parade of heroes, Anchises draws a
     lesson of Rome's mission:

For other peoples will, I do not doubt,
still cast their bronze to breathe with softer
     features,   1130
or draw out of the marble living lines,
plead causes better, trace the ways of heaven
with wands and tell the rising constellations;
but yours will be the rulership of nations,
remember, Roman, these will be your arts: 1135
to teach the ways of peace to those you conquer,
to spare defeated peoples, tame the proud."

Aeneas returns from the underworld inspired with love
for the future greatness of his people. He is now more
Roman than Trojan, and the rest of the epic will be devoted to his feats in "arms" necessary to the founding
of Rome.

The cultural values asserted in this epic are clearly
Roman. The Romans were on the whole a practical
people, conscious that their real genius was not in the
cult of individualism or in art for its own sake, but in
the art of administrating and ruling. They did not see
their imperialism in moralistic terms, as did European
imperialists in Africa and Asia in the nineteenth century, who believed that destiny had sent them to "civilize" heathens. The Romans knew that the cultures
they ruled in Greece, the Near East, and North Africa
were in most cases more highly developed than their
own. But they knew, too, that they gave the world an
unparalleled peace and a system of law that could not
have been obtained without their particular kind of
imperialism. Europeans often compare Americans to
ancient Romans because of the practical, administrative genius of both. The United States has even been
accused of trying to establish a *pax americana*.

Roman Satire   The other great poet of the Augustan Age was Horace (Quintus Horatius Flaccus, 65–8
B.C.). Horace was the son of an uneducated freedman (a
former slave) who saw to it that his son received the
best schooling that Rome could provide. Horace was in
his early years an ardent republican but became just as
ardent a supporter of the emperor. He is, in fact, often
called Augustus' "poet laureate" because his later
poems celebrate the emperor's policies and ideals. Interested, among other things, in literary criticism and
theory, Horace formulated the basic tenet for Roman
poets: poetry must be both *dulce* (pleasing) and *utile*
(useful). The poem should combine patriotic, moral, or
philosophical messages with sensuous beauty of
rhythm and language. This idea that poetry should be
useful is certainly more Roman than Greek.

Horace wrote lyrics (the *Epodes* and *Odes*) and later
on *Epistles*, including *The Art of Poetry*. Here we have
printed two examples from one of the early works, the
Satires. Although satire as a mode of human expression
had been in existence long before the Romans, the
Romans developed it into a literary form, just as the
Greeks did for comedy. Satire is in fact the only
uniquely Roman contribution to literary genre.

The nonliterary origins of the mode are related to
those of the *komos*. The desire to ridicule, or to expose
human vices and follies, seems universal. In certain cultures, the process of ridiculing one's enemy with particularly vicious words was believed to have magical effects. It could actually injure the enemy or even cause
him to kill himself and thus be used as a weapon of war.
For example, the pre-Islamic Arabs, especially women,
used invectives hurled against their enemies as magical,
deadly curses. We still use words like caustic, biting,
and venomous to describe words used in satire and ridicule. The magical and ritual origins of satire are evident
here if we bear in mind that such descriptions were for
many peoples not merely *metaphorical*.

The ancient Greeks also seem to have used satire for
magical purposes. At the phallic ceremonies, which we
mentioned in connection with old comedy, two ritual
purposes were involved. One ceremony was intended
to ensure fertility of land and people through the
power of the phallus; the other was to expel evil spirits
and influence through abuse. Out of the latter practice
grew a tradition of composing *iambs*, short invective
verses directed against a particular person. The practice
of this kind of satire certainly influenced old comedy.
Aristophanes held many important public figures, in-

cluding Socrates and Euripides, up to devastating ridicule. In *Lysistrata* the invectives that the choruses of old men and old women hurl against each other are in the same satirical tradition.

No word for satire as such existed until the Romans gave it one: *satura*, which means both "full" and "a mixture of different things." In comparison to more refined and subtle forms of literature, satire is down-to-earth, hearty, and full of all kinds of things, like a good stew. For example, the satires of Horace contain lyrical poetry, philosophical arguments, folk tales, descriptions of everyday life, slapstick comedy, and obscene jokes. It is not surprising that this literary type should have developed among a people whose tastes were more practical and realistic than contemplative and abstract. Although the Roman writers of satire no longer believed in its magical effects, they believed that the function of satire to expose the vices and follies of individuals and society could be greatly therapeutic.

Roman verse satire, as we have already implied, is a particular literary form. Satires were written in hexameters, the six-foot Latin line (the translator of the Horace passage has attempted to imitate the original), and are of two types. One, represented by Horace, is mild, humorous, and fundamentally optimistic. Horace claimed that the actions of some of his contemporaries impelled him to satirize—"fools rush into my head, and so I write"—but that his purpose was to enable the "fools" to reform by exposing their foolishness rather than to punish them. Horace's satires are usually in two parts: the first part exposes or attacks some kind of foolishness or viciousness, and the second part upholds a norm or a virtue that contrasts with it. Often the poem is framed by a conflict between a satirist and an enemy. The dialogue between Horace and his slave, Davus, illustrates this well.

The scene for Horace's satire is the Roman holiday at the end of December, the *Saturnalia*, which was characterized by a general freedom from work, normal duties, and normal social restraints. Slaves, during the Saturnalia, were supposed to be treated with great indulgence. Horace uses this setting to treat a theme prevalent in Stoicism: the true nature of freedom. Is the man of material wealth, apparently free, but enslaved to his greed and his passions, any freer than a slave? For the Stoics, only the philosopher, or the man whose mind was unencumbered by material wants, is truly free. A slave, in this sense, could be freer than his master. The Stoics were particularly fond of such paradoxes or apparent contradictions. As the slave lectures the master on freedom, the philosophical paradox becomes good material for satire. Here, the object of the satire is the writer himself. During the course of the satire, Horace's portrayal of himself changes from that of a liberal to that of a tyrant. Like everyone else, he finds that the blows of satire, especially when they contain truth, can be wounding. (The translation is by Smith Palmer Bowie.)

HORACE

My Slave Is Free to Speak Up for Himself

> Iamdudum ausculto et cupiens tibi dicere servus

Davus. I've been listening for quite some time now, wanting to have
A word with you. Being a slave, though, I haven't the nerve.
   Horace. That you, Davus?
   Dav.   Yes, it's Davus, slave as I am.
Loyal to my man, a pretty good fellow: *pretty* good,
I say. I don't want you thinking I'm too good to live.
   Hor. Well, come on, then. Make use of the freedom traditionally yours
At the December holiday season. Speak up, sound off!
   Dav. Some people *like* misbehaving: they're persistent and consistent.
But the majority waver, trying at times to be good,
At other times yielding to evil. The notorious Priscus
Used to wear three rings at a time, and then again, none.
He lived unevenly, changing his robes every hour.
He issued forth from a mansion, only to dive
Into the sort of low joint your better-class freedman
Wouldn't want to be caught dead in. A libertine at Rome,
At Athens a sage, he was born, and he lived, out of season.
   When Volanerius, the playboy, was racked by the gout
In the joints of his peccant fingers (so richly deserved),

He hired a man, by the day, to pick up the dice
For him and put them in the box. By being consistent
In his gambling vice, he lived a happier life
Than the chap who tightens the reins and then lets
     them flap.
     Hor. Will it take you all day to get to the bottom of
          this junk,
You skunk?
     Dav.   But I'm saying, *you're* at the bottom.
     Hor.   How so, you stinker?
     Dav. You praise the good old days, ancient fortunes,
          and manners,
And yet, if some god were all for taking you back,
You'd hang back, either because you don't really think
That what you are praising to the skies is all that
     superior
Or because you defend what is right with weak
     defenses
And, vainly wanting to pull your foot from the mud,
Stick in it all the same. At Rome, you yearn
For the country, but, once in the sticks, you praise to
     high heaven
The far-off city, you nitwit. If it happens that no one
Asks you to dinner, you eulogize your comfortable
     meal
Of vegetables, acting as if you'd only go out
If you were dragged out in chains. You hug yourself,
Saying how glad you are not to be forced to go out
On a spree. But Maecenas *suggests*, at the very last
     minute,
That you be his guest: "Bring some oil for my lamp,
     somebody!
Get a move on! Is everyone deaf around here?" In a
     dither
And a lather, you charge out. Meanwhile, your
     scrounging guests,
Mulvius & Co., make their departure from your place
With a few descriptive remarks that won't bear
     repeating—
For example, Mulvius admits, "Of course, I'm fickle,
Led around by my stomach, and prone to follow my nose
To the source of a juicy aroma, weak-minded, lazy,
And, you may want to add, a gluttonous souse.
But you, every bit as bad and perhaps a bit worse,
Have the gall to wade into me, as if you were better,

And cloak your infamy in euphemism?"
                         What if you're found out
To be a bigger fool than me, the hundred-dollar slave?
Stop trying to browbeat me! Hold back your hand,
And your temper, while I tell you what Crispinus'
     porter
Taught me.
               Another man's wife makes you her slave.
A loose woman makes Davus hers. Of us two sinners,
Who deserves the cross more? When my passionate
     nature
Drives me straight into her arms, she's lovely by
     lamplight,
Beautifully bare, all mine to plunge into at will,
Or, turning about, she mounts and drives me to death.
And after it's over, she sends me away neither
     shamefaced
Nor worried that someone richer or better to look at
Will water the very same plant. But when you go out
     for it,
You really come in for it, don't you? Turning yourself
     into
The same dirty Dama you pretend to be when you take
     off
Your equestrian ring and your Roman robes, and
     change
Your respectable self, hiding your perfumed head
Under your cape?
                    Scared to death, you're let in the house,
And your fear takes turns with your hope in rattling
     your bones.
What's the difference between being carted off to be
     scourged
And slain, in the toils of the law (as a gladiator is),
And being locked up in a miserable trunk, where the
     maid,
Well aware of her mistress' misconduct, has stored you
     away,
With your knees scrunched up against your head?
     Hasn't the husband
Full power over them both, and even more over the
     seducer?
For the wife hasn't changed her attire or her location,
And is not the uppermost sinner. You walk open-eyed
Right under the fork, handing over to a furious master

Your money, your life, your person, your good
   reputation.
   Let's assume that you got away: you learned your
      lesson,
I trust, and will be afraid from now on, and be careful?
Oh, no! You start planning how to get in trouble again,
To perish again, enslave yourself over and over.
But what wild beast is so dumb as to come back again
To the chains he has once broken loose from?
                              "But I'm no adulterer,"
You say. And I'm not a thief when I wisely pass up
Your good silver plate. But our wandering nature will
   leap
When the reins are removed, when the danger is taken
   away.
   Are you my master, you, slave to so many
Other people, so powerful a host of other things, whom
   no
Manumission could ever set free from craven anxiety,
Though the ritual were conducted again and again?
   And besides,
Here's something to think about: whether a slave who's
   the slave
Of a slave is a plain fellow slave or a "subslave," as you
   masters
Call him, what am I your?[1] You, who command me,
Cravenly serve someone else and are led here and there
Like a puppet, the strings held by others.
                              Who, then, is free?
The wise man alone, who has full command of
   himself,
Whom poverty, death, or chains cannot terrify,
Who is strong enough to defy his passions and scorn
Prestige, who is wholly contained in himself, well
   rounded,
Smooth as a sphere on which nothing external can
   fasten,
On which fortune can do no harm except to herself.
   Now which of those traits can you recognize as one
      of yours?
Your woman asks you for five thousand dollars,
   needles you,

---

[1] If Horace is himself a slave, Davus wonders what status he, as a
slave of a slave, has.

Shuts the door in your face and pours out cold water,
Then calls you back. Pull your neck from that yoke!
Say, "I'm free, I'm free!" Come on, say it. You can't! A
   master
Dominates your mind, and it's no mild master who
   lashes
You on in spite of yourself, who goads you and guides
   you.
   Or when you stand popeyed in front of a painting by
      Pausias,
You madman, are you less at fault than I am who
   marvel
At the posters of athletes straining their muscles in
   combat,
Striking out, thrusting, and parrying, in red chalk and
   charcoal,
As if they were really alive and handling these
   weapons?
But Davus is a no-good, a dawdler, and you? Oh,
   MONSIEUR
Is an EXPERT, a fine CONNOISSEUR of antiques, I ASSURE
   you.
   I'm just a fool to be tempted by piping-hot pancakes.
Does your strength of character and mind make much
   resistance
To sumptuous meals? Why is it worse for me
To supply the demands of my stomach? My back will
   pay for it,
To be sure. But do you get off any lighter, hankering
After delicate, costly food? Your endless indulgence
Turns sour in your stomach, your baffled feet won't
   support
Your pampered body. Is the slave at fault, who
   exchanges
A stolen scraper for a bunch of grapes, in the dark?
Is there nothing slavish in a man who sells his estate
To satisfy his need for rich food?
                              Now, add on these items:
(1) You can't stand your own company as long as an
   hour;
(2) You can't dispose of your leisure in a decent
   fashion;
(3) You're a fugitive from your own ego, a vagabond
   soul,
Trying to outflank your cares by attacking the bottle

Or making sorties into sleep. And none of it works:
The Dark Companion rides close along by your side,
Keeps up with and keeps on pursuing the runaway
    slave.
    Hor. "Where's a stone?"
    Dav.   "What use do you have for it?"
    Hor.   "Hand me my arrows!"
    Dav. The man is either raving or satisfying his
    craving
For creative writing.
    Hor.   If you don't clear out, instanter,
I'll pack you off to the farm to be my ninth planter.

COMMENTS AND QUESTIONS

1. What proofs does Davus use to show that Horace is
   more enslaved than he?
2. How is the nature of "true freedom" defined, and in
   what context? Relate this to what you know of stoicism.
3. What aspects of Horace's self-satire do you find particularly comic? Why?
4. What are the difficulties involved in writing a self-
   satire?
5. Compare Horace's concepts and techniques of satire
   to contemporary examples from television, film,
   and writing.
6. Is it possible to define which characteristics of a personality are most often targets for satire?

The verses of a later Roman writer, Juvenal (died c.
130 A.D.), who lived in a period when Roman society
was more corrupt, represent the second type of satire.
Juvenal's satire is truly biting: it exposes and cas-
tigates. Satirists like Juvenal seem to believe that evil
is inherent in human nature and in the structure of
society. It can be identified but not easily cured. The
two selections which follow—on the daily life of the
rich woman and on teaching by example—typify
Juvenal's ruthless social criticism. (The translation is
by Peter Green.) It should be observed, in conclusion,
that the two types of satire discussed here—we might
call them simply optimistic and pessimistic—can be
found throughout the history of literature, in stage and
media entertainment, and in ordinary conversation.

JUVENAL
The Roman Matron

Worse still is the well-read menace, who's hardly
    settled for dinner   1
Before she starts praising Virgil, making a moral
    case
For Dido (death justifies all), comparing,
    evaluating
Rival poets, Virgil and Homer suspended
In opposite scales, weighed up one against the
    other.   5
Critics surrender, academics are routed, all
Fall silent, not a word from lawyer or auctioneer—
Or even another woman. Such a rattle of talk,
You'd think all the pots and bells were being
    clashed together
When the moon's in eclipse. No need now for
    trumpets or brass: 10
One woman can act, single-handed, as lunar
    midwife.°
But wisdom imposes limits, even on virtue, and if
She's so determined to prove herself eloquent,
    learned,
She should hoist up her skirts and gird them
    above the knee,
Offer a pig to Silvanus (female worshippers
    banned) and   15
Scrub off in the penny baths.° So avoid a dinner-
    partner
With an argumentative style, who hurls well-
    rounded
Syllogisms like slingshots, who has all history
    pat:
Choose someone rather who doesn't understand
    all she reads.

---

11. Eclipses were supposedly caused by witchcraft. By spells the
    witch would torture and reduce the moon. If enough noise
    was made, however, the spells could not be heard. The wax-
    ing of the moon was associated with pregnancy. This woman
    is so noisy that in time of eclipse no other noise is needed to
    bring the moon back to its full size.
16. Wearing skirts above the knees, worshipping Silvanus, and
    going to the public baths were attributes of males.

I hate these authority-citers, the sort who are
    always thumbing   20
Some standard grammatical treatise, whose every
    utterance
Observes all the laws of syntax, who with
    antiquarian zeal
Quote poets I've ever heard of. Such matters are
    men's concern.
If she wants to correct someone's language, she can
    always
Start with her unlettered girl-friends. A husband
    should be allowed   25
His solecisms in peace.
                   There's nothing a woman
Baulks at, no action that gives her a twinge of
    conscience
Once she's put on her emerald choker, weighted
    down her ear-lobes
With vast pearl pendants. What's more
    insufferable
Than your well-heeled female? But earlier in the
    process   30
She presents a sight as funny as it's appalling,
Her features lost under a damp bread face-pack,
Or greasy with vanishing-cream that clings to her
    husband's
Lips when the poor man kisses her—though it's
    all
Wiped off for her lover. She takes no trouble
    about   35
The way she looks at home: those imported
    Indian
Scents and lotions she buys with a lover in
    mind.
First one layer, then the next: at last the contours
    emerge
Till she's almost recognizable. Now she freshens
Her complexion with asses' milk. (If her
    husband's posted   40
To the godforsaken North, a herd of she-asses
Will travel with them.) But all these medicaments
And various treatments—not least the damp
    bread-poultice—
Make you wonder what's underneath, a face or a
    boil.

It's revealing to study the details of such a
    woman's   45
Daily routine, to see how she occupies her time.
If her husband, the night before, has slept with
    his back to her, then
The wool-maid's had it, the dressers are stripped
    and flogged,
The litter-bearer's accused of coming late. One
    victim
His rods broken over his back, another bears
    bloody stripes   50
From the whip, a third is lashed with a cat-o'-
    nine-tails:
Some women pay their floggers an annual salary.
While the punishment's carried out she'll be
    fixing her face,
Gossiping with her friends, giving expert
    consideration
To the width of the hem on some gold-
    embroidered robe—   55
Crack! Crack!—or skimming through the daily
    gazette;
Till at last, when the flogger's exhausted, she
    snaps 'Get out!'
And for one day at least the judicial hearing is
    over.
Her household's governed with all the savagery
Of a Sicilian court.° If she's made some
    assignation   60
That she wants to look her best for, and is in a
    tearing hurry
Because she's late, and her lover's waiting for her
In the public gardens, or by the shrine (bordello
Might be a more accurate term) of Isis°—why then,
    the slave-girl
Arranging her coiffure will have her own hair torn
    out,   65
Poor creature, and the tunic ripped from her
    shoulders and breasts.

---

60. The ancient tyrants of Sicilian city-states were notorious for
    their cruelty.
64. One aspect of the worship of the Eastern Goddess Isis was
    ritualistic prostitution connected with a fertility cult.

'Why isn't this curl in place?' the lady screams, and her rawhide
Lash inflicts chastisement for the offending ringlet.
But what was poor Psecas's° crime? How could you blame an attendant
For the shape of your own nose? Another maid   70
Combs out the hair on her left side, twists it round the curlers;
The consultative committee is reinforced by
An elderly lady's-maid inherited from Mama,
And now promoted from hairpins to the wool department. She
Takes the floor first, to be followed by her inferiors   75
In age and skill, as though some issue of reputation
Or life itself were at stake, so obsessionally they strive
In beauty's service. See the tall edifice
Rise up on her head in serried tiers and storeys!
See her heroic stature—at least, that is, from in front: 80
Her back view's less impressive, you'd think it belonged
To a different person. The effect is ultra-absurd
If she's lacking in inches, the sort who without stilettos
Resembles some sawn-off pygmy, who's forced to stand
On tiptoe for a kiss.   85
                        Meantime she completely
Ignores her husband, gives not a moment's thought
To all she costs him. She's less a wife than a neighbor—
Except when it comes to loathing his friends and slaves,
Or running up bills. . . .

---

69. Psecas: A slave girl's name.

QUESTIONS

1. What is Juvenal's position on female learning?
2. What suggests that the poet might have personal motives for his criticism?
3. Why does the lady's dressing up affect her conscience?
4. How does the lady conduct herself differently with husband and lover?
5. Juvenal's satires generally reveal the arbitrary cruelty of Rome's slave economy. What motivates the lady's cruelty here?

JUVENAL

As the Tree Is Bent

A great many things, Fuscinus, of deservedly ill repute,   1
Things that would leave an indelible stain on the brightest fortune,
Children acquire from their parents. Bad examples are catching:
If Papa's a ruinous gambler, then his son and heir is bound
To be rattling a miniature dice-box by early adolescence;   5
Nor need the family expect better things from any youth
Whose spendthrift father, a hoary old glutton, has taught him
To appreciate peeled truffles, and the proper sort of sauce
On mushrooms; who's learnt to tuck into quails and plovers°
Served up with their natural juices. By the time that he's seven,   10
With quite a few milk-teeth left still, a boy like this has got
His character fixed for life. Set a thousand bearded tutors
On either side of him, he'll never give up his passion

---

9. Plover: A species of bird excellent for eating.

For luxurious meals, or lower his standards of
    haute cuisine.
    Take Rutilus, now: does his conduct encourage
    a lenient   15
Temper, a sense of restraint when dealing with
    peccadilloes?°
Does he hold that slaves are fashioned, body and
    soul, from the same
Elements as their masters? Not on your life.
    What he teaches
Is sadism, pure and simple: there's nothing
    pleases him more
Than a good old noisy flogging, no siren song to
    compare   20
With the crack of the lash. To his quaking
    household he's
A monster, a mythical ogre, never so happy as
    when
The torturer's there on the job, and some poor
    wretch who's stolen
A couple of towels is being branded with red-hot
    irons. What
Effect on the young must he have, with his yen
    for clanking chains,   25
For dungeons, and seared flesh, and field-gang
    labour camps?
    How can you hope, you bumpkin, that the
    daughter won't sleep around
When however fast she gabbles the list of her
    mother's lovers
She must stop to get her breath back a score of
    times and more?
As a schoolgirl she shared Mummy's secrets, and
    now she composes   30
Billets-doux° on her own account—though
    Mummy dictates them—
And sends them round to her lover by the same
    fag go-between,
Such, though, is Nature's order: we're sooner,
    more swiftly corrupted

16. Peccadilloes: Delicacies for the palate.
31. Billets-doux: Love letters.

By examples of vice in the home, since they enter
    our minds
With high authority's sanction. Perhaps you'll
    find one or two   35
Youths who despise such conduct, whose spirits
    have been formed
From finer clay, with a kindlier touch in the
    firing; but
The rest troop off down the path where their
    father's unsavoury
Footsteps lead them, they're dragged through the
    ruts of familiar vice.
    So we've got one powerful motive at least for
    steering clear of   40
All reprehensible acts—lest the crimes we
    commit are copied
By the children we raise. We're all too willing to
    model ourselves
On vice and depravity: you'll find some rebellious
    traitor
Wherever you look, in every country and clime,
    but
A righteous, inflexible statesman—that's quite
    another matter.   45
Let no foul sight or utterance ever approach the
    threshold
Of a father's dwelling-place: may this house be
    free from call-girls
And noisy all-night parties. If you're planning any
    misdeed,
Never forget that a child has first claim on your
    respect:
Don't disregard the tender years of your son, but
    rather   50
Let his presence serve to dissuade you from the
    sin you contemplate.
for if, in time to come, he earns officialdom's
    wrathful
Attention, and proves himself your son in more
    than looks
And physical build, if he's the child of your moral
    actions,
And while following where you lead him, sinks
    deeper still in crime—   55
Then, I don't doubt, you'll revile him, you'll read
    him a bitter

And furious lecture, and cut him out of your will.
   But how
Can you assume the mien and privileges of a
   father
When your old age is marred with worse
   indiscretions than his,
And the cupping-glass° hasn't found any brains in
   your vacuous noddle   60
Since heaven knows when? If a visitor is expected,
Then none of your household's idle. 'Get the floors
   swept,' you shout,
'Burnish the columns, fetch down those spiders'
   webs up there!
You, clean the silver plate, and you, the embossed
   vessels—'
Hark at the voice of the master, standing over them,
   whip in hand!   65
You're all of a dither, poor creature: your friend's
   eye might be offended
By a dog's turd in the lobby, or some splashes of
   mud
Down the covered colonnade—things that one
   small slave-boy
Could fix with a bucket of sawdust. Then why
   take no trouble
To ensure that your son will enjoy the sanctity of
   the home   70
Unmarred, without blemish? Yes, it's a fine thing
   to present
Another citizen to your country and people—
   provided
You raise him to be what your country needs, a
   capable
Farmer, who's equally skilled in the arts of peace
   and war.

So it makes a great difference what practical,
   what moral   75
Education you give your son. The stork scours
   the countryside
For snakes and lizards to feed its young ones; and
   when they've learnt

To fly, they go off in search of the same creatures
   themselves.
The vulture hastens home from dead cattle and
   dogs, or the gibbet,
Bearing carrion plunder to share with its chicks:
   and so   80
When the chick's grown-up, when it's built a nest
   of its own in another
Tree, when it's self-supporting, it feeds on carrion
   still.
But Jupiter's noble eagle goes hunting hare and
   hind through
The upland pastures, this is the prey it brings
   home
To its eyrie: so when the eaglets reach full
   maturity   85
And leave the nest, at the dictates of hunger
   they'll swoop
Down on the self-same prey they first ate when
   they burst the shell.
   X had a passion for building: he ran up multi-
   storeyed
Mansions all over the place—at the seaside, in
   mountain resorts
Like Praeneste, on Tivoli's hillsides—done up
   with marble imported   90
From Greece, or still further afield, piles that
   eclipsed the local
Temples in splendour (just like that eunuch
   nabob, the freedman
Of Claudius,° whose town house far outshone the
   Capitol).°
Such grandiose schemes made inroads in his
   fortune, frittered away
His ready cash; yet somehow he kept a quite
   substantial   95
Proportion intact—for his crazy son to
   squander
On building more stately homes with even
   costlier marble.

---

60. Cupping-glasses: Cups of pottery or glass heated and placed
   on body parts to draw out fluids, usually harmful ones.

---

93. Claudius: Roman Emperor (41–54 A.D.).
93. Capitol: The group of buildings forming the center of political
   life of Old Rome were grouped on the Capitoline Hill.

Some, whose lot it is to have Sabbath-fearing
    fathers,
Worship nothing but clouds and the *numen* of the
    heavens,°
And think it as great a crime to eat pork, from
    which their parents   100
Abstained, as human flesh. They get themselves
    circumcised,
And look down on Roman law, preferring instead
    to learn
And honour and fear the Jewish commandments,
    whatever
Was handed down by Moses in that arcane tome
    of his—

Never to show the way to any but fellow-
    believers   105
(If they ask where to get some water, find out if
    they're foreskinless).°

QUESTIONS

1. What is the essential message of the satire?
2. What does Juvenal mean when he writes: "Never forget that a child has first claims on your respect"?
3. What vices of the rich Romans are criticized here?
4. What purpose do the comparisons with other animals and their offspring serve? (lines 76–87)?
5. What criticism is Juvenal making of the Jews?

99. Numen of the heavens: Probably the phrase means that Jews worshipped some impalpable divine spirit and no concrete diety. They did not worship the heavens, but "the spirit" of the heavens.

106. Alternatively the whole line could be translated: "leading none but the circumcised to the desired fountain." This would suggest the rite of baptism which became common among Jews of the first century A.D.

THE GRECO-ROMAN ROOT: CONTINUITIES

The Classical Ideal The classical cultures, Greece and Rome, in spite of many differences, form together a unified system of cultural values and creations that has profoundly influenced the course of Western culture and is still with us today. In our focus on the "classical" phase of "classical" culture—Athens in the fifth century B.C.—we witnessed the aesthetic and moral values associated with the term. The Greek mentality of that century looks to human reason as the force giving order to the world. It is humanistic in that it stresses the dignity and worth of human individuals as such more than as part of a social or divine order. Yet it cautions against the dangers of human pride, *hubris.* "Nothing in excess" were the words of the oracle at Delphi, and we see this applied to Oedipus when he tries to outwit fate; in Pericles' description of the equilibrium between private and public good in Athens; in the historians' demonstrations of the evils entailed by extreme action; in the sculptural and architectural monuments that strive to balance or harmonize the real and the ideal; in Aristotle's golden mean. Classical art is dynamic and pleasing because its proportions and symmetry represent an attempt to harmonize forces like body and soul, man and the gods, reason and emotion. When a classical work is copied and calculated from reason alone, it becomes lifeless. The Greeks very much admired the power of reason, but they were deeply interested in the *whole* human being.

Greek Logic and Mathematics The Greeks were the first to elaborate the logical structures of our thought, structures that have become so natural to the modern mind that we take them for granted. Greek logicians laid down the basic rules for determining when arguments are valid or invalid; that is, when conclusions follow from a given set of premises and when they do not. Greek terminology still predominates in textbooks of logic. Perhaps more significantly, the Greeks were the first to utilize logic and its companion mathematics for the systematic understanding of nature. These instruments of human reason were be-

lieved to work because the world was viewed as by nature intelligible and its functioning capable of being reduced to laws. Something of this same trust in the capability of man's intellect to solve the mysteries of nature motivates numbers of scientists and their supporters today. Even those of us less optimistic about the potentialities of man's mental faculties recognize the ability of intellect to organize large segments of human experience through the use of rational powers.

Greek Science and Politics Modern culture owes to the ancient Greeks most of the basic categories for ordering knowledge into disciplines, like physics, ethics, politics, and poetic (all Greek words). The Greeks also defined and distinguished the methodologies or ways of investigating truth appropriate to various disciplines. Utilizing these methodologies, the Greeks made such advances that, in the sciences at least, Western Europe was not to surpass them until after roughly 1600. Greek political theorists provided an analysis of the basic constitutional forms of monarchy, tyranny, aristocracy, oligarchy, republican government, and democracy that still informs modern political science. The Aristotelian idea that true liberty is to be found in a republic, or a state where men rule themselves, lies at the basis of our American political system.

Greek Literature, Architecture, and Sculpture The Greeks created basic literary forms that influenced not only the course of Western literature but also the ways in which we think about life. The English language acknowledges its debt to Greek concepts with terms like *epic, lyric, tragedy,* and *comedy.* In much the same way, Greek architectural orders and the temple form and Roman arch and dome construction are the basic elements of a major architectural language that has persisted to the present. Similarly, the accomplishments of the Greeks and Romans in sculpture and painting provided the archetypes for early Christian art. The remembered greatness of Rome was a major impetus for the artists of Renaissance Italy who sought to equal the ancients. Through the Renaissance, ideas on Greek and Roman art and architecture were to be a goad and support for artistic development in the West.

Roman Expansion of Greek Culture   Although the Greeks were undoubtedly the originators of most of the cultural forms we have been studying here, the term Greco-Roman makes sense because of what the Romans did with Greek culture. As the last and the greatest of the Hellenistic (Greeklike) empires, Rome spread Greek culture to the considerable area of the world that it occupied. Without Rome, Greek culture would have remained limited to a parochial group of city-states. The Romans, adding their own cultural forms to the Greek ones, adapted Greek culture to the needs of a larger world. The Greeks saw the world as divided between "Greek" and "barbarian"; the Romans were more cosmopolitan in outlook. The Greeks philosophized about the laws of nature, but the Romans realized them as a code of laws that became the basis for legal systems in the Western world. The Romans adapted Greek sculptural and artistic forms to more practical uses: the portrait, the forum, the triumphal arch, the colosseum. Our engineering and city planning derive from Roman innovation.

Latin Language and Literature   The Romans reworked the Greek literary forms to their own taste and added a new one, verse satire. Because of the spread of the Roman empire, the Greek innovations were transmitted to modern Western culture. Latin became the literary language of the West and the official language of the Roman catholic church for many centuries. The Latin language had a direct influence on the growth of the Romance languages and played an important part in the development of English and other European languages.

Greek/Roman Cultural Values   The differences between Homer's *Iliad* and Virgil's *Aeneid* are indicative of the shift in emphasis between Greek and Roman cultural values. Achilles is a hero because of his pride, strength, and daring: he may embody Greek cultural values but is still primarily an individual. Aeneas is praised for his *pietas*, or loyalty to family and nation. It is his task to serve the destiny of Rome, not primarily to excel himself. Our concept of patriotism (from the Latin *patria*) is primarily Roman.

It has been argued that the Greco-Roman emphasis on man, human reason, and secular glory has had detrimental as well as beneficial effects on Western culture. Pushed to its extreme, it can result in a spiritual vacuum. Hebraic cultural values, at the base of the Judeo-Christian root, are, as we shall see, of a different order.

PART TWO

The Judeo-Christian Root

6

Judaism and Early Christianity

In moving to the second root culture of the Western world, we shift from a culture primarily centered on man to one primarily centered on an all-powerful, unique God. The creators of this world-view and its system of values were the ancient Hebrews, who have left their legacy in the Bible and in the other cultural manifestations of Judaism. As Christianity developed from Judaism, it brought elements of Greco-Roman culture to bear on the Hebraic core. We will examine a few important monuments of the culture of Christianity in our focal point for Part Two, the European High Middle Ages. First we will look briefly at the seminal Hebraic culture.

The Ancient Hebrews and the Bible

Modern Christian versions of the Bible include the scriptures of Judaism, called the Old Testament, and the scriptures of Christianity called the New Testament. Originally, however, the Bible referred only to the Old Testament. It can be defined as a collection of religious literature written in Hebrew (with some parts in other Middle Eastern languages) from about 1000 B.C. to 100 A.D. Like the Homeric epics, biblical literature first existed as *oral* narratives and poetry. The written Bible contains a wealth of different kinds of literature: history, short stories, drama, lyric poetry, and philosophical meditation.

What of the people who composed these greatly influential works? The Hebrews were originally a Middle Eastern tribe belonging to the racial group known as Semites, a group that includes the Arabs. Their early history can be divided into three parts: (1) the period of the patriarchs or founding fathers: Abraham, his son Isaac, and his son Jacob; (2) the captivity of the Hebrews (now called Israelites) in Egypt; and (3) the Exodus or deliverance from Egypt to the promised land of Canaan.

Abraham   Abraham, who probably lived about four thousand years ago, is traditionally looked on as the original founder of the Jewish people. His most important contribution was to establish the worship of one God—not a god of nature, of the sun, wind, or rain, as was common in other Middle Eastern religions, but a truly personal God who took a direct interest in His chosen people, the Israelites. God himself initiates a contractual relationship with Abraham. The relationship between Abraham and his God came to be known as the covenant.

According to this agreement, God promised that Abraham's clan would be led to a new land and would become a great nation. In return, the Israelites were to place their trust and faith in God. Abraham's grandson Jacob, driven by famine out of the Israelites' land of Canaan, settled with his clan in Egypt. Although the Egyptians were originally tolerant of them, the Israelites eventually became slaves until they were delivered by Moses, around 1200 B.C.

Moses   Moses led the Israelites to Mount Sinai, where a new covenant between the God of Israel and His people was made. God revealed Himself to Moses under the name of "Jahweh," which means in Hebrew "he brings into existence." Jahweh was not only the creator of everything but could also enter into history to influence the course of human events. Israel itself was a creation of divine action in time. It was felt that God not only cared for his people but He ordered events for the good. History was not, as the pagans conceived of it, meaningless change or a series of endlessly repeating cycles of events. Rather, it was the means through which God revealed his will. This conception of God gave the Israelites their strong sense of destiny. They were the chosen people—God would take care of them. In the covenant at Mount Sinai, Jahweh promised His protection and gave the Israelites the Ten Commandments to follow. The first of these is, of course, "Thou shalt have no other gods before me." The principle of one supreme personal God was firmly established, as it has been in Judaism ever since.

The Kings   Moses' successor, Joshua, brought his people to the promised land of Canaan, and at that point the Israelites became a settled, rather than a nomadic people. The next phase of their history is called the period of kings, for they had not had one king over them earlier. The first king was Saul; the second and most famous, David. David founded the capital at Jerusalem, establishing a splendid court there with a luxury never known to the Israelites previously. It is during the reign of David that the Hebrew literature we know as the Bible was first written down. Up until that time, the legends of the patriarchs, the account of the creation, and so on, had been passed along orally.

Solomon   Writing of biblical literature continued under the reign of the next king, Solomon. Solomon's court and kingdom were the most lavish and splendid that Israel ever knew. He taxed the people heavily for his extravagant building and also maintained a harem —although the hundred wives attributed to him is probably an exaggeration. He was reputed to be the wisest man in the world and a poet as well. Most scholars now think that this is probably a legend and especially that the Song of Songs, the great Hebrew poem also called the Song of Solomon, was not written by Solomon but by a later author; still, it seems to fit the splendor of Solomon's court. Solomon's power and splendor did not continue after him. When he died in 922 B.C., Israel was split into two kingdoms and foreign conquests of the Israelites began again. The Jews were exiled in Babylonia, then conquered by the Egyptians, by the Syrians, and finally, shortly before the birth of Jesus, by the Romans.

Genesis   The first biblical text included here is one that may appear all too familiar, but a student of the humanities should approach it with new questions. All cultures of the world have myths of creation. Compare this Hebrew account of the beginnings of things (the meaning of the Latin word *genesis*) with the Greek one summarized in the section on Greek mythology in Chapter 1 and with the African accounts in Part Four. All of the biblical passages are from the King James translation of 1611, itself a cultural monument of great importance to the formation of the English language.

GENESIS

The Creation

CHAPTER 1

1 In the beginning God created the heaven and the earth.

2 And the earth was without form, and void; and darkness was upon the face of the deep. And the Spirit of God moved upon the face of the waters.

3 And God said, Let there be light: and there was light.

4 And God saw the light, that it was good: and God divided the light from the darkness.

5 And God called the light Day, and the darkness he called Night. And the evening and the morning were the first day.

6 And God said, Let there be a firmament in the midst of the waters, and let it divide the waters from the waters.

7 And God made the firmament, and divided the waters which were under the firmament from the waters which were above the firmament: and it was so.

8 And God called the firmament Heaven. And the evening and the morning were the second day.

9 And God said, Let the waters under the heaven be gathered together unto one place, and let the dry land appear: and it was so.

10 And God called the dry land Earth; and the gathering together of the waters called he Seas: and God saw that it was good.

11 And God said, Let the earth bring forth grass, the herb yielding seed, and the fruit tree yielding fruit after his kind, whose seed is in itself, upon the earth: and it was so.

12 And the earth brought forth grass, and herb yielding seed after his kind, and the tree yielding fruit, whose seed was in itself, after his kind: and God saw that it was good.

13 And the evening and the morning were the third day.

14 And God said, Let there be lights in the firmament of the heaven to divide the day from the night; and let them be for signs, and for seasons, and for days, and years:

15 And let them be for lights in the firmament of the heaven to give light upon the earth: and it was so.

16 And God made two great lights; the greater light to rule the day, and the lesser light to rule the night: he made the stars also.

17 And God set them in the firmament of the heaven to give light upon the earth,

18 And to rule over the day and over the night, and to divide the light from the darkness: and God saw that it was good.

19 And the evening and the morning were the fourth day.

20 And God said, Let the waters bring forth abundantly the moving creature that hath life, and fowl that may fly above the earth in the open firmament of heaven:

21 And God created great whales, and every living creature that moveth, which the waters brought forth abundantly, after their kind, and every winged fowl after his kind: and God saw that it was good.

22 And God blessed them, saying, Be fruitful, and multiply, and fill the waters in the seas, and let fowl multiply in the earth.

23 And the evening and the morning were the fifth day.

24 And God said, Let the earth bring forth the living creature after his kind, cattle, and creeping thing, and beast of the earth after his kind: and it was so.

25 And God made the beast of the earth after his kind, and cattle after their kind, and every thing that creepeth upon the earth after his kind: and God saw that it was good.

26 And God said, Let us make man in our image, after our likeness: and let them have dominion over the fish of the sea, and over the fowl of the air, and over the cattle, and over all the earth, and over every creeping thing that creepeth upon the earth.

27 So God created man in his own image, in the image of God created he him; male and female created he them.

28 And God blessed them, and God said unto them, Be fruitful, and multiply, and replenish the earth, and subdue it: and have dominion over the fish of the sea, and over the fowl of the air, and over every living thing that moveth upon the earth.

29 And God said, Behold, I have given you every herb bearing seed, which is upon the face of all the earth, and every tree, in the which is the fruit of a tree yielding seed; to you it shall be for meat.

30 And to every beast of the earth, and to every fowl of the air, and to every thing that creepeth upon the earth, wherein there is life, I have given every green herb for meat: and it was so.

31 And God saw every thing that he had made, and, behold, it was very good. And the evening and the morning were the sixth day.

CHAPTER 2

1 Thus the heavens and the earth were finished, and all the host of them.

2 And on the seventh day God ended his work which he had made; and he rested on the seventh day from all his work which he had made.

3 And God blessed the seventh day, and sanctified it: because that in it he had rested from all his work which God created and made.

4 These are the generations of the heavens and of the earth when they were created, in the day that the Lord God made the earth and the heavens,

5 And every plant of the field before it was in the earth, and every herb of the field before it grew: for the Lord God had not caused it to rain upon the earth, and there was not a man to till the ground.

6 But there went up a mist from the earth, and watered the whole face of the ground.

7 And the Lord God formed man of the dust of the ground, and breathed into his nostrils the breath of life; and man became a living soul.

8 And the Lord God planted a garden eastward in Eden; and there he put the man whom he had formed.

9 And out of the ground made the Lord God to grow every tree that is pleasant to the sight, and good for food; the tree of life also in the midst of the garden, and the tree of knowledge of good and evil.

10 And a river went out of Eden to water the garden; and from thence it was parted, and became into four heads.

11 The name of the first is Pison: that is it which compasseth the whole land of Havilah, where there is gold;

12 And the gold of that land is good: there is bdellium and the onyx stone.

13 And the name of the second river is Gihon: the same is it that compasseth the whole land of Ethiopia.

14 And the name of the third river is Hiddekel: that is it which goeth toward the east of Assyria. And the fourth river is Euphrates.

15 And the Lord God took the man, and put him into the garden of Eden to dress it and to keep it.

16 And the Lord God commanded the man, saying, Of every tree of the garden thou mayest freely eat:

17 But of the tree of the knowledge of good and evil, thou shalt not eat of it: for in the day that thou eatest thereof thou shalt surely die.

18 And the Lord God said, It is not good that the man should be alone; I will make him a help meet for him.

19 And out of the ground the Lord God formed every beast of the field, and every fowl of the air; and brought them unto Adam to see what he would call them: and whatsoever Adam called every living creature, that was the name thereof.

20 And Adam gave names to all cattle, and to the fowl of the air, and to every beast of the field; but for Adam there was not found a help meet for him.

21 And the Lord God caused a deep sleep to fall upon Adam, and he slept; and he took one of his ribs, and closed up the flesh instead thereof.

22 And the rib, which the Lord God had taken from man, made he a woman, and brought her unto the man.

23 And Adam said, This is now bone of my bones, and flesh of my flesh: she shall be called Woman, because she was taken out of man.

24 Therefore shall a man leave his father and his mother, and shall cleave unto his wife: and they shall be one flesh.

25 And they were both naked, the man and his wife, and were not ashamed.

COMMENTS AND QUESTIONS

1. The two different accounts of creation in Genesis have caused biblical scholars to believe that each was written at a different time and by a different author. What are the two accounts? Where does one end and the other begin?
2. Does God create from nothing? Does it seem that anything was there before God?
3. How does the role of the Hebrew God of creation differ from that of God in the Greek and African myths?
4. How do the two accounts of the creation of woman differ? How might these accounts have influenced ways in which we think about the nature of woman?

The following text is central to the Judaic and Christian concepts of man's relationship to God and to the problem of evil. Whereas the first two chapters of Genesis show man as a part of the totality of creation and in harmony with it, in this chapter the human beings, quite unlike the other living things in the created world, begin to act on their own: to make their own decisions apart from God. They have *free will:* they are given an orderly and harmonious world but are capable of creating disorder in it.

GENESIS

The Fall

CHAPTER 3

1 Now the serpent was more subtile than any beast of the field which the Lord God had made. And he said unto the woman, Yea, hath God said, Ye shall not eat of every tree of the garden?

2 And the woman said unto the serpent, We may eat of the fruit of the trees of the garden:

3 But of the fruit of the tree which is in the midst of the garden, God hath said, Ye shall not eat of it, neither shall ye touch it, lest ye die.

4 And the serpent said unto the woman, Ye shall not surely die:

5 For God doth know that in the day ye eat thereof, then your eyes shall be opened, and ye shall be as gods, knowing good and evil.

6 And when the woman saw that the tree was good for food, and that it was pleasant to the eyes, and a tree to be desired to make one wise, she took of the fruit thereof, and did eat, and gave also unto her husband with her; and he did eat.

7 And the eyes of them both were opened, and they knew that they were naked; and they sewed fig leaves together, and made themselves aprons.

8 And they heard the voice of the Lord God walking in the garden in the cool of the day: and Adam and his wife hid themselves from the presence of the Lord God amongst the trees of the garden.

9 And the Lord God called unto Adam, and said unto him, Where art thou?

10 And he said, I heard thy voice in the garden, and I was afraid, because I was naked; and I hid myself.

11 And he said, Who told thee that thou wast naked? Hast thou eaten of the tree, whereof I commanded thee that thou shouldest not eat?

12 And the man said, The woman whom thou gavest to be with me, she gave me of the tree, and I did eat.

13 And the Lord God said unto the woman, What is this that thou hast done? And the woman said, The serpent beguiled me, and I did eat.

14 And the Lord God said unto the serpent, Because thou hast done this, thou art cursed above all cattle, and above every beast of the field; upon thy belly shalt thou go, and dust shalt thou eat all the days of thy life:

15 And I will put enmity between thee and the woman, and between thy seed and her seed; it shall bruise thy head, and thou shalt bruise his heel.

16 Unto the woman he said, I will greatly multiply thy sorrow and thy conception; in sorrow thou shalt bring forth children; and thy desire shall be to thy husband, and he shall rule over thee.

17 And unto Adam he said, Because thou hast hearkened unto the voice of thy wife, and hast eaten of the tree, of which I commanded thee, saying, Thou shalt not eat of it: cursed is the ground for thy sake; in sorrow shalt thou eat of it all the days of thy life;

18 Thorns also and thistles shall it bring forth to thee; and thou shalt eat the herb of the field:

19 In the sweat of thy face shalt thou eat bread, till thou return unto the ground; for out of it wast thou taken: for dust thou art, and unto dust shalt thou return.

20 And Adam called his wife's name Eve; because she was the mother of all living.

21 Unto Adam also and to his wife did the Lord God make coats of skins, and clothed them.

22 And the Lord God said, Behold, the man is become as one of us, to know good and evil: and now, lest he put forth his hand, and take also of the tree of life, and eat, and live for ever:

23 Therefore the Lord God sent him forth from the garden of Eden, to till the ground from whence he was taken.

24 So he drove out the man: and he placed at the east of the garden of Eden cherubim, and a flaming sword which turned every way, to keep the way of the tree of life.

COMMENTS AND QUESTIONS

1. How does this story reconcile the idea of God's infinite justice with the presence of evil in the world?
2. How does God appear in this story in relation to man?
3. What, specifically, tempts Eve and then Adam to eat the forbidden fruit? What does this tell you about the Hebrews' concept of the nature of human beings?
4. Compare the relationship between human curiosity and divine power here with the treatment of the same theme in *Oedipus Rex*.
5. Do you as a reader feel admiration or scorn for the human desire to eat the fruit?

Genesis goes on to recount the rise of the tribe of Israel. The following passage is illustrative of God's relationship with His "chosen people," here in the person of their founding father, Abraham.

GENESIS

The Sacrifice of Isaac

CHAPTER 22

1 And it came to pass after these things, that God did tempt Abraham, and said unto him, Abraham: and he said, Behold, here I am.

2 And he said, Take now thy son, thine only son Isaac, whom thou lovest, and get thee into the land of Moriah; and offer him there for a burnt offering upon one of the mountains which I will tell thee of.

3 And Abraham rose up early in the morning, and saddled his ass, and took two of his young men with him, and Isaac his son, and clave the wood for the burnt offering, and rose up, and went unto the place of which God had told him.

4 Then on the third day Abraham lifted up his eyes, and saw the place afar off.

5 And Abraham said unto his young men, Abide ye here with the ass; and I and the lad will go yonder and worship, and come again to you.

6 And Abraham took the wood of the burnt offering, and laid it upon Isaac his son; and he took the fire in his hand, and a knife; and they went both of them together.

7 And Isaac spake unto Abraham his father, and said, My father: and he said, Here am I, my son. And he said, Behold the fire and the wood: but where is the lamb for a burnt offering?

8 And Abraham said, My son, God will provide himself a lamb for a burnt offering: so they went both of them together.

9 And they came to the place which God had told him of; and Abraham built an altar there, and laid the

wood in order, and bound Isaac his son, and laid him on the altar upon the wood.

10 And Abraham stretched forth his hand, and took the knife to slay his son.

11 And the Angel of the Lord called unto him out of heaven, and said, Abraham, Abraham: and he said, Here am I.

12 And he said, Lay not thine hand upon the lad, neither do thou any thing unto him: for now I know that thou fearest God, seeing thou hast not withheld thy son, thine only son, from me.

13 And Abraham lifted up his eyes, and looked, and behold behind him a ram caught in a thicket by his horns: and Abraham went and took the ram, and offered him up for a burnt offering in the stead of his son.

14 And Abraham called the name of that place Jehovah-jireh: as it is said to this day, In the mount of the Lord it shall be seen.

15 And the Angel of the Lord called unto Abraham out of heaven the second time,

16 And said, By myself have I sworn, saith the Lord, for because thou hast done this thing, and hast not withheld thy son, thine only son,

17 That in blessing I will bless thee, and in multiplying I will multiply thy seed as the stars of the heaven, and as the sand which is upon the sea shore; and thy seed shall possess the gate of his enemies;

18 And in thy seed shall all the nations of the earth be blessed; because thou hast obeyed my voice.

COMMENTS AND QUESTIONS

1. This is a *narrative*: a tight, brief and simple one based on the old principle of suspense. In order to understand simply how it functions as a narrative, it may be useful to break it down into parts as follows:
   1. (verses 1–6) A straightforward account of events.
   2. (verses 7–8) *Almost* a breakdown. Suspense introduced.
   3. (verses 9–12) The climax.
   4. (verses 13–19) The resolution, a happy ending.
2. Analyze the contrast between the simple way in which the events are narrated and the underlying emotions. What are these emotions, and how does the writer convey them?

3. Why is God testing Abraham? What is Abraham's reaction?
4. Would the story be more or less effective if the writer described Abraham's inner feelings in more detail?
5. What attitude on the part of man in relation to God is advocated here? Compare this attitude with the Greek one.
6. Refer back to Matthew Arnold's distinction between Hebraic "right acting" and Hellenic "right thinking" in Chapter 1, page 13. Does this story, contrasted with Greek attitudes, support that distinction?

The Covenant and Divine Law

As liberator and savior of Israel, God brought His people out of bondage in Egypt and into the wilderness, where he forged them into a community under the leadership of Moses. In the very first days of their desert sojourn He led them to Mount Sinai where, through Moses, He declared His offer of a covenant with them and sealed the agreement with the revelation of His laws.

EXODUS

The Ten Commandments

CHAPTER 19

1 In the third month, when the children of Israel were gone forth out of the land of Egypt, the same day came they into the wilderness of Sinai.

2 For they were departed from Rephidim, and were come to the desert of Sinai, and had pitched in the wilderness; and there Israel camped before the mount.

3 And Moses went up unto God, and the Lord called unto him out of the mountain, saying, Thus shalt thou say to the house of Jacob, and tell the children of Israel;

4 Ye have seen what I did unto the Egyptians, and how I bare you on eagles' wings, and brought you unto myself.

5 Now therefore, if ye will obey my voice indeed, and keep my covenant, then ye shall be a peculiar treasure unto me above all people: for all the earth is mine:

6 And ye shall be unto me a kingdom of priests, and an holy nation. These are the words which thou shalt speak unto the children of Israel.

7 And Moses came and called for the elders of the people, and laid before their faces all these words which the Lord commanded him.

8 And all the people answered together, and said, All that the Lord hath spoken we will do. And Moses returned the words of the people unto the Lord.

9 And the Lord said unto Moses, Lo, I come unto thee in a thick cloud, that the people may hear when I speak with thee, and believe thee for ever. And Moses told the words of the people unto the Lord.

10 And the Lord said unto Moses, Go unto the people, and sanctify them to day and to morrow, and let them wash their clothes.

. . .

14 And Moses went down from the mount unto the people, and sanctified the people; and they washed their clothes.

15 And he said unto the people, Be ready against the third day: come not at your wives.

16 And it came to pass on the third day in the morning, that there were thunders and lightnings, and a thick cloud upon the mount, and the voice of the trumpet exceeding loud; so that all the people that was in the camp trembled.

17 And Moses brought forth the people out of the camp to meet with God; and they stood at the nether part of the mount.

18 And mount Sinai was altogether on a smoke, because the Lord descended upon it in fire: and the smoke thereof ascended as the smoke of a furnace, and the whole mount quaked greatly.

19 And when the voice of the trumpet sounded long, and waxed louder and louder, Moses spake, and God answered him by a voice.

20 And the Lord came down upon mount Sinai, on the top of the mount; and the Lord called Moses up to the top of the mount; and Moses went up.

21 And the Lord said unto Moses, Go down, charge the people, lest they break through unto the Lord to gaze, and many of them perish.

22 And let the priests also, which come near to the Lord, sanctify themselves, lest the Lord break forth upon them.

23 And Moses said unto the Lord, The people cannot come up to mount Sinai: for thou chargedst us, saying, Set bounds about the mount, and sanctify it.

24 And the Lord said unto him, Away, get thee down, and thou shalt come up, thou, and Aaron with thee: but let not the priests and the people break through to come up unto the Lord, lest he break forth upon them.

25 So Moses went down unto the people, and spake unto them.

CHAPTER 20

1 And God spake all these words, saying,

2 I am the Lord thy God, which have brought thee out of the land of Egypt, out of the house of bondage.

3 Thou shalt have no other gods before me.

4 Thou shalt not make unto thee any graven image, or any likeness of any thing that is in heaven above, or that is in the earth beneath, or that is in the water under the earth:

5 Thou shalt not bow down thyself to them, nor serve them: for I the Lord thy God am a jealous God, visiting the iniquity of the fathers upon the children unto the third and fourth generation of them that hate me;

6 And shewing mercy unto thousands of them that love me, and keep my commandments.

7 Thou shalt not take the name of the Lord thy God in vain; for the Lord will not hold him guiltless that taketh his name in vain.

8 Remember the sabbath day, to keep it holy.

9 Six days shalt thou labour, and do all thy work:

10 But the seventh day is the sabbath of the Lord thy God: in it thou shalt not do any work, thou, nor thy son, nor thy daughter, thy manservant, nor thy maidservant, nor thy cattle, nor thy stranger that is within thy gates:

11 For in six days the Lord made heaven and earth, the sea, and all that in them is, and rested the seventh day: wherefore the Lord blessed the sabbath day, and hallowed it.

12 Honour thy father and thy mother: that thy days may be long upon the land which the Lord thy God giveth thee.

13 Thou shalt not kill.

14 Thou shalt not commit adultery.

15 Thou shalt not steal.

16 Thou shalt not bear false witness against thy neighbour.

17 Thou shalt not covet thy neighbour's house, thou shalt not covet thy neighbour's wife, nor his manserv-

ant, nor his maidservant, nor his ox, nor his ass, nor any thing that is thy neighbour's.

18 And all the people saw the thunderings, and the lightnings, and the noise of the trumpet, and the mountain smoking: and when the people saw it, they removed, and stood afar off.

19 And they said unto Moses, Speak thou with us, and we will hear: but let not God speak with us, lest we die.

20 And Moses said unto the people, Fear not: for God is come to prove you, and that his fear may be before your faces, that ye sin not.

21 And the people stood afar off, and Moses drew near unto the thick darkness where God was.

22 And the Lord said unto Moses, Thus thou shalt say unto the children of Israel, Ye have seen that I have talked with you from heaven.

QUESTIONS

1. What previous event does God use to gain credibility for His promise?
2. What is God's promise to the Israelites?
3. In what sense is a covenant established between them and God?
4. The Ten Commandments, or Decalogue, is divided into two parts. The first four relate to the individual's relationship with God, while the last six deal with the sphere of human relationships. Why is the command to honor parents often described as the "bridge" commandment between the two parts?
5. Why, according to Moses, did God reveal Himself in a cloud?

The Decalogue formed the core of Israel's law, but over the centuries an elaborate code of legislation developed around it, dealing with all aspects of ritual, moral, and civil life. The so-called "Holiness Code," *Leviticus 17–26*, received this title because the laws it embodied were designed to preserve a level of conduct worthy of the people whom God had elected over all others. Although written down in this form in the sixth century B.C., it is presented in the Bible as part of the legislation made during the period of desert wanderings six hundred years earlier. Nonetheless, like the previous legislation of the Israelites, these laws contrast with those of other contemporary Near Eastern

peoples in placing greater emphasis on people than on property. They also tend to ignore the distinctions between classes so prominent in the codes of other traditions. In its concern for the downtrodden, the "Holiness Code" reflects the continuing folk memory of the liberation of the Israelites themselves from bondage in Egypt. Leviticus 19 may be considered perhaps the ultimate development in ethics in the Old Testament.

LEVITICUS

The "Holiness Code"

CHAPTER 19

1 And the Lord spake unto Moses, saying,

2 Speak unto all the congregation of the children of Israel, and say unto them, Ye shall be holy: for I the Lord your God am holy.

3 Ye shall fear every man his mother, and his father, and keep my sabbaths: I am the Lord your God.

. . .

9 And when ye reap the harvest of your land, thou shalt not wholly reap the corners of thy field, neither shalt thou gather the gleanings of thy harvest.

10 And thou shalt not glean thy vineyard, neither shalt thou gather every grape of thy vineyard; thou shalt leave them for the poor and stranger: I am the Lord your God.

11 Ye shall not steal, neither deal falsely, neither lie one to another.

12 And ye shall not swear by my name falsely, neither shalt thou profane the name of thy God: I am the Lord.

13 Thou shalt not defraud thy neighbour, neither rob him: the wages of him that is hired shall not abide with thee all night until the morning.

14 Thou shalt not curse the deaf, nor put a stumbling block before the blind, but shalt fear thy God: I am the Lord.

15 Ye shall do no unrighteousness in judgment: thou shalt not respect the person of the poor, nor honour the person of the mighty: but in righteousness shalt thou judge thy neighbour.

16 Thou shalt not go up and down as a talebearer among thy people: neither shalt thou stand against the blood of thy neighbour: I am the Lord.

17 Thou shalt not hate thy brother in thine heart: thou shalt in any wise rebuke thy neighbour, and not suffer sin upon him.

18 Thou shalt not avenge, nor bear any grudge against the children of thy people, but thou shalt love thy neighbor as thyself: I am the Lord.

. . .

33 And if a stranger sojourn with thee in your land, ye shall not vex him.

34 But the stranger that dwelleth with you shall be unto you as one born among you, and thou shalt love him as thyself; for ye were strangers in the land of Egypt: I am the Lord your God.

QUESTIONS

1. On what grounds does God base His demand that the Israelites be holy?
2. What provisions should be made for the poor?
3. By implication, according to verse 14, how were the handicapped sometimes treated in ancient society?
4. Why should the Israelites especially be kind to strangers?

The Psalms

No other Old Testament book has enjoyed the perennial success of the Psalms in appealing to readers. A few of the one hundred fifty poems composing the book may go back in some form to the period of King David in the tenth century B.C., but others were doubtless composed centuries later. These poetic works were designed to fulfill specific purposes in temple ritual. More than fifty years ago the German biblical scholar Hermann Gunkel[1] distinguished five major categories of psalms according to function: (1) hymns of praise, (2) communal laments, (3) royal psalms, (4) individual laments, and (5) individual thanksgiving psalms.

The following hymn of praise has as its object the praise of God, but closely associated with the idea of divine greatness here is that of the dignity of man. Human beings have a unique relationship with the

Creator, and to them He has committed the government of the earth. Consequently, in the biblical tradition, the worth of the individual is grounded directly in God's personal love and in the responsibilities created by that love.

PSALMS

PSALM 8

1 O Jehovah, our Lord,
  How excellent is thy name in all the earth,
  Who hast set thy glory upon the heavens!
2 Out of the mouth of babes and sucklings hast
      thou established strength,
  Because of thine adversaries,
  That thou mightest still the enemy and the
      avenger.
3 When I consider thy heavens, the work of thy
      fingers,
  The moon and the stars, which thou hast
      ordained;
4 What is man, that thou art mindful of him?
  And the son of man, that thou visitest him?
5 For thou hast made him but little lower than God,
  And crownest him with glory and honor.
6 Thou makest him to have dominion over the
      works of thy hands;
  Thou hast put all things under his feet:
7 All sheep and oxen,
  Yea, and the beasts of the field,
8 The birds of the heavens, and the fish of the sea,
  Whatsoever passeth through the paths of the seas.
9 O Jehovah, our Lord,
  How excellent is thy name in all the earth!

QUESTIONS

1. What is meant by the mouths of babes and infants chanting God's glory?
2. A famous saying praising the dignity of man is attributed to the fifth-century B.C. Greek philosopher Protagoras: "Man is the measure of all things." Compare the basis for human dignity suggested by this statement with that found in the Psalms, which begins: "What is man that thou art mindful of him?"

---

[1](*The Psalms*, trans. Thomas M. Horner [Philadelphia: Fortress Press, 1967].)

The Prophet Amos

From the mid-eighth to the sixth century B.C., the spiritual life of Jews was dominated by a succession of prophets. Men who considered themselves inspired by God, the prophets took it as their mission to warn kings and their people of the divine punishment to be inflicted upon those who failed to fulfill the duties and moral standards imposed on the chosen people of God. Generally speaking, these were centuries of great difficulty for the Jews. They saw their kingdom—divided in two since the death of Solomon in 922—pressured first by the Assyrians and then by the Babylonians. The northern kingdom, Israel, with its capital at Samaria, finally fell to the Assyrians in 722, while the southern kingdom, Judah, centered at Jerusalem, held out until conquered by the Babylonians in 587.

The first in this line of prophets, Amos, lived in the mid-eighth century. During his lifetime, the northern kingdom, to which he primarily directed his words, still enjoyed peace and prosperity. Landed estates expanded; costly homes were built; religious shrines were richly endowed; and the arts flourished. To Amos, however, the scrupulous insistence on religious rites, which was characteristic of the period, masked wholesale immorality: sexual liberty, oppression of the poor, bribery of judges, and corruption in government and business. Amos's emphasis on the spirit rather than the letter of religion and his burning sense of social justice also characterized the prophets who followed him.

AMOS

CHAPTER 5

. . .

10 They hate him that reproveth in the gate, and they abhor him that speaketh uprightly.

11 Forasmuch therefore as ye trample upon the poor, and take exactions from him of wheat: ye have built houses of hewn stone, but ye shall not dwell in them: ye have planted pleasant vineyards, but ye shall not drink the wine thereof.

12 For I know how manifold are your transgressions, and how mighty are your sins—ye that afflict the just, that take a bribe, and that turn aside the needy in the gate from their right.

13 Therefore he that is prudent shall keep silence in such a time; for it is an evil time.

14 Seek good, and not evil, that ye may live; and so Jehovah, the God of hosts, will be with you, as ye say.

15 Hate the evil, and love the good, and establish justice in the gate: it may be that Jehovah, the God of hosts, will be gracious unto the remnant of Joseph.

16 Therefore thus saith Jehovah, the God of hosts, the Lord: Wailing shall be in all the broad ways; and they shall say in all the streets, Alas! alas! and they shall call the husbandman to mourning, and such as are skilful in lamentation to wailing.

17 And in all vineyards shall be wailing; for I will pass through the midst of thee, saith Jehovah.

18 Woe unto you that desire the day of Jehovah! Wherefore would ye have the day of Jehovah? It is darkness, and not light.

19 As if a man did flee from a lion, and a bear met him; or went into the house and leaned his hand on the wall, and a serpent bit him.

20 Shall not the day of Jehovah be darkness, and not light? even very dark, and no brightness in it?

21 I hate, I despise your feasts, and I will take no delight in your solemn assemblies.

22 Yea, though ye offer me your burnt-offerings and meal-offerings, I will not accept them; neither will I regard the peace-offerings of your fat beasts.

23 Take thou away from me the noise of thy songs; for I will not hear the melody of thy viols.

24 But let justice roll down as waters, and righteousness as a mighty stream.

QUESTIONS

1. How does Amos expect his prophesy to be received? What does the prudent man say in such dangerous times?
2. What is meant in verse 12 when the poor in the gate are said to be turned aside "from their right"? What does "the gate" refer to here and elsewhere in this selection?
3. Why will the Lord not accept the sacrifices and prayers of His people?
4. What threats does Amos make?

The Song of Songs　Hebraic literature has greatly influenced our culture, primarily through the religious views that are developed in it and, along with them, a concept of morality. One book of the Bible, however, has been influential in quite different ways and represents a unique form of biblical literature. This is the Song of Songs, called in the King James Bible the Song of Solomon. Its authorship is unknown, but because of King Solomon's reputation for wisdom and poetic gifts, it was attributed to him. It is unique in the Bible in that God is never mentioned in it. What it appears to be is a passionate love poem, or more likely several love lyrics that were at some point (scholars speculate by the fifth century B.C.) collected together. Sometimes the speaker is the lover, or bridegroom, sometimes the beloved, or bride. In the course of the poems they are united, separated, sought by each other, found. The awakening of love is closely allied with the awakening of nature in springtime. The lovers celebrate each other's physical beauty and the marvel of being in love, all with a direct and sensuous imagery.

One may well ask how such a poem found its way into a collection of sacred scripture. No one has the definitive answer to this question, but it has puzzled scholars for centuries. Both Jewish and Christian commentators have attempted to explain away its sensuous, physical aspects by *allegorical* interpretations. In the Jewish tradition, the lover was said to represent Jahweh and the beloved his people, Israel. In the Christian version of the *allegory*, the lover becomes Christ; the beloved, his church. This allegorical way of thinking came to be of great importance to the medieval Christian mentality, as we shall discover in later chapters.

More recent scholars believe that the poems in the Song of Songs are what they appear to be—celebrations of human love. They were probably originally folk poems, and they may have been sung at weddings. In any case, they have become a part of our lyric tradition and have influenced the ways in which we express love between man and woman.

The Song of Songs

CHAPTER 1

1 The Song of songs, which is Solomon's.

2 Let him kiss me with the kisses of his mouth: for thy love is better than wine.

3 Because of the savour of thy good ointments thy name is as ointment poured forth, therefore do the virgins love thee.

4 Draw me, we will run after thee: the King hath brought me into his chambers: we will be glad and rejoice in thee, we will remember thy love more than wine: the upright love thee.

5 I am black, but comely, O ye daughters of Jerusalem, as the tents of Kedar, as the curtains of Solomon.

6 Look not upon me, because I am black, because the sun hath looked upon me: my mother's children were angry with me; they made me the keeper of the vineyards; but mine own vineyard have I not kept.

7 Tell me, O thou whom my soul loveth, where thou feedest, where thou makest thy flock to rest at noon: for why should I be as one that turneth aside by the flocks of thy companions?

8 If thou know not, O thou fairest among women, go thy way forth by the footsteps of the flock, and feed thy kids beside the shepherds' tents.

9 I have compared thee, O my love, to a company of horses in Pharaoh's chariots.

10 Thy cheeks are comely with rows of jewels, thy neck with chains of gold.

11 We will make thee borders of gold with studs of silver.

12 While the King sitteth at his table, my spikenard sendeth forth the smell thereof.

13 A bundle of myrrh is my well beloved unto me; he shall lie all night betwixt my breasts.

14 My beloved is unto me as a cluster of camphire in the vineyards of Engedi.

15 Behold, thou art fair, my love; behold, thou art fair; thou hast doves' eyes.

16 Behold, thou art fair, my beloved, yea, pleasant: also our bed is green.

17 The beams of our house are cedar, and our rafters of fir.

CHAPTER 2

1 I am the rose of Sharon, and the lily of the valleys.

2 As the lily among thorns, so is my love among the daughters.

3 As the apple tree among the trees of the wood, so is my beloved among the sons. I sat down under his shadow with great delight, and his fruit was sweet to my taste.

4 He brought me to the banqueting house, and his banner over me was love.

5 Stay me with flagons, comfort me with apples: for I am sick of love.

6 His left hand is under my head, and his right hand doth embrace me.

7 I charge you, O ye daughters of Jerusalem, by the roes, and by the hinds of the field, that ye stir not up, nor awake my love, till he please.

8 The voice of my beloved! behold, he cometh leaping upon the mountains, skipping upon the hills.

9 My beloved is like a roe or a young hart: behold, he standeth behind our wall, he looketh forth at the windows, shewing himself through the lattice.

10 My beloved spake, and said unto me, Rise up, my love, my fair one, and come away.

11 For, lo, the winter is past, the rain is over and gone;

12 The flowers appear on the earth; the time of the singing of birds is come, and the voice of the turtle is heard in our land;

13 The fig tree putteth forth her green figs, and the vines with the tender grape give a good smell. Arise, my love, my fair one, and come away.

14 O my dove, that art in the clefts of the rock, in the secret places of the stairs, let me see thy countenance, let me hear thy voice; for sweet is thy voice, and thy countenance is comely.

15 Take us the foxes, the little foxes, that spoil the vines: for our vines have tender grapes.

16 My beloved is mine, and I am his: he feedeth among the lilies.

17 Until the day break, and the shadows flee away, turn, my beloved, and be thou like a roe or a young hart upon the mountains of Bether.

COMMENTS AND QUESTIONS

1. The best known, most often quoted part of this poem is in Chapter 2, verses 10–17. How would you explain its appeal?
2. The association between love and spring is, of course, by now an overworked cliché. Is the statement made here nevertheless still fresh and powerful?
3. Compare these love lyrics with those of Sappho (Chapter 1). Which is richer in imagery? If you were to paint your impressions of them, which would have more color and more varied *textures?*
4. How would you describe the relationship between man and woman as it appears in these two chapters of the Song of Songs?
5. Do you see any justification for the Jewish or the Christian allegorical interpretations?

There are many other types of biblical literature that we do not have space to represent here. The book of Job, which deals with human suffering in a way similar to Greek tragedy but in an Hebraic context, makes an interesting comparison with *Oedipus.* The "wisdom" literature, such as the books of Proverbs and Ecclesiastes, has been influential throughout the Western tradition. For Christianity the most important books of the Old Testment were those of the prophets (see for example Isaiah 11), who predicted that from the house of David would come the Messiah, or Savior, who would redeem Israel and bring about an era of peace and justice on earth. It is this promise that the followers of Jesus of Nazareth found that their leader fulfilled. The hope of a Messiah yet to come, however, still remains at the core of Judaism.

Early Christianity

Jesus of Nazareth was born during the age of the Emperor Augustus. Nazareth was a part of Judea, a Roman province ruled over by a Roman governor; but Judea was also the kingdom of the Jews and had a Jewish king, Herod. The followers of Jesus were all Jews and did not intend to establish a separate religion but to carry out a radical reform of Judaism. Not only did they view him as the Messiah prophesied to redeem Israel, they also wanted to extend the message of salvation beyond God's chosen people to all mankind.

After Jesus' crucifixion his disciples became an active sect in Jerusalem among their fellow Jews. It was Saint Paul, a convert to the sect of Jesus, who spread the word of the resurrected Christ (a Greek word meaning "anointed") throughout the Greek-speaking world. Coming to Rome in 60 A.D., Paul had much success there. The followers of Jesus, who now included more non-Jews than Jews, were by this time called Christians, after the name of their founder. In 64 A.D. much of Rome was destroyed by fire. The emperor,

Nero, may have set it himself (to clear large areas in the center city where he intended to build a new palace complex); but he blamed the destruction on the Christians, whom he accused of "hatred of the human race." Christianity then became illegal and went underground. The Christians were accused of disloyalty to the emperor; of refusing to worship the state gods; of practicing incest, black magic, and cannibalism ("eating" their god in the communion rite); and of generally causing all sorts of misfortunes. The Roman persecution of Christian martyrs is well known, especially in its popular film versions. To be Christian in Rome was to be an antiestablishment, radical member of an underground organization—to risk imprisonment or death. If this was so, why did Christianity appeal to so many people and spread so rapidly? To answer this question is also to determine why the Christians were so easily marked out for harassment by the Roman authorities, who were usually tolerant of religious differences.

Official Roman religion at the time that the Christian message was being spread was fairly similar to the Greek religion. Generally, while adding a few state gods of their own, the Romans simply took over most of the Greek gods, giving them Latin names. Like the Greek gods and goddesses, the Roman ones were blown-up people who had their favorites among mortals and their sexual adventures. To have a happy love affair, an easy childbirth, a safe trip, or a good business deal, one might pray for help to one god or another but would not expect much more of them. The average lower-class person, for example, would not get any help from the gods at the hour of death. The pagan Greeks and Romans believed in something resembling a heaven called the Elysian Fields—a sort of happy hunting ground—but it was off-limits for the lower classes. The slave or former slave (freedman) could only hope to cross a dark river and then, as a shade, to wander eternally in the kingdom of the dead. This kind of religion had obviously satisfied the Romans for hundreds of years, but already in the last century of the Roman Republic before the advent of Caesar Augustus a change in religious interests was beginning to take place.

The change occurring in Greek religious and philosophical thought from the third century B.C. on has already been noted. The spread of Greek culture to the East was balanced by a gradual penetration of Eastern mystery religions into Europe. These religions extended to their adherents hope for a personal immortality beyond the grave and tended to deemphasize the importance of success in this earthly life. Philosophies too, like Stoicism, increasingly came to look on God not merely as some kind of principle of rationality needed to explain the nature of the world as it was but also as a personality who exercised a providential power over man's destiny.

By the reign of Augustus, while the official religion remained centered on the pagan gods, this same movement was well underway in the western half of the Roman empire as well. It affected men and women at all levels of society. Large numbers of Romans were rejecting the classical ethos that death in the service of the motherland was the highest moral end of the citizen. Even members of the upper class began to regard the state as a primarily negative force designed to keep order so that men could go about their central task of finding spiritual fulfillment in religious worship or philosophical contemplation of a divine being who promised individual salvation.

With so many mystery religions to choose from, like the worship of the "Great Mother" Isis or Persian Mithraism, why did Christianity prove so attractive to so many and ultimately triumph over its competitors? The Christians saw in their victory the vindication of their claims to be the true religion, but there are obvious historical explanations for the rapid growth of the sect and the intensive persecution of its members.

Of the Eastern mystery religions only Christianity was exclusive. Adherents to Isis, Mithras, or Cybele could belong to cults worshiping these gods and at the same time sacrifice to the gods of Rome. Christians forbade any worship of other gods. More than this, they condemned all other religions as sinful and inferior. Thus, while they offered their membership eternal life, Christians also claimed that theirs was the only way to heaven. This exclusiveness must have attracted many, while it made enemies of others who could not understand Christian intolerance.

In a sense the Christians were like the Jews in their unwillingness to participate in public religious ceremonies and to take an oath of loyalty to the emperor. But Judaism was an established religion with a limited potential for membership. Christians by contrast were bursting with missionary zeal. They claimed that the souls of all, whether slave or free, Jew or Gentile, man or woman, were equal in God's sight. This message of equality, love, and charity had a tremendous attraction, especially among the poor and enslaved.

That Christianity welcome all to its membership was not the intention of many of the leaders of the movement in the decades immediately following Jesus' death. A powerful group centered at Jerusalem fervently believed that proselytizing should be limited only to Jews or to those who were willing to convert to Judaism, accepting circumcision along with the other rules of the faith. Opposed to this position was Saul of Tarsus, whose Roman name was Paul.

Raised in a strict orthodox Jewish family in apparently comfortable circumstances—his father was a Roman citizen—Paul initially viewed the Christians as dangerous fanatics bent on destroying Judaism, and he joined in their persecution. Then, about 35 A.D., during a journey to Jerusalem on an errand of persecution, he had a vision in which Jesus called him to His service. Transformed by the experience, Paul became an ardent Christian and for the rest of his life devoted himself to missionary work, founding churches all over the eastern half of the Roman Empire.

To the converted Paul, Jesus had died for everyone and Christians enjoyed a freedom from all laws, including those of Judaism. "All things," he wrote to the church at Corinth (I Cor. 6:12), "are lawful for me," and, in I Cor. 2:15, "But he that is spiritual judgeth all things, and he himself is judged of no man." Paul was in no way proclaiming absolute license. Rather, he believed that one who had Jesus for lord would of his own accord do what was right, and that adherence to elaborate dietary practices and other rituals had no spiritual value for the believer.

Despite a number of efforts on both sides to reach a reconciliation that would allow Paul to continue his missionary work among the Gentiles and also allow the Jerusalem congregation to proselytize Jews exclusively, the issue was never settled in Paul's lifetime. Nevertheless, Paul's universalistic interpretation quickly triumphed throughout the empire, and Christianity emerged as a religion in its own right rather than as a sect of Judaism.

However, because of its broad appeal, Christianity appeared to pose a menace to Roman authority. Rome was a society founded on the institution of slavery; its upper classes could never forget the horrors of the great slave revolt of Spartacus, in the last century of the Republic, that had threatened to incite slaves throughout Italy to murder their masters. If mere yokels—workers and slaves—became preoccupied with the personal salvation of their souls and believed that they possessed truth through their religion, would this not endanger their obedience to their masters and thus endanger the whole structure of Roman society? The new religion must be destroyed. But the more the state persecuted, the more the faith grew.

With the growth of that faith we find the first stirrings of an art that gives expression to the central ideas of the movement. Unlike the Greeks and Romans, or the Jews with their synagogues, the early Christians had no specific building or architectural setting for their celebrations. Without money or power, all they had was their sense of separateness and community within the great world. They met then in homes or rented rooms; but, as persecution grew, it became necessary to seek a safer place for the celebration of the Eucharist (Holy Communion)—the central rite that affirmed fellowship and God's presence among men.

Outside Rome were underground chambers for burial; in these catacombs the Christians met in secret. The walls were decorated with paintings that tell stories from the Old and New Testaments, especially about miracles, persecutions, and Christ's saving grace. The painting reproduced here (Fig. 6-1) shows Christ as the Good Shepherd. What is the motive behind this representation? Compare the figure with other male figures that we have seen. Is he like an emperor or more like a young athlete? This person, the Good Shepherd, who "lays down" his life for his sheep is the same Christ who speaks in the Sermon on the Mount, the New Testament text that best introduces the Christian message.

MATTHEW

The Sermon on the Mount

CHAPTER 5

1 And seeing the multitudes, he went up into a mountain: and when he was set, his disciples came unto him:

2 And he opened his mouth, and taught them, saying,

3 Blessed are the poor in spirit: for theirs is the kingdom of heaven.

4 Blessed are they that mourn: for they shall be comforted.

5 Blessed are the meek: for they shall inherit the earth.

6 Blessed are they which do hunger and thirst after righteousness: for they shall be filled.

7 Blessed are the merciful: for they shall obtain mercy.

8 Blessed are the pure in heart: for they shall see God.

9 Blessed are the peacemakers: for they shall be called the children of God.

10 Blessed are they which are persecuted for righteousness' sake: for theirs is the kingdom of heaven.

11 Blessed are ye, when men shall revile you, and persecute you, and shall say all manner of evil against you falsely, for my sake.

12 Rejoice, and be exceeding glad: for great is your reward in heaven: for so persecuted they the prophets which were before you.

13 Ye are the salt of the earth: but if the salt have lost his savour, wherewith shall it be salted? it is thenceforth good for nothing, but to be cast out, and to be trodden under foot of men.

14 Ye are the light of the world. A city that is set on an hill cannot be hid.

15 Neither do men light a candle, and put it under a bushel, but on a candlestick; and it giveth light unto all that are in the house.

16 Let your light so shine before men, that they may see your good works, and glorify your Father which is in heaven.

17 Think not that I am come to destroy the law, or the prophets: I am not come to destroy, but to fulfill.

18 For verily I say unto you, Till heaven and earth pass, one jot or one tittle shall in no wise pass from the law, till all be fulfilled.

19 Whosoever therefore shall break one of these least commandments, and shall teach men so, he shall be called the least in the kingdom of heaven: but whosoever shall do and teach them, the same shall be called great in the kingdom of heaven.

20 For I say unto you, That except your righteousness shall exceed the righteousness of the scribes and Pharisees, ye shall in no case enter into the kingdom of heaven.

21 Ye have heard that it was said by them of old time, Thou shalt not kill; and whosoever shall kill shall be in danger of the judgment:

22 But I say unto you, That whosoever is angry with his brother without a cause shall be in danger of the judgment: and whosoever shall say to his brother, Raca, shall be in danger of the council: but whosoever shall say, Thou fool, shall be in danger of hell fire.

23 Therefore if thou bring thy gift to the altar, and there rememberest that thy brother hath ought against thee;

24 Leave there thy gift before the altar, and go thy way; first be reconciled to thy brother, and then come and offer thy gift.

25 Agree with thine adversary quickly, whiles thou art in the way with him; lest at any time the adversary

6–1 "The Good Shepherd." Catacomb of St. Callixtus, Rome. (Hirmer Fotoarchiv München)

deliver thee to the judge, and the judge deliver thee to the officer, and thou be cast into prison.

26 Verily I say unto thee, Thou shalt by no means come out thence, till thou hast paid the uttermost farthing.

27 Ye have heard that it was said by them of old time, Thou shalt not commit adultery:

28 But I say unto you, That whosoever looketh on a woman to lust after her hath committed adultery with her already in his heart.

29 And if thy right eye offend thee, pluck it out, and cast it from thee: for it is profitable for thee that one of thy members should perish, and not that thy whole body should be cast into hell.

30 And if thy right hand offend thee, cut it off, and cast it from thee: for it is profitable for thee that one of thy members should perish, and not that thy whole body should be cast into hell.

31 It hath been said, Whosoever shall put away his wife, let him give her a writing of divorcement:

32 But I say unto you, That whosoever shall put away his wife, saving for the cause of fornication, causeth her to commit adultery: and whosoever shall marry her that is divorced committeth adultery.

33 Again, ye have heard that it hath been said by them of old time, Thou shalt not forswear thyself, but shalt perform unto the Lord thine oaths:

34 But I say unto you, Swear not at all; neither by heaven; for it is God's throne:

35 Nor by the earth; for it is his footstool: neither by Jerusalem; for it is the city of the great King.

36 Neither shalt thou swear by thy head, because thou canst not make one hair white or black.

37 But let your communication be, Yea, yea; Nay, nay: for whatsoever is more than these cometh of evil.

38 Ye have heard that it hath been said, An eye for an eye, and a tooth for a tooth:

39 But I say unto you, That ye resist not evil: but whosoever shall smite thee on thy right cheek, turn to him the other also.

40 And if any man will sue thee at the law, and take away thy coat, let him have thy cloke also.

41 And whosoever shall compel thee to go a mile, go with him twain.

42 Give to him that asketh thee, and from him that would borrow of thee turn not thou away.

43 Ye have heard that it hath been said, Thou shalt love thy neighbour, and hate thine enemy.

44 But I say unto you, Love your enemies, bless them that curse you, do good to them that hate you, and pray for them which despitefully use you, and persecute you;

45 That ye may be the children of your Father which is in heaven: for he maketh his sun to rise on the evil and on the good, and sendeth rain on the just and on the unjust.

46 For if ye love them which love you, what reward have ye? do not even the publicans the same?

47 And if ye salute your brethren only, what do ye more than others? do not even the publicans so?

48 Be ye therefore perfect, even as your Father which is in heaven is perfect.

CHAPTER 6

1 Take heed that ye do not your alms before men, to be seen of them: otherwise ye have no reward of your Father which is in heaven.

2 Therefore when thou doest thine alms, do not sound a trumpet before thee, as the hypocrites do in the synagogues and in the streets, that they may have glory of men. Verily I say unto you, They have their reward.

3 But when thou doest alms, let not thy left hand know what thy right hand doeth:

4 That thine alms may be in secret: and thy Father which seeth in secret himself shall reward thee openly.

5 And when thou prayest, thou shalt not be as the hypocrites are: for they love to pray standing in the synagogues and in the corners of the streets, that they may be seen of men. Verily I say unto you, They have their reward.

6 But thou, when thou prayest, enter into thy closet, and when thou hast shut thy door, pray to thy Father which is in secret; and thy Father which seeth in secret shall reward thee openly.

7 But when ye pray, use not vain repetitions, as the heathen do: for they think that they shall be heard for their much speaking.

8 Be not ye therefore like unto them: for your Father knoweth what things ye have need of, before ye ask him.

9 After this manner therefore pray ye: Our Father which art in heaven, Hallowed be thy name.

10 Thy kingdom come. Thy will be done in earth, as it is in heaven.

11 Give us this day our daily bread.

12 And forgive us our debts, as we forgive our debtors.

13 And lead us not into temptation, but deliver us from evil: For thine is the kingdom, and the power, and the glory, for ever. Amen.

14 For if ye forgive men their trespasses, your heavenly Father will also forgive you:

15 But if ye forgive not men their trespasses, neither will your Father forgive your trespasses.

16 Moreover when ye fast, be not, as the hypocrites, of a sad countenance: for they disfigure their faces, that they may appear unto men to fast. Verily I say unto you, They have their reward.

17 But thou, when thou fastest, anoint thine head, and wash thy face;

18 That thou appear not unto men to fast, but unto thy Father which is in secret: and thy Father, which seeth in secret, shall reward thee openly.

19 Lay not up for yourselves treasures upon earth, where moth and rust doth corrupt, and where thieves break through and steal:

20 But lay up for yourselves treasures in heaven, where neither moth nor rust doth corrupt, and where thieves do not break through nor steal:

21 For where your treasure is, there will your heart be also.

22 The light of the body is the eye: if therefore thine eye be single, thy whole body shall be full of light.

23 But if thine eye be evil, thy whole body shall be full of darkness. If therefore the light that is in thee be darkness, how great is that darkness!

24 No man can serve two masters: for either he will hate the one, and love the other; or else he will hold to the one, and despise the other. Ye cannot serve God and mammon.

25 Therefore I say unto you, Take no thought for your life, what ye shall eat, or what ye shall drink; nor yet for your body, what ye shall put on. Is not the life more than meat, and the body than raiment?

26 Behold the fowls of the air: for they sow not, neither do they reap, nor gather into barns; yet your heavenly Father feedeth them. Are ye not much better than they?

27 Which of you by taking thought can add one cubit unto his stature?

28 And why take ye thought for raiment? Consider the lilies of the field, how they grow; they toil not, neither do they spin:

29 And yet I say unto you, That even Solomon in all his glory was not arrayed like one of these.

30 Wherefore, if God so clothe the grass of the field, which to day is, and to morrow is cast into the oven, shall he not much more clothe you, O ye of little faith?

31 Therefore take no thought, saying, What shall we eat? or, What shall we drink? or, Wherewithal shall we be clothed?

32 For after all these things do the Gentiles seek: for your heavenly Father knoweth that ye have need of all these things.

33 But seek ye first the kingdom of God, and his righteousness; and all these things shall be added unto you.

34 Take therefore no thought for the morrow: for the morrow shall take thought for the things of itself. Sufficient unto the day is the evil thereof.

CHAPTER 7

1 Judge not, that ye be not judged.

2 For with what judgment ye judge, ye shall be judged: and with what measure ye mete, it shall be measured to you again.

3 And why beholdest thou the mote that is in thy brother's eye, but considerest not the beam that is in thine own eye?

4 Or how wilt thou say to thy brother, Let me pull out the mote out of thine eye; and, behold, a beam is in thine own eye?

5 Thou hypocrite, first cast out the beam out of thine own eye; and then shalt thou see clearly to cast out the mote out of thy brother's eye.

6 Give not that which is holy unto the dogs, neither cast ye your pearls before swine, lest they trample them under their feet, and turn again and rend you.

7 Ask, and it shall be given you; seek, and ye shall find; knock, and it shall be opened unto you:

8 For every one that asketh receiveth; and he that

seeketh findeth; and to him that knocketh it shall be opened.

9 Or what man is there of you, whom if his son ask bread, will he give him a stone?

10 Or if he ask a fish, will he give him a serpent?

11 If ye then, being evil, know how to give good gifts unto your children, how much more shall your Father which is in heaven give good things to them that ask him?

12 Therefore all things whatsoever ye would that men should do to you, do ye even so to them: for this is the law and the prophets.

13 Enter ye in at the strait gate: for wide is the gate, and broad is the way, that leadeth to destruction, and many there be which go in thereat:

14 Because strait is the gate, and narrow is the way, which leadeth unto life, and few there be that find it.

15 Beware of false prophets, which come to you in sheep's clothing, but inwardly they are ravening wolves.

16 Ye shall know them by their fruits. Do men gather grapes of thorns, or figs of thistles?

17 Even so every good tree bringeth forth good fruit; but a corrupt tree bringeth forth evil fruit.

18 A good tree cannot bring forth evil fruit, neither can a corrupt tree bring forth good fruit.

19 Every tree that bringeth not forth good fruit is hewn down, and cast into the fire.

20 Wherefore by their fruits ye shall know them.

21 Not every one that saith unto me, Lord, Lord, shall enter into the kingdom of heaven; but he that doeth the will of my Father which is in heaven.

22 Many will say to me in that day, Lord, Lord, have we not prophesied in thy name? and in thy name have cast out devils? and in thy name done many wonderful works?

23 And then will I profess unto them, I never knew you: depart from me, ye that work iniquity.

24 Therefore whosoever heareth these sayings of mine, and doeth them, I will liken him unto a wise man, which built his house upon a rock:

25 And the rain descended, and the floods came, and the winds blew, and beat upon that house; and it fell not: for it was founded upon a rock.

26 And every one that heareth these sayings of mine, and doeth them not, shall be likened unto a foolish man, which built his house upon the sand:

27 And the rain descended, and the floods came, and the winds blew, and beat upon that house; and it fell: and great was the fall of it.

28 And it came to pass, when Jesus had ended these sayings, the people were astonished at his doctrine:

29 For he taught them as one having authority, and not as the scribes.

QUESTIONS

1. What does Jesus demand of his followers, and what does he promise?
2. What kind of a leader, what kind of personality, is Jesus?
3. Why do you think he speaks in parables and "similitudes"? What is the effect of the comparisons made?
4. To what extent does Jesus, in his views, reject the Jewish heritage?

Paul has frequently been referred to as the founder of Christian theology. His mind well-trained in Jewish law and clearly influenced by late Hellenistic culture, Paul was sure to offer a highly developed interpretation of what came to him as the simple faith of primitive Christianity. His emphasis on the central significance of Christ's death and resurrection for human salvation was doubtless original. By nature children of Adam, we share in the heritage of sin. We are Christ's, on the other hand, by adoption—a concept of Roman Law— and thereby share in God's kingdom. Through the suffering and death of Christ, man's sins are forgiven, and the belief in that redemptive act becomes the source for a new life of love: "Far be it from me to glory save in the Cross of our Lord Jesus Christ" (Gal. 6:10). Christ's resurrection, moreover, is proof that Jesus was God's own son and that we, as believers, after leading a rich spiritual life, will also live eternally in paradise. Thus Paul proclaims (I Cor. 2:2): "For I decided to know nothing . . . except Jesus Christ and Him crucified."

Paul declares emphatically that no one has a *right* to become a child of Christ. Adoption is a gift of God, that is, an act of divine grace. God decides on whom he will bestow the privilege. The condition for the reception of grace is faith. As Paul writes (Rom. 10:2): "If thou shalt confess with thy mouth Jesus as Lord, and shalt believe in thy heart that God raised Him from the dead, thou shalt be saved." The essence of Christian life, therefore, lies in a vital, personal relationship between man and Christ. For Paul, Christ, the Son of God, is his Lord and Redeemer.

SAINT PAUL

Letter to the Ephesians

CHAPTER 2

1 And you did he make live when ye were dead through your trespasses and sins,

2, wherein ye once walked according to the course of this world, according to the prince of the powers of the air, of the spirit that now worketh in the sons of disobedience;

3 among whom we also all once lived in the lusts of our flesh, doing the desires of the flesh and of the mind, and were by nature children of wrath, even as the rest:

4 but God, being rich in mercy, for his great love wherewith he loved us,

5 even when we were dead through our trespasses, made us alive together with Christ (by grace have ye been saved),

6 and raised us up with him, and made us to sit with him in the heavenly places, in Christ Jesus:

7 that in the ages to come he might show the exceeding riches of this grace in kindness toward us in Christ Jesus:

8 for by grace have ye been saved through faith; and that not of yourselves, it is the gift of God;

9 not of works, that no man should glory.

10 For we are his workmanship, created in Christ Jesus for good works, which God afore prepared that we should walk in them.

11 Wherefore remember, that once ye, the Gentiles in the flesh, who are called Uncircumcision by that which is called Circumcision, in the flesh, made by hands;

12 that ye were at that time separate from Christ, alienated from the commonwealth of Israel, and strangers from the covenants of the promise, having no hope and without God in the world.

13 But now in Christ Jesus ye that once were far off are made nigh in the blood of Christ.

14 For his is our peace, who made both one, and brake down the middle wall of partition,

15 having abolished in his flesh the enmity, even the law of commandments contained in ordinances; that he might create in himself of the two one new man, so making peace;

16 and might reconcile them both in one body unto God through the cross, having slain the enmity thereby:

17 and he came and preached peace to you that were far off, and peace to them that were nigh:

18 for through him we both have our access in one Spirit unto the Father.

19 So then ye are no more strangers and sojourners, but ye are fellow-citizens with the saints, and of the household of God,

20 being built upon the foundation of the apostles and prophets, Christ Jesus himself being the chief corner stone;

21 in whom each several building, fitly framed together, groweth into a holy temple in the Lord;

22 in whom ye also are builded together for a habitation of God in the Spirit.

CHAPTER 3

1 For this cause I Paul, the prisoner of Christ Jesus in behalf of you Gentiles,

2 if so be that ye have heard of the dispensation of that grace of God which was given me to you-ward;

3 how that by revelation was made known unto me the mystery, as I wrote before in few words,

4 whereby, when ye read, ye can perceive my understanding in the mystery of Christ;

5 which in other generations was not made known unto the sons of men, as it hath now been revealed unto his holy apostles and prophets in the Spirit;

6 to wit, that the Gentiles are fellow-heirs, and fellow-members of the body, and fellow-partakers of the promise in Christ Jesus through the gospel,

7 whereof I was made a minister, according to the gift of that grace of God which was given me according to the working of his power.

8 Unto me, who am less than the least of all saints, was this grace given, to preach unto the Gentiles the unsearchable riches of Christ;

9 and to make all men see what is the dispensation of the mystery which for ages hath been hid in God who created all things;

10 to the intent that now unto the principalities and the powers in the heavenly places might be made known through the church the manifold wisdom of God,

11 according to the eternal purpose which he purposed in Christ Jesus our Lord:

12 in whom we have boldness and access in confidence through our faith in him.

QUESTIONS

1. How does Paul characterize the life of the individual before coming to Christ?
2. For what motive did God give us eternal life?
3. The Church of Ephesus in Asia Minor was composed primarily of Gentiles. How did they become, according to Paul, one with the commonwealth of Israel? That is, how was peace established between Jew and Gentile?
4. How did Christ abolish the "law of commandments and ordinances"?

At the center of the new spiritual life of the Christian is love. In the following passage from I Cor. 12–13, Paul strikingly dramatizes the emphasis Christ placed on the love toward God and one's neighbor that he expected from his followers.

SAINT PAUL

First Letter to the Corinthians

CHAPTER 13

1 If I speak with the tongues of men and of angels, but have not love, I am become sounding brass, or a clanging cymbal.

2 And if I have the gift of prophecy, and know all mysteries and all knowledge; and if I have all faith, so as to remove mountains, but have not love, I am nothing.

3 And if I bestow all my goods to feed the poor, and if I give my body to be burned, but have not love, it profiteth me nothing.

4 Love suffereth long, and is kind; love envieth not; love vaunteth not itself, is not puffed up,

5 doth not behave itself unseemly; seeketh not its own, is not provoked, taketh not account of evil;

6 rejoiceth not in unrighteousness, but rejoiceth with the truth;

7 beareth all things, believeth all things, hopeth all things, endureth all things.

8 Love never faileth: but whether there be prophecies, they shall be done away; whether there be tongues, they shall cease; whether there be knowledge, it shall be done away.

9 For we know in part, and we prophesy in part;

10 but when that which is perfect is come, that which is in part shall be done away.

11 When I was a child, I spake as a child, I felt as a child, I thought as a child: now that I am become a man, I have put away childish things.

12 For now we see in a mirror, darkly; but then face to face: now I know in part; but then shall I know fully even as also I was fully known.

13 But now abideth faith, hope, love, these three; and the greatest of these is love.

QUESTIONS

1. Why are the power of tongues, prophetic powers, faith, and self-denial nothing without love?
2. What does Paul mean when he writes: "When I was a child, I spake as a child?"

The End of Antiquity

While Christianity grew ever stronger in the first three centuries after the death of its founder, the Roman empire itself in the third century began a rapid decline. The middle half of the century saw almost continuous civil war between at least fifty claimants to the imperial throne.

The decline of Rome was temporarily halted in the last quarter of the century by a number of strong emperors who, through a series of reforms and careful management of resources, kept the empire together for another hundred years. However, the move of the capital from Rome to Constantinople by Emperor Constantine (280?–337) indicates the displacement of political and economic power from the western to the eastern half of the empire by the fourth century.

Foundation of the Christian Church   Given the divisive tendencies at work in the empire in the third century, the conversion of Emperor Constantine to Christianity in the early fourth century strikes the observer as politically opportune. In the three hundred years of its growth the Church under the pressure of persecution had created a kind of state within a state. Christians settled disputes among themselves within the Christian community; treasuries were created for the purposes of providing for the poor, orphans, and widows. By A.D. 200 almost every major city in the empire had its bishop and its body of priests, chosen by the community. From this time as well, the bishop of Rome, the Roman pope, asserted his claim to be the spiritual leader of the whole church. His claim rested on the scriptural passage in which Christ tells Peter, his disciple:

> Thou art Peter . . . and upon this rock I will build my church; and the gates of hell shall not prevail against it. And I will give unto thee the keys of the Kingdom of heaven; and whatsoever thou shalt bind on earth shall be bound in heaven; and whatsoever thou shalt loose on earth shall be loosed in heaven. (Matthew 16:18–19)

Saint Peter was believed to have been the first bishop of Rome; as a result, his successors in that office were thought to have inherited this power of binding and loosing men's souls on earth and in heaven. Although these claims were hotly disputed, especially by bishops in the eastern half of the empire, by the fourth century the leadership of Rome was generally recognized in the western portion.

At the time of Constantine's conversion, only about 10 percent of the population in the Roman empire, most of them city dwellers, were Christian. Constantine and his successors were able to support the failing imperial machine with the vital, dynamic organization of the Christian Church. From the beginning the emperors looked on the Church as another branch of the imperial government. They influenced the election of

bishops and even that of the pope himself. Clerics were treated as public officials, and the emperors drew on the various Church treasures when the need arose. Thus Christianity developed into something totally different from its beginnings: from an underground sect it became a state religion.

The First Church Buildings   The alliance of Christianity with the state is immediately evident in the appearance of churches–specific complexes for the preaching, teaching, and propagation of the faith. Old Saint Peter's in Rome (Fig. 6-2) was built in the early fourth century (333). Archaeological reconstructions show us a complex of buildings—a great gate, an open courtyard, a roofed porch (narthex), and then the church itself—a large simple building with a central space, the nave, for the congregation. Parallel to the nave on each side are two passageways, aisles. These reinforce the directional quality of the nave that focuses on the altar at the east end, supposedly placed above the bones of Saint Peter. Columns separating the nave and aisles support the roof and walls rising above. The roofs of the aisles do not rise the full height of the nave so that there is a story left free for windows before we reach the combinations of beams called trusses of the roof. These windows, in what is called the clerestory, provided light. Candles and lamps were used for night services.

Before the east end is reached, another space crosses the nave at right angles. The transept was for the pulpit

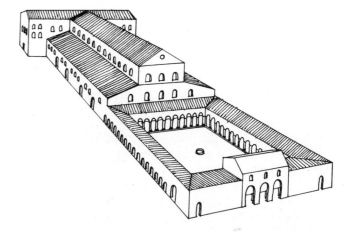

6–2   Reconstruction of Old St. Peter's, Rome.

and separated the nave from the altar. The semicircular east end, called the *apse*, had a half-dome above it. The clerics and the bishop would sit here during services.

In addition to the church and courtyard there was a round building called a *baptistery*. Walls were probably painted with stories like those of the catacombs. The exterior would have been fairly plain since the significant events took place in the interior space.

Compare this building plan (Fig. 6-3) with that of a Roman basilica (Fig. 5-15). How are they different? Why do you think the law court plan might have been a source for this kind of building? What is particularly Greek? Roman?

Early Christian Sculpture Other important monuments that document the spread and power of Christianity are the numerous *sarcophagi* (caskets) that were found in Rome and in other Christian sites. Decorated with scenes from the Christian story, they emphasize the importance of its association with life,

death, and afterlife. An excellent example is the sarcophagus of Junius Bassus, a Roman noble (Fig. 6-4). Along the side represented here we see scenes that will appear again and again in Christian art.

The sarcophagus is divided into two registers or rows with five scenes each; each scene is separated by a column giving each a strong architectural framework. In the top register from left to right are the sacrifice of Isaac; Saint Peter taken prisoner; Christ enthroned between Saint Peter and Saint Paul; and Christ before Pontius Pilate (the last two scenes). In the bottom register we see Job and his comforters; Adam, Eve, and the serpent (the Fall of Man); Christ's entry into Jerusalem; Daniel in the lions' den; and Saint Paul led to his martyrdom. The artist has combined Old and New Testament scenes emphasizing sin, martyrdom, and death. These are mitigated by the two central scenes— Christ the heavenly king (he sits on a personification of the firmament) and Christ the earthly king, cheered as he enters Jerusalem. How does this sculpture differ from that we have considered? Is it classical? Do you feel the presence of other needs and aims in the presentation of these scenes? How is Christ presented—youthful or dignified, imperial or divine? How do the nude bodies of Adam and Eve compare with the Greek *Spearbearer* or the Cnidian *Aphrodite?* What accounts for the differences?

If these questions are difficult to answer, it is because art and architecture were at this point in a state of transition. Artists and thinkers were searching for the best means to convey new and important ideas at a time when there were no clear patterns for the presentation of these ideas. Greek and Roman art were sources that acted as strong influences but were not the perfect match for making images of Christianity's beliefs. Moreover, what does faith, Christianity's basic tenet, look like? Visual art could only provide examples of the acts of people who had taken the path of faith.

The Barbarian Influence in the Roman World The barbarians, who invaded the Roman empire in the fifth century, left many of these art objects and buildings intact. Primarily of Germanic origin, they had been in contact with Roman civilization for centuries. Their intention was not to destroy a civilization but to garner its fruits for themselves. In the eastern half of

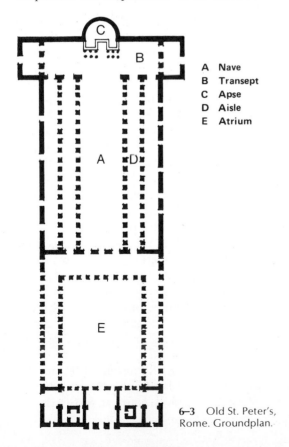

A   Nave
B   Transept
C   Apse
D   Aisle
E   Atrium

6–3   Old St. Peter's, Rome. Groundplan.

6–4   Sarcophagus of Junius Bassus, c. 359 A.D. Vatican Museums. (Alinari—Scala)

the empire the emperors were strong enough to resist the attackers; there the empire survived until its destruction by the Turks in 1453. But in the western provinces the emperors lost control; barbarian rulers assumed the position of authority in different areas.

Most of the barbarians were already Christian or were converted to Christianity soon after settling on Roman soil. Those converting in the homeland, however, had done so largely under the influence of heretical preachers and, once in the empire, had to be converted to the Catholic faith. Although the central role of kings in the tribe was a religious one and war chiefs supervised military expeditions, the pressures of invading the empire created a need for more central direction and led to a significant increase in the king's military powers. To an extent, the conversion of the various tribes to Christianity reduced the significance of the king as a religious leader, although throughout most of the Middle Ages the office retained something of its sacred, priestly qualities.

In the wreckage of the old imperial structure, what had been the Roman empire became a series of smaller kingdoms (see map). Because of their original Germanic religious associations, the kings were able not only to assert control over the churches but also over another important religious institution, the monastery.

Monasticism   From the first century of Christianity men and women who rejected life in the world had moved out into the wilderness individually to worship God in isolation. They called themselves hermits. Others who would have liked to withdraw from the world, however, felt unable to endure the loneliness of such a retreat or believed that isolation contradicted the Christian's duty to love one's neighbor. A communal retreat seemed to such Christians preferable to a solitary one. Thus, by the second century, communities of like-minded men and women came into existence, normally founded in remote places, and emphasizing common worship and mutual service. Often these *monasteries*, as they were eventually called, became the object of rich donations in land and money and grew to be powerful economic and political forces in the society.

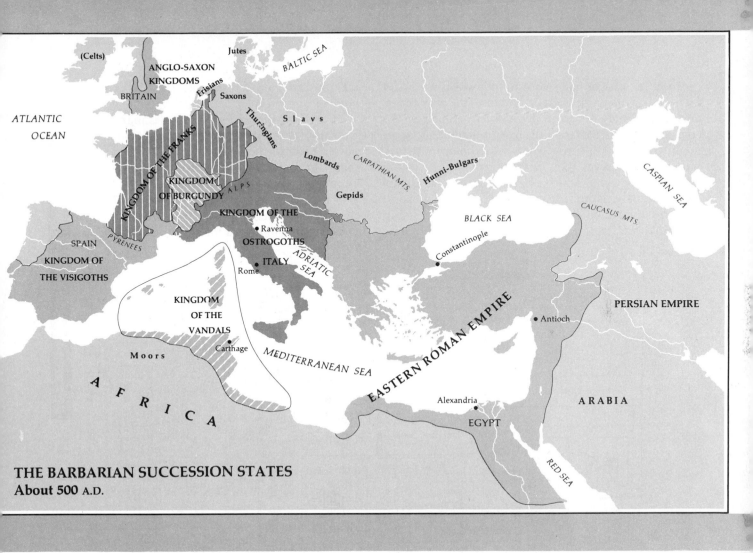

THE BARBARIAN SUCCESSION STATES
About 500 A.D.

In the confusion following the disintegration of the western Roman empire, monasticism flourished as never before. Centers of learning sometimes as well as of piety, offering physical as well as spiritual safety, monasteries were places of refuge in a dangerous world. An ideal plan for a monastery, drawn up about 800, the Saint Gaul plan (Fig. 6-5) shows a basilica, dormitories, dining room, library, hospital, hostel, cemetery, and gardens. It resembles a small, self-contained city. Given the wealth and importance of the great monasteries, it is easy to understand why the kings in the centuries after the invasions were concerned to assert some control over the resources of these foundations and to regulate the election of abbots.

Decline of Roman Centralization Yet, even with the support of the local churches and monasteries, the barbarian rulers after A.D. 500 proved unable to keep the old Roman institutions running. The Roman conception of political power enshrined in the imperial institutions of government was a public one; that is, the Romans considered political authority to be a series of magistracies. Obedience was owed to a magistrate not as a person but as an official representing the majesty of the Roman people. The most effective political bonds in Germanic society were, on the other hand, the personal ones between a war chief and his followers, established by an oath. The warrior obeyed the chief not because the latter represented the tribe but because the warrior had sworn to follow this particular man. As has been seen, the tendency to local autonomy had already set in under the late emperors; the coming of the barbarians only accentuated the development. In a period of insecurity, when men must seek protection wherever they can, the private conception of political power almost inevitably comes to dominate governmental relationships. By the seventh and eighth centuries a large portion of Europe's population found itself involved in a welter of political and economic relationships founded on oaths involving promises to obey or to protect.

The Germanic and surviving Roman aristocracies were the chief beneficiaries of this proliferation of power because they alone had the military might to maintain order at the local level. This group also seized control of churches and monasteries in their various regions, using them to advance their families. Whereas under the late empire and the early barbarian kings, the Church had been a tool in the hands of the central

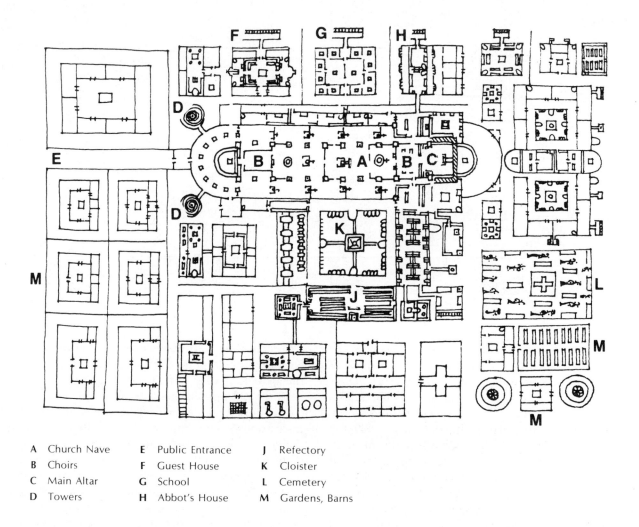

A	Church Nave	**E** Public Entrance	**J** Refectory
B	Choirs	**F** Guest House	**K** Cloister
C	Main Altar	**G** School	**L** Cemetery
D	Towers	**H** Abbot's House	**M** Gardens, Barns

6–5 Schematic plan for an ideal monastery at St. Gall, Switzerland, c.819 A.D. (Drawing after a 9th century manuscript, Chapter Library, St. Gall, Switzerland)

governments, now it had ten thousand masters. The papacy at Rome as well fell under the control of the Roman nobility. The effort of the Carolingian rulers of France in the eighth and early ninth centuries to reunite authority over a large expanse of territory had only a temporary effect on the process of political disintegration in most areas. Central government required a vigorous economic basis, but until the eleventh century Western Europe had, generally speaking, a localized subsistence economy.

7

Medieval Europe:
Culture and
the Cathedral

> The focus of our treatment of the Judeo-Christian root falls roughly on the period 1000 to 1350, sometimes called the High Middle Ages. Within this time period we can speak with some assurance of a civilization of the Middle Ages. Before 1000 medieval culture was still in formation, while after 1350 new currents (which historians generally label as characteristic of the Renaissance) were becoming dominant. Medieval society was doubtless affected by survivals of primitive Germanic, Italic, and Celtic folk culture, together with admixtures of sophisticated pagan philosophy and literature; but the informing ideas centered around belief in a transcendent, all-powerful God who, through the God-man Christ, offered redemption to the sinful race of men. Most cultural forms tended to be manifestations and expressions of this Christian (as developed from the Judaic) conception of God and the human predicament.

Prior to examining the productions in the arts and literature of this society, we will take up medieval developments in economics, in the Church, in political history, and in intellectual history generally. The early eleventh century in all these four areas initiated revivals that were interrelated. After five hundred years of progressive decline and relative stabilization at a low plateau, Western Europe by 1000 began to stir with new life.

Medieval Revivals

Economic Revival   Already by the end of the tenth century the tempo of economic life was changing. The development of the castle had finally provided the population with a source of security. Agricultural techniques and inventions like the horse collar gradually came into widespread use, leading to an increase in agricultural productivity and ultimately to an enormous population rise between 1000 and 1250. The distribution of the population was also altered; because food was easier to produce, a portion of the population could be spared from direct employment in agriculture for other things. Established towns grew in size, and new ones were founded. While by 1300 only about 10 percent of Europe's population lived in towns over 2000, nonetheless, the towns, serving as they did as focuses of economic and cultural life, played a role in medieval society much greater than this percentage would suggest. Silver deposits were exploited by mining; and when the bullion produced poured into the economy as currency, there was further expansion. International markets developed again, and large-scale production was encouraged.

Religious Revival   This renewed vitality in the economy was paralleled by a revival of religious interests. The great outpouring of European crusades toward the East from the end of the eleventh century is a reflection of a society bursting with creative energy and religious enthusiasm. In the decades after 1050 the popes at Rome initiated a program to dislodge the churches and monasteries from the hands of secular powers and to make them independent. The whole present relationship of the Church to the secular power, they argued, was sinful. Men of the world dominated the men of God. The soul is superior to the body, yet those who by divine command are to control bodily

things now dominate heavenly ones. The priest is in fact superior to the king because his realm is higher. The priest controls the sacraments, that is, rites like baptism and communion, which are the channels through which divine, life-giving grace pours. The pope, at the very pinnacle of the channels of grace, can let it flow or cut it off from whom he deems unworthy. The other priests act by his authority. For all his earthly power, the greatest monarch of Christendom will perish eternally if he is separated from the divine source; it depends on the priest and, first of all, the pope to decide whether he is worthy to receive the sacraments.

On the basis of this theory the papacy from the mid-eleventh century embarked on a policy of removing secular lords—kings and princes included—from power over the churches in their areas. Bishops, priests, abbots and monks were to give ultimate obedience to the pope, the vicar of Christ in Rome. Every Christian was commanded to follow divine law as it was interpreted by the papacy, and kings who disobeyed God's rule were to cease being kings. The result of the development was that by the early thirteenth century the Roman pope was the most powerful figure in Christendom. Not only did he effectively supervise all the churches and monasteries, but he also acted as the conscience of the secular rulers and their governments.

Political Revival   These same centuries also witnessed a political revival. The economic revival intensified contact between the different regions of a kingdom and created a tendency for political integration. In the long run this served the cause of the secular rulers. Princes came increasingly to stress the public nature of political power and the obligations of subjects to obey them not on the basis of a personal oath but because the ruler was the prince in a given territory. In the course of the twelfth and thirteenth centuries the monarchies gradually asserted their authority at the local level and subordinated that of the nobility.

Increased central government, however, required money to pay for an army, a bureaucracy, and a royal court. This meant taxes. The king could not seize the money of his subjects. The Germanic conception of private political power founded on an oath was coupled with an implicit understanding that the leader would protect his follower's person and property. By the eleventh century there was a general recognition of the lord's right to demand aid from his followers in certain cases, but both the lord and his men had to agree in council when such circumstances existed and to work out the obligations of each man to his lord. Roman law, studied in Europe again from the eleventh century, also stipulated that "what touches all must be approved of by all." This was interpreted to mean, that when levying a tax for the good of the country, the king had to consult with important individuals and with representatives of various segments of the population. Thus, the desire of the monarchs to increase their power over the country led to the need for taxation, and this called into being consultative assemblies. Almost everywhere in Europe a tradition of consent of the people to taxation was developing.

By the fourteenth century the political revival would significantly hinder the effectiveness of papal intervention in international politics. Already in the twelfth, monarchies were diverting loyalties of their peoples to themselves not only away from local nobility but also away from the Christian republic led by the pope. But even by the first half of the thirteenth century this process was still only underway: if the glory was a fragile one, the papacy remained the most important political force in Europe.

Intellectual Revival   Along with the political, economic, and religious revival beginning in the eleventh century came an intellectual revival. In its early stages in the eleventh and twelfth centuries, this revival can generally be described as a process of ordering knowledge in an effort to control experience. The initial step in this development around the year 1000 was the introduction of elementary texts of Aristotle's logic. From the ancient Greek system of logic, Europeans learned the idea of subordinating one idea to another, the part to the whole. Logic instructed them in the process of arriving at new truth and of organizing their knowledge into categories. Trained in logic, Europeans were able to present systematically pieces of knowledge that before were a confused jumble. A great European logician, Peter Abelard, wrote a book in the first half of the twelfth century called *Yes and No* in which he asked hundreds of central questions regarding human life and theology such as, "Is it right to murder another?" and "Does God exist?" After each ques-

tion he placed the answers given by ancient great authorities, both pagan and Christian writers. Logic was also an aid in the reorganization of the highly confused laws of the Church. The scholars of the twelfth century gave an ordered form to church or canon law, besides systematically presenting in concise fashion the fruits of numerous commentaries on the Holy Bible. All these endeavors gave men a confidence in the power of reason to understand the universe and offered them a possibility of eventually controlling it.

In the centuries between the fall of Rome and the eleventh century, learning was centered in the monasteries of Europe. With the revival of the towns, however, the cathedral came to dominate intellectual life. As we have seen, Catholic Christianity was divided into hundreds of administrative units called dioceses. The major church of the diocese and the residence of the bishop was the cathedral. Almost without exception located in an urban center, the cathedral contained a school in which the young clergy of the diocese could learn Latin and the proper way of performing their future religious functions. The reinvigoration of town life was accompanied by a new concern for learning in these cathedral schools. The first organized teaching of Aristotle's basic logical works occurred around the year 975 in a cathedral school, that of Rheims. From this point until the twelfth century the initiative in education belonged to these schools. By the twelfth century the number of students had increased to such a degree that in places like Paris and Oxford the cathedral was no longer able to contain the classes; then private teachers opened up their own schools in the vicinity. In the next century, as organization was given to this diversified instruction, the university was born.

The term *scholasticism* is usually applied to the scientific, theological, and philosophical learning taught in these schools and universities. First of all, this kind of learning was a monopoly of the schools, rather than of private scholars or secluded groups. The method, moreover, of presenting the thought in question-and-answer form was that followed in actual schoolroom teaching. But the term also applied to a common assumption of the thinkers of this three-hundred-year period. There was among them an implicit confidence that there was no conflict between the conclusions produced by reason and those accepted on faith, that the two sets of truth were compatible.

Initially with the introduction of Aristotelian logic the primary question became: to what extent could reason be employed to understand faith? As Christians, Europeans were committed to belief in the need of divine revelation to know certain truths. By the fifth century A.D. the basic doctrines of the Christian Church had been worked out on the basis of God's revealed word in the Bible, as follows: (1) the belief in a Trinity composed of Father, Son, and Holy Ghost, three persons in one divine substance. How this could be without making them three separate gods was acknowledged as divine mystery. (2) The belief in the creation of the universe out of nothing by an all-powerful God. (3) The doctrine of the fall of man into evil through his own free will. (4) The belief in heaven as a final resting place for the good and in a hell as the place for punishment of the evil. (5) The belief in Christ, human and divine, as the redeemer of man. Because he was God, he could live on earth without sin, and by virtue of his humanity he could redeem sinful, fallen mankind. (6) The doctrine of eternal life for the soul in paradise and the resurrection of the body through redemption. (7) Redemption was promised to those who believed in Christ as the Lord and who did good work on earth. (8) The necessity of God's grace for salvation. Whether some men are predestined by God to believe in Christ and do good work with God's grace doing everything, or whether grace is offered to all and men must cooperate with it in the process of salvation, was a debated point. The overwhelming tendency in the Church, however, was to stress the power and responsibility of men to cooperate.

The most congenial philosophic school of antiquity for early Christian thinkers had been that of Plato and his followers. Christians were attracted by the Platonic doctrine of two levels of reality, the world of the Ideas and that of the senses. Plato embraced the idea of the immortality of the soul; and the negative attitude of Platonists to the body, which they considered a prison, also proved attractive to Christians eager to dominate bodily lusts. The Christians were so influenced by these ascetic impulses that they often overlooked their own doctrine that the body, too, would be raised to heaven with the soul. Plato seemed so close to Christianity in some things he wrote that many Christian scholars believed that he had written either under the influence of the Holy Ghost or with knowledge of the work of the Hebrew prophets.

Stoicism also proved attractive to Christians, at least in its moral doctrines. Stoic stress on indifference to worldly success or failure seemed to be helpful to believers in their efforts to turn to God from the false joys of the world. The late Stoic view of government as having largely negative functions of keeping order reappeared in the works of the Church Fathers. As reformulated by the latter, the duty of the state was to prevent sinners from killing one another while the Church went about saving men's souls. The sword of kings was to be at the service of the Church: monarch and bishop were to work in harmony to bring men to seek righteousness.

The Church Fathers of the second to the fifth century, therefore, utilized the writings of Platonists and Stoics both as aids in elaborating Christian theological, philosophical, and moral ideas and as witnesses to the truth of Christian doctrine. While the writings of ancient Latin Stoics like Seneca survived in numbers between the fifth and the eleventh century, almost all of Plato was lost; and the Europeans' knowledge of his thought came mainly from what the Church Fathers had written about him. Aristotle's thought had not been popular in late antiquity and had had little effect on Christian doctrine in its formative stages. However, the craze for Aristotelian logic beginning in the eleventh century added a third ancient Greek influence to Christian thought. Working with Latin translations of Aristotle's elementary logic texts and ancient commentaries on these, European scholars were eager to sharpen their newfound intellectual instruments on the Christian faith. The danger to divine mystery was clearly perceived by critics of such efforts. Pious Christians in the twelfth century were especially alarmed at what appeared to be the assumption of some theologians that God's mind, working by the same processes, was subject to the same rules and conditions in its operations as was the human mind and that it was thus possible for the human mind to understand why God had operated as he did. Did this not detract from God's all-powerful nature and will? But what, then, were the limits of reason?

The recovery in the course of the thirteenth century of all of Aristotle's philosophical, moral, and scientific writings made the problem of faith and reason even more acute. Aristotle's logical works had been only an introduction to this masterpiece of thought. Medieval Europe was particularly weak in scientific work; but, with the introduction of Aristotle's body of writings, Europeans became aware of a system of thinking, ultimately reducible to a few basic principles, that had something to say about almost everything in the universe. Aristotle answered questions that they had not yet even learned to ask.

In the course of the thirteenth century, as they came to understand what Aristotle had written—and his work was and is very difficult to read—Christian thinkers came, however, to see that Aristotle believed in an eternal world and in a God who did not create the universe but who served only to explain why things in it moved. Moreover, he also seemed to believe that the human soul died with the human body. Aristotle appeared to be the culmination of the power of human reason; yet the results of his investigation, conducted according to the procedures of his logic (on which they too relied), seemed to point to some conclusions that contradicted the faith. Was the Christian faith therefore irrational? God was supposed to be truth, yet reason's conclusions apparently were not those of revelation.

Thomas Aquinas   The most influential attempt to reconcile reason and revelation in the thirteenth century was that of Thomas Aquinas (died 1274). Thomas showed, first of all, that Aristotle's proof for the eternity of the world was not a conclusive one. In fact, he maintained that there is no way by reason to prove either the eternity or the creation of the universe. We know that it was created, but that knowledge comes from faith. In the matter of Aristotle's position on the immortality of the human soul, Aquinas argued that Aristotle himself is ambiguous. Thus, he concluded, there is no proof that reason contradicts faith. Quite the contrary.

There are, according to Thomas Aquinas, many truths about the world that reason can discover: the causes of the rainbow, the source of locomotion in animals, and the like. More than this, there are certain truths revealed to us by God that could also be known by reason; for instance, that God exists and that he is

one God. After all, some ancient pagans knew this through the use of their reason. Then there are truths about God that no pagan could have known, such as the existence of the Trinity. Thus, for Aquinas the two spheres of truth, that established by reason and that by revelation, overlap.

If we follow reason according to the rules of logic, we can know many things about God and heaven; and, at the very pinnacle of this kind of truth, reason duplicates the lowest truths of revelation. Moreover, even the truths of revelation not open to human reason are not in themselves illogical, irrational. When reason examines them, in fact, they are quite reasonable. If man utilizes his reason according to the proper procedures of logic, he will gradually define a body of truth that at its greatest heights demands to be completed by the truths of faith.

Accordingly Aquinas and thinkers like him were able to construct enormous systems of thought beginning with our awareness of ourselves and the world and integrating all aspects of our internal and external experience. Every natural phenomenon from the falling of the raindrops to the movement of the stars can be set within a framework of explanation that literally requires the truths of revelation to cap it with ultimate meaning. Just as these edifices of human thought presented a world where all truth pointed heavenward, so did the great stone cathedrals that dotted the landscape of Western Europe in the thirteenth century.

Medieval Art and the Church: The Gothic Cathedral

Art in the ninth, tenth, and eleventh centuries, like learning, was centered in the court and monastery. These two institutions had the means, personnel, and time to produce creative work. Painting, sculpture, and architecture were viewed as ways to enhance and explain Christian doctrine. It is also true that both princes and churchmen realized the power of beauty and wealth to enhance their respective positions.

Along with the economic, religious, political, and intellectual revivals of Europe in the twelfth and thirteenth centuries, an artistic growth flourished. This gave rise to the Gothic style in art and architecture, a style whose forms and conventions would be practiced

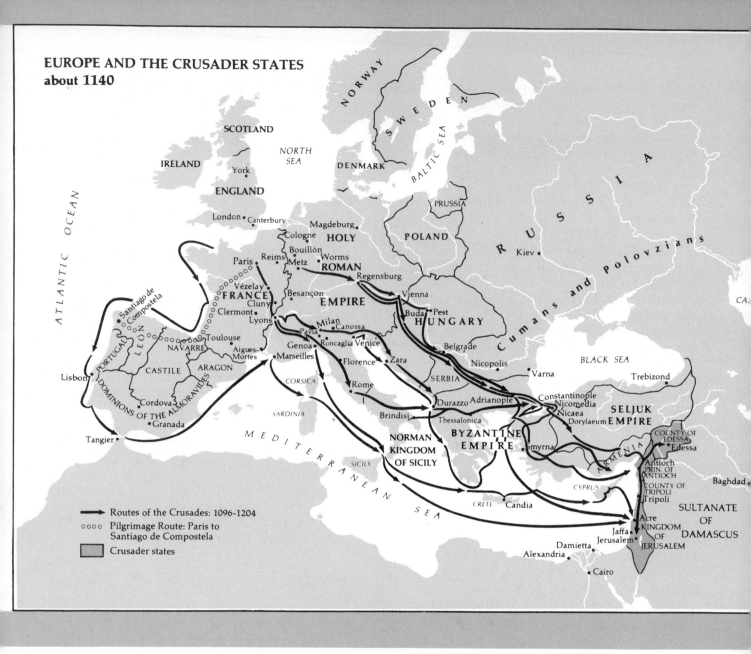

EUROPE AND THE CRUSADER STATES
about 1140

NORWAY
SWEDEN
SCOTLAND
NORTH SEA
IRELAND
DENMARK
BALTIC SEA
York
ENGLAND
PRUSSIA
London • Canterbury
Magdeburg
POLAND
Cologne
HOLY
Bouillon
ROMAN
Worms
Paris
Reims
Metz
Kiev
RUSSIA
Vézelay
FRANCE
Besançon
EMPIRE
Regensburg
Vienna
Cluny
Clermont
Canossa
Buda
Pest
Lyons
Milan
HUNGARY
Santiago de
Compostela
Pavia
Roncaglia
Venice
Cumans and Polovzians
LEÓN
Toulouse
Genoa
Belgrade
NAVARRE
Aigues-
Mortes
Marseilles
Florence
Zara
Nicopolis
Varna
BLACK SEA
PORTUGAL
CASTILE
ARAGON
CORSICA
Rome
SERBIA
Trebizond
Lisbon
Brindisi
Durazzo
Adrianople
Constantinople
DOMINIONS OF THE ALMORAVIDES
SARDINIA
Thessalonica
Nicomedia
SELJUK
Cordova
NORMAN
Nicaea
EMPIRE
Granada
KINGDOM
BYZANTINE
Dorylaeum
OF SICILY
EMPIRE
COUNTY OF
Tangier
SICILY
Smyrna
ARMENIA
EDESSA
MEDITERRANEAN
Edessa
SEA
Antioch
PRIN. OF
ANTIOCH
Baghdad
CYPRUS
COUNTY OF
CRETE
Candia
TRIPOLI
Tripoli
SULTANATE
Acre
OF
Jaffa
KINGDOM
DAMASCUS
Damietta
Jerusalem
OF
Alexandria
JERUSALEM
Cairo

→ Routes of the Crusades: 1096-1204
oooo Pilgrimage Route: Paris to
     Santiago de Compostela
▨ Crusader states

all over northern Europe and in the British Isles. Two particular occurrences were of great significance for this development: the pilgrimage and the crusades. Both activities united people and provided them with profound new experiences.

Pilgrimages Since every Christian could not be a monk, nun, priest, or in some other way directly affili-

ated with the church, it fell to the great numbers of lay Catholics to seek other ways to ensure their salvation. The immediate means open was the performance of good works, which usually meant contributions of time and wealth to the local church, cathedral, or monastery. Another was the route of penance—the undertaking of a pilgrimage to Rome, the Holy Land, or another shrine to seek the aid of a saint or saints. Along the route, the pilgrim could visit the relics and shrines of important local saints, who would then act on behalf of the sinner.

For Frenchmen and Germans one of the most favored pilgrimages was to Santiago de Compostela in northern Spain. This was the site of the tomb of Saint James, the son of Zebedee, one of Christ's chosen disciples. We know of it as a pilgrimage site as early as the mid-ninth century. By the mid-tenth century, clerics and laity were making the journey in increasing numbers. The map shows the route followed. Chaucer's *Canterbury Tales*, set on an English pilgrimage to Thomas à Becket's shrine, reflects the spirit of comradeship that pilgrimages instilled.

Movement in a pilgrimage was slow, fifteen or twenty miles a day, mostly on foot. Monasteries and churches provided accommodations along the road and broke the monotony of the trip by their beauty. As pilgrims came from many directions to Santiago, churches and cathedrals began to develop specific regional types. In the great burst of building activity many architectural ideas were tried, discarded, and elaborated.

A brief look at one of the great pilgrimage churches in France will be of help in understanding the Gothic tradition that developed after the eleventh and twelfth centuries. Saint Sernin, located at Toulouse, in southern France, was one of many great churches built in the eleventh and twelfth centuries in response to the pilgrimages and to growing wealth, mobility, and ambition. All over France and Germany and in England, many builders employed the means of Roman architecture to create new feelings and form. We generally call this art *Romanesque* because of its relation to Roman architecture (Fig. 7-1).

The plan of Saint Gaul (Fig. 6-5) showed a church with rounded ends, nave, and two apses. Entrance was from the side, with no clearly defined transepts. Two round stair towers were located at one end outside the apse. Local parish churches were even simpler. They might have an apse; a crypt below ground for treasure, burial, and relics; and a simple nave with entry at the west end.

The plan of Saint Sernin at Toulouse (Fig. 7-2) represents a shape called the Latin cross. There is a clearly defined entrance porch that opens into a nave with

7–1 St. Sernin, Toulouse, east end. (© ARCH. PHOT. PARIS/ S.P.A.D.E.M., 1980)

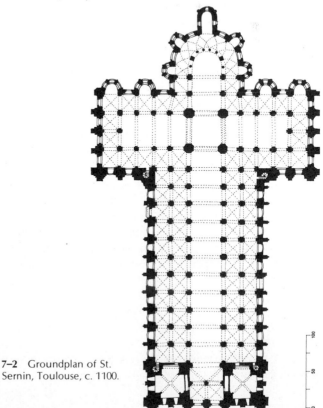

7–2 Groundplan of St. Sernin, Toulouse, c. 1100.

double aisles on each side. The transept and apse are sharply defined. On the east side of the transept and around the apse are separate, clearly defined small apses, which are called chapels. These are all related to each other by an aisle which goes all the way around the transept arms and around the apse itself. This passageway is called an *ambulatory*. From the outside we see that Saint Sernin is a brick and stone building with clearly defined roof forms. There is the nave roof and, lower down, the roofs over the aisles and the separately roofed apse and chapels.

On entering, we would see a church meant to accommodate not only the monastery (of which it was a part) but also crowds of pilgrims. The arrangement of nave and aisles is comparable to that of Old Saint Peter's (Fig. 6-2), but the ceiling is composed of barrel and groin vaults like those used in the Colosseum (Fig. 5-10).

Crusades　The Crusades, those holy wars designed to free the great sites of Christianity from "heathen" hands, afforded another opportunity for churchmen and laity to gain wider knowledge of buildings and building techniques. Churches in Jerusalem, Constantinople, and southern Italy encouraged builders to seek greater splendor. The medieval crusades, like the pilgrimages fostering exchange of ideas and expertise from one region to another, similarly contributed to the rise of the Gothic style (see map).

The Rise of Gothic Architecture　Many villages in France today still give the impression that an enormous church dominates the small houses, shops, and other buildings around it. Fantastic energy was put into the construction of these great stone works. Usually everyone in the village, from the lords and ladies down to the peasants, joined the professional stonemasons in doing their part to construct an edifice to the glory of God and to the representation of the Church on earth (Fig. 7-3).

Why did medieval people devote such time, energy, and money to the construction of these huge and complex buildings? It is hard to find anything comparable in the lives of modern people. We must try to remember that churches were not merely places to go on Sunday or decorations for a town; they represented a vital

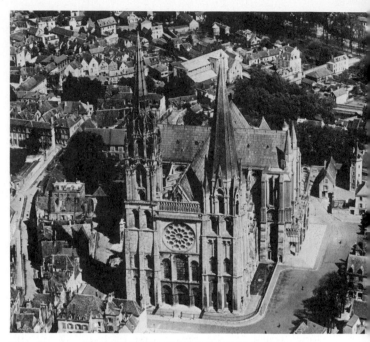

7–3　Chartres. (© ARCH. PHOT. PARIS/S.P.A.D.E.M., 1980)

aspect of everyone's spiritual life. They were not only dwellings for God on earth but also a kind of bridge between the physical and spiritual realms. They began as heavy stone set on the ground, but they soared upward toward heaven. They contained something for everyone. For the common people, many of whom could neither read nor write, they offered a kind of visual religious education.

The stained-glass windows, the sculptures, and the architectural design of the churches built in the twelfth and thirteenth centuries tell us a great deal about the values and beliefs of the people who built them and worshiped in them. The term *Gothic*, used to describe their style, was coined in the Renaissance. Until the eighteenth century it was a derogatory term, implying that a style created by the descendants of the Goths, one of the barbarian tribes that overran the Roman empire, was uncivilized and greatly inferior to the classical style. (In a similar way, Westerners once considered African art barbaric until European artists in the early part of our century began to appreciate its originality.) Certainly one can say that the aesthetic impression felt inside a Gothic cathedral is *different* from the im-

7–4 Chartres, west front. (Lauros-Giraudon, Paris)

7–5 Chartres, nave. (Giraudon, Paris)

pression one has inside a Roman building like the Pantheon, but most modern viewers would not at all agree with the Renaissance belief that this difference constitutes inferiority. Preference here is largely a matter of taste and temperament. Before we begin our analysis of some of the technical and artistic features of the Gothic cathedral, formulate some of your own impressions by comparing the interior and exterior of the Pantheon (Figs. 5-12, 5-13, 5-14) with Notre Dame of Chartres (Figs. 7-4, 7-5). Consider the actual size, the importance of interior or exterior for the user, the purpose of each, the arrangement of interior spaces, and the materials.

Gothic buildings, like all other architecture, evolved from the technology, needs, and ideals of a particular time and place. The patrons and master craftsmen who created these great churches drew on the current architectural solutions and skills while experimenting with and expanding both structural and formal capabilities.

Masons, carpenters, and other craftsmen followed the routes of the crusades and pilgrimages.

The monastery church of Saint Denis (Fig. 7-6), in the Ile-de-France, near Paris, and the cathedral of Notre Dame (Our Lady) of Chartres, which we will consider in this chapter, document the origin and extraordinary capacities of the period for visual expression of metaphysical and deeply religious ideas.

Suger and Saint Denis   In 1120 a monk named Suger was named abbot of the Abbey of Saint Denis, one of the oldest and most venerable monastic foundations in France. Named for the founding saint of French Catholicism, it was also associated with the Capets, successors to Charlemagne, many of whom were buried there. Suger had been at Saint Denis since childhood and had grown up with Louis VI, the Capetian king. A dynamic, ambitious, and highly intelligent individual, he had already distinguished himself as a diplomat for the papacy before becoming abbot. In 1147, when Louis VII left for the Second Crusade, Suger was made regent of the kingdom. But Suger did not seek power for its own sake. His association of the abbey with secular power came from his Christian desire to bring order and spiritual enlightenment to the poor and to the powerful. These beliefs, in combination with other factors (the church was in disrepair and crowded on feast days), caused Suger to begin to work on rebuilding the church at Saint Denis.

Descriptions of churches seen on Crusades provided Suger with some ideas; but most important were those derived from his own theology, which developed in the years before the work at Saint Denis began. It was heavily Neoplatonic, for it was based on the writing of Dionysius, a sixth-century Greek mystic who was mistakenly associated with Saint Denis (A.D. 200s), the patron saint of France. Suger's ideas were also related to those of Aristotle and the scholastics. The two central themes with which he worked were harmony and light. Suger believed that all matter in some degree partakes of God and in some way reflects ultimate reality. Visible light is, therefore, the analogy for the light of God, and thus symbolic of the unity of all creation. As natural light infuses and transforms, so we are transformed by this heavenly light, illumination, knowledge. Suger also believed that the contemplation of the truly beautiful "worthy materials" of gold, gemstones, chalices, and altars could transport one from the world here below to the heavenly one. In 1144 he wrote:

> Thus, when out of my delight in the beauty of the house of God—the loveliness of the many-colored gems has called me away from external cares, and worthy meditation has induced me to reflect, transferring that which is material to that which is immaterial, on the diversity of the sacred virtues—then it seems to me that I see myself dwelling, as it were, in some strange region of the universe which neither exists entirely in the slime of the earth nor entirely in the purity of Heaven; and that, by the grace of God, I can be transported from this inferior to that higher world.

It became his ambition to make his church such a means of transcendence, to fill it with light and to give it a spiritual significance as great as that of its saint and the French kingdom.

We do not know how Suger conveyed his ideas to

7–6   St. Denis, west front. (Giraudon, Paris)

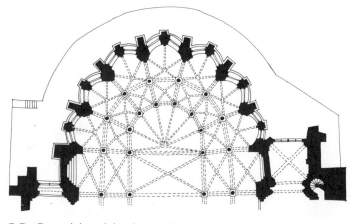

7–7   Groundplan of the choir, St. Denis, near Paris, c. 1140.

the master builders who undertook the work. But we do know the combination of his visions and the hired technical skill produced a number of important changes in church design and construction that were absorbed at once by builders in the area around Saint Denis.

Perhaps the most significant innovation was a new system of *piers* and *vaults*, employing pointed arches that allowed the enlargement of the east end, creating a large *choir* (a rectangular space for the clergy between the transept and apse) surrounded by an aisle (ambulatory) with seven chapels spaced equidistantly on its outer edge (Fig. 7-7). These were roofed with vaults. Most important of all, however, the outside walls of the chapel and the clerestory above were now largely glass. This glass was richly colored—reds, blues, yellows, and some white. The small pieces of glass were arranged in patterns, figures, and stories. Joined together by lead strips, the panels were then set within a framework of stone. The east end of the church became a vessel for the transmission of divine, transforming light.

> Once the new rear part [east end] is joined to the part in front, the church shines with its middle part brightened. For bright is that which is brightly coupled with the bright. And bright is the noble edifice that is prevaded by the new light.

The church, filled with light, was a bridge to the ultimate reality of divine revelation, the harmonious and orderly world. The windows transformed light, as God's light transformed the dull heaviness of matter. Uplifted by this created light within the church, the worshipers' souls would rise to seek God, its uncreated source.

This new way of building will be explored further in the rebuilding of the cathedral of Notre Dame of Chartres (Fig. 7-4), which is among the finest examples of Gothic design and construction.

The Cathedral at Chartres   The village of Chartres seems almost inundated by the fields of grain that spread out from the town, but the cathedral dominates the horizon. The church, dedicated to the Virgin, was founded before 743 (the first sure date associated with it). Its chief relic, the tunic of the Virgin, had been given by King Charles the Bald. This gift made Chartres the center of the cult of the Virgin in Western Europe, and the deep devotion it engendered is revealed by the successive buildings on the site. Documents tell of numerous fires, and we can follow successive rebuildings up to this great monument. A new

basilica had been erected in the eleventh century. In the early twelfth century another fire occasioned the erection of the three entrances and tower bases at the west end. Then in June 1194 a fire devastated the basilica and town, leaving only the west front intact. From this anonymous account, written early in the thirteenth century, we can get a good idea of the role of this church in the life of the people.

> Therefore, in the year 1194 after the Incarnation of the Lord, since the church at Chartres had been devastated on the third of the Ides of June [June 10] by an extraordinary and lamentable fire making it necessary later, after the walls had been broken up and demolished and leveled to the ground, to repair the foundations and then erect a new church.... The inhabitants of Chartres, clerics as well as laymen, ... considered as their chief misfortune, the fact that they, unhappy wretches, in justice for their own sins, had lost the palace of the Blessed Virgin, the special glory of the city, the showpiece of the entire region, the incomparable house of prayer...
>
> Indeed, when for several days they had not seen the most sacred reliquary of the Blessed Mary, the population of Chartres was seized with incredible anguish and grief, concluding that it was unworthy to restore the structures of the city or the church, if it had lost such a precious treasure, [which was] indeed the glory of the whole city. At last, on a particular holy day, when the entire populace had assembled by order of the clergy at the spot where the church had stood, the above mentioned reliquary was brought forth from the crypt.... The fact must not be passed over that when, at the time of the fire, the reliquary frequently referred to had been moved by certain persons into the lower crypt (whose entrance the laudable foresight of the ancients had cut near the altar of the Blessed Mary), and they had been shut up there, not daring to go back out because of the fire now raging, they were so preserved from mortal danger under the protection of the Blessed Mary that neither did the rain of burning timbers falling from above shatter the iron door covering the face of the crypt, nor did the drops of melted lead penetrate it, nor the heap of burning coals overhead injure it.... And after such a fierce conflagration, when men who were considered already dead from smoke or excessive heat had come back unharmed, all present were filled with such gladness that they rejoiced together, weeping affectionately with them.
>
> ...When, following the ruin of the walls mentioned above, necessity demanded that a new church be built and the wagons were at last ready to fetch the stone, all beckoned as well as exhorted each other to obey instantly and

do without delay whatever they thought necessary for this construction or [whatever] the master workers prescribed. But the gifts or assistance of the laymen would never have been adequate to raise such a structure had not the bishop and the canons contributed so much money, as stated above, for three years from their own revenues. For this became evident to everyone at the end of the three-year period when all finances suddenly gave out, so that the supervisors had no wages for the workmen, nor did they have in view anything that could be given otherwise. But I recall that at that moment someone said—I know not by what spirit of prophecy—that the purses would fail before the coins needed for the work on the church of Chartres [were obtained]. What is there to add? Since, in view of the utter failure of human resources, it was necessary for the divine to appear, the blessed Mother of God, desiring that a new and incomparable church be erected in which she could perform her miracles, stirred up the power of this son of hers by her merits and prayers. When there was a large gathering of people there, she openly and clearly exhibited a certain new miracle, one unheard of for a long time past, seen by all for the first time. As a result, news of the miracle spread far and wide through the whole of Gaul and made it easier to give credence to succeeding miracles.

Out of despair the people, clerics, and nobility of Chartres created an enduring act of devotion by making this palace for the queen of heaven. The new church was occupied by 1220 and dedicated in 1260—an astonishingly short time given the technology of the age. Its form embraced the changes that Suger had made at Saint Denis, creating a harmonious, substantial expression of belief rendered into visible form.

Standing before the west front (Fig. 7-8), you feel that the building looks somewhat familiar. The central doors suggest that the nave and aisles lie behind, and at the end of the nave may be seen an apse. Turning to the right, moving across the front, and looking down the south side, you see a wing that joins the nave at right angles. The church has a transept that can be entered through a graceful three-part porch and doors. Standing before the porch of the transept, looking west, toward the front towers, you see the wall of the aisle, its roof sloping up slightly to meet the walls of the nave and clerestory that rise above it (Figs. 7-9, 7-12).

Extension of the Building Topping the aisle wall is a row of columns carrying arches and a lintel. This *parapet* partially conceals the aisle roof. The aisle wall is divided into seven regular intervals expressed by six large, single, pointed windows and a passageway. The wall of the nave rising above the aisle repeats the intervals, but the single window is replaced by pairs of

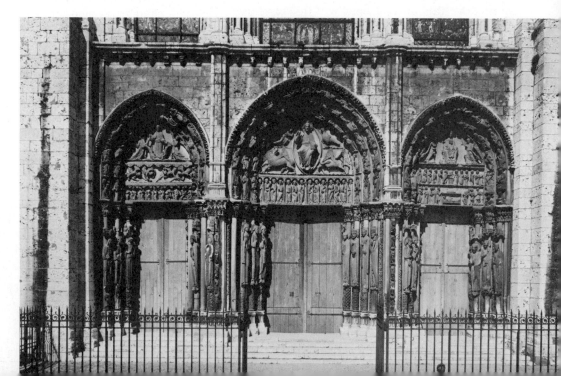

7-8 Chartres, west front. Left tympanum, Ascension of Christ; central tympanum, Second Coming of Christ; right tympanum, Incarnation of Christ. (Lauros-Giraudon, Paris)

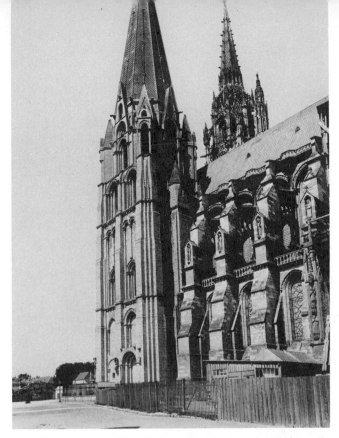

7-9 Chartres, south aisle. Windows of aisle are separated by wall buttresses that rise to the parapet. (LEFEVRE-PONTALIS/© ARCH. PHOT. PARIS/S.P.A.D.E.M., 1980)

7-10 Chartres, detail of nave showing wall buttresses between aisle windows. These rise above aisle parapet as detached and flying buttresses of clerestory arcade. (Lauros-Giraudon, Paris)

7-11 Chartres, choir, west end. Aisle, clerestory and flying buttresses between windows. (© ARCH. PHOT. PARIS/S.P.A.D.E.M., 1980)

tall pointed windows topped with a round one. These are the windows of the clerestory of the nave with its sharply pointed lead-covered roof. The exterior walls, however, seem less like walls than elaborate piers, and in the spaces between each window are carefully cut and laid towers of stone called *buttresses* (Fig. 7-10). Each buttress continues to rise vertically but becomes thinner and lighter as it is stepped in toward the clerestory wall. Beginning at the gabled opening with its figure, a section of stone arch reaches out to join the stone pier between the clerestory windows. Finally, as each buttress towers almost to the parapet of the nave roof, another arch reaches out to the clerestory pier. These are the *flying buttresses*, arches of stone reaching across space to help transfer the weight of wall and roof to the foundations. This is the building framework: a great skeleton of stone. Light and air pass over it freely, moving among the details of moldings, angles, and arches and over the surfaces of the great windows themselves. As you move around the apse (Fig. 7-11), you note that the walls and windows deflect in and out, responding to the location of the chapels around the apse. There are also flying buttresses around the apse, supporting its great windows that rise, like the nave clerestory, above the ambulatory below. The exterior of Saint Denis may have looked like this; Chartres resembles it in plan and, in all probability, idea. Walking around the choir to the north, you reach the other entrance to the transept. Both transept entrances are towered and columned, quite different from the west front, which was built before the fire of 1194, and therefore long before the north and south transepts. Completing the circuit of the church shows its familiar basilican plan (Fig. 7-12) but also demonstrates that it is realized in a new way: in a structure that seems to stand outside the walls of windows, windows that fill the interior with light.

To understand the physical achievement that made the building possible, we must remind ourselves of Roman vaulting. The *barrel* and *groin vaults* of the Romans were semicircular in section, and the *bay* had to be regular (Fig. 7-13). Moreover, the tops of the arches had to be the same height. Piers, columns, and walls

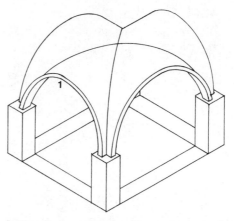

7–13a Groin vaults normally require square bays. When a rectangular bay is needed, the arches on the shorter sides (1) must be raised to keep the four sides of the vault equal in height. This is not a very satisfactory solution.

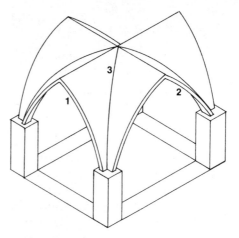

7–13b The pointed arch permits the arches of the short (1), long (2), and diagonal (3) spans to accommodate a rectangular bay with greater efficiency.

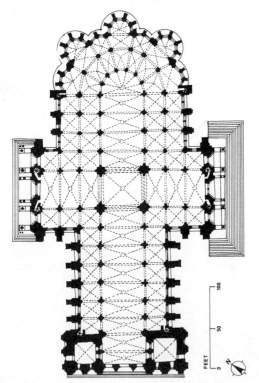

7–12 Groundplan, Chartres.

carried the vaults, and windows were small. Centering was used to erect the vaults; and, as a basilica grew, bay by bay, it became a series of separate units of space.

Study the plan of the apse of Chartres (Fig. 7-12). Pay particular attention to the dots and dark areas that indicate columns and piers. The diagonal lines on the plan indicate the joining of sections of the vaults. There are seven vaults of four sections each for the ambulatory; each of the side chapels contains vaults of five parts, but the bays of the ambulatory and chapels are irregular—they become larger as one moves from the apse out to the bounding wall. Regular Roman vaults would not permit this, nor would the system permit such irregularity in the size of pier and column. What permitted this new configuration in the plan? First, the arches of the vaults are not semicircular in section, but pointed, second, the vaults are joined by pointed ribs that act as a permanent centering for the vaults (Figs. 7-5, 7-13).

It is not as if pointed arches were unknown. They had been used before and have the advantage of being more self-supporting: the two sides lean on each other. Ribs had been used before. What was important was the combination of pointed arch and rib to make a vaulting system that was lighter and much more flexible, permitting more and more wall to be opened for glass. The outward, downward thrust of the vaults is carried away from the walls by the pier and flying buttresses that rise above the roofs. The new system makes Chartres' ambulatory a space with no sharp delineations, as between ambulatory and chapel, or apse and aisle. The separate cells of space made by the chapels at Saint Sernin (Fig. 7-2) have been replaced by a greater unity—a whole greater than its parts. This system of pointed arches, ribs, and flying buttresses made possible this accomplishment.

At the west front again, the towers seem to squeeze the portals between them, and the airy complexity of the south and north porches is replaced by a majestic weightiness, reinforced by the three round arched windows above the doors and the single huge, round window (Fig. 7-4). The south tower was finished about 1155, but the north tower spire was added only in the early sixteenth century. The three entrance doors are decorated with sculpted figures; and, as we examine the sculpture of the west front, we can begin to understand more about the church as a whole, this palace for the Virgin, this place of transportation from earthly to heavenly life.

For modern man it is difficult to think of art as a teaching tool; but for the man of the Middle Ages, art, like everything else, had a purpose in the divine scheme of things. The cathedral, like the philosophical system of Thomas Aquinas, was concerned with God, the world, and man—with the accumulation of human knowledge and speculation and their relation to divine knowledge and revelation.

Exterior Sculptures The three doors of the west front, called the Royal Portal (Fig. 7-8), sit in round

arches deep in the thick wall. The wall from the door to the outer wall face, the *jamb*, is slanted outward; these jambs are decorated with columns and figures. The columns have richly decorated bases, and their *capitals* are carved, providing a horizontal contrast to the jamb figures (Fig. 7-8). Above the doors are sculptured lintels, and above the lintel is the *tympanum*, the sculpture-filled panels that reach to the top of the opening. In the slanted area above the lintel from the arch to the wall's outer surface are stones called *archivolts*, also sculpted. All these sculptures, like Greek sculpture, would have been painted, gilded, and decorated to enhance and intensify the specific qualities of figure and setting.

The sculptures of the west front present the fundamentals of the Christian dogma with directness and clarity. Let us look more closely at each section to see

7–14 Chartres, west front, right tympanum, Incarnation of Christ. (Giraudon, Paris)

how the sculptor presents his images and relates them to each other and to the architectural framework. You might also ask how this sculpture differs from that we saw in Athens on the Parthenon and in Rome.

Beginning with the tympanum of the right door, we see a crowned, haloed Virgin seated on a throne, the Christ Child in her lap (Fig. 7-14). On either side of the central figures is an angel swinging a censer, a container for burning incense. The Virgin and Child face us directly; the folds of their garments fall symmetrically and emphasize this frontality. The angels, seen in profile, are almost identical, their poses giving the composition great repose. These heavenly attendants, the throne, and the pose tell us that we are before the Virgin as the queen of heaven.

The lintel below is divided into two registers containing the following scenes: lower register, left to right, the Annunciation (Gabriel visits Mary to tell her that she will conceive and bear a son, Jesus); the Visitation (Mary visits Elizabeth, the mother of John the Baptist); the Nativity and the angels announcing Jesus' birth to the shepherds; in the upper register, the presentation of Jesus in the temple. All the figures in the scenes seem stocky and somewhat ill-proportioned; their clothes are simplified, and the faces all resemble each other. The figures in both rows share a simple rhythmical relation, spaced equidistantly apart and almost symmetrically. Was naturalism this artist's goal? What was his goal? Can we read the story with clarity and ease?

In addition to the apparent subjects, these representations were filled with much deeper meaning for medieval man—meanings that have been discovered in medieval treatises and sermons. For example, seeing Christ as child and in young manhood reminds us that he was human and present with us, as well as being God. Mary, his mother, is human and divine also, the queen of heaven and the motherly intercessor for us. In the nativity scene we see Mary resting on what looks like a bed. The medieval person would have recognized it as an altar, and placing the child in the manger on the bed's top edge alludes to Christ, the sacrifice, the Eucharist. The scene of the presentation in the temple repeats the idea; Christ stands in the center on an altarlike form. Thus, the sculptures not only represent scenes from the life of Jesus, they also serve as remind-

ers of the complex nature of Christ, as God made man and as the sacrifice for mankind's salvation.

In the archivolts around the tympanum are personifications of the seven liberal arts: grammar, dialectic, rhetoric, arithmetic, music, geometry, and astronomy. The cathedral at Chartres was a seat of great learning, and the inclusion of the liberal arts in the sculptural program is a natural allusion to this and the major concern of the schools: to forge the links in knowledge from the human to the divine, from the systematics of Aristotle to the mystical transcendence of faith. These sculptures should also remind us that Christ is wisdom incarnate, the *logos*, the word of God made man.

The other two tympana expand the story begun in the right portal. In the left portal is the Ascension of Christ. In its tympanum, Christ, supported by angels, is drawn up into heaven on a cloud (Fig. 7-15). In the upper register of the lintel four angels announce his second coming to the Apostles seated below. The archivolts are carved with signs of the zodiac and the labors of the months—Christ as man was in time; Christ as God *is* time, the beginning and the end—seasons, la-

7–15 Chartres, west front, left tympanum, Ascension of Christ. (Lauros-Giraudon, Paris)

7–16 Chartres, west front, central tympanum, Second Coming of Christ. (Giraudon, Paris)

bors, and life will stop at his coming again. Compare these figures to those on the right, Incarnation portal. Do words like simplicity, order, clarity, symmetry apply? Look at the clouds and the angels' drapery. How do these figures compare with the Panathenaic festival? Those on the *Ara Pacis*?

The central tympanum shows Christ in majesty, one hand raised in blessing, surrounded by the four symbols of the Evangelists: Mark's lion, John's eagle, Matthew's man (or angel), and Luke's bull (Fig. 7-16). Angels and church elders in the archivolts and the apostles in the lintel witness the Second Coming—to judge the quick and the dead. Christ is seated and crowned with a halo, his ultimate kingship emphasized by the two angels who hold the crown at the top of the archivolts.

The capitals on the columns below show scenes from the life of Mary and Jesus. They connect the subjects of the three portals both narratively and visually. This is indeed a presentation of sacred history.

The remaining figures are the elongated columnar ones on the jambs. Only nineteen remain of the original twenty-four, male and female, crowned and uncrowned, neither ancient nor youthful. They share the

stylized drapery and physical simplification of the other portal figures. But their scale and location give them a vibrating tension as they seem poised before the doors (Fig. 7-17).

The absolute identification of these figures has never been agreed upon, but we think them to be kings and prophets of the Old Testament. It is as if these are the ancestors of the sacred history of the New Testament revealed above. In these figures we may also perceive the close ties between church and state, kingship and priesthood. The crowned and uncrowned figures may refer to heavenly rule—earthly kingship and priesthood. The female figures may be the ancestors of the Virgin.

Our knowledge of the subject matter of the sculpture and windows and the architecture at Chartres derives not only from it but also from the programs of decoration at numerous other cathedrals and churches. It is important to know that the work at Chartres is not an isolated phenomenon but reaches backward to earlier programs at other buildings and is subsequently in-

7–17 Chartres, west front, Old Testament figures. (Lauros-Giraudon, Paris)

fluential in the creation of later programs, both in form and content. Chartres is a paradigm for many such buildings—the cathedrals at Rheims, Amiens, Paris, Rouen, Laon, Cologne, and Strasbourg and for churches in Paris and many other cities in France, Germany, and England.

These great doors on the west, illuminated by the setting sun, must have been perceived as palatial, heavenly gates, the entry to the court of Mary, the queen of heaven, for one enters acutely aware of the majesty and presence of this person and her Son.

Interior   Passing from the exterior into the nave is like leaving one world to enter another. The nave arcade rises to support a row of shallow arched openings, and above these the clerestory rises to the vaults 118 feet above the floor (Fig. 7-5). The great piers that make up the nave arcade and separate the nave from the aisles are not single columns, like those of the Parthenon, but seem to be created from a collection of individual shafts. Each pier has a central shaft, and centered on each face is a smaller shaft: one faces the aisle, one faces the nave, and one faces the pier behind or in front of it. These are gathered at the base, rise to the capital, and then disperse in the nave and aisle vaults. The nave is seven bays long, the transept spreads left and right, and the choir, apse, and ambulatory seem distant and light-filled. As you move down the nave, radiant with the colored light spilling in from the stained-glass windows of the clerestory above, you remember the complex and weighty stone skeleton that supports this light-filled and awesome space. The interior is the final expression of the diversity and unity of a system of building with arches and ribs, piers and columns.

Look at one pier and one bay of the nave (Fig. 7-5). Compare it with a column of the Parthenon and the bay of the pilgrimage church, Saint Sernin. What is immediately different? The base of the Gothic pier has not one, but a variety of simple moldings that unite the small shafts attached to the central column. Because of the attached columns and their capitals, the pier does not seem to face squarely into the nave or aisle. The different locations of the attached columns cause your eyes to move across, around, and behind the pier so that the nave and aisle interlock. Follow the attached

shafts as they rise upward. Those two that face each other and decorate the arch of the nave arcade carry a series of curved moldings (Fig. 7-5). The shaft facing in the aisle carries smaller shafts that rise to become the aisle vault ribs. The shaft facing the nave bursts into five clearly articulated smaller shafts that rise to become the ribs of the nave vault. One shaft reaches the vault and crosses transversely; another crosses the vault diagonally to a pier on the other side of the bay. Where the two diagonal ribs meet, their flow is gathered into a circular *keystone.* Moreover, as each rib springs across the vault, it is multiplied into three or more curving ribs—not a flat rib. Between the ribs are the smooth surfaces of the vaults. Looking up, you see the vault of a single bay, which looks like this $\times$; yet it merges into the next bay in a shape that looks like this $\diamondsuit$. The experience produced is one of a constant fluid merging of separate but totally dependent units of space. The bays of the aisles, like those of the nave, melt into a whole. Reaching the light-filled apse, you experience an absorbing, objective order and consistency of building form that does not intimidate or overwhelm but absorbs you as an integral part of the whole, just as every base, shaft, capital, and molding is essential.

The structural knowledge and expertise that produced the cathedral is not a matter of speculation. It was the product of the guilds and lodges of master masons who worked for the cathedral or monastery. These men were conversant with the knowledge of engineering, stone masonry, and mathematics necessary to make the building stand up. More specifically, we can say that the medieval mason proportioned his cathedral on a sure foundation of mathematics. The mason worked from a constant proportion, established in the beginning and capable of determining the measure of every member and element. This was not just a pragmatic tool; the mason, like the philosopher and theologian, believed that numbers and therefore harmony were reflections of the divine order of the world. From Aristotle and Pythagoras the mason drew knowledge of certain simple ratios as being the most sure reflections of that harmony, and these he applied to plan and elevation. If we do not immediately see, we sense overriding appropriateness of height to width and of equal correctness of division within. Thus, the Gothic cathedral is a concrete example of the use of reason in the service of faith, comparable to the philosophies of Abelard and Aquinas mentioned earlier in this chapter. The culture of the High Middle Ages was both practical and intellectual, but these two aspects were subordinated to man's primary purpose in life: the aspiration of the soul toward salvation by God, to be accomplished through the Church.

Stained-Glass Windows Harmony and light, then, are the two binding physical motifs of Chartres: harmony of building—its spaces and forms—and light, the luminescence of the translucent window wall, stretching thin webs between the stones. These two values, harmony and light, are presented perhaps most completely in the stained glass of Chartres, where the art reached a level of unusual perfection. Unlike a painting, which reflects light, the windows transmit and transform light. The varicolored light conceals, reveals, and warms the spare stone of the building. The jewellike windows adorn the building as gold and gems adorn the vessels of the sacrament and cross of the altar. The Madonna herself is enthroned in the central window of the west front, and she is the subject of the windows of the north transept. But it is in a window in the south ambulatory, called *Notre Dame de la Belle Verrière* (Color Plate I), that we sense the profound adoration that her people felt for her. This window is the oldest and was probably saved from the debris of the fire. Like the Virgin on the west front, she sits enthroned, holding her child on her knees. Angels bearing censers and candles fill the panels on either side. We see a loving and supporting intercessor. The deep ruby glass seems to fall slightly behind the blue of the Virgin's robe and warms the air around her. The deep, intense-blue side panels have ruby niches that house the angels. Their smaller scale, the more intricate gowns and poses give them an animation and vitality contrasting with the stable order that they surround. Mother and child, heavenly and earthly love are permanent images.

The other windows in the basilica organize and present all facets of medieval knowledge—Old and New Testament, lives of the saints, fundamentals of Christian doctrine, labors of the months, signs of the zodiac, vices and virtues, and the activities of the guilds. Like the sculpture on the west front, and that on the north and south transepts (which we will consider finally), the same events are repeated and elaborated—man and God in time and at the end of time.

Moreover, in the windows at Chartres we see once again the deep relationship between churchman and lay person. The townspeople depended for their economic vitality on the cathedral, the fairs, and the pilgrims who came because of the relics of the Virgin. They held meetings on the church's steps, sold wine from the crypt, gathered to seek jobs in the nave, attended plays presented before the west front, socialized, loved, and were baptized and buried from Our Lady's chapels. To these people we owe many of the windows. The five great windows of the apse honoring the Virgin were paid for largely by the butchers and bakers. The Saint James Major window was given by the merchant tailors who appear in the bottom corners in two scenes from a tailor's shop (Color Plate II). In another window a banner with a red stocking tells us that the hosiers gave it, while the Charlemagne window, which relates the origins of the French monarchy, was given by the furriers.

Perhaps it seems unfair to say so little about the glass at Chartres, particularly because the architectural arrangements seem to evolve in order to permit the creation of more and more windows. But it is the most magical of the aspects of the building and the least susceptible to reproduction, either visual or verbal. The subjects of the windows are high up and not easily read; rather what is supremely important are the rich patterns of light that fall on the floors and play over the piers and ribs, transforming the entire space into a light-filled, unearthly one meant for contemplation and celebration. In the morning light the east end is filled with the new day, the church brightens with the noonday light, and the windows at the west end glow in the low setting sun. They reflect the passage of time, the church triumphant in this world, and beyond this world.

Transept Door Sculptures While it is not really possible to bring the experience of Chartres to a conclusion, it is appropriate to end with the latest sculpture (ca. 1250–1270), that of the transept doors. The climactic scenes are found in the central tympana of each, and their meaning is enhanced by the subsidiary scenes in the doors on either side.

On the north portal concentration is on the *Virgin's* life, death, and assumption into heaven. The south portal presents the Christian Church on earth, in heaven, and ending in time on the day of the Last Judgment. The central portal shows the Last Judgment in the tympanum, the Twelve Apostles along the jambs, with Christ standing on the post between the doors. The left portal is dedicated to the *martyrs* (persons killed for their beliefs) and the right one to the *confessors* (persons who gave special witness to the faith).

Formally, the figures of both the north and south portals show a steady increase in the degree of humanization, naturalism, and individuality. Compared to the much earlier figures of the west front, they grow in bulk, gain weight and volume, and fill the space. The drapery articulates the forms of the body. Faces, hands, and feet become more convincing, yet a balance is always maintained between these figures and their architectural setting. Like the great stone framework itself, these figures are individual yet integral, separate parts of a great whole.

The complex of building, sculpture, and stained glass at Chartres is, for many who have experienced it, an almost perfect harmony between reason and emotion, order and complexity, the spiritual and the worldly.

Music and Drama in the Cathedral:
THE PLAY OF DANIEL

The combined visual arts of the great Gothic cathedrals—architecture, painting, sculpture, and stained glass—exemplify the medieval Catholic belief (quite opposed to later, puritanical ones) that spiritual truths could be apprehended through physical, sensuous beauty. This same belief seems to underlie the service of the mass and the music developed for it. Earlier, in the monasteries, one-voiced (*monophonic*) chants, called Gregorian chants (after Pope Gregory the Great) were sung at masses and at the monks' spiritual exercises during the day. In the Gothic period, individual singers were used along with a choir, and a many-voiced (*polyphonic*) type of music for the mass developed. The resonance provided by the soaring vaults of

the cathedral gave this music a special richness that it would not have in another setting. The performance of the mass, with its procession of priests and choirs, the play of light through the stained glass, the burning of incense, and the reverberations of music and oratory from the stones must have been an experience to delight both senses and spirit.

Each cathedral, as mentioned earlier, had a school for instructing the young clerics who sang in the choir and performed other services in the church. The school and the rest of the cathedral were administered and cared for by the chapter, a group of clergy associated with the cathedral and subject to a rule, or canon, that ordered their way of life. One of the duties of the chapter, and the boys in its school, was to provide music for the services of the church. Medieval musicians were always part of a community, either religious or secular; and the music they wrote and performed was composed for purposes other than a purely musical one, just as the purposes of medieval sculptors, painters, and architects were never purely artistic. In this regard they were unlike modern composers and performers who sell their wares as individuals to the public on an open market, for it was the community that imposed rules and requirements both on their daily lives and on their musical activities.

The demands of the community did not seem to restrict the musicians' creativity—on the contrary, medieval people seemed to be eager for more and more elaborate forms. It is perhaps because of this kind of demand that a type of drama developed out of the mass. This form, called *liturgical drama* because it was probably a part of the worship service, represented the same religious stories from the Old and New Testaments as were represented on the windows, walls, and niches of the cathedral; it acted on the imaginations of the faithful in much the same way. *The Play of Daniel*, which we will study here, is an example of liturgical drama; it must be understood both as music and as drama. This would, of course, ideally be true of Greek drama too, but at least we are fortunate enough to have manuscripts of medieval music (preserved in monasteries and cathedral schools) that give us some idea, if not a totally accurate one, of how it was performed. Medieval liturgical drama, in some ways stranger to the modern mind than Greek tragedy, is an important phenomenon in our cultural history because it developed at a time when the theater was all but dead in the Western world and thus made possible the growth of modern drama.

The theater, as it was known in the classical world, was in effect killed by the combined influence of barbarians and Christianity. The invaders of the Roman empire had no idea what a theater was, and by the time of the "fall" of Rome, drama survived only in the form of bloody spectacles or rituals associated with pagan feasts. Seeing these survivals as corruptions of the body and spirit, Christians attempted to wipe them out; actors were, in fact, excommunicated from the Church. Nevertheless, it is a tribute to the human desire to participate in or to observe shows—to mime the outside world—that some form of dramatic activity continued throughout the early Middle Ages. Wandering minstrels, jugglers, tumblers, and other showmen continued to entertain willing audiences in village squares.

Ironically, after centuries of hostility, it was within the Church itself that drama was reborn as an art form. It is as if the Church at last recognized the human need for imitation and spectacle and thus incorporated it for spiritual purposes. The mass itself is dramatic in character: it is a reenactment of the sacrifice of Christ. Processions, such as those held on Palm Sunday and Easter, added to its spectacular qualities. In line with the Gothic tendency to elaborate and enrich, evident in the art of the cathedral, the mass itself became more complex and decorative. Choirs began to sing in alternation with one another, a process called *antiphony* that is already somewhat dramatic. Then, in the early tenth century, lengthened musical passages and elaborations on the text of the mass were added. These *tropes*, as they were called, are credited with the rebirth of drama. A trope used in the Easter Mass, referred to as "Quem Quaeritis?" (Whom do you seek?) is, as far as we know, the first "drama" ever to be performed within the church. Here (translated from Latin) is the entire text:

Angel: Whom do you seek in the tomb, O Christians?
The Three Marys: Jesus of Nazareth, the crucified,
           O celestial ones.
Angel: He is not here, he is risen as he predicted.
       Go and tell that he is risen from the tomb.

Probably this text was sung by antiphonal choirs and did not involve actors. It is admittedly not much of a drama, but from it an entire new tradition was born. By the twelfth century, musical drama as part of the mass reached the point at which it involved characters, choruses, and real dramatic action, as in *The Play of Daniel*. This musical drama was created in the twelfth century for the cathedral of Beauvais, a flourishing city of medieval France just northwest of Paris.

According to the prologue of *The Play of Daniel*, this music was written by the young scholars of Beauvais.

Ad honorem tui, Christe,   In your honor, Christ,
Danielis ludus iste,   This play of Daniel
In Belvaco est inventus,   Was created in Beauvais;
Et invenit hunc juventus.   The youth created it.

The language is Latin (with some phrases in Old French), and this is not surprising, for the affairs of the church were conducted in Latin as, most likely, were the classes that these young men attended. At the end of the play appears the rubric, or performance instruction:

Hic auditis, cantores   After hearing this, the singers
incipient Te Deum   intone the "O God,
Laudamus.   We praise Thee."

This is the clue informing us that this play was probably performed at Matins, a religious service celebrated daily by the chapter in the early hours of the morning before dawn. Matins is normally a long service, for it contains the chanting of nine complete Psalms and their antiphons as well as the reading of nine scriptural lessons and the singing of nine Responses and the Te Deum. Obviously, the addition of a complete drama would occur only for a special holiday; and, from references in the text, including the final prophecy of Daniel (which Christians interpret as foretelling the birth of Christ), we conclude that it was written for the Christmas season, probably performed at the end of matins for Christmas morning.

The Play of Daniel has many features that made it particularly attractive to twelfth-century Christians. Coming at the time of the first Crusades, the story includes the great historical personages of the Persian empire, King Belshazzar and King Darius, a subject most in keeping with current political interest. Then, the story of the miracle of Daniel's salvation from the terror of the lions' den provides an opportunity for the dramatization of a spectacular event for people who fervently believed in the miraculous. The pageantry of the processions and the rituals of the Persian court were also affairs that could be related to the regular activities of the chapter but that were elevated to a higher level by being unusual or extraordinary. Lastly, the music itself had its own fascination. Each of these elements, when understood within the context of the whole, can speak to us directly when we listen to, and witness a performance of, *The Play of Daniel*.[1]

The music of the play is divided into nine sections, and it is possible that it substituted for, or replaced parts of, the nine sections of matins. The following divisions outline the Daniel story:

1. Prologue. Introduction of characters and synopsis of the story.
2. Belshazzar commands a feast and orders his wise men to interpret the riddle, "Mene, Tekel, Peres," which a mysterious hand has written on the wall.
3. The queen arrives, suggests asking Daniel, and he is called before the king.
4. Daniel prophesies doom for Belshazzar but is rewarded for having spoken the truth.
5. The procession of Darius the Great arrives, Belshazzar is slain, and the musicians celebrate the ascendancy of the new ruler.
6. Darius calls for Daniel, raises him to high office, and Daniel pledges allegiance.
7. The jealous counselors find a way to force the king to condemn Daniel.
8. Daniel is saved from the lions by an angel, and he delivers his prophecy of the coming of the Son of Man.
9. Epilogue. An angel announces the birth of Christ, and the Te Deum is sung.

---

[1] The reader is advised to listen to *A Twelfth Century Music Drama: The Play of Daniel*, recorded by the New York Pro Musica directed by Noah Greenberg (Decca DL 9402). Specific listening assignments refer to this album. The text of the play (in Latin and in English) is included in the album.

What about the music of the play? After all, it is radically different from current musical sounds. If we take the version recorded by the New York Pro Musica as a fair representation of the way it might have been performed during the twelfth century,[2] we are immediately struck by the presence of instruments no longer used in modern orchestras, a singing style that is certainly not common now, music that does not use *harmony*, and a language that is no longer spoken. Where does one begin in order to understand and enjoy? Perhaps first with the *dynamics*, the volume level of the performance.

Nothing in *The Play of Daniel* is loud. Europeans of the twelfth century were accustomed to a quiet unknown to us, and their hearing was sensitive to minute aural detail. The words of a solo voice at speaking level are much easier to understand and carry the excitement of the story line more effectively and intimately than an amplified voice artificially enhanced with electronic reverberation. Besides, the cathedral walls were reverberant enough. The listeners had no ear pollution from electronic rock music, jet landings, and freeway traffic, or from background sounds of air conditioning, electric typewriters, and screaming radio disc jockeys. This awareness of subtle variations in melody, in the *timbre* (or tonal color) of instruments, and in performer *inflection* is reflected in the music that they composed to glorify their world and their God. Medieval man did not need volume to hear; he was more interested in finesse and detail.

Even the instruments play softly. The straight trumpet (fifteenth century!) used for this performance could in no way match the gross dynamics of a twentieth-century orchestral trumpet. What does play a significant role in medieval orchestration and replaces volume as an important factor of instrumental sonority is timbre, or tone color. Medieval musicians delighted in the variety, rather than the unity, of the instrumental sounds. The rebec is a little bowed fiddle with a thin nasal sound; the vielle a larger bowed string instrument with a more open tone; the minstrel's harp a stringed instrument that is plucked rather than

---

[2] The scoring and editing is a modern reconstruction, for the original source does not indicate instruments, dynamics, voices, and so on.

bowed, and the psaltery another type of plucked string instrument. There were many different sounds from the percussion: jingles, triangles, finger cymbals, cymbals, tambourine, bells, and drums of varying size and pitch; likewise with the wind instruments: portative organ, recorders, and bagpipes. These instruments were not designed to blend but to stand apart and remain distinct. Medieval people heard and enjoyed the differences, and we can, too. Perhaps nineteenth-century America was striving for sameness, but twentieth-century America is beginning to cultivate, preserve, and appreciate individuality that is much in keeping with the way that medieval man—and medieval musicians—viewed their world.

In the same way that twelfth-century listeners would distinguish individual voices and separate timbres, they could also isolate different song types. Some kinds of music were appropriate for one action or emotion; other kinds were suitable for different situations. In *The Play of Daniel* two distinct musical types are easily discerned: songs and processionals. There are others, but let us study those two as the most important in this work. Daniel's lament, upon being condemned to the lions, reads:

Heu, heu, heu!	Woe, woe, woe!
Quo casu sortis venit haec damnatio mortis?	By what chance of fate do I receive this condemnation to death?
Heu, heu, heu!	Woe, woe, woe!
Scelus infandum!	Unspeakable calamity!
Cur me dabit ad lacerandum	Why will this savage multitude
Haec fera turba feris?	Give me to be torn by wild beasts?
Sic me, Rex, perdere quaeris?	Thus, O King, do you seek to kill me?
Heu!	Woe!
Qua morte mori me cogis?	To what death do you compel me?
Parce furori.	Spare your fury.

The music is *through-composed* to emphasize the emotional intensity of each portion of the text. No repeated passages appear that would use the same music for different words, and, in this case, the beginning is nonme-

lodic (that is, it opens on a monotone) to underline the cry of despair, *"Heu, heu, heu!"*

As you listen to the recording, note that the composers further clarify the text of this lament by basically setting the text one syllable to one pitch. In ecstatic passages of celebration and jubilation, it was customary to sing florid groups of notes, thus giving the music a sense of freedom and release. Here the opposite is true, for the sense of fear, uncertainty, and self-doubt calls for restraint and reflection.

A contrasting type of composition is a *conductus* or processional, and an excellent example is the procession of the queen coming to King Belshazzar: *"Cum doctorum."*

Cum doctorum et magorum omnis adsit contio	All the throng of learned and wise men is present.
Secum volvit, neque solvit, quae sit manus visio.	They ponder, but cannot explain, the appearance of the hand.
Ecce prudens, styrpe cluens, dives cum potentia;	Behold the prudent, well-born, rich in power,
In vestitu deaurato coniunx adest regia.	Gold-clad spouse of the King is here.
Haec latentem promet vatem per cujus inditium	She will reveal the unknown prophet by whose information
Rex describi suum ibi noverit exitium.	The King will learn and know of his destruction.
Laetis ergo haec virago comitetur plausibus;	Let this heroine be accompanied with joyful applause;
Cordis, orisque sonoris personetur vocibus.	With strings and voices, let loud songs resound.

First notice that the Latin text is strophic; that is, it is written in verse form. The words are both metrical and rhymed, and so is the music. The meter for the first verse is:

```
/ ˘ / ˘ / ˘ / ˘
/ ˘ / ˘ / ˘ /
/ ˘ / ˘ / ˘ / ˘
/ ˘ / ˘ / ˘ /
```

This is the basic meter of all the verses, but a few poetic changes in verses 3 and 4 are regularized by the music, which was probably composed with verse 1 in mind.

In listening, notice that the melody for *"Cum doctorum"* (the first stanza) is the same as that for the following three stanzas. In other words, the form is similar to some folk songs, modern hymns, a few "pop" songs, and many Country and Western tunes in which several verses are sung to the same melody. Music written this way is easily remembered; and, if it has a good beat (as this one does), it carries the listener along in a forward movement of insistent rhythm. It cannot express the precise meaning of the text as well as a through-composed piece, but that is not important in this case, for this *conductus* was not written to express deep feelings and heighten a monologue but to accompany a parade. In other words, the medieval composer used different compositional means to accomplish quite different artistic ends.

It should be apparent by now that the music of this play is not just one long, continuous, undifferentiated monophonic song but a logical series of discrete artistic songs, balanced and blended into a recipe that produces effective music drama. The wedding of drama with music was certainly not new—we saw it with the Greeks, although their music is lost to us. (It is, rather, drama without music that is a recent form.) Both medieval liturgical drama and Greek drama have influenced modern drama, musical theater, and opera. Medieval music is, of course, still found within the Mass. But the music of the cathedral was only one side of the medieval contribution; the court would produce its own music.

The Play of Daniel

(Prologue)

BELSHAZZAR'S PRINCE:
   In your honor, Christ,
   This Play of Daniel
   Was created in Beauvais;
   The youth created it.

THE COURT:
   To the Almighty One who holds the stars,
   The crowd of men and mob of boys
   Gives praise.

   For they hear how faithful Daniel
   Undergoes and bears many things
   With constancy.

   The King calls the wise men to him
   That they may explain
   The handwriting.

   But they could not solve it,
   And they fell silent, on the spot,
   Before the King.

But to Daniel, upon reading the writing,
The words, which had been a mystery to them,
Soon became clear.

Because Belshazzar saw him surpass them,
He was exalted in the assembly,
It is told.

An insufficient case, brought to trial,
Delivered him to the lions' mouths
To be torn apart.

But you, O God,
Wanted Daniel's enemies
To be good to him.

Also, that he might not hunger,
You sent a prophet on wings
To give him food.

(The Play Proper Begins)

THE COURT:
  O King, live forever!

BELSHAZZAR:
  You who obey my voice,
  Bring, for my use, the vessels
  Which my father carried off from the temple
  When he smote Judaea mightily.

THE COURT:
  Let us rejoice in our King, great and powerful!
  Let us sing his worthy praise in a suitable voice!
  Let the joyous crowd resound with solemn odes!
  Let them play harps, clap hands, make a thousand
    noises.

His father, who destroyed the temple of the Jews,
Did great things, and this one rules by his example.
His father despoiled the kingdom of the Jews;
This one celebrates, appropriately, with their vessels.

These are royal vessels, which were plundered
From Jerusalem to enrich royal Babylon.
Let us present them to Belshazzar our King,
Who has adorned his servants with purple.

He is mighty, he is strong, he is glorious,
Virtuous, courtly, handsome, and fair.
Let us rejoice in such a King with melodious voice;
Let all resound his loud praises in unison;
Babylon applauds, laughing, Jerusalem weeps.
The latter is despoiled; the former, triumphant,
  worships Belshazzar.
Let us all, therefore, exult in such a mighty one,
Offering the King's vessels to His Majesty.

Behold, here they are before you.

(A hand writes "MENE, TEKEL, PERES" on the wall)

BELSHAZZAR:
  Call the Chaldean mathematicians and astrologers.
  Find the soothsayers,
  And bring the wise men in!

TWO WISE MEN:
  O King, live forever!
  Here we are.

BELSHAZZAR:
  Whoever shall read this writing
  And disclose its meaning,
  Under his power
  Babylonia shall be placed,
  And he shall wear purple
  And a golden necklace.

THE TWO WISE MEN:
  We do not know, nor can we explain,
  What the writing is, nor what the hand means.

THE QUEEN AND HER ATTENDANTS:
  All the throng of learned
    and wise men is present.
  They ponder, but cannot explain,
    the appearance of the hand.

  Behold the prudent, well-born,
    rich in power,
  Gold-clad spouse
    of the King is here.

  She will reveal the unknown prophet
    by whose information
  The King will learn and know
    of his destruction.

  Let this heroine be accompanied
    with joyful applause;
  With strings and voices,
    let loud songs resound.

THE QUEEN:
  O King, live forever!

  That you may know the writer's meaning,
  King Belshazzar, hear my advice.
  With the captive people of Judaea,
  Daniel, learned in prophetic oracles,
  Was brought from his country,

A prisoner of your father's victory.
He lives here under your rule,
And reason demands that he be called.
Therefore send for him without delay,
For he will show you what the vision conceals.

BELSHAZZAR:
Seek Daniel and bring him here
When he has been found.

THE COURTIERS:
O Daniel, man and prophet of God
Come to the King.
Come, he wishes
To speak to you.
He is fearful and disturbed, Daniel,
Come to the King.
He wants to learn from you what is a secret to us,
He will make you rich with gifts, Daniel,
Come to the King.
If he can learn from you the meaning of the writing.

DANIEL:
I wonder greatly by whose advice
The King's command seeks me out.
I will go, however, and he shall know from me,
At no cost, what is hidden.

THE COURTIERS:
This is God's true servant,
Whom all people praise,
The fame of whose prudence
Is known in the King's court.
The King sends for him by us.

DANIEL:
Poor, and an exile, I go to the King by your request.

THE COURTIERS:
In the glory of youth,
Full of heavenly grace,
He greatly excels all men
In virtue, in living, in his habits.
The King sends for him by us.

DANIEL:
Poor, and an exile, I go to the King by your request.

THE COURTIERS:
This is he whose help
Will explain that vision,
In which the writing of a hand
Disturbed the King deeply.
The King sends for him by us.

DANIEL:
Poor, and an exile, I go to the King by your request.

(Daniel appears before the King)
O King, live forever!

BELSHAZZAR:
Are you he who is called Daniel,
Brought here with the wretched of Judaea?
They say that you have the spirit of God,
And that you know whatever is hidden.
If, therefore, you can explain the writing,
Huge rewards will be given to you.

DANIEL:
King, I do not want your rewards.
The writings will be explained for no fee.
Now this is the solution:
Your destruction is at hand.
Your father was once mighty
Above all others.
Greatly puffed up with pride,
He was cast down from his glory.
For not walking with God,
But making himself like God,
He snatched the vessels from the temple
For his own use.
But after many excesses,
He finally lost his riches,
And divested of human form,
He ate grass for fodder.
You too, his son,
Are no less impious,
For you follow after his deeds
And use his vessels.

But whatever displeases God
Has a time for retribution,
And now the handwriting
Threatens a punishment.
And God says, MENE,
Your reign is at an end.
TEKEL means scales,
Which show you to be lacking.
PERES is distribution,
Your rule is given to another.

BELSHAZZAR:
  Let him who thus has solved the mystery
  Be clothed in a royal garment.
  Take away the vessels, prince of the army,
  Lest they be a source of misery to me.

THE QUEEN AND HER ATTENDANTS:
  There is recorded, in the book of Solomon,
  Fitting and proper praise of woman.
  Her value is that of a strong man
  From far and distant lands.
  Her husband's heart trusts in her;
  He possesses abundant riches.
  Let this woman be compared
  To one whose king is worthy of support.
  For the eloquence of her words
  Overcomes the wisdom of the learned.
  Let us who are performing this play
  On this solemn day
  Give to her devout praise;
  Let the ends of the earth come and sing.

THE MEN OF THE COURT:
  Carrying the vessels of the King
  Before whom the peoples of Judae tremble,
  And giving praise to Daniel,
  Let us rejoice! Fitting praises
  Let us bear him!
  He foretold the King's downfall
  When he explained the writing;
  He proved the witnesses guilty
  And freed Susannah.
  Let us rejoice!
  Fitting praises
  Let us bear him!

Babylon exiled him,
When the Jews were taken captive
Whom Belshazzar honors.
Let us rejoice!
Fitting praises
Let us bear him!
He is a holy prophet of God.
Honored by Chaldeans
And Gentiles and Jews.
Therefore, making merry before him,
Let us rejoice!
Fitting praises
Let us bear him!

(King Darius and his soldiers and courtiers now enter,
having overthrown Belshazzar)

DARIUS'S SOLDIERS AND COURT:
  Behold! King Darius
  Comes with his princes,
  The noble one with his nobles.
  And his court
  Resounds with joy,
  And there is dancing.
  He is awesome,
  Venerated by all.
  Empires are
  His tributaries.
  All honor him as King
  And worship him.
  The land of Babylonia
  Fears him, also.
  With his armed troops,
  Descending like a whirlwind,
  He crushes armies
  And destroys the strong.
  Honesty and nobility
  Are his endowments.
  He is the noble King,
  Darius of Babylonia.
  Let this throng
  Rejoice in him with dancing
  And praise with joy
  His mighty deeds,
  So wondrous.
  Let us all be glad together;

Let the drums sound,
Let harpists pluck their strings;
Let the musicians' instruments
Resound his praises.

(Darius is seated on the throne. All acclaim him, saying)

O King, live forever!

TWO COUNSELORS:
Hear us, you princes of the King's court,
Who administer the laws throughout the land.
There is a certain wise man in Babylonia,
Who by the gods' grace reveals secret things.
His advice pleased the King,
For he explained the writing to Belshazzar.
So quickly, let there be no delay—
We want to make use of his counsel.
If he will come, let him be made counselor
To the King, and he shall rank third in the kingdom.

(Three messengers are sent to Daniel)

MESSENGERS:
Our embassy comes by command of the King,
O servant of God.
Your uprightness is praised to the King;
Your amazing skill commends you.
Through you alone was explained
The apparition of a hand which was a mystery to
    everyone.
The King calls you to his court,
That he may acknowledge your discretion.
You shall be, according to what Darius says,
His principal adviser.
Therefore come, for the whole court
Is being readied for your pleasure.

DANIEL:
I will go to the King.

(Daniel is led before Darius)

COUNSELORS, MESSENGERS, COURTIERS:
With great rejoicing let us celebrate the Christmas
    solemnities;

God's Wisdom has now redeemed us from death.
He who created all things is born man, in the flesh;
His birth was foretold by the words of the prophet.
The old anointing of Daniel's time had ended;
The dispensation of the Jews is over.
On this Christmas,
With joy, O Daniel,
This crowd praises you.
You freed Susannah from a capital charge;
God inspired you by his holy spirit.
You proved the witnesses guilty by their own
    accusations;
You destroyed the dragon Bel in the sight of the
    people.
And God guarded you from the lion's pit.
Therefore, praised by the Word of God, born of a
    Virgin.

DANIEL:
O King, live forever!

DARIUS:
Because I know your prudence,
Daniel, I give you responsibility
Over the entire kingdom
And award you the highest place.

DANIEL:
King, if you trust in me,
You will do no evil by following my advice.

TWO ENVIOUS ADVISERS:
O King, live forever!
It was decreed in your court
By the rulers who are glorious
That, by the power of your name,
Every god should be rejected
For the space of thirty days,
And that you should be adored as God by all, O
    King!
If anyone should be so rash
As to disregard your command
And to prefer another god above you,
The punishment should be
That he be delivered to the lion's pit;

Let this be proclaimed throughout your realm, O
    King!

DARIUS:
    I command and ordain
    That this decree be obeyed. Hear it!

(*Daniel worships his own God in spite of the decree*)

TWO ENVIOUS ADVISERS:
    Do you remember, Darius, the observance you
        commanded,
    That whoever is guilty of praying to any god but you
    For anything will be given to the lions?
    This law was proclaimed by your princes.

DARIUS:
    It is true that I commanded
    All people to worship me.

TWO ENVIOUS ADVISERS:
    We saw this Jew, Daniel, worshiping
    And praying to his God in defiance of your laws.

DARIUS:
    May it never be granted you
    That that holy man should be so destroyed.

TWO ENVIOUS ADVISERS:
    The law of the Medes and the Persians in the annals
        commands
    That whoever scorns the King's decree be given to
        the lions.

DARIUS:
    If he has disobeyed the law that I made,
    Let him receive the punishment that I decreed.

(*Daniel is seized and brought to the lions' den*)

DANIEL:
    Woe, woe, woe!
    By what chance of fate do I receive this
        condemnation to death?
    Woe, woe, woe!

Unspeakable calamity!
    Why will this savage multitude
    Give me to be torn by wild beasts?
    Thus, O King, do you seek to kill me?
    Woe!
    To what death do you compel me?
    Spare your fury.

DARIUS:
    The God whom you worship so faithfully
    Will deliver you miraculously.

(*Daniel is thrown into the lions' den*)

DANIEL:
    I am not guilty of this crime;
    God have mercy on me, eleyson.
    To this place, O God, send a defender
    Who will restrain the power of the lions, eleyson.

(*An angel is sent to protect Daniel from the lions. Another
    angel comes to Habakkuk, far away*)

ANGEL:
    Habakkuk, pious old man,
    Bring food to Daniel,
    To the pit in Babylonia;
    The King of all commands it of you.

HABAKKUK:
    God in his wisdom knows
    That I know nothing of Babylon,
    Nor of the pit
    Into which Daniel has been put.

(*The angel leads him there*)

HABAKKUK:
    Arise, brother, and take food;
    God has seen your sufferings;
    God has sent me, give thanks to him
    Who made you.

DANIEL:
    You have remembered me, Lord;
    I accept this in your name, Alleluiah!

(Darius approaches the pit)

DARIUS:

> Do you think, Daniel,
> That he whom you revere and worship
> Will save you and rescue you
> From the death to which you are sent?

DANIEL:

> O King, live forever!
> With his accustomed pity, God sent an angelic
>   protection
> To close the lions' mouths for the time being.

DARIUS:

> Bring Daniel out,
> And throw the envious ones in.

(His princes proclaim the command)

> Bring Daniel out,
> And throw the envious ones in.

THE TWO ENVIOUS ADVISERS:

> We suffer this deservedly, for we have
> Sinned against a holy man of God;
> We have acted unjustly
> And have done evil.

DARIUS:

> I command all people to worship
> Daniel's God, who rules the world.

DANIEL:

> Behold, the holy one shall come,
> The holiest of the holy,
> Whom this king, powerful and mighty,
> Commands us to worship.

> Temples, anointings,
> This kingdom shall cease;
> The end of the Kingdom of Judaea,
> And of its oppression, is at hand.

(An angel appears to announce the fulfillment of Daniel's
*   prophecy)*

ANGEL:

> I bring you a message from on high:
> Christ, the ruler of the world, is born
> In Bethlehem in Judah,
> As the Prophet foretold.

(The entire company sings the "Te Deum laudamus")

> We praise thee, O God;
> We acknowledge thee to be the Lord.
> All the earth doth worship thee,
> The Father everlasting.
> To thee all Angels cry aloud;
> The Heavens and all the Powers therein;
> To thee Cherubim and Seraphim continually do cry:

> Holy, holy, holy,
> Lord God of Sabaoth;
> Heaven and earth are full of the Majesty of thy glory.
> The glorious company of the Apostles praise thee.
> The goodly fellowship of the Prophets praise thee.
> The noble army of Martyrs praise thee.
> The holy Church throughout all the world doth
>   acknowledge thee;
> The Father of an infinite Majesty;
> Thine adorable true and only Son;
> Also the Holy Ghost the Comforter.
> Thou art the King of Glory, O Christ.
> Thou art the everlasting Son of the Father.
> When thou tookest upon thee to deliver man,
> Thou didst humble thyself to be born of a Virgin.
> When thou hadst overcome the sharpness of death,
> Thou didst open the Kingdom of Heaven to all
>   believers.
> Thou sittest at the right hand of God, in the glory of
>   the Father.
> We believe that thou shalt come to be our Judge.
> We therefore pray thee help thy servants,
> Whom thou hast redeemed with thy precious blood.
> Make them to be numbered with thy Saints in glory
>   everlasting.
> O Lord, save thy people
> And bless thine heritage.
> Govern them, and lift them up for ever.
> Day by day we magnify thee;
> And we worship thy Name ever world without end.

Vouchsafe, O Lord, to keep us this day without sin.
Have mercy upon us, O Lord, have mercy upon us.
O Lord, let thy mercy be upon us,
As our trust is in thee.
O Lord, in thee have I trusted;
Let me never be confounded.

COMMENTS AND QUESTIONS

1. Read the Book of Daniel in the Old Testament, asking yourself what the author has done with the biblical story. Has he Christianized any of its specifically Jewish aspects? Has he added anything to the various characters or depicted them more clearly than they are in the story?

2. In noting the differences between the story of Daniel in the Bible and the way that it is handled in the play, you may be able to see something of the same process of transformation of myth into drama that was at work in Sophocles' creation of *Oedipus Rex*. Does the hero of *The Play of Daniel* show the same internal development or character transformations Oedipus does? Are the other characters as well defined? Why or why not?

3. From a comparison of these two plays, what inferences can you make concerning the differences between the classical and the medieval aesthetic, particularly concerning the view of the place of human beings held by each culture?

4. Could *Daniel* have been written as a tragedy? What keeps it from being a tragedy? Would a tragic view of life be alien to the Judeo-Christian view of the world?

5. In what ways do the lack of harmony and orchestration affect the function of the melody in the *Daniel* play?

6. Even though you might not recognize distinctive melodies as such in *The Play of Daniel*, do you hear sounds that are more appropriate for one kind of action or emotion than for another?

8

Divine And
Human Love

The Cult of the Virgin Mary

The cathedral of Notre Dame de Chartres, built as a palace for the queen of heaven, containing a relic of her tunic, full of images of her in stone and stained glass, is, among other things, a testament to the enormous importance that the mother of Jesus had in the spiritual and daily lives of medieval men and women. And Chartres was not the only such palace. Romanesque churches were dedicated to a variety of saints, but in the Gothic period the greatest cathedrals of France—Amiens, Rheims, Laon, Rouen, and Paris—were named for the Virgin *Notre Dame* (our lady). Why did Mary play such an important part in medieval lives, and what were the effects of this cult?

The devotion to Mary was part of a general humanizing trend in religion that began in the eleventh and twelfth centuries. Monastic literature of this time began to emphasize the theme of tenderness and compassion for

Jesus's sufferings. In art, Jesus was portrayed as more and more human. Whereas early medieval portrayals of the Christ Child had been somewhat allegorical, making the baby look already like the king of the world, twelfth-century artists began to portray a more child-like child and with him a mother who could express the tenderness of human, as well as divine, love. The artists who represented this divine mother took care to represent her as a lady of great beauty, combining physical attractiveness with a more ethereal quality. In the language of Mary's devotees, the praise of spiritual and physical beauty was often intermingled. Mary was seen as a queen but also as a mother—a kind and warm woman full of compassion for human sufferings and shortcomings, able and willing to intercede between individuals and God and thereby to save souls. A great many stories about miracles done by the Virgin circulated orally in the twelfth century; some were written down. The following examples illustrate the common man's view of the Virgin's compassion and power.

> A clerk at Chartres led an unchaste life, but often prayed to the Virgin. When he died, he was buried outside the churchyard because of his bad reputation. The Virgin appeared to one of his colleagues, asked him why her "chancellor" had been so badly treated, and ordered that he be reburied in the churchyard.

> A certain thief named Ebbo was devoted to the Virgin, and even hailed her when he went out to steal. He was finally arrested and hanged [a common punishment for thieves] but the Virgin supported him for two days and when the hangmen tried to tighten the rope, she put her hands around his throat and prevented them. Finally he was let go.

One of the spiritual leaders most responsible for promoting the cult of the Virgin in theology, along with popular devotion, was Saint Bernard (1090–1153). Bernard, abbot of Clairvaux and a close associate of the abbot Suger, was a Cistercian monk who emphasized in his teachings the value of the inner life and self-knowledge as part of a mystical ascension to God. Divine love, the essential attribute of the Virgin, could aid the soul in its progressive ascent from the love of bodily things, to the love of spiritual things, to the selfless love of God. The Virgin, human and yet the mother of God, could aid human beings in their progress from carnal to spiritual love. St. Bernard's spiritual devotion to Mary was immortalized by Dante Alighieri's representation of his hymn to the virgin near the end of the *Divine Comedy.*

Although written in the fifteenth century, the French poet François Villon's ballad about his mother vividly portrays the simple faith, in particular the devotion to the Virgin Mary, characteristic of the common people throughout the medieval period. In the latter part of the poem we observe how the wall paintings (probably of a romanesque church) served to educate and to heighten religious emotion. The translation is by William Frederic Giese.

FRANCOIS VILLON

Ballade

For His Mother to Our Lady

Queen of the skies and regent of the earth
And sovran empress of the realms of hell,
Receive me, Mary, though of little worth,
Yet heavenward bent, a child of Christian birth;
Through your grace only can I enter in—
For your great goodness, as I know full well,
Is greater than the burden of my sin.
O queen of heaven, your servitor am I,
And in this faith I mean to live and die.

Tell your blest Son I am His own, and thus,
Even as Egyptian Mary was forgiven
Or that most learnèd clerk, Theophilus,
Who once did seal a compact with the devil—
May God forbid I fall into like evil!—
So may I also be absolved and shriven;
For I hold true, howe'er unworthily,
Since I am weak, and sinful too alas,
The holy things that I have heard at Mass,
And in this faith I mean to live and die.

I am a woman poor and very old,
Who cannot read and nothing know at all,
But in the cloister, when my beads I've told,

I see God's paradise upon the wall,
All gay with harps and lutes, and, underneath,
A flaming hell where damned souls boil and seethe.
Hell frightens me, and heaven fills with joy:
O heavenly goddess, let the joy be mine,
For you to every sinner are benign
Whose faith is free of weakness and alloy—
And in this faith I mean to live and die.

Envoi

Virgin and blest princess without stain,
Thy Son was He who shall forever reign,
Jesus, who, wrought on by our feebleness,
Left His bright heaven to succor our distress
And offered on the cross His lovely youth.
Our Lord is He: this do I hold for sooth—
And in this faith I mean to live and die.

Representations of the Virgin Mary in medieval art and literature had many facets. Queen of heaven, loving mother, sister of the humble, she also appeared as a beautiful lady. The expression of mystical love for the Virgin began, in the twelfth century, to influence secular love poetry, so that poets began to write of their lady loves in terms more religious than amorous, as if they were worshiping them. In turn, love poetry had its influence on devotional poetry, so that the modern reader senses a confusion between the two realms. The following poem by the provençal troubadour Guiraut Riquier (fl. 1252–1294) may serve as a transition between the art of the cathedral and the art of the court.

GUIRAUT RIQUIER

Song to the Virgin

Often in times past I thought that I was singing of love; yet I knew it not, for what I called love was my folly. But now love brings me to love such a lady that I can neither honor her nor fear her nor cherish her to the measure of her worth. But I hope that her love will hold me until the hope that I have in her is fulfilled.

For by her love I hope to increase in worth and honor and riches and joy. To nothing else, then, should I

turn my thought or my desire. For, since all that I want I can have through her, I must do all that I can to serve her. For I have her love, if only I behave toward her as true love teaches me to do.

And so I must try my best: since she loves me, let me, too, love, for I could not love her if she did not give me the power. Hence it is only right that, for her love, I should give mine. For without her I am good for nothing. I can do nothing for her except to honor her. God, who has the power, grant that I may hold before my lady the banner of true lovers among whom love reigns.

I have neither wit nor knowledge to praise her; such is her honor that there is room for no more, such her virtue that nothing can increase it. How, then, can my praise honor her? The honor is mine, for I can only speak what is true. Hence I must do my best to tell the truth of her from morning to evening; for I can never fail in anything that I should do, if only I remember my lady.

So great is her beauty that it can never lessen, there is no imperfection in it, it shines night and day. So great is her power that it cannot fail. Such are her kindness and charity and wisdom and knowledge and pity and mercy that I hope her love—since she deigns to love me—will keep me joyful, if only I truly come to her.

Representations of the Virgin Mary

The Virgin Mary was naturally a great subject for artists of all kinds. In the sculpture and glass at Chartres she is majestic and beautiful, portrayed as the Mother of Christ and, therefore, the Queen of Heaven. Somewhat later, in the jamb sculptures on the west portal of Notre Dame de Reims (Fig. 8-1) she is depicted as a young, shy, innocent girl when visited by the archangel Gabriel. On the adjacent jamb she is the pregnant matron who greets her cousin Elizabeth, pregnant with the child who will be John the Baptist. Both women have a weight and gravity in their bearing, conveyed by pose and drapery, that is almost classical in feeling, and highly appropriate to the roles that God has assigned them.

The association of Mary with Christian and

8-1   Annunciation and Visitation, jamb statues, west portal, Cathedral of Reims, c. 1225–45 (Giraudon/Art Resource)

courtly love, and thus with majesty and divinity, provided the inspiration for Simone Martini's late-Gothic *Annunciation*, painted in 1333 (Color Plate III). Martini (1283–1344) was born in Siena, but one of his chief patrons was Robert of Anjou, King of Naples (d. 1343). Through the Neapolitan court Martini was exposed to French art. The consequences of this contact are to be found in his stunning, glittering altarpieces executed in these years. The *Annunciation* is divided into panels that seem to echo the elaborate designs and proportions of the east portals of a French Gothic cathedral with its portals, finials, and carved, embossed, and double-curved arches. In this frame Martini has placed a most retiring, but nevertheless sinuous, sensuous Mary shrinking from the splendid beauty of the archangel Gabriel who has just alighted, his drapery still fluttering in the air.

This Mary annunciate is not a simple woman like the one depicted at Reims (Fig. 8-1), but rather a demure, decorous, young princess with slender hands and delicate features. This is the Mary of the Court of Heaven, where she is seated on a marble throne, reads from a beautiful book, and is separated from her visitor by a gilded vase with unfading lilies, symbolic of her virtue and purity. Martini's careful attention to the things of the experienced world—the gold embroidered border of Mary's gown, the plaid pattern of Gabriel's drapery, the minute varicolored feathers of his wings—links us to the temporal world, which courtly love is to enlighten and inform with virtue like that of Mary's.

The Literature and Music of Courtly Love

The graceful reverence for Mary apparent in both Simone Martini's painting and Guiraut Riquier's song reflect the tradition that has come to be known as "courtly love." Although it represented a literary vision of love rather than a reflection of contemporary reality, this style was associated with the new princely courts that first appeared in southern France in the early twelfth century and subsequently in northern France, England, and southern Germany. By this period, the economic revival had enriched rulers enough that they were able to maintain a modest group of friends and retainers around them. Like courts everywhere and at all times, these courts were marked by the effort to make an art of leisure and by the prominence of women in this attempt. The strong desire for entertainment and novelty was fulfilled either through the nobles' creativity and ingenuity or through attracting to the court someone endowed with these gifts.

One of the chief means of entertainment and artistic expression was literature, particularly songs and stories of love. Although the medieval nobles usually knew no Latin, both men and women were literate in the vernacular—that is, the modern European languages. Although stories about heros, or epics, had been composed from as early as the seventh century in Anglo-Saxon and then in the other European tongues, the main literary language of the early Middle Ages was still Latin. By the twelfth century, however, the vernacular was increasingly the vehicle for literature, and love became the main theme. Formed primarily from classical expressions of ideal friendship (Cicero's *On Friendship*) and of destructive passion (Ovid's *Heroides* and *Metamorphoses*), combined with biblical expressions of mystical love (Song of Songs) and of charity (I Corinthians), this courtly literature took a variety of forms.

The court of William of Aquitaine (d. 1131) was probably the first center for this new literature. Himself a poet, this prince of the southern French principality of Aquitaine encouraged the writing of vernacular literature in his entourage, as did his more famous daughter, Elinor of Aquitaine (d. 1204). Surely one of the greatest women of the Middle Ages, Elinor—beautiful, passionate and wilful—became first the wife of Louis VII, King of France, and then of Henry II, King of England. Patroness of a number of poets, including Bernart de Ventadorn, son of a mercenary soldier and a serving lady, she proved a significant influence in the diffusion of love literature to northern France and to England.

The Romance   One of the new genres of literature, the *romance*, a term originally signifying a composition in a romance (from Roman) language—French, Italian, or Spanish—was fast becoming the dominant form of narrative. In romances the main characters were knights and ladies, and the concerns were chivalry and love rather than heroic combat (as in the epic). But though the characters may have suggested ideals of courtesy and nobility, neither they nor their actions should be thought of as reflecting daily life at the time. They, their deeds of chivalry, and their loves were all fictions. And though the love that dominates these romances, as well as the new vernacular lyric poetry, is easily taken at face value, it was grounded more in fiction than in fact. The knight languishing in love for years and unable to bring himself to tell his lady of his feelings was a conventional literary figure. Around the fifteenth century, it is true that men started acting as they were described in the romances, but this was a case of life imitating art.

The medieval view of man, grounded in the classical and Christian insistence on the need to be guided by reason, would hardly permit an audience to find admirable a swooning lover, unable to act or even to think clearly. Such a figure would represent a ridiculous distortion of man created in the image of God and provide a vivid example of the folly of allowing passion to overcome reason. Whereas the language of what has been popularly known as courtly love (though the term is a modern invention) was at times similar to that used to express love of God or devotion to the Virgin, the application of such language to earthly love, necessarily transitory and changing, served neither to elevate the earthly nor to lower the divine. Rather, instead of making the earthly lady appear like the Virgin Mary, this effusive praise emphasized the inappropriateness of the comparison. The use of religious language to describe a lady love could only seem like a strange, distorted overstatement. The fiction of courtly love, with the lady functioning as an object of adoration and the man acting as her humble servant, parodied not only the veneration of the Virgin but also the sacrament of marriage, in which the woman promised to love, honor, and obey her husband, who was properly her lord. For man to be controlled by woman was, in the medieval view, for him to give up his responsibilities, as asserted by his religion, and to create a situation that would have been regarded as inverted and perverted, hardly one to be taken seriously.

There exist several medieval handbooks on love. One of the most popular, by Andreas Capellanus (late twelfth century), contains two parts on seduction (with instructions and models). In the third and final part, however, Andreas writes that if one is concerned with his salvation, he should forsake all such loves and turn to God. That man, even in the twelfth century, was not about to give up readily the pleasures of the flesh was clear to medieval writers: and one of the most important books of the Middle Ages, the thirteenth-century French narrative called *The Romance of the Rose*, shows in its dream *allegory* the lover ignoring the advice of Reason and continuing to pursue his earthly love. The final consummation—on the literal level a happy ending—is especially ironic, for the lover has allowed his passion to overcome his reason and has even jeopardized his salvation.

Even when the lover and the beloved are in accord, and even when their love seems good, it will fail—as medieval writings insist over and over—if they view it as the most important thing in their lives. As medieval Christianity emphasized, human love is properly a way of loving God and is good when it uses love of created things as a way of loving the Creator. If, on the other hand, the love is so consuming that it makes the lovers oblivious of anything outside themselves, including God, then it is what in Church tradition was called cupidity, wrong loving, not at all an expression of right loving, or charity.

Though from the twelfth century well into the Renaissance love provided the dominant subject of narratives and lyrics, the literature should not be viewed as celebrating this passion or sentiment. Rather, love provided a focal point for examining human folly and self-destruction; and the lover who regarded his own good ahead of what his religion taught him to be the common good was to be laughed at for his folly rather than pitied for his frustration.

The "Ways of Love"   The following medieval English poems, in a modern version by Edmund Reiss, were found on the same page of a thirteenth-century manuscript. They illustrate well the interrelationship in medieval literature of the religious and the secular. Whatever the precise relationship between the two pieces—whether the first, urging love of God, provides a basis for understanding the earthly love of the second, or whether the complaint of earthly love is a parody of the overtly religious poem, simultaneously calling up ideal love and making clear the inadequacy of earthly passion—it is clear that the two together offer two sides of an issue, two perspectives that must be taken into account by the audience. Together, especially through their parallel language and verses, they create an ambiguous statement of love that demands solution or reconciliation.

The Troubadour Song   One of the most stylized expressions of courtly love is found in the poetry and the music of the troubadours. The troubadours were poet-composers who worked and entertained in the region of southern France known as Provence, and they wrote in the regional dialect, Provençal, or *langue d'oc*. The themes of troubadour love poetry are nearly always the same: they concern a beautiful, idealized lady for whom the poet languishes with love but who does not return his love. Like the poets of ancient Greece and the modern folk singer, these artists entertained their (usually aristocratic) audience with solo voice, accompanied by a stringed instrument, the lute.

Perhaps the most famous troubadour was Bernart de Ventadorn, son of a mercenary soldier and a serving lady in the castle of the earl of Ventadorn. As an adult, he worked as a member of the court of Elinor of Aquitaine, so his presence was known in northern France as well. Bernart's travel surely contributed to the spread of the troubadour's art throughout France.

Although the poems of the troubadours concerned themselves with many subjects—morality, courtly love, politics—the preserved songs of Bernart seem to deal only with love. The stylized notions of chivalric love are matched by the stylized poetic and musical forms employed by the troubadours. Bernart's chanson, *Be m'an perdut*, has only three musical *phrases*—that is, only three very short melodic ideas—and the first two are identical. This construction results in an *AAB* musical form, a common secular music pattern known in the Middle Ages as *barform*. Notice in the music that the end of the third phrase is repeated and that

The Way of Christ's Love

Little knows any man
The love by which he is bound,
Whose heart's blood for us ran
And who saved us with his wound.
His love for us has made us sound
And cast the devil to the ground.
    Ever and always, he has us in his thought;
    He will not lose what he so dearly bought.

He bought us with his holy blood,
What could he do more?
He is so meek and mild and good
That he never sinned therefore.
The sins we do we should rue sore,
And cry to Jesus, "Christ, thy ore!"
    Ever and always, etc.

He saw his father full of pain
At man's most grievous fall.
With sad heart he swore again
That we should pay for all.
His sweet son he did call
And prayed him die for us all.
    Ever and always, etc.

He brought us all out of death
And did a friend's good deed.
Sweet Jesus of Nazareth,
You give us heaven's meed.
Why do we not of him take heed?
His fresh wounds so grimly bleed.
    Ever and always, etc.

His deep wounds bleed so fast,
We ought to care for him.
Out of hell he has us cast
And brought us out of sin.
For love of us his cheeks grow thin
His heart's blood he gave for his kin.
    Ever and always, etc.

The Way of Woman's Love

Little knows any man
How secret love can be,
Until he desires a fair woman
Who has been loved previously.
The love of such does not last long;
She promises love but treats me with wrong.
    Ever and always sorrow weighs on me,
    I long for her whom I seldom see.

Today I would utter her name
If to say it I should dare.
She has by far the greatest fame
Of all those who are fair.
Unless she love me she will sin;
Woe is he who loves what he cannot win.
    Ever and always, etc.

Before her I fall on my knees
And cry, "Lady, thy grace!"
Lady, give my love some ease
And show me a fair face.
Unless you do, it will grieve me sore;
Love afflicts me so, I can live no more.
    Ever and always, etc.

Merry it is inside her tower
With knights and servants attending.
So it is in her bower
With mirth and pleasure unending.
Unless she love me, it will me rue;
Woe is he who loves a love untrue.
    Ever and always, etc.

Fairest creature of all such,
My good love, I salute you,
As many times and as much
As there are drops of dew,
Or stars in the sky, or grasses sweet and sour;
Whose love is untrue is seldom content an hour.
    Ever and always, etc.

these are the same notes as the endings of the first two phrases. All this repetition creates easily remembered tunes, and, after all, we are dealing with song that is somewhat analogous to today's popular music. If the tune is not catchy, it will fail in its function of light and pleasant entertainment music.

The poet uses the same approach and care with the poetic devices of rhyme and *meter* in his composition. These qualities disappear in the translation, but their presence in the original allows an easy match of words and music as well as creating an ingenious and clever "way with words."

Be m'an perdut lai enves Ventadorn
   Tuih mei amic, pois ma domna no m'ama;
Et es be dreihz que jamais lai no torn,
   C'ades estai vas me salvatj' e grama.

  ˘ ˊ / ˘ / ˘ / ˘ / ˘ /
  ˘ / ˘ / ˘ / ˘ / ˘ / ˘
  ˘ / ˘ / ˘ / ˘ / ˘ /
  ˘ / ˘ / ˘ / ˘ / ˘ / ˘

BERNART DE VENTADORN

Be m'an perdut

I am indeed lost from the region of Ventadorn
To all my friends, for my lady loves me not;
With reason I turn not back again,
For she is bitter and ill-disposed toward me.
See why she turns a dark and angry countenance
   to me:
Because I take joy and pleasure in loving her!
Nor has she aught else with which to charge me.

So, like the fish who rushes to the lure
And suspects nothing until caught upon the hook,
Once I rushed to the overpowering love
And was not aware until I was in the flame
That burns hotter than ever furnace did.
And yet I cannot free my hands from it,
So greatly does my love hold and chain me.

I marvel not that love holds me fast,
For a more entrancing form, I believe, was never seen;
Beautiful and white she is, and fresh and smooth,
And wholly as I wish and desire her.
I can say no ill of her, for there is none in her;
Yet gladly would I say it if I knew any,
But I know none, and so forbear to speak it.

Ever shall I wish her honor and good,

The syllables in each line are grouped by units of length (short–long, short–long . . .), and this is matched to the metrical style of the day, the *modal* rhythm of long–short groupings.

Like many popular songs and folk songs of today that tell a story, this piece has several verses sung to the same melody. Notice in the translation (by Carl Parrish) that the male singer, the troubadour, sings about a rather unapproachable lady and refers to familiar images (the regions of Ventadorn and Provence as well as the lord of Beaucaire) in addition to fanciful creations of his imagination.

Obviously a song of this kind might use four verses or ten, depending on the patron's disposition, the poet's

And shall be her aid, her friend and servant,
And shall love her whether it please her or not,
For one cannot gainsay one's heart without
   destroying it.
I know no lady, whether she will or nor,
Whom I could not love if I wished.
They all can bring one to grief, though.

To others, then, I am in forfeit;
Whichever will can draw me to her
On condition that what honor and benefit
She thinks to do me will not be sold too dearly,
For the seeking is grievous if sought in vain.
From experience I speak, for I have suffered,
And beauty has betrayed me badly.

To Provence I send joy and greeting
And more of good than I could speak.
And it is a wonder that I do this;
For I send that which I have not;
I have no joy save what is brought me
By my beauteous vision, and Sire Enchantment, my
   confident,
And Sire Pleasure, the Lord of Beaucaire.

  Tornada

My beauteous vision, God works such wonder
   through you
That no one seeing you would not be enraptured
Who knew what to tell you and what to do.

BERNART DE VENTADORN

Be m'an perdut

improvisational ability, and other circumstances of the moment; but whenever the last verse is sung, the musician uses a closing device, the *tornada*, a set of words sung to the music of the last phrase signaling the end by breaking the regular pattern.

The music (p. 237) is tuneful, easily sung, rhythmically simple, and generally memorable. It fits the conditions required for courtly entertainment, and the music exemplified in this song, *Be m'an perdut*, is typical of much of the art of the medieval courtly singers. The techniques of the troubadour, having originated in southern France, spread to many parts of Europe, and the musicians became known by different names—*trouvère* and *Minnesinger*. The origins of the troubadour song remain unknown, but this genre of extemporized vocal music surely had a history in Europe long before our earliest notated examples. By the time of Bernart, the courtly love song was a highly refined art, and it has had a deep and long-lasting influence on the secular songs of Europe and America. The music of *Be m'an perdut* is singable, easily playable on any instrument, and available on a professional recording.[1] With familiarity, it can be almost as enjoyable today as it was six hundred years ago.

The *Lais* of Marie de France   While the musician-poets of southern France excelled in the short lyric, those of Brittany, in northern France, specialized in longer narrative songs called *lais*. These were probably composed orally, and none of them has survived, but a woman of exceptional education (for her time) and talent made the *lai* into a written literary form. Her name was Marie de France, and we know nothing more about her except that she wrote in French at the Norman court in England during the late twelfth century. She probably derived the plots of her twelve *lais* from those of the Breton singers. All were written in verse, and they represent different explorations of love and its effects on men and women. "Equitan," which appears here in a modern prose translation by Edmund Reiss, demonstrates especially vividly the destructiveness of illicit passion that was, as mentioned

earlier, a prime concern in this period. By being so concerned with pleasure, the king in this story is unable to rule justly. Not only does he seek to murder his loyal seneschal, or field marshal, he also ultimately brings about his own death as well as that of his lady.

The tale also shows a blend of the courtly and the ludicrous, especially at the end with the action centering on the bath. Here what had seemed noble and even beautiful is undercut so successfully that the deaths of the lovers do not result in our feeling any sense of tragedy. In fact, the fate of the two lovers may be seen as a *parody* of the conventional tragic ending of lovers who are ultimately ennobled by being joined together in death.

MARIE DE FRANCE

Equitan

Many noble lords have lived in Brittany. In times past, through their prowess, courtesy, and nobility they would compose lays of various adventures that they had heard so that these could be held in mind and not forgotten. They made one, which I have heard told and which should not be neglected, about Equitan, lord of Nantes, who was very courteous, just, and royal.

Equitan was held in great esteem and loved much in his country. He delighted in pleasure and love-making, which to him constituted chivalry. Those who love without sense or measure place their lives at nought; such is the rule of love that no one who feels passion can maintain his reason.

Equitan had a seneschal, a good knight, worthy and loyal, who administered all his land and ruled it justly, for the king was concerned only with hunting, hawking, and love-making, and would not leave these pursuits except to wage war.

The seneschal had married a woman from whom great evil came to the country. The lady was exceptionally beautiful and of very good breeding. She had a fine body and a lovely figure which Nature had taken pains to fashion. Her eyes were clear and her face beautiful, her mouth lovely, and her nose well shaped. There was none her equal in the entire kingdom. The king often heard her praised, and frequently he sent her his greet-

---

[1] *A Treasury of Early Music*, Vol. 1 (Haydn Society Records HSE 7-9100), No. 6 [side 2, band 1].

ings as well as gifts. Even though he had never seen her, he desired her and wished that he could speak with her.

One day, to amuse himself, he secretly went hunting in the country where the seneschal lived. At night, when the king returned from his sport, he took his lodging at the castle where the lady was. There he could talk with her as much as he wished and reveal to her his heart and his desire. He found her to be very courteous and wise, beautiful of body and of face, well-mannered and cheerful. Love had taken him into His household. Love had shot an arrow at him, which made a great wound where it lodged in his heart. Love had no need for craft or subtlety. The king was so overcome by the lady that he became mournful and pensive. Now when he needed most to understand, he could not help himself. That night he neither slept nor rested, but blamed and accused himself.

"Alas!" he said. "What destiny has brought me into this country? Because of this lady whom I have seen I have an ache in my heart and all my body is trembling. I thought I would never fall in love, and if I love now I shall do evil. This is the wife of my seneschal. I should love and keep faith with him just as I wish him to do with me. If through some mishap he should learn of my passion, I know well that it would disturb him greatly. Nevertheless, it would be worse for me if I should go mad because of him. And it would be a shame if such a beautiful lady was without a lover. What would happen to her courtesy if she did not have a lover? There is no man on earth who would not benefit greatly from her love. Even if the seneschal should hear about it, he should not be too heavy-hearted. He should not have all of that treasure for himself alone; indeed, I wish to share it with him."

When he had said these things, the king sighed, then tossed and turned, and thought more. Finally he said, "Why am I so upset and so afraid? I still do not know, and have not tried to learn, whether she will have me for her lover. I will soon find out, and if she feels what I feel, I will be rid of this sorrow. God, it is so long until daylight! I still cannot sleep, and it has been so long since I went to bed last night."

The king stayed awake until dawn, which he awaited with great discomfort. He went out as though he planned to hunt, but soon he returned, saying that

he felt ill. He went to his room and went to bed. The seneschal was concerned about him; he did not know what the sickness was that was causing the king to tremble so. But his wife was the real cause of it. The seneschal had her go talk with the king in order to amuse and comfort him. The king opened his heart to her and let her know that he was dying because of her. She could either bring him comfort or give him death.

"Sir," the lady replied, "I must have some time to think. This is the first time I have been in this position. You are a king of great nobility. I am not so rich that you should approach me with love. If you do take your desire, I know truly that it will lead to nothing. You will soon leave me, and I will be ruined. If it should be that I love you and grant your request, love would not be equally divided between the two of us, for you are a powerful king, and my husband is one of your vassals. You would think to have mastery in this love, and love is not worthy if it is not among equals. A poor man who is honest, if he has sense and worth, is better than a prince or king who is not honest; the poor man will also have greater joy in love. She who loves above her station will be insecure in every way. The rich man believes that nothing can take away from him the love that he has acquired through his position."

Equitan replied, "Lady, please! Say no more to me! These words are not refined or courteous but are rather the business dealings of a merchant, who for gain or property devotes his efforts to an unworthy cause. There is no lady on earth, if she is wise, courteous, and generous of heart, provided she set a high value on her love and not be fickle, who, if she had nothing more than a rich prince of a castle under her mantle, would not suffer for him and love him loyally and well. Those who are fickle in love and who turn to deceit are in turn scorned and deceived. We have seen several of these false lovers; it is no wonder that they lose what they have earned through their efforts. My dear lady, I surrender myself to you. Do not take me as your king, but as your servant and your friend. I swear to you that I will do your pleasure. Do not cause me to die for you. You will be the lady and I the servant, you the proud lord and I the suppliant."

The king spoke to her so long and begged mercy so much that she finally assured him of her love and gave up her body to him. With their rings they pledged themselves to each other and swore their loyalty to each other. They desired each other greatly and loved each other fervently. Through their passion they died and came to their end.

For a long time their love affair lasted, for it was not known by anyone. At the time of their meetings—when they would speak together—the king told his people that he was to be bled privately. The doors of his chamber were closed, and you could not have found a man so daring as to enter unless summoned by the king. The seneschal held the court to hear the various pleas and petitions.

The king loved the lady for a long time and desired no other woman. He did not wish to marry anyone; indeed he did not wish to hear the subject spoken of. The people disliked this greatly, so much so that the wife of the seneschal often heard about it. It weighed on her heavily, and she feared losing the king. When she was able to speak with him—at a time when she should have been happy kissing, hugging, embracing, and playing with him—she wept sorely and expressed great sadness. The king asked what was wrong.

The lady answered, "Sir, I weep for our love which for me has turned to great sorrow. You will take a wife, the daughter of a king, and so you will leave me. I have heard it said often, and I know it well. And alas, what will become of me? Because of you I will die, for I know no other comfort."

The king said to her with great love, "Fair friend, do not be afraid. Indeed, I will not take a wife or leave you for another. Know this truly and believe it. If your husband were dead, I would make you my wife and queen. I swear, for no other will I leave you."

The lady thanked him and said he had made her very happy. And since he had assured her that he would not leave her for another, she would bring about the death of her husband right away. It would be easy to accomplish if the king would help her. He answered that he would do so. In fact there was nothing he would not do for her if it lay in his power, no matter whether it were wise or foolish.

"Sir," she said, "if it please you, come to hunt in the forest in the country where I live. Stay at the castle of my lord; there you will be bled and, three days later, bathed. My husband will be bled and also bathed along with you. Be sure to command him, without fail, to accompany you. And I will have the baths heated and the

two tubs brought. His bath will be so boiling hot that no man on earth could sit in it without being scalded and killed. As soon as he is dead, call your men and his, and show them how he died suddenly in his bath."

The king agreed that he would do her will in everything.

Not three months passed before the king went hunting in the country. He had himself bled, on account of his illness. Along with him went his seneschal. On the third day the king said that he wished to bathe; the seneschal wished likewise.

"Bathe with me," said the king.

The seneschal said, "Gladly."

The lady had the baths heated and the two tubs brought and placed by each bed as planned. She had the boiling water poured in the seneschal's tub. That gentleman had arisen and gone out for his ease. The lady came to speak to the king who sat her down beside him. They lay on the bed of the seneschal and amused themselves playing with each other. They played together by the tub of scalding water which was in front of them. They had posted a servant girl to guard the door. The seneschal returned shortly and found his way blocked. He became so angry that he flung it open and discovered the king and his wife lying on the bed embracing each other. The king saw the seneschal as soon as he came in, and to cover up his villainy, he jumped into the tub with his feet together. There he was scalded and died. All his evil came back on them, and the seneschal remained safe and well. He had seen what happened to the king and immediately seized his wife and pushed her head first into the same bath. There both died, the king first and the lady after him.

Whoever wishes to understand the meaning of this can discover a lesson here. Those who pursue evil toward another will find all this evil returned on them. This happened as I have told you. The Bretons made a lay of it, about Equitan, how he and the lady whom he loved so much came to their end.

QUESTIONS

1. What feelings, as a reader, do you have toward the two lovers? Is the author's portrayal of them ambivalent in any way?
2. Do you find any contradiction between the story and the moral?

3. What elements of comedy or parody do you see in this story, and what do you think medieval people would have seen?

4. Could you write a modern version of this tale? How do you think the portrayal of love here might have influenced our ideas of love?

5. How did our term *romance* derive from such stories?

6. What meanings are attached to terms like *refined* and *courteous,* and what have these values to do with the idea of courtly love?

Courtly Love in a Bawdy Version: Chaucer's "Miller's Tale"

The love of noble knights for noble ladies was not the only aspect of passion that interested medieval people. As we indicated earlier, they were well aware of the comic aspects of romantic entanglements. Sex, as we saw with *Lysistrata,* has universal potential for comedy. Geoffrey Chaucer, writing in England at the end of the Middle Ages, was interested in a wide range of people and topics, among them the comedy of sex.

It has been said that if we possessed nothing of medieval literature other than Chaucer's narrative poem *The Canterbury Tales* (1390–1400), we would still have represented all the major types of medieval narrative. Representing three days of tale telling by pilgrims on their way to Canterbury Cathedral, *The Canterbury Tales* develop by presenting apparent truths that are then undercut to seem not entirely valid. Chaucer's method enables him both to give *mirthe* and to provide *doctryne* or instruction. By insisting that his audience be aware of the complexities and ramifications of actions, especially those having moral significance, he forces them to participate in the creation of meaning and to look beyond the surface appearance of things.

Each of the tales is told by a different pilgrim, reflecting its narrator's personality in its tone and content. Our selection is a modern verse translation, by Neville Coghill, of the tale told by the miller. Although the Miller's Tale might seem to be on the surface a bawdy tale, Chaucer has used this unlikely vehicle to undercut the noble appearance of courtly love, as brought out in "The Knight's Tale," which immediately precedes it. The situation of the piece is one typically ripe for sexual hanky-panky, with the old husband, John, married to the young woman, Alison. But even though John is jealous and worried about being cuckolded, he is apparently oblivious of their lodger, the young cleric Nicholas. In a sense John's unconcern is understandable, for clerics were supposed to be contemplatives, loving God and the Virgin, and being beyond the concerns of the flesh. But when Nicholas casts his eyes heavenward, it is only to deceive. Instead of using things of this world as means of getting to eternal verities, Nicholas ironically reverses the process, using the other world as a means of obtaining his love in this world. The incongruous blend of contemplative and worldly may be seen when Nicholas embraces Alison and at the same time speaks to her as a subservient courtly lover and also when he uses a fictitious vision of the Second Deluge to effect his deception of the old husband. Although Noah's Flood was a traditional symbol of cleansing and purification, it is here ironically used as a vehicle for lechery. But John, the old husband, is so foolish that he cannot be pitied, for he does not even know God's covenant with man after the original Deluge that He would never again flood the earth.

The illicit love of Nicholas and Alison is not only contrasted with the inadequate but licit marriage, it is also the basis for the love expressed by Absolon, another cleric. When Absolon sings outside the bedroom window urging Alison to love, he employs language clearly recognizable from the Song of Songs. Chaucer's point is far from burlesquing this mystical love; rather, by including it in an obviously inappropriate situation, he calls up the ideal love lacking in the bawdy sexuality at hand and makes the amorous passion of Absolon seem as inadequate as Absolon himself is ridiculous. It is at least as inappropriate for him to refer to Alison in terms of the imagery of mystical love as it is for Nicholas at the beginning of the tale to ask her for the "mercy" traditionally associated with prayers to the Virgin.

GEOFFREY CHAUCER

The Miller's Tale

Some time ago there was a rich old codger
Who lived in Oxford and who took a lodger.

The fellow was a carpenter by trade,
His lodger a poor student who had made   105
Some studies in the arts, but all his fancy
Turned to astrology and geomancy,°
And he could deal with certain propositions
And make a forecast under some conditions
About the likelihood of drought or showers   110
For those who asked at favourable hours,
Or put a question how their luck would fall
In this or that, I can't describe them all.
    This lad was known as Nicholas the Gallant,
And making love in secret was his talent,   115
For he was very close and sly, and took
Advantage of his meek and girlish look.
He rented a small chamber in the kip°
All by himself without companionship.
He decked it charmingly with herbs and fruit   120
And he himself was sweeter than the root
Of liquorice, or any fragrant herb.
His astronomic text-books were superb,
He had an astrolabe to match his art
And calculating counters laid apart   125
On handy shelves that stood above his bed.
His press was curtained coarsely and in red;
Above there lay a gallant harp in sight
On which he played melodiously at night
With such a touch that all the chamber rang;   130
It was *The Virgin's Angelus*° he sang,
And after that he sang *King William's Note*,°
And people often blessed his merry throat.
And that was how this charming scholar spent
His time and money, which his friends had sent. 135
    This carpenter had married a young wife
Not long before, and loved her more than life.
She was a girl of eighteen years of age.
Jealous he was and kept her in the cage,
For he was old and she was wild and young;   140
He thought himself quite likely to be stung.
    He might have known, were Cato on his shelf,
A man should marry someone like himself;
A man should pick an equal for his mate.

---

107. Divination
118. An inn
131, 132. *The Virgin's Angelus, King William's Note:* two popu-
    lar religious songs.

Youth and old age are often in debate.   145
His wits were dull, he'd fallen in the snare
And had to bear his cross as others bear.
    She was a pretty creature, fair and tender,
And had a weasel's body, softly slender.
She used to wear a girdle of striped silk,   150
Her apron was a white as morning milk
To deck her loins, all gusseted and pleated.
Her smock was white; embroidery repeated
Its pattern on the collar front and back,
Inside and out; it was of silk, and black.   155
And all the ribbons on her milky mutch
Were made to match her collar, even such.
She wore a broad silk fillet rather high,
And certainly she had a lecherous eye.
And she had plucked her eyebrows into bows,   160
Slenderly arched they were, and black as sloes.
And a more truly blissful sight to see
She was than blossom on a cherry-tree,
And softer than the wool upon a wether.
And by her girdle hung a purse of leather,   155
Tasselled in silk, with metal droplets, pearled.
If you went seeking up and down the world
The wisest man you met would have to wrench
His fancy to imagine such a wench.
She had a shining colour, gaily tinted,   170
And brighter than a florin newly minted,
And when she sang it was as loud and quick
As any swallow perched above a rick.
And she would skip or play some game or other
Like any kid or calf behind its mother.   175
Her mouth was sweet as mead or honey—say
A hoard of apples lying in the hay.
Skittish she was, and jolly as a colt,
Tall as a mast and upright as a bolt
Out of a bow. Her collaret revealed   180
A brooch as big as boss upon a shield.
High shoes she wore, and laced them to the top.
She was a daisy, O a lollypop
For any nobleman to take to bed
Or some good man of yeoman stock to wed.   185
    Now, gentlemen, this Gallant Nicholas
Began to romp about and make a pass
At this young woman, happening on her one day,
Her husband being out, down Osney way.
Students are sly, and giving way to whim,   190

He made a grab and caught her by the quim
And said, "O God, I love you! Can't you see
If I don't have you it's the end of me?"
Then held her haunches hard and gave a cry
"O love-me-all-at-once or I shall die!"   195
She gave a spring, just like a skittish colt
Boxed in a frame for shoeing, and with a jolt
Managed in time to wrench her head away,
And said, "Give over, Nicholas, I say!
No, I won't kiss you! Stop it! Let me go   200
Or I shall scream! I'll let the neighbours know!
Where are your manners? Take away your paws!"
    Then Nicholas began to plead his cause
And spoke so fair in proffering what he could
That in the end she promised him she would,   205
Swearing she'd love him, with a solemn promise
To be at his disposal, by St Thomas,
When she could spy an opportunity.
"My husband is so full of jealousy,
Unless you watch your step and hold your breath   210
I know for certain it will be my death,"
She said, "So keep it well under your hat."
"Oh, never mind about a thing like that,"
Said he; "A scholar doesn't have to stir
His wits so much to trick a carpenter."   215
    And so they both agreed to it, and swore
To watch their chance, as I have said before,
When things were settled thus as they thought fit,
And Nicholas had stroked her loins a bit
And kissed her sweetly, he took down his harp   220
And played away, a merry tune and sharp.
    It happened later she went off to church,
This worthy wife, one holiday, to search
Her conscience and to do the works of Christ.
She put her work aside and she enticed   225
The colour to her face to make her mark;
Her forehead shone. There was a parish clerk
Serving the church, whose name was Absalon.
His hair was all in golden curls and shone;
Just like a fan it strutted outwards, starting   230
To left and right from an accomplished parting.
Ruddy his face, his eyes as grey as goose,
His shoes cut out in tracery, as in use
In old St Paul's. The hose upon his feet
Showed scarlet through, and all his clothes were
    neat   235

And proper. In a jacket of light blue,
Flounced at the waist and tagged with laces too,
He went, and wore a surplice just as gay
And white as any blossom on the spray.
God bless my soul, he was a merry knave!   240
He knew how to let blood, cut hair and shave,
And draw up legal deeds; at other whiles
He used to dance in twenty different styles
(After the current school at Oxford though,
Casting his legs about him to and fro)   245
He played a two-stringed fiddle, did it proud,
And sang a high falsetto rather loud;
And he was just as good on the guitar.
There was no public-house in town or bar
He didn't visit with his merry face   250
If there were saucy barmaids round the place.
He was a little squeamish in the matter
Of farting, and satirical in chatter.
This Absalon, so jolly in his ways,
Would bear the censer round on holy days   255
And cense the parish women. He would cast
Many a love-lorn look before he passed,
Especially at this carpenter's young wife;
Looking at her would make a happy life
He thought, so neat, so sweet, so lecherous.   260
And I dare say if she had been a mouse
And he a cat, she'd have been pounced upon.
    In taking the collection Absalon
Would find his heart was set in such a whirl
Of love, he would take nothing from a girl,   265
For courtesy, he said, it wasn't right.
    That evening, when the moon was shining
        bright
He ups with his guitar and off he tours
On the look-out for any paramours.
Larky and amorous, away he strode   270
Until he reached the carpenter's abode
A little after cock-crow, took his stand
Beside the casement window close at hand
(It was set low upon the cottage-face)
And started singing softly and with grace,   275

Now dearest lady, if there pleasure be
In thoughts of love, think tenderly of me!

On his guitar he plucked a tuneful string.
    This carpenter awoke and heard him sing

And turning to his wife said, "Alison!   280
Wife! Do you hear him? There goes Absalon
Chanting away under our chamber wall."
And she replied, "Yes, John, I hear it all."
If she thought more of it she didn't tell.
   So things went on. What's better than "All's
     well"?   285
From day to day this jolly Absalon.
Wooing away, became quite woe-begone;
He lay awake all night, and all the day
Combed his thick locks and tried to pass for gay,
Wooed her by go-between and wooed by proxy,   290
Swore to be page and servant to his doxy,
Trilled and rouladed° like a nightingale,
Sent her sweet wine and mead and spicy ale,
And wafers piping hot and jars of honey,
And, as she lived in town, he offered money.°   295
For there are some a money-bag provokes
And some are won by kindness, some by strokes.
   Once, in the hope his talent might engage,
He played the part of Herod on the stage.
What was the good? Were he as bold as brass,   300
She was in love with gallant Nicholas;
However Absalon might blow his horn
His labour won him nothing but her scorn.
She looked upon him as her private ape
And held his earnest wooing all a jape.   305
   There is a proverb—and it is no lie—
You'll often hear repeated: "Nigh and Sly
Wins against Fair and Square who isn't there."
For much as Absalon might tear his hair
And rage at being seldom in her sight,   310
Nicholas, nigh and sly, stood in his light.
Now, show your paces, Nicholas you spark!
And leave lamenting to the parish clerk.
   And so it happened that one Saturday,
When the old carpenter was safe away   315
At Osney, Nicholas and Alison
Agreed at last in what was to be done.
Nicholas was to exercise his wits
On her suspicious husband's foolish fits,
And, if so be the trick worked out all right,   320
She then would sleep with Nicholas all night,

---

292. Sang
295. As you would to a whore.

For such was his desire and hers as well;
And even quicker than it takes to tell,
Young Nicholas, who simply couldn't wait,
Went to his room on tip-toe with a plate   325
Of food and drink, enough to last a day
Or two, and Alison was told to say,
In case her husband asked for Nicholas,
That she had no idea where he was,
And that she hadn't set eyes on him all day   330
And thought he must be ill, she couldn't say;
And more than once the maid had given a call
And shouted but no answer came at all.
   So things went on the whole of Saturday
Without a sound from Nicholas, who lay   335
Upstairs, and ate or slept as pleased him best
Till Sunday when the sun went down to rest.
   This foolish carpenter was lost in wonder
At Nicholas; what could have got him under?
He said, "I can't help thinking, by the Mass,   340
Things can't be going right with Nicholas.
What if he took and died? God guard his ways!
A ticklish place the world is, nowadays.
I saw a corpse this morning borne to kirk
That only Monday last I saw at work.   345
Run up," he told the serving-lad, "be quick,
Shout at his door, or knock it with a brick.
Take a good look and tell me how he fares."
   The serving-boy went sturdily upstairs.
Stopped at the door and, standing there, the lad 350
Shouted away and, hammering like mad,
Cried, "Ho! What's up? Hi! Master Nicholay!
How can you lie up there asleep all day?"
   But all for nought, he didn't hear a soul.
He found a broken panel with a hole   355
Right at the bottom, useful to the cat
For creeping in; he took a look through that,
And so at last by peering through the crack
He saw this scholar gaping on his back
As if he'd caught a glimpse of the new moon.   360
Down went the boy and told his master soon
About the state in which he found the man.
   On hearing this the carpenter began
To cross himself and said, "St. Frideswide bless
     us!
We little know what's coming to distress us.   365
The man has fallen, with this here astromy,

Into a fit, or lunacy maybe.
I always thought that was how it would go.
God has some secrets that we shouldn't know.
How blessed are the simple, aye, indeed,   370
That only know enough to say their creed!
Happened just so with such another student
Of astromy and he was so imprudent
As to stare upwards while he crossed a field,
Busy foreseeing what the stars revealed;   375
And what should happen but he fell down flat
Into a marl-pit. He didn't foresee that!
But by the Saints we've reached a sorry pass;
I can't help worrying for Nicholas.
He shall be scolded for his studying   380
If I know how to scold, by Christ the King!
Get me a staff to prise against the floor.
Robin, you put your shoulder to the door.
We'll shake the study out of him, I guess!"

    The pair of them began to heave and press   385
Against the door. Happened the lad was strong
And so it didn't take them very long
To heave it off its hinges; down it came.
Still as a stone lay Nicholas, with the same
Expression, gaping upwards into air.   390
The carpenter supposed it was despair
And shook him by the shoulders with a stout
And purposeful attack, and gave a shout:
"What, Nicholas! Hey! Look down! Is that a
    fashion
To act? Wake up and think upon Christ's passion. 395
I sign you with the cross from elves and sprites!"
And he began the spell for use at nights
In all four corners of the room and out
Across the threshold too and round about:

    Jesu Christ and Benedict Sainted   400
    Bless this house from creature tainted,
    Drive away night-hags, white Pater-noster,
    Where did you go St Peter's soster?°
And in the end the dandy Nicholas
Began to sigh, "And must it come to pass?"   405
He said, "Must all the world be cast away?"
The carpenter replied, "What's that you say?
Put trust in God as we do, working men."

Nicholas answered, "Fetch some liquor then,
And afterwards, in strictest secrecy,   410
I'll speak of something touching you and me,
But not another soul must know, that's plain."
    This carpenter went down and came again
Bringing some powerful ale—a largeish quart.
When each had had his share of this support   415
Young Nicholas got up and shut the door
And, sitting down beside him on the floor,
Said to the carpenter, "Now, John, my dear,
My excellent host, swear on your honour here
Not to repeat a syllable I say,   420
For here are Christ's intentions, to betray
Which to a soul puts you among the lost,
And vengeance for it at a bitter cost
Shall fall upon you. You'll be driven mad!"
"Christ and His holy blood forbid it, lad!"   425
The silly fellow answered. "I'm no blab,
Though I should say it, I'm not given to gab.
Say what you like, for I shall never tell
Man, woman or child by Him° that harrowed
    Hell!"
    "Now, John," said Nicholas, "believe you me,   430
I have found out by my astrology,
And looking at the moon when it was bright,
That Monday next, a quarter way through night,
Rain is to fall in torrents, such a scud
It will be twice as bad as Noah's Flood.   435
This world," he said, "in just about an hour,
Shall all be drowned, it's such a hideous shower,
And all mankind, with total loss of life,"
    The carpenter exclaimed, "Alas, my wife
My little Alison! Is she to drown?"   440
And in his grief he very near fell down.
"Is there no remedy," he said, "for this?"
"Thanks be to God," said Nicholas, "there is,
If you will do exactly what I say
And don't start thinking up some other way.   445
In wise old Solomon you'll find the verse
'Who takes advice shall never fare the worse,'
And so if good advice is to prevail
I undertake with neither mast nor sail
To save her yet, and save myself and you.   450
Haven't you heard how Noah was saved too

---

403. *soster:* a medieval chant used to drive away evil spirits.

429. Christ

When God forewarned him and his sons and
    daughters
That all the world should sink beneath the
    waters?'
"Yes," said the carpenter, "a long time back."
"Haven't you heard," said Nicholas, "what a
    black   455
Business it was, when Noah tried to whip
His wife (who wouldn't come) on board the ship?
He'd have been better pleased, I'll undertake,
With all that weather just about to break,
If she had had a vessel of her own.   460
Now, what are we to do? We can't postpone
The thing; it's coming soon, as I was saying,
It calls for haste, not preaching or delaying."
    "I want you, now, at once, to hurry off
And fetch a shallow tub or kneading-trough   465
For each of us, but see that they are large
And such as we can float in, like a barge.
And have them loaded with sufficient victual
To last a day—we only need a little.
The waters will abate and flow away   470
Round nine o'clock upon the following day.
Robin the lad mayn't know of this, poor knave,
Nor Jill the maid, those two I cannot save.
Don't ask me why; and even if you do
I can't disclose God's secret thoughts to you.   475
You should be satisfied, unless you're mad,
To find as great a grace as Noah had.
And I shall save your wife, you needn't doubt it,
Now off you go, and hurry up about it."
    "And when the tubs have been collected, three, 480
That's one for her and for yourself and me,
Then hang them in the roof below the thatching
That no one may discover what we're hatching.
When you have finished doing what I said
And stowed the victuals in them overhead,   485
Also an axe to hack the ropes apart,
So, when the water rises, we can start,
And, lastly, when you've broken out the gable,
The garden one that's just above the stable,
So that we may cast free without delay   490
After the mighty shower has gone away,
You'll float as merrily, I undertake,
As any lily-white duck behind her drake.
And I'll call out, 'Hey, Alison! Hey, John!

Cheer yourselves up! The flood will soon be
    gone.'   495
And you'll shout back, 'Hail, Master Nicholay!
Good morning! I can see you well. It's day!'
We shall be lords for all the rest of life
Of all the world, like Noah and his wife."
    "One thing I warn you of; it's only right.   500
We must be very careful on the night,
Once we have safely managed to embark,
To hold our tongues, to utter no remark,
No cry or call, for we must fall to prayer.
This is the Lord's dear will, so have a care."   505
    "Your wife and you must hang some way apart,
For there must be no sin before we start,
No more in longing looks than in the deed.
Those are your orders. Off with you! God speed!
To-morrow night when everyone's asleep   510
We'll all go quietly upstairs and creep
Into our tubs, awaiting Heaven's grace.
And now be off. No time to put the case
At greater length, no time to sermonize;
The proverb says, 'Say nothing, send the wise.'   515
You're wise enough, I do not have to teach you.
Go, save our lives for us, as I beseech you."
    This silly carpenter then went his way
Muttering to himself, "Alas the day!"
And told his wife in strictest secrecy.   520
She was aware, far more indeed than he,
What this quaint stratagem might have in sight,
But she pretended to be dead with fright.
"Alas!" she said. "Whatever it may cost,
Hurry and help, or we shall all be lost.   525
I am your honest, true and wedded wife,
Go, dearest husband, help to save my life!"
    How fancy throws us into perturbation!
People can die of mere imagination,
So deep is the impression one can take.   530
This silly carpenter began to quake,
Before his eyes there verily seemed to be
The floods of Noah, wallowing like the sea
And drowning Alison his honey-pet.
He wept and wailed, his features were all set   535
In grief, he sighed with many a doleful grunt.
He went and got a tub, began to hunt
For kneading-troughs, found two, and had them
    sent

Home to his house in secret; then he went
And, unbeknowns, he hung them from a rafter.   540
With his own hands he made three ladders after,
Uprights and rungs, to help them in their scheme
Of climbing where they hung upon the beam.
He victualled tub and trough, and made all snug
With bread and cheese, and ale in a large jug,   545
Enough for three of them to last the day,
And, just before completing this array,
Packed off the maid and his apprentice too
To London on a job they had to do.
And on the Monday when it drew to night   550
He shut his door and dowsed the candle-light
And made quite sure all was as it should be
And shortly, up they clambered, all the three,
Silent and separate. They began to pray
And *"Pater Noster*° mum," said Nicholay,   555
And "mum" said John, and "mum" said Alison
The carpenter's devotions being done,
He sat quite still, then fell to prayer again
And waited anxiously to hear the rain.

    The carpenter, with all the work he'd seen,   560
Fell dead asleep—round curfew, must have been,
Maybe a little later on the whole.
He groaned in sleep for travail of his soul
And snored because his head was turned awry.

    Down by their ladders, stalking from on high   565
Came Nicholas and Alison, and sped
Softly downstairs, without a word, to bed,
And where this carpenter was wont to be
The revels started and the melody.
And thus lay Nicholas and Alison   570
At busy play in eager quest of fun,
Until the bell for lauds had started ringing
And in the chancel Friars began their singing.

    This parish clerk, this amorous Absalon,
Love-stricken still and very woe-begone,   575
Upon the Monday was in company
At Osney with his friends for jollity,
And chanced to ask a resident cloisterer
What had become of John the carpenter.
The fellow drew him out of church to say,   580
"Don't know; not been at work since Saturday.

I can't say where he is; I think he went
To fetch the Abbot timber. He is sent
Often enough for timber, has to go
Out to the Grange° and ston° a day or so;   585
If not he's certainly at home to-day,
But where he is I can't exactly say,"
    Absalon was a jolly lad and light
Of heart; he thought, "I'll stay awake to-night;
I'm certain that I haven't seen him stirring   590
About his door since dawn; it's safe inferring
That he's away. As I'm alive I'll go
And tap his window softly at the crow
Of cock—the sill is low-set on the wall.
I shall see Alison and tell her all   595
My love-longing, and I can hardly miss
Some favour from her, at the least a kiss.
I'll get some satisfaction anyway;
There's been an itching in my mouth all day
And that's a sign of kissing at the least.   600
And all last night I dreamt about a feast.
I think I'll go and sleep an hour or two,
Then wake and have some fun, that's what I'll
    do,"
    The first cock crew at last, and thereupon
Up rose this jolly lover Absalon   605
In gayest clothes, garnished with that and this;
But first he chewed a grain of liquorice
To charm his breath before he combed in hair.
Under his tongue the comfit nestling there
Would make him gracious. He began to roam   610
To where old John and Alison kept home
And by the casement window took his stand.
Breast-high it stood, no higher than his hand.
He gave a cough, no more than half a sound:
"Alison, honey-comb, are you around?   615
Sweet cinnamon, my little pretty bird,
Sweetheart, wake up and say a little word!
You seldom think of me in all my woe,
I sweat for love of you wherever I go!
No wonder if I do, I pine and bleat   620
As any lambkin hungering for the teat,
Believe me, darling, I'm so deep in love
I croon with longing like a turtle-dove,

555. Our Father

585. farm, stay

I eat as little as a girl at school."
"You go away," she answered, "you Tom-fool!   625
There's no come-up-and-kiss-me here for you.
I love another and why shouldn't I too?
Better than you, by Jesu, Absalon!
Take yourself off or I shall throw a stone.
I want to get some sleep. You go to Hell!"   630
"Alas!" said Absalon. "I knew it well;
True love is always mocked and girded at;
So kiss me, if you can't do more than that,
For Jesu's love and for the love of me!"
"And if I do, will you be off?" said she.   635
"Promise you, darling," answered Absalon.
"Get ready then; wait, I'll put something on,"
She said and then she added under breath
To Nicholas, "Hush . . . we shall laugh to death!"
   This Absalon went down upon his knees;   640
"I am a lord!" he thought, "And by degrees
There may be more to come; the plot may
      thicken."
"Mercy, my love!" he said, "Your mouth, my
      chicken!"
   She flung the window open then in haste
And said, "Have done, come on, no time to
      waste,   645
The neighbours here are always on the spy."
   Absalon starting wiping his mouth dry.
Dark was the night as pitch, as black as coal,
And at the window out she put her hole,
And Absalon, so fortune framed the farce,   650
Put up his mouth and kissed her naked arse
Most savorously before he knew of this.
   And back he started. Something was amiss;
He knew quite well a woman had no beard,
Yet something rough and hairy had appeared.   655
"What have I done?" he said. "Can that be you?"
"Teehee!" she cried and clapped the window to.
Off went poor Absalon sadly through the dark.
"A beard! a beard!" cried Nicholas the Spark.
"God's body, that was something like a joke!"   660
And Absalon, overhearing what he spoke,
Bit on his lips and nearly threw a fit
In rage and thought, "I'll pay you back for it!"
   Who's busy rubbing, scraping at his lips
With dust, with sand, with straw, with cloth,
      with chips,   665

But Absalon? He thought, "I'll bring him down!
I wouldn't let this go for all the town.
I'd take my soul and sell it to the Devil
To be revenged upon him! I'll get level.
O God, why did I let myself be fooled?"   670
   The fiery heat of love by now had cooled,
For from the time he kissed her hinder parts
He didn't give a tinker's° curse for tarts;°
His malady was cured by this endeavour
And he defied all paramours whatever.   675
   So, weeping like a child that has been whipped,
He turned away; across the road he slipped
And called on Gervase. Gervase was a smith;
His forge was full of things for ploughing with
And he was busy sharpening a share.   680
   Absalon knocked, and with an easy air
Called, "Gervase! Open up the door, come on!"
"What's that? Who's there?" "It's me, it's
      Absalon."
"What, Absalon? By Jesu's blessed tree
You're early up! Hey, *benedicite,*°   685
What's wrong? Some jolly girl as like as not
Has coaxed you out and set you on the trot.
Blessed St Neot! You know the thing I mean."
   But Absalon, who didn't give a bean
For all his joking, offered no debate.   690
He had a good deal more upon his plate
Than Gervase knew, and said, "Wout it be fair
To borrow that coulter° in the chimney there,
The hot one, see it? I've a job to do;
It won't take long, I'll bring it back to you."   695
Gervase replied, "Why, if you asked for gold,
A bag of sovereigns or for wealth untold,
It should be yours, as I'm an honest smith.
But, Christ, why borrow that to do it with?"
"Let that," said Absalon, "be as it may;   700
You'll hear about it all some other day."
   He caught the coulter up—the haft was cool—
And left the smithy softly with the tool,
Crept to the little window in the wall
And coughed. He knocked and gave a little call   705

---

673. gypsy's
673. whores
685. a blessing
693. plow blade

Under the window as he had before.
  Alison said, "There's someone at the door.
Who's knocking there? I'll warrant it's a thief."
"Why, no," said he, "my little flower-leaf,
It's your own Absalon, my sweety-thing!   710
Look what I've brought you—it's a golden ring
My mother gave me, as I may be saved.
It's very fine, and prettily engraved;
I'll give it to you, darling, for a kiss."
  Now Nicholas had risen for a piss,   715
And thought he could improve upon the jape
And make him kiss his arse ere he escape,
And opening the window with a jerk,
Stuck out his arse, a handsome piece of work,
Buttocks and all, as far as to the haunch.   720
  Said Absalon, all set to make a launch,
"Speak, pretty bird, I know not where thou art!"
This Nicholas at once let fly a fart
As loud as if it were a thunder-clap.
He was near blinded by the blast, poor chap,   725
But his hot iron was ready; with a thump
He smote him in the middle of the rump.
  Off went the skin a hand's-breadth round about
Where the hot coulter struck and burnt it out.
Such was the pain, he thought he must be dying   730
And, mad with agony, he started crying,
"Help! Water! Water! Help! For Heaven's love!"
  The carpenter, startled from sleep above,
And hearing shouts for water and a thud,
Thought, "Heaven help us! Here comes Nowel's
    Flood!"   735
And up he sat and with no more ado
He took his axe and smote the ropes in two
And down went everything. He didn't stop
To sell his bread and ale, but came down flop
Upon the floor and fainted right away.   740
  Up started Alison and Nicholay
And shouted, "Help!" and "Murder!" in the
    street.
The neighbours all came running up in heat
And stook there staring at the wretched man.
He lay there fainting, pale beneath his tan;   745
His arm in falling had been broken double.

___

735. Noah's Flood

But still he was obliged to face his trouble,
For when he spoke he was at once borne down
By Nicholas and his wife. They told the town
That he was mad, there'd got into his blood   750
Some sort of nonsense about "Nowel's Flood,"
That vain imaginings and fantasy
Had made him buy the kneading-tubs, that he
Had hung them in the rafters up above
And that he'd begged them both for heaven's love 755
To sit up in the roof for company.
  All started laughing at this lunacy
And streamed upstairs to gape and pry and poke,
And treated all his sufferings as a joke.
No matter what the carpenter asserted   760
It went for nothing, no one was converted;
With powerful oaths they swore the fellow down
And he was held for mad by all the town;
Even the learned said to one another,
"The fellow must be crazy, my dear brother."   765
So to a general laughter he succumbed.
  That's how the carpenter's young wife was
    plumbed
For all the tricks his jealousy could try,
And Absalon has kissed her nether eye
And Nicholas is branded on the bum.   770
And God bring all of us to Kingdom Come.

QUESTIONS

1. How do you react to "The Miller's Tale"? Does it have appeal for modern readers?
2. How deeply do you become involved with each of the characters? Is it necessary to remain detached from them? Why or why not?
3. Are these characters more or less realistic than those in earlier medieval literature, such as *The Play of Daniel?*
4. Compare the comedy of sex in this tale with that in *Lysistrata.* What differences are attributable to the differences in culture?
5. What impact does Chaucer's Christianity have on his comedy?
6. Compare the expressions of love in this tale with those in "Equitan." What justification can you find for the interpretation that this tale represents a parody of "courtly" love?

Dante Alighieri (1265–1321)

No study of the many varieties of love in the Middle Ages would be complete without at least a partial reading of what is undoubtedly the greatest love poem ever written, Dante Alighieri's *Divina Commedia* (*Divine Comedy*). Although human and divine love act as the impetus and the goal of this poem, the poem also encompasses a great deal more, especially politics and theology, and it is necessary to know something of Dante's life and times in order to understand it.

Thirteenth-Century Florence and Dante's Early Life   Although he was born seventy-five years before Chaucer, Dante was, like the English poet, the product of a society in transition from rural and courtly to urban and mercantile, from medieval to Renaissance. Although he was to know the bitterness of exile from his native city, Dante was, like Chaucer, a town-dweller, profoundly urban and Florentine. The Florence of his youth was just entering into its period of greatness. In the course of his lifetime, the city on the Arno River established its international reputation as the producer of the finest woolen fabrics made. The soundness of its gold coin, the florin, made it the standard of the western world. By 1300, Florence's population of about 100,000 people equalled that of Venice, making them the two largest cities in Europe.

Legally, Florence, together with much of the upper half of Italy, formed the Kingdom of Italy, which in turn was part of the Holy Roman Empire. This Empire, consisting of the kingdoms of Germany, Italy, and Arles (principally what is now eastern France) had, since the tenth century, been ruled by a German prince. The German Emperor's capability to exert power over Italy had always been sporadic, so that Italian cities had, for long periods of time, found themselves, for all practical purposes, independent. Naturally, the stronger cities tended to expand and to create around themselves a ring of dependent little towns and cities over which they ruled, just as Athens and Sparta had done in ancient Greece. Although the governments of these city-states were not democratic, as those in Greece had been, by the thirteenth century most could be classified as republican—that is, they were ruled by a large body of citizens, though with the lower social elements ex-

cluded. In the Florence of Dante's time, the basis for citizenship and political participation in government was membership in one of the numerous guilds in the city.

The German emperors rarely exerted much real power over their Italian kingdom, but when they took their authority seriously and came into Italy with an army, the result was usually political chaos. At those times, the bulwark of Italian independence became the Roman papacy. A secular prince over a band of territories that straddled the central portion of the peninsula, the pope had good reason to fear the emperor's presence. Both pope and emperor had rival claims to certain areas, and friction between the two was almost inevitable. From the late twelfth century, when the German Emperor Frederick Barbarossa had been exceptionally active in Italy, this struggle became institutionalized in Italian politics through the development of two political parties, the Guelf party, loyal to the pope, and the Ghibellines, loyal to the emperor. Within decades, the political life of every major Italian city-state was disrupted by a struggle between the two parties. Clearly, although the papal-imperial rivalry provided a kind of ideological umbrella for the parties throughout Italy, in each city-state local issues counted more in determining party loyalty.

The party struggle dividing Florence in the thirteenth century was particularly bitter. In 1267, the leaders of the Guelf party, who had been exiled by the Ghibellines, returned triumphantly to the city, drove out their enemies, and established an enduring Guelf domination in Florence. But the Guelf victory did not bring peace, because within decades the Guelfs themselves divided into two parties called the White and Black Guelfs, and the struggle of parties resumed. Dante's involvement in this factional struggle was to change the course of his life, and his involvement in the political struggles of his time would also have a profound impact on his great work, the *Divina Commedia*.

Relatively little is known of the life of Dante. Born in 1265, he was the son of a family that, on his father's side, claimed descent from the Romans. Although the family was at the time in modest circumstances, Dante never had to seek gainful employment, and in early manhood managed to devote his time to study. In an early work, the *Vita Nuova* (the "new life") Dante recounts the great influence on his life and on the *Commedia* of his love for a girl named Beatrice.

Dante tells us that he first met Beatrice when he was nine and she eight, and from that moment his heart was possessed by a passionate and enduring love. Nine years later he saw her again, dressed all in white, walking in the street between two older ladies. On this occasion she turned and greeted him. Overjoyed, Dante promptly retired to the solitude of his bedroom where, thinking of Beatrice, he fell asleep and had a marvelous vision. When he woke, he composed the poem, "To every captive soul, and gentle heart," his earliest known composition. To conceal his love for Beatrice, he paid attention to another lady, but this caused Beatrice to deny him her glance and plunged Dante into the deepest grief. When he saw her next at a wedding feast, perhaps her own in 1288, he could not keep from looking at her, whereupon Beatrice and the ladies about her began to whisper and make fun of him. Dante had to be led from the house by a friend.

Dante by this time was already married to a rich banking heiress to whom he had been betrothed since he was twelve. His wife, who ultimately bore him three or four children, could not have failed to notice her husband's utter desolation when in 1290 his beloved Beatrice died. Dante tells us that for a time he could do nothing, but finally, through the study of philosophy, he regained enough control to set down, in a mixture of prose and verse, the story of his love. Composed between 1292 and 1293, the *Vita Nuova* recounts Dante's moral regeneration through his pure love for Beatrice. At the end of this work, the author vows that he will write of her what has never yet been written of any woman, a resolve he was to carry out in the *Divina Commedia*.

The Sonnet and a New Vision of Love From very early in his life, Dante had been one of a group of Florentine writers of poetry who wrote love poetry in the "vulgar" language—that is, in Tuscan Italian, Latin being still the official literary language of Italy. Influenced by the French and Provencal poets of courtly love, this *dolce stil nuovo* (sweet new style) celebrated the lofty, idealized figure of the beloved woman. Its poetry differed from the French, however, in placing heavier emphasis on the woman's redemptive role.

Whereas the troubadours emphasized their ladies' social position and refinements, the Italian poets, in their less hierarchical urban society, tended to interpret "nobility" in terms of moral qualities and beauty. Perhaps the greatest contrast with the older, courtly-love tradition lay in the psychological sophistication of the Florentine poets, their concentration on the details of the effect of love on inner life.

The form most often used and indeed perfected by this group of poets, the *sonnet*, probably originated in Sicily, at the court of Frederick II, although some claim that its origins are Provençal. The sonnet, several important examples of which we will study, is practically the only fixed form of medieval poetry to continue to be used by modern poets. The many sonnets in the *Vita Nuova*, interspersed with the prose narrative of Dante's relationship with Beatrice, express a vision of love that seems to originate in the courtly praise of the beloved, and to extend beyond this to a religious awe resembling literature, praising the Virgin and preparing the religious role that Beatrice will play in *The Divine Comedy*. The following two sonnets, in the famous translation by the English poet Dante Gabriel Rossetti, illustrate this new vision of love. Rossetti has kept both the original rhyme scheme and the traditional division of the Italian sonnet—two quatrains, or the octave (eight lines), and two tercets, or the sestet (six lines).

Love and the gentle heart are one same thing,
  Even as the wise man° in his ditty saith:
  Each, of itself, would be such life in death
As rational soul bereft of reasoning.
'T is Nature makes them when she loves: a king   5
  Love is, whose palace where he sojourneth
  Is called the Heart; there draws he quiet breath
At first, with brief or longer slumbering.
Then beauty seen in virtuous womankind
  Will make the eyes desire, and through the heart   10
  Send the desiring of the eyes again;
Where often it abides so long enshrin'd
  That Love at length out of his sleep will start.
  And women feel the same for worthy men.

---

2. Guido Guinicelli, in the canzone which begins, "Within the gentle heart Love shelters him."

My lady carries love within her eyes;   15
  All that she looks on is made pleasanter;
  Upon her path men turn to gaze at her;
He whom she greeteth feels his heart to rise,
And droops his troubled visage, full of sighs,
  And of his evil heart is then aware: 20
  Hate loves, and pride becomes a worshipper.
O women; help to praise her in somewise.
Humbleness, and the hope that hopeth well,
  By speech of hers into the mind are brought,
  And who beholds is blessèd oftenwhiles.   25
    The look she hath when she a little smiles
Cannot be said, nor holden in the thought;
'T is such a new and gracious miracle.

Dante's Later Life Because Dante, during the years immediately following his composition of the *Vita Nuova*, spent his time writing and studying, he played only a minor role in Florentine political life. Then in 1300 he was chosen to serve on the *Signoria*, the highest executive body of the Florentine Republic. Hardly a political partisan, Dante nevertheless felt that, in the tense situation created by rivalry between the Black and White Guelfs, the latter had the interests of the city more at heart. Dante's identification with the Whites led to his exile when in 1302 the Blacks, supported by a French prince and Pope Boniface VIII, took over the city by violence. Moving periodically from city to city in northern and central Italy, leading a life of poverty, he produced a remarkable series of works in prose and poetry.

Dante's one formal contribution to political theory, *On Monarchy*, was written between 1310 and 1313 in the period when Henry VII, the German emperor, was attempting to reassert control over the Italian kingdom in the name of peace. Dante's work reflects his thoughts on Italian politics after years of exile. Over the centuries the papacy had developed the doctrine that because the king ruled over the body and the Church over the soul, the ecclesiastical authority was not only morally superior but also had the prerogative to command the royal power. This position was closely linked to the view that the earth was a vale of tears and that the king's main task was to keep sinners from interrupting the Church as it went about the really important task of showing souls the way to the transcendent world. Essen-

tially, royal power was negative, aimed at punishing evildoing. Given the central religious goal of the society, the Church expected Christian kings to look for guidance to the pope, who headed the great salvific enterprise.

Dante became convinced that the only way to stop factional divisions rending the fabric of Italian political and social life was to have a strong emperor, who would establish order. The arrival in Italy, in 1310, of Emperor Henry VII, who refused to recognize either the Guelf or the Ghibelline Party, raised his hopes. Everywhere, however, the papacy was trying to thwart Henry's policies, justifying itself on the grounds that the emperor was disobedient to the pope. Consequently, Dante felt it necessary to attack directly the claim of the papacy for a supervisory role over the emperor. The two powers, the emperor and the pope, he declared, have authority in two separate realms, the worldly and the religious. The role of the emperor is to use his authority to help his subjects attain "terrestrial beatitude," whereas the pope seeks their "celestial beatitude." Thus, there is no justification for one power to interfere with the other's work.

Clearly, what Dante has done is to reject the almost-unquestioned medieval assumption that the Church has a monopoly on moral and spiritual values. In contrast, Dante argues that life in this world, though of short duration, has its own integrity, significance, and rewards. Over this realm the secular power reigns supreme. The pope, on the other hand, rules the other sphere, that concerned with religious values, in which the goal can be reached only beyond the grave. This view of the separation of church and state was to have an impact on modern political ideas. The significance of the Roman empire in God's design for man, and the importance of life on earth, are extremely important for an understanding of the *Divine Comedy*.

The Divine Comedy

Shortly before his death, Dante finished the work he called his "comedy" (the adjective "divine" was added by later admirers). This is certainly no comedy in the ordinary sense, but Dante so named it because it was written in the "vulgar" (Italian, rather than Latin) tongue and because, in contrast to tragedy, it begins in despair and ends in bliss. The work is also akin to comedy in its realistic view of human nature and in its inclusiveness of a wide variety of human types. It might best be described as a spiritual epic, for it is essentially the story of the poet's quest for salvation. In his "comedy," Dante developed a motif found in the sixth book of the *Aeneid* and in much medieval literature—a journey by a living man through the realm of the dead.

The *Divine Comedy* is composed of three books, or "canticles," each divided into thirty-three "cantos," with one introductory canto. In addition, the entire poem is composed in a verse scheme called *terza rima*—stanzas of three lines with interlocking rhymes. Multiples of three appear throughout the poem. The emphasis on the number three, symbol of the holy trinity, is quite intentional. Part of Dante's genius was to combine abstract forms of medieval symbolism with a new realism. In its overall design, the work is often compared to the philosophical system of Thomas Aquinas and to the great cathedrals, such as Chartres. Like them, it is an edifice that embraces and builds upon almost every conceivable aspect of life, in this world and the next, with the whole pointing toward God. And yet Dante's graphic interest in individual human dilemmas and in the intricacies of Florentine politics reveals an artistic sensibility that has gone beyond the medieval view.

Dante intended his readers to read his poetic journey on both a literal and an allegorical level. It is at the same time the story of Dante himself and of the people he meets during the course of his journey and the representation of Everyman's quest for salvation. The introductory canto begins with the poet's description of himself at age 35 on Good Friday in the year 1300, "midway through life's journey" and "lost in a dark wood." The dark wood may symbolize the corruption in Florence that had so dismayed Dante, or his turning away from the pure love of Beatrice to baser loves, or a spiritual confusion resulting from neglect of religion. On a universal level, for the modern reader, the dark wood may signify something like a "mid-life crisis," or any form of mental and spiritual confusion. In the depths of despair, Dante meets the shade of Virgil, who tells him that in order to find his way out of the dark wood he must first journey through the three parts of the catholic afterlife—hell, purgatory, and paradise. Virgil will serve as his guide through the first two. Allegorically,

Virgil represents human reason. Reason can understand the nature of sin, punishment, and purgation, but not the divine mysteries of faith. In paradise, therefore, Virgil will be replaced by the shade of Beatrice, at once Dante's long-lost love and a symbol of Divine Revelation.

In the first canticle, the *Inferno* (hell), Dante, guided by Virgil, witnesses the gamut of human sins and their punishments, suffering intensely himself. Dante's order of sins comes partly from classical sources, partly from other medieval texts, and is partly his own invention. Hell is shaped like a cone, with the lesser sins at the wide top and the gravest sins in the narrow bottom, where Satan resides. The sins of passion are lighter than the sins of the intellect, and the worst sins of all are treachery to the two important powers in God's plan for earth, the Church and the Roman empire. Thus the three heads of Satan, in the icy depths of hell, chew on the shades of Brutus and Cassius, traitors to the empire, and Judas, traitor to Christ. The law of punishment for sins in hell, as in purgatory, is defined by what Dante calls *contrapasso*, or retribution: sinners pay for their sins with a punishment of the same nature. Thus the lustful, who let themselves be carried away by stormy passions, are blown about by a violent wind, the gluttons who "made pigs" of themselves wallow in the mud, murderers are steeped in rivers of boiling blood, and so forth.

Once Dante has passed through the depths of hell, he must climb the mountain of purgatory (see Fig. 8-2). Here, in the second book, *Purgatorio*, the sinners are not merely being punished, they are also purging themselves of sin for eventual entrance into paradise. On top of the mountain, in the earthly paradise, Beatrice comes to take Dante into heaven. The third book, *Paradiso*, recounts this final journey and assures Dante's salvation.

In the medieval world-view that Dante held, earth was believed to be at the center of the universe and the heavens a series of spheres around it from the closest sphere of the moon to the farthest Empyrean sphere, the dwelling place of God. When Dante and Beatrice reach the Empyrean, she prepares to leave the pilgrim to return to her place in heaven, entrusting him to Saint Bernard (Bernard of Clairvaux, devotee of Mary). Dante sings his final song of praise for Beatrice,

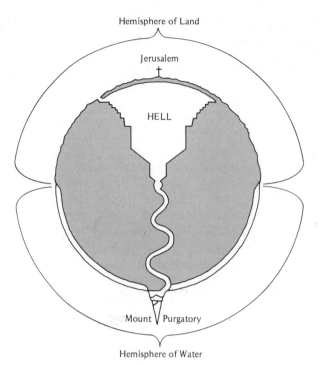

Hemisphere of Land

Jerusalem

HELL

Mount Purgatory

Hemisphere of Water

8-2 Dante's Earth, showing Hell and Purgatory. (Reprinted with permission of David Higham Associates Limited, London, from Dante Alighieri, *The Divine Comedy*, trans. Dorothy L. Sayers, © 1949 by Dorothy L. Sayers.)

conceding (though he praises his own poetic powers in the *Inferno*) that her heavenly beauty utterly undoes his art. Bernard promises Dante a vision of God, to be attained through the intercession of the Virgin Mary. Dante raises his eyes to the center of the mystic rose (a symbol of Mary, like the rose windows in the cathedrals) and, while experiencing unearthly bliss, sees the queen of heaven herself enthroned. Saint Bernard then offers a prayer to the Virgin, asking her to intercede for Dante, and Dante experiences a final rapture as he gazes directly on God. God is the source of all love—"the Love that moves the Sun and the other stars" are the final words of the poem—and the Eternal Light. Light, bearing much the same significance as it did for Suger when he created his cathedral, is the dominant image in paradise. It is a tribute to Dante's genius that he was able to render the ineffable in human language.

Because the *Inferno* is the book most accessible to modern readers, and because it best illustrates Dante's realism, we have chosen most of our selections from it. From *Purgatorio* we have chosen Canto XXX, in which

Dante is at last reunited with the long-lost Beatrice. The *Paradiso* is represented by the last canto, XXXIII, in which Saint Bernard leads Dante to a vision of the Virgin Mary, and at last to a vision of God. The translation, as well as the introductions and notes, are by the American poet John Ciardi. The note references refer to line numbers.

From *Inferno*

CANTO I

The Dark Wood of Error

Midway in his allotted threescore years and ten, Dante comes to himself with a start and realizes that he has strayed from the True Way into the Dark Wood of Error (Worldliness). As soon as he has realized his loss, Dante lifts his eyes and sees the first light of the sunrise (the Sun is the Symbol of Divine Illumination) lighting the shoulders of a little hill (The Mount of Joy). It is the Easter Season, the time of resurrection, and the sun is in its equinoctial rebirth. This juxtaposition of joyous symbols fills Dante with hope and he sets out at once to climb directly up the Mount of Joy, but almost immediately his way is blocked by the Three Beasts of Worldliness: THE LEOPARD OF MALICE AND FRAUD, THE LION OF VIOLENCE AND AMBITION, *and* THE SHE-WOLF OF INCONTINENCE. *These beasts, and especially the She-Wolf, drive him back despairing into the darkness of error. But just as all seems lost, a figure appears to him. It is the shade of* VIRGIL, *Dante's symbol of* HUMAN REASON.

*Virgil explains that he has been sent to lead Dante from error. There can, however, be no direct ascent past the beasts: the man who would escape them must go a longer and harder way. First he must descend through Hell (The Recognition of Sin), then he must ascend through Purgatory (The Renunciation of Sin), and only then may he reach the pinnacle of joy and come to the Light of God. Virgil offers to guide Dante, but only as far as Human Reason can go. Another guide (*BEATRICE, *symbol of* DIVINE LOVE) *must take over for the final ascent, for Human Reason is self-limited. Dante submits himself joyously to Virgil's guidance and they move off.*

Midway in our life's journey, I went astray
   from the straight road and woke to find myself
   alone in a dark wood. How shall I say   3

---

[1] *midway in our life's journey:* The Biblical life span is three-score years and ten. The action opens in Dante's thirty-fifth year, i.e., 1300 A.D.

what wood that was! I never saw so drear,
   so rank, so arduous a wilderness!
   Its very memory gives a shape to fear.   6

Death could scarce be more bitter than that place!
   But since it came to good, I will recount
   all that I found revealed there by God's grace.   9

How I came to it I cannot rightly say,
   so drugged and loose with sleep had I become
   when I first wandered there from the True Way.   12

But at the far end of that valley of evil
   whose maze had sapped my very heart with fear!
   I found myself before a little hill   15

and lifted up my eyes. Its shoulders glowed
   already with the sweet rays of that planet
   whose virtue leads men straight on every road,   18

and the shining strengthened me against the fright
   whose agony had wracked the lake of my heart
   through all the terrors of that piteous night.   21

Just as a swimmer, who with his last breath
   flounders ashore from perilous seas, might turn
   to memorize the wide water of his death—   24

so did I turn, my soul still fugitive
   from death's surviving image, to stare down
   that pass that none had ever left alive.   27

And there I lay to rest from my heart's race
   till calm and breath returned to me. Then rose
   and pushed up that dead slope at such a pace   30

each footfall rose above the last. And lo!
   almost at the beginning of the rise
   I faced a spotted Leopard, all tremor and flow   33

and gaudy pelt. And it would not pass, but stood
   so blocking my every turn that time and again
   I was on the verge of turning back to the wood.   36

This fell at the first widening of the dawn
   as the sun was climbing Aries with those stars
   that rode with him to light the new creation.   39

Thus the holy hour and the sweet season
   of commemoration did much to arm my fear
   of that bright murderous beast with their good
      omen.   42

Yet not so much but what I shook with dread
   at sight of a great Lion that broke upon me
   raging with hunger, its enormous head   45

held high as if to strike a mortal terror
   into the very air. And down his track,
   a She-Wolf drove upon me, a starved horror   48

ravening and wasted beyond all belief.
   She seemed a rack for avarice, gaunt and craving.
   Oh many the souls she has brought to endless
      grief!   51

---

every footfall carried him above the last despite the steepness of the climb. At a slow pace, on the other hand, the rear foot might be brought up only as far as the forward foot. This device of selecting a minute but exactly-centered detail to convey the whole of a larger action is one of the central characteristics of Dante's style.

THE THREE BEASTS: These three beasts undoubtedly are taken from *Jeremiah* v, 6. Many additional and incidental interpretations have been advanced for them, but the central interpretation must remain as noted. They foreshadow the three divisions of Hell (incontinence, violence, and fraud) which Virgil explains at length in Canto XI, 16–111. I am not at all sure but what the She-Wolf is better interpreted as Fraud and the Leopard as Incontinence. Good arguments can be offered either way.

38-9 *Aries . . . that rode with him to light the new creation:* The medieval tradition had it that the sun was in Aries at the time of the Creation. The significance of the astronomical and religious conjunction is an important part of Dante's intended allegory. It is just before dawn of Good Friday 1300 A.D. when he awakens in the Dark Wood. Thus his new life begins under Aries, the sign of creation, at dawn (rebirth) and in the Easter season (resurrection). Moreover the moon is full and the sun is in the equinox, conditions that did not fall together on any Friday of 1300. Dante is obviously constructing poetically the perfect Easter as a symbol of his new awakening.

---

17 *that planet:* The sun. Ptolemaic astronomers considered it a planet. It is also symbolic of God as He who lights man's way.

31 *each footfall rose above the last:* The literal rendering would be: "So that the fixed foot was ever the lower." "Fixed" has often been translated "right" and an ingenious reasoning can support that reading, but a simpler explanation offers itself and seems more competent: Dante is saying that he climbed with such zeal and haste that

She brought such heaviness upon my spirit
  at sight of her savagery and desperation,
  I died from every hope of that high summit.   54

And like a miser—eager in acquisition
  but desperate in self-reproach when Fortune's wheel
  turns to the hour of his loss—all tears and
    attrition   57

I wavered back; and still the beast pursued,
  forcing herself against me bit by bit
  till I slid back into the sunless wood.   60

And as I fell to my soul's ruin, a presence
  gathered before me on the discolored air,
  the figure of one who seemed hoarse from long
    silence.   63

At sight of him in that friendless waste I cried:
  "Have pity on me, whatever thing you are,
  whether shade or living man." And it replied: 66

"Not man, though man I once was, and my blood
  was Lombard, both my parents Mantuan.
  I was born, though late, *sub Julio*, and bred   69

in Rome under Augustus in the noon
  of the false and lying gods. I was a poet
  and sang of old Anchises' noble son   72

who came to Rome after the burning of Troy.
  But you—why do *you* return to these distresses
  instead of climbing that shining Mount of Joy   75

which is the seat and first cause of man's bliss?"
  "And are you then that Virgil and that fountain
  of purest speech?" My voice grew tremulous: 78

"Glory and light of poets! now may that zeal
  and love's apprenticeship that I poured out
  on your heroic verses serve me well!   81

For you are my true master and first author,
  the sole maker from whom I drew the breath
  of that sweet style whose measures have brought
    me honor.   84

See there, immortal sage, the beast I flee.
  For my soul's salvation, I beg you, guard me from
    her,
  for she has struck a mortal tremor through me."   87

And he replied, seeing my soul in tears:
  "He must go by another way who would escape
  this wilderness, for that mad beast that fleers   90

before you there, suffers no man to pass.
  She tracks down all, kills all, and knows no glut,
  but, feeding, she grows hungrier than she was.   93

She mates with any beast, and will mate with more
  before the Greyhound comes to hunt her down.
  He will not feed on lands nor loot, but honor   96

and love and wisdom will make straight his way.
  He will rise between Feltro and Feltro, and in him
  shall be the resurrection and new day   99

of that sad Italy for which Nisus died,
  and Turnus, and Euryalus, and the maid Camilla.
  He shall hunt her through every nation of sick
    pride   102

till she is driven back forever to Hell
  whence Envy first released her on the world.
  Therefore, for your own good, I think it well   105

---

95 *The Greyhound . . . Feltro and Feltro:* Almost certainly refers to
Can Grande della Scala (1290–1329), great Italian leader born in
Verona, which lies between the towns of Feltre and Montefeltro.

100-101 *Nisus, Turnus, Euryalus, Camilla:* All were killed in the war
between the Trojans and the Latians when, according to legend, Aeneas led the survivors of Troy into Italy. Nisus and
Euryalus (*Aeneid* IX) were Trojan comrades-in-arms who died
together. Camilla (*Aeneid* XI) was the daughter of the Latian
king and one of the warrior women. She was killed in a horse
charge against the Trojans after displaying great gallantry.
Turnus (*Aeneid* XII) was killed by Aeneas in a duel.

---

69 *sub Julio:* In the reign of Julius Caesar.

you follow me and I will be your guide
  and lead you forth through an eternal place.
  There you shall see the ancient spirits tried   108

in endless pain, and hear their lamentation
  as each bemoans the second death of souls.
  Next you shall see upon a burning mountain   111

souls in fire and yet content in fire,
  knowing that whensoever it may be
  they yet will mount into the blessed choir.   114

To which, if it is still your wish to climb,
  a worthier spirit shall be sent to guide you.
  With her shall I leave you, for the King of Time,
                                      117

who reigns on high, forbids me to come there
  since, living, I rebelled against his law.
  He rules the waters and the land and air   120

and there holds court, his city and his throne.
  Oh blessed are they he chooses!" And I to him:
  "Poet, by that God to you unknown,   123

lead me this way. Beyond this present ill
  and worse to dread, lead me to Peter's gate
  and be my guide through the sad halls of Hell."
                                      126

And he then: "Follow." And he moved ahead
  in silence, and I followed where he led.   128

---

[110] *the second death:* Damnation. "This is the second death, even the lake of fire." (*Revelation* xx, 14)

[118] *forbids me to come there since, living, etc.:* Salvation is only through Christ in Dante's theology. Virgil lived and died before the establishment of Christ's teachings in Rome, and cannot therefore enter Heaven.

[125] *Peter's gate:* The gate of Purgatory. (See *Purgatorio* IX, 76 ff.) The gate is guarded by an angel with a gleaming sword. The angel is Peter's vicar (Peter, the first Pope, symbolized all Popes; i.e., Christ's vicar on earth) and is entrusted with the two great keys.
  Some commentators argue that this is the gate of Paradise, but Dante mentions no gate beyond this one in his ascent to Heaven. It should be remembered, too, that those who pass the gate of Purgatory have effectively entered Heaven.
  The three great gates that figure in the entire journey are: the gate of Hell (Canto III, 1–11), the gate of Dis (Canto VIII, 79–113, and Canto IX, 86–87), and the gate of Purgatory, as above.

CANTO III

THE VESTIBULE OF HELL: The Opportunists

The Poets pass the Gate of Hell and are immediately assailed by cries of anguish. Dante sees the first of the souls in torment. They are THE OPPORTUNISTS, *those souls who in life were neither for good nor evil but only for themselves. Mixed with them are those outcasts who took no sides in the Rebellion of the Angels. They are neither in Hell nor out of it. Eternally unclassified, they race round and round pursuing a wavering banner that runs forever before them through the dirty air; and as they run they are pursued by swarms of wasps and hornets, who sting them and produce a constant flow of blood and putrid matter which trickles down the bodies of the sinners and is feasted upon by loathsome worms and maggots who coat the ground.*

The law of Dante's Hell is the law of symbolic retribution. As they sinned so are they punished. They took no sides, therefore they are given no place. As they pursued the evershifting illusion of their own advantage, changing their courses with every changing wind, so they pursue eternally an elusive, ever-shifting banner. As their sin was a darkness, so they move in darkness. As their own guilty conscience pursued them, so they are pursued by swarms of wasps and hornets. And as their actions were a moral filth, so they run eternally through the filth of worms and maggots which they themselves feed.

Dante recognizes several, among them POPE CELESTINE V, *but without delaying to speak to any of these souls, the Poets move on to* ACHERON, *the first of the rivers of Hell. Here the newly-arrived souls of the damned gather and wait for monstrous* CHARON *to ferry them over to punishment. Charon recognizes Dante as a living man and angrily refuses him passage. Virgil forces Charon to serve them, but Dante swoons with terror, and does not reawaken until he is on the other side.*

I AM THE WAY INTO THE CITY OF WOE.
I AM THE WAY TO A FORSAKEN PEOPLE.
I AM THE WAY INTO ETERNAL SORROW.   3

SACRED JUSTICE MOVED MY ARCHITECT.
I WAS RAISED HERE BY DIVINE OMNIPOTENCE,
PRIMORDIAL LOVE AND ULTIMATE INTELLECT.   6

ONLY THOSE ELEMENTS TIME CANNOT WEAR
WERE MADE BEFORE ME, AND BEYOND TIME I STAND.
ABANDON ALL HOPE YE WHO ENTER HERE.   9

These mysteries I read cut into stone
  above a gate. And turning I said: "Master,
  what is the meaning of this harsh inscription?"   12

And he then as initiate to novice:
  "Here must you put by all division of spirit
  and gather your soul against all cowardice.   15

This is the place I told you to expect.
  Here you shall pass among the fallen people,
  souls who have lost the good of intellect."   18

So saying, he put forth his hand to me,
  and with a gentle and encouraging smile
  he led me through the gate of mystery.   21

Here sighs and cries and wails coiled and recoiled
  on the starless air, spilling my soul to tears.
  A confusion of tongues and monstrous accents
    toiled   24

in pain and anger. Voices hoarse and shrill
  and sounds of blows, all intermingled, raised
  tumult and pandemonium that still   27

whirls on the air forever dirty with it
  as if a whirlwind sucked at sand. And I,
  holding my head in horror, cried: "Sweet Spirit,   30

what souls are these who run through this black haze?"
  And he to me: "These are the nearly soulless
  whose lives concluded neither blame nor praise.   33

They are mixed here with that despicable corps
  of angels who were neither for God nor Satan,
  but only for themselves. The High Creator   36

scourged them from Heaven for its perfect beauty,
  and Hell will not receive them since the wicked
  might feel some glory over them." And I: 39

"Master, what gnaws at them so hideously
  their lamentation stuns the very air?"
  "They have no hope of death," he answered me,   42

"and in their blind and unattaining state
  their miserable lives have sunk so low
  that they must envy every other fate.   45

No word of them survives their living season.
  Mercy and Justice deny them even a name.
  Let us not speak of them: look, and pass on."   48

I saw a banner there upon the mist.
  Circling and circling, it seemed to scorn all pause.
  So it ran on, and still behind it pressed   51

a never-ending rout of souls in pain.
  I had not thought death had undone so many
  as passed before me in that mournful train.   54

And some I knew among them; last of all
  I recognized the shadow of that soul
  who, in his cowardice, made the Great Denial.   57

---

⁷⁻⁸ *Only those elements time cannot wear:* The Angels, the Empyrean, and the First Matter are the elements time cannot wear, for they will last to all time. Man, however, in his mortal state, is not eternal. The Gate of Hell, therefore, was created before man. The theological point is worth attention. The doctrine of Original Sin is, of course, one familiar to many creeds. Here, however, it would seem that the preparation for damnation predates Original Sin. True, in one interpretation, Hell was created for the punishment of the Rebellious Angels and not for man. Had man not sinned, he would never have known Hell. But on the other hand, Dante's God was one who knew all, and knew therefore that man would indeed sin. The theological problem is an extremely delicate one.

It is significant, however, that having sinned, man lived out his days on the rind of Hell, and that damnation is forever below his feet. This central concept of man's sinfulness, and, opposed to it, the doctrine of Christ's ever-abounding mercy, are central to all of Dante's theology. Only as man surrenders himself to Divine Love may he hope for salvation, and salvation is open to all who will surrender themselves.

⁸ *and to all time I stand:* So odious is sin to God that there can be no end to its just punishment.

⁹ *Abandon all hope ye who enter here:* The admonition, of course, is to the damned and not to those who come on Heaven-sent errands. The Harrowing of Hell (Canto IV) provided the only exemption from this decree, and that only through the direct intercession of Christ.

⁵⁷ *who, in his cowardice, made the Great Denial:* This is almost certainly intended to be Celestine V, who became Pope in 1294. He was a man of saintly life, but allowed himself to be convinced by a priest named Benedetto that his soul was in danger since no man could live in the world without being damned. In fear for his soul he withdrew from all worldly affairs and renounced the papacy. Benedetto promptly assumed the mantle himself and became Boniface VIII, a Pope who became for Dante a symbol of all the worst corruptions of the church. Dante also blamed Boniface and his intrigues for many of the evils that befell Florence. We shall learn in Canto XIX that the fires of Hell are waiting for Boniface in the pit of the Simoniacs, and we shall be given further evidence of his corruption in Canto XXVII. Celestine's great guilt is that his cowardice (in selfish terror for his own welfare) served as the door through which so much evil entered the church.

At once I understood for certain: these
 were of that retrograde and faithless crew
 hateful to God and to His enemies.   60

These wretches never born and never dead
 ran naked in a swarm of wasps and hornets
 that goaded them the more the more they fled,   63

and made their faces stream with bloody gouts
 of pus and tears that dribbled to their feet
 to be swallowed there by loathsome worms and
  maggots.   66

Then looking onward I made out a throng
 assembled on the beach of a wide river,
 whereupon I turned to him: "Master, I long   69

to know what souls these are, and what strange usage
 makes them as eager to cross as they seem to be
 in this infected light." At which the Sage: 72

"All this shall be made known to you when we
  stand
 on the joyless beach of Acheron." And I
 cast down my eyes, sensing a reprimand   75

in what he said, and so walked at his side
 in silence and ashamed until we came
 through the dead cavern to that sunless tide.   78

There, steering toward us in an ancient ferry
 came an old man with a white bush of hair,
 bellowing: "Woe to you depraved souls! Bury   81

here and forever all hope of Paradise:
 I come to lead you to the other shore,
 into eternal dark, into fire and ice.   84

And you who are living yet, I say begone
 from these who are dead." But when he saw me
  stand
 against his violence he began again: 87

"By other windings and by other steerage
 shall you cross to that other shore. Not here! Not
  here!
 A lighter craft than mine must give you passage."
    90

And my Guide to him: "Charon, bite back your
  spleen:
 this has been willed where what is willed must be,
 and is not yours to ask what it may mean."   93

The steersman of that marsh of ruined souls,
 who wore a wheel of flame around each eye,
 stifled the rage that shook his woolly jowls.   96

But those unmanned and naked spirits there
 turned pale with fear and their teeth began to
  chatter
 at sound of his crude bellow. In despair   99

they blasphemed God, their parents, their time on
  earth,
 the race of Adam, and the day and the hour
 and the place and the seed and the womb that
  gave them birth.   102

But all together they drew to that grim shore
 where all must come who lose the fear of God.
 Weeping and cursing they come for evermore,   105

and demon Charon with eyes like burning coals
 herds them in, and with a whistling oar
 flails on the stragglers to his wake of souls.   108

As leaves in autumn loosen and stream down
 until the branch stands bare above its tatters
 spread on the rustling ground, so one by one   111

88-90 *By other windings:* Charon recognizes Dante not only as a living
 man but as a soul in grace, and knows, therefore, that the Infernal Ferry was not intended for him. He is probably referring to
 the fact that souls destined for Purgatory and Heaven assemble
 not at his ferry point, but on the banks of the Tiber, from which
 they are transported by an Angel.

100 *they blasphemed God:* The souls of the damned are not permitted
 to repent, for repentance is a divine grace.

---

80 *an old man:* Charon. He is the ferryman of dead souls across the
 Acheron in all classical mythology.

the evil seed of Adam in its Fall
 cast themselves, at his signal, from the shore
 and streamed away like birds who hear their call.
           114

So they are gone over that shadowy water,
 and always before they reach the other shore
 a new noise stirs on this, and new throngs gather.
           117

"My son," the courteous Master said to me,
 "all who die in the shadow of God's wrath
 converge to this from every clime and country. 120

And all pass over eagerly, for here
 Divine Justice transforms and spurs them so
 their dread turns wish: they yearn for what they
  fear.   123

No soul in Grace comes ever to this crossing;
 therefore if Charon rages at your presence
 you will understand the reason for his cursing."
           126

When he had spoken, all the twilight country
 shook so violently, the terror of it
 bathes me with sweat even in memory: 129

the tear-soaked ground gave out a sigh of wind
 that spewed itself in flame on a red sky,
 and all my shattered senses left me. Blind, 132

like one whom sleep comes over in a swoon,
 I stumbled into darkness and went down. 134

---

[123] *they yearn for what they fear:* Hell (allegorically Sin) is what the souls of the damned really wish for. Hell is their actual and deliberate choice, for divine grace is denied to none who wish for it in their hearts. The damned must, in fact, deliberately harden their hearts to God in order to become damned. Christ's grace is sufficient to save all who wish for it.

[133-34] DANTE'S SWOON: This device (repeated at the end of Canto V) serves a double purpose. The first is technical: Dante uses it to cover a transition. We are never told how he crossed Acheron, for that would involve certain narrative matters he can better deal with when he crosses Styx in Canto VII. The second is to provide a point of departure for a theme that is carried through the entire descent: the theme of Dante's emotional reaction to Hell. These two swoons early in the descent show him most susceptible to the grief about him. As he descends, pity leaves him, and he even goes so far as to add to the torments of one sinner. The allegory is clear: we must harden ourselves against every sympathy for sin.

CANTO V

CIRCLE TWO: The Carnal

The Poets leave Limbo and enter the SECOND CIRCLE. *Here begin the torments of Hell proper, and here, blocking the way, sits* MINOS, *the dread and semi-bestial judge of the damned who assigns to each soul its eternal torment. He orders the Poets back; but Virgil silences him as he earlier silenced Charon, and the Poets move on.*

They find themselves on a dark ledge swept by a great whirlwind, which spins within it the souls of the CARNAL, *those who betrayed reason to their appetites. Their sin was to abandon themselves to the tempest of their passions: so they are swept forever in the tempest of Hell, forever denied the light of reason and of God. Virgil identifies many among them.* SEMIRAMIS *is there, and* DIDO, CLEOPATRA, HELEN, ACHILLES, PARIS, *and* TRISTAN. *Dante sees* PAOLO *and* FRANCESCA *swept together, and in the name of love he calls to them to tell their sad story. They pause from their eternal flight to come to him, and Francesca tells their history while Paolo weeps at her side. Dante is so stricken by compassion at their tragic tale that he swoons once again.*

So we went down to the second ledge alone;
 a smaller circle of so much greater pain
 the voice of the damned rose in a bestial moan. 3

There Minos sits, grinning, grotesque, and hale.
 He examines each lost soul as it arrives
 and delivers his verdict with his coiling tail. 6

That is to say, when the ill-fated soul
 appears before him it confesses all,
 and that grim sorter of the dark and foul 9

---

[2] *a smaller circle:* The pit of Hell tapers like a funnel. The circles of ledges accordingly grow smaller as they descend.

[4] *Minos:* Like all the monsters Dante assigns to the various offices of Hell, Minos is drawn from classical mythology. He was the son of Europa and of Zeus who descended to her in the form of a bull. Minos became a mythological king of Crete, so famous for his wisdom and justice that after death his soul was made judge of the dead. Virgil presents him fulfilling the same office at Aeneas' descent to the underworld. Dante, however, transforms him into an irate and hideous monster with a tail. The transformation may have been suggested by the form Zeus assumed for the rape of Europa—the monster is certainly bullish enough here—but the obvious purpose of the brutalization is to present a figure symbolic of the guilty conscience of the wretches who come before it to make their confessions. Dante freely reshapes his materials to his own purposes.

decides which place in Hell shall be its end,
  then wraps his twitching tail about himself
  one coil for each degree it must descend.   12

The soul descends and others take its place:
  each crowds in its turn to judgment, each
      confesses,
  each hears its doom and falls away through space.
                                                 15

"O you who come into this camp of woe,"
  cried Minos when he saw me turn away
  without awaiting his judgment, "watch where you
      go   18

once you have entered here, and to whom you turn!
  Do not be misled by that wide and easy passage!"
  And my Guide to him: "That is not your
      concern;   21

it is his fate to enter every door.
  This has been willed where what is willed must
      be,
  and is not yours to question. Say no more."   24

Now the choir of anguish, like a wound,
  strikes through the tortured air. Now I have come
  to Hell's full lamentation, sound beyond sound. 27

I came to a place stripped bare of every light
  and roaring on the naked dark like seas
  wracked by a war of winds. Their hellish flight 30

of storm and counterstorm through time foregone,
  sweeps the souls of the damned before its charge.
  Whirling and battering it drives them on,   33

and when they pass the ruined gap of Hell
  through which we had come, their shrieks begin
      anew.
  There they blaspheme the power of God eternal.   36

And this, I learned, was the never ending flight
  of those who sinned in the flesh, the carnal and
      lusty
  who betrayed reason to their appetite.   39

As the wings of wintering starlings bear them on
  in their great wheeling flights, just so the blast
  wherries these evil souls through time foregone. 42

Here, there, up, down, they whirl and, whirling,
      strain
  with never a hope of hope to comfort them,
  not of release, but even of less pain.   45

As cranes go over sounding their harsh cry,
  leaving the long streak of their flight in air,
  so come these spirits, wailing as they fly.   48

And watching their shadows lashed by wind, I cried:
  "Master, what souls are these the very air
  lashes with its black whips from side to side?"   51

"The first of these whose history you would know,"
  he answered me, "was Empress of many tongues.
  Mad sensuality corrupted her so   54

---

[8] *it confesses all:* Just as the souls appeared eager to cross Acheron, so they are eager to confess even while they dread. Dante is once again making the point that sinners elect their Hell by an act of their own will.

[27] *Hell's full lamentation:* It is with the second circle that the real tortures of Hell begin.

---

[34] *the ruined gap of Hell:* At the time of the Harrowing of Hell a great earthquake shook the underworld shattering rocks and cliffs. Ruins resulting from the same shock are noted in Canto XII, 34, and Canto XXI, 112 ff. At the beginning of Canto XXIV, the Poets leave the *bolgia* of the Hypocrites by climbing the ruined slabs of a bridge that was shattered by this earthquake.

THE SINNERS OF THE SECOND CIRCLE (THE CARNAL): Here begin the punishments for the various sins of Incontinence (The sins of the She-Wolf). In the second circle are punished those who sinned by excess of sexual passion. Since this is the most natural sin and the sin most nearly associated with love, its punishment is the lightest of all to be found in Hell proper. The Carnal are whirled and buffeted endlessly through the murky air (symbolic of the beclouding of their reason by passion) by a great gale (symbolic of their lust).

[53] *Empress of many tongues:* Semiramis, a legendary queen of Assyria who assumed full power at the death of her husband, Ninus.

that to hide the guilt of her debauchery
  she licensed all depravity alike,
  and lust and law were one in her decree.   57

She is Semiramis of whom the tale is told
  how she married Ninus and succeeded him
  to the throne of that wide land the Sultans hold.   60

The other is Dido; faithless to the ashes
  of Sichaeus, she killed herself for love.
  The next whom the eternal tempest lashes   63

is sense-drugged Cleopatra. See Helen there,
  from whom such ill arose. And great Achilles,
  who fought at last with love in the house of
    prayer.   66

And Paris. And Tristan." As they whirled above
  he pointed out more than a thousand shades
  of those torn from the mortal life by love.   69

I stood there while my Teacher one by one
  named the great knights and ladies of dim time;
  and I was swept by pity and confusion.   72

At last I spoke: "Poet, I should be glad
  to speak a word with those two swept together
  so lightly on the wind and still so sad."   75

And he to me: "Watch them. When next they pass,
  call to them in the name of love that drives
  and damns them here. In that name they will
    pause."   78

Thus, as soon as the wind in its wild course
  brought them around, I called: "O wearied souls!
  if none forbid it, pause and speak to us."   81

As mating doves that love calls to their nest
  glide through the air with motionless raised wings,
  borne by the sweet desire that fills each breast—   84

Just so those spirits turned on the torn sky
  from the band where Dido whirls across the air;
  such was the power of pity in my cry.   87

"O living creature, gracious, kind, and good,
  going this pilgrimage through the sick night,
  visiting us who stained the earth with blood,   90

were the King of Time our friend, we would pray
    His peace
  on you who have pitied us. As long as the wind
  will let us pause, ask of us what you please.   93

The town where I was born lies by the shore
  where the Po descends into its ocean rest
  with its attendant streams in one long murmur.   96

---

61 *Dido:* Queen and founder of Carthage. She had vowed to remain faithful to her husband, Sichaeus, but she fell in love with Aeneas. When Aeneas abandoned her she stabbed herself on a funeral pyre she had had prepared.

According to Dante's own system of punishments, she should be in the Seventh Circle (Canto XIII) with the suicides. The only clue Dante gives to the tempering of her punishment is his statement that "she killed herself for love." Dante always seems readiest to forgive in that name.

65 *Achilles:* He is placed among this company because of his passion for Polyxena, the daughter of Priam. For love of her, he agreed to desert the Greeks and to join the Trojans, but when he went to the temple for the wedding (according to the legend Dante has followed) he was killed by Paris.

---

74 *those two swept together:* Paolo and Francesca (PAH-oe-loe: Frahn-CHAY-ska).

Dante's treatment of these two lovers is certainly the tenderest and most sympathetic accorded any of the sinners in Hell, and legends immediately began to grow about this pair.

The facts are these. In 1275 Giovanni Malatesta (Djoe-VAH-nee Mahl-ah-TEH-stah) of Rimini, called Giovanni the Lame, a somewhat deformed but brave and powerful warrior, made a political marriage with Francesca, daughter of Guido da Polenta of Ravenna. Francesca came to Rimini and there an amour grew between her and Giovanni's younger brother Paolo. Despite the fact that Paolo had married in 1269 and had become the father of two daughters by 1275, his affair with Francesca continued for many years. It was sometime between 1283 and 1286 that Giovanni surprised them in Francesca's bedroom and killed both of them.

Around these facts the legend has grown that Paolo was sent by Giovanni as his proxy to the marriage, that Francesca thought he was her real bridegroom and accordingly gave him her heart irrevocably at first sight. The legend obviously increases the pathos, but nothing in Dante gives it support.

Plate VII Della Francesca, *Resurrection*. Pinacoteca Communale, Sansepolcro. (Scala/Art Resource)

I 420-1492   Plate 1450's

Plate VIII Botticelli, *Primavera*. Galleria degli Uffizi, Florence. (Scala/Art Resource)

1444-1510   1477-1485

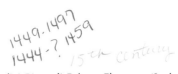

Plate IX   Gozzoli, *The Journey of the Magi*. Medici-Riccardi Palace, Florence. (Scala/Art Resource)

Plate X Da Vinci, *The Madonna of the Rocks*. The Louvre, Paris.
(Clichés Musées Nationaux, Paris)

1483

Plate XI Da Vinci, *The Madonna of the Rocks* (detail). The Louvre, Paris.
(Cliches Musées Nationaux, Paris)

1452-1519

Love, which in gentlest hearts will soonest bloom
   seized my lover with passion for that sweet body
   from which I was torn unshriven to my doom.   99

Love, which permits no loved one not to love,
   took me so strongly with delight in him
   that we are one in Hell, as we were above.   102

Love led us to one death. In the depths of Hell
   Caïna waits for him who took our lives."
   This was the piteous tale they stopped to tell.   105

And when I had heared those world-offended lovers
   I bowed my head. At last the Poet spoke:
   "What painful thoughts are these your lowered
      brow covers?"   108

When at length I answered, I began: "Alas!
   What sweetest thoughts, what green and young
      desire
   led these two lovers to this sorry pass."   111

Then turning to those spirits once again,
   I said: "Francesca, what you suffer here
   melts me to tears of pity and of pain.   114

But tell me: in the time of your sweet sighs
   by what appearances found love the way
   to lure you to his perilous paradise?"   117

And she: "The double grief of a lost bliss
   is to recall its happy hour in pain.
   Your Guide and Teacher knows the truth of this.
      120

But if there is indeed a soul in Hell
   to ask of the beginning of our love
   out of his pity, I will weep and tell: 123

On a day for dalliance we read the rhyme
   of Lancelot, how love had mastered him.
   We were alone with innocence and dim time.   126

Pause after pause that high old story drew
   our eyes together while we blushed and paled;
   but it was one soft passage overthrew   129

our caution and our hearts. For when we read
   how her fond smile was kissed by such a lover,
   he who is one with me alive and dead   132

breathed on my lips the tremor of his kiss.
   That book, and he who wrote it, was a pander.
   That day we read no further." As she said this,   135

the other spirit, who stood by her, wept
   so piteously, I felt my senses reel
   and faint away with anguish. I was swept   138

by such a swoon as death is, and I fell,
   as a corpse might fall, to the dead floor of Hell.   140

---

[102] *that we are one in Hell, as we were above:* At many points of *The Inferno* Dante makes clear the principle that the souls of the damned are locked so blindly into their own guilt that none can feel sympathy for another, or find any pleasure in the presence of another. The temptation of many readers is to interpret this line romantically: *i.e.,* that the love of Paolo and Francesca survives Hell itself. The more Dantean interpretation, however, is that they add to one another's anguish (a) as mutual reminders of their sin, and (b) as insubstantial shades of the bodies for which they once felt such great passion.

[104] *Caïna waits for him:* Giovanni Malatesta was still alive at the writing. His fate is already decided, however, and upon his death, his soul will fall to Caïna, the first ring of the last circle (Canto XXXII), where lie those who performed acts of treachery against their kin.

[124-5] *the rhyme of Lancelot:* The story exists in many forms. The details Dante makes use of are from an Old French version.

[126] *dim time:* The original simply reads "We were alone, suspecting nothing." "Dim time" is rhyme-forced, but not wholly outside the legitimate implications of the original, I hope. The old courtly romance may well be thought of as happening in the dim ancient days. The apology, of course, comes after the fact: one does the possible then argues for justification, and there probably is none.

[134] *that book, and he who wrote it, was a pander:* "Galeotto," the Italian word for "pander," is also the Italian rendering of the name of Gellehault, who in the French Romance Dante refers to here, urged Lancelot and Guinevere on to love.

CANTO XXXIII

CIRCLE NINE: Cocytus   Compound Fraud
ROUND TWO: Antenora   The Treacherous to Country
ROUND THREE: Ptolomea   The Treacherous to Guests and Hosts

In reply to Dante's exhortation, the sinner who is gnawing his companion's head looks up, wipes his bloody mouth on his victim's hair, and tells his harrowing story. He is COUNT

THE CLASSIFICATIONS OF SIN IN LOWER HELL

HERESY   CIRCLE VI

THE VIOLENT AND BESTIAL (CIRCLE VII) (SINS OF THE LION)
- ROUND 1. AGAINST NEIGHBORS. (MURDERERS AND WAR-MAKERS)
- ROUND 2. AGAINST SELF. (SUICIDES AND DESTROYERS OF THEIR OWN SUBSTANCE)
- ROUND 3. AGAINST GOD, ART, AND NATURE. (BLASPHEMERS, PERVERTS, AND USURERS)

THE FRAUDULENT AND MALICIOUS (SINS OF THE LEOPARD)

(CIRCLE VIII) (SIMPLE FRAUD)
- BOLGIA 1. SEDUCERS AND PANDERERS.
- BOLGIA 2. FLATTERERS.
- BOLGIA 3. SIMONIACS.
- BOLGIA 4. FORTUNE TELLERS AND DIVINERS.
- BOLGIA 5. GRAFTERS.
- BOLGIA 6. HYPOCRITES.
- BOLGIA 7. THIEVES.
- BOLGIA 8. EVIL COUNSELORS.
- BOLGIA 9. SOWERS OF DISCORD.
- BOLGIA 10. COUNTERFEITERS AND ALCHEMISTS.

(CIRCLE IX) (COMPOUND FRAUD)
- CAÏNA. TREACHERY AGAINST KIN.
- ANTENORA. TREACHERY AGAINST COUNTRY.
- PTOLEMEA. TREACHERY AGAINST GUESTS AND HOSTS.
- JUDECCA. TREACHERY AGAINST LORDS AND BENEFACTORS.

LOWER HELL: The structure of Dante's Hell is based on Aristotle (as Virgil makes clear in his exposition), but with certain Christian symbolisms, exceptions, and misconstructions of Aristotle's text. The major symbolisms are the three beasts met in Canto I. The exceptions are the two peculiarly Christian categories of sin: Paganism and Heresy. The misconstructions of Aristotle's text involve the classification of ''bestiality.'' Aristotle classified it as a different thing from vice or malice, but medieval commentators construed the passage to mean ''another sort of malice.'' Dante's intent is clear, however; he understood Aristotle to make three categories of sin: Incontinence, Violence and Bestiality, and Fraud and Malice. Incontinence is punished in the Upper Hell. The following chart sets forth the categories of the Lower Hell.

UGOLINO *and the wretch he gnaws is* ARCHBISHOP RUGGIERI. *Both are in Antenora for treason. In life they had once plotted together. Then Ruggieri betrayed his fellow-plotter and caused his death, by starvation, along with his four ''sons.'' In the most pathetic and dramatic passage of the* INFERNO, UGOLINO *details how their prison was sealed and how his ''sons'' dropped dead before him one by one, weeping for food. His terrible tale serves only to renew his grief and hatred, and he has hardly finished it before he begins to gnaw Ruggieri again with renewed fury. In the immutable Law of Hell, the killer-by-starvation becomes the food of his victim.*

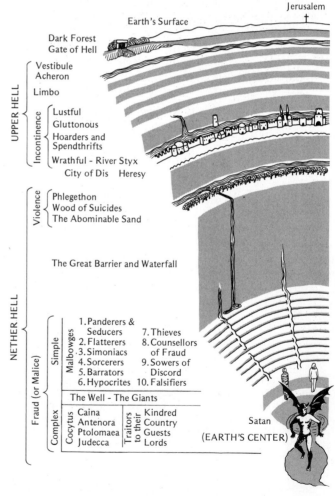

8-3   Cross-Section of Dante's Circular Hell. (Reprinted with permission of David Higham Associates Limited, London, from Dante Alighieri, *The Divine Comedy*, trans. Dorothy L. Sayers, © 1949 by Dorothy L. Sayers.)

The Poets leave Ugolino and enter PTOLOMEA, *so named for the Ptolomaeus of* MACCABEES, *who murdered his father-in-law at a banquet. Here are punished those who were* TREACHEROUS AGAINST THE TIES OF HOSPITALITY. *They lie with only half their faces above the ice and their tears freeze in their eye sockets, sealing them with little crystal visors. Thus even the comfort of tears is denied them. Here Dante finds* FRIAR ALBERIGO *and* BRANCA D'ORIA, *and discovers the terrible power of Ptolomea: so great is its sin that the souls of the guilty fall to its torments even before they die, leaving their bodies still on earth, inhabited by Demons.*

The sinner raised his mouth from his grim repast
    and wiped it on the hair of the bloody head
    whose nape he had all but eaten away. At last   3

he began to speak: "You ask me to renew
    a grief so desperate that the very thought
    of speaking of it tears my heart in two.   6

But if my words may be a seed that bears
    the fruit of infamy for him I gnaw,
    I shall weep, but tell my story through my tears.   9

Who you may be, and by what powers you reach
    into this underworld, I cannot guess,
    but you seem to me a Florentine by your speech.   12

I was Count Ugolino, I must explain;
    this reverend grace is the Archbishop Ruggieri:
    now I will tell you why I gnaw his brain.   15

That I, who trusted him, had to undergo
    imprisonment and death through his treachery,
    you will know already. What you cannot know—   18

that is, the lingering inhumanity
    of the death I suffered—you shall hear in full:
    then judge for yourself if he has injured me.   21

A narrow window in that coop of stone
    now called the Tower of Hunger for my sake
    (within which others yet must pace alone)   24

had shown me several waning moons already
    between its bars, when I slept the evil sleep
    in which the veil of the future parted for me.   27

This beast appeared as master of a hunt
    chasing the wolf and his whelps across the
        mountain
    that hides Lucca from Pisa. Out in front   30

of the starved and shrewd and avid pack he had
        placed
    Gualandi and Sismondi and Lanfranchi
    to point his prey. The father and sons had raced   33

1-90 *Ugolino and Ruggieri:* (Oog-oh-LEE-noe: Roo-DJAIR-ee) Ugolino, Count of Donoratico and a member of the Guelph family della Gherardesca. He and his nephew, Nino de' Visconti, led the two Guelph factions of Pisa. In 1288 Ugolino intrigued with Archbishop Ruggieri degli Ubaldini, leader of the Ghibellines, to get rid of Visconti and to take over the command of all the Pisan Guelphs. The plan worked, but in the consequent weakening of the Guelphs, Ruggieri saw his chance and betrayed Ugolino, throwing him into prison with his sons and his grandsons. In the following year the prison was sealed up and they were left to starve to death. The law of retribution is clearly evident: in life Ruggieri sinned against Ugolino by denying him food; in Hell he himself becomes food for his victim.

---

18 *you will know already:* News of Ugolino's imprisonment and death would certainly have reached Florence, *what you cannot know:* No living man could know what happened after Ugolino and his sons were sealed in the prison and abandoned.

22 *coop:* Dante uses the word *muda,* in Italian signifying a stone tower in which falcons were kept in the dark to moult. From the time of Ugolino's death it became known as The Tower of Hunger.

25 *several waning moons:* Ugolino was jailed late in 1288. He was sealed in to starve early in 1289.

28 *This beast:* Ruggieri.

29-30 *the mountain that hides Lucca from Pisa:* These two cities would be in view of one another were it not for Monte San Giuliano.

32 *Gualandi and Sismondi and Lanfranchi:* (Gwah-LAHN-dee . . . Lahn-FRAHN-kee) Three Pisan nobles, Ghibellines and friends of the Archbishop.

a brief course only when they failed of breath
    and seemed to weaken; then I thought I saw
    their flanks ripped open by the hounds' fierce
       teeth.   36

Before the dawn, the dream still in my head,
    I woke and heard my sons, who were there with me,
    cry from their troubled sleep, asking for bread.   39

You are cruelty itself if you can keep
    your tears back at the thought of what foreboding
    stirred in my heart; and if you do not weep,   42

at what are you used to weeping?—The hour when
      food
    used to be brought, drew near. They were now
      awake,
    and each was anxious from his dream's dark
      mood.   45

And from the base of that horrible tower I heard
    the sound of hammers nailing up the gates:
    I stared at my sons' faces without a word.   48

I did not weep: I had turned stone inside.
    They wept. 'What ails you, Father, you look so
      strange,'
    my little Anselm, youngest of them, cried.   51

But I did not speak a word nor shed a tear:
    not all that day nor all that endless night,
    until I saw another sun appear.   54

When a tiny ray leaked into that dark prison
    and I saw staring back from their four faces
    the terror and the wasting of my own,   57

I bit my hands in helpless grief. And they,
    thinking I chewed myself for hunger, rose
    suddenly together. I heard them say: 60

'Father, it would give us much less pain
    if you ate us: it was you who put upon us
    this sorry flesh; now strip it off again.'   63

I calmed myself to spare them. Ah! hard earth,
    why did you not yawn open? All that day
    and the next we sat in silence. On the fourth,   66

Gaddo, the eldest, fell before me and cried,
    stretched at my feet upon that prison floor:
    'Father, why don't you help me?' There he died.   69

And just as you see me, I saw them fall
    one by one on the fifth day and the sixth.
    Then, already blind, I began to crawl   72

from body to body shaking them frantically.
    Two days I called their names, and they were
      dead.
    Then fasting overcame my grief and me.''   75

His eyes narrowed to slits when he was done,
    and he seized the skull again between his teeth
    grinding it as a mastiff grinds a bone.   78

Ah, Pisa! foulest blemish on the land
    where "si" sounds sweet and clear, since those
      nearby you
    are slow to blast the ground on which you stand,
          81

may Caprara and Gorgona drift from place
    and dam the flooding Arno at its mouth
    until it drowns the last of your foul race!   84

51-71 UGOLINO'S "SONS": Actually two of the boys were grandsons
and all were considerably older than one would gather from
Dante's account. Anselm, the younger grandson, was fifteen.
The others were really young men and were certainly old
enough for guilt despite Dante's charge in line 90.

---

75 *Then fasting overcame my grief and me:* i.e., He died. Some interpret the line to mean that Ugolino's hunger drove him to cannibalism. Ugolino's present occupation in Hell would certainly support
that interpretation but the fact is that cannibalism is the one major
sin Dante does not assign a place to in Hell. So monstrous would it
have seemed to him that he must certainly have established a special punishment for it. Certainly he could hardly have relegated it
to an ambiguity. Moreover, it would be a sin of bestiality rather
than of fraud, and as such it would be punished in the Seventh
Circle.

79-80 *the land where "si" sounds sweet and clear:* Italy.

82 *Caprara and Gorgona:* These two islands near the mouth of the
Arno were Pisan possessions in 1300.

For if to Ugolino falls the censure
    for having betrayed your castles, you for your part
    should not have put his sons to such a torture: 87

you modern Thebes! those tender lives you spilt—
    Brigata, Uguccione, and the others
    I mentioned earlier—were too young for guilt! 90

We passed on further, where the frozen mine
    entombs another crew in greater pain;
    these wraiths are not bent over, but lie supine. 93

Their very weeping closes up their eyes;
    and the grief that finds no outlet for its tears
    turns inward to increase their agonies: 96

for the first tears that they shed knot instantly
    in their eye-sockets, and as they freeze they form
    a crystal visor above the cavity. 99

And despite the fact that standing in that place
    I had become as numb as any callus,
    and all sensation had faded from my face, 102

somehow I felt a wind begin to blow,
    whereat I said: "Master, what stirs this wind?
    Is not all heat extinguished here below?" 105

And the Master said to me: "Soon you will be
    where your own eyes will see the source and cause
    and give you their own answer to the mystery."
                                    108

And one of those locked in that icy mall
    cried out to us as we passed: "O souls so cruel
    that you are sent to the last post of all, 111

relieve me for a little from the pain
    of this hard veil; let my heart weep a while
    before the weeping freeze my eyes again." 114

And I to him: "If you would have my service,
    tell me your name; then if I do not help you
    may I descend to the last rim of the ice." 117

"I am Friar Alberigo," he answered therefore,
    "the same who called for the fruits from the bad
        garden.
    Here I am given dates for figs full store." 120

"What! Are you dead already?" I said to him.
    And he then: "How my body stands in the world
    I do not know. So privileged is this rim 123

of Ptolomea, that often souls fall to it
    before dark Atropos has cut their thread.
    And that you may more willingly free my spirit
                                    126

of this glaze of frozen tears that shrouds my face,
    I will tell you this: when a soul betrays as I did,
    it falls from flesh, and a demon takes its place,
                                    129

---

[86] *betrayed your castles:* In 1284, Ugolino gave up certain castles to Lucca and Florence. He was at war with Genoa at the time and it is quite likely that he ceded the castles to buy the neutrality of these two cities, for they were technically allied with Genoa. Dante, however, must certainly consider the action as treasonable, for otherwise Ugolino would be in Caïna for his treachery to Visconti.

[88] *you modern Thebes:* Thebes, as a number of the foregoing notes will already have made clear, was the site of some of the most hideous crimes of antiquity.

[91] *we passed on further:* Marks the passage into Ptolomea.

[105] *is not all heat extinguished:* Dante believed (rather accurately, by chance) that all winds resulted from "exhalations of heat." Cocytus, however, is conceived as wholly devoid of heat, a metaphysical absolute zero. The source of the wind, as we discover in the next Canto, is Satan himself.

[117] *may I descend to the last rim of the ice:* Dante is not taking any chances; he has to go on to the last rim in any case. The sinner, however, believes him to be another damned soul and would interpret the oath quite otherwise than as Dante meant it.

[118] *Friar Alberigo:* (Ahl-beh-REE-ghoe) Of the Manfredi of Faenza. He was another Jovial Friar. In 1284 his brother Manfred struck him in the course of an argument. Alberigo pretended to let it pass, but in 1285 he invited Manfred and his son to a banquet and had them murdered. The signal of the assassins was the words: "Bring in the fruit." "Friar Alberigo's bad fruit," became a proverbial saying.

[125] *Atropos:* The Fate who cuts the thread of life.

ruling the body till its time is spent.
The ruined soul rains down into this cistern.
So, I believe, there is still evident   132

in the world above, all that is fair and mortal
of this black shade who winters here behind me.
If you have only recently crossed the portal   135

from that sweet world, you surely must have known
his body: Branca D'Oria is its name,
and many years have passed since he rained
down."   138

"I think you are trying to take me in," I said,
"Ser Branca D'Oria is a living man;
he eats, he drinks, he fills his clothes and his
bed."   141

"Michel Zanche had not yet reached the ditch
of the Black Talons," the frozen wraith replied,
"there where the sinners thicken in hot pitch,   144

when this one left his body to a devil,
as did his nephew and second in treachery,
and plumbed like lead through space to this dead
level.   147

But now reach out your hand, and let me cry."
And I did not keep the promise I had made,
for to be rude to him was courtesy.   150

Ah, men of Genoa! souls of little worth,
corrupted from all custom of righteousness,
why have you not been driven from the earth?   153

For there beside the blackest soul of all
Romagna's evil plain, lies one of yours
bathing his filthy soul in the eternal   156

glacier of Cocytus for his foul crime,
while he seems yet alive in world and time!   158

---

[137] *Branca d'Oria:* (DAW-ree-yah) A Genoese Ghibelline. His sin is identical in kind to that of Friar Alberigo. In 1275 he invited his father-in-law, Michel Zanche (see Canto XXII), to a banquet and had him and his companions cut to pieces. He was assisted in the butchery by his nephew.

CANTO XXXIV

CIRCLE NINE (Cocytus):   Compound Fraud
ROUND FOUR (Judecca):   The Treacherous to Their Masters
THE CENTER: Satan

"On march the banners of the King," Virgil begins as the Poets face the last depth. He is quoting a medieval hymn, and to it he adds the distortion and perversion of all that lies about him. "On march the banners of the King—of Hell." And there before them, in an infernal parody of Godhead, they see Satan in the distance, his great wings beating like a windmill. It is their beating that is the source of the icy wind of Cocytus, the exhalation of all evil.

All about him in the ice are strewn the sinners of the last round, JUDECCA, *named for Judas Iscariot. These are the* TREACHEROUS TO THEIR MASTERS. *They lie completely sealed in the ice, twisted and distorted into every conceivable posture. It is impossible to speak to them, and the Poets move on to observe Satan.*

He is fixed into the ice at the center to which flow all the rivers of guilt; and as he beats his great wings as if to escape, their icy wind only freezes him more surely into the polluted ice. In a grotesque parody of the Trinity, he has three faces, each a different color, and in each mouth he clamps a sinner whom he rips eternally with his teeth. JUDAS ISCARIOT *is in the central mouth:* BRUTUS *and* CASSIUS *in the mouths on either side.*

Having seen all, the Poets now climb through the center, grappling hand over hand down the hairy flank of Satan himself—a last supremely symbolic action—and at last, when they have passed the center of all gravity, they emerge from Hell. A long climb from the earth's center to the Mount of Purgatory awaits them, and they push on without rest, ascending along the sides of the river Lethe, till they emerge once more to see the stars of Heaven, just before dawn on Easter Sunday.

"On march the banners of the King of Hell,"
my Master said. "Toward us. Look straight ahead:
can you make him out at the core of the frozen
shell?"   3

---

[1] *On march the banners of the King:* The hymn (*Vexilla regis prodeunt*) was written in the sixth century by Venantius Fortunatus, Bishop of Poitiers. The original celebrates the Holy Cross, and is part of the service for Good Friday to be sung at the moment of uncovering the cross.

Like a whirling windmill seen afar at twilight,
  or when a mist has risen from the ground—
  just such an engine rose upon my sight   6

stirring up such a wild and bitter wind
  I cowered for shelter at my Master's back,
  there being no other windbreak I could find.   9

I stood now where the souls of the last class
  (with fear my verses tell it) were covered wholly;
  they shone below the ice like straws in glass.   12

Some lie stretched out; others are fixed in place
  upright, some on their heads, some on their soles;
  another, like a bow, bends foot to face.   15

When we had gone so far across the ice
  that it pleased my Guide to show me the foul
    creature
  which once had worn the grace of Paradise,   18

he made me stop, and, stepping aside, he said:
  "Now see the face of Dis! This is the place
  where you must arm your soul against all dread."
    21

Do not ask, Reader, how my blood ran cold
  and my voice choked up with fear. I cannot write
    it:
  this is a terror that cannot be told.   24

I did not die, and yet I lost life's breath:
  imagine for yourself what I became,
  deprived at once of both my life and death.   27

The Emperor of the Universe of Pain
  jutted his upper chest above the ice;
  and I am closer in size to the great mountain   30

the Titans make around the central pit,
  than they to his arms. Now, starting from this
    part,
  imagine the whole that corresponds to it!   33

---

17 *the foul creature:* Satan.

If he was once as beautiful as now
  he is hideous, and still turned on his Maker,
  well may he be the source of every woe!   36

With what a sense of awe I saw his head
  towering above me! for it had three faces:
  one was in front, and it was fiery red;   39

the other two, as weirdly wonderful,
  merged with it from the middle of each shoulder
  to the point where all converged at the top of the
    skull;   42

the right was something between white and bile;
  the left was about the color that one finds
  on those who live along the banks of the Nile.   45

Under each head two wings rose terribly,
  their span proportioned to so gross a bird:
  I never saw such sails upon the sea.   48

They were not feathers—their texture and their form
  were like a bat's wings—and he beat them so
  that three winds blew from him in one great
    storm: 51

it is these winds that freeze all Cocytus.
  He wept from his six eyes, and down three chins
  the tears ran mixed with bloody froth and pus.   54

In every mouth he worked a broken sinner
  between his rake-like teeth. Thus he kept three
  in eternal pain at his eternal dinner.   57

For the one in front the biting seemed to play
  no part at all compared to the ripping: at times
  the whole skin of his back was flayed away.   60

---

38 *three faces:* Numerous interpretations of these three faces exist. What is essential to all explanation is that they be seen as perversions of the qualities of the Trinity.

54 *bloody froth and pus:* The gore of the sinners he chews which is mixed with his slaver.

"That soul that suffers most," explained my Guide,
  "is Judas Iscariot, he who kicks his legs
  on the fiery chin and has his head inside.   63

Of the other two, who have their heads thrust
    forward,
  the one who dangles down from the black face
  is Brutus: note how he writhes without a word.   66

And there, with the huge and sinewy arms, is the
    soul
  of Cassius.—But the night is coming on
  and we must go, for we have seen the whole."   69

Then, as he bade, I clasped his neck, and he,
  watching for a moment when the wings
  were opened wide, reached over dexterously   72

and seized the shaggy coat of the king demon;
  then grappling matted hair and frozen crusts
  from one tuft to another, clambered down.   75

When we had reached the joint where the great
    thigh
  merges into the swelling of the haunch,
  my Guide and Master, straining terribly,   78

turned his head to where his feet had been
  and began to grip the hair as if he were climbing;
  so that I thought we moved toward Hell again.   81

"Hold fast!" my Guide said, and his breath came
    shrill
  with labor and exhaustion. "There is no way
  but by such stairs to rise above such evil."   84

At last he climbed out through an opening
  in the central rock, and he seated me on the rim;
  then joined me with a nimble backward spring.   87

I looked up, thinking to see Lucifer
  as I had left him, and I saw instead
  his legs projecting high into the air.   90

Now let all those whose dull minds are still vexed
  by failure to understand what point it was
  I had passed through, judge if I was perplexed.   93

"Get up. Up on your feet," my Master said.
  "The sun already mounts to middle tierce,
  and a long road and hard climbing lie ahead."   96

It was no hall of state we had found there,
  but a natural animal pit hollowed from rock
  with a broken floor and a close and sunless air.   99

"Before I tear myself from the Abyss,"
  I said when I had risen, "O my Master,
  explain to me my error in all this: 102

where is the ice? and Lucifer—how has he
  been turned from top to bottom: and how can the
    sun
  have gone from night to day so suddenly?"   105

And he to me: "You imagine you are still
  on the other side of the center where I grasped
  the shaggy flank of the Great Worm of Evil   108

which bores through the world—you *were* while I
    climbed down,
  but when I turned myself about, you passed
  the point to which all gravities are drawn.   111

You are under the other hemisphere where you
    stand;
  the sky above us is the half opposed
  to that which canopies the great dry land.   114

---

[62] *Judas:* Note how closely his punishment is patterned on that of the Simoniacs (Canto XIX).

[67] *huge and sinewy arms:* The Cassius who betrayed Caesar was more generally described in terms of Shakespeare's "lean and hungry look." Another Cassius is described by Cicero (*Catiline* III) as huge and sinewy. Dante probably confused the two.

[68] *the night is coming on:* It is now Saturday evening.

[82] *his breath came shrill:* CF. Canto XXIII, 85, where the fact that Dante breathes indicates to the Hypocrites that he is alive. Virgil's breathing is certainly a contradiction.

---

[95] *middle tierce:* In the canonical day tierce is the period from about six to nine A.M. Middle tierce, therefore, is seven-thirty. In going through the center point, they have gone from night to day. They have moved ahead twelve hours.

Under the mid-point of that other sky
    the Man who was born sinless and who lived
    beyond all blemish, came to suffer and die.   117

You have your feet upon a little sphere
    which forms the other face of the Judecca.
    There it is evening when it is morning here.   120

And this gross Fiend and Image of all Evil
    who made a stairway for us with his hide
    is pinched and prisoned in the ice-pack still.   123

On this side he plunged down from heaven's height,
    and the land that spread here once hid in the sea
    and fled North to our hemisphere for fright;   126

and it may be that moved by that same fear,
    the one peak that still rises on this side
    fled upward leaving this great cavern here."   129

Down there, beginning at the further bound
    of Beelzebub's dim tomb, there is a space
    not known by sight, but only by the sound   132

of a little stream descending through the hollow
    it has eroded from the massive stone
    in its endlessly entwining lazy flow.   135

My Guide and I crossed over and began
    to mount that little known and lightless road
    to ascend into the shining world again.   138

He first, I second, without thought of rest
    we climbed the dark until we reached the point
    where a round opening brought in sight the blest
       141

---

128 *the one peak:* The Mount of Purgatory.

129 *this great cavern:* The natural animal pit of line 98. It is also "Beelzebub's dim tomb," line 131.

133 *a little stream:* Lethe. In classical mythology, the river of forgetfulness, from which souls drank before being born. In Dante's symbolism it flows down from Purgatory, where it has washed away the memory of sin from the souls who are undergoing purification. That memory it delivers to Hell, which draws all sin to itself.

and beauteous shining of the Heavenly cars.
    And we walked out once more beneath the Stars.
       143

From *Purgatorio*

(Dante and Virgil have climbed the mountain.)

CANTO XXX

THE EARTHLY PARADISE: **Beatrice**

(Virgil Vanishes)

The procession halts and the Prophets turn to the chariot and sing "Come, my bride, from Lebanon." They are summoning BEATRICE, *who appears on the left side of the chariot, half-hidden from view by showers of blossoms poured from above by* A HUNDRED ANGELS. *Dante, stirred by the sight, turns to Virgil to express his overflowing emotions, and discovers that* VIRGIL HAS VANISHED.

Because he bursts into tears at losing Virgil, DANTE IS REPRIMANDED BY BEATRICE. *The Angel Choir overhead immediately breaks into a Psalm of Compassion, but Beatrice, still severe, answers by detailing Dante's offenses in not making proper use of his great gifts. It would violate the ordering of the Divine Decree, she argues, to let Dante drink the waters of Lethe, thereby washing all memory of sin from his soul, before he had shed the tears of a real repentance.*

When the Septentrion of the First Heaven,
    which does not rise nor set, and which has never
    been veiled from sight by any mist but sin,   3

---

143 *Stars:* As part of his total symbolism Dante ends each of the three divisions of the *Commedia* with this word. Every conclusion of the upward soul is toward the stars, God's shining symbols of hope and virtue. It is just before dawn of Easter Sunday that the Poets emerge—a further symbolism.

1 *the Septentrion of the First Heaven:* The Septentrion is the seven stars of the Big Dipper. Here Dante means the seven candelabra. They are the Septentrion of the First Heaven (the Empyrean) as distinct from the seven stars of the dipper which occur lower down in the Sphere of the Fixed Stars.

2 *which does not rise nor set:* The North Star does not rise or set north of the equator, but the Septentrion, revolving around the North Star, does go below the horizon in the lower latitudes. This Septentrion of the First Heaven, however, partaking of the perfection and constancy of Heaven, neither rises nor sets but is a constant light to mankind. So these unchanging lights guide the souls of man on high, as the "lower Seven" (line 5), in their less perfect way, guide the earthly helmsmen to their earthly ports.

and which made every soul in that high court
  know its true course (just as the lower Seven
  direct the helmsman to his earthly port),   6

had stopped; the holy prophets, who till then
  had walked between the Griffon and those lights,
  turned to the car like souls who cry "Amen."   9

And one among them who seemed sent from Heaven
  clarioned: "*Veni, sponsa, de Libano,*"
  three times, with all the others joining in.   12

As, at the last trump every saint shall rise
  out of the grave, ready with voice new-fleshed
  to carol *Alleluliah* to the skies;   15

just so, above the chariot, at the voice
  of such an elder, rose a hundred Powers
  and Principals of the Eternal Joys,   18

all saying together: "*Benedictus qui venis*";
  then, scattering flowers about on every side:
  "*Manibus o date lilia plenis.*"   21

Time and again at daybreak I have seen
  the eastern sky glow with a wash of rose
  while all the rest hung limpid and serene,   24

and the Sun's face rise tempered from its rest
  so veiled by vapors that the naked eye
  could look at it for minutes undistressed.   27

Exactly so, within a cloud of flowers
  that rose like fountains from the angels' hands
  and fell about the chariot in showers,   30

a lady came in view: an olive crown
  wreathed her immaculate veil, her cloak was
    green,
  the colors of live flame played on her gown.   33

My soul—such years had passed since last it saw
  that lady and stood trembling in her presence,
  stupefied by the power of holy awe—   36

now, by some power that shone from her above
  the reach and witness of my mortal eyes,
  felt the full mastery of enduring love.   39

The instant I was smitten by the force,
  which had already once transfixed my soul
  before my boyhood years had run their course,   42

I turned left with the same assured belief
  that makes a child run to its mother's arms
  when it is frightened or has come to grief,   45

to say to Virgil: "There is not within me
  one drop of blood unstirred. I recognize
  the tokens of the ancient flame." But he,   48

he had taken his light from us. He had gone.
  Virgil had gone. Virgil, the gentle Father
  to whom I gave my soul for its salvation!   51

---

[7] *the holy prophets:* The twenty-four elders who represent the books of the Old Testament.

[10] *one among them: The Song of Solomon.*

[11] *Veni, sponsa, de Libano:* "Come [with me] from Lebanon, my spouse." *Song of Solomon,* iv, 8. This cry, re-echoed by choirs of angels, summons Beatrice, who may be taken here as revelation, faith, divine love, hence as the bride of the spirit, to Dante (man's redeemed soul).

[17-18] *a hundred Powers and Principals:* Angels.

[19] *Benedictus qui venis:* "Blessed is he who cometh." (*Matthew,* xxi, 9.)

[21] *Manibus o date lilia plenis:* "Oh, give lilies with full hands." These are the words of Anchises in honor of Marcellus. (*Aeneid,* VI, 883.) Thus they are not only apt to the occasion but their choice is a sweetly conceived last literary compliment to Virgil before he vanishes.

---

[31] *a lady:* Beatrice. She is dressed in the colors of Faith (white), Hope (green), and Charity (red).

[34] *since last it saw:* Beatrice died in 1290. Thus Dante has passed ten years without sight of her.

[36] *stupefied:* Dante describes the stupor of his soul at the sight of the living Beatrice in *La Vita Nuova,* XIV and XXIV. Then, however, it was mortal love; here it is eternal, and the effect accordingly greater.

Not all that sight of Eden lost to view
 by our First Mother could hold back the tears
 that stained my cheeks so lately washed with dew.
                                                        54

"Dante, do not weep yet, though Virgil goes.
 Do not weep yet, for soon another wound
 shall make you weep far hotter tears than those!"
                                                        57

As an admiral takes his place at stern or bow
 to observe the handling of his other ships
 and spur all hands to do their best—so now,   60

on the chariot's left side, I saw appear
 when I turned at the sound of my own name
 (which, necessarily, is recorded here),   63

that lady who had been half-veiled from view
 by the flowers of the angel-revels. Now her eyes
 fixed me across the stream, piercing me through. 66

And though the veil she still wore, held in place
 by the wreathed flowers of wise Minerva's leaves,
 let me see only glimpses of her face,   69

her stern and regal bearing made me dread
 her next words, for she spoke as one who saves
 the heaviest charge till all the rest are read.   72

"Look at me well. I am she. I am Beatrice.
 How dared you make your way to this high
   mountain?
 Did you not know that here man lives in bliss?"   75

I lowered my head and looked down at the stream.
 But when I saw myself reflected there,
 I fixed my eyes upon the grass for shame.   78

I shrank as a wayward child in his distress
 shrinks from his mother's sternness, for the taste
 of love grown wrathful is a bitterness.   81

She paused. At once the angel chorus sang
 the blessed psalm: *In te, Domine, speravi.*
 As far as *"pedes meos"* their voices rang.   84

As on the spine of Italy the snow
 lies frozen hard among the living rafters
 in winter when the northeast tempests blow;   87

then, melting if so much as a breath stir
 from the land of shadowless noon, flows through
   itself
 like hot wax trickling down a lighted taper—   90

just so I froze, too cold for sighs or tears
 until I heard that choir whose notes are tuned
 to the eternal music of the spheres.   93

---

[54] *washed with dew:* By Virgil. I, 124.

[55] *Dante:* This is the only point in the *Commedia* at which Dante mentions his own name. Its usage here suggests many allegorical possibilities. Central to all of them, however, must be the fact that Dante, in ending one life (of the mind) and beginning a new one (of faith) hears his name. The suggestion of a second baptism is inevitable. And just as a child being baptized is struck by the priest, so Beatrice is about to strike him with her tongue before he may proceed to the holy water.

[64] *that lady:* There are thirty-four Cantos in the *Inferno* and this is the thirtieth of the *Purgatorio*, hence the sixty-fourth Canto of the *Commedia*. This is the sixty-fourth line of the sixty-fourth Canto. In Dante's numerology such correspondences are always meaningful. Six plus four equals ten and ten equals the sum of the square of trinity and unity. Obviously there can be no conclusive way of establishing intent in such a structure of mystic numbering, but it certainly is worth noting that the line begins with "that lady." The Italian text, in fact, begins with *vidi la donna, i.e.,* I saw the lady [who represents the sum of the square of trinity plus unity?]. The lady, of course, is Beatrice.

[68] *wise Minerva's leaves:* The olive crown.

[80] *his mother's sternness:* Beatrice appears in the pageant as the figure of the Church Triumphant. The Church is the mother of the devout and though she is stern, as law decrees, her sternness is that of a loving mother.

[83-84] *In te, Domine, speravi . . . pedes meos:* In mercy the angel chorus sings Psalm XXXI, 1–8, beginning "In thee, O Lord, do I put my trust" and continuing as far as "thou hast set my feet in a large room."

[85-90] *the spine of Italy:* The Apennines. *the living rafters:* The trees. *the land of shadowless noon:* Africa. In equatorial regions the noonday sun is at the zenith over each point twice a year. Its rays then fall straight down and objects cast no shadows.

But when I heard the voice of their compassion
   plead for me more than if they had cried out:
   "Lady, why do you treat him in this fashion?";   96

the ice, which hard about my heart had pressed,
   turned into breath and water, and flowed out
   through eyes and throat in anguish from my
      breast.   99

Still standing at the chariot's left side,
   she turned to those compassionate essences
   whose song had sought to move her, and replied:
            102

"You keep your vigil in the Eternal Day
   where neither night nor sleep obscures from you
   a single step the world takes on its way;   105

but I must speak with greater care that he
   who weeps on that far bank may understand
   and feel a grief to match his guilt. Not only   108

by the workings of the spheres that bring each seed
   to its fit end according to the stars
   that ride above it, but by gifts decreed   111

in the largesse of overflowing Grace,
   whose rain has such high vapors for its source
   our eyes cannot mount to their dwelling place;   114

this man, potentially, was so endowed
   from early youth that marvelous increase
   should have come forth from every good he sowed.
            117

---

101 *compassionate essences:* The Angel chorus.

106 *greater care:* For his understanding than for your intercession.

109-11 *the working of the spheres . . . . :* The influence of the stars in
   their courses which incline men at birth to good or evil ends
   according to the astrological virtue of their conjunctions.

114 *our eyes:* Beatrice is still replying to the plea of the Angel choir.
   Hence "our eyes" must refer not to mortal eyes, but to the eyes of
   the blessed. Not even such more-than-human eyes may mount to
   the high place of those vapors, for that place is nothing less than
   the Supreme Height, since Grace flows from God Himself.

But richest soil the soonest will grow wild
   with bad seed and neglect. For a while I stayed
   him
   with glimpses of my face. Turning my mild   120

and youthful eyes into his very soul,
   I let him see their shining, and I led him
   by the straight way, his face to the right goal.   123

The instant I had come upon the sill
   of my second age, and crossed and changed my
   life,
   he left me and let others shape his will.   126

When I rose from the flesh into the spirit,
   to greater beauty and to greater virtue,
   he found less pleasure in me and less merit.   129

He turned his steps aside from the True Way,
   pursuing the false images of good
   that promise what they never wholly pay.   132

Not all the inspiration I won by prayer
   and brought to him in dreams and meditations
   could call him back, so little did he care.   135

He fell so far from every hope of bliss
   that every means of saving him had failed
   except to let him see the damned. For this   138

I visited the portals of the dead
   and poured my tears and prayers before that spirit
   by whom his steps have, up to now, been led.   141

The seal Almighty God's decree has placed
   on the rounds of His creation would be broken
   were he to come past Lethe and to taste   144

124-126 *my second age:* Beatrice's womanhood. When she had reached
   the full bloom of youth Dante turned from her and wrote to
   his *donna gentile.* Allegorically, he turned from divine "sciences" to an overreliance upon philosophy (the human "sciences"). For this sin he must suffer.

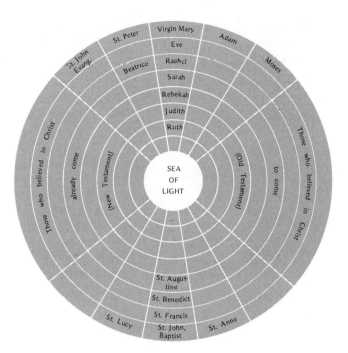

8-4   Dante's Circular Heaven.

the water that wipes out the guilty years
    without some scot of penitential tears!''   146

From *Paradiso*

CANTO XXXIII

THE EMPYREAN: St. Bernard

Prayer to the Virgin

The Vision of God

ST. BERNARD *offers a lofty* PRAYER TO THE VIRGIN, *asking her to intercede in Dante's behalf, and in answer Dante feels his soul swell with new power and grow calm in rapture as his eyes are permitted the* DIRECT VISION OF GOD.

There can be no measure of how long the vision endures. It passes, and Dante is once more mortal and fallible. Raised

by God's presence, he had looked into the Mystery and had begun to understand its power and majesty. Returned to himself, there is no power in him capable of speaking the truth of what he saw. Yet the impress of the truth is stamped upon his soul, which he now knows will return to be one with God's Love.

"Virgin Mother, daughter of thy son;
    humble beyond all creatures and more exalted;
    predestined turning point of God's intention;   3

thy merit so ennobled human nature
    that its divine Creator did not scorn
    to make Himself the creature of His creature.   6

The Love that was rekindled in Thy womb
    sends forth the warmth of the eternal peace
    within whose ray this flower has come to bloom.   9

Here, to us, thou art the noon and scope
    of Love revealed; and among mortal men,
    the living fountain of eternal hope.   12

Lady, thou art so near God's reckonings
    that who seeks grace and does not first seek thee
    would have his wish fly upward without wings.   15

Not only does thy sweet benignity
    flow out to all who beg, but oftentimes
    thy charity arrives before the plea.   18

144-145 *were he to come past Lethe:* In passing Lethe and drinking its waters, the soul loses all memory of guilt. This, therefore, is Dante's last opportunity to do penance.

1-39 ST. BERNARD'S PRAYER TO THE VIRGIN MARY. No reader who has come this far will need a lengthy gloss of Bernard's prayer. It can certainly be taken as a summarizing statement of the special place of Mary in Catholic faith. For the rest only a few turns of phrase need underlining. 3. *predestined turning point of God's intention:* All-foreseeing God built his whole scheme for mankind with Mary as its pivot, for through her He would become man. 7. *The Love that was rekindled in thy womb:* God. In a sense He withdrew from man when Adam and Eve sinned. In Mary He returned and Himself became man. 35. *keep whole the natural bent of his affections:* Bernard is asking Mary to protect Dante lest the intensity of the vision overpower his faculties. 37. *Protect him from the stirrings of man's clay:* Protect him from the stirrings of base human impulse, especially from pride, for Dante is about to receive a grace never before granted to any man and the thought of such glory might well move a mere mortal to an hybris that would turn glory to sinfullness.

In thee is pity, in thee munificence,
  in thee the tenderest heart, in thee unites
  all that creation knows of excellence!   21

Now comes this man who from the final pit
  of the universe up to this height has seen,
  one by one, the three lives of the spirit.   24

He prays to thee in fervent supplication
  for grace and strength, that he may raise his eyes
  to the all-healing final revelation.   27

And I, who never more desired to see
  the vision myself than I do that he may see It,
  add my own prayer, and pray that it may be   30

enough to move you to dispel the trace
  of every mortal shadow by thy prayers
  and let him see revealed the Sum of Grace.   33

I pray thee further, all-persuading Queen,
  keep whole the natural bent of his affections
  and of his powers after his eyes have seen.   36

Protect him from the stirrings of man's clay;
  see how Beatrice and the blessed host
  clasp reverent hands to join me as I pray."   39

The eyes that God reveres and loves the best
  glowed on the speaker, making clear the joy
  with which true prayer is heard by the most blest.
                                                            42

Those eyes turned then to the Eternal Ray,
  through which, we must indeed believe, the eyes
  of others do not find such ready way.   45

And I, who neared the goal of all my nature,
  felt my soul, at the climax of its yearning,
  suddenly, as it ought, grow calm with rapture.   48

Bernard then, smiling sweetly, gestured to me
  to look up, but I had already become
  within myself all he would have me be.   51

Little by little as my vision grew
  it penetrated further through the aura
  of the high lamp which in Itself is true.   54

What then I saw is more than tongue can say.
  Our human speech is dark before the vision.
  The ravished memory swoons and falls away.   57

As one who sees in dreams and wakes to find
  the emotional impression of his vision
  still powerful while its parts fade from his mind—
                                                            60

just such am I, having lost nearly all
  the vision itself, while in my heart I feel
  the sweetness of it yet distill and fall.   63

So, in the sun, the footprints fade from snow.
  On the wild wind that bore the tumbling leaves
  the Sybil's oracles were scattered so.   66

O Light Supreme who doth Thyself withdraw
  so far above man's mortal understanding,
  lend me again some glimpse of what I saw;   69

---

50 *but I had already become:* i.e., "But I had already fixed my entire
attention upon the vision of God." But if so, how could Dante have
seen Bernard's smile and gesture? Eager students like to believe they
catch Dante in a contradiction here. Let them bear in mind that
Dante is looking directly at God, as do the souls of Heaven, who
thereby acquire—insofar as they are able to contain it—God's own
knowledge. As a first stirring of that heavenly power, therefore,
Dante is sharing God's knowledge of St. Bernard.

54 *which in Itself is true:* The light of God is the one light whose
source is Itself. All others are a reflection of this.

65-66 *tumbling leaves . . . oracles:* The Cumean Sybil (Virgil describes
her in *Aeneid*, III, 441 ff.) wrote her oracles on leaves, one letter
to a leaf, then sent her message scattering on the wind. Presumably, the truth was all contained in that strew, could one only
gather all the leaves and put the letters in the right order.

---

40 *the eyes:* Of Mary.

make Thou my tongue so eloquent it may
    of all Thy glory speak a single clue
    to those who follow me in the world's day;   72

for by returning to my memory
    somewhat, and somewhat sounding in these verses,
    Thou shalt show man more of Thy victory.   75

So dazzling was the splendor of that Ray,
    that I must certainly have lost my senses
    had I, but for an instant, turned away.   78

And so it was, as I recall, I could
    the better bear to look, until at last
    my vision made one with the Eternal Good.   81

Oh grace abounding that had made me fit
    to fix my eyes on the eternal light
    until my vision was consumed in it!   84

I saw within Its depth how It conceives
    all things in a single volume bound by Love,
    of which the universe is the scattered leaves;   87

substance, accident, and their relation
    so fused that all I say could do no more
    than yield a glimpse of that bright revelation.   90

I think I saw the universal form
    that binds these things, for as I speak these words
    I feel my joy swell and my spirits warm.   93

Twenty-five centuries since Neptune saw
    the Argo's keel have not moved all mankind,
    recalling that adventure, to such awe   96

as I felt in an instant. My tranced being
    stared fixed and motionless upon that vision,
    ever more fervent to see in the act of seeing.   99

Experiencing that Radiance, the spirit
    is so indrawn it is impossible
    even to think of ever turning from It.   102

For the good which is the will's ultimate object
    is all subsumed in It; and, being removed,
    all is defective which in It is perfect.   105

Now in my recollection of the rest
    I have less power to speak than any infant
    wetting its tongue yet at its mother's breast;   108

and not because that Living Radiance bore
    more than one semblance, for It is unchanging
    and is forever as it was before;   111

rather, as I grew worthier to see,
    the more I looked, the more unchanging semblance
    appeared to change with every change in me.   114

Within the depthless deep and clear existence
    of that abyss of light three circles shown—
    three in color, one in circumference: 117

the second from the first, rainbow from rainbow;
    the third, an exhalation of pure fire
    equally breathed forth by the other two.   120

76-81 How can a light be so dazzling that the beholder would swoon if he looked away for an instant? Would it not be, rather, in looking at, not away from, the overpowering vision that the viewer's senses would be overcome? So it would be on earth. But now Dante, with the help of all heaven's prayers, is in the presence of God and strengthened by all he sees. It is by being so strengthened that he can see yet more. So the passage becomes a parable of grace. Stylistically it once more illustrates Dante's genius: even at this height of concept, the poet can still summon and invent new perceptions, subtlety exfoliating from subtlety.

The simultaneous metaphoric statement, of course, is that no man can lose his good in the vision of God, but only in looking away from it.

85-87 The idea here is Platonic: the essence of all things (form) exists in the mind of God. All other things exist as exempla.

88 *substance:* Matter, all that exists in itself. *accident:* All that exists as a phase of matter.

92 *these things:* Substance and accident.

109-114 In the presence of God the soul grows ever more capable of perceiving God. Thus, the worthy soul's experience of God is a constant expansion of awareness. God appears to change as He is better seen. Being perfect, He is changeless within himself, for any change would be away from perfection.

But oh how much my words miss my conception,
   which is itself so far from what I saw
   that to call it feeble would be rank deception!   123

O Light Eternal fixed in Itself alone,
   by Itself alone understood, which from Itself
   loves and glows, self-knowing and self-known;   126

that second aureole which shone forth in Thee,
   conceived as a reflection of the first—
   or which appeared so to my scrutiny—   129

seemed in Itself of Its own coloration
   to be painted with man's image. I fixed my eyes
   on that alone in rapturous contemplation.   132

Like a geometer wholly dedicated
   to squaring the circle, but who cannot find,
   think as he may, the principle indicated—   135

so did I study the supernal face.
   I yearned to know just how our image merges
   into that circle, and how it there finds place;   138

130-144 The central metaphor of the entire *Comedy* is the image of God and the final triumphant inGodding of the elected soul returning to its Maker. On the mystery of that image, the metaphoric symphony of the *Comedy* comes to rest.

   In the second aspect of Trinal-unity, in the circle reflected from the first, Dante thinks he sees the image of mankind woven into the very substance and coloration of God. He turns the entire attention of his soul to that mystery, as a geometer might seek to shut out every other thought and dedicate himself to squaring the circle. In *Il Convivio*, II, 14, Dante asserted that the circle could not be squared, but that impossibility had not yet been firmly demonstrated in Dante's time and mathematicians still worked at the problem. Note, however, that Dante assumes the impossibility of squaring the circle as a weak mortal example of mortal impossibility. How much more impossible, he implies, to resolve the mystery of God, study as man will.

   The mystery remains beyond Dante's mortal power. Yet, there in Heaven, in a moment of grace, God revealed the truth to him in a flash of light—revealed it, that is, to the God-enlarged power of Dante's emparadised soul. On Dante's return to the mortal life, the details of that revelation vanished from his mind but the force of the revelation survives in its power on Dante's feelings.

   So ends the vision of the *Comedy*, and yet the vision endures, for ever since that revelation, Dante tells us, he feels his soul turning ever as one with the perfect motion of God's love.

8-5 Giotto's portrait of Dante as a young man included in the crowd in one of Giotto's frescoes (Museo Nazionale, Florence).

but mine were not the wings for such a flight.
   Yet, as I wished, the truth I wished for came
   cleaving my mind in a great flash of light.   141

Here my powers rest from their high fantasy,
   but already I could feel my being turned—
   instinct and intellect balanced equally   144

as in a wheel whose motion nothing jars—
by the Love that moves the Sun and the other stars.

QUESTIONS ON THE *DIVINE COMEDY*

1. Describe the ordering of sins in Dante's vision of hell. How does this fit with your own religious or moral beliefs?
2. How does the law of *contrapasso* (retribution) work in the punishment of each sin?

3. Describe the portrayals of Virgil and of Beatrice, and Dante's relationship with them. Do they seem real as well as allegorical?

4. Compare the story of Paolo and Francesca (canto V of the *Inferno*) to Marie de France's *Equitan*. What seems to be Dante's attitude toward "courtly love"? How can Dante fall into a swoon out of sympathy for Francesca and still judge the lovers to be deserving of hell? Does he show this double attitude elsewhere?

5. Primo Levi, an Italian writer deported to Auschwitz during the second world war, found that one means of survival was reciting the canto of Ulysses (Inferno XXVI) by memory. Do you see any relationship?

6. Describe Dante's portrayal of the depths of hell. Why is it made of ice rather than fire?

7. Describe the reunion of Dante and Beatrice. What understanding of love is communicated by each of them?

8. Give examples of the imagery Dante uses in the *Inferno* and that used in *Paradiso*. Is Dante successful, in the latter, in portraying a mystic experience?

THE JUDEO-CHRISTIAN ROOT: CONTINUITIES

Judeo-Christian and Greco-Roman   In some ways it does not make sense to speak of "Judeo-Christian" as a continuum, or as a cultural root in opposition to the Greco-Roman one. If the Hellenic/Hebraic distinction is fairly clear, one must remember that Christianity (and, for that matter, Judaism from the second century B.C.) was strongly influenced by Greek ways of thinking. The New Testament is itself a document of Greek literature, containing Greek philosophical terms; and the influence of Plato and Aristotle on the development of Catholic theology was enormous. Nor can one neglect the Roman contribution to Christian culture. The economic, political, and legal structures provided by the Roman Empire facilitated communication and helped make Christianity the dominant cultural influence in Europe. We have seen how the Christian church, God's house on earth, grew out of the Roman basilica.

Once this is said, however, it is nonetheless evident that certain aspects of Christianity, deriving from Judaism, differentiate it profoundly from the classical values of Greece and Rome. Foremost of these is the Hebraic concept of Jahweh, the one, supreme God who takes a personal interest in His chosen people, Israel: "Thou shalt have no other gods before me." The God of the Jews and the Christians is a creator who made the world as we know it from nothing and a law-giver who dictates to His creation, man, the fundamental principles of morality. Socrates determined what is right and good according to the dictates of reason; the Jew or Christian accepts the Ten Commandments or the Sermon on the Mount as moral law because it is the word of God. The contrast between Protagoras' dictum "Man is the measure of all things" and the words of the psalmist, "What is man, that Thou art mindful of him?" is indicative: one culture is man-centered, the other God-centered.

Opposing itself to the values of the Greco-Roman world as a small, radical group, Christianity demanded allegiance to Christ before allegiance to the Roman emperor and the gods of the state. Yet Paul had molded it into a potentially universalist faith. Once Emperor Constantine converted, it was able to use the empire to its advantage. The Middle Ages witnessed the growth of two spheres of allegiance for every European, the spiritual and the temporal. In his great synthesis of medieval thought, Dante outlined the proper sphere of each.

Culture and the Church   In the twelfth and thirteenth centuries, our focus of attention here, the Church claimed the right to act as the conscience of Christian rulers and their subjects, to determine proper Christian belief, and to judge offenses against the faith. While allowing discussion within broad limits, the Church permitted no questioning of basic doctrines. As it was, few had any desire to do so. Temporal rulers were advised not to interfere in matters of belief and morals and to support the judgment of the spiritual in such cases.

By the end of the thirteenth century, Church efforts to intervene insecular matters became so frequent that some thinkers reacted by insisting that the Church's domain was limited to religion proper and that civil morality, the dealings of men with one another, was in the control of secular rulers. Underlying this distinction was a new, more positive view of human existence on earth. Dante even dared speak of a "terrestrial beatitude."

Nevertheless, recognition of a certain area of consciousness as off limits to temporal powers survived in later centuries, even after the Reformation, when religious authorities were no longer able to exercise close control over it. In the eighteenth and nineteenth centuries, thinkerscame to define this spiritual sphere as within the province of the individualconscience and independent of the constraints of government action. Although the Reformation itself had, as we will see, a great deal of influenceon this evolution, the origins of this demand for freedom of individual conscience really lie with the Church's demarcation of its sphere of authority.

Monarchy and the Modern State By the twelfth and thirteenth centuries a new form of temporal power, the medieval monarchy, had developed; it was to serve as the basis for our modern state. There were essentially two kinds of states in the ancient period, the small, tightly knit city-state and the sprawling empire that controlled a variety of separate peoples by means of a relatively small elite. To expand as the city-states Athens and Rome did was to become an empire, because the city-state had no means of integrating the new populations into its intensive political life. Thus, it had to govern subject peoples with a corps of officials sent out from the mother city.

The medieval monarchy, on the other hand, was both larger than the city-state and more cohesive than the empire. Closely tied to the rise of the monarch's power was the development of representative institutions both at the local level and at the center, ultimately making subjects feel part of a greater whole. When a new area was incorporated into the country, *its* population, too, became involved in the political processes and a sense of common identity arose. Utilizing this sense of identity, the monarch could mobilize a far greater population than could the rulers of the city-state; he could demand a greater degree of loyalty from them than could the emperor. While in the centuries since the Middle Ages the supreme executive has become at least nominally an elected official, the European medieval monarchy with its representative element has served as the ancestor for the modern state adopted throughout the world.

Germanic Contributions We have not emphasized the Germanic or "barbarian" contributions to our cultural roots, but we have at least mentioned their importance in the formation of medieval civilization. The personal sense of loyalty to the lord and the lord's responsibility to his men were essential ingredients in the rise of the medieval monarchy. The ruler could expect obedience, but the follower would normally be consulted in the decision process. Together with principles of Roman law, Germanic custom limited the ruler's freedom of action and encouraged him to cooperate with larger and larger groups of his subjects in order to extend the operations and influence of the state.

The Cathedral as Center We have centered much of our study of medieval culture on the cathedral because it was such an important part of medieval life. We have looked at four cultural forms connected with the cathedral: the schools and the philosophy taught there; the Gothic architecture, sculpture, stained-glass painting, and theory behind them; the music performed at worship services; and the cult of the Virgin Mary, to whom the cathedrals were dedicated.

The art and thought in and around the cathedral show an extraordinary diversity and creativity and a love of elaboration quite different from the simplicity and restraint of classical art and thought. Three of the great systems of the Middle Ages—the philosophy of Thomas Aquinas, Chartres Cathedral, and Dante Alighieri's *Divine Comedy*—seem to encompass everything in this world and the next in their province, while organizing their edifice so that the whole is directed toward God. The belief that the sensual and intellectual realms of being can serve as steps into the spiritual realm is at the heart of all three of these systems. This belief also explains the medieval love of *symbolism*, *allegory*, and suggestion. Modern art forms owe much to their medieval predecessors, both in their use of symbols (that is, the suggestion of "another world" through physical reality) and in their use of form to express feeling. The neoclassicists of the eighteenth century thought the distorted sculptures on medieval cathedrals much inferior to the naturalistic, proportioned Greek and Roman ones. In the twentieth century we are well aware that apparent distortion is one means for expression.

"Gothic" was a disparaging term given by the neoclassicists to medieval architecture. But the nineteenth century rediscovered its beauty to such an extent that the United States, like other Western countries, became dotted with neo-Gothic churches, cathedrals, and universities. Today, when most people think of a religious edifice, they think of some form of Gothic style. Our universities, not only the neo-Gothic ones, stand as testimonies that the roots in the cathedral schools have flourished.

Medieval and Modern Music and Drama The vocal and instrumental music composed in the monasteries and cathedral schools was the first truly Western music. Much of it is still used in religious services today; and the great musical elaboration of medieval Europe, *polyphony*, is not only the basis of all modern music but is also the distinctive feature identifying Western music from all other forms. While legend labels chant as the gift of God, history records polyphony as the creation of man. The drama written along with medieval chant was also the first European drama, emerging within the cathedral at a time when the dramatic form in the Western world was almost dead.

Views of Women   The cult of the Virgin Mary, a major element in medieval art and life and in Catholicism, has profoundly influenced our society's conception of women. We have seen how the Virgin was represented in twelfth- and thirteenth-century literature and art as a divine mother, an object of the highest form of spiritual love, an intercessor between man and God. The portrayal of earthly ladies in the same period, strongly influenced by the cult of the Virgin, became either so etherealized that the lady became a symbol and the lover's feeling for her purely spiritual, or else she became a parody of the Virgin and the lover—an example of the destructiveness of earthly passion. Later centuries, however, took these parodies of swooning lovers worshiping their ladies quite seriously. As life began to imitate art, women became in a sense objects of veneration. In order to merit this attitude, they were supposed to be pure, chaste, and unattainable, not creatures of flesh and blood. Men developed the idea that women could be placed in two categories: pure (on a pedestal) and "fallen," so corrupted and irresponsible that they had to be controlled by men. We are only now changing the residues of this attitude.

Some of the gestures that stem from the courtly or chivalric tradition—men opening doors for women, holding out chairs for them, paying for their entertainment on dates—are still with us. So are some of our notions about love. Later centuries, as we shall see, took seriously the literary "courtly" type that presented love as an all-consuming, irresistible passion. From this came the "romantic" search for constant ecstasy and the resultant idea that adultery is necessarily more passionate than marriage. The idealization of the power and value of romantic love is very much a Western cultural value. More stable, traditional societies (as we will see in our study of Africa) view romantic love as exaggerated.

Transition to Renaissance   Although in the hierarchical vision of his great epic Dante faithfully reflected the integrated vision of the medieval universe and in his elaborate allegories captured the age's sense of its profound mysteries, he drew for his realistic description of many of the figures in his drama not from the culture of the cathedral or the court but from that of the city's marketplace. Although in Beatrice he elevated the ideal of spiritual love far beyond what it was in the work of the troubadour, the personalities he encountered on his journey to the depths of hell and his ascent through purgatory are men and women of flesh and blood. In much the same way Giotto, for all his medieval attachments, through his ability to capture body weight and individual expression in his figures opens the path toward the more human-centered art of the Renaissance. By Chaucer's time, the period we call medieval was also drawing to a close in the north. The fleshed-out characters in his stories mark the transition there as well to a more realistic, less symbolic vision of man and the universe.

PART THREE

Renaissance and Reformation: Fusion of the Roots

9

Humanism and the Early Italian Renaissance

Students of history used to learn that everything in the Middle Ages was "obscure" or "superstitious," or that the minds of people were dominated by the Church and that suddenly in the Renaissance "light" burst forth, and culture, as in antiquity, flourished once again. The Middle Ages are now seen as a culture with its own values and creations, highly important ones, in fact, for our cultural roots. Many scholars also see the change from the Middle Ages to the Renaissance as gradual rather than revolutionary. There are continuities to be found in philosophy, politics, and the fine arts; and, despite the much-publicized shift from God to man, the culture of the European Renaissance remained fundamentally within the Judeo-Christian tradition. The subjects of painting, sculpture, music, and the other arts during the Renaissance were predominantly religious. At least in its early stage, humanism, the period's leading intellectual movement, viewed its major task as making the men and women of the time better Christians. Daily life in the Renaissance, as in the Middle Ages, was intimately tied to the rituals and calendar of the Church.

Nevertheless, despite these continuities, there is no doubt that something new happened in Western culture in the years 1350–1600. Our whole modern view of reality would not be the same without the Renaissance. What was this new view of the world, and how did it manifest itself in cultural achievements?

An Italian Phenomenon   Whereas the center of medieval culture was located in northern France and southern Germany, the Renaissance from 1350 to 1500 was dominated by Italy. Throughout the previous two centuries Italy had been the leading commercial power of Europe, and by 1300 the peninsula became the center of industry as well. Italy was far more urbanized than the North: in 1300 half a dozen cities of more than 50,000 people dotted the Italian landscape, while north of the Alps only Paris could boast of a population above that number. Although lay literacy was relatively high in urbanized sections of the peninsula, education before 1300 had largely been oriented toward practical goals, primarily medicine and law. The figure of Dante, coming at the end of the thirteenth century, therefore, is an exception and harbinger of great things to come. In contrast to its secondary role in medieval culture, Italy dominated in the Renaissance. Although after 1500 the Renaissance was to become a European movement, during the first 150 years it was largely an Italian phenomenon.

The Crisis of the Fourteenth Century   The fourteenth century was a time of trouble for Europe. By 1300 Western Europe was overpopulated for the technological level of the society. The costs of food and food-bearing land were high, wages were low, and a good percentage of the population was undernourished. When a terrible famine, the worst of the Middle Ages, struck the subcontinent between 1314 and 1318, about 10 percent of the people died and the losses were not made up. Beginning in 1348 the Black Death struck repeatedly over a wide area for the next fifty years. By 1400 Europe had only about 60 percent of the population that it had in 1300. The population was to remain

at this low level until the last decades of the century, when a spectacular rise in population began. This great human loss resulted in an economic contraction, a rise in labor costs, and a drop in rents and food prices. The overall effect on the upper classes of Europe who earned their income from trade or agriculture was adverse.

Although, like the rest of Europe, Italy was affected by the plague and the economic contraction, it remained the commercial and industrial center and did not suffer economic stagnation to the same degree as the North. Indeed, it appears that an imbalance in trade favorable to Italy existed in the fourteenth and fifteenth centuries. Quantities of gold and silver flowed into the peninsula from the North in exchange for luxury goods that Italians produced or imported from the East. The drain from the North could not go on forever; and, as purchases of Italian goods by northerners slowed down, investment opportunities in business narrowed in Italy. Some of the stocks of surplus precious metals, with no profitable outlet available, were subsequently funneled into culture; they paid for architecture, for art objects, and for patronage to scholars and writers.

The Rise of Mysticism   Not coincidentally, the fourteenth century, a period of enormous loss of life and dislocation, was the time when intellectual forces critical of the scholastic synthesis of faith and reason made themselves heard. The scholastic systems made sense in a period of economic and political integration like the twelfth and thirteenth centuries, but the great famine and the holocaust of the Black Death made a mockery of such approaches. In the North, theological and philosophical movements assaulted scholasticism for its attempt to build bridges of reason reaching up to God himself. These movements rejected the possibility of defining God through an analysis of His creation. For these new thinkers there was no way to argue back from what God created to Him as creator because, had He willed, He could have made everything in the universe different from what it is. The realms of faith and reason were seen to be absolutely separate. Human beings could know of God only what He had decided to tell in the Bible and through the subsequent operations of the Holy Spirit. Reason's work was limited to the created world. Aquinas' neat conception of continuity and overlap between the two was, therefore, rejected.

Confronted with famine and repeated outbreak of plague, the thinkers of the fourteenth century understandably magnified God as absolute will and the world as completely dependent on Him at every moment. Understandable, too, is the importance of *mysticism* in the fourteenth century. Mysticism was an effort to transcend outward experience in order to join oneself immediately with the divine while still within the body. Although mysticism was throughout the Middle Ages an acceptable element in the spiritual life of the Church, the misery and high mortality of this century made the mystic ascent very desirable.

Humanism

Another response to the crisis of the fourteenth century was humanism. The inhabitants of the Italian city-state were in many ways the most likely to appreciate the achievements and spirit of the ancient world. Roman and Greek monuments dotted the peninsula as nowhere else in Europe, and Roman law was the basic law of all the city-states; politically, Italy in the fourteenth century was organized like the ancient world around the city-state. Whereas northern European culture was primarily agricultural, the Italian, like the ancient, was urban. Consequently, it was easy for the Italian humanists of the fourteenth to the sixteenth centuries to see themselves as the descendants of the ancient Roman orators and writers who dominated the intellectual lives of their own cities.

Essentially, the humanists were literary scholars interested in Greek and Latin literature, grammar, history, and ethics. These subjects, therefore, constituted the *studia humanitatis*—that is, the disciplines that made man truly human. Man, for the humanist, distinguished himself from all other animals in his capacity to use words to express himself. If this was the basic human characteristic, then the man who best expressed himself in words was the most human. The humanists also assumed that outer speech was a reflection of one's inner state. If the inner man was calm and in harmony with his nature, then his speech would be fluent and harmonious. True eloquence stemmed from a fine soul just as the highest degree of moral virtue

was closely tied to eloquence. Of course, one could be virtuous and still stutter, but virtue could be realized only by helping others to become virtuous as well. The individual Christian had a responsibility to other men to help them to be good Christians; this could best be done by eloquent speech that inspired the will and heart to do the right.

Since the humanists considered the ancient pagan writers to have achieved excellence in speaking and writing, they believed that the study of Greek and Roman literature could best teach effective oral and written expression. They also thought that the writings of the pagans contained moral teachings urged with such forcefulness that they could not but influence their readers to become virtuous. In reading these writings, therefore, the humanists sharpened their moral sensibilities as well as their literary technique. They, in turn, would use their eloquence and virtue to persuade and train others.

Admittedly, the truth found in the pagan authors—fragmentary and based on reason—had to be interpreted in the context of the overarching truths of the Judeo-Christian tradition. The humanists, however, saw no incompatibility between what the Bible told man about God and about the nature of the human soul and the moral lessons taught by the ancient writers. The eloquence and learning of the ancients, consequently, coupled with the greater vision provided by divine revelation, could be a tremendous force for Christian reform.

On the whole, the humanists were hostile to scholasticism. Unlike the northern critics of the movement, who attacked scholasticism because it seemed to limit God's free will (by assuming that human reason could define His basic nature through an examination of the created world), the humanists simply felt that elaborate philosophical and theological systems were unnecessary. God gives us in revelation what we need to know about Christian truth: the real task of man is not to make systems but to live better Christian lives. The humanists also attacked the language of the scholastics as too technical and awkward. Such a style could never inspire men to improve their lives. There was an enormous difference between knowing the truth and carrying out its lessons in practice. Eloquent speech was the means of making truth active in the world.

Humanism was clearly an outgrowth of the urban culture of central and northern Italy. Dante had already shown the creative vigor present in this maturing urban society, but he had written in medieval Latin as well as in Tuscan. This new movement, as we have seen, took the ancients and their Latin as its models. Once initiated, imitation of the ancient Romans seemed natural to Italians.

The Use of Classical Authors Because ancient eloquence was central to their scheme of education, the humanists from the fourteenth century on devoted enormous energy not only to recovering lost ancient writings but also to preparing good editions of those inherited from the Middle Ages. In the more than eleven or twelve hundred years since ancient Roman times, the works of the pagans, especially the most popular ones, had been copied thousands of times by thousands of scribes; thus, texts were terribly corrupted. It fell to the humanists to restore as fully as possible the words and phrases of the pagan writers by a systematic comparison of surviving manuscripts. If ancient eloquence was to serve as a basis of inspiration to the present generation, the texts must be restored to their original purity.

Medieval writers used the classics as a kind of quarry from which to borrow words and ideas in order to adorn and support their own schemes of thought. On the other hand, while concerned with using the ancient writers for their own purposes, the humanists were also interested in defining the personalities of the great men of antiquity. Rather than attribute attitudes and ideas to pagan writers on a piecemeal basis, they tried to form an integrated picture of their thought and personalities by a careful analysis of all of an individual writer's works. Because of the similarities between their own and the ancient culture, they were able to appreciate the thoughts and actions of the ancients as the Middle Ages never could. This awareness of an interest in the totality of a personality, moreover, motivated their approach not merely to historical personages but also to men of their own time.

Furthermore, all the comparison of words and phrases in the effort to obtain accurate texts taught the humanists a concept not well understood in the Middle Ages: languages change; they have a history. The same is true of institutions, customs, and ideas. Thus, the scholarly endeavors of the humanists led them gradually to develop a sense of change and development, of historicity. This deepened their appreciation of the nature of human personality, permitting them to see the extent to which individuals were conditioned by circumstances of time and place. It also led them to a growing awareness that men are responsible for their history in large part and, subsequently, for their future as well. They came to see man as a doer, a maker, endowed with the godlike powers of reason and will to create his own culture.

Humanism and Science While by no means discarding the medieval ethos, which emphasized compassion, suffering, and humility, humanism in its essential tendencies moved toward a reevaluation of the human predicament by accenting the active, dynamic aspect of human nature. Originally biased against the natural sciences because of their focus in nature rather than man, the humanists nonetheless furnished the scientists with better texts of antiquity on which to base their investigations. By the sixteenth century, they were largely responsible for providing a vision of man and his creative capacities that encouraged scientific inquiry. Through the joint efforts of humanism and natural science, the task of improving human life materially as well as spiritually through a better understanding of man and his environment became increasingly viewed as a prime goal of learning.

Florence and Civic Humanism By the early fifteenth century Florence became the unrivaled center of humanistic studies as well as the artistic capital of Italy. Its population, varying between forty and sixty thousand throughout the century, was about half of what it had been before the Black Death of 1348. Although its cloth industry was suffering from the enormous population decline, it had become the undisputed financial center of Europe.

By 1400 Florentine republican institutions were deteriorating. Whereas the main form of government in the Italian towns of the northern and central portions of the peninsula in the thirteenth century had been republican, it became common in the next century for these popular regimes to be replaced by the rule of one man or one family. Florence was one of a dwindling number of cities still governed by republican methods, but even in Florence the sphere of active citizens had in effect narrowed to less than a hundred families. Although hundreds of other families shared in the more than two thousand public offices that had to be filled annually in the Florentine state, a narrower group of families controlled the key positions.

Petrarch   Francesco Petrarca (1304–1374) is generally considered the first of the Italian humanists. Although he was Florentine by descent and his first teacher was an exiled Florentine like his own father, Petrarch grew to manhood in France, not Italy. In the last half of his life, which he spent primarily in Italy, Petrarch saw the city of his ancestors only twice on brief visits. Petrarch's pioneering achievement was to formulate the basic humanistic conception of the intimate connection between ethics and eloquence just described and to develop an appreciation for ancient life and thought in its historical context.

In certain respects, however, Petrarch was still closely linked to medieval traditions. Medieval thinkers were fully committed to the belief that the contemplative life was the best form of existence for man and that monarchy was the best form of government. Like these thinkers, Petrarch, who spent most of his mature life in proximity to the new princely courts of northern Italy, considered the life of the citizen—the married man with business and civic responsibilities—unquestionably inferior to that of the solitary scholar or monk, who devoted his energies to the contemplation of divine truth. Moreover, like them he believed that monarchy was the ideal political constitution and that the Roman emperors had been established by God to replace the decaying Roman Republic.

Whereas Petrarch's scholarly contemporaries and Petrarch himself believed that his principal claim to enduring fame lay in his Latin writings (he was made poet laureate for his Latin epic poem *Africa*), subsequent generations have been most influenced by the poems he wrote in Tuscan Italian, the *Rime sparse*. These include both longer poems and sonnets, and it is especially as master of the sonnet form that Petrarch's

impact was felt on all European poetry. Petrarch's sonnets were inspired by those of Dante and the poets of the *dolce stil nuovo* (see p. 251). Like Dante's theme in the *Vita Nuova*, Petrarch's major theme in his sonnets is the poet's love for a beautiful and inaccessible lady, and like Dante, he writes of this love both during her lifetime and after her death. But Petrarch's Laura, often pictured in nature, among spring flowers, is less symbolic and medieval than Dante's Beatrice. Although there is no hard evidence for her actual existence, most scholars assume that she was a married French noblewoman whom Petrarch encountered while living in the south of France. In the sonnets, Petrarch not only speaks of Laura's beauty but also analyzes the whole range of his emotions as a lover, from elation to despair. It is this interest in the problems of human nature and in man as an individual that differentiates Petrarch from medieval writers. Although Petrarch sometimes strives to present Laura as the transcendental ideal in imitation of Dante's Beatrice, this effort is constantly undercut by an ambivalent mixture of the sacred and the erotic.

Petrarch explores the possibilities of symmetry and contrast in the formal aspects of the sonnet with great ingenuity. The octave usually presents a situation, event, image, or generalization, and the sestet a reflection, result, or application. The first sonnet printed below exemplifies Petrarch's love of technical ingenuity, his artificiality. He puns on each syllable of Laura's name in two forms (Laureta and Laure). Note, too, the classical reference, frequent in Petrarch, to the myth of Apollo and the laurel tree. Another sonnet plays with the word *aura* (breeze) and its relation to Laura. Although some of Petrarch's sonnets seem natural in their use of imagery, others, such as the one that develops the complex metaphor of the prison, are highly ingenious in their attempt to portray the sufferings and joys of love. The translation, which keeps the original rhyme scheme, is by Anna Maria Armi.

V

When I summon my sighs to call you near
With the name that Love wrote within my heart,
"LAUdable," one seems suddenly to hear
The sound of its first sweet melodies start.

Your REgal state that I wish to define
Doubles my valour to the enterprise;
"TAcitly," for her honour, the end cries,
Is load for other shoulders than are thine.

Thus to LAUd and REvere teaches and vows
The voice itself, if someone tries to call,
O worthy of all praise and reverence;

Unless perhaps Apollo take offence
That mortal tongue his ever-verdant boughs
Presumptuously endeavour to extol.

LXXVI

Love with his promises and flattery
Directed me again to my old prison,
And gave the keys to that same enemy
Who keeps me locked, divided from my reason.

I noticed it, alas! only when I
Was in their power; and now in agony
(Who will believe it, though I will not lie?)
And weary I return to liberty.

Like to a true, afflicted captive, now
I carry a great number of my chains,
And my heart is imprinted on my brow.

When you observe how all my colour wanes,
You will say:—If I can judge from his head,
He has not far to go before he's dead.—

XC

The golden hair was loosened in the breeze
That in many sweet knots whirled it and reeled,
And the dear light seemed ever to increase
Of those fair eyes that now keep it concealed:

And the face seemed to colour, and the glance
To feel pity, who knows if false or true;
I who had in my breast the loving cue,
Is it surprising if I flared at once?

Her gait was not like that of mortal things,
But of angelic forms; and her words' sound
Was not like that which from our voices springs;

A divine spirit and a living sun
Was what I saw; if such it is not found,
The wound remains, although the bow is gone.

CCXXVII

Aura that fold her blond and curly hair,
And move it softly and are moved by it,
And scatter that sweet gold as you think fit,
Then gather it and bind in knots so fair,

You fill her eyes from where some loving wasp
Stings me so that I feel it here, and grumble,
And, wavering, my treasure seek to clasp,
Like animals that often shy and stumble.

I think I have it, and I realize
That I am far from it, and fall and rise
Seeing now what I wish, now what is true.

Happy air, stay with the ray of her look,
Life-giving, fair. And you, clear running brook,
Why can I not change my journey with you?

CCXXVIII

Love with his right hand opened my left side
And planted in the middle of my heart
A laurel green that by its colour's art
Would casue every emerald to hide.

Ploughshare of pen with sighing of the breast,
And the pouring of sweet rain from the eyes,
Adorned it so that a scent reached the skies
Such as no other leaves ever expressed.

Fame, honour, virtue and enchantment,
A chaste beauty in heavenly array,
Are the roots from which rises the great bay.

Such I find it in me, no matter where
I am, my lovely load; and with deep prayer
I worship and revere it as a saint.

QUESTIONS

1. Note the divisions between octave and sestet in
   each poem. What are the advantages and disadvan-

tages of the sonnet as a poetic form? In what respect do Petrarch's sonnets differ from Dante's?

2. How does Petrarch develop images such as the prison and the laurel tree? How do they acquire meaning?

3. How would you define the Petrarchan concept of love? of woman?

Salutati and Bruni   After the death of Petrarch, the humanist and chancellor of Florence, Coluccio Salutati (1331–1406), helped to make Florence the center for humanistic studies. Both in his official work as Florentine secretary of state or chancellor and in his more scholarly writings, Salutati began to challenge the medieval theory of the superiority of monarchy. His disciple, Leonardo Bruni (1370–1444), was primarily responsible for formulating a theory of republican government that was to remain a living force down to the nineteenth century and beyond. He considered the rule of one man harmful to the common good. Since men realize themselves to the fullest in serving the state, republican government is natural to man and inherently stronger than monarchy. Rome reached its highest power under the Republic, not under the emperors; in fact, while some emperors might have been personally good men, as a group they destroyed Rome. Florence, founded in the days of the Roman Republic, inherited that tradition of liberty, and in contemporary Italy it served as the leader in the struggle of free men against *tyranny*.

The origins of Bruni's theory can be traced to the writings of Aristotle and Cicero. But Bruni's capacity to sense the republican spirit of these writers, which his predecessors had not perceived, stems from his personal experience as a part of a living republican society. His arguments rested both on his understanding of human nature and on the lessons he believed were found in history. The first European to formulate republican ideas with such clarity, he was followed over the next hundred years by a whole succession of writers, mainly Florentine, urging similar views.

Bruni was also one of the first of the humanists to learn Greek. Eminent Latin scholars like Petrarch and Salutati in the previous century did not know the other classic language. Aristotle's works had been translated hundreds of years before into Latin, but Bruni's knowl-

edge of Greek gave him access to the rest of extant Greek literature. This learning was especially valuable to him in his work in political theory, as indicated in the following excerpt from one of Bruni's Latin orations (translated by Ronald Witt). This is a funeral oration written by Bruni in 1428 in honor of the Florentine general, Nanni Strozzi, who died fighting against Milan, Florence's bitter enemy. Pericles' funeral oration as reported by Thucydides was clearly an influence. The Florentine orator ascribes to the dead man and to Florence many of the virtues and qualities attributed by Pericles to the Athenian war dead and to the city for which they sacrificed their lives.

BRUNI

Funeral Oration

This is an exceptional funeral oration because it is appropriate neither to weep nor lament. For we should be sorry for those who die having accomplished nothing which might bring comfort to those left behind. The life of this man was most enviable and his death was most glorious. We would be ungrateful to mourn a man who lived and died enjoying such a wealth of advantages. But in explaining the nature of his good fortune we must acknowledge that a good many things, the most important ones, were his by a kind of divinely ordained destiny. His first claim to fame is conferred on him because of his country's merit. For the homeland is the first and chief basis of human happiness and more worthy of our veneration than even our own parents. If we begin therefore by praising the motherland, we will be starting in the right order.

He was born in the most spacious and greatest of cities, wide-ruling and endowed with the mightiest power, without question the foremost of all the Etruscan cities.[1] Indeed, it is second to none of the cities of Italy either in origin, wealth, or size. The two most noble

---

[1] Cities of the ancient Etruscans (as we saw in the section on Roman architecture in Chapter 5) dominated the central portion of the Italian peninsula before the rise of Rome. There is little indication that Florence was an Etruscan city, but Fiesole, a town on the heights above Florence, was founded by that people.

and outstanding races of people in Italy cooperated in its foundation, that is, the Tuscans, the former lords of Italy, and the Romans, who acquired domination of the whole world through their virtue and their military prowess. For our city was a Roman colony integrated with the native Tuscan population.[2] The Tuscans had been the chief people of Italy and supreme both in authority and wealth. Before the foundation of the Roman empire their power was so great that this one people gave its name to both the seas that encircle Italy and governed the whole length of the country from the Alps to the Straits of Sicily for many centuries. Finally, this one people diffused the worship of the immortal gods as well as learning and letters throughout Italy. Other peoples of Italy borrowed their symbols of war and peace. As for the power of the Romans, their excellence, virtue, glory, magnanimity, wisdom and the size of their empire, it is better to say nothing than to have said only a few words.

What city, therefore, can be more excellent, more noble? What descended from more glorious antecedents? Among all the powerful cities, what one can be compared with our own on these grounds? Our fathers, moreover, are worthy of commendation because inheriting this city in their turn, they so established and governed it that they were in no way inferior to their own fathers in virtue. Sustained by the most sacred laws, the state was ruled by them with such wisdom that they served as an example of good moral behavior for other peoples and had no need to take others as their model. With constant vigilance they either conserved their authority and power or even increased it. The result is that in the memory of man this city has always been the foremost in Tuscany.

Worthy of praise as well are those who are its present-day citizens. They have augmented the power received from their predecessors even more by adding Pisa[3] and a number of other great cities to their empire through their virtue and valor in arms. But there is not time here to recall wars, battles, and feats of arms. This is ex-

tensive material indeed, and such things demand the labor and attention of not one day but many years. However, at this point with the discussion of external affairs either laid aside or already considered, let us stop to view and investigate in some detail the very body, so to speak, of the city.

Our form of governing the state aims at achieving liberty and equality for each and every citizen. Because it is equal in all respects, it is called a popular government. We tremble before no lord nor are we dominated by the power of a few. All enjoy the same liberty, governed only by law and free from fear of individuals. Everyone has the same hope of attaining honors and of improving his condition provided he is industrious, has talent and a good sober way of life. For our city requires virtue and honesty in its citizens. It considers anyone with these qualities to be noble enough to govern the state. The pride and haughtiness of the powerful are so hated that the city has passed more numerous and stringent laws against this kind of men than against anything else. As a result it has conquered the proud, as if binding them with unbreakable chains of the law, forcing them to bow their necks and to humble themselves to a moderate status. The result is that it is considered a benefit to transfer from the great families into the ranks of the common people.

This is true liberty and equality in a city: to fear the power of no one nor dread injury from them; to experience equality of law among the citizens and the same opportunity of ruling the state. These advantages cannot be had where one man rules or a few. For those who espouse kingly rule seem to imagine a degree of virtue in a king which they admit no man ever had. Has there ever been a king who did all of those things which are accomplished in a state on behalf of the people? Was there ever one who wanted nothing for himself except the empty glory of the name? Thus it is that praise of monarchy is like a thing false and shadowy, not clear and solid. Both good and evil people, says the historian,[4] are suspected by kings. The virtue of another is always frightening to them. Nor is it much different under the rule of a few.

---

[2] The date of Florence's foundation is still controversial. It occurred sometime in the first century B.C.

[3] Pisa was captured in 1406.

[4] Refers to the Roman historian Sallust (86–34 B.C.).

Thus the popular remains the only legitimate form of governing the state. In a popular government are found true liberty and equity for all citizens; in it the desires for virtue can thrive without suspicion. This capacity for a free people to attain honors and this ability to pursue one's goals serve in a marvelous way to excite men's talents. For with the hope of honors extended, men raise themselves and surge upward; excluded they become lifeless. Since in our state men have this hope and the opportunity is offered, no wonder that talents and industry abound so exceedingly. Indeed our city has such a numerous multitude of citizens that, in addition to the countless population living in the homeland, an infinite number are diffused throughout the world. . . . There is no place in the world so remote or out of the way where some Florentine does not live . . . Wherefore, if the whole multitude of our absent citizens variously diffused throughout the world be joined to those present in the city, an absolutely infinite and innumerable multitude would result, which no city in Italy could match. Our citizens excel so greatly in talents and intelligence that few equal them and none surpass them. They have vivacity and industry and alacrity and agility in acting with a greatness of spirit equal to all challenges.

We thrive not only in governing the republic, in domestic arts, and in engaging in business everywhere, but we are also distinguished for military glory. For our ancestors splendidly fought many wars on the dusty battlefield, overcoming all neighboring people with their military prowess. They shattered a thousand enemy battle wedges and set up almost innumerable trophies. Besides our city has furnished generals to the most powerful kings and produced skillful leaders of military science.

What now shall I say about literature and scholarship in which all concede that Florence is the chief and most splendid leader? Nor am I now speaking about those popular arts executed for money—although in these as well our people are foremost. But I am speaking about those more civilized and lofty studies which are considered more excellent and worthy of everlasting immortal glory. For who is able to name a poet in our generation or in the last one who is not Florentine?

Who but our citizens recalled this skill at eloquence, already lost, to light, to practical use, and to life? Who but they understood Latin literature, already abject, prostrate and almost dead, and raised it up, restored and reclaimed it from destruction? Camillus[5] is rightly said to be the founder of the city of Rome, not because he established it at the beginning, but because he restored it when it was defeated and occupied by the enemy. For the same reason, should our city not merit being proclaimed the parent of the Latin language, which a short time ago it found lost and cast down, and which it restored to its brilliance and dignity? Furthermore, just as we attribute to Triptolemus,[6] who first produced wheat, whatever has grown since, so whatever literature and cultivated learning takes root anywhere ought to be credited to our city. Now even the knowledge of Greek literature, which had decayed in Italy for more than seven hundred years, has been revived and restored by our city. Now we are able to confront the greatest philosophers, the admirable orators, and other men of outstanding learning, not through the obscurity of clumsy interpretations[7] but face to face. Finally, these humanistic studies [studia humanitatis] most excellent and of highest value, especially relevant for human beings, necessary both for private and public life, adorned with a knowledge of letters worthy of free men, have originated in our city and are now thriving throughout Italy. The city enjoys such resources and wealth that I fear to arouse jealousy by referring to its inexhaustible supply of money. This is demonstrated by the long Milanese war[8] waged at an almost incredible cost, in which we spent over 3,500,000 florins. Now at the end of the war men are more prompt in paying their taxes than they were at the beginning. As if miraculously, the abundance of money seems to increase in the city daily.

Therefore, the man we praise belonged by birth to this most noble, laudably established, most populous, spir-

---

[5] Camillus freed Rome from the Gauls in the early fourth century B.C.

[6] According to legend Triptolemus was the founder of agriculture.

[7] Refers to the Latin scholastic translations of the twelfth and thirteenth centuries, for example, those of the works of Aristotle.

[8] This particular war with Milan began in 1425 and ended in 1429.

ited, rich and glorious homeland. By the will of the immortal gods he (Strozzi) achieved in this way at the very beginning the greatest part of his happiness. . . . In this regard he could not have been more fortunate than he was in fact. . . .

QUESTIONS

1. Compare this praise of Florence with Pericles' praise of Athens (Chapter 2) and Virgil's praise of Rome in the *Aeneid* (Chapter 5). In what respects does Bruni seem to consider Florence comparable to the classical cities, and what new elements does he add?
2. Does any part of Bruni's speech sound as though it could have been made by an American statesman? In what respects?
3. How does Bruni define the humanities? Why does he consider them vital to the life of the city?
4. Why does he think that popular government is superior to the rule of one or of a few?

The Medici; Neoplatonism   In the last decade of Bruni's life Florence came under the control of the Medici family and their supporters. An old Florentine banking family, the Medici by the early fifteenth century were the richest family in the city. In the early 1430s the head of the family, Cosimo, quarreled with the other leading members of the Florentine government and was sent into exile in 1433. The following year, when his enemies in the government proved themselves clearly incompetent, they were driven out and Cosimo was recalled. Though the republican institutions continued to function and Cosimo remained a private citizen, for all practical purposes he and his close friends were usually able to control both the internal and external policies of the republic.

When Cosimo died in 1466, his son, Piero the Gouty, inherited the authority; and, when three years later Piero died, he in turn was succeeded by his two sons, Lorenzo and Giuliano, then twenty and eighteen respectively. After the assassination of Giuliano in 1478, Lorenzo alone directed the political life of the city until his own death in 1492. The years of Lorenzo's domination in Florence were also years of some of the highest cultural achievements in the city. Because of his exquisite taste and personal talents, Lorenzo be-

came known in his own lifetime as Lorenzo the Magnificent.

The rise of the Medici and their political control over Florentine institutions rendered Bruni's emphasis on the active life of the citizen unrealistic. While a republican current persisted in the city, the mood was generally one of political quietism. Not by chance the last half of the fifteenth century marked the progress of a movement usually labeled Florentine Platonism.

As we have already seen, Greek studies were introduced in Florence at the beginning of the fifteenth century. One of the first goals of Greek scholars was to translate the complete works of Plato. Whereas Aristotle had been translated into Latin in the thirteenth century, until this time only a handful of Plato's writings were in that language. Now, along with Plato's works, writings of Plato's ancient followers were also put into Latin. The most famous of these followers was Plotinus, an Egyptian of the second century A.D., who had given Plato's philosophy a clearly mystical bent. Plotinus stressed that through proper training the soul, whose true home was beyond this world, could at times in this life return by a mystic ascent to the world of the Ideas. The ultimate step was to merge totally with the Platonic One or Idea of the Good. Besides those of Plotinus, other Platonic writings, many of them of a magical nature, became popular with late fifteenth-century intellectuals. This kind of literature fitted an age that was no longer interested in active participation in politics.

The following selection, translated by Ronald Witt, is taken from *Oration on the Dignity of Man*, by Pico della Mirandola (1463–1494). Pico was not a Florentine by birth but, heavily influenced by Florentine Platonism, spent the last years of his short life in the city. An ideal Renaissance type, Pico was handsome, brilliant, and heir to a little Italian principality. He knew Latin, Greek, Hebrew, and Arabic. This oration was written as the introduction to a list of nine hundred theological and philosophical propositions that (at the age of twenty) he volunteered to debate in Rome with anyone. The debate never occurred.

The oration begins with the presentation of an extraordinary conception of the creative free will of man. Formerly, in line with the doctrines of Plotinus, Florentine Platonists had conceived of man midway on a chain of being between the lowest material objects and God. They believed that man had the power either to rise to the highest reaches of being or to fall to the lowest depths. Pico's achievement was to view man as outside the chain of being linking earth with heaven. Man contains within himself the potentiality of being anything. His free will is complete. His being, in fact, is a microcosm of the whole universe.

PICO DELLA MIRANDOLA

Oration on the Dignity of Man

I have read, O venerable fathers, in the records of the Arabs that Abdala the Saracen,[1] when asked what he believed was the most admirable thing on the stage of this world, as it were, replied that there was nothing more admirable than man. Hermes Trismegistus supported this opinion when he said, "O Asclepius, man is a great miracle!" Yet when I consider the grounds for such sayings, the many justifications, given by many, for the outstanding qualities of human nature do not satisfy me: that man is intermediary between the creatures, a friend of the higher powers, king of the lower regions; capable of understanding nature with the sharpness of his senses, the penetration of his reason, and the light of his intelligence; the space between unchanging eternity and the flux of time, and (as the Persians say) the bond of the world, nay rather, its marriage bond, and, as David testifies, only less than the angels.[2] Indeed these are great qualities but not the principal ones, that is, those which rightly serve as the basis for such extraordinary admiration. But why should we not admire the very angels and the blessed chorus of the heavens more? At length I seemed to myself to have understood why man is the most fortunate animal and therefore worthy of universal admiration and what his place in the order of the universe is that makes him an object of envy not only by brutes or by the stars, but even by minds beyond this world. It is an unbelievable and wonderful thing. Why should it not be? For on this account man is properly said to be a great miracle and a wondrous being. But now hear, Fathers, what it is and out of your kindness lend me your full attention.

The supreme father, God the architect, had already fabricated this house of the world which we see, the most illustrious temple of the divinity, according to the laws of His secret wisdom. He had adorned the place above the heavens with minds and animated the heavenly spheres with eternal souls; He had filled the excrementary and filthy places of the lower world with all manner of animals. But, with the work finished, the artisan wanted there to be someone who could contemplate the nature of so great a work, love its beauty and admire its magnitude. For this reason with all these things finished (as Moses and Timeaus[3] bear witness) only then did He think of creating man. But there was nothing among the archetypes from which He could model a new creature, nor in His treasuries was there an inheritance to bestow on His new son; nor was there any place left in the whole world where this contemplator of the universe could sit. Everything was already full; everything in the highest, middle, and lowest orders of being was already given out. But it was not in the Father's nature to fail as if worn out in this last creation; nor was His wisdom to waver without a plan in such a serious situation. Nor was it a part of His loving kindness that He, who would praise divine liberality in others, would condemn Himself for His lack of it. At length the consummate artificer decreed that the creature whom He could endow with no properties of its own should share in all those which the others possessed individually for themselves. Therefore, He took man, a creation of indeterminate form, and placing him at the midpoint of the world spoke to him in this way: "I have given you no fixed abode, no form of your own, no gifts peculiarly yours, O Adam, so that you might have and possess the abode, form and gifts you yourself desire according to your will and judgment. The defined nature of other beings is confined by laws which I have prescribed. You, compelled by no limitations, according to your free choice in whose hands I have placed you, shall prescribe your own limits. I have set you in the center of the world, that you might more

---

[1] Abdala was presumably the cousin of Mohammed.
[2] Psalms 8:5.

[3] Plato, *Timaeus*.

easily observe whatever there is in the world. We have made you neither heavenly nor terrestrial, neither mortal nor immortal, so that, free of constraint and more honorable as your own moulder and maker, you might give yourself whatever form you prefer. You can degenerate toward lower beings, which are brutes, or, if you will, you can be reborn among higher beings, which are divine."

Oh, the magnificent generosity of God the Father! Oh, the extraordinary and wondrous felicity of man, who was given the power to be that which he wanted! Brutes as soon as they are born bring with them from the mother's womb everything they are to have. The highest spiritual beings either from the beginning or soon thereafter are that which they will be for eternity. In the case of man, the Father bestowed on him at birth manifold seeds and germs of every kind of life. Whichever ones he cultivates will grow and bear their fruit in him. If he cultivates vegetative seeds, then he becomes a plant; if sensual ones, then a brute; if rational seeds, then he becomes a heavenly being. If intellectual ones,

then he will be an angel and son of God. And if, unhappy with being a creature of any sort, he draws into the center of his own unity, his spirit will be made one with God, and in the solitary darkness of the Father, Who is above all things, he will distinguish himself beyond all things. Who does not admire this our chamelon? Could anything else be more an object of wonder?

QUESTIONS

1. What different sources does Pico appear to use in establishing the dignity of man?
2. Compare Pico's account of man's creation with that in Genesis (Chapter 6). To what extent does he remain within the Judeo-Christian tradition, and how does he differ?
3. What is the basis for man's dignity? In what respect is man more wonderful than the angels?
4. Compare Pico's glorification of man to that of Sophocles in the choral ode from *Antigone* (see the section "Humanism and Tragedy" in Chapter 3).

10

Art, Architecture, and Music in Florence

Innovation Based on Antiquity In 1436 when Leon Battista Alberti (1404–1472) published the Italian version of his Latin treatise *On Painting* (1435), he added a prologue, praising the great Florentine artists Donatello, Ghiberti, and Masaccio, and the architect Brunelleschi. These men, says Alberti, are responsible for returning to the study of nature as the source of art and have consequently brought great fame to Florence. In a passage that parallels Bruni's in the *Funeral Oration*, Alberti compares Florentine accomplishments in art to those of the ancients, reserving the greatest praise for the Florentines, since they had to create by first discovering the knowledge that the ancients had already attained.

This point of view stresses the sense of departure from the immediate past and that of courageous experiment and exploration which, to Alberti and his contemporaries, must have seemed characteristic of Florence in the mid-fifteenth century. Wealth, power, and the association of free men had produced the republic; these same conditions fostered the new forms and conventions in art and architecture.

Similarly, the successful artists of the fifteenth century had roots in Roman antiquity. Brunelleschi, Florence's architect, is reported to have visited Rome in the early 1400s, studying and measuring the remains of the Forum. He returned to create a conspicuously new architecture. Alberti, who knew Brunelleschi, was also an architect who studied ancient texts; he wrote about the ideals and intentions that made Roman and fifteenth-century architecture so different from that of the Middle Ages. His theory and Brunelleschi's practice were, as we will see, representative of the changes taking place in Florence and were largely responsible for the transmission of new ideas to the future.

The City of Florence   It is difficult to imagine the events of the fifteenth century without some feeling for the physical setting of Florence itself (Color Plate IV). In the center of Italy, the city sits in a plain at the foothills of the Apennine Mountains, bisected by the Arno River. From almost any vantage point outside or within the city, one's view is dominated by the red-tiled octagonal dome of Saint Mary of the Flowers, or the *Duomo*, the cathedral of the city. The feeling created by this cathedral and its place within the city is vastly different from that of Notre Dame at Chartres. The *Duomo* sits in its own square *(piazza)* but within a city of other squares that belong to equally important old Christian churches or civic and mercantile enterprises. The *Palazzo Vecchio* (the old city hall) with its battlements and tower reminds one of the Gothic period (Fig. 10-1). It dominates the square where Michelangelo's *David* was originally placed.

The city has many centers of activity; there are distinguishable quarters for artisans, and the *Ponte Vecchio* (the old bridge) spanning the Arno still carries the many shops for luxury items that were there in the 1400s. Florence bustles with business activity—with the precious industries of gold, silver, silk, and leather still practiced today. The great food market near San Lorenzo and the small street stalls give the city an air of tantalizing fecundity.

Florence is dominated by narrow, cobbled streets and

10–1   Palazzo Vecchio, Florence. (Alinari/Editorial Photocolor Archives)

the thick walls of the palaces, banks, and apartments that rise three and four stories, keeping the blistering summer sun from the streets. In the winter the reds, yellows, browns, and tans of marble, stone, stucco, and brick glow wetly, contrasting with the black and white, gray, or green marble of the façades of many of the churches (Fig. 10-2). The city has a this-worldly intensity, a presence of now that is surely both a condition and creation of her fifteenth-century efflorescence.

Florentine Architecture

The cathedral dome that dominates Florence was designed by Filippo Brunelleschi (1377–1446), who won a competition for the commission. While not the most significant of Brunelleschi's accomplishments, it introduces the scientist, inventor, and designer that Brunelleschi had become. Technically he employed a system that suspended an interior shell from the exterior structure of ribs and concealed buttresses that originated in Roman and Gothic technology. Of almost equal importance to the city fathers were the machines and devices that Brunelleschi invented to erect the dome without an enormous quantity of wooden centering (see Roman and Gothic architecture). The *lantern* (cupola) based on his design was put in place after his death. Brunelleschi's influence on architecture was enormous. We can better appreciate some of the new ideas and vitality he gave to the art by considering two other works: the interior of San Lorenzo and the Pazzi Chapel.

10–2 Baptistry, Florence. (Alinari/Editorial Photocolor Archives)

The Church of San Lorenzo   Brunelleschi designed a sacristy for the Medici family to be added to San Lorenzo, an essentially Gothic church. The Medici were so delighted with it that he was then commissioned to remodel the interior of the church (Fig. 10-3), a project that began in 1421 and went on for many years. San Lorenzo's great simplicity and directness emphasize the contrast between the Renaissance and the Middle Ages. The interior seems almost early Christian, but with a substantial difference. Imposed on the traditional plan of nave and aisles (Fig. 10-4) is a sense of mathematical harmony, the repetition of sizes and shapes that derive from, but achieve a form different from, that of Gothic or Roman buildings.

Perhaps the most significant obvious difference is the sense of definite measured units of space, individual and independent. The nave is separated from the aisles by arcades of smooth Corinthian columns that carry semicircular arches. Above the arches is an entablature marking off the clerestory walls that are broken by arched windows centered above the arches. The columns, arches, and entablature are all in a gray stone that contrasts sharply with the smooth white plaster walls. The aisles are roofed by shallow vaults, and shallow side chapels line the walls. These have semicircular arched openings with a decorative keystone and are

10–3 Interior, San Lorenzo, Florence. (Alinari/Editorial Photocolor Archives)

also flanked by pilasters with Corinthian capitals, thus repeating the column-arch combination of the nave arcade. The aisles are lit by small round windows, one centered above each side chapel (Fig. 10-5).

The division of the wall planes of the aisles and the nave arcade are reinforced by the pavement, which is arranged in squares (see plan, Fig. 10-4)—thus, two squares form a bay of the nave and equal the height of a column; one square equals a bay of the aisle and one-half square a chapel. The transept is made of four large squares that are approximately equal to four square bays of the aisles. The nave roof is flat and decorated with square coffers.

Space in San Lorenzo is clear and limited, strongly directional but ordered into a rigorous sequence of bays. Each column, perfectly articulated, marks the beginning and end of a bay, a space. The light is dim but not mysterious. The transept is a specific and different space, as is the square apse at the east end. The feeling is one of intellectual control, not mystic transcendence.

Alberti, the architectural theorist, wrote that a church should induce contemplation through order and harmony, reflecting the mathematical perfection of the universe. It should, he said, be plain and encourage one to focus inward on control of self for the attainment of right, Christian actions. Windows should be high, so that one could see only the sky and not be distracted by the external world. Brunelleschi seems to have anticipated these ideals.

The Pazzi Chapel   The Pazzi Chapel was commissioned by the wealthy Pazzi family for their own use and for the use of the monastery of which it is a part. Located in the cloister of Santa Croce, it forms a strong contrast to the church that is one of the few Gothic buildings in Florence. The façade, with its columns and portico, clearly recalls Roman architecture (Fig. 10-6).

Structurally the interior of the chapel is familiar also (Fig. 10-7). Brunelleschi has used a post and lintel and load-bearing wall system to carry barrel vaults and an arrangement of domes. The plan shows two major axes; that formed by the domical space of the portico (which is repeated in the dome over the apse) and that formed by the rectangular spaces of the barrel vaults that support the central dome (Fig. 10-8). The directional quality of each axis is resolved under the great dome of the

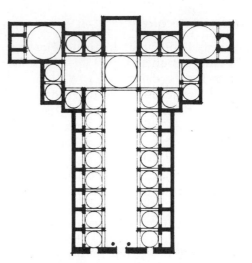

10–4   Groundplan, San Lorenzo, Florence.

10–5   Nave, San Lorenzo, Florence. (Alinari/Editorial Photocolor Archives)

hall. The resultant feeling is one of quiet serenity reinforced by the articulation of the wall planes, windows, door, and apse opening. Applied pilasters rising from a base carry an entablature on which rest the arches of the vaults. These members, like the other decorative elements (the blind arches opposite the windows, for

10-6   Pazzi Chapel, Florence. (Alinari/Editorial Photocolor Archives)

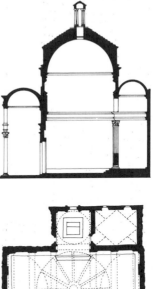

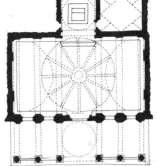

10-7   Groundplan and cross section, Pazzi Chapel, Florence.

10-8   Interior, Pazzi Chapel, Florence. (Alinari/Editorial Photocolor Archives)

example), are made of *pietra serena*, the gray stone that is also used on the interior surfaces of San Lorenzo. They form a strong contrast with the white plastered walls and the terra cotta plaques, which are predominantly blue and white. The impression of the interior is one of cool elegance, for each element is paired, or repeated, except for the central dome, which in its singularity acts to arrest all motion. Does the chapel remind you of Roman buildings that we have seen? How does it differ from a Greek temple, a Roman one? Can you compare this building with San Lorenzo, with Chartres?

It is easy to understand how Brunelleschi's work must have appeared to his colleagues. With its order, clarity, and use of elements from the antique, it must have seemed like Rome revived. Yet it is not based on simply copying from ruins that Brunelleschi had seen, or from later uses of antique forms in early Christian and Romanesque buildings. Like Gothic art and architecture, the art and architecture of fifteenth-century Florence depend for their forms and ideals on a structure of knowledge and value, on a society that was not in ignorance of the meaning to be found in building. Alberti's Latin treatise *On Architecture* presents some of the ideas and principles that he certainly believed capable of communication in building. The model for his treatise was the text by Vitruvius, the first-century B.C. Roman architect and engineer, but the book itself was very much the product of Alberti and fifteenth-century Florentine thought. It is another important way to understand the art and architecture of that century.

Leon Battista Alberti and the Theory of Architecture   Alberti wrote that the architecture and the planning of cities should be based on a rational analysis of problems, needs, site, and climate. The city, he felt, would inspire its citizens through its propriety, order, harmony, and control. Buildings should be considered in a hierarchy based on significance. The ornaments of a city should be its churches. Of second importance are buildings of civic and mercantile nature, like guild halls, bridges, and squares; finally, one should consider housing. Private dwellings should constitute a self-effacing background for the public monuments to Christian and civic virtues.

Alberti not only advocated public housing for the lower classes but also admonished the city fathers to prevent conspicuous consumption. Rich men, he said, should not be permitted to call attention to themselves by the creation of lavish, individual buildings but should live in houses only somewhat better than the less fortunate city dwellers. Wealth should be used to create buildings that all could share, and buildings would contribute to the public good.

These ideas are consistent with Bruni's concept of man as a civic person whose ambitions and skills, intellect and passion should be turned to the benefit of the republic. Moreover, there is almost a parallel between the humanists' belief that eloquence should be cultivated to speak and persuade for the truth of Christian virtue and Alberti's idea that eloquent architecture, based on the great principles of nature, will enable a person to discover and lead a harmonious life.

In Alberti's text we find these proposals for eloquent architecture derived from a study of nature and of the antique. Man, Alberti says, is a creature of reason and appetite, of intellect and will. If he succumbs only to the forces of appetite and will, he may enjoy his life briefly but will not achieve goodness and virtue, the attributes of greatness. In fact, he says, it is only by use of reason and intellect that one can know how to act. These tools are sharpened and trained through the study of nature.

Perfection in architecture is achieved for Alberti by emulation of perfect forms—the square and circle—and by the application of the rules of harmony that govern that of music. Both geometrical and musical forms are divine in origin and occur throughout the universe. Beauty, says Alberti, is the result of the correct observation and application of rules of proportion derived from Pythagoras' system of musical harmony. Beauty is the creation of a whole to which nothing can be added and from which nothing can be subtracted without the destruction of that whole. Our minds, understanding that perfection intuitively, respond to harmony and order, producing actions that will grace life as monuments grace a city.

The belief that good buildings can make a good life is highly debatable. What cannot be denied is that the application of reason to art was one of the most powerful forces in the Renaissance. This will emerge more clearly as we study the other arts.

Sculpture in Florence in the Fifteenth Century

Sculpture, like architecture, was considered a preeminent manifestation of civil and religious pride. As in the case of other artists, sculptors of this period drew inspiration from antiquity, nature, and thirteenth- and fourteenth-century achievements in their medium. There are many whose work might be considered—Brunelleschi, Ghiberti, Nanno di Banco, Luca della Robbia—but, as with painters, no single sculptor represents all the energy and accomplishment of this period. Donatello (1386–1466), however, created a body of work that covers the range of sculptural possibilities—low relief to free-standing sculpture in the round, carved marble and cast bronze, and a variety of subjects that provided enormous intellectual and psychological challenge. Because he was a powerful individual creator in his own right, Donatello was a natural forebearer to Michelangelo.

Among his earliest commissions were two sculptures of saints, George and Mark, for niches on the exterior of a church, Orsanmichele (Fig. 10-9). These larger-than-life figures have the vitality and presence of particular, individual human beings. This effect is achieved through Donatello's clear articulation of the body under its clothing and the definite sense of personality carved in the face. These two elements are combined in the total composition of the body and its attire.

Donatello's skill and innovative ability is no better exhibited than in his gilded bronze relief for the baptismal font of the cathedral of Siena, executed in 1425. The subject is the *Feast of Herod*, and in it Donatello makes use of a new formal tool—one-point perspective—which will also be used by Masaccio and other painters and sculptors to render the illusion of three-dimensional space (Fig. 10-10). Organized in an architectural setting, which provides the diminution in space that creates the illusion of light and distance, this dramatic moment is presented in all its emotional horror and intensity. In the center of the composition is a vacuum, created as people scatter before the presentation of the severed head of the Baptist. Donatello's observations of the human body in movement, of drapery, of emotion are all demonstrated here.

Accomplishments like these surely convinced the Florentines of the dynamism of their own time and

10-9 Donatello, *Saint George*, from Orsanmichele, Florence (where it has been replaced by a bronze copy), c. 1415–16, marble, height 6'10". (Museo Nazionale del Bargello, Florence—Alinari/Art Resource)

10-10 Donatello, *Feast of Herod*, c. 1425, gilded bronze relief, 23⅝ × 23⅝", baptismal font, Cathedral of Siena. (Alinari/Art Resource)

gave them a particular consciousness of their accomplishments and their shortcomings.

New Developments in Painting

Painting and sculpture in the Middle Ages depended upon formulas and conventions for the presentation of visual equivalents of important ideas and beliefs. The makers of stained glass increased the size of significant persons in their glass and ignored any illusions of weight or volume in the representation of figures. The illuminators who made manuscript plates emphasized intense color, flat surface, complex linear patterns, and stylized gestures to create their pictures. Also, the size and location of figures were determined by their importance. Rarely do we feel that the rules for making—the formal conventions—are inappropriate to or detract from the information to be conveyed. Fifth-century-B.C. Athenians considered ideal representation of the human body the best means of commemorating or perpetuating important events and beliefs. The sculptors of the Royal Portal at Chartres subordinated the visible world to symmetry, pattern, flatness, and distortion, in order to teach and inform viewers of Christian dogma. At times the rules and their results may seem strange to us, but it is the successful marriage of means and ends that makes great art and architecture. In the art of fifteenth-century Florence we meet a new set of rules, of conventions for making, that were arrived at experimentally through trial and error, as were the other conventions we have studied. Alberti wrote about painting, describing the rules for making successful pictures. Giorgio Vasari (1511–1574), who was among the first biographers of artists and architects of the Renaissance, was also an important critic of the intentions and development of their art. Like Alberti, he praised artists for their return to, and successful conquest of, the representation of nature.

Giotto (1267?–1337)

If we follow the example of Vasari, the first artist who must be considered in the development of painting in Renaissance Florence is not a fifteenth-century painter at all but Giotto, who, as Dante noted in the *Purgatorio*, eclipsed Cimabue (1271–1302), who was considered the best painter of his day.

In painting Cimabue thought indeed
To hold the field; now Giotto has the cry,
So that the fame of the other few now heed.
(Canto 11, 94–96)

Legend has it that Cimabue saw the poor young shepherd Giotto drawing on a rock with a stone and was so impressed by his talent that he brought him to Florence, where he was apprenticed to a painter. In Florence, Giotto found himself in the cultural and artistic center of Europe, and after absorbing all he needed, he rose to fame as the inventor of a new style of painting.

There was much for Giotto to absorb. In addition to the established, late-medieval art of Florence, there were ideas from the East, from Christian Byzantium, and from the flowering of Gothic art in France. The many different approaches and realizations of Mary, which we have seen in sculptures and glass at Chartres, and the figures from Reims are indicative of the many ways in which artists were conveying ideas and meanings. What Giotto seemed particularly successful in achieving, however, was a sense of drama, a moment stopped in real time, which the observer could then participate in for all time. Giotto combined a keen observation of human movement, gesture, and expression with a growing ability to depict figures whose weight, form, and pose convey a sense of space in which a drama is acted out.

When one first sees work by Giotto, the impact of his formal innovations is not immediately apparent. The *Madonna and Child Enthroned* (Fig. 10-11), painted (c. 1310) for the Church of the Ognissanti in Florence, has the kinds of discrepancies in scale that one expects in medieval painting. For example, the angels are one size, Mary and Jesus are another. The figures are placed in front of a traditional gold ground, long used by both Byzantine artists and many medieval illuminators and painters. But a closer examination shows that Mary and the Child occupy a gothic throne that sits heavily in space. Mary *sits;* her knees show under the folds of her robe, and the Baby, though not exactly a baby, is not a little old man, either. He is round and firm, and his cheeks are the fat cheeks of babyhood. This Mary and Child are quite different from the frontal, hierarchical Madonna and Child of the right portal of the West Porch at Chartres (Fig. 7-14).

traditional themes. The scenes painted in fresco on the walls are "living" tableaux, acted out in shallow con stricted spaces, but they are spaces that are nonetheless based on observation of the experienced world. The participants, presented in simple drapery—the density of which seems to emphasize weight, gravity, and the physical body underneath—gesture, move, and give expression to the changing emotional content of each scene. The composition of each scene seems accidental—as if seen at a glance, and yet studied—as if designed to emphasize the significant action of the moment. In *The Lamentation* (Color Plate V) the action falls from the right to the lower left corner, where the Virgin cradles the head and shoulders of her dead Son on her knees. The actions and gestures of each of the figures and the shape of the landscape reinforce the movement into the corner, a movement that is both a visual and psychological decline and dead end. The mourners have the self-contained and controlled gestures of disbelieving grief, from the woman who tenderly holds Jesus's feet, to the stylized gesture of the standing figure (St. John) whose arms fly back, to the onlooker who stands in the right corner, hands mutely folded. This exposition of the stages of grief acted out by heavy, somewhat lumpy figures is extraordinarily eloquent. Grief is presented as painful, timeless, and almost silent; yet the faces and hands tell us that folded into these bodies that cluster around the dead Christ is soft, muffled weeping. Then, looking into the sky, the viewer sees the angels who give themselves up to grief, wailing and keening. It is impossible to see these paintings and not be deeply moved. The stories of the Virgin and Christ are given a new humanity and power that transcends this world by being so clearly of it.

The simple intensity and power of Giotto's work disguises the monumental effort required to break with tradition and to create new formal conventions. He is still far from using the paint, color, line, light, and shade one associates with the art of fifteenth- and sixteenth-century Florence. His paintings reveal his limited knowledge of the rules of perspective, and his landscapes are as stylized as those of the older schools. None of his paintings have a secular theme. Nevertheless, no one can differ seriously with the judgment of Vasari, who traced the artistic revival that culminated in his day back to Giotto two hundred and fifty years before,

10-11   Giotto, *Madonna and Child Enthroned,* tempera on panel, 10′8″ × 6′8¼″, from the Church of the Ognissanti, Florence, c. 1310 Galleria degli Uffizi, Florence, (Alinari/Art Resource)

Vasari tells us that Giotto's accomplishments were based on his observation of nature and his abandonment of the existing formal language of tradition. Whether a result of nature, the influence of French art, or a combination of these, Giotto's achievement in the Arena Chapel cycle is evident.

The Arena Chapel in Padua is decorated with scenes from the life of the Virgin and the life of Christ, both for it was he who led art back to "a path which may be called the true one." Although the path is not a direct one, his work is a major basis for the art of Masaccio.

Masaccio (1401–1428?)

Giotto's accomplishment, which filled his contemporaries with admiration, was dependent upon the success with which he captured the human presence through bodily form, gesture, and emotion. A few visual clues placed the scenes in the experienced world, but his technique did not extend to creating a convincing facsimile of the light, shade, and space of the three-dimensional world in which people live. This was to be the accomplishment of the many painters of fifteenth-century Florence.

One of those painters was Masaccio, who painted expressive human bodies in palpable space. The work for which he is most famous is the series of *frescos* for the Brancacci Chapel in Santa Maria delle Carmine in Florence. Recently cleaned and restored, these works reveal Masaccio's close observation of nature and of the human form. The *Expulsion from Eden* (Fig. 10-12) on a side wall of the Chapel presents a powerfully human, sorrowful, nude Adam and Eve as they leave paradise. Adam covers his face, but Eve seems to wail. Their muscular, substantial bodies are depicted through contrasts of light, shade, and shadow. These figures have the presence of the nudes of antiquity.

The central painting of the chapel, *The Tribute Money*, recounts a story from Christ's life as told in Matthew 17:24–27 (Color Plate VI and detail, Fig. 10-13). A tax collector has approached Jesus, who then instructs Peter to catch a fish from the Sea of Galilee; in its mouth will be a coin sufficient for the tax to be paid. The action of the story is stretched out in the painting. Compare Giotto's *Lamentation* (Color Plate V) with this work. What are the major differences between Masaccio's fresco and that of Giotto? Is there a greater illusion of space around the figures and in which the figures move? What role does the landscape play? Is it day or night? Are weather conditions important? What is important to conveying the action? Do the figures casting shadows that fall around each other, on faces, and on hands focus our attention? Where is Masaccio's light source? Does light seem to come into the space of the painting from the sky, or does it seem to originate outside the painting? What kind of people are the disciples? Do they have personalities, or are they simply twelve images who stand for the Twelve? What has happened to enable Masaccio to delineate so easily a world similar to the one we see?

Masaccio, it would seem, has transformed the wall plane into a transparent curtain that reveals a stage space in which he can present a dramatic event. We see into the space where people move; light falls from the sky; figures cast shadows; people have personalities and are therefore like us, like the visible world of experienced reality. These people are also not self-conscious actors but are convincing as Adam and Eve, who notice neither angel nor audience in the pain of their degradation. Like Donatello's sculpture *David* (Fig. 10-14) the human body is expressive, sensuous, and filled with life.

Masaccio and Donatello both had the use of a new artistic language, which had been developed by Brunelleschi, the cathedral architect. *Linear perspective* is a tool for the accurate translation of three-dimensional space onto the two-dimensional plane of paper, panel, or wall (Fig. 10-15). Masaccio, learning from Giotto the importance of gesture and the feeling of weight, combined the two with his own ideas about shade and shadow, volume and location, to create his dramatic scenes. Obviously, Masaccio did not achieve this in one day (equally obviously, he was not alone in his endeavors), but he gives us scenes that seem suddenly familiar to us. His work both transforms and presents a series of new conventions, which we will further explore.

There is a close parallel between the development of perspective in painting and sculptural relief and the humanists' growing sense of the historical past. The fifteenth-century humanists were coming to understand the past as composed of a group of successive societies leading down to their own time. Increasingly they became aware of the differences between pagan Roman society and Christian Rome and of the changes that had occurred in thinking in the Middle Ages located between their own time and antiquity. In a sense they viewed history as a series of temporal planes corresponding to the spatial planes defined by the linear perspective. Just as the artist objectified space from the

10-13 Detail of Masaccio, *The Tribute Money*. (Brancacci Chapel, Florence— Scala/Editorial Photocolor Archives)

10-12 Masaccio, *Explusion from Eden*, fresco, c. 1425, Brancacci Chapel, Sta. Maria del Carmine, Florence

point of view of his eye, so the humanist defined the past in relationship to his own time. Similarly the humanists utilized this objectified time for their own purposes, in their case, the improvement of the present and the shaping of the future.

It is not enough, however, that we celebrate the conquest of illusion. To assume that this was the goal of Renaissance painting is to miss the point of this artistic development. Just as Brunelleschi and Alberti wanted to learn the principles of antique architecture in order to create new forms in response to new ideas, so perspective was a principle, a tool to enhance the purpose of Christian art. The purpose of creating art with Christian subjects was to teach, enlighten, and persuade people in the ways of right moral action. Viewers are therefore expected to not merely *observe* an event but to be moved by it toward repentance and salvation. The illusion of weight and volume, and of the visible world itself, and the creation of splendid individuals, all serve this purpose.

Piero della Francesca To fully appreciate the extent to which painters, sculptors, and other artisans served the church and their faith through their art, it is

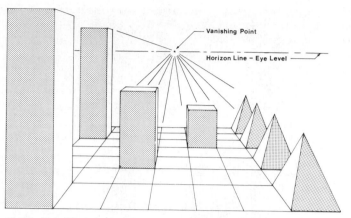

10-15   Simplified single-point perspective (after Brunelleschi).

10-14   Donatello, *David*, c. 1430–32. Bronze, height 62¼″. (Museo Nazionale del Bargello, Florence—Alinari/Art Resource)

necessary to consider the work of other painters and the ways in which they explored the new ideas. Such a painter was Piero della Francesca (1420–1492). Born in southeastern Tuscany, he came to Florence as a painter's apprentice. He left a few years later, never to return, but worked in the vicinity of his birth, Arezzo, Borgo San Sepolcro, and finally in Urbino, a small but wealthy mountain principality. The origins of his art lie in Masaccio, but his intellectual capacity and artistic study created an art of severe harmony, clarity, and cool detachment.

Piero's *Resurrection* (Color Plate VII) fresco, painted for the town hall in Borgo San Sepolcro in the late 1450s, presents an unforgettable image of the resurrected Christ. This Christ is a heroic figure of powerful proportions. He stands, one bare foot inside the other on the front edge of the sepulchre, a shroud covering one arm, the other bare and muscular, holding the flag of the church triumphant. He confronts the viewer directly and seems to see beyond. There is little emotional drama here; the four soldiers sleep on in the tight, constricted, but perfectly articulated space between the picture plane and the sarcophagus. Light is cool and even, revealing a body whose wounds no longer bleed but are simply revealed for our contemplation. The hush of morning fills the stony Italian landscape. To the right of Christ the trees are foliage-covered; to the left there is barrenness; and at the center, the focus of our salvation and eternal resurrection. The powerful emotional energy of Masaccio's Adam and Eve (Fig. 10-12) contrasts with the still psychological drama Piero presents.

Piero did many drawings for this and every work. His investigations led to a treatise in which he demonstrated the uses of perspective to delineate bodies and architectural forms. These he reduced to their most abstract geometrical components, seeing forms as variations on or combinations of spheres, cylinders, cones, cubes, and pyramids. Like Alberti, he sought nature's perfect forms, and like Leonardo after him, he learned much from that study.

Botticelli   Sandro Botticelli (1444–1510) was more interested in the expressive possibilities of a graceful and energetic line than in the structural problems of perspective. He had been apprenticed to an engraver and from his experiences with those conventions came his reliance on draftsmanship. The favorite painter of the Medici family, Botticelli was very much interested in the ideas of humanism and Neoplatonism prevailing in the intellectual circles around Lorenzo. He was one of the first Florentine painters to represent subjects from classical mythology. Just as the humanists attempted to fuse Greco-Roman myths and ideas with Christian theology, Botticelli endowed his pagan subjects with a spirituality that derives from medieval painting and sculpture.

The large painting called *Primavera (Springtime)* or *The Realm of Venus* is an *allegory* of the rebirth of nature in spring under the power of love (Color Plate VIII). In the center stands Venus, who looks more like a madonna than a Greek love goddess. The fusion of the pagan goddess and the Christian saint would not have surprised the Neoplatonists, who believed that both could aid the soul in its ascent to God. Venus appears to give her blessing to the three Graces, who are dancing in a circle to her right. The rhythmical line for which Botticelli was so well known is nowhere more apparent than here. The folds of flowing drapery make one feel the movement of the dance. The seminude bodies are another classical inspiration—they could never have appeared in medieval art. Next to the Graces stands Mercury, raising his wand to the skies. To the viewer's right is Flora, in a dress abundantly covered with flowers, and another almost-nude nymph representing springtime, who is about to be seized by a young man personifying Zephyr, the wind. Above everyone flies the blindfolded Cupid with his bow and arrow. What about the setting of this painting? Although the flowers are exact copies of flowers that grow around Tuscany, Botticelli has certainly not portrayed a realistic natural setting. What kind of nature is he portraying, and what is he attempting to suggest by it? How would you characterize the colors? Make a schematic drawing to show how the *composition* works. Are the various elements of the painting held together in some way? Does the right side of the painting convey a different sort of feeling from that conveyed by the left side? How? Compare your reactions to this painting to your reactions to Piero della Francesca's paintings.

Primavera is the work that best states in visual terms the spirit of the Florentine Renaissance under Lorenzo de' Medici. Botticelli was inspired by a poem on the subject written by one of the Medici friends, Poliziano, and the painting decorated the Medici palace. It celebrates youth, beauty, and love with the same underlying melancholy that characterizes Lorenzo's own poems and carnival songs.

Lorenzo de' Medici's Carnivals and Carnival Songs

During the fifteenth century the city of Florence developed a tradition of outdoor public celebrations, feasts that probably had their intellectual origins in the pre-Christian pagan festivals celebrating the victory of spring over winter, the returning fertility of the earth. By the time of Lorenzo the Magnificent, two major carnivals occurred each year—a season of pre-Lenten revelry (which has its modern version in the Mardi Gras activities of New Orleans) and the *Calendimaggio*, which was an extended May Day celebration (from May 1 to June 24!).

The grandeur of Lorenzo's style of life earned him his nickname, "the Magnificent," and the carnivals received his strong encouragement because of his taste for opulence and probably also for political reasons. The Medicis' love of pageantry is represented by Gozzoli's mural *Journey of the Magi* (Color Plate IX). Carnivals kept the populace happy. Lorenzo, an accomplished poet and an ardent lover of music and display, hired a musician from Flanders of international reputation, Heinrich Isaac, as his court composer and as tutor of his children.

Torchlight processions in which decorated wagons were pulled through the streets were the main feature of the carnivals. The wagons, or *carri*, were decorated by some of the best artists of the time in a manner similar to today's parade floats, and the themes of the decoration often represented stories from classical antiquity and popular legends. Lorenzo wrote carnival songs in Italian (many humanist poets wrote for an elite, in Latin), the most famous of which was "The Song of Bacchus," a poem written for a float depicting the triumph of Bacchus and Ariadne. According to a Greek myth Ariadne, a princess of Crete, ran off with her lover, Theseus of Athens. She was abandoned by him on an island but later rescued by Bacchus (Dionysus, the Greek god of love and wine), who fell in love with her and married her.

The usual themes associated with the "triumphs" depicted on the carnival floats were love, pleasure, and the enjoyment of life, but among them there was always a macabre "triumph of death," a terrifying float including men dressed as skeletons drawn by a team of black oxen. Thus during a part of the gaiety people were urged to repent—a Renaissance fascination with death amidst a proclamation of joy in life on earth is evident here. Even in Lorenzo's "Song of Bacchus," one can sense the urgent fear of time running out beneath the exhortation to love and pleasure. (The translation is by Mary Ann Witt.)

LORENZO DE' MEDICI

The Song of Bacchus

What a lovely time is youth,
  Yet how it slips away!
Be happy, if you will, today,
  Tomorrow is unsure.

Here are Bacchus and Ariadne,
  So fair, so deep in love,
Because time flies and cheats,
  They stay together happily.
These nymphs and other folk
  Are always merry and gay.
Be happy, if you will, today,
  Tomorrow is unsure.

These joyful little satyrs
  Enamoured of the nymphs,
Have for them in cave and wood
  Set a hundred traps.
Now, enflamed by Bacchus,
  They dance, they jump every way.
Be happy, if you will, today,
  Tomorrow is unsure.

The nymphs won't mind being caught,
  They're ripe for traps,
For only the rude and ungrateful
  Can guard against love.
Now mingling with one another,
  They pipe and sing alway.
Be happy, if you will, today,
  Tomorrow is unsure.

Here comes a big load, riding an ass.
  It's Silenus,
Old and drunk and glad,
  By now he's full of flesh and years.
He can't stand straight,
  But he'll laugh and play.
Be happy, if you will, today,
  Tomorrow is unsure.

Here comes Midas after them:
  Whatever he touches turns to gold.
What good does treasure do a man
  If it can't bring him joy?
And what contentment can Midas feel
  Who's thirsty forever, night and day?
Be happy, if you will, today,
  Tomorrow is unsure.

Everyone: open wide your ears!
  Let no one feed on tomorrow;
Men and women, young and old,
  Be happy today, each one!
Banish every sad thought
  But let the festival stay.
Be happy, if you will, today,
  Tomorrow is unsure.

Sweet ladies and young lovers, come,
  Long live Bacchus and long live love!
Let everyone play and dance and sing,
  And fill your hearts with joy.
Do not toil and do not grieve,
  What's to be will come anyway.
Be happy, if you will, today,
  Tomorrow is unsure.

Although we are uncertain about the identity of the composer of the music for "The Song of Bacchus," it is likely that Isaac himself composed this carnival song. Not only was he in the employ of Lorenzo during the last years of the patron's life (the most likely time for the creation of this work), but also the music reflects a mastery of technique that indicates the hand of a professional composer. The lilting melody and smooth-flowing harmonies reflect the best style of Italian secular music of the late fifteenth century.

QUESTIONS

1. How does the poet use characters from classical mythology to convey a message for the present?
2. Describe the *tone* of this poem and its music. How is a sense of the fear of death blended with that of joy in life?
3. Contrast the attitude expressed here with the medieval Christian doctrine that patient suffering in this life is necessary in order to achieve happiness in the afterlife.
4. Compare the feeling conveyed by this song with that conveyed by Botticelli's *Primavera.*

Music for the Death of Lorenzo

During the same year that Columbus made his first voyage to the New World, Lorenzo de' Medici died. He had been the ideal Renaissance prince: a consummate diplomat, intellectual leader, connoisseur and patron of the arts. His loss was felt deeply and personally by those poets and musicians who knew and worked for him and also loved and respected him.

One of the most beautiful and moving musical compositions written in the last years of the fifteenth century, the beginning of the High Renaissance in music, was Heinrich Isaac's *threnody*, a dirge or funeral song, in the Italian style on Angelo Poliziano's Latin verse lamenting the death of Lorenzo.

ANGELO POLIZIANO

Quis Dabit Capiti

Quis dabit capiti meo aquam?
Quis oculis meis fontem
   lachrimarum dabit?
Ut nocte fleam,
Ut luce fleam?

Sic turtur viduus solet,
Sic cygnus moriens solet,
Sic luscinia conqueri.
Heu miser, miser,
O dolor, dolor!

Laurus impetu fulminis
Illa illa jacet subito,
Laurus omnium celebris
Musarum choris,
Nympharum choris.

Who will give my head water?
Who will give my eyes
   a fountain of tears?
That I may weep by night,
That I may weep by day?

Thus the lonely turtle-dove mourned,
Thus the dying swan,
Thus the nightingale.
Ah wretched, wretched me,
Oh grief, oh grief.

The laurel [Lorenzo] lies there,
Lies there, struck suddenly by a thunderbolt,
The laurel honored by the choir
Of all the Muses,
And all the nymphs.

The Song of Bacchus

Sub cuius patula coma
Et Phebi lira blandius
Insonat et vox blandius,
Nunc muta omnia,
Nunc surda omnia.

Beneath whose spreading branches
The lyre of Phoebus more charmingly
Sounds and his voice more sweetly sings.
Now all is silent,
Now all is deaf.

Isaac's genius and sensitivity created a *motet* (a *polyphonic* composition for unaccompanied chorus based on a Latin sacred text) of moving solemnity, a four-voice composition scored in a low register to dramatize its function as a dirge. An intimate bond between word and tone was the goal of Renaissance composers working in the company of the Italian humanists, and Isaac masterfully sculpted his sounds in this musical elegy.

To make the opening statement incisive, to be certain the listener could understand every word, Isaac declaimed the text of the beginning syllabically in slow-moving chords, at first in hollow *open fifths*, all voices enunciating the syllables at the same time—"Who will give my head . . ." Then, as the singers reach the word "water," the chords dissolve into flowing polyphonic lines, a musical gesture symbolizing the text being set.

He begins the second phrase in like manner but sets the "fountain of tears" with a base of three chordal notes (the solid base of an actual fountain comes to mind) over which, or out of which, flows a curving, almost liquid, soprano melodic line.

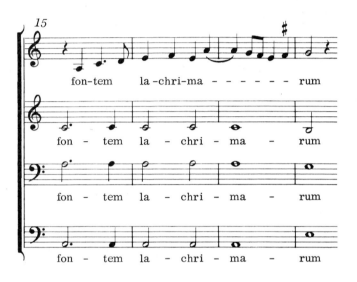

Harmonic modulation, as we know it today, was not a part of the composer's art in the late fifteenth century; but Renaissance *chromaticism*, the use of accidentals (flats and sharps) to displace the music slightly out of the regular *tonal* order of the style, was an expressive device reserved for moments of intense emotion. Isaac's harmonic progression from A to F to C and then B-flat strains and wrings the phrase *Sic cygnus moriens solet* ("Thus [mourns] the dying swan").

Although the motet begins with four vocal parts, the second section of the work beginning *Laurus impetu fulminis* ("The laurel, struck [suddenly] by a thunderbolt") uses only three vocal parts. However, in the original Renaissance choirbook in which this work is notated, a space with no notes is set aside in which is written *Laurus tacet* ("The Laurel is silent"). Lorenzo's absence, therefore, was painted graphically in music by a device detectable primarily by the composer and the singers but also by those who were trained and skilled in detecting the subtleties of Renaissance tone painting. Four-voice music and three-voice music have distinctive qualities that are identifiable aurally, and the

absence of a part could be felt by those in attendance who heard the change in *texture* and comprehended the meaning of the words.

At the same time that the texture of the piece drops from four to three parts, the lowest voice is given a part to sing whose words are neither the same as those being sung by the other singers nor from the text of Poliziano's poem. Instead, Isaac composed an insertion referring to the requiem service of the Church, *Et requiescamus in pace* ("And let us rest in peace"). The composer took this phrase, set it to a short bass melody, and slowly repeated it over and over as an *ostinato*, one step lower each time it enters—a certain symbolic representation of Lorenzo descending step by step into the grave. The emotion of the event, the words, and the music are focused and concentrated into a dramatic setting of intense grief.

When, in the third and final section of the motet, the fourth voice reenters, it is no longer a regular part but a single, unmoving note (which is held for eighteen measures in the modern edition), quite likely an aural *image* of death in a tomb. When finally this note is given a rest (literally a rest in the music), the other three parts sing of Phoebus Apollo's sweet-sounding voice, a godly song whose magic, according to Greek mythology, could give peace and healing to those in the underworld. Then, "Now all is silent, Now all is deaf," and the motet ends.[1]

QUESTIONS

1. In what ways are the polyphonic carnival song and the funeral motet more or less expressive than the monophonic *Play of Daniel* or the troubadour song *Be m'an perdut*?
2. How might the change in society with an emerging middle class affect the role of the composer?
3. Scientific advances of the Renaissance had an effect on music. What would the invention of printing do for composers? How might this affect the music they wrote?

---

[1] Two excellent, but different, recordings of Isaac's motet are available: *Ceremonial Music of the Renaissance* (Das alte Werk, SAWT 9524-B) and *Fifteenth-Century Netherlands Masters* (Decca DL 79413). The former employs chorus and antique instruments; the latter performs the work with voices only.

Renaissance man experienced his world passionately, and he proclaimed himself master of all he could touch, taste, see, and hear. Lorenzo (and Isaac?) expressed the joys of youth in *Quant'è bella giovinezza*, while Poliziano and Isaac voiced the bitterness of death in *Quis dabit capiti meo aquam*. But the latter did not portray the fear of judgment and punishment—concepts ever present in the thoughts of medieval man. It was the sadness of loss of life, of parting from the pleasures of this world that stirred the Renaissance man's soul to anguish. One can see, therefore, that both these compositions, as unlike as a carnival song and a dirge might seem at first glance, are similar in their philosophic basis. They both celebrate the joys of life and lament the end that comes all too quickly.

11

The End of the Florentine Renaissance: Machiavelli, Leonardo, Michelangelo, and Raphael

The death of Lorenzo the Magnificent in 1492 came in a very troubled time not only for Florence but for the whole of Italy (see map). In 1495 the French invaded Italy, sweeping the length of the peninsula with their powerful armies. This was only the first of a whole series of foreign invasions over the next fifty years, during which time Italy became the battleground between the two rising national monarchies, France and Spain. The Medici were toppled from power with the arrival of the French in 1495, and a republic under French rule was established. But the waning of French influence over Italy in the following decade spelled the doom of the new regime, and the Medici returned to power in 1512. Except for a brief three-year interruption (1527–1530), they were to remain rulers of Tuscany down to the eighteenth century.

Already by Lorenzo's last years, Florence was sharing its position of cul-

tural dominance with Rome. From the early decades of the sixteenth century, moreover, France and northern Europe began to rival Italy's position of cultural leadership. The Florentine efflorescence was to be given new forms in art, architecture, and political thought. Four individuals—Niccolo Machiavelli (1469–1527), Leonardo da Vinci (1452–1519), Michelangelo Buonarotti (1475–1564), and Raffaello Sanzio (1483–1520)—represent aspects of the transformation of the confidence of the fifteenth century into the doubt of the sixteenth

century, when Italy was invaded and the Papacy came under siege from Martin Luther and the princes of northern Europe.

Niccolo Machiavelli (1469–1527)

The ease with which the Italians succumbed to Spanish and French arms shocked Italian thinkers and caused them to seek explanations. Many focused on the chaotic political structure of the peninsula as the major factor in Italian weakness. This atmosphere of questioning produced one of the greatest political theorists of all time, the Florentine Niccolò Machiavelli. Born in Florence in 1469, Machiavelli rose to a position of prominence in the republican government established in the city after 1495. Closely associated with that regime, Machiavelli fell into disfavor after the reestablishment of Medici power in 1512. He spent most of the last fifteen years of his life as a private citizen, composing his works on history and political theory.

At heart a republican, Machiavelli faced squarely the problem that confronts any political thinker, the conflict between liberty and order. To what extent can individuals be given freedom without disrupting authority? Although he would like to have seen Florence and other Italian states republican, he recognized that, given the corruption of Italian society, only a strong ruler was capable of establishing order; until order had been established, there was no hope of reforming the people to make them capable of self-government. He realized the risk: the kind of ruler ruthless enough to establish order was not likely to be the kind of prince willing to train the people in self-government. But in a peninsula divided into fifty to a hundred power centers, a prey to foreign invasions, strong authority had priority. Thus, although raised in the tradition of Florentine civic humanism derived from Bruni, Machiavelli gave first place to political realities.

Machiavelli's most famous work, *The Prince*, written in 1513, was designed to give lessons in statecraft to a prince with an eye to creating an authority capable of driving out the invaders and bringing peace to Italy. Although throughout the work Machiavelli appeals to the selfish desire of the prince for power, in the final chapter Machiavelli's own altruistic motives on behalf of Italian unity become manifest. *The Prince* is intended to be a revolutionary "mirror of the prince," based on a medieval form of literature designed to instruct the prince on how to be a good ruler. However, whereas the traditional mirror of the prince endeavored to make the prince conform to common principles of Christian morality in his rule, the thesis of *The Prince* is that the morality of the successful ruler is unlike that of the private citizen; indeed, the conduct required of a prince would frequently be reprehensible in a private

individual. Nevertheless, as Chapter 17 suggests, in the long run actions that would be immoral in an ordinary citizen may very well be the best means for achieving a goal that serves the common good.

When Machiavelli came to sketch the character of the ideal prince, he defined *virtù* as his essential quality. Not to be confused with virtue, Machiavelli defined the term as "the ability to measure oneself." At points in *The Prince* he appears to consider the prince as a kind of artist imposing a form (his particular regime) on matter (the people). The quality of *virtù* will help the prince to understand the nature of the particular matter he is working with and thus know the limits of what can be done with it. Realization of political ends, however, is not merely a product of executing a rationally determined course of action. The ability to measure oneself also entails taking account of the whims of fortune. Against her unpredictability, the prince can only construct dikes to protect himself when she rages. This does not mean that cautiousness is the best policy; rather, Machiavelli urges a bold attitude, modified by self-restraint.

That Machiavelli considered the ruthless Cesare Borgia (1475?–1507), bastard son of Alexander VI, something approaching the ideal prince, shocked many in his own generation, as it does in ours. But the fascination of Machiavelli remains, for he is telling us something that might be true but that we cannot bear to hear. This is especially true for Americans, who have always nourished the belief that at some point public morality can be forced to coincide with private morality, that statesmen can be judged by the same standards as average citizens. What Machiavelli tells us is that this will never be the case, nor ought it to be; there is a fundamental difference between the rules of the game of politics and those of ordinary life. The translation of *The Prince* is by Ninian Hill Thompson.

The Prince
CHAPTER XV

Of the qualities in respect of which men, and most of all Princes, are praised or blamed

It now remains for us to consider what ought to be the conduct and bearing of a Prince in relation to his subjects and friends. And since I know that many have written on this subject, I fear it may be thought presumptuous in me to write of it also; the more so, because in my treatment of it I depart widely from the views that others have taken.

But since it is my object to write what shall be useful to whosoever understands it, it seems to me better to follow the real truth of things than an imaginary view of them. For many Republics and Princedoms have been imagined that were never seen or known. It is essential, therefore, for a Prince who would maintain his position, to have learned how to be other than good, and to use or not to use his goodness as necessity requires.

Laying aside, therefore, all fanciful notions concerning a Prince, and considering those only that are true, I say that all men when they are spoken of, and Princes more than others from their being set so high, are noted for certain of those qualities which attach either praise or blame. Thus one is accounted liberal, another miserly (which word I use, rather than *avaricious*, to denote the man who is too sparing of what is his own, *avarice* being the disposition to take wrongfully what is another's); one is generous, another greedy; one cruel, another tender-hearted; one is faithless, another true to his word; one effeminate and cowardly, another high-spirited and courageous; one is courteous, another haughty; one lewd, another chaste; one upright, another crafty; one firm, another facile; one grave, another frivolous; one devout, another unbelieving; and the like. Every one, I know, will admit that it would be most laudable for a Prince to be endowed with all of the above qualities that are reckoned good; but since it is impossible for him to possess or constantly practise them all, the conditions of human nature not allowing it, he must be discreet enough to know how to avoid the reproach of those vices that would deprive him of his government, and, if possible, be on his guard also against those which might not deprive him of it; though if he cannot wholly restrain himself, he may with less scruple indulge in the latter. But he need never hesitate to incur the reproach of those vices without which his authority can hardly be preserved; for if he well consider the whole matter, he will find that there may be a line of conduct having the appearance of virtue, to follow which would be his ruin, and

that there may be another course having the appearance of vice, by following which his safety and well-being are secured.

CHAPTER XVII

Of Cruelty and Clemency, and whether it is better to be Loved or Feared

Passing to the other qualities above mentioned, I say that every Prince should desire to be accounted merciful and not cruel. Nevertheless, he should be careful not to abuse this quality of mercy. Cesare Borgia was reputed cruel, yet his cruelty restored Romagna, united it, and brought it to order and obedience; so that if we look at things in their true light, it will be seen that he was in reality far more merciful than the people of Florence, who, to avoid the imputation of cruelty, suffered Pistoja to be destroyed by factions.[1]

A Prince should therefore disregard the reproach of cruelty where it enables him to keep his subjects united and faithful. For he who quells disorder by a very few signal examples will in the end be more merciful than he who from excessive leniency suffers things to take their course and so result in rapine and bloodshed; for these hurt the entire State, whereas the severities of the Prince injure individuals only.

And for a new Prince, above all others, it is impossible to escape a name for cruelty, since new States are full of dangers. Wherefore Virgil, by the mouth of Dido:—

'Res dura et regni novitas me talia cogunt
Moliri, et late fines custode tueri.'[2]

Nevertheless, the new Prince should not be too ready of belief, nor too easily set in motion; nor should he himself be the first to raise alarms; but should so temper prudence with kindliness that too great confidence

---

[1] Florence attempted to govern Pistoia by encouraging the disputes between the two major factions. When in 1501–1502 it attempted finally to end the civil conflict, it caused untold bloodshed and destruction.

[2] 'A fate unkind, and newness in my reign Compel me thus to guard a wide domain.'

in others shall not throw him off his guard, nor groundless distrust render him insupportable.

And here comes in the question whether it is better to be loved rather than feared, or feared rather than loved. It might be answered that we should wish to be both; but since love and fear can hardly exist together, if we must choose between them, it is far safer to be feared than loved. For of men it may generally be affirmed that they are thankless, fickle, false, studious to avoid danger, greedy of gain, devoted to you while you confer benefits upon them, and ready, as I said before, while the need is remote, to shed their blood, and sacrifice their property, their lives, and their children for you; but when it comes near they turn against you. The Prince, therefore, who without otherwise securing himself builds wholly on their professions, is undone. For the friendships we buy with a price, and do not gain by greatness and nobility of character, though fairly earned are not made good, but fail us when we need them most.

Moreover, men are less careful how they offend him who makes himself loved than him who makes himself feared. For love is held by the tie of obligation, which, because men are a sorry breed, is broken on every prompting of self-interest; but fear is bound by the apprehension of punishment which never loosens its grasp.

Nevertheless a Prince should inspire fear in suchwise that if he do not win love he may escape hate. For a man may very well be feared and yet not hated, as will always be the case so long as he does not intermeddle with the property or with the women of his citizens and subjects. And if constrained to put any one to death, he should do so only when there is manifest cause or reasonable justification. But, above all, he must abstain from the property of others. For men will sooner forget the death of their father than the loss of their patrimony. Moreover, pretexts for confiscation are never to seek, and he who has once begun to live by rapine always finds reasons for taking what is not his; whereas reasons for shedding blood are fewer, and sooner exhausted.

But when a Prince is with his army, and has many soldiers under his command, he must entirely disregard the reproach of cruelty, for without such a reputation in its Captain, no army can be held together or kept ready for every emergency. Among other things remarkable in Hannibal[3] this has been noted, that having a very great army, made up of men of many different nations and brought to serve in a foreign country, no dissension ever arose among the soldiers themselves, nor any mutiny against their leader, either in his good or in his evil fortunes. This we can only ascribe to the transcendent cruelty, which, joined with numberless great qualities, rendered him at once venerable and terrible in the eyes of his soldiers; for without this reputation for cruelty his other virtues would not have effected the like results.

Unreflecting writers, indeed, while praising his achievements, have condemned the chief cause of them; but that his other merits would not by themselves have been so efficacious we may see from the case of Scipio, one of the greatest Captains, not of his own time only but of all times whereof we have record,[4] whose armies rose against him in Spain from no other cause than his excessive leniency in allowing them freedoms inconsistent with military discipline. With which weakness Fabius Maximus taxed him in the Senate House, calling him the corrupter of the Roman soldiery.[5] Again, when the Locrians were shamefully outraged by one of his lieutenants, he neither avenged them, nor punished the insolence of his officer;[6] and this from the natural easiness of his disposition. So that it was said in the Senate by one who sought to excuse him, that there were many who knew better how to refrain from doing wrong themselves than how to correct the wrong-doing of others. This temper, however, must in time have marred the name and fame even of Scipio, had he continued in it, and retained his command. But living as he did under the control of the

---

[3] Hannibal (247–183 B.C.) almost succeeded in destroying Rome in the Second Carthaginian War. Machiavelli often uses him as an example of efficacious cruelty. He is compared with Scipio (236?–184 B.C.), the Roman general, whose humanity was equally successful.

[4] Scipio (see note above) defeated Hannibal decisively at Zama in 202 B.C.

[5] Fabius Maximus, called the Delayer, wore Hannibal's army out by delaying tactics in 217 B.C., but, knowing his army was weak, refused to do open battle with him.

[6] Locri, a Greek colony in southern Italy, was bled white by its supposed governor, Quintus Pleminus. Scipio, although knowing of his misdeeds, did nothing to punish his subordinate.

Senate, this hurtful quality was not merely veiled, but came to be regarded as a glory.

Returning to the question of being loved or feared, I sum up by saying, that since his being loved depends upon his subjects, while his being feared depends upon himself, a wise Prince should build on what is his own, and not on what rests with others. Only, as I have said, he must do his best to escape hatred.

CHAPTER XIX

That a Prince should seek to escape
Contempt and Hatred

Having now spoken of the chief of the qualities above referred to, the rest I shall dispose of briefly with these general remarks, that a Prince, as has already in part been said, should consider how he may avoid such courses as would make him hated or despised; and that whenever he succeeds in keeping clear of these, he has performed his part, and runs no risk though he incur other reproaches.

A Prince, as I have said before, sooner becomes hated by being rapacious and by interfering with the property and with the women of his subjects, than in any other way. From these, therefore, he should abstain. For so long as neither their property nor their honour is touched, the mass of mankind live contentedly, and the Prince has only to cope with the ambition of a few, which can in many ways and easily be kept within bounds.

A Prince is despised when he is seen to be fickle, frivolous, effeminate, pusillanimous, or irresolute, against which defects he ought therefore to guard most carefully, striving so to bear himself that greatness, courage, wisdom, and strength may appear in all his actions. In his private dealings with his subjects his decisions should be irrevocable, and his reputation such that no one would dream of over-reaching or cajoling him.

The Prince who inspires such an opinion of himself is greatly esteemed, and against one who is greatly esteemed conspiracy is difficult; nor, when he is known to be an excellent Prince and held in reverence by his subjects, will it be easy to attack him. For a Prince is exposed to two dangers, from within in respect of his subjects, from without in respect of foreign powers.

Against the latter he will defend himself with good arms and good allies, and if he have good arms he will always have good allies; and when things are settled abroad, they will always be settled at home, unless disturbed by conspiracies; and even should there be hostility from without, if he has taken those measures, and has lived in the way I have recommended, and if he never despairs, he will withstand every attack; as I have said was done by Nabis the Spartan.[7]

As regards his own subjects, when affairs are quiet abroad, a Prince has to fear they may engage in secret plots; against which he best secures himself when he escapes being hated or despised, and keeps on good terms with his people; and this, as I have already shown at length, it is essential he should do. Not to be hated or despised by the body of his subjects, is one of the surest safeguards that a Prince can have against conspiracy. For he who conspires always reckons on pleasing the people by putting the Prince to death: but when he sees that instead of pleasing he will offend them, he cannot summon courage to carry out his design. For the difficulties that attend conspirators are infinite, and we know from experience that while there have been many conspiracies, few of them have succeeded.

He who conspires cannot do so alone, nor can he assume as his companions any save those whom he believes to be discontented; but so soon as you impart your design to a discontented man, you supply him with the means of removing his discontent, since by betraying you he can procure for himself every advantage; so that seeing on the one hand certain gain, and on the other a doubtful and dangerous risk, he must either be a rare friend to you, or the mortal enemy of the Prince, if he keep your secret.

To put the matter shortly, I say that on the side of the conspirator there are distrust, jealousy, and dread of punishment to deter him, while on the side of the Prince there are the laws, the majesty of the throne, the protection of friends and of the government to defend him; to which if the general good-will of the people be added, it is hardly possible that any should be rash enough to conspire. For while in ordinary cases, the conspirator has ground for fear only before the execu-

---

[7] He was tyrant of Sparta 205–192 B.C.

tion of his villany, in this case he has also cause to fear after, since he has the people for his enemy, and is thus cut off from all hope of shelter.

Of this, endless instances might be given, but I shall content myself with one that happened within the recollection of our fathers. Messer Annibale Bentivoglio, Lord of Bologna and grandsire of the present Messer Annibale, was conspired against and slain by the Canneschi, leaving behind none belonging to him save Messer Giovanni, then an infant in arms. Immediately upon the murder, the people rose and put all the Canneschi to death. This resulted from the goodwill then generally felt towards the House of the Bentivogli in Bologna; which feeling was so strong, that when upon the death of Messer Annibale no one was left who could govern the State, there being reason to believe that a descendant of the family (who up to that time had been thought to be the son of a smith) was living in Florence, the citizens of Bologna went there to fetch him, and entrusted him with the government of their city; which he retained until Messer Giovanni was old enough to govern.

To be brief, a Prince has little to fear from conspiracies when his subjects are well affected towards him; but when they are hostile and hold him in abhorrence, he has then reason to fear everything and every one. And well ordered States and wise Princes have provided with extreme care that the nobility shall not be driven to desperation, and that the commons shall be kept satisfied and contented; for this is one of the most important matters that a Prince has to look to.

Among the well ordered and governed Kingdoms of our day is that of France, wherein we find an infinite number of wise institutions, upon which depend the freedom and security of the King, and of which the most important are the Parliament and its authority. For he who gave its constitution to this Realm, knowing the ambition and arrogance of the nobles, and judging it necessary to bridle and restrain them, and on the other hand knowing the hatred, originating in fear, entertained against them by the commons, and desiring that they should be safe, was unwilling that the responsibility for this should rest on the King; and to relieve him of the ill-will which he might incur with the nobles by favouring the commons, or with the commons by favouring the nobles, appointed a third party to arbi-

trate, who without committing the King, might depress the nobles and uphold the commons. Nor could there be any better or wiser remedy than this, nor any surer safeguard for the King and Kingdom. And hence we may draw another notable lesson, namely, that Princes should devolve on others those matters which entail responsibility, and reserve to themselves those that relate to grace and favour. And again I say that a Prince should esteem the great, but must not make himself odious to the people. . . .

CHAPTER XXV

What Fortune can effect in human affairs,
and how she may be withstood

I am not ignorant that many have been and are of the opinion that human affairs are so governed by Fortune and by God, that men cannot alter them by any prudence of theirs, and indeed have no remedy against them; and for this reason have come to think that it is not worth while to labour much about anything, but that they must leave everything to be determined by chance.

Sometimes when I turn the matter over, I am in part inclined to agree with this opinion, which has had the readier acceptance in our own times from the great changes in things which we have seen, and every day see, happen contrary to all human expectation. Nevertheless, that our free will be not wholly set aside, I think it may be the case that Fortune is the mistress of one half our actions, and yet leaves the control of the other half, or a little less, to ourselves. And I would liken her to one of those wild torrents which, when angry, overflow the plains, sweep away trees and houses, and carry off soil from one bank to throw it down upon the other. Every one flees before them, and yields to their fury without the least power to resist. And yet, though this be their nature, it does not follow that in seasons of fair weather, men cannot, by constructing weirs and moles, make such provision as will cause them when again in flood to pass off by some artificial channel, or at least prevent their course from being so uncontrolled and destructive. And so it is with Fortune, who displays her might where there is no prepared strength to resist her, and directs her onset where she knows there is neither barrier nor embankment to confine her.

And if you look at Italy, which has been at once the seat of these changes and their cause, you will perceive that it is a field without embankment or barrier. For if, like Germany, France, and Spain, it had been guarded with sufficient skill, this inundation, if it ever came upon us, would never have wrought the violent changes we have witnessed.

This I think enough to say generally touching resistance to Fortune. But confining myself more closely to the matter in hand, I note that one day we see a Prince prospering and the next overthrown, without detecting any change in his nature or conduct. This, I believe, comes chiefly from a cause already dwelt upon, namely, that the Prince who rests wholly on Fortune is ruined when she changes. Moreover, I believe that he will prosper most whose mode of acting best adapts itself to the character of the times; and conversely that he will be unprosperous, with whose mode of acting the times do not accord. For we see that men in those matters which lead to the end each has before him, namely, glory and wealth, proceed by different ways, one with caution, another with impetuosity, one with violence, another with subtlety, one with patience, another with its contrary; and that by one or other of these different courses each may succeed.

Again, of two who act cautiously, you shall find that one attains his end, the other not, and that two of different temperament, the one cautious, the other impetuous, are alike successful. All which happens from no other cause than that the character of the times accords or does not accord with their methods of acting. And hence it comes, as I have already said, that two operating differently arrive at the same result, and two operating similarly, the one succeeds, the other not. On this likewise depend the shifts of Fortune. For if to one who conducts himself with caution and patience, time and circumstance are propitious, so that his method of acting is good, he goes on prospering; but if these change he is ruined, because he does not change his method of acting.

For no man is found prudent enough to adapt himself to these changes, both because he cannot deviate from the course to which nature impels him, and because, having always prospered while pursuing one path, he cannot be persuaded that it would be well for him to leave it. And so when occasion requires the cautious man to act impetuously, he cannot do so and is undone: whereas, had he changed his nature with time and circumstances, his fortune would have been unchanged.

Pope Julius II acted with impetuosity in all his affairs, and found time and circumstance in such harmony with his mode of acting that he always obtained happy results. Witness his first expedition against Bologna, when Messer Giovanni Bentivoglio was yet living.[8] The Venetians were not favourable to the enterprise; nor was the King of Spain. Negotiations respecting it with France were still open. Nevertheless, the Pope with his wonted hardihood and impetuosity marched in person on the expedition, and by this movement brought the King of Spain and the Venetians to a stay, the latter through fear, the former from his eagerness to recover the entire Kingdom of Naples; at the same time, he dragged after him the King of France, who, desiring to have the Pope for an ally in humbling the Venetians, and finding him already in motion, saw that he could not refuse him his soldiers without openly offending him. By the impetuosity of his movements, therefore, Julius effected what no other Pontiff endowed with the highest human prudence could. For had he, as any other Pope would have done, put off his departure from Rome until terms had been settled and everything duly arranged, he never would have succeeded. For the King of France would have found a thousand pretexts to delay him, and the others would have menaced him with a thousand alarms. I shall not touch upon his other actions, which were all of a like character, and all of which had a happy issue, since the shortness of his life did not allow him to experience reverses. But if times had overtaken him, rendering a cautious line of conduct necessary, his ruin must have ensued, since he never would have deviated from those methods to which nature inclined him.

To be brief, I say that since Fortune changes and men stand fixed in their old ways, they are prosperous so long as there is congruity between them, and unprosperous when there is not. Of this, however, I am well persuaded, that it is better to be impetuous than cautious. For Fortune is a woman who to be kept under

---

[8] Pope Julius attacked in 1506.

must be beaten and roughly handled; and we see that she suffers herself to be more readily mastered by those who so treat her than by those who are more timid in their approaches. And always, like a woman, she favours the young, because they are less scrupulous, and fiercer, and command her with greater audacity.

CHAPTER XXVI

An Exhortation to liberate Italy from the Barbarians

Turning over in my mind all the matters which have above been considered, and debating with myself whether in Italy at the present hour the times are such as might serve to win honour for a new Prince, and whether fit opportunity now offers for a prudent and valiant leader to bring about changes glorious for himself and advantageous for the whole Italian people, it seems to me that so many conditions combine to further such an enterprise, that I know of no time so favourable to it as now. And if, as I have said, it was necessary in order to display the valour of Moses that the children of Israel should be slaves in Egypt, to know the greatness and courage of Cyrus that the Persians should be oppressed by the Medes,[9] and to illustrate the excellence of Theseus that the Athenians should be scattered and divided,[10] so at this hour, to prove the worth of some Italian hero, it was required that Italy should be brought to her present abject condition, to be more enslaved than the Hebrews, more oppressed than the Persians, more disunited than the Athenians, without a head, without order, beaten, spoiled, torn in pieces, over-run and abandoned to destruction in every shape.

For although, heretofore, glimmerings may have been discerned in this man or that, whence it might be conjectured that he was ordained by God for her redemption, nevertheless it has afterwards been seen at the very height of his career that Fortune has disowned him; so that our country, left almost without life, still waits to know who it is that is to heal her bruises, to put an end to the devastation and plunder of Lombardy, to the exactions and imposts of Naples and Tuscany, and to stanch those wounds of hers which long neglect has changed into running sores.

We see how she prays God to send some one to rescue her from these barbarous cruelties and oppressions. We see, too, how ready and eager she is to follow any standard were there only some one to raise it. But at present we see no one except in your illustrious House (pre-eminent by its virtues and good fortune, and favoured by God and by the Church whose headship it now holds), who could assume the part of a deliverer.[11]

But for you this will not be too hard a task, if you keep before your eyes the lives and actions of those whom I have named above. For although these men were singular and extraordinary, after all they were but men, not one of whom had so great an opportunity as now presents itself to you. For their undertakings were not more just than this, nor more easy, nor was God more their friend than yours. The justice of the cause is conspicuous; for that war is just which is necessary, and those arms are sacred wherein lies our only hope. Everywhere there is the strongest disposition to engage in this enterprise; and where the disposition is strong the difficulty cannot be great, provided you follow the methods observed by those whom I have set before you as models.

Moreover, we see here extraordinary and unexampled proofs of Divine favour. The sea has been divided; the cloud has attended you on your way; the rock has flowed with water; the manna has rained from heaven; everything has concurred to promote your greatness. What remains to be done must be done by you; since not to deprive us of our free will and such share of glory as belongs to us, God will not do everything himself.

Nor is it to be marvelled at if none of those Italians I have spoken of has been able to effect what we hope to see effected by your illustrious House; or that amid so many revolutions and so many warlike movements it should always seem as though the military virtue of Italy were spent; for this comes from her old system being defective, and from no one being found among us

---

[9] Cyrus (559–529 B.C.) was king of the Medes.
[10] Theseus was a mythological figure who became king of Athens after slaying the Minotaur of Crete.

[11] *The Prince* is dedicated to Lorenzo de' Medici (1492–1519), whose grandfather was Lorenzo the Magnificent.

who has known to strike out anew. Nothing confers such honour on a new ruler, as do the new laws and institutions he devises; for these when they stand on a solid basis and have a greatness in their scope, make him admired and venerated. And in Italy material is not wanting for improvement in every form. If the head be weak the limbs are strong, and we see daily in single combats, or where few are engaged, how superior are the vigour, dexterity, and intelligence of Italians. But when it comes to armies, they are nowhere, and this from no other reason than the defects of their leaders. For those who know are not obeyed, and every one thinks he knows, since hitherto we have had none among us so raised by merit or by fortune above his fellows that they should recognize him as their superior. Whence it happens that for the long period of twenty years, during which so many wars have taken place, whenever there has been an army purely Italian it has always been beaten. To this testify, first Taro, then Alessandria, Capua, Genoa, Vaïla, Bologna, Mestri.[12]

If, then, your illustrious House should seek to follow the example of those great men who have delivered their country in past ages, it is before all things necessary, as the true foundation of every such attempt, to be provided with national troops, since you can have no braver, truer, or more faithful soldiers; and although every single man of them be good, collectively they will be better, seeing themselves commanded by their own Prince, and honoured and maintained by him. That you may be able, therefore, to defend yourself against the foreigner with Italian valour, the first step is to provide yourself with an army such as this.

And although the Swiss and the Spanish infantry are each accounted formidable,[13] there are yet defects in both, by reason of which troops trained on a different system might not merely withstand them, but be confident of defeating them. For the Spaniards cannot resist cavalry, and the Swiss will give way before infantry if they find them as resolute as themselves at close quarters. Whence it has been seen, and may be seen again, that the Spaniards cannot sustain the onset of the French men-at-arms, and that the Swiss are broken by the Spanish foot. And though of this last we have no complete instance, we have yet an indication of it in the battle of Ravenna,[14] where the Spanish infantry confronted the German companies, who have the same formation as the Swiss; on which occasion the Spaniards by their agility and with the aid of their bucklers forced their way over the pikes, and stood ready to close with the Germans, who were no longer in a position to defend themselves; and had they not been charged by cavalry, they must have put every German to the sword. Knowing, then, the defects of each of these kinds of troops, you can train your men on some different system, to withstand cavalry and not to fear infantry. This will be effected by the use of other weapons, and a change in the order of battle. And these are matters in reforming which the new Prince acquires reputation and importance.

This opportunity, then, for Italy at last to look on her deliverer, ought not to be allowed to pass away. With what love he would be received in all those Provinces which have suffered from the foreign inundation, with what thirst for vengeance, with what fixed fidelity, with what devotion, and what tears, no words of mine can declare. What gates would be closed against him? What people would refuse him obedience? What jealousy would stand in his way? What Italian but would yield him homage? This barbarian tyranny stinks in all nostrils.

Let your illustrious House therefore take upon itself this charge with all the courage and all the hopes with which a just cause is undertaken; so that under your standard this our country may be ennobled, and under your auspices be fulfilled the words of Petrarch:

Brief will be the strife
When valour arms against barbaric rage;
For the bold spirit of a bygone age
Still warms Italian hearts with life.[15]

---

[12] The battle of Fornovo on the Taro occurred in 1496; that of Alessandria in 1499; that of Capua in 1501; of Genoa in 1507; of Vaila, or Agnadello, in 1509; of Bologna in 1511; and of Mestri in 1513.

[13] The Swiss mercenaries fought for whoever would pay them but primarily for the French. The Spanish infantry was a national army.

[14] The Battle of Ravenna was fought in April 1512 between the French under Gaston of Foix and the Spanish under Raimondo of Cardona.

[15] Petrarca, Canzone beginning: 'Italia mia, benchè 'l parlar sia indarno.'

QUESTIONS

1. Do you consider Machiavelli's advice immoral or merely practical?
2. What is the author's opinion of human nature?
3. Why should the prince not fear being feared but avoid being hated?
4. To what extent can the prince conquer fortune?
5. To what motives does Machiavelli appeal to encourage Lorenzo to drive out the "barbarians"?
6. How would Machiavelli judge Bruni's *Oration*?

In Machiavelli's view the state was not a product of undirected growth of authority; rather, it was a work of art, the creation of the prince who skillfully imposed a form of political order on the people, who served as the matter for his work. This kind of imagery indeed reflects the Renaissance preoccupation with defining the nature of the artist and his activity. It was in this period that people first began to take the word *artist* seriously and to look on the artist with respect.

The Renaissance Artist   Who is an artist? Is he a maker, a thinker, a craftsman, a technician, a manipulator of emotions, a teacher? Is he a worldly, extroverted, confident, sophisticated personality or lonely, introverted, filled with self-doubt and scorn? These questions were asked by writers and artists in the Renaissance, and it is to them that we owe concepts of the artist and architect, as well as the inclusion of these arts in the "fine" or "liberal" as opposed to the mechanical arts. Not only theory but also the works of the artists themselves produced these ideas. In the contrasts between two of the greatest figures of Italian Renaissance art, we find two very different images of the artist.

Leonardo da Vinci (1452–1519)

Both Leonardo and Michelangelo were Florentine, near contemporaries, and undeniable geniuses. Leonardo was splendidly handsome; Michelangelo was at times obsessed with his ugliness. When Leonardo offered his services to the duke of Milan, he gave primacy to his qualifications as a military and hydraulic engineer, architect, and sculptor, mentioning painting

last. When Pope Julius II commanded Michelangelo to paint the frescoes on the ceiling of the Sistine Chapel (in the Vatican Palace), he replied that he was not a painter but a sculptor. Nevertheless, he fulfilled the commission and later became noted not only for his genius in painting and sculpture, but also in architecture. Both men seem to possess enormous ego and incredible versatility. In both we find characteristics that have contributed to our idea of the "Renaissance man"—a person of broad learning and skill.

Although Leonardo viewed painting as the least of his talents, until recently we knew him principally as painter and courtier. Now, since the discovery and publication of his notes and drawings, begun in the late nineteenth century, we can call him a scientist with equal correctness. Perhaps, above all, he was an investigator of nature through observation and practice. He was an architect, engineer, botanist, and musician; he studied hydraulics, geology, and human anatomy. The pages of his notebooks reveal a man obsessed with nature's beauty, power, and functional complexity. He sought answers to his questions neither in the Church nor in antiquity but in nature—that which was observable—and in the mind—that which asked and imagined. He studied the motion of water to capture its power to operate engines, but his drawings also reveal his respect for its awesome natural power in a flood or storm. He dissected bodies to understand human anatomy, which then became the source for the mighty bodies in a drawing or painting. But muscles were abstracted into the ropes of levers and pulleys (Fig. 11-1). He drew the fetus in the womb and anticipated Harvey's discovery of the circulation of the blood. His botanical drawings created a style for scientific illustration, and the plants reappear, lovingly delineated in his pictures. It is as if Leonardo could not satisfy a longing to know, to understand the principles of life—birth, transformation, change, and decay operating in the natural world. It is as if what he saw constantly assailed him with its incredible diversity, beauty, simplicity, and ugliness; and he sought rationally to control, order, and understand the vast potentialities open to human experience. He *attended* to *his* world; he wanted nothing to escape that questing, loving eye.

In his lifetime Leonardo finished few paintings. The *Mona Lisa* (or *La Gioconda*), a portrait of the enig-

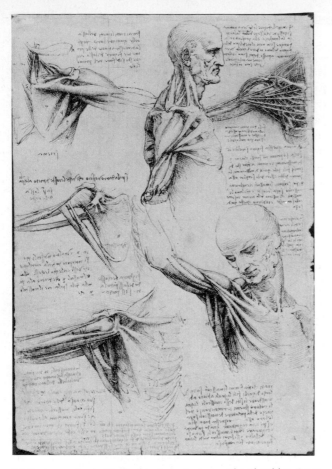

11-1 Leonardo da Vinci, drawing: *Anatomy of a Shoulder, Transformation into Levers.* (Royal Library, Windsor Castle, copyright reserved)

matic lady of the sublime smile, is perhaps the most familiar. Even more enigmatic to many is *The Madonna of the Rocks* (1483) in the Louvre—a soft, slightly mist-filled representation of the Virgin with the Christ Child, who, supported by an angel, blesses the kneeling John the Baptist presented by the Virgin (Color Plates X and XI).

The Madonna of the Rocks Set in a curious cavelike opening on a ledge in a rocky landscape, the four figures interact with each other; yet the viewer is hard pressed to define the interaction. The light is soft and vague, the landscape shadowy and moist. The edges of the figures, their drapery, and their expressions lack clear definition. We do not doubt their presence in space, for the figures have a weight and volume that

originated with Masaccio; yet there is a sense of fragility that is shared with Botticelli's *Primavera.* Nor do these figures possess Piero's intense abstraction—we are not sure what to look at in them. We seem forced by gesture and glance to look from face to face. The landscape itself is ambivalent, rocky, yet filled with beautiful plants and flowers. Light penetrates from behind and falls in the foreground. Where are we? Precisely what do we see? Academically we know the picture may deal with the doctrine of the virgin birth of Christ, but that knowledge does not begin to explain the picture. Rather it is almost a sacred conversation—a moment suspended in time that alludes to events years hence. Or is time, in a chronological sense, of any consequence? This is a picture rich in ambivalences. Its brilliant *illusionism* is dependent on the experienced world, and on a technical mastery of the creation of subtle nuances of shade and shadow that was one of Leonardo's great accomplishments. Similarly, it is a knowledge of anatomy, the study of faces and gestures, of falling light, of air suffused with light that makes the vision possible. But technical expertise cannot account for the experience of the picture—a profound religious silence—where children who are touchingly childlike imitate the roles of their adulthood, and a mother's protective gesture reaches all of us. This splendid vision is so rich in nuance and idea that it is ever fresh to the eye and imagination. This is the end attained by the means that the fifteenth-century Florentines made possible—an end so filled with resonances that we are still compelled to discuss the picture and we struggle to know the painter's mind.

The Madonna of the Rocks is one of the few almost finished paintings by Leonardo. It is because of such a painting as this that we study the complex, unfinished *Adoration of the Magi* or the ruined *Last Supper* hoping to reconstruct not just the means but also the purpose of an artist who presents both a final statement and a vision of potentiality, of transformation. The vision is complete by Alberti's definition, but also ever ready, like nature itself, to provide a new experience, to stimulate the imagination with fresh questions. It is as if reason, finally, is not enough. One can control the will, guide intuition, define problems, comprehend mathematical harmonies, and draw the structure of the body; but one cannot determine the source of the life force or define the power of experience. Nor can one rule the imagination as it seeks knowledge of the work through the world. In this capacity, man is Godlike and transcendent, free of everything except death.

Leonardo's art raises some problems that are still with us. What is it in the combination of nature, imagination, skill, and communication that creates a successful or a great painting or, for that matter, any work of art? How does a work of art evoke resonance and sympathy in the viewer? We may agree that a particular painting moves us, yet not on why that happens. With Masaccio's paintings, it may be the still drama, enacted in a space that we share. Piero della Francesca certainly presents clarified images, harmonized in a world that he has made both more abstract and orderly. Botticelli speaks to our sensitivities with delicate color and linear harmonies. The powerful visual experience evoked by *The Madonna of the Rocks* is more difficult to define precisely. Leonardo's predecessors and peers reinstated the nude, the portrait, and the landscape; moreover, they created conventions of form and technique to achieve the presentation of Christian and pagan themes for personal edification. The possibilities for the artist must have seemed unlimited to them, maybe frightening in their limitlessness. Perhaps, in Leonardo's mind, it was the limits imposed by sculpture that made this art seem inferior, yet it was his greatest peer, Michelangelo, who defined limits so wide and so demanding that they changed the course of sculpture.

Michelangelo Buonarotti (1475–1564)

In contrast to Leonardo, the handsome, graceful courtier with polished manners and mellifluous voice, Michelangelo seems like a difficult child. He was secretive, rude, dirty, and offensive. Leonardo passionately embraced nature, while Michelangelo seems to have embraced his own genius, then God, as the path to immortality (both concerns far removed from Leonardo's elevation of the artist to the status of the gentleman). But both artists shared to the status of the gentleman). But both artists shared the power to imagine, make, and move. Both used nature—the visible world—but they transformed it, filling the objects made with immediate and universal meaning.

Michelangelo was a writer as well as an artist, and his sonnets use the traditional form for concerns beyond those of Dante and Petrarch. The following two sonnets express Michelangelo's belief that there is a sphere in which Love and art become one. The sculptor's art is to release the power already contained in the stone, as beautiful forms on earth express the eternal beauty of God. (The translation is by Dante Gabriel Rossetti.)

MICHELANGELO

XV

The Lover and the Sculptor

Non ha l' ottimo artista.

The best of artists hath no thought to show
    Which the rough stone in its superfluous shell
    Doth not include: to break the marble spell
    Is all the hand that serves the brain can do.
The ill I shun, the good I seek, even so
    In thee, fair lady, proud, ineffable,
    Lies hidden: but the art I wield so well
    Works adverse to my wish, and lays me low.
Therefore not love, nor thy transcendent face,
    Nor cruelty, nor fortune, nor disdain,
    Cause my mischance, nor fate, nor destiny;
Since in thy heart thou carriest death and grace
    Enclosed together, and my worthless brain
    Can draw forth only death to feed on me.

LXI

AFTER THE DEATH OF VITTORIA
COLONNA
Irreparable Loss.

Se'l mie rozzo martello.

When my rude hammer to the stubborn stone
    Gives human shape, now that, now this, at will,
    Following his hand who wields and guides it
    still,
    It moves upon another's feet alone:
But that which dwells in heaven, the world doth fill
    With beauty by pure motions of its own;
    And since tools fashion tools which else were
    none,

Its life makes all that lives with living skill.
Now, for that every stroke excels the more
   The higher at the forge it doth ascend,
   Her soul that fashioned mine hath sought the
    skies:
Wherefore unfinished I must meet my end,
   If God, the great artificer, denies
   That aid which was unique on earth before.

The squares of Florence were decorated by some of the city's great sculptors. The Loggia dei Lanzi, a great open porch to the right of the Palazzo Vecchio, is still filled with sculpture. To the left is the Neptune fountain, whose splashing water invigorates the humid summer air. Directly in front, on the raised terrace before the Palazzo is a copy of Michelangelo's *David* (the original was moved inside a museum in 1873). Light is intense in the square, and the high walls and tower of the Palazzo Vecchio intensify the experience. The figure silently commands the busy space and challenges your passage into the palace.

The *David* is marble, over thirteen feet tall (Fig. 11-2). The figure is completely nude; the limbs and torso, now aged by rain and sun, once had a smoothness that remains only on the surface of the face. Never painted or decorated, unlike the statuary of former times, its first impact is of intractable stone formed into a super-human figure. But what is the boy like? The *Kritios Boy* (Fig. 2-8) and *The Spearbearer* (Fig. 2-12) are obvious idealizations of the human figure. How is David different from these two? Compare his face with that of Augustus and with a prophet from the doors at Chartres. Is this David an idealization of youth? His face is not symmetrical, the hands are enormous, and the arms and legs are too long. The body is awkward, like that of a tough youth, streetwise and confident. The brooding face is reticent but filled with a fierce courage. The body turns, a knee flexed; does the boy search the horizon for Goliath? The muscles of the neck and torso are tense, standing forth under the skin. The veins in arms, elbows, and hands rise to enliven the surface of the skin. The toes on one foot grasp the ground, while the toes of the other play over the rocky ledge. Has the stone been thrown, or does it lie in his curved fingers?

11-2 Michelangelo, *David* (Academy, Florence—Alinari/Editorial Photocolor Archives)

Does he ready the sling, or does it lie on his shoulder, no longer useful, but used?

If you are unable to decide the precise moment or motivation, you have begun to experience the *David*—an experience deriving its power from ambiguity. He is splendidly beautiful without being idealized. The torso and limbs flow into his pose with ease and grace, yet show the tension of movement. He is youthful but confident, brooding but able to act. His face has an intellectual intensity, and his body is its physical complement. Over all lies a feeling of potential—to make, do, dream, and be—to live in the world, to challenge with mind and body the limits of our human nature. That is the enemy—not the giant Goliath but the struggle between intellect and will, self-interest and unselfishness, love and hate.

The *David* was placed before the entrance to the Florentine city hall in 1504, during the restoration of the Republic, as a visible sign of courage and purpose—qualities that had made the Republic possible. After the ascendancy of the Medici, it might have been a reminder of what had been and might be again. The shepherd boy became king, only to be destroyed by his pride.

Michelangelo populated Florence and Rome with giants like this one. He loved the stone that was his medium and hated the demands that it made. In his sonnets he writes of the conflict between his art with its glorification of the human body and his personal quest for the salvation of his soul, a quest that he felt his art contradicted. The great commissions produced in the sixty years after the *David* reflect stages not only in his art but also in the bent of his mind. There were the great papal commissions like the unfinished tomb for Julius II and the frescoes for the Sistine Chapel ceiling (1508–1512) and *The Last Judgment* (1536–1541) behind its high altar. Although he became the architect for the new Saint Peter's, redesigned the Capitoline Hill, and executed other architectural and painted commissions, his greatest vehicle for expression was the human body. In some figures he was able to attain a classicism almost Greek (Color Plate XII). In other figures, like the unfinished *Captive Slave* (1527–28), whose body is still contained in the block, the imperfect stone seems expressive of those faults that must fall away if man is to become good and filled with grace (Fig. 11-3).

There was no artistic convention that Michelangelo could not turn to his use. He was capable of making architecture as evocative as sculpture and painting. In the entry corridor to the Laurentian Library (Fig. 11-4), the walls push out between the paired columns and the columns seem to float above the ground, separated from a base or plinth by the molding and the volutes, which break out beneath them; thus the supporting members

11-3 Michelangelo, *Captive Slave*. Louvre, Paris. (© ARCH. PHOT. PARIS/S.P.A.D.E.M., 1980)

appear decorative and the decorative members structural. Similarly, the stairway denies the feeling of ascension by heavy curving steps which seem to ooze downward. Michelangelo deliberately transforms familiar elements of classical architecture not only to expand their potential meaning but also to change the viewer's perception of their value and importance as elements of building.

In his unfinished works, like those of Leonardo, we sense the skill needed to manipulate the medium and the potential of the object for interpretations that reach beyond the accepted meaning. The bust of Brutus (the assassin of Julius Caesar), although made after 1537 (thus after the final demise of the Republic and return

11-4 Michelangelo, Laurentian Library, Florence. (Alinari/ Editorial Photocolor Archives)

that it comes from sacrifice. Our responses to this face are varied, rich, and resonant. In it are recorded the marks of life and the need for meaning.

Raphael (1483–1520)

Raffaello Sanzio (anglicized as Raphael) is the youngest of these four individuals whose ideas were born and matured in the intensely creative, confident atmosphere of late-fifteenth-century Florence. Taught by his father, then by the painter Perugino in sophisticated, worldly Urbino, Raphael traveled to Florence, then to Rome. Raphael's vision of the nature of painting seems to have been founded on a desire to make paintings that presented an ideal and harmonious moment in which time and change are suspended. This vision contrasts sharply with the ideas of Michelangelo and Leonardo, but its presence emphasizes the rich possibilities inherent in Florentine art. Just as Giotto and Simone Martini represented alternatives in the fourteenth century, Raphael, with Leonardo and Michelangelo, presented alternatives that artists explored well into the nineteenth century.

Among Raphael's first important works, *The Marriage of the Virgin* (Fig. 11-6) was painted for the church in Città di Castello about 1504. Before a circular, domed templelike building, a group of young

of the Medici to power), seems to carry on the spirit of republican Florence (Fig. 11-5). The head and face are unfinished, the drape completed by one of Michelangelo's assistants. Compare it with similar works that we have seen. The ridges left by the chisel do not detract from the strong, heavy face. The folds of flesh that extend from the nostrils to the small but sensuous mouth, as well as the hollows of the cheeks, give the face a tension and purpose that come with age. The deep hollows of the simplified eyes hold shadow; they contrast with the broad ridge of the nose. This face could be that of any man with courage who has known fear, with purpose who has known discouragement. He is neither the purely detached imperial Augustus (Fig. 5-2) nor the political Arringatore (Fig. 5-1). He asks questions and seeks answers. He loves life but knows that death will come. He wants salvation but knows

11-5 Michelangelo, *Brutus*. (Alinari/Editorial Photocolor Archives)

11-6 Raphael, *Marriage of the Virgin*, panel painting, 1504
Pinacoteca di Brera, Milan (Alinari/Art Resource)

men and women stand in the foreground of a spacious, light-filled piazza. The paving pattern on the ground connects the foreground to the background as it diminishes in the distance.

The arch of the frame, almost touching the dome of the temple, is one curve in a repeating pattern of curves and rectangles, which focus attention on Joseph, who places a ring on the finger of the Virgin. Their bodies and heads incline inward toward each other, as do all the figures. Everything in the work quietly conspires to concentrate on this precise moment in time. The principal characters stand as silently as their attendants; their elegant profiles and the curves of their rich drapery repeat each other. The light in the piazza is clear

and golden; figures in the middle distance and background move easily through this spacious, ordered world.

The successful marriage of figures with their setting was and remains a problem for the artist. The setting must reinforce the motif of the painting, but it must not be so contrived as to be incredible. Raphael's painting *The School of Athens* (Color Plate XIII), executed for the Stanza della Segnatura in the papal apartments in Rome (1510–11), presents another solution and one that should be compared with Michelangelo's Sistine ceiling frescoes (Color Plate XII).

In *The School of Athens*, Raphael places the great philosophers of antiquity in a barrel-vaulted and domed hall lined with sculpture in niches, open to the air, light filled. Plato and Aristotle are framed by the central arches as they stand in the sunlight at the top of steps, between groups of auditors. In the upper left, Socrates holds the attention of some youths; in the lower left, Pythagoras computes on a slate and Euclid, lower right, draws a geometrical demonstration.

The groups of figures form a circle in the space and color, and gesture and overlapping figures move the eye around the composition in an even rhythm. In spite of all the movement, discussion, and implied noise, the painting seems to portray a dream of antiquity concentrated in a golden moment of time. The figures and the architecture are idealizations, like the subject itself, an occasion that could have never occurred.

On the opposite wall of the apartment, Raphael placed the complex *Disputation of the Sacrament*, an exposition of the doctrine of the Eucharist. These two subjects seem to symbolize Renaissance thought, which sought to reconcile antiquity and Christianity.

At the same time that Raphael was executing these frescoes, Michelangelo was working in the Sistine Chapel on the ceiling decorations that were to tell the story of Creation. These paintings are directly overhead, at quite a distance from the viewer. Michelangelo was faced with a problem. What could be seen—figures, setting, both? Discarding any but the barest architectural framework, the barest landscape, Michelangelo concentrated all his effort on creating a series of idealized, heroic figures, a canopy of giants. The ceiling is given over to the human body, which is the sole carrier of meaing. These are the figures of a sculptor, translated into painting. But the difference is more than one of the physical location of the work. Raphael was more interested in attaining a completely harmonious moment in a harmonized world, whereas Michelangelo was more interested in the human power of the narrative. (The cleaning of the Sistine Chapel frescoes, a massive project that has aroused controversy in the art world, has revealed Michelangelo's work in an entirely new light.)

Raphael, like Michelangelo, could not ignore the realities of this world, or the people in it. His stunning portrait of Pope Leo X (Color Plate XIV), painted about 1517, presents this Renaissance prelate in all his corpulent power. A shrewd man, given to worldly things, Leo excommunicated Martin Luther in 1520. There was no golden moment to capture here, but there was the reality of earthly power. Raphael's ability to see this, along with the ideal, gave his art its lasting vitality.

12

Northern Humanism and The Protestant Reformation

By 1500 humanism had northern European adherents. Generally speaking, northern humanism differed from the Italian variety in directing its attention to the ancient texts of the Christian religion rather than to the writings of Roman and Greek antiquity. Humanist philological techniques developed in preparing editions of Cicero, Plato, and others were now applied to editing the Bible and the writings of the Latin and Greek Church Fathers. Thus, the humanists in the north were responsible for directing the attention of learned men to the early history of Christianity and the sources of the Christian faith.

Erasmus

The leading northern humanist and doubtless the most important humanist of his generation was Desiderius Erasmus (1463–1536). Though born in the Low Countries, Erasmus lived most of his mature life in France, England, and Switzerland. Like his Italian humanist predecessors, he believed that ethics were more important than elaborate systems of philosophy and theology. Coupled with his extremely critical attitude toward current Church abuses, this insistence on the primacy of moral action became a powerful weapon for the reform of Christian life.

In Erasmus's opinion, the Church had overemphasized rituals and outward manifestations of piety. It had made too sharp a distinction between the status of a cleric and that of a layman. The central focus of Christianity should be on the spirit, on the cultivation of deep religious feeling rather than depending on its ceremonies. While not attacking the principle of monasticism as evil, he nevertheless maintained that the lay life, doing God's work in the world, was just as effective in serving Christ as was the life of the cloistered monk. Moreover, laymen, too, needed and had the right to read and discuss the sources of their faith. In short, as Erasmus himself said at one point: "The world has become my monastery."

Like the texts of pagan antiquity, those of Christian antiquity were highly defective. Erasmus chose as his first task the preparation of a new edition of the Greek New Testament with Latin translation, which he published in 1516. It was a courageous task to undertake. Over a thousand years of Christian scholarship had been based on the Vulgate, composed of early translations of the books of the Bible; now Erasmus showed that some of the key passages on which countless interpretations had been made were not actually in the Greek original or were mistranslated. In the same year he published his nine-volume edition of the works of Saint Jerome. This was one of the first humanist editions of the complete works of a Church Father, but many were to follow.

Erasmus was the first great European writer to make use of an important invention, the printing press. Although printing had been developed before his time— the Gutenberg Bible first appeared in 1455—the earlier books were primarily luxury items. Erasmus distributed his editions and his polemical pamphlets throughout Europe. Writing in Latin, he could be read by educated people in all countries; thus, he helped to create a culture of the printed word that has since dominated Western intellectual life.

Erasmus firmly believed that if all the sources of Christian truth could be published in an accurate form, the eloquence of the words, as they were originally written under the inspiration of the Holy Spirit, could not fail to move men to become better Christians. The goal of Erasmus's Christian scholarship was, therefore, to reform both individual Christians and the Church itself. He did not attack the dogma of the Church, but he did attack the effort of theologians to elaborate on the dogma and to claim certainty for their deductions. For him there were only a few absolutely certain principles in the Bible, and these were all men needed to believe in order to be saved. What was important for him was that Christian belief be reflected in one's life. True Christians acted like Christians. This was Erasmus's "philosophy of Christ" in essence. Accordingly, he was exceedingly tolerant of differing views of theology but severely critical of evil conduct.

The *Colloquies* were originally conceived by Erasmus as a device to teach children the art of Latin conversation, but he soon realized that the dialogue form could be an effective means for teaching his reform program. The following colloquy, "The Shipwreck," is one of the most popular. A skillful satire of superficial piety and religious superstition, the work delighted most of its readers. Conservative theologians, however, criticized Erasmus as impious in what they felt was his mockery of the invocation of saints and of the Virgin Mary. In his defense Erasmus argued that he was only satirizing extravagant abuses of traditional religious practices. His critics remained unconvinced. This translation is by Craig R. Thompson.

The Shipwreck

ANTONY, ADOLPH

ANTONY   Terrible tales you tell! That's what going to sea is like? God forbid any such notion should ever enter *my* head!

ADOLPH   Oh, no, what I've related up to this point is mere sport compared with what you'll hear now.

ANTONY   I've heard more than enough of disasters. When you're recalling them I shudder as if I myself were sharing the danger.

ADOLPH   To me, on the contrary, troubles over and done with are enjoyable.—On that same night something happened which in large part robbed the skipper of his hope of safety.

ANTONY   What, I beseech you?

ADOLPH   The night was partially clear, and on the topmast, in the "crow's-nest" (as I think they call it), stood one of the crew, looking out for land. Suddenly a fiery ball[1] appeared beside him—a very bad sign to sailors when it's a single flame, lucky when it's double. Antiquity believed these were Castor and Pollux.

ANTONY   What's their connection with sailors? One was a horseman, the other a boxer.

ADOLPH   This is the poets' version. The skipper, who was by the helm, spoke up: "Mate"—that's what sailors call one another—"see your company alongside there?" "I see it," the man replied, "and I hope it's good luck." Soon the blazing ball slid down the ropes and rolled straight up to the skipper.

ANTONY   Wasn't he scared out of his wits?

ADOLPH   Sailors get used to marvels. After stopping there a moment, it rolled the whole way round the ship, then dropped through the middle hatches and disappeared. Toward noon the storm began to rage more and more. Ever seen the Alps?

ANTONY   Yes, I've seen them.

ADOLPH   Those mountains are warts compared with the waves of the sea. Whenever we were borne on the crest, we could have touched the moon with a finger; whenever dipped, we seemed to plunge through the gaping earth to hell.

ANTONY   What fools they are who trust themselves to the sea!

ADOLPH   Since the crew's struggle with the storm was hopeless, the skipper, pale as a ghost, at last came up to us.

ANTONY   His pallor forebodes some great disaster.

ADOLPH   "Friends," he says, "I'm no longer master of my ship; the winds have won. The only thing left to do is to put our hope in God and each one prepare himself for the end."

ANTONY   Truly a Scythian[2] speech.

ADOLPH   "But first of all," he says, "the ship must be unloaded. Necessity, a stern foe, demands it. Better to save life at the cost of goods than for both to perish together." This was undeniable. A lot of luggage filled with costly wares was tossed overboard.

ANTONY   This was sacrificing for sure!

ADOLPH   On board was a certain Italian who had served as legate to the King of Scotland. He had a chest full of silver plate, rings, cloth, and silk robes.

ANTONY   He didn't want to come to terms with the sea?

ADOLPH   No, instead he wanted to go down with his beloved treasures or else be saved along with them. So he protested.

ANTONY   What did the skipper do?

ADOLPH   "We're quite willing to let you perish alone with your goods," said he, "but it's not fair for all of us to be endangered because of your chest. What's more, we'll throw you and the chest together into the sea."

ANTONY   True sailor's lingo!

ADOLPH   So the Italian, too, threw his goods overboard, cursing away by heaven and hell because he had entrusted his life to so barbarous an element.[3]

ANTONY   I recognize the Italian accent.

ADOLPH   Soon afterward the winds, unappeased by our offerings, broke the ropes and tore the sails to pieces.

ANTONY   Catastrophe!

ADOLPH   At that moment the skipper comes to us again.

ANTONY   To make a speech?

ADOLPH   "Friends"—he begins by way of greeting— "the hour warns each of us to commend himself to God and prepare for death." Questioned by some who were ignorant of seamanship as to how many

---

[1] Saint Elmo's Fire.

[2] Blunt, harsh.

[3] As Erasmus remarks in his *Praise of Folly*, everything foreign was "barbarous" to Italians.

hours he thought he could keep the ship afloat, he replied that he couldn't promise anything, but not more than three hours.

ANTONY   This speech was even sterner than the first one.

ADOLPH   After saying this, he orders all the shrouds to be slashed and the mast sawn off down to its socket and thrown into the sea, together with the spars.

ANTONY   Why this?

ADOLPH   With the sail ruined or torn, the mast was a useless burden. Our whole hope was in the tiller.

ANTONY   What about the passengers meanwhile?

ADOLPH   There you'd have seen what a wretched plight we were in: the sailors singing *Salve Regina*, praying to the Virgin Mother, calling her Star of the Sea, Queen of Heaven, Mistress of the World, Port of Salvation, flattering her with many other titles the Sacred Scriptures nowhere assign to her.[4]

ANTONY   What has she to do with the sea? She never went voyaging, I believe.

ADOLPH   Formerly Venus was protectress of sailors, because she was believed to have been born to the sea. Since she gave up guarding them, the Virgin Mother has succeeded this mother who was not a virgin.

ANTONY   You're joking.

ADOLPH   Prostrating themselves on the deck, some worshiped the sea, pouring whatever oil they had on the waves, flattering it no differently from the way we do a wrathful sovereign.

ANTONY   What did they say?

ADOLPH   "O most merciful sea, O most kind sea, O most splendid sea, O most lovely sea, have pity on us! Save us!" Many songs of this kind they sang to the sea—which was deaf.

ANTONY   Absurd superstition! What did the rest do?

ADOLPH   Some did nothing but get sick. Many made vows. There was an Englishman who promised

heaps of gold to the Virgin of Walsingham[5] if he reached shore alive. Some promised many things to the wood of the Cross at such and such a place; others, again, to that in some other place. The same with respect to the Virgin Mary, who reigns in many places; and they think the vow worthless unless you specify the place.

ANTONY   Ridiculous! As if saints don't dwell in heaven.

ADOLPH   Some pledged themselves to become Carthusians. There was one who promised to journey to St. James at Compostella[6] barefoot, bareheaded, clad only in a coat of mail, begging his bread besides.

ANTONY   Did nobody remember Christopher?[7]

ADOLPH   I couldn't help laughing as I listened to one chap, who in a loud voice (for fear he wouldn't be heard) promised a wax taper as big as himself to the Christopher in the tallest church in Paris—a mountain rather than a statue. While he was proclaiming this at the top of his lungs, insisting on it again and again, an acquaintance who chanced to be standing by nudged him with his elbow and cautioned: "Be careful what you promise. Even if you sold all your goods at auction, you couldn't pay for it." Then the other, lowering his voice—so St. Christopher wouldn't overhear him, of course!—said, "Shut up, you fool. Do you suppose I'm serious? If I once touch land, I won't give him a tallow candle."

ANTONY   O stupid! I suspect he was a Batavian.[8]

ADOLPH   No, but he was a Zeelander.

ANTONY   I'm surprised nobody thought of the Apostle Paul, who was once shipwrecked himself, and when the ship broke, jumped overboard and

---

[4] Erasmus' ecclesiastical and academic enemies denounced this and other passages in "The Shipwreck" as impious. Erasmus retorted that he was attacking superstitions (*Opera Omnia*, Leiden edition, IX, 942C-943F, 1086C-F, 1163C-E).

[5] On the gold at the shrine of Walsingham, and the wood of the Cross, see Erasmus' colloquy "A Pilgrimage for Religion's Sake," in *The Ten Colloquies of Erasmus*, Trans. Craig R. Thompson (New York: Macmillan, 1957).

[6] In northwestern Spain. One of the favorite places of pilgrimage in the Middle Ages.

[7] Patron saint of travelers. The statue mentioned a few lines later once stood in the entrance of the Church of Notre Dame.

[8] Erasmus enjoyed a joke at the expense of his fellow Hollanders, but note his remark, at the end of the colloquy, about their character.

reached land.[9] No stranger to misfortune, he knew how to help those in distress.

ADOLPH   Paul wasn't mentioned.

ANTONY   Did they pray all the while?

ADOLPH   Strenuously. One chanted *Salve Regina,* another *Credo in Deum.* Some had certain queer beads,[10] like charms, to ward off danger.

ANTONY   How devout men are made by suffering! In prosperity the thought of God or saint never enters their heads.

What were you doing all this time? Making vows to any of the saints?

ADOLPH   Not at all.

ANTONY   Why?

ADOLPH   Because I don't make deals with saints. For what else is that but a bargain according to the form "I'll give this if you do that" or "I'll do this if you'll do that"; "I'll give a taper if I can swim"; "I'll go to Rome if you save me."

ANTONY   But you called on some saint for help?

ADOLPH   Not even that.

ANTONY   But why?

ADOLPH   Because heaven's a large place. If I entrust my safety to some saint—St. Peter, for example, who perhaps will be the first to hear, since he stands at the gate—I may be dead before he meets God and pleads my cause.

ANTONY   What did you do, then?

ADOLPH   Went straight to the Father himself, reciting the Pater Noster. No saint hears sooner than he, or more willingly grants what is asked.

ANTONY   But didn't your conscience accuse you when you did this? Weren't you afraid to entreat the Father, whom you had offended by so many sins?

ADOLPH   To speak frankly, my conscience did deter me somewhat. But I soon recovered my spirits, thinking to myself, "No father is so angry with his son that, if he sees him in danger in a stream or lake, he won't grasp him by the hair and pull him out." Of all the passengers, none behaved more calmly than a certain woman who was suckling a baby.

ANTONY   What did she do?

ADOLPH   She was the only one who didn't scream, weep, or make promises; she simply prayed in silence, clasping her little boy. While the ship was continually battered by the sea, the skipper undergirded it with ropes both fore and aft, for fear it might break to pieces.

ANTONY   Miserable protection!

ADOLPH   Meantime an old priest, a man of sixty named Adam, jumped up. Stripped to his underclothes, and with his shoes and leggings removed, he urged us all to prepare likewise for swimming. And standing so in the middle of the ship, he preached to us a sermon from Gerson[11] on the five truths concerning the benefit of confession. He urged everyone to be ready both for life and for death. A Dominican was there, too. Those who wished confessed to these two.

ANTONY   What did you do?

ADOLPH   Seeing everything in an uproar, I confessed silently to God, condemning my unrighteousness before him and imploring his mercy.

ANTONY   Where would you have gone if you had died in that condition?

ADOLPH   That I left to God the judge, for I was unwilling to be judge of my own cause; nevertheless a strong hope possessed my mind the whole time. While all this is going on, the captain tearfully returns to us. "Get ready," says he, "because the ship will be useless to us in a quarter of an hour." For it was already shattered in some places, and was drawing water. Soon afterwards a sailor reports seeing a church tower in the distance, and beseeches us to appeal to whichever saint took that church under his protection. Everyone falls to his knees and prays to the unknown saint.

ANTONY   Had you invoked him by name, he might have heard.

ADOLPH   We didn't know his name. As much as he could, meantime, the skipper steered the ship in that direction. It was already breaking up, taking in water everywhere and clearly about to fall to pieces if it hadn't been undergirded with ropes.

---

[9] Acts 27:9–44.
[10] Rosaries.

[11] The great churchman and chancellor of the University of Paris (1363–1429); famous as a theologian and preacher.

ANTONY   A bad state of affairs!

ADOLPH   We were carried far enough in for the inhabitants of the place to see our plight. Groups of them rushed to the shore, and taking off hats and coats and sticking them on poles, urged us towards themselves, and by lifting their arms to heaven indicated their pity for our lot.

ANTONY   I'm waiting to hear what happened.

ADOLPH   The whole ship was filled with water now, so that thereafter we would be no safer in ship than in sea.

ANTONY   At that moment you had to fall back on your last hope.

ADOLPH   On suffering, rather. The crew released the lifeboat and lowered it into the sea. Everyone tried to hurl himself into it, the sailors protesting in the uproar that the lifeboat would not hold such a crowd, but everybody should grab what he could and swim. The situation did not allow leisurely plans. One person snatched an oar, another a boathook, another a tub, another a bucket, another a plank; and, each relying on his own resources, they committed themselves to the waves.

ANTONY   What happened during this time to that poor little woman who alone did not weep and wail?

ADOLPH   She was the first of them all to reach shore.

ANTONY   How could she do that?

ADOLPH   We put her on a curved plank and tied her in such a way that she couldn't easily fall off. We gave her a small board to use as a paddle, and, wishing her luck, shoved her off into the waves, pushing with a pole to get her clear of the ship, where the danger lay. Holding her baby in her left hand, she paddled with the right.

ANTONY   Brave woman!

ADOLPH   Since nothing else remained, one man seized a wooden statue of the Virgin Mother, now rotten and mouse-eaten, and, putting his arms around it, began to swim.

ANTONY   Did the lifeboat come through safely?

ADOLPH   The first to go down. And thirty people had thrown themselves into it.

ANTONY   What mishap caused that?

ADOLPH   Before it could get away it was overturned by the lurching of the big ship.

ANTONY   A cruel business! What then?

ADOLPH   While looking out for others, I nearly perished myself.

ANTONY   How so?

ADOLPH   Because there was nothing left for me to swim on.

ANTONY   Cork would have been useful there.

ADOLPH   In that emergency I would rather have had plain cork tree than golden candlestick. Casting about, I finally thought of the stump of the mast. Since I couldn't pry it loose by myself, I enlisted the help of another man. Supporting ourselves on this, we put to sea, I holding on to the right end and he to the left. While we were tossing about in this way, that priest who preached on board threw himself in our midst—on our shoulders. Big fellow, too. "Who's the third?" we yell. "He'll be the death of us all." He, on the other hand, says calmly, "Cheer up, there's plenty of room. God will help us."

ANTONY   Why was he so late in starting to swim?

ADOLPH   Oh, he was to be in the lifeboat along with the Dominican (for everybody conceded this much honor to him), but although they had confessed to each other on the ship, nevertheless some condition—I don't know what—had been forgotten. There on the edge of the ship they confess anew, and each lays his hand on the other. While they're doing this, the lifeboat goes down. Adam told me this.

ANTONY   What became of the Dominican?

ADOLPH   According to Adam, after entreating the aid of the saints he threw off his clothes and began to swim.

ANTONY   Which saints did he invoke?

ADOLPH   Dominic, Thomas, Vincent, and I don't know which Peter, but first and foremost he placed his trust in Catherine of Siena.

ANTONY   Christ didn't come to mind?

ADOLPH   This is what the priest told me.

ANTONY   He'd have swum better if he hadn't thrown off his sacred cowl. With that put aside, how could Catherine of Siena recognize him? But go on with what happened to you.

ADOLPH   While we were still tossing beside the ship, which was rolling from side to side at the will of the waves, the broken rudder smashed the thigh of the man who was holding on to the left end of the stump. So he was torn away. The priest, saying a prayer *Requiem aeternam* for him, took his place, urging me to keep hold of my end with confidence and kick my feet vigorously. We were swallowing a lot of salt water all this while. Thus Neptune saw to it that we had not only a salty bath but even a salty drink, though the priest showed us a remedy for that.

ANTONY   What, please?

ADOLPH   Every time a wave came rushing upon us, he turned the back of his head to it and kept his mouth closed.

ANTONY   A doughty old fellow you tell me of.

ADOLPH   When we'd made some progress after swimming a while, the priest, who was very tall, said, "Cheer up, I'm touching bottom!" I didn't dare hope for such great luck. "We're too far from shore to hope for bottom." "Oh, no," he replied, "I feel land with my feet." "Maybe it's something from the chests that the sea has rolled this way." "No," he said, "I feel land plainly by the scraping of my toes." After we had swum a while longer in this direction and he again touched bottom, "Do what you think best," he said, "I'm giving up the whole mast to you and trusting myself to the bottom"; and thereupon, after waiting for the waves to subside, he went on foot as fast as he could. When the waves overtook him again, he resisted by clasping his knees with his hands and putting his head under water, as divers and ducks do; when the waves receded, up he popped and rushed on. When I saw he was successful at this, I imitated him. Standing on the coast were men—hardy fellows, and used to the water—who by means of extremely long poles, held out from one to the other, braced themselves against the force of the waves; so that the one farthest out held his pole to the swimmer. When this was grasped, all heaved toward shore and the swimmer was hauled safely to dry land. A number were rescued by this device.

ANTONY   How many?

ADOLPH   Seven, but two of these died when brought to a fire.

ANTONY   How many were you in the ship?

ADOLPH   Fifty-eight.

ANTONY   O cruel sea! At least it might have been satisfied with a tenth,[12] which is enough for priests. From so large a number how few returned!

ADOLPH   We were treated with wonderful kindness by the people there, who looked after our needs with astonishing eagerness: lodging, fire, food, clothing, money for travel.

ANTONY   What people were they?

ADOLPH   Hollanders.

ANTONY   No people could be more kindly, though they do have savage neighbors. I guess you won't visit Neptune very soon again after this.

ADOLPH   No, not unless God takes my reason from me.

ANTONY   And I for my part would rather hear such tales than experience the events at first hand.

QUESTIONS

1. What role does the description of Saint Elmo's fire at the beginning of the colloquy play?
2. How, according to Adolph, did the Virgin Mary, who "never went voyaging," become the protectress of sailors? Why might Erasmus's enemies consider the passage irreverent?
3. How did Adolph's comportment during the storm compare with that of most of the other passengers? Why did these others hesitate to pray directly to God the Father? Why is Erasmus ridiculing the invocation of the saints?
4. How might Erasmus be seen as criticizing the rite of confession? How could Erasmus defend himself from this charge?
5. Why is Erasmus in the conclusion so generous in his praise of the Hollanders who rescued some of the ship's company?

Erasmus remained a Catholic despite every effort of the Lutherans to convince him to join their sect. Nonetheless, the sweeping criticism he made of abuses in the Church had a devastating effect and has led some

---

[12] This refers to the tithe. A tenth of all goods produced—normally agricultural in nature—was to be given to the Church for its support.

scholars to say that "Erasmus laid the egg that Luther hatched."

The Protestant Reformation

The reform tendencies present in Erasmus and other northern humanists were not unique to them. Rather, by 1500 in northern Europe a broad spirit of Christian reform prevailed, of which humanism was only one reflection. Intensive efforts were underway to reform monastic orders, and new orders were founded devoted to strict enforcement of the monastic vows. Pietistic movements like the Brethren of the Common Life, which included both laymen and clerics, aimed at infusing in the daily life of all Christians a deep spirit of devotion. Against this background the Lutheran reform could be interpreted as only another manifestation of a universal concern. Martin Luther (Fig. 12-1) was different from the other reformers, however, in that he attacked not only abuses but doctrines as well.

Martin Luther   For Luther (1483–1546), the Church, for the past thousand and more years had distorted the truth found in the Bible. In practice the Church had exalted the pronouncements of Church councils, popes, and learned men to a level equal to that of Scripture. For him these "truths" were human ones; men made mistakes and only the Bible was unquestionably true. Hence, he rejected the authoritative interpretations that the Church had placed on each passage of the Bible as concealing rather than revealing the Word of God found therein. Each man should have the power of coming to the text and reading it according to the dictates of his own conscience. When in 1521 Luther was called before the Catholic emperor, Charles V of Germany, at Augsburg to renounce his deviation from Catholic truth, he exalted the majesty of the individual human conscience in refusing:

Since then Your Majesty and your lordships desire a simple reply, I will answer without horns and without teeth. Unless I am convicted by Scripture and plain reason—I do not accept the authority of popes and councils, for they have contradicted each other—my conscience is captive to the Word of God. I cannot and I will not recant anything, for to go against conscience is neither right nor safe. God help me. Amen.

By this, however, he did not mean that everyone's opinion about religion should be respected. The truth on important issues of the faith was so evident for Luther that no fair-minded person could differ with his interpretation. Accordingly, he was perfectly willing to persecute others who did not share his understanding of the basic principles found in the Bible.

A dominant tradition of the medieval Church had been, as we have seen, the belief that men could cooperate with God's grace in earning their own salvation. Through a succession of good works, product of the joint efforts of human will and grace, the individual could build up enough merits to earn a place in

12-1   Lucas Cranach, the Elder, *Portrait of Luther as an Augustinian Friar*, engraving, 1520. (Courtesy of Fogg Art Museum, Harvard University. Francis Calley Gray Collection)

heaven. The sacraments controlled by the Church hierarchy were viewed as the channels through which life-giving grace poured to believers. The clerics (the priests who administered the sacraments and had care of souls) and the monks and friars (who had taken special vows to devote their life to God) were considered as a group to be on a higher spiritual level than were laymen. Their average chances for entering heaven were considered better than those of nonclerics; they were more likely to build up merits because of their profession.

Luther attacked the central thesis of this belief. No man can cooperate with God in his own salvation. Mortals are too sinful. God predestines some individuals from all eternity to salvation. These men and women know who they are because they have faith that Christ's merits have been imputed to them for their salvation. They themselves did absolutely nothing to win this salvation; it was a free gift of God. In saying this he firmly believed that he was truly interpreting the words of Christ and Paul. Therefore, gone was the need for pilgrimages, penance, masses for the dead, and all the other rituals of the medieval Church designed to build up a sum of the good works requisite for salvation. Only after an individual is justified and knows that Christ is his savior can be really begin to do good works. Yet these count nothing for salvation: they are merely the fruits of knowing that God has already chosen one to be saved. The good works pour out as a product of love for God and one's fellow men because Christ is at work in the depths of the soul.

Consequently, no one is saved because of what he or she does. From this it follows that a shoemaker has just as good a chance of being saved as does the pope. In Luther's view, the whole spiritual hierarchy with the bishops, archbishops, cardinals, and pope was a man-made construction. He denied that Christ in committing the keys to Peter intended to make the bishop of Rome the head of the whole Church. The present hierarchical Church was a work of man, not God; and, since it was loaded with corruption and led by blind men, the edifice had to be destroyed. Luther's solution was that the territorial prince in each area should be the governor of the territorial Church.

The sources for Luther's thought, in addition to the Bible, included Saint Augustine and northern European critics of medieval scholasticism. Unlike Thomas Aquinas, Luther had little faith in the ability of human reason to establish truths about the divine nature. Luther's God was primarily Will, and men had no power to know anything more of him than the Bible conveyed. The reformer's insistence on the importance of the inner life as opposed to ceremonies was perhaps in part an inheritance from northern mysticism, but humanists like Erasmus also exercised an influence here. To humanism as well, Luther owed his training in the three major ancient languages, Latin, Greek and Hebrew, and his confidence in his critical powers when confronted with a text. Humanism placed at his disposal a set of philological tools and a tradition of independent judgment; Luther fearlessly applied these in an examination of the whole body of Christian doctrine.

Like Erasmus, Luther made extensive use of the medium of printing to distribute his ideas. The impact of his message was much greater, however, because whereas Erasmus wrote only in Latin, Luther championed his appeal to reform in eloquent German. To make the Bible more accessible to the layman, he translated the whole of the Old and New Testaments, a translation that served as the basis for the modern German language. A musician and poet, Luther composed literally hundreds of hymns, thus establishing the Protestant tradition of hymn singing in church. Through music and the popular word, Luther's thought had a widespread and profound influence.

While Luther embraced the doctrine of the freedom of conscience to interpret the Bible—confident that the Bible clearly supported his views—other reformers, using the same principle, held very different positions with similar certainty. For more than ten centuries the holy book of the Christian faith had been protected by authoritative commentaries on key words and phrases. And now Luther proclaimed a doctrine of interpretation that, contrary to his intention, encouraged religious anarchy.

John Calvin   Next to the Lutherans the single most important Protestant group were the Calvinists. John Calvin (1509–1564), a Frenchman, came to Geneva in Switzerland after the city had already converted from Catholicism; after 1540 under his able direction the city became the center of that variety of Protestantism bearing his name. A second-generation reformer, Calvin believed with Luther in God's predestination of the human soul either to heaven or to hell and in the uselessness of man's good works for salvation. But whereas Luther's preoccupation had been with the salvation of the sinner and its consequences for the individual, Calvin focused on the duty of the "elect" to glorify God in all their actions as instruments of God's work. The result of the difference was that, while Lutherans stressed the need of the saved to live as Christians in their daily life, the Calvinists viewed themselves as charged with responsibility to reform society so as to make it acceptable in the Lord's eyes. As exemplified in Geneva, Calvinism was against taverns, whorehouses, elaborate clothing, and any form of behavior that would detract from God's glory. For the same reason Calvinists proved much more active missionaries than did Lutherans. Moreover, although Calvin himself was politically conservative, his followers were born revolutionaries in countries where rulers were not Calvinists. After the founder's death, Calvinism was rapidly diffused in France and England as well as in Eastern Europe, especially Poland.

There is no place here to discuss the multitude of more radical Protestant sects that sprang up in the sixteenth century along with Lutheranism and Calvinism. Suffice it to say that throughout the century Catholics and Protestants, conservative Protestants and radical Protestants, tortured and killed one another in the name of their religious convictions. Religious toleration would come in the next century only because most of the European population was tired of civil wars and of anarchy created by religious struggles.

Cultural Relativism and Scepticism

Surely part of the reason for the massive participation of Europeans in the religious wars of the sixteenth century can be traced to the economic development of the subcontinent in that century and to the enormous population increases. The only previous European-wide religious phenomenon to match it was that of the Crusades in the twelfth and thirteenth centuries, the last great age of general economic boom and population in-

crease. As in the earlier case, the vigor felt in the expanding society of the sixteenth century found an outlet to an extent in religious warfare, this time within Europe itself.

Economic Expansion The causes of the economic expansion were various. Certainly the population increase itself was a major factor. But one element that cannot be discounted was the enormous increase in bullion stocks, which multiplied the currency of Europe, causing a price rise and stimulating production. From the early fourteenth century the Spanish and the Portuguese had been exploring the coast of Africa. By the end of the fifteenth century they managed to round the dangerous Cape of Good Hope and establish contact with the Far East. By the second half of that century significant supplies of gold were being imported into Europe from the gold mines south of the Sahara.

Through the voyages of Christopher Columbus from 1492 on, the crown of Castille laid claim to a whole new world beyond the Atlantic Ocean. In the sixteenth century the New World provided an almost unlimited stream of precious metals for Europe, raising prices and fueling the economy. Both agricultural and industrial production expanded. While most of the industrial goods were still produced in homes and small shops, an increasing number of people were involved in their manufacture. In a few areas like paper, glass, and cannon making, the mining of coal, ship building, and printing, there was significant investment made in the modes of production. The forerunners of modern factories were constructed.

The new discoveries in Africa, Asia, and the Americas had profound cultural as well as economic effects on Europeans. Contact with different systems of religion, thought, government, and new customs challenged their view of what was "natural" to human nature. In a word, exploration encouraged cultural relativism.

Montaigne The writings of one of the great minds of the late sixteenth century show the effects both of the geographical discoveries and of the religious wars. Michel de Montaigne (1533–1592) came to doubt not only the possibility of establishing any certitude in re-

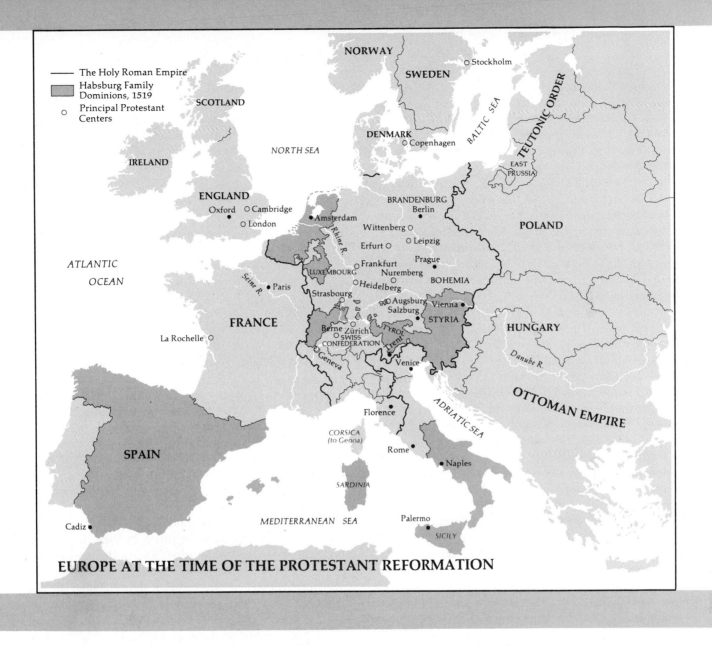

EUROPE AT THE TIME OF THE PROTESTANT REFORMATION

Map legend:
— The Holy Roman Empire
▨ Habsburg Family Dominions, 1519
○ Principal Protestant Centers

ligion, but also the power of reason to establish laws of nature and society in the world. He was one of the few thinkers in history up to his time who seriously raised the question *What do I know?*

Son of a Catholic father and a Protestant-Jewish mother, Montaigne served for a time as the mayor of the modest French city of Bordeaux, but he preferred to remain away from the centers of power. His favorite place for his major activities—reading, writing, and thinking—was his book-lined study located in a tower.

There, he not only read and commented on classical philosophers but also, in a more modern vein, looked inward in an attempt to understand himself. This he did, not because he considered himself an exceptional individual, but because he thought that an understanding of oneself could lead to an understanding of the human predicament. He certainly had no intention of establishing laws for human beings. Reason could not do that; men were each one different from the other. But, at least by the last years of his life, he came to believe that nature through pain and pleasure gives us some guidance in the conduct of our lives. While he relished his own peculiarities, he felt a kinship with other humans and a need to communicate his thoughts to them: "Every man bears the whole form of the human condition."

Montaigne called his writings essays, meaning "trials" or "experiences." He does not claim to impose a lesson but rather to invite the reader to participate in his "tryouts," his observations, his experiences. The essays might be called the journal of a man seeking wisdom. Although each one has a definite subject, Montaigne does not hesitate to go off on tangents when his reflections so lead him. The subjects he chooses may be philosophical, personal, or social. His essay on cannibals, most of which is reprinted below, represents one of his most daring social criticisms. He uses a society from a newly discovered land—in this case Indians in Brazil—to comment on the false sense of moral superiority in his own countrymen, or in Europeans in general. The theme of the "noble savage" (contrasted with decadent and corrupt "civilized" human beings) will become, as we will see, an even more popular theme in the eighteenth century. Montaigne was one of the first Europeans to understand and portray the cultural relativism that the new travels and discoveries made possible.

Montaigne's *Essays* were translated into English in 1603 by an Englishman of Italian extraction named John Florio. They were then widely read in England, most notably by Shakespeare, who quoted from them in at least one of his plays. Florio's English has the robust, somewhat rambling quality of Montaigne's French. It is essentially the English of Shakespeare and the King James Bible. The translation of the selection below is mostly Florio's, with spelling modernized and a few phrases simplified.

MICHEL DE MONTAIGNE

Of Cannibals

When King Pyrrhus came into Italy, after he had surveyed the marshalling of the army which the Romans sent against him, he said: "I know not what barbarous men these are" (for so the Greeks called all foreign na-

tions) "but the disposition of this army, which I see, is nothing barbarous." . . . Thus should a man take heed, lest he follow vulgar opinions, which should be measured by the rule of reason, and not by the common report. I have had for a long time dwelling with me a man, who for the space of ten or twelve years had dwelt in that other world, which in our age was lately discovered in those parts where Villegaignon first landed, and surnamed Antarctic France.[1] The discovery of so infinite and vast a country seems worthy of great consideration. . . .[2]

This servant I had was a simple and rough-hewn fellow, a condition fit to yield a true testimony. For subtle people may indeed . . . observe things more exactly, but they amplify and gloss them, the better to persuade . . . they never represent things truly, but fashion and mask them according to the visage they saw them in. . . . I would have every man write what he knows, and no more. . . .

Now (to return to my purpose) I find (as far as I have been informed) there is nothing in that nation, that is either barbarous or savage, unless men call that barbarism which is not common to them. As indeed, we have no other measure of truth and reason, than the example and idea of the opinions and customs of the country we live in. There is ever the perfect religion, the perfect government, perfect and complete customs in all things. We call people savage, as we call fruits wild, which nature has produced by herself. Indeed, however, we should rather term savage those which we ourselves have altered by our artificial devices and diverted from their common order. In the former are the true and most profitable virtues, and natural properties most lively and vigorous, which in the latter we have bastardized, applying them to the pleasure of our corrupted taste. And if notwithstanding we find that the fruits of those lands that were never tilled are still more excellent, compared to ours, there is no reason why art should win the point of honor over our great and powerful mother nature. We have so much by our inventions surcharged the beauties and riches of her works

---

[1] Villegaignon landed in Brazil in 1557.

[2] In the passage omitted here, Montaigne recounts Plato's account of the "lost continent," Atlantis, and wonders if the "new world" could once have been connected with the old.

that we have altogether overchoked her: yet wherever her purity shines, she makes our vain and frivolous enterprises wonderfully ashamed. . . . All our endeavor or wit cannot so much as represent the nest of the least little bird, its contexture, beauty, profit and use, nor even the web of a frail spider. "All things" (says Plato) "are produced, either by nature, by fortune, or by art. The greatest and fairest by one or other of the two first, the least and imperfect by the last."

Those nations therefore seem to me barbarous thus: they have received very little fashioning from human ingenuity, and are yet near their original natural state. The laws of nature do yet command them, but little bastardized by ours, and that with such purity, that I am sometimes grieved that the knowledge of it no sooner came to light, when men better than we could have judged of it. I am sorry that Lycurgus and Plato had it not, for it seems to me that what in those nations we see by experience . . . exceeds all the pictures with which poetry has embellished the golden age. . . . They could not imagine a genuineness so pure and simple as we see by experience, nor ever believe our society might be maintained by so little art and human combination. It is a nation, I would answer Plato, that has no kind of traffic, no knowledge of letters, no intelligence of numbers, no name of magistrate, nor of political superiority, no use of service, of riches or of poverty; no contracts, no successions, no partitions, no occupation but idle, no kinship but common, no apparel but natural, no manuring of lands, no use of wine, corn or metal. The very words that import lying, falsehood, treason, dissimulations, covetousness, envy, belittling and pardon were never heard of amongst them. How different would he find his imaginary commonwealth from this perfection: *Men but recently born of the gods.*[3]

Furthermore, they live in a country of so exceeding pleasant and temperate situation, that as my testimonies have told me, it is very rare to see a sick body amongst them; and they have further assured me they never saw any man there, either shaking with the palsy, toothless, with eyes dropping, or crooked and stooped with age. They are situated along the sea

coast. . . . They have great abundance of fish and flesh, that have no resemblance at all with ours, and eat them without any sauces, or skill of cookery, but plain boiled or broiled. The first man that brought a horse thither, although he had in many other voyages conversed with them, bred so great a horror in the land, that before they could take notice of him, they slew him with arrows. . . . They spend the whole day dancing. Their young men go hunting after wild beasts with bows and arrows. Their women busy themselves meanwhile with warming their drink—that is their main occupation. Some of their old men, in the morning before they go to eat, preach in common to all the household, walking from one end of the house to the other, repeating the same sentence many times . . . . The preacher commends but two things to his listeners: first, courage against their enemies, and second, lovingness to their wives. . . . They are shaven all over, much closer and cleaner than we are, with no other razors than of wood and stone. They believe their souls to be eternal, and those that have deserved well of their gods to be placed in that part of heaven where the sun rises, and the cursed ones toward the west. They have certain prophets and priests which normally live in the mountains and very seldom show themselves to the people. When they do come down, a great feast is prepared . . . . The prophet speaks to the people in public, exhorting them to embrace virtue and follow their duty. All their moral discipline contains but these two articles: first an undaunting resolution in war, and second an inviolable affection to their wives. . . .

They war against the nations that lie beyond their mountains, to which they go naked, having no other weapons than bows, or wooden swords, sharp at one end as our broaches are. It is an admirable thing to see the constant resolution of their combats, which never end but by effusion of blood and murder, for they know not what fear and routs are. Every victor brings home the head of the enemy he has slain as a trophy of his victory, and fastens it to the entrance of his dwelling. After they have treated their prisoners well for a long time, with all commodities, the master of them summons together a great assembly of his acquaintance, ties a cord to one of the prisoner's arms, by the end of which he holds him fast, though at some distance, for fear of being hurt. He then gives the other

---

[3] Seneca, *Epistles,* XC, 44. Montaigne uses many classical quotations in this essay (as in his others), some of which are omitted here.

arm, bound in like manner, to his dearest friend, and both in the presence of all the assembly kill him with swords. This done, they roast and then eat him in common, and send some slices of him to their friends who are absent. It is not, as some imagine, to nourish themselves with it (as anciently the Scythians[4] used to do), but to represent an extreme revenge. We can prove it thus: some of them saw the Portuguese, who had allied themselves with their adversaries, use another kind of death when they took them prisoners, which was to bury them up to the middle, and shoot arrows against the upper part of the body, and then when they were almost dead to hang them. They supposed that these people of the other world, they who had sowed the knowledge of many vices among their neighbors, and were much more cunning in all kinds of evil and mischief, did not undertake this manner of revenge without cause, and that consequently it was more painful and cruel than theirs. Thereupon they began to leave their old fashion to follow this one.

I am not sorry that we note the barbarous horror of such an action, but grieved that in prying so narrowly into their faults we are so blinded in ours. I think there is more barbarism in eating men alive than to feed upon them being dead; to mangle by tortures and torments a body full of lively sense, to roast him in pieces, to make dogs and swine gnaw and tear him (as we have not only read, but seen very recently, not among ancient enemies, but among our neighbors and fellow citizens, and what is worse, under the pretext of piety and religion[5]) than to roast and eat him after he is dead. Chrysippus and Zeno, arch-pillars of the Stoic sect, thought that there was no harm at all, in time of need, to make use of our carrion bodies, and to feed upon them, as did our forefathers, who being besieged by Caesar in the City of Alexia, resolved to sustain the famine of the siege with the bodies of old men, women, and other persons unserviceable and unfit to fight.

> Gascons (as fame reports)
> Liv'd with meats of such sorts.[6]

---

[4] An ancient, nomadic, and warlike people who lived in southeastern Europe and Asia.
[5] Montaigne refers here to the tortures inflicted by both Protestants and Catholics on their enemies.
[6] Juvenal, *Satires*, XV, 93–94. The Gascons were a people of southwestern France (Montaigne's own region).

. . . We may then well call these people barbarous in respect to the rules of reason, but not in respect to ourselves, who exceed them in all kinds of barbarism.

Their wars are noble and generous, and have as much excuse and as much beauty as this human infirmity can: they aim at nothing but rivalry in valor. They do not contend for the gaining of new lands, for to this day they still enjoy that natural abundance and fruitfulness which without laboring toil furnishes them in plenteous abundance with all necessary things so that they need not enlarge their limits. They are still in that happy state of desiring no more than their natural necessities: anything beyond is superfluous to them.

Those that are about the same age call each other brethren, those that are younger are called children, and the aged are esteemed as fathers to the rest. They leave full possession of goods in common, without division, to their heirs, and no other claim or title but that which nature gives to all creatures as she brings them into the world.

If their neighbors chance to come over the mountains to invade them and are victorious over them, the victors' conquest is glory and the advantage to be and remain superior in valor and virtue. Otherwise, they have nothing to do with the goods and spoils of the vanquished, and so return to their country where they are not lacking in any necessary thing, and know how to enjoy their condition happily and be content with what nature supplies them. The others do the same when their turn comes. They require no other ransom of their prisoners but an acknowledgement and confession that they are vanquished. But it is impossible to find one in a whole century who would not rather embrace death than either by word or countenance yield one jot from the grandeur of an invincible courage. There is not one who would not rather be slain and devoured than to beg for his life or show any fear. . . .

The reputation and worth of a man consists in his heart and will: therein lies true honor. Valor is in the strength, not of arms and legs, but of mind and courage; not in the spirit and courage of our horse, nor of our arms, but in our own. He who falls persistent in his courage, "If he slip or fall, he fights upon his knee."[7]

---

[7] Seneca, *On Providence*, II.

He who, in danger of imminent death, is in no way daunted in his assuredness, he that in yielding up his ghost beholds his enemy with a scornful and fierce look, he is vanquished, not by us but by fortune; he is slain, but not conquered. The most valiant are often the most unfortunate. So are there triumphant losses that rival victories. . . .

To return to our story, the prisoners, no matter how they are dealt with, are so far from yielding that during the two or three months they are kept they always keep cheerful and urge and defy their keepers to hasten their trial. They upbraid them with their cowardliness and with the number of battles they have lost. I have a song made by a prisoner which contains this clause: "Let them boldly come together and flock in multitudes to feed on him; for with him they shall feed upon their fathers and grandfathers that heretofore have served his body for food and nourishment. These muscles, this flesh, these veins, are your own, fools that you are, know you not that the substance of your forefathers' limbs is still tied to ours? Taste them well, for in them you shall find the relish of your own flesh." This is an invention that shows no barbarism. Those who describe them dying say that when they are put to execution, the prisoners spit in their executioners' faces and scowl at them. Truly, as long as breath is in their body, they never cease to brave and defy them, both in speech and countenance. Surely, in respect to us these are very savage men, for either they must be so or we must be so. There is a wondrous difference between their style and ours.

Their men have many wives; the more valiant they are reputed to be, the greater the number. The manner and beauty of their marriages is wondrously strange and remarkable. Just as our wives jealously try to keep us from the love and affection of other women, their try to obtain it. Being more concerned for their husbands' honor than for anything else, they endeavor to have as many rivals as they possibly can, since that is a testimony to their husbands' valor. Our women would count it a wonder, but it is not so. It is a properly matrimonial virtue, of the highest kind. In the Bible, Leah, Rachel, Sarah, and Jacob's wives brought their fairest maid servants to their husbands' beds. . . . And lest anyone should think that this is done out of simple and servile duty to custom, . . . or because they are so block-

ish and dull spirited . . . I must cite an example of their abilities. Besides what I have said of one of their war songs, I have a love song which begins like this: "Adder stay, stay good adder, that my sister may by the pattern of thy many-colored coat draw the fashion and work of a rich lace for me to give unto my love; so may thy beauty, thy nimbleness and disposition be ever preferred before all other serpents." The first couplet is the refrain of the song. I am familiar enough with poetry that I may judge that this invention has no barbarism at all in it, but is altogether Anacreontic.[8] Their language is a kind of pleasant speech, and has a pleasing sound, and some affinity with Greek in its endings.

Three of that nation, ignorant of how costly the knowledge of our corruptions will one day be to their repose, security and happiness, and how their ruin shall proceed from this commerce, which I imagine is already well advanced (miserable as they are to have let themselves be so deceived by a desire for new-fangled novelties and to have left the calmness of their climate to come and see ours) were at Rouen at the time of our late King Charles the ninth[9] who talked with them a great while. They were shown our fashions, our pomp, and the way a beautiful city looks. Afterwards, some demanded their opinion, and wished to know of them what noteworthy and admirable things they had observed among us. They answered three things, the last of which I have forgotten, and am very sorry for it, the other two I yet remember. They said that first they found it very strange that so many tall men with long beards, strong and well armed, around the person of the king (very likely they meant his Swiss guards) would submit themselves to obey a beardless child, and they wondered why we did not rather choose one among them to command the rest. Secondly, (they have a way of speaking whereby they call men "halves" of one another) they had perceived that there were men among us full gorged with all sorts of commodities, and others which hunger-starved, and bare with need and poverty, begged at their gates, and they found it strange that these needy "halves" could endure such an injustice,

---

[8] Anacreon was a Greek lyric poet who lived about a century later than Sappho.
[9] King Charles IX was only about twelve years old at the time.

and that they did not take the others by the throat or set fire to their houses.

I talked a good while with one of them but had such a bad interpreter who understood my meaning so badly and was so foolish in his conceptions of my ideas, that I did not learn a great deal from him. When I asked him what good he received from the superior position he had among his countrymen (for he was a captain and our sailors called him king) he told me that it was to march foremost in any war charge. When I asked him how many men followed him, he showed me a space of ground to signify as many as might be contained there which I guessed to be about four or five thousand men. Moreover, I asked, when all wars were ended, did his authority expire? He answered that only this much was left, that when he visited the villages dependent on him, the inhabitants prepared paths across the hedges of their woods for him to pass through at ease. All this is not very bad, but what of that? They wear no kind of breeches nor hose.

QUESTIONS AND COMMENTS

1. What does Montaigne seem to mean by "nature"? Would a modern anthropologist agree with his observations on people in a "natural" state?

2. Montaigne uses a great deal of irony in contrasting the cannibals' "natural" state with the European "civilized" one. Point out some specific examples of irony.

3. What criticisms, implicit and explicit, does Montaigne make of his own culture? How does he convince the reader that cannibalism is a relative value rather than an absolute "barbarous" evil?

4. What seem to be Montaigne's positive values? His views on morality and religion? Would you call Montaigne a humanist?

5. Montaigne's references to Greek and Roman events or thinkers often have the effect of allying the ancients with the Brazilian Indians against modern Europeans, to the detriment of the latter. Show how this is done. Why would this be an effective technique for Montaigne's readers?

6. What is the impact of the last sentence of the essay?

7. Is the main subject of the essay really the cannibals? What would you say it is?

8. With Montaigne, we have obviously come a long way from Pico della Mirandola and Erasmus, with their faith in the achievements and potential of man in general and of European culture in particular. What specific differences can you point out between Montaigne and these earlier thinkers?

13

Shakespeare and the Late Renaissance

The world of Montaigne, fraught with religious dissension, stimulated and enlarged by travels and discoveries, was also fundamentally the world of Shakespeare, though England under the reign of Queen Elizabeth I had a dynamic culture very much its own. More has been written about Shakespeare than about any other writer, and with good reason. The universality of his genius is such that it is difficult not to fall into what Bernard Shaw called "bardolatry" when discussing him. There are writers whose works are more unified, more even, certainly more "classical" than Shakespeare's; but the dramatic power, the philosophical depth, and the superb characterization in Shakespeare's major plays have never been equaled. For English-speaking people, the way in which his poetry has enriched and amplified our language assures his place in our cultural roots. His language may seem difficult to us today; but, as we read Shakespeare, we become aware of his enormous impact on our everyday speech and writing.

While Shakespeare remains a writer for all times, he was also very much a man of his time. Many of the cultural and intellectual trends that we have seen developing throughout the Renaissance are synthesized in this playwright of Elizabethan England. He shares Montaigne's skeptical and relativistic view of the human condition, and he often displays a deep pessimism and doubt that would have been impossible under the more unified, God-centered culture of the Middle Ages. Yet he had also been influenced by the earlier humanists' glorification of human beings. This passage from one of Hamlet's soliloquies illustrates the two tendencies:

> What a piece of work is a man! how noble in reason! how infinite in faculty! in form and moving how express and admirable! in action how like an angel! in apprehension how like a god! the beauty of the world! the paragon of animals! And yet, to me, what is this quintessence of dust? Man delights not me.

Compare this portrayal of man to that in the passage from *Antigone* that we quoted in Chapter 3 and from Pico della Mirandola in Chapter 9. The whole span of Renaissance-Reformation culture is found in Shakespeare: the early humanistic confidence in human powers, bolstered by the revival of classical texts, and the doubt, deepened by the Reformation, that man's endeavors amounted to very much at all.

Shakespeare's Sonnets

Shakespeare's vision of the human condition may be approached through his collection of 142 sonnets. In the wake of Petrarch (see p. 289) and the school of poets influenced by him in France, sonnet-writing came into vogue in England during the sixteenth century. Many of these "sonneteers," as they were called, wrote in a derivative manner, writing sterile imitations of love poems to imaginary golden-haired ladies resembling Laura. In Shakespeare's hands, however, the sonnet became an original and vital English form. Not only did he ridicule the conventional Petrarchan lover in his sonnets, proposing another, more earthly vision of love for a "dark lady" instead of an elusive blonde; he also

used the sonnet form for meditations of a philosophical nature, most notably on the passage of time. The first two sonnets reprinted here are two such meditations on time; the third is a meditation on love and lust; and the fourth, an anti-Petrarchan sonnet using a series of comparisons to describe his ladylove. In reading these sonnets, compare Shakespeare's rhyme scheme and his use of the octave and the sestet to those of Petrarch.

15

When I consider everything that grows
Holds in perfection but a little moment,
That this huge stage presenteth nought but shows
Whereon the stars in secret influence comment;
When I perceive that men as plants increase,   5
Cheerèd and checked even by the selfsame sky,
Vaunt in their youthful sap, at height decrease,
And wear their brave state out of memory;
Then the conceit of this inconstant stay
Sets you most rich in youth before my sight,   10
Where wasteful Time debateth with Decay
To change your day of youth to sullied night;
   And, all in war with Time for love of you,
   As he takes from you, I ingraft you new.

60

Like as the waves make towards the pebbled
   shore,
So do our minutes hasten to their end;
Each changing place with that which goes before,
In sequent toil all forwards do contend.
Nativity, once in the main of light,   5
Crawls to maturity, wherewith being crowned,
Crookèd eclipses 'gainst his glory fight,
And Time that gave doth now his gift confound.
Time doth transfix the flourish set on youth
And delves the parallels in beauty's brow,   10
Feeds on the rarities of nature's truth,
And nothing stands but for his scythe to mow;
   And yet to times in hope my verse shall stand,
Praising thy worth, despite his cruel hand.

129

Th' expense of spirit in a waste of shame
Is lust in action; and, till action, lust
Is perjured, murd'rous, bloody, full of blame,

Savage, extreme, rude, cruel, not to trust;
Enjoyed no sooner but despisèd straight;   5
Past reason hunted, and no sooner had,
Past reason hated, as a swallowed bait
On purpose laid to make the taker mad;
Mad in pursuit, and in possession so;
Had, having, and in quest to have, extreme;   10
A bliss in proof—and proved, a very woe;
Before, a joy proposed; behind, a dream.
   All this the world well knows; yet none knows
     well
   To shun the heaven that leads men to this hell.

130

My mistress' eyes are nothing like the sun;
Coral is far more red than her lips' red;
If snow be white, why then her breasts are dun;
If hairs be wires, black wires grow on her head.
I have seen roses damasked, red and white,   5
But no such roses see I in her cheeks;
And in some perfumes is there more delight
Than in the breath that from my mistress reeks.
I love to hear her speak, yet well I know
That music hath a far more pleasing sound.   10
I grant I never saw a goddess go:
My mistress when she walks treads on the
    ground;
   And yet by heaven I think my love as rare
   As any she belied with false compare.

QUESTIONS

1. What concept of time does Shakespeare express in these sonnets? How is it conveyed poetically?
2. How do paradox and contradiction function in Sonnet 129? What is its subject?
3. In what respects is Sonnet 130 anti-Petrarchan? (See p. 289.)

Shakespeare and the Theater

It is, of course, because of his plays that Shakespeare is now considered the greatest English writer in history. The era in which he lived, Elizabethan England, was a time in which broad interests and creativity could flourish. Although Elizabeth, the Protestant daughter of Henry VIII, came to the throne when there was great rivalry between Protestant and Catholic factions, she was beloved by her subjects and proved to be a powerful and able ruler. Under the reign of Elizabeth, England changed from an island kingdom to an expanding empire that controlled the seas after the naval defeat of the greatest European power, Spain. England grew rich through trade. Sixteenth-century Englishmen traveled to the New World and to Africa. Music, dance, poetry, painting, and architecture flourished; but the art form in which Elizabethan England surpassed the rest of Europe (except perhaps Spain) was the theater.

In order to understand the development of this theater, we should go back for a moment to the discussion of medieval drama. There we saw that the theater, which had practically disappeared from Europe after the Roman empire, was revived as a part of the church service. As the plays representing stories from the Bible grew more elaborate, they moved to the exterior of the church. No longer a part of the service, the "mystery plays," as they were called, responded to popular taste by adding more and more comical elements, often gross ones. In England these were sponsored by various trade guilds and presented on stage-wagons that went from place to place. When the mystery plays began to lose their appeal, they were replaced by "morality" plays that had allegorical characters (such as Fellowship, Good Deeds, Beauty, Death) and always taught a moral. The best of these, *Everyman*, shows man preparing himself for death and God's judgment. Farces and clowning of various sorts continued alongside this more serious theater. In Italy these grew into the *commedia dell'arte*, an improvisational form with stock characters that would greatly influence the development of modern comedy.

The impact of the humanist resurrection of classical texts on the theater was great. Humanists in Italy translated Latin and Greek plays; then they wrote their own tragedies and comedies in the classical manner, first in Latin and, by the sixteenth century, in Italian. French, German, and Spanish writers turned to the classical models. In England schools and universities began to produce comedies and tragedies by Plautus, Terence, and Seneca. In spite of a contemporary's remark that Shakespeare knew "a little Latin and less Greek," he was well grounded in the classical humanities through his own reading as well as through formal education. Certainly he knew the Roman tragedies of Seneca and the comedies of Plautus, which served as models for his own drama. In characteristic Renaissance fashion, his interests ranged beyond book learning to practical knowledge of military strategy, seafaring, business affairs, and the new geographical discoveries, all evident in his plays.

Writers associated with the universities in England began to write plays in English that combined classical and medieval, Roman and English elements. Companies of "strolling players" who had specialized in morality plays began to stage the new plays. Professional actors, who had been viewed by English society as little better than vagrants or criminals, gradually came under the protection of the nobility. Licensed theater companies were formed; Shakespeare belonged to one of these, where in addition to his writing, he acquired a wide experience in acting and theater management.

The theater grew in popularity, despite disapproval by the Puritans and others. Public theaters were built, not inside the city limits but just outside, along with the brothels, taverns, and other places of entertainment. Theaters in Elizabethan England, like theaters in ancient Greece, were patronized by all social classes. The Globe Theatre, built in 1599, where many of Shakespeare's plays were performed, had a platform stage jutting out into a central courtyard. The audience sat around three sides of this platform—the lower-class people (who each paid a penny) in the "pit" and the wealthier spectators in the galleries above. The orchestra was on stage, as music was usually a significant part of the production. It is important to keep in mind as one reads the script that the *spectacle*—the costumes, scenery, singing, playing, and dancing, as well as the acting—was (and of course still is) essential to the total show. There was no lighting, however; plays were performed in the afternoon. Shakespeare knew his audience: his theater is addressed not just to the elite and educated but to all segments of society.

Shakespeare's plays have been classified in four categories: comedies, histories, tragedies, and romances. None of these are "pure" forms. The tragedies, for example, nearly all contain elements of history and comedy. We will concentrate here on Shakespeare's use of

the tragic form in one of his major works, *Othello, the Moor of Venice*, first produced in 1604.

Tragedy in the Renaissance   One question often asked by literary historians is: what permitted tragedy, a dead form in the Middle Ages, to revive in the Renaissance? In the scheme of Judeo-Christian values, tragedy is hardly possible. The story of Adam and Eve's fall is basically tragic, but the believer sees it as part of a greater whole, a promise of redemption. Isaac's sacrifice is almost tragic, but Jahweh intervenes just in time. The passion of Jesus would be tragic without the knowledge of God's design. The literary work closest to tragedy in the Bible is the Book of Job, but it was amended by later authors to have a happy ending. *The Play of Daniel* is typical of medieval art: it portrays a near catastrophe that is averted by the power of God. It is not by accident that the greatest literary work of the Middle Ages was called *The Divine Comedy*. It is a "comedy" not because it is funny but because it ends in happiness, in fact in paradise.

Renaissance culture, as we have seen, remained basically Christian; but, with the revival of Greco-Roman elements, one often perceives in it a tension between the two sets of values. Shakespeare, for example, refers to Christian doctrines and symbols but at times almost seems to believe in something like the classical Fate. In any case, he was able to write of the fall of his heroes without reference to their possible redemption. *Othello*, while it contains references to religion, takes place in a secular scheme of things. Some commentators have argued that Shakespeare was without any religious belief, or at least was as skeptical toward religion as was Montaigne. His audience, in a theater freed from attachment to the Church, accepted non-Christian tragedy.

The sources of Shakespeare's plays range from classical history to contemporary romances. Like the Greek dramatists, he did not make up the basic plots himself but shaped those he found for his own purposes. The source that he used for *Othello* is a rather badly told tale by an Italian writer named Cinthio. Because Renaissance Italy interested Shakespeare greatly, as it did his countrymen, many of his plays are set there. *Othello* had an even more exotic element for the English audience: a black man as its hero. To understand the background of the tragedy, it will be helpful to know something about Venice and about Moors.

Venice   Venice was an independent Italian city-state that reached the height of its power in the fifteenth century. It was ruled by a duke *(doge)* with a senate. Its colonies included Crete, the Dalmatian coast (now part of Yugoslavia), and the island of Cyprus, in which most of *Othello* is set. The Venetians were frequently at war with the Turks, who finally captured their colonies. Venice as a trade center was full of people from faraway lands; it was a center of culture as well, especially noted for its painting. Italy, and Venice in particular, seemed to Englishmen a place of luxuriousness, corruption, and subtle political intrigue. It is no surprise that Iago, the most intelligent and the most evil of Shakespeare's villains, is a Venetian.

Europeans and Blacks   Renaissance Europeans called the people of North Africa "tawny Moors" and the people of sub-Saharan Africa "black Moors." Othello is clearly one of the latter. By the time Shakespeare wrote his tragedy, black people were not uncommon on the streets of London. Several Englishmen had been to Africa; various European travel accounts had found their way to England. Most of these are a mixture of fantasy and reality. There are tales of "headless men," descriptions of the legendary kingdom of Prester John, and what seem to be fairly accurate accounts of the splendor of the court of Benin (see Chapter 14). Some of the stereotypes that would inflame prejudices are present in these accounts: black Moors, or Negroes, were said to be "naked," "without religion," "uncivilized," "cruel." They were thought to be hot-blooded and highly sexed because they lived so near the sun. In addition, the term *black* in the English language already had strong connotations of unclean, evil, and ugly, contrasted with the pure and ideally beautiful white.[1]

These associations and stereotypes served the Elizabethan dramatists who created the Moor as something of a stage type. Usually the Moor was portrayed as a villain, lusty and cruel.[2] Cinthio, Shakespeare's source, emphasizing Othello's "hot-bloodedness" and weakness, moralizes that blacks should not marry whites.

Shakespeare's Use of Black and White   It was then something of a feat for Shakespeare, and a testimony to his genius, to present a black man as the hero of a tragedy. Playing upon his audience's preconceptions, Shakespeare makes an original, rich use of black and white symbolism throughout the play. It is the black man who is inwardly pure, and it is a seemingly honest white man (and a soldier, a type usually portrayed as genuinely honest) who is inwardly evil. The difficulty of distinguishing being from seeming is a major theme in the play, brought out in part by the black-white symbolism. The alleged supersexuality of Africans also figures in the play: Iago calls Othello the "lusty Moor," describing him with images of animal sexuality. Once again, the popular stereotype is turned around. Othello loves his Venetian wife Desdemona (though by no means platonically) with romantic devotion; Iago is totally unable to understand that love is not simple lust. Othello's overriding concern with sex appears only when he has been infected by Iago's "poison" (another important type of image in the play). This gradual mental and emotional poisoning of Othello by Iago is the motivating force of the tragedy.

Othello as Tragic Hero   Othello, a typical tragic figure, moves from a position of power and good fortune to a degraded state in which he can no longer endure his life. Like Oedipus he experiences a powerful revelation of truth and self-knowledge; like Oedipus he turns his own hand on himself. But the combination of fate and character that caused Oedipus' tragedy is here replaced by the combination of Othello's character and the carefully plotted malignancy carried out by Iago. *Othello*, very tightly constructed, is in many ways the most classical of Shakespeare's tragedies, yet it differs substantially from Greek tragedy.

Poetic Form   The poetic form of most of this tragedy is *blank verse*, the verse line introduced in the six-

---

[1] See Winthrop D. Jordan, *White Over Black*, (Chapel Hill; University of North Carolina Press, 1968), Chapter 1.

[2] See Eldred Jones, *Othello's Countrymen*, (London: Oxford University Press, 1965).

teenth century and still considered the most natural to the English language. It consists of unrhymed lines in *iambic pentameter*, that is, five strong stresses and five weak stresses. For example:

It is the cause, it is the cause, my soul,—
Let me not name it to you, you chaste stars!

Not all of *Othello* is in blank verse, however; Shakespeare uses prose and rhyming verse for various purposes in the play.

WILLIAM SHAKESPEARE

Othello, the Moor of Venice[1]

CHARACTERS

DUKE OF VENICE
BRABANTIO [*a senator*] *father to Desdemona*
[*Other*] *Senators*
GRATIANO [*brother to Brabantio*] ⎱ *two noble*
LODOVICO [*kinsman to Brabantio*] ⎰ *Venetians*
OTHELLO, *the Moor* [*in the military service of Venice*]
CASSIO, *an honourable lieutenant*
IAGO [*an ensign*], *a villain*
RODERIGO, *a gulled gentleman*
MONTANO, *governor of Cyprus* [*before Othello*]
CLOWN [*servant to Othello*]
DESDEMONA [*daughter to Brabantio and*] *wife to Othello*
EMILIA, *wife to Iago*
BIANCA, *a courtezan*
Gentlemen of Cyprus, Sailors [*Officers, Messenger, Herald, Musicians, and Attendants*]

[SCENE: *Venice; a sea-port in Cyprus.*]

ACT ONE

SCENE 1.   [*Venice. A street.*][2]

Enter RODERIGO *and* IAGO.

RODERIGO.   [Tush]! never tell me! I take it much unkindly
That thou, Iago, who hast had my purse
As if the strings were thine, shouldst know of this.
IAGO.   ['Sblood], but you'll not hear me.
If ever I did dream of such a matter,   5
Abhor me.
RODERIGO.   Thou told'st me thou didst hold him in thy hate.
IAGO.   Despise me if I do not. Three great ones of the city,
In personal suit to make me his lieutenant,
Off-capp'd to him; and, by the faith of man,   10
I know my price; I am worth no worse a place.
But he, as loving his own pride and purposes,
Evades them with a bombast circumstance
Horribly stuff'd with epithets of war,
[And, in conclusion,]   15
Nonsuits my mediators; for, "Certes," says he,
"I have already chose my officer."
And what was he?
Forsooth, a great arithmetician,
One Michael Cassio, a Florentine,   20
(A fellow almost damn'd in a fair wife)
That never set a squadron in the field,
Nor the division of a battle knows
More than a spinster, unless the bookish theoric,
Wherein the [toged] consuls can propose   25
As masterly as he. Mere prattle without practice
Is all his soldiership. But he, sir, had th' election;
And I, of whom his eyes had seen the proof
At Rhodes, at Cyprus, and on other grounds
Christen'd and heathen, must be be-lee'd
and calm'd   30
By debitor and creditor; this counter-caster,
He, in good time, must his lieutenant be,
And I—[God] bless the mark!—his Moorship's ancient.

[1] "The text of the present edition [of *Othello*] is based upon the Folio [1623], with deference to the Quarto [1622] where a better reading can be supplied." In the notes, passages from the Folio are designated with a capital F, from the Quarto with a capital Q.
   Lines have been renumbered for this volume.
[2] "Stage directions, if modern, are enclosed in [brackets]; when they are substantially those of editions not later than 1623, they are unbracketed, or are set aside by a single bracket only, or, when occurring within a line, are enclosed in (parentheses)." (Neilson and Hill, p. v.)

Act I, Scene i, line 1. [*Tush*] Q. Omitted in F.
3. *this:* Desdemona's elopement.   4. [*'Sblood*] Q. Om. F. Profane exclamations in brackets, such as this and that in I.i.33, were ommited in F on account of the Act of 1605 against swearing. Frequently *Heaven* was substituted for *God.*   13. *circumstance:* discourse.   15. [*And . . . conclusion*] Q. Om F.   23. *division:* array.   25. [*toged*] Q. wearing a toga. *tongued* F.   31. *counter-caster:* accountant.   33. [God] Q. Om. F.

RODERIGO. By heaven, I rather would have been his
   hangman.
IAGO. Why, there's no remedy. 'Tis the curse of
   service,   35
   Preferment goes by letter and affection,
   And not by old gradation, where each second
   Stood heir to th' first. Now, sir, be judge yourself
   Whether I in any just term am affin'd
   To love the Moor.
RODERIGO. I would not follow him then.   40
IAGO. O, sir, content you;
   I follow him to serve my turn upon him.
   We cannot all be masters, nor all masters
   Cannot be truly follow'd. You shall mark
   Many a duteous and knee-crooking knave   45
   That, doting on his own obsequious bondage,
   Wears out his time, much like his master's ass,
   For nought but provender, and when he's old,
      cashier'd.
   Whip me such honest knaves. Others there are
   Who, trimm'd in forms and visages of duty,   50
   Keep yet their hearts attending on themselves,
   And, throwing but shows of service on their lords,
   Do well thrive by them and, when they have lin'd
      their coats,
   Do themselves homage. These fellows have some
      soul;
   And such a one do I profess myself. For, sir,   55
   It is as sure as you are Roderigo,
   Were I the Moor, I would not be Iago.
   In following him, I follow but myself;
   Heaven is my judge, not I for love and duty,
   But seeming so, for my peculiar end;   60
   For when my outward action doth demonstrate
   The native act and figure of my heart
   In compliment extern, 'tis not long after
   But I will wear my heart upon my sleeve
   For daws to peck at. I am not what I am.   65
RODERIGO. What a full fortune does the thick-lips
   owe,

If he can carry't thus!
IAGO. Call up her father,
   Rouse him. Make after him, poison his delight,
   Proclaim him in the streets. Incense her kinsmen,
   And, though he in a fertile climate dwell,   70
   Plague him with flies. Though that his joy be joy,
   Yet throw such [changes] of vexation on't,
   As it may lose some colour.
RODERIGO. Here is her father's house; I'll call aloud.
IAGO. Do, with like timorous accent and dire
      yell   75
   As when, by night and negligence, the fire
   Is spied in populous cities.
RODERIGO. What, ho, Brabantio! Signior Brabantio,
   ho!
IAGO. Awake! what, ho, Brabantio! thieves! thieves!
   Look to your house, your daughter, and your
      bags!   80
   Thieves! thieves!

   BRABANTIO [*appears*] *above, at a window.*

BRABANTIO. What is the reason of this terrible sum-
   mons?
   What is the matter there?
RODERIGO. Signior, is all your family within?
IAGO. Are your doors lock'd?
BRABANTIO. Why, wherefore ask you this?   85
IAGO. ['Zounds], sir, you're robb'd! For shame, put on
   your gown.
   Your heart is burst, you have lost half your soul;
   Even now, now, very now, an old black ram
   Is tupping your white ewe. Arise, arise!
   Awake the snorting citizens with the bell,   90
   Or else the devil will make a grandsire of you.
   Arise, I say!
BRABANTIO. What, have you lost your wits?
RODERIGO. Most reverend signior, do you know my
   voice?
BRABANTIO. Not I. What are you?
RODERIGO. My name is Roderigo.
BRABANTIO. The worser welcome;   95
   I have charg'd thee not to haunt about my doors.

---

36. *letter:* i.e., of recommendation.   37. *old gradation:* seniority.
39. *affin'd:* bound.   48. *cashier'd:* dismissed.   50. *visages:*
semblances.   60. *peculiar:* private.   63. *compliment extern:* external show.   66. *thick-lips:* i.e., the Moor.   *owe:* own.

72. [*changes*] Q. *chances* F.   75. *timorous:* terrifying.
90. *snorting:* snoring.

In honest plainness thou hast heard me say
My daughter is not for thee; and now, in madness,
Being full of supper and distemp'ring draughts,
Upon malicious [bravery] dost thou come   100
To start my quiet.
RODERIGO. Sir, sir, sir,—
BRABANTIO. But thou must needs be sure
My spirits and my place have in their power
To make this bitter to thee.
RODERIGO. Patience, good sir.
BRABANTIO. What tell'st thou me of robbing? This is
Venice;   105
My house is not a grange.
RODERIGO. Most grave Brabantio,
In simple and pure soul I come to you.
IAGO. ['Zounds], sir, you are one of those that will not
serve God, if the devil bid you. Because we come to
do you service and you think we are ruffians, you'll
have your daughter cover'd with a Barbary horse;
you'll have your nephews neigh to you; you'll have
coursers for cousins, and gennets for germans. 112
BRABANTIO. What profane wretch art thou?
IAGO. I am one, sir, that comes to tell you your daugh-
ter and the Moor are [now] making the beast with
two backs.   115
BRABANTIO. Thou art a villain.
IAGO. You are—a senator.
BRABANTIO. This thou shalt answer; I know thee,
Roderigo.
RODERIGO. Sir, I will answer anything. But, I beseech
you,
If't be your pleasure and most wise consent,
As partly I find it is, that your fair daughter,   120
At this odd-even and dull watch o' th' night,
Transported, with no worse nor better guard
But with a knave of common hire, a gondolier,
To the gross clasps of a lascivious Moor,—
If this be known to you and your allowance,   125
We then have done you bold and saucy wrongs;
But if you know not this, my manners tell me

We have your wrong rebuke. Do not believe
That, from the sense of all civility,
I thus would play and trifle with your
reverence.   130
Your daughter, if you have not given her leave,
I say again, hath made a gross revolt,
Tying her duty, beauty, wit, and fortunes
In an extravagant and wheeling stranger
Of here and everywhere. Straight satisfy
yourself.   135
If she be in her chamber or your house,
Let loose on me the justice of the state
For thus deluding you.
BRABANTIO. Strike on the tinder, ho!
Give me a taper! Call up all my people!
This accident is not unlike my dream;   140
Belief of it oppresses me already.
Light, I say! light! [Exit [above].
IAGO. Farewell; for I must leave you.
It seems not meet, nor wholesome to my place,
To be produc'd—as, if I stay, I shall—
Against the Moor; for, I do know, the state,   145
However this may gall him with some check,
Cannot with safety cast him, for he's embark'd
With such loud reason to the Cyprus wars,
Which even now [stand] in act, that, for their souls,
Another of his fathom they have none   150
To lead their business; in which regard,
Though I do hate him as I do hell-pains,
Yet, for necessity of present life,
I must show out a flag and sign of love,
Which is indeed but sign. That you shall surely find
him,   155
Lead to the Sagittary the raised search;
And there will I be with him. So, farewell. [Exit.

Enter [below,] BRABANTIO in his night-gown, and
Servants with torches.

---

99. distemp'ring: intoxicating.   100. [bravery] Q: swaggering.
knavery F.   101. start: startle.   106. grange: isolated farm.
111. nephews: grandsons.   112. gennets: Spanish horses. germans:
relatives.   115. [now] Q. Om F.   121. odd-even: midnight.
dull: dead.   125. your allowance: has your approval.

---

129. from: contrary to.   134. extravagant: vagabond.   wheeling:
roving.   146. check: rebuke.   147. cast: dismiss.   149. [stand].
stands QF.   150. fathom: capacity.   156. Sagittary: an inn (with a
Centaur on its sign). It has also been proposed that the word is a
translation of Frezzaria, the Street of the Arrow-makers in Venice.
158. S.D. night-gown: dressing gown.

BRABANTIO.   It is too true an evil; gone she is;
   And what's to come of my despised time
   Is nought but bitterness. Now, Roderigo,   160
   Where didst thou see her? O unhappy girl!
   With the Moor, say'st thou? Who would be a father!
   How didst thou know 'twas she? O, she deceives me
   Past thought! What said she to you? Get moe tapers;
   Raise all my kindred. Are they married, think
     you?   165
RODERIGO.   Truly, I think they are.
BRABANTIO.   O heaven! How got she out? O treason of
   the blood!
   Fathers, from hence trust not your daughters' minds
   By what you see them act. Is there not charms
   By which the property of youth and
     maidhood   170
   May be abus'd? Have you not read, Roderigo,
   Of some such thing?
RODERIGO.   Yes, sir, I have indeed.
BRABANTIO.   Call up my brother.—O, would you had
   had her!—
   Some one way, some another.—Do you know
   Where we may apprehend her and the Moor?   175
RODERIGO.   I think I can discover him, if you please
   To get good guard and go along with me.
BRABANTIO.   Pray you, lead on. At every house I'll call;
   I may command at most. Get weapons, ho!
   And raise some special officers of [night].   180
   On, good Roderigo; I'll deserve your pains.

   [*Exeunt.*

SCENE 2.   [*Another street.*]

   Enter OTHELLO, IAGO, *and* Attendants *with torches.*

IAGO.   Though in the trade of war I have slain men,
   Yet do I hold it very stuff o' th' conscience
   To do no contriv'd murder. I lack iniquity
   Sometimes to do me service. Nine or ten times   4
   I'd thought to have yerk'd him here under the ribs.
OTHELLO.   'Tis better as it is.

---

170. *property:* nature.   171. *abus'd:* deceived.   180. [*night*]
Q. *might* F.   181. *deserve:* reward.

Scene ii, 5. *yerk'd:* stabbed.

IAGO.   Nay, but he prated,
   And spoke such scurvy and provoking terms
   Against your honour
   That, with the little godliness I have,
   I did full hard forbear him. But, I pray you, sir,   10
   Are you fast married? Be assur'd of this,
   That the magnifico is much belov'd,
   And hath in his effect a voice potential
   As double as the Duke's. He will divorce you,
   Or put upon you what restraint or grievance   15
   The law, with all his might to enforce it on,
   Will give him cable.
OTHELLO.   Let him do his spite;
   My services which I have done the signiory
   Shall out-tongue his complaints. 'Tis yet to know,—
   Which, when I know that boasting is an
     honour,   20
   I shall promulgate—I fetch my life and being
   From men of royal siege, and my demerits
   May speak unbonneted to as proud a fortune
   As this that I have reach'd; for know, Iago,
   But that I love the gentle Desdemona,   25
   I would not my unhoused free condition
   Put into circumscription and confine
   For the sea's worth. But, look! what lights come yond?

   Enter CASSIO, *with lights,* Officers, *and torches.*

IAGO.   Those are the raised father and his friends.
   You were best go in.
OTHELLO.   Not I; I must be found.   30
   My parts, my title, and my perfect soul
   Shall manifest me rightly. Is it they?
IAGO.   By Janus, I think no.
OTHELLO.   The servants of the Duke, and my
   lieutenant.
   The goodness of the night upon you, friends!   35
   What is the news?
CASSIO.   The Duke does greet you, general,
   And he requires your haste-post-haste appearance,
   Even on the instant.
OTHELLO.   What is the matter, think you?
CASSIO.   Something from Cyprus, as I may divine;

---

14. *double:* strong.   22. *siege:* rank.   *demerits:* deserts.   23. *unbonneted:* without taking my hat off, on equal terms.   26. *unhoused:* unconfined.   31. *perfect soul:* clear conscience.

It is a business of some heat. The galleys   40
Have sent a dozen sequent messengers
This very night at one another's heels,
And many of the consuls, rais'd and met,
Are at the Duke's already. You have been hotly call'd
  for;
When, being not at your lodging to be found,   45
The Senate hath sent about three several quests
To search you out.
OTHELLO.   'Tis well I am found by you.
  I will but spend a word here in the house.
  And go with you. [*Exit.*
CASSIO.   Ancient, what makes he here?
IAGO.   Faith, he to-night hath boarded a land
    carack.   50
  If it prove lawful prize, he's made for ever.
CASSIO.   I do not understand.
IAGO.   He's married.
CASSIO.   To who?

[*Re-enter* OTHELLO.]

IAGO.   Marry, to—Come, captain, will you go?
OTHELLO.   Have with you.
CASSIO.   Here comes another troop to seek for you.

Enter BRABANTIO, RODERIGO, *and* Officers *with torches
  and weapons.*

IAGO.   It is Brabantio. General, be advis'd;   55
  He comes to bad intent.
OTHELLO.   Holla! stand there!
RODERIGO.   Signior, it is the Moor.
BRABANTIO.   Down with him, thief!

[*They draw on both sides.*]

IAGO.   You, Roderigo! come, sir, I am for you.
OTHELLO.   Keep up your bright swords, for the dew will
    rust them.
  Good signior, you shall more command with
    years   60
  Than with your weapons.
BRABANTIO.   O thou foul thief, where hast thou stow'd
    my daughter?

Damn'd as thou art, thou hast enchanted her;
For I'll refer me to all things of sense,
If she in chains of magic were not bound,   65
Whether a maid so tender, fair, and happy,
So opposite to marriage that she shunn'd
The wealthy curled darlings of our nation,
Would ever have, t' incur a general mock,
Run from her guardage to the sooty bosom   70
Of such a thing as thou—to fear, not to delight.
Judge me the world, if 'tis not gross in sense
That thou hast practis'd on her with foul charms,
Abus'd her delicate youth with drugs or minerals
That weakens motion. I'll have 't disputed on;   75
'Tis probable, and palpable to thinking.
I therefore apprehend and do attach thee
For an abuser of the world, a practiser
Of arts inhibited and out of warrant.
Lay hold upon him; if he do resist,   80
Subdue him at his peril.
OTHELLO.   Hold your hands,
  Both you of my inclining, and the rest.
  Were it my cue to fight, I should have known it
  Without a prompter. [Where] will you that I go
  To answer this your charge?
BRABANTIO.   To prison, till fit time   85
  Of law and course of direct session
  Call thee to answer.
OTHELLO.   What if [I] do obey?
  How may the Duke be therewith satisfi'd,
  Whose messengers are here about my side
  Upon some present business of the state   90
  To bring me to him?
OFFICER.   'Tis true, most worthy signior.
  The Duke's in council; and your noble self,
  I am sure, is sent for.
BRABANTIO.   How! the Duke in council!
  In this time of the night! Bring him away;
  Mine's not an idle cause. The Duke himself,   95
  Or any of my brothers of the state,

---

40. *galleys:* i.e., officers of the galleys.
50. *carack:* large trading ship.

---

72. *gross in sense:* perfectly clear.   75. *motion:* will power.
disputed on: argued legally.   77. *attach:* arrest.   79. *inhibited:*
prohibited.   *out of warrant:* unjustifiable.   82. *inclining:*
party.   84. [*Where*] Q. *Weather* F. *Whither* F₂.   86. *course . . . session:* due course of law.   87. [*I*] Q. Om. F.

Cannot but feel this wrong as 'twere their own;
For if such actions may have passage free,
Bond-slaves and pagans shall our statesmen be.

[*Exeunt.*

SCENE 3.   [*A council-chamber.*]

The DUKE *and* SENATORS *set at a table, with lights;* Officers *attending.*

DUKE.   There is no composition in [these] news
That gives them credit.
FIRST SENATOR.   Indeed, they are disproportion'd;
My letters say a hundred and seven galleys.
DUKE.   And mine, a hundred forty.
SECOND SENATOR.   And mine, two hundred!
But though they jump not on a just account,—   5
As in these cases, where the aim reports,
'Tis oft with difference—yet do they all confirm
A Turkish fleet, and bearing up to Cyprus.
DUKE.   Nay, it is possible enough to judgement.
I do not so secure me in the error,   10
But the main article I do approve
In fearful sense.
SAILOR (*within*).   What, ho! what, ho! what, ho!

Enter a SAILOR.

OFFICER.   A messenger from the galleys.
DUKE.   Now, what's the business?
SAILOR.   The Turkish preparation makes for Rhodes;
So was I bid report here to the state   15
By Signior Angelo.
DUKE.   How say you by this change?
FIRST SENATOR.   This cannot be,
By no assay of reason; 'tis a pageant,
To keep us in false gaze. When we consider
Th' importancy of Cyprus to the Turk,   20
And let ourselves again but understand
That, as it more concerns the Turk than Rhodes,
So may he with more facile question bear it,

For that it stands not in such warlike brace,
But altogether lacks th' abilities   25
That Rhodes is dress'd in; if we make thought of this,
We must not think the Turk is so unskilful
To leave that latest which concerns him first,
Neglecting an attempt of ease and gain
To wake and wage a danger profitless.   30
DUKE.   Nay, in all confidence, he's not for Rhodes.
OFFICER.   Here is more news.

Enter a MESSENGER.

MESSENGER.   The Ottomites, reverend and gracious,
Steering with due course towards the isle of Rhodes,
Have there injointed them with an after fleet.   35
FIRST SENATOR.   Ay, so I thought. How many, as you
guess?
MESSENGER.   Of thirty sail; and now they do restem
Their backward course, bearing with frank appearance
Their purposes toward Cyprus. Signior Montano,
Your trusty and most valiant servitor,   40
With his free duty recommends you thus,
And prays you to believe him.
DUKE.   'Tis certain, then, for Cyprus.
Marcus Luccicos, is not he in town?
FIRST SENATOR.   He's now in Florence.   45
DUKE   Write from us to him; post-post-haste dispatch.
FIRST SENATOR.   Here comes Brabantio and the valiant
Moor.

Enter BRABANTIO, OTHELLO, CASSIO, IAGO,
RODERIGO, *and* Officers.

DUKE.   Valiant Othello, we must straight employ you
Against the general enemy Ottoman.
    [*To* BRABANTIO.] I did not see you; welcome, gentle signior;   50
We lack'd your counsel and your help to-night.
BRABANTIO.   So did I yours. Good your Grace, pardon
me;
Neither my place nor aught I heard of business
Hath rais'd me from my bed, nor doth the general
care
Take hold on me; for my particular grief   55

Scene iii, 1. *composition:* consistency [*these*] Q. *this* F.

5. *jump:* agree.   *just:* exact.   6. *the . . . reports:* the reports
are conjectural.   10. *so . . . error:* take such assurance from the
disagreement.   11. *approve:* assent to.   18. *pageant:* pretense.   23. *with . . . it:* capture it more easily.

24. *brace:* defense.   35. *after:* i.e., sent after.   55. *particular:* personal.

Is of so flood-gate and o'erbearing nature
That it engluts and swallows other sorrows
And it is still itself.
DUKE.   Why, what's the matter?
BRABANTIO.   My daughter! O, my daughter!
SENATOR.   Dead?
BRABANTIO.   Ay, to me;
   She is abus'd, stol'n from me, and corrupted   60
   By spells and medicines bought of mountebanks;
   For nature so prepost'rously to err,
   Being not deficient, blind, or lame of sense,
   Sans witchcraft could not.
DUKE.   Whoe'er he be that in this foul proceeding   65
   Hath thus beguil'd your daughter of herself
   And you of her, the bloody book of law
   You shall yourself read in the bitter letter
   After your own sense, yea, though our proper son
   Stood in your action.
BRABANTIO.   Humbly I thank your Grace.   70
   Here is the man,—this Moor, whom now, it seems,
   Your special mandate for the state affairs
   Hath hither brought.
ALL.   We are very sorry for't.
DUKE [to OTHELLO].   What, in your own part, can
   you say to this?
BRABANTIO.   Nothing, but this is so.   75
OTHELLO.   Most potent, grave, and reverend signiors,
   My very noble and approv'd good masters,
   That I have ta'en away this old man's daughter,
   It is most true; true, I have married her:
   The very head and front of my offending   80
Hath this extent, no more. Rude am I in my
   speech,
And little bless'd with the soft phrase of peace;
For since these arms of mine had seven years' pith
Till now, some nine moons wasted, they have us'd
Their dearest action in the tented field,   85
And little of this great world can I speak
More than pertains to feats of broils and battle,
And therefore little shall I grace my cause
In speaking for myself. Yet, by your gracious pa-
   tience,
I will a round unvarnish'd tale deliver   90

Of my whole course of love—what drugs, what
   charms,
   What conjuration, and what mighty magic,
   (For such proceeding I am charg'd withal,)
   I won his daughter.
BRABANTIO.   A maiden never bold;
   Of spirit so still and quiet that her motion   95
   Blush'd at herself; and she, in spite of nature,
   Of years, of country, credit, everything,
   To fall in love with what she fear'd to look on!
   It is a judgment maim'd and most imperfect
   That will confess perfection so could err   100
   Against all rules of nature, and must be driven
   To find out practices of cunning hell,
   Why this should be. I therefore vouch again
   That with some mixtures powerful o'er the blood,
   Or with some dram conjur'd to this effect,   105
   He wrought upon her.
[DUKE.]   To vouch this is no proof,
   Without more wider and more overt test
   Than these thin habits and poor likelihoods
   Of modern seeming do prefer against him.
[FIRST] SENATOR.   But, Othello, speak.   110
   Did you by indirect and forced courses
   Subdue and poison this young maid's affections?
   Or came it by request and such fair question
   As soul to soul affordeth?
OTHELLO.   I do beseech you,
   Send for the lady to the Sagittary,   115
   And let her speak of me before her father.
   If you do find me foul in her report,
   The trust, the office I do hold of you,
   Not only take away, but let your sentence
   Even fall upon my life.
DUKE.   Fetch Desdemona hither.   120

[Exeunt two or three.

OTHELLO.   Ancient, conduct them; you best know the
   place.

[Exit IAGO.]

And, till she come, as truly as to heaven
I do confess the vices of my blood,

---

90. round: plain.

95. motion: impulses.   106. [DUKE] Q. Om. F.
108. thin habits: slight semblances.   109. modern: ordinary, trivial.

So justly to your grave ears I'll present
How I did thrive in this fair lady's love,   125
And she in mine.
DUKE.   Say it, Othello.
OTHELLO.   Her father lov'd me; oft invited me;
Still question'd me the story of my life
From year to year, the battles, sieges,
    fortunes,   130
That I have pass'd.
I ran it through, even from my boyish days
To the very moment that he bade me tell it;
Wherein I spoke of most disastrous chances,
Of moving accidents by flood and field,   135
Of hair-breadth scapes i' th' imminent deadly breach,
Of being taken by the insolent foe
And sold to slavery, of my redemption thence
And portance in my travel's history;
Wherein of antres vast and deserts idle,   140
Rough quarries, rocks, [and] hills whose heads touch
    heaven,
It was my hint to speak,—such was my process,—
And of the Cannibals that each other eat,
The Anthropophagi, and men whose heads
[Do grow] beneath their shoulders. These to
    hear   145
Would Desdemona seriously incline;
But still the house-affairs would draw her thence,
Which ever as she could with haste dispatch,
She'd come again, and with a greedy ear
Devour up my discourse: which I observing,   150
Took once a pliant hour, and found good means
To draw from her a prayer of earnest heart
That I would all my pilgrimage dilate,
Wherof by parcels she had something heard,
But not [intentively]. I did consent,   155
And often did beguile her of her tears
When I did speak of some distressful stroke
That my youth suffer'd. My story being done,
She gave me for my pains a world of [sighs].

She swore, in faith, 'twas strange, 'twas passing
    strange,   160
'Twas pitiful, 'twas wondrous pitiful.
She wish'd she had not heard it; yet she wish'd
That Heaven had made her such a man. She thank'd
    me,
And bade me, if I had a friend that lov'd her,
I should but teach him how to tell my story,   165
And that would woo her. Upon this hint I spake:
She lov'd me for the dangers I had pass'd,
And I lov'd her that she did pity them.
This only is the witchcraft I have us'd.
Here comes the lady; let her witness it.   170

Enter DESDEMONA, IAGO, *and* Attendants.

DUKE.   I think this tale would win my daughter too.
    Good Brabantio,
Take up this mangled matter at the best;
Men do their broken weapons rather use
Than their bare hands.
BRABANTIO.   I pray you, hear her speak.   175
If she confess that she was half the wooer,
Destruction on my head if my bad blame
Light on the man! Come hither, gentle mistress.
Do you perceive in all this noble company
Where most you owe obedience?
DESDEMONA.   My noble father,   180
I do perceive here a divided duty.
To you I am bound for life and education;
My life and education both do learn me
How to respect you; you are the lord of duty;
I am hitherto your daughter. But here's my
    husband;   185
And so much duty as my mother show'd
To you, preferring you before her father,
So much I challenge that I may profess
Due to the Moor, my lord.
BRABANTIO.   God be with you! I have done.
Please it your Grace, on to the state-affairs.   190
I had rather to adopt a child than get it.
Come hither, Moor.
I here do give thee that with all my heart
Which, but thou hast already, with all my heart
I would keep from thee. For your sake, jewel,   195

139. *portance:* behavior.   140. *antres:* caves.   *idle:* barren.
141. [*and*] Q. Om. F.   142. *hint:* occasion.   145. [*Do grow*]
Q. *Grew* F.   *These* Q₂. *These things* F.   151. *pliant:* convenient.   155. [*intentively*] Q: attentively.   *instinctively* F.
159. [*sighs*] Q. kisses F.

166. *hint:* opportunity (not consciously given). Cf. 1.142.

I am glad at soul I have no other child;
For thy escape would teach me tyranny,
To hang clogs on them. I have done, my lord.
DUKE.   Let me speak like yourself, and lay a
    sentence,
Which, as a grise or step, may help these lovers 200
[Into your favour].
When remedies are past, the griefs are ended
By seeing the worst, which late on hopes
   depended.
To mourn a mischief that is past and gone
Is the next way to draw new mischief on.   205
What cannot be preserv'd when fortune takes,
Patience her injury a mock'ry makes.
The robb'd that smiles steals something from the
   thief;
He robs himself that spends a bootless grief.
BRABANTIO.   So let the Turk of Cyprus us beguile
We lose it not, so long as we can smile.   211
He bears the sentence well that nothing bears
But the free comfort which from thence he hears,
But he bears both the sentence and the sorrow
That, to pay grief, must of poor patience borrow.
These sentences, to sugar or to gall   216
Being strong on both sides, are equivocal.
But words are words; I never yet did hear
That the bruis'd heart was pierced through the ear.
I humbly beseech you, proceed to the affairs of state.
                                220
DUKE.   The Turk with a most mighty preparation
    makes for Cyprus. Othello, the fortitude of the
    place is best known to you; and though we have
    there a substitute of most allowed sufficiency, yet
    opinion, a sovereign mistress of effects, throws a
    more safer voice on you. You must therefore be
    content to slubber the gloss of your new fortunes
    with this more stubborn and bois'trous expedition.
                                  226
OTHELLO.   The tyrant custom, most grave senators,
Hath made the flinty and steel couch of war

My thrice-driven bed of down. I do agnize
A natural and prompt alacrity   230
I find in hardness, and do undertake
These present wars against the Ottomites.
Most humbly therefore bending to your state,
I crave fit disposition for my wife,
Due reference of place and exhibition,   235
With such accommodation and besort
As levels with her breeding.
DUKE.   [If you please,
Be 't at her father's.]
BRABANTIO.   I'll not have it so.
OTHELLO.   Nor I.
DESDEMONA.   Nor I; [I would not] there reside,
To put my father in impatient thoughts   240
By being in his eye. Most gracious Duke,
To my unfolding lend your prosperous ear;
And let me find a charter in your voice
To assist my simpleness.
DUKE.   What would you, Desdemona?   245
DESDEMONA.   That I [did] love the Moor to live with
    him,
My downright violence and storm of fortunes
May trumpet to the world. My heart's subdu'd
Even to the very quality of my lord.
I saw Othello's visage in his mind,   250
And to his honours and his valiant parts
Did I my soul and fortunes consecrate.
So that, dear lords, if I were left behind,
A moth of peace, and he go to the war,
The rites for [which] I love him are
   bereft me,   255
And I a heavy interim shall support
By his dear absence. Let me go with him.
OTHELLO.   Let her have your voice.
Vouch with me, Heaven, I therefore beg it not
To please the palate of my appetite,   260
Nor to comply with heat, the young affects

---

199. *like yourself:* as you should.   200. *grise:* degree.
201. [*Into . . . favour*] Q. Om. F.   216. *sentences:* maxims.
217. *equivocal:* equal.   222. *fortitude:* strength, fortification.
223. *allowed:* admitted.   223–224. *sovereign* Q. *more sovereign* F.
225. *slubber:* sully.

229. *thrice-driven:* thoroughly sifted. *agnize:* acknowledge.
235. *reference:* assignment.   *exhibition:* provision.
236. *besort:* company.   237. *levels with:* befits.   237–238. [*If
. . . father's*] Q. *Why at her Fathers?* F.   239. [*I . . . not*] Q.
would I F.   242. *prosperous:* propitious.   243. *charter:* privilege.   246. [*did*] Q. Om. F.   247. *My . . . fortunes:* my pre-
cipitate assault upon my fortunes.   255. [*which*] Q. *why* F.

In my defunct and proper satisfaction,
But to be free and bounteous to her mind;
And Heaven defend your good souls, that you think
I will your serious and great business scant   265
When she is with me. No, when light-wing'd toys
Of feather'd Cupid seel with wanton dullness
My speculative and offic'd instruments
That my disports corrupt and taint my business,
Let housewives make a skillet of my helm,   270
And all indign and base adversities
Make head against my estimation!

DUKE.   Be it as you shall privately determine,
Either for her stay or going. Th' affair cries haste,
And speed must answer it.

FIRST SENATOR.   You must away to-night.   275

[DESDEMONA.   To-night, my lord?

DUKE.   This night.]

OTHELLO.   With all my heart.

DUKE.   At nine i' th' morning here we'll meet again.
Othello, leave some officer behind,
And he shall our commission bring to you,
And such things else of quality and respect   280
As doth import you.

OTHELLO.   So please your Grace, my ancient;
A man he is of honesty and trust.
To his conveyance I assign my wife,
With what else needful your good Grace shall think
To be sent after me.

DUKE.   Let it be so.   285
Good-night to every one. [To BRABANTIO.] And,
    noble signior,
If virtue no delighted beauty lack,
Your son-in-law is far more fair than black.

FIRST SENATOR.   Adieu, brave Moor; use Desdemona
    well.

BRABANTIO.   Look to her Moor, if thou hast eyes to
    see;   290
She has deceiv'd her father, and may thee.

[*Exeunt* [DUKE, Senators, Officers, *etc.*].

OTHELLO.   My life upon her faith! Honest Iago,
My Desdemona must I leave to thee.
I prithee, let thy wife attend on her;
And bring them after in the best advantage.   295
Come, Desdemona; I have but an hour
Of love, of worldly matters and direction,
To spend with thee. We must obey the time.

[*Exeunt* OTHELLO *and* DESDEMONA.]

RODERIGO.   Iago,—

IAGO.   What say'st thou, noble heart?   300

RODERIGO.   What will I do, think'st thou?

IAGO.   Why, go to bed and sleep.

RODERIGO.   I will incontinently drown myself.

IAGO.   If thou dost, I shall never love thee after.
Why, thou silly gentleman!   305

RODERIGO.   It is silliness to live when to live is torment; and then have we a prescription to die when
Death is our physician.

IAGO.   O villanous! I have look'd upon the world for
four times seven years; and since I could distinguish betwixt a benefit and an injury, I never
found man that knew how to love himself. Ere I
would say I would drown myself for the love of a
guinea-hen, I would change my humanity with a
baboon.   312

RODERIGO.   What should I do? I confess it is my shame
to be so fond, but it is not in my virtue to amend it.

IAGO.   Virtue! a fig! 'tis in ourselves that we are thus or
thus. Our bodies are our gardens, to the which our
wills are gardeners; so that if we will plant nettles
or sow lettuce, set hyssop and weed up thyme, supply it with one gender of herbs or distract it with
many, either to have it sterile with idleness or
manured with industry, why, the power and corrigible authority of this lies in our wills. If the
[balance] of our lives had not one scale of reason
to poise another of sensuality, the blood and
baseness of our natures would conduct us to most

---

262. *defunct:* The modern meaning is here excluded, and no convincing explanation has been found.   264. *defend:* forbid.
267. *seel:* blind (from falconry)   268. *My . . . instruments:* my faculties whose office is to perceive.   271. *indign:* unworthy.   272. *estimation:* reputation.   276. [DESDEMONA. *To-night . . . night*] Q. Om. F.
281. *import:* concern.   287. *delighted:* delightful.

295. *advantage:* opportunity.   303. *incontinently:* straightway.
317. *hyssop:* fragrant herb.   318. *gender:* kind.   319–320. *corrigible
authority:* corrective power.   320. [*balance*] Q. *braine* F.

preposterous conclusions; but we have reason to cool our raging motions, our carnal stings, our unbitted lusts, whereof I take this that you call love to be a sect or scion.

RODERIGO.   It cannot be.   325

IAGO.   It is merely a lust of the blood and a permission of the will. Come, be a man! Drown thyself? drown cats and blind puppies! I have profess'd me thy friend, and I confess me knit to thy deserving with cables of perdurable toughness; I could never better stead thee than now. Put money in thy purse; follow thou the wars; defeat thy favour with an usurp'd beard. I say, put money in thy purse. It cannot be long that Desdemona should continue her love to the Moor,—put money in thy purse,—nor he his to her. It was a violent commencement in her, and thou shalt see an answerable sequestration. Put but money in thy purse. These Moors are changeable in their wills—fill thy purse with money;—the food that to him now is as luscious as locusts, shall be to him shortly as bitter as coloquintida. She must change for youth; when she is sated with his body, she will find the error of her choice; [she must have change, she must:] therefore put money in thy purse. If thou wilt needs damn thyself, do it a more delicate way than drowning. Make all the money thou canst. If sanctimony and a frail vow betwixt an erring barbarian and a super-subtle Venetian be not too hard for my wits and all the tribe of hell, thou shalt enjoy her; therefore make money. A pox of drowning thyself! it is clean out of the way. Seek thou rather to be hang'd in compassing thy joy than to be drown'd and go without her.   345

RODERIGO.   Wilt thou be fast to my hopes, if I depend on the issue?

IAGO.   Thou art sure of me. Go, make money. I had told thee often, and I re-tell thee again and again, I hate the Moor. My cause is hearted; thine hath no less reason. Let us be conjunctive in our revenge against him. If thou canst cuckold him, thou dost thyself a pleasure, me a sport. There are many events in the womb of time which will be delivered. Traverse! go, provide thy money. We will have more of this to-morrow. Adieu.

RODERIGO.   Where shall we meet i' th' morning?

IAGO.   At my lodging.   355

RODERIGO.   I'll be with thee betimes.

IAGO.   Go to; farewell. Do you hear, Roderigo?

[RODERIGO.   What say you?]

IAGO.   No more of drowning, do you hear?

RODERIGO.   I am chang'd;] I'll sell all my land.   [Exit.

IAGO.   Thus do I ever make my fool my purse;   361
For I mine own gain'd knowledge should profane
If I would time expend with such a snipe
But for my sport and profit. I hate the Moor;
And it is thought abroad that 'twixt my sheets 365
He has done my office. I know not if 't be true;
But I, for mere suspicion in that kind,
Will do as if for surety. He holds me well;
The better shall my purpose work on him.
Cassio's a proper man: let me see now: 370
To get his place and to plume up my will
In double knavery—How, how?—Let's see:—
After some time, to abuse Othello's ear
That he is too familiar with his wife.
He hath a person and a smooth dispose   375
To be suspected, fram'd to make women false.
The Moor is of a free and open nature,
That thinks men honest that but seem to be so,
And will as tenderly be led by th' nose
As asses are.   380
I have't. It is engend'red. Hell and night
Must bring this monstrous birth to the world's light.
      [Exit.

ACT TWO

SCENE 1.   [A sea-port in Cyprus. An open place near the quay.]

---

323. *motions:* appetites.   324. *sect or scion:* cutting or off-shoot.
329. *perdurable:* eternal.   330. *defeat thy favour:* disguise thy face.   334. *sequestration:* separation.   336. *locusts:* the fruit of the carob tree.   337. *coloquintida:* a bitter fruit.
338–339. [*she . . . she must*] Q. Om. F.   346. *depend . . . issue:* rely on the outcome.   348. *hearted:* heartfelt.   349. *conjunctive:* united.

---

352. *Traverse:* forward.   358–360. [RODERIGO. *What . . . chang'd*] Q. Om. F.   363. *snipe:* woodcock, a silly bird.   370. *proper:* handsome.   371–372. *plume . . . In:* brace myself to.   375. *dispose:* disposition.

Enter MONTANO *and two* Gentlemen.

MONTANO.   What from the cape can you discern at
   sea?

FIRST GENTLEMAN.   Nothing at all; it is a high-wrought
   flood.
   I cannot, 'twixt the heaven and the main,
   Descry a sail.

MONTANO.   Methinks the wind hath spoke aloud at
   land;   5
   A fuller blast ne'er shook our battlements.
   If it hath ruffian'd so upon the sea,
   What ribs of oak, when mountains melt on them,
   Can hold the mortise? What shall we hear of this?

SECOND GENTLEMAN.   A segregation of the Turkish
   fleet.   10
   For do but stand upon the foaming shore,
   The chidden billow seems to pelt the clouds;
   The wind-shak'd surge, with high and monstrous
   mane,
   Seems to cast water on the burning Bear
   And quench the guards of th' ever-fixed Pole.   15
   I never did like molestation view
   On the enchafed flood.

MONTANO.   If that the Turkish fleet
   Be not enshelter'd and embay'd, they are drown'd;
   It is impossible to bear it out.

Enter a third Gentleman.

THIRD GENTLEMAN.   News, lads! our wars are done.
   The desperate tempest hath so bang'd the Turks, 21
   That their designment halts. A noble ship of Venice
   Hath seen a grievous wreck and sufferance
   On most part of their fleet.

MONTANO.   How! is this true?

THIRD GENTLEMAN.   The ship is here put in.   25
   A Veronese, Michael Cassio,
   Lieutenant to the warlike Moor Othello,
   Is come on shore; the Moor himself at sea,
   And is in full commission here for Cyprus.

MONTANO.   I am glad on't; 'tis a worthy governor. 30

THIRD GENTLEMAN.   But this same Cassio, though he
   speak of comfort
   Touching the Turkish loss, yet he looks sadly
   And prays the Moor be safe, for they were parted
   With foul and violent tempest.

MONTANO.   Pray heavens he be;
   For I have serv'd him, and the man commands 35
   Like a full soldier. Let's to the seaside, ho!
   As well to see the vessel that's come in
   As to throw out our eyes for brave Othello,
   Even till we make the main and th' aerial blue
   An indistinct regard.

THIRD GENTLEMAN.   Come, let's do so;   40
   For every minute is expectancy
   Of more arrivance.

Enter CASSIO.

CASSIO.   Thanks, you the valiant of this warlike isle,
   That so approve the Moor! O, let the heavens
   Give him defence against the elements,   45
   For I have lost him on a dangerous sea.

MONTANO.   Is he well shipp'd?

CASSIO.   His bark is stoutly timber'd, and his pilot
   Of very expert and approv'd allowance;
   Therefore my hopes, not surfeited to death, 50
   Stand in bold cure.

   [*Within*, "A sail, a sail, a sail!" *Enter a* [*fourth*
   Gentleman].

CASSIO.   What noise?

[FOURTH] GENTLEMAN.   The town is empty; on the
   brow o' th' sea
   Stand ranks of people, and they cry, "A sail!"

CASSIO.   My hopes do shape him for the governor. 55

   [*A shot.*

SECOND GENTLEMAN.   They do discharge their shot of
   courtesy.
   Our friends at least.

CASSIO.   I pray you, sir, go forth,
   And give us truth who 'tis that is arriv'd.

SECOND GENTLEMAN.   I shall. [*Exit.*

Act II, Scene i, 9. hold the mortise: hold their joints together.   10. *segregation:* dispersion.   15. *guards:* stars in the
Little Bear in line with the polestar.   24. *sufferance:* disaster.
26. *A Veronese.* In I.i.20 Cassio is called a Florentine.

49. *approv'd allowance:* tested repute.   50–51. *my hopes . . .
cure.* The sense seems to be: "My hopes, though far from being
nourished to excess, yet stand a good chance of being fulfilled."

MONTANO.   But, good Lieutenant, is your General
    wiv'd?   60
CASSIO.   Most fortunately. He hath achiev'd a maid
    That paragons description and wild fame;
    One that excels the quirks of blazoning pens,
    And in th' essential vesture of creation
    Does tire the [ingener].

Re-enter second Gentleman.

How now! who has put in?   65
SECOND GENTLEMAN.   'Tis one Iago, ancient to the
    general.
CASSIO.   He has had most favourable and happy speed.
    Tempests themselves, high seas, and howling winds,
    The gutter'd rocks and congregated sands,
    Traitors ensteep'd to enclog the guiltless keel,   70
    As having sense of beauty, do omit
    Their mortal natures, letting go safely by
    The divine Desdemona.
MONTANO.   What is she?
CASSIO.   She that I spake of, our great captain's captain,
    Left in the conduct of the bold Iago,   75
    Whose footing here anticipates our thoughts
    A se'nnight's speed. Great Jove, Othello guard,
    And swell his sail with thine own powerful breath,
    That he may bless this bay with his tall ship,
    Make love's quick pants in Desdemona's arms,   80
    Give renew'd fire to our extincted spirits,
    [And bring all Cyprus comfort!]

Enter DESDEMONA, EMILIA, IAGO, RODERIGO [*and*
    Attendants].

O, behold,
The riches of the ship is come on shore!
You men of Cyprus, let her have your knees.
Hail to thee, lady! and the grace of heaven,   85
Before, behind thee, and on every hand,
Enwheel thee round!
DESDEMONA.   I thank you, valiant Cassio.
    What tidings can you tell [me] of my lord?

CASSIO.   He is not yet arriv'd; nor know I aught
    But that he's well and will be shortly here.   90
DESDEMONA.   O, but I fear—How lost you company?
CASSIO.   The great contention of sea and skies
    Parted our fellowship.—But, hark! a sail.

[*Within,* "A sail, a sail!" [*Guns heard.*]

SECOND GENTLEMAN.   They give [their] greeting to
    the citadel.   95
    This likewise is a friend.
CASSIO.   See for the news.

[*Exit Gentleman.*]

Good ancient, you are welcome. [*To* EMILIA.] Wel-
    come, mistress.
Let it not gall your patience, good Iago,
That I extend my manners; 'tis my breeding
That gives me this bold show of courtesy. [*Kissing
    her.*]   100
IAGO.   Sir, would she give you so much of her lips
    As of her tongue she oft bestows on me,
    You'd have enough.
DESDEMONA.   Alas, she has no speech.
IAGO.   In faith, too much;
    I find it still, when I have [list] to sleep.   105
    Marry, before your ladyship, I grant,
    She puts her tongue a little in her heart,
    And chides with thinking.
EMILIA.   You have little cause to say so.
IAGO.   Come on, come on; you are pictures out of
    door,   110
    Bells in your parlours, wild-cats in your kitchens,
    Saints in your injuries, devils being offended,
    Players in your housewifery, and housewives in your
    beds.
DESDEMONA.   O, fie upon thee, slanderer!
IAGO.   Nay, it is true, or else I am a Turk.   115
    You rise to play and go to bed to work.
EMILIA.   You shall not write my praise.
IAGO.   No, let me not.
DESDEMONA.   What wouldst thou write of me, if thou
    shouldst praise me?

---

62. *paragons:* excels.   63. *quirks:* flourishes.   *blazoning:* praising.   64. *essential . . . creation:* i.e., just as she is, in her essential quality.   65. [*ingener*] (conjecture): inventor (of praise).
Ingeniver F. For *tire the* [*ingener*] Q reads *beare an excellency.*
69. *gutter'd:* furrowed, jagged.   70. *ensteep'd:* submerged.
72. *mortal:* deadly.   82. [*And . . . comfort*] Q. Om. F.
88. [*me*] Q. Om. F.

---

95. [*their*] Q. *this* F.   105. [*list*] Q: inclination. *leave* F.
108. *with thinking:* i.e., without words.   110–113. *Come . . .
beds.* So Q. Prose in F.   111. *Bells:* i.e., clanging tongues.
112. *Saints . . . injuries:* i.e., you offend sanctimoniously.
113. *Players:* triflers. *housewives:* hussies.

IAGO.   O gentle lady, do not put me to't;
  For I am nothing if not critical.   120

DESDEMONA.   Come on, assay.—There's one gone to
  the harbour?

IAGO.   Ay, madam.

DESDEMONA.   I am not merry; but I do beguile
  The thing I am by seeming otherwise.—
  Come, how wouldst thou praise me?   125

IAGO.   I am about it; but indeed my invention
  Comes from my pate as birdlime does from frieze;
  It plucks out brains and all. But my Muse labours,
  And thus she is deliver'd:
  If she be fair and wise, fairness and wit,   130
  The one's for use, the other useth it.

DESDEMONA.   Well prais'd! How if she be black and
  witty?

IAGO.   If she be black, and thereto have a wit,
  She'll find a white that shall her blackness fit.

DESDEMONA.   Worse and worse.   135

EMILIA.   How if fair and foolish?

IAGO.   She never yet was foolish that was fair;
  For even her folly help'd her to an heir.

DESDEMONA.   These are old fond paradoxes to make
  fools laugh i' th' alehouse. What miserable praise
  hast thou for her that's foul and foolish?   140

IAGO.   There's none so foul and foolish thereunto,
  But does foul pranks which fair and wise ones do.

DESDEMONA.   O heavy ignorance! thou praisest the
  worst best. But praise couldst thou bestow on a deserving woman indeed, one that, in the authority
  of her merit, did justly put on the vouch of very
  malice itself?   146

IAGO.   She that was ever fair and never proud,
  Had tongue at will and yet was never loud,
  Never lack'd gold and yet went never gay,
  Fled from her wish and yet said, "Now I may;"   150
  She that being ang'red, her revenge being nigh,
  Bade her wrong stay and her displeasure fly;
  She that in wisdom never was so frail
  To change the cod's head for the salmon's tail;
  She that could think and ne'er disclose her mind,
                                155

  See suitors following and not look behind,
  She was a wight, if ever such wights were,—

DESDEMONA.   To do what?

IAGO.   To suckle fools and chronicle small beer.   159

DESDEMONA.   O most lame and impotent conclusion!
  Do not learn of him, Emilia, though he be thy husband. How say you, Cassio? Is he not a most profane and liberal counsellor?

CASSIO.   He speaks home, madam. You may relish him
  more in the soldier than in the scholar.   164

IAGO. [aside].   He takes her by the palm; ay, well said,
  whisper. With as little a web as this will I ensnare
  as great a fly as Cassio. Ay, smile upon her, do; I
  will gyve thee in thine own courtship.—You say
  true; 'tis so, indeed.—If such tricks as these strip
  you out of your lieutenantry, it had been better
  you had not kiss'd your three fingers so oft, which
  now again you are most apt to play the sir in. Very
  good; well kiss'd! an excellent curtsy! 'Tis so, indeed. Yet again your fingers to your lips? Would
  they were clyster-pipes for your sake!

(Trumpet within.)

—The Moor! I know his trumpet.   173

CASSIO.   'Tis truly so.

DESDEMONA.   Let's meet him and receive him.

CASSIO.   Lo, where he comes!

Enter OTHELLO and Attendants.

OTHELLO.   O my fair warrior!

DESDEMONA.   My dear Othello!

OTHELLO.   It gives me wonder great as my content
  To see you here before me. O my soul's joy!
  If after every tempest come such calms,   180
  May the winds blow till they have waken'd death!
  And let the labouring bark climb hills of seas
  Olympus-high, and duck again as low
  As hell's from heaven! If it were now to die,
  'Twere now to be most happy; for, I fear,   185
  My soul hath her content so absolute

126–129. *I am . . . deliver'd.* So Q. Prose in F.   132. *black:* bru-
nette.   134. *white:* with a pun on *wight* (person).   145. *put
. . . vouch:* compel the testimony.   154. *To . . . tail:* to take the
worthless in exchange for the worthy.

159. *chronicle small beer:* i.e., to keep petty accounts.   162. *liberal:* free-spoken.   165. *well said:* well done.   167. *gyve:* fetter,
entangle. *courtship:* courtesy.   170. *sir:* gentleman.
172. *clyster-pipes:* syringes.

That not another comfort like to this
Succeeds in unknown fate.

DESDEMONA.   The heavens forbid
But that our loves and comforts should increase,
Even as our days do grow!

OTHELLO.   Amen to that, sweet powers!   190
I cannot speak enough of this content;
It stops me here; it is too much of joy.
And this, and this, the greatest discords be [*Kissing
her.*
That e'er our hearts shall make!

IAGO [*aside*].   O, you are well tun'd now!   195
But I'll set down the pegs that make this music,
As honest as I am.

OTHELLO.   Come, let us to the castle.
News, friends: our wars are done, the Turks are
drown'd.
How does my old acquaintance of this isle?
Honey, you shall be well desir'd in Cyprus;   200
I have found great love amongst them. O my sweet,
I prattle out of fashion, and I dote
In mine own comforts. I prithee, good Iago,
Go to the bay and disembark my coffers.
Bring thou the master to the citadel;   205
He is a good one, and his worthiness
Does challenge much respect. Come, Desdemona,
Once more, well met at Cyprus.

[*Exeunt* OTHELLO, DESDEMONA [*and* Attendants.]

IAGO.   Do thou meet me presently at the harbour.—
Come [hither]. If thou be'st valiant,—as, they say,
base men being in love have then a nobility in
their natures more than is native to them,—list
me. The lieutenant to-night watches on the court
of guard;—first, I must tell thee this: Desdemona is
directly in love with him.

RODERIGO.   With him! why, 'tis not possible.   214

IAGO.   Lay thy finger thus, and let thy soul be instructed. Mark me with what violence she first
lov'd the Moor, but for bragging and telling her
fantastical lies. To love him still for prating,—let

not thy discreet heart think it. Her eye must be
fed; and what delight shall she have to look on the
devil? When the blood is made dull with the act of
sport, there should be, [again] to inflame it and to
give satiety a fresh appetite, loveliness in favour,
sympathy in years, manners, and beauties; all
which the Moor is defective in. Now, for want of
these requir'd conveniences, her delicate tenderness will find itself abus'd, begin to heave the gorge,
disrelish and abhor the Moor. Very nature will instruct her in it and compel her to some second
choice. Now, sir, this granted,—as it is a most pregnant and unforc'd position—who stands so eminent in the degree of this fortune as Cassio does? a
knave very voluble; no further conscionable than
in putting on the mere form of civil and humane
seeming, for the better compassing of his salt and
most hidden loose affection? Why, none; why,
none; a slipper and subtle knave, a finder of occasion, that has an eye can stamp and counterfeit
advantages, though true advantage never present
itself; a devilish knave. Besides, the knave is handsome, young, and hath all those requisites in him
that folly and green minds look after; a pestilent
complete knave, and the woman hath found him
already.   235

RODERIGO.   I cannot believe that in her; she's full of
most bless'd condition.

IAGO.   Bless'd fig's-end! The wine she drinks is made
of grapes. If she had been bless'd, she would never
have lov'd the Moor. Bless'd pudding! Didst thou
not see her paddle with the palm of his hand? Didst
not mark that?   241

RODERIGO.   Yes, that I did; but that was but courtesy.

IAGO.   Lechery, by this hand; an index and obscure
prologue to the history of lust and foul thoughts.
They met so near with their lips that their breaths
embrac'd together. Villanous thoughts, Roderigo!
When these [mutualities] so marshal the way,

---

200. *desir'd:* beloved.   205. *master:* ship's master.
209. [hither] Q. *thither* F.

---

220. [*again*] Q. *a game* F.   223. *heave the gorge:* be nause-
ated.   226. *pregnant:* evident.   228. *conscionable:* conscien-
tious.   229. *salt:* lewd.   230. *slipper:* slippery.   236–
237. *condition:* character.   246. [*mutualities*] Q: exchanges.
mutabilities F.

hard at hand comes the master and main exercise, th' incorporate conclusion. Pish! But, sir, be you rul'd by me; I have brought you from Venice. Watch you to-night; for the command, I'll lay 't upon you. Cassio knows you not. I'll not be far from you. Do you find some occasion to anger Cassio, either by speaking too loud, or tainting his discipline; or from what other course you please, which the time shall more favourably minister.

RODERIGO. Well?   253

IAGO. Sir, he's rash and very sudden in choler, and haply may strike at you. Provoke him, that he may; for even out of that will I cause these of Cyprus to mutiny, whose qualification shall come into no true taste again but by the displanting of Cassio. So shall you have a shorter journey to your desires by the means I shall then have to prefer them; and the impediment most profitably removed, without the which there were no expectation of our prosperity.   260

RODERIGO. I will do this, if you can bring it to any opportunity.

IAGO. I warrant thee. Meet me by and by at the citadel; I must fetch his necessaries ashore. Farewell.

RODERIGO. Adieu. [Exit.

IAGO. That Cassio loves her, I do well believe 't;   265
That she loves him 'tis apt and of great credit;
The Moor, howbeit that I endure him not,
Is of a constant, loving, noble nature,
And I dare think he'll prove to Desdemona
A most dear husband. Now, I do love her too;   270
Not out of absolute lust, though peradventure
I stand accountant for as great a sin,
But partly led to diet my revenge,
For that I do suspect the lusty Moor
Hath leap'd into my seat; the thought whereof   275
Doth, like a poisonous mineral, gnaw my inwards;
And nothing can or shall content my soul
Till I am even'd with him, wife for [wife];
Or failing so, yet that I put the Moor
At least into a jealousy so strong   280
That judgement cannot cure. Which thing to do,

If this poor trash of Venice, whom I [trash]
For his quick hunting, stand the putting on,
I'll have our Michael Cassio on the hip,
Abuse him to the Moor in the [rank] garb—   285
For I fear Cassio with my night-cap too—
Make the Moor thank me, love me, and reward me
For making him egregiously an ass
And practising upon his peace and quiet
Even to madness. 'Tis here, but yet confus'd;   290
Knavery's plain face is never seen till us'd. [Exit.

SCENE 2. [A street.]

Enter OTHELLO'S Herald, with a proclamation [People following.]

HERALD. It is Othello's pleasure, our noble and valiant general, that, upon certain tidings now arriv'd importing the mere perdition of the Turkish fleet, every man put himself into triumph; some to dance, some to make bonfires, each man to what sport and revels his [addiction] leads him; for, beside these beneficial news, it is the celebration of his nuptial. So much was his pleasure should be proclaimed. All offices are open, and there is full liberty of feasting from this present hour of five till the bell have told eleven. [Heaven] bless the isle of Cyprus and our noble general Othello!   9

[Exeunt.

[Scene 3. A hall in the castle.]

Enter OTHELLO, DESDEMONA, CASSIO, and Attendants.

OTHELLO. Good Michael, look you to the guard to-night.
Let's teach ourselves that honourable stop,
Not to outsport discretion.

CASSIO. Iago hath direction what to do;
But, notwithstanding, with my personal eye   5
Will I look to 't.

---

282. *trash:* worthless fellow. [*trash*] (Steevens): check: *trace* F. crush Q.   283. *putting on:* inciting.   285. [*rank*] Q: gross. right F. *garb:* manner.   289. *practising upon:* plotting against.

Scene ii, 2. *mere:* utter.   4. [*addiction*] Q₂: inclination. *addition* F. minde Q. 6. *offices:* kitchens, etc.   8. [*Heaven*] Q. Om. F.

---

256. *qualification:* appeasement.   266. *apt:* natural. *of . . . credit:* most credible.   278. [*wife*] Q. *wist* F.

OTHELLO.   Iago is most honest.
Michael, good-night; to-morrow with your earliest
Let me have speech with you. [*To* DESDEMONA.]
Come, my dear love;
The purchase made, the fruits are to ensue;
That profit's yet to come 'tween me and you.   10
Good-night.

[*Exeunt* [OTHELLO, DESDEMONA, *and* Attendants.]
Enter IAGO.

CASSIO.   Welcome, Iago; we must to the watch.
IAGO.   Not this hour, Lieutenant; 'tis not yet ten o' th'
clock. Our general cast us thus early for the love of
his Desdemona; who let us not therefore blame.
He hath not yet made wanton the night with her;
and she is sport for Jove.   16
CASSIO.   She's a most exquisite lady.
IAGO.   And, I'll warrant her, full of game.
CASSIO.   Indeed, she's a most fresh and delicate crea-
ture.
IAGO.   What an eye she has! Methinks it sounds a par-
ley to provocation.   21
CASSIO.   An inviting eye; and yet methinks right modest.
IAGO.   And when she speaks, is it not an alarum to
love?
CASSIO.   She is indeed perfection.
IAGO.   Well, happiness to their sheets! Come, lieutenant, I have a stoup of wine; and here without are a
brace of Cyprus gallants that would fain have a
measure to the health of black Othello.   27
CASSIO.   Not to-night, good Iago. I have very poor and
unhappy brains for drinking; I could well wish
courtesy would invent some other custom of entertainment.
IAGO.   O, they are our friends. But one cup; I'll drink
for you.   31
CASSIO.   I have drunk but one cup to-night, and that
was craftily qualified too, and, behold, what innovation it makes here. I am unfortunate in the infirmity, and dare not task my weakness with any
more.

IAGO.   What, man! 'tis a night of revels. The gallants
desire it.   35
CASSIO.   Where are they?
IAGO.   Here at the door; I pray you, call them in.
CASSIO.   I'll do't; but it dislikes me. [*Exit.*
IAGO.   If I can fasten but one cup upon him,
With that which he hath drunk to-night already,
40
He'll be as full of quarrel and offence
As my young mistress' dog. Now, my sick fool
Roderigo,
Whom love hath turn'd almost the wrong side out,
To Desdemona hath to-night carous'd
Potations pottle-deep; and he's to watch.   45
Three [lads] of Cyprus, noble swelling spirits
That hold their honours in a wary distance,
The very elements of this warlike isle,
Have I to-night fluster'd with flowing cups,
And they watch too. Now, 'mongst this flock of
drunkards   50
Am I to put our Cassio in some action
That may offend the isle. But here they come.

Re-enter CASSIO; *with him* MONTANO *and* Gentlemen
[Servants *follow with wine.*]

If consequence do but approve my dream,
My boat sails freely, both with wind and stream.
CASSIO.   'Fore [God], they have given me a rouse al-
ready.   55
MONTANO.   Good faith, a little one; not past a pint, as
I am a soldier.
IAGO.   Some wine, ho! [*Sings.*]
    "And let me the canakin clink, clink;
      And let me the canakin clink.
        A soldier's a man;   60
        O, man's life's but a span;
      Why, then, let a soldier drink."
Some wine, boys!
CASSIO.   'Fore [God], an excellent song.   64
IAGO.   I learn'd it in England, where, indeed, they are
most potent in potting; your Dane, your German,

Scene iii, 14. *cast:* dismissed.   32–33. *craftily qualified:* slyly
diluted.

38. *it dislikes me:* I don't want to.   45. *pottle-deep:* to the bottom of the tankard.   46. [*lads*] Q. *else* F.   47. *hold . . . distance:* i.e., are quick to quarrel.   48. *very elements:* true representatives.   55. *rouse:* bumper.

and your swag-belli'd Hollander—Drink, ho!—are
nothing to your English.

CASSIO.   Is your Englishman so exquisite in his drink-
ing?   68

IAGO.   Why, he drinks you, with facility, your Dane
dead drunk; he sweats not to overthrow your
Almain; he gives your Hollander a vomit ere the
next pottle can be fill'd.

CASSIO.   To the health of our general!

MONTANO.   I am for it, Lieutenant; and I'll do you justice.

IAGO.   O sweet England!
    "King Stephen was and-a worthy peer,   75
        His breeches cost him but a crown;
    He held them sixpence all too dear,
        With that he call'd the tailor lown.

    "He was a wight of high renown,
        And thou art but of low degree.   80
    'Tis pride that pulls the country down;
        And take thy auld cloak about thee."

    Some wine, ho!

CASSIO.   Why, this is a more exquisite song than the
other.

IAGO.   Will you hear 't again?   85

CASSIO.   No; for I hold him to be unworthy of his place
that does those things. Well, [God's] above all; and
there be souls must be saved, and there be souls
must not be saved.

IAGO.   It's true, good Lieutenant.

CASSIO.   For mine own part—no offence to the general,
nor any man of quality—I hope to be saved.

IAGO.   And so do I too, Lieutenant.   92

CASSIO.   Ay, but, by your leave, not before me; the
Lieutenant is to be saved before the ancient. Let's
have no more of this; let's to our affairs.—[God]
forgive us our sins!—Gentlemen, let's look to our
business. Do not think, gentlemen, I am drunk.
This is my ancient; this is my right hand, and this
is my left. I am not drunk now; I can stand well
enough, and I speak well enough.   98

GENTLEMEN.   Excellent well.

CASSIO.   Why, very well then; you must not think
then that I am drunk. [Exit.

MONTANO.   To the platform, masters; come, let's set
the watch.

IAGO.   You see this fellow that is gone before:
He is a soldier fit to stand by Cæsar
And give direction; and do but see his vice.   105
'Tis to his virtue a just equinox,
The one as long as th' other; 'tis pity of him.
I fear the trust Othello puts him in,
On some odd time of his infirmity,
Will shake this island.

MONTANO.   But is he often thus?   110

IAGO.   'Tis evermore his prologue to his sleep.
He'll watch the horologe a double set
If drink rock not his cradle.

MONTANO.   It were well
The general were put in mind of it.
Perhaps he sees it not; or his good nature   115
Prizes the virtue that appears in Cassio,
And looks not on his evils. Is not this true?

Enter RODERIGO.

IAGO [*aside to him*].   How now, Roderigo!
I pray you, after the lieutenant; go.

[*Exit* RODERIGO.

MONTANO.   And 'tis great pity that the noble Moor
Should hazard such a place as his own second   121
With one of an ingraft infirmity.
It were an honest action to say
So to the Moor.

IAGO.   Not I, for this fair island.
I do love Cassio well; and would do much   125
To cure him of this evil.—But, hark! what noise?

[*Cry within:* "Help! help!"] *Re-enter* CASSIO, *pursuing*
RODERIGO.

CASSIO.   'Zounds, you rogue! you rascal!

MONTANO.   What's the matter, Lieutenant?

CASSIO.   A knave teach me my duty!
I'll beat the knave into a twiggen bottle.   130

RODERIGO.   Beat me!

CASSIO.   Dost thou prate, rogue? [*Striking* RODERIGO.]

---

70. *Almain:* German.   78. *lown:* fellow, rascal.

106. *equinox:* counterpart, equivalent.   112. *horologe . . . set:*
clock twice around.   130. *twiggen:* wicker-covered.

MONTANO.   Nay, good Lieutenant [*staying him*];
I pray you, sir, hold your hand.
CASSIO.   Let me go, sir,
Or I'll knock you o'er the mazzard.
MONTANO.   Come, come, you're drunk.
CASSIO.   Drunk!

[*They fight.*

IAGO [*aside to* RODERIGO].   Away, I say; go out, and
cry a mutiny.

[*Exit* RODERIGO.

Nay, good Lieutenant,—[God's will], gentlemen;—
Help, ho!—Lieutenant,—sir,—Montano,—[sir];—
Help, masters!—Here's a goodly watch indeed!   137

[*Bell rings.*

Who's that which rings the bell?—Diablo, ho!
The town will rise. Fie, fie, Lieutenant, [hold]!
You will be sham'd for ever.

Re-enter OTHELLO *and* Attendants.

OTHELLO.   What is the matter here?   140
MONTANO.   ['Zounds], I bleed still; I am hurt to the
death. He dies!
OTHELLO.   Hold, for your lives!
IAGO.   Hold, ho! Lieutenant,—sir,—Montano,—gen-
tlemen,—
Have you forgot all [sense of place] and duty?
Hold! the general speaks to you; hold, for shame!
OTHELLO.   Why, how now, ho! from whence ariseth
this?   146
Are we turn'd Turks, and to ourselves do that
Which Heaven hath forbid the Ottomites?
For Christian shame, put by this barbarous brawl
He that stirs next to carve for his own rage   150
Holds his soul light; he dies upon his motion.
Silence that dreadful bell; it frights the isle
From her propriety. What is the matter, masters:
Honest Iago, that looks dead with grieving,   154
Speak, who began this? On thy love, I charge thee.

IAGO.   I do not know. Friends all but now, even now,
In quarter, and in terms like bride and groom
Devesting them for bed; and then, but now—
As if some planet had unwitted men—
Swords out, and tilting one at other's breast,   160
In opposition bloody. I cannot speak
Any beginning to this peevish odds;
And would in action glorious I had lost
Those legs that brought me to a part of it!
OTHELLO.   How comes it, Michael, you are thus
forgot?   165
CASSIO.   I pray you, pardon me; I cannot speak.
OTHELLO.   Worthy Montano, you were wont to be
civil;
The gravity and stillness of your youth
The world hath noted, and your name is great
In mouths of wisest censure. What's the matter   170
That you unlace your reputation thus,
And spend your rich opinion for the name
Of a night-brawler? Give me answer to it.
MONTANO.   Worthy Othello, I am hurt to danger.
Your officer, Iago, can inform you—   175
While I spare speech, which something now offends
me—
Of all that I do know; nor know I aught
By me that's said or done amiss this night,
Unless self-charity be sometimes a vice,
And to defend ourselves it be a sin   180
When violence assails us.
OTHELLO.   Now, by heaven,
My blood begins my safer guides to rule;
And passion, having my best judgement collied,
Assays to lead the way. If I once stir
Or do but lift this arm, the best of you   185
Shall sink in my rebuke. Give me to know
How this foul rout began, who set it on;
And he that is approv'd in this offence,
Though he had twinn'd with me, both at a birth,
Shall lose me. What! in a town of war,   190
Yet wild, the people's hearts brimful of fear,
To manage private and domestic quarrel,

---

133. *mazzard:* head.   135. [*God's will*] Q. *Alas* F.   136. [*sir*]
Q. Om. F.   139. [*hold*] Q. Om. F.   141. [*sense of place*]
(Hammer). *place of sense.* QF.   150. *carve . . . rage:* act on his
own impulse.

157. *quarter:* peace.   162. *peevish odds:* stupid quarrel.
170. *censure:* judgment.   172. *opinion:* reputation.
176. *offends:* pains.   183. *collied:* darkened.   188. *approv'd:*
found guilty.   192. *manage:* carry on.

In night, and on the court and guard of safety!
'Tis monstrous. Iago, who began 't?

MONTANO.   If partially affin'd, or leagu'd in office,
Thou dost deliver more or less than truth,   196
Thou art no soldier.

IAGO.   Touch me not so near.
I had rather have this tongue cut from my mouth
Than it should do offence to Michael Cassio;
Yet, I persuade myself, to speak the truth   200
Shall nothing wrong him. [Thus] it is, General:
Montano and myself being in speech,
There comes a fellow crying out for help;
And Cassio following him with determin'd sword
To execute upon him. Sir, this gentleman   205
Steps in to Cassio and entreats his pause;
Myself the crying fellow did pursue,
Lest by his clamour—as it so fell out—
The town might fall in fright. He, swift of foot,
Outran my purpose; and I return'd the rather   210
For that I heard the clink and fall of swords,
And Cassio high in oath; which till to-night
I ne'er might say before. When I came back—
For this was brief—I found them close together,
At blow and thrust; even as again they were   215
When you yourself did part them.
More of this matter cannot I report.
But men are men; the best sometimes forget.
Though Cassio did some little wrong to him,
As men in rage strike those that wish them best,
Yet surely Cassio, I believe, receiv'd   221
From him that fled some strange indignity
Which patience could not pass.

OTHELLO.   I know, Iago,
Thy honesty and love doth mince this matter,
Making it light to Cassio. Cassio, I love thee;   225
But never more be officer of mine.

Re-enter DESDEMONA, *attended.*

Look, if my gentle love be not rais'd up!
I'll make thee an example.

DESDEMONA.   What's the matter, dear?

OTHELLO.   All's well [now], sweeting; come away to
bed.

Sir, for your hurts, myself will be your surgeon.—
Lead him off. [*To* MONTANO, *who is led off.*]   231
Iago, look with care about the town,
And silence those whom this vile brawl distracted.
Come, Desdemona; 'tis the soldiers' life
To have their balmy slumbers wak'd with strife.
                                                     235

[*Exeunt all but* IAGO *and* CASSIO.

IAGO.   What, are you hurt, Lieutenant?

CASSIO.   Ay, past all surgery.

IAGO.   Marry, God forbid!

CASSIO.   Reputation, reputation, reputation! O, I have
lost my reputation! I have lost the immortal part of
myself, and what remains is bestial. My reputation,
Iago, my reputation!   241

IAGO.   As I am an honest man, I thought you had received some bodily wound; there is more sense in
that than in reputation. Reputation is an idle and
most false imposition; oft got without merit, and
lost without deserving. You have lost no reputation
at all, unless you repute yourself such a loser.
What, man! there are more ways to recover the
general again. You are but now cast in his mood, a
punishment more in policy than in malice; even so
as one would beat his offenceless dog to affright an
imperious lion. Sue to him again, and he's yours.
                                                     249

CASSIO.   I will rather sue to be despis'd than to deceive
so good a commander with so slight, so drunken,
and so indiscreet an officer. Drunk? and speak parrot? and squabble? swagger? swear? and discourse
fustian with one's own shadow? O thou invisible
spirit of wine, if thou hast no name to be known
by, let us call thee devil!   254

IAGO.   What was he that you follow'd with your
sword? What had he done to you?

CASSIO.   I know not.

IAGO.   Is't possible?

CASSIO.   I remember a mass of things, but nothing distinctly; a quarrel, but nothing wherefore. O [God],
that men should put an enemy in their mouths to

---

195. *partially affin'd:* biased because of ties.   201. [Thus] Q.
This F.   229. [now] Q. Om. F.

242. *thought* Q. *had thought* F.   246. *recover:* regain favor
with.   252. *parrot:* nonsense.   *fustian:* nonsense.

steal away their brains! That we should, with joy, pleasance, revel, and applause, transform ourselves into beasts!   262

IAGO.   Why, but you are now well enough. How came you thus recovered?

CASSIO.   It hath pleas'd the devil drunkenness to give place to the devil wrath. One unperfectness shows me another, to make me frankly despise myself.
                                                                                          267

IAGO.   Come, you are too severe a moraler. As the time, the place, and the condition of this country stands, I could heartily wish this had not befallen; but since it is as it is, mend it for your own good.

CASSIO.   I will ask him for my place again; he shall tell me I am a drunkard! Had I as many mouths as Hydra, such an answer would stop them all. To be now a sensible man, by and by a fool, and presently a beast! O strange! Every inordinate cup is unbless'd and the ingredient is a devil.   275

IAGO.   Come, come, good wine is a good familiar creature, if it be well us'd; exclaim no more against it. And, good Lieutenant, I think you think I love you.

CASSIO.   I have well approved it, sir. I drunk!   279

IAGO.   You or any man living may be drunk at a time, man. [I'll] tell you what you shall do. Our general's wife is now the general;—I may say so in this respect, for that he hath devoted and given up himself to the contemplation, mark, and [denotement] of her parts and graces;—confess yourself freely to her; importune her help to put you in your place again. She is of so free, so kind, so apt, so blessed a disposition, she holds it a vice in her goodness not to do more than she is requested. This broken joint between you and her husband entreat her to splinter; and, my fortunes against any lay worth naming, this crack of your love shall grow stronger than it was before.   289

CASSIO.   You advise me well.

IAGO.   I protest, in the sincerity of love and honest kindness.

CASSIO.   I think it freely; and betimes in the morning I will beseech the virtuous Desdemona to undertake for me. I am desperate of my fortunes if they check me [here].   294

IAGO.   You are in the right. Good-night, Lieutenant; I must to the watch.

CASSIO.   Good-night, honest Iago.   [Exit.

IAGO.   And what's he then that says I play the villain?
When this advice is free I give and honest,
Probal to thinking and indeed the course   300
To win the Moor again? For 'tis most easy
Th' inclining Desdemona to subdue
In any honest suit; she's fram'd as fruitful
As the free elements. And then for her
To win the Moor, [were't] to renounce his baptism,
All seals and symbols of redeemed sin,   306
His soul is so enfetter'd to her love,
That she may make, unmake, do what she list,
Even as her appetite shall play the god
With his weak function. How am I then a villain
To counsel Cassio to this parallel course,   311
Directly to his good? Divinity of hell!
When devils will the blackest sins put on,
They do suggest at first with heavenly shows,
As I do now; for whiles this honest fool   315
Plies Desdemona to repair his fortune
And she for him pleads strongly to the Moor,
I'll pour this pestilence into his ear,
That she repeals him for her body's lust;
And by how much she strives to do him good,   320
She shall undo her credit with the Moor.
So will I turn her virtue into pitch,
And out of her own goodness make the net
That shall enmesh them all.

Re-enter RODERIGO.

How now, Roderigo!   324

RODERIGO.   I do follow here in the chase, not like a hound that hunts, but one that fills up the cry. My money is almost spent; I have been tonight exceedingly well cudgell'd; and I think the issue will be, I shall have so much experience for my pains; and

---

280. [*I'll*] Q. *I* F.   283. [*denotement*] Q₂. *devotement* QF.
287. *splinter:* bind with splints.   288. *lay:* wager.

294. [*here*] Q. Om. F.   300. *Probal:* probable.   303. *fruitful:* generous.   305. [*were't*] Q. *were* F.   310. *function:* mental faculties.   313. *put on:* incite.

so, with no money at all and a little more wit, return again to Venice.

IAGO.   How poor are they that have not patience.   330
What wound did ever heal but by degrees?
Thou know'st we work by wit, and not by witchcraft;
And wit depends on dilatory time.
Does't not go well? Cassio hath beaten thee,
And thou, by that small hurt, hast cashier'd Cassio.
Though other things grow fair against the sun,   336
Yet fruits that blossom first will first be ripe.
Content thyself a while. In troth, 'tis morning;
Pleasure and action make the hours seem short.
Retire thee; go where thou art billeted.   340
Away, I say; thou shalt know more hereafter.
Nay, get thee gone.

[Exit RODERIGO.]

Two things are to be done:
My wife must move for Cassio to her mistress;
I'll set her on;
Myself a while to draw the Moor apart,   345
And bring him jump when he may Cassio find
Soliciting his wife. Ay, that's the way;
Dull not device by coldness and delay. [Exit.

ACT THREE

SCENE 1.   [Cyprus before the castle.]

Enter CASSIO, with Musicians.

CASSIO.   Masters, play here; I will content your pains;
Something that's brief; and bid "Good morrow, general."

[They play. Enter CLOWN.

CLOWN.   Why, masters, have your instruments been
in Naples, that they speak i' th' nose thus?
FIRST MUSICIAN.   How, sir, how?   5
CLOWN.   Are these, I pray you, wind-instruments?
FIRST MUSICIAN.   Ay, marry, are they, sir?
CLOWN.   O, thereby hangs a tail.
FIRST MUSICIAN.   Whereby hangs a tale, sir?   9
CLOWN.   Marry, sir, by many a wind-instrument that I

know. But, masters, here's money for you; and the
General so likes your music, that he desires you,
for love's sake, to make no more noise with it.
FIRST MUSICIAN.   Well, sir, we will not.
CLOWN.   If you have any music that may not be heard,
to't again; but, as they say, to hear music the Gen-
eral does not greatly care.   15
FIRST MUSICIAN.   We have none such, sir.
CLOWN.   Then put up your pipes in your bag, for I'll
away. Go, vanish into air, away!

[Exeunt Musicians.

CASSIO.   Dost thou hear mine honest friend?
CLOWN.   No, I hear not your honest friend; I hear
you.   20
CASSIO.   Prithee, keep up thy quillets. There's a poor
piece of gold for thee. If the gentlewoman that at-
tends the [General's wife] be stirring, tell her
there's one Cassio entreats her a little favour of
speech. Wilt thou do this?
CLOWN.   She is stirring, sir. If she will stir hither, I shall
seem to notify unto her.   26
CASSIO.   [Do, good my friend.]

[Exit CLOWN. Enter IAGO.

In happy time, Iago.
IAGO.   You have not been a-bed, then?
CASSIO.   Why, no; the day had broke
Before we parted. I have made bold, Iago,   30
To send in to your wife. My suit to her
Is that she will to virtuous Desdemona
Procure me some access.
IAGO.   I'll send her to you presently;
And I'll devise a mean to draw the Moor
Out of the way, that your converse and business   35
May be more free.
CASSIO.   I humbly thank you for't.

[Exit IAGO.]

I never knew
A Florentine more kind and honest.

Enter EMILIA.

Act III, Scene i, 1. content: requite.

19. *hear* Q. *hear me* F.   21. *quillets:* quibbles.   22. [General's
wife] Q. *general* F.   27. [Do . . . friend] Q. Om F.

EMILIA.   Good morrow, good Lieutenant. I am sorry
For your displeasure; but all will sure be well.   40
The General and his wife are talking of it,
And she speaks for you stoutly. The Moor replies
That he you hurt is of great fame in Cyprus
And great affinity, and that in wholesome wisdom
He might not but refuse you; but he protests he
loves you,   45
And needs no other suitor but his likings
[To take the safest occasion by the front]
To bring you in again.
CASSIO.   Yet, I beseech you,
If you think fit, or that it may be done,
Give me advantage of some brief discourse   50
With Desdemon alone.
EMILIA.   Pray you, come in.
I will bestow you where you shall have time
To speak your bosom freely.
CASSIO.   I am much bound to you.

[*Exeunt,*

SCENE 2.   [*A room in the castle.*]

Enter OTHELLO, IAGO, *and* Gentlemen.

OTHELLO.   These letters give, Iago, to the pilot;
And by him do my duties to the Senate.
That done, I will be walking on the works;
Repair there to me.
IAGO.   Well, my good lord, I'll do't.
OTHELLO.   This fortification, gentlemen, shall we
see't?   5
GENTLEMEN.   We'll wait upon your lordship.

[*Exeunt.*

SCENE 3.   [*The garden of the castle.*]

Enter DESDEMONA, CASSIO, *and* EMILIA.

DESDEMONA.   Be thou assur'd, good Cassio, I will do
All my abilities in thy behalf.
EMILIA.   Good madam, do. I warrant it grieves my hus-
band
As if the cause were his.

DESDEMONA.   O, that's an honest fellow. Do not doubt,
Cassio,   5
But I will have my lord and you again
As friendly as you were.
CASSIO.   Bounteous madam,
Whatever shall become of Michael Cassio,
He's never anything but your true servant.
DESDEMONA.   I know't; I thank you. You do love my
lord;   10
You have known him long; and be you well assur'd
He shall in strangeness stand no farther off
Than in a politic distance.
CASSIO.   Ay, but, lady,
That policy may either last so long,
Or feed upon such nice and waterish diet,   15
Or breed itself so out of circumstances,
That, I being absent and my place supplied,
My general will forget my love and service.
DESDEMONA.   Do not doubt that; before Emilia here
I give thee warrant of thy place. Assure thee,   20
If I do vow a friendship, I'll perform it
To the last article. My lord shall never rest;
I'll watch him tame, and talk him out of patience;
His bed shall seem a school, his board a shrift;
I'll intermingle everything he does   25
With Cassio's suit. Therefore be merry, Cassio;
For thy solicitor shall rather die
Than give thy cause away.

Enter OTHELLO *and* IAGO.

EMILIA.   Madam, here comes my lord.
CASSIO.   Madam, I'll take my leave.   30
DESDEMONA.   Why, stay, and hear me speak.
CASSIO.   Madam, not now; I am very ill at ease,
Unfit for mine own purposes.
DESDEMONA.   Well, do your discretion.

[*Exit* CASSIO.

IAGO.   Ha! I like not that.
OTHELLO.   What dost thou say?   35
IAGO.   Nothing, my lord; or if—I know not what.
OTHELLO.   Was not that Cassio parted from my wife?

---

40. *displeasure:* disgrace.   44. *affinity:* connections.   47. [*To
. . . front*] Q. Om. F. *front:* forelock.
Scene ii, 3. *works:* fortifications.

Scene iii, 12. *strangeness:* aloofness.   19. *doubt:* fear.
23. *watch him tame:* keep him awake till he gives in.
24. *shrift:* confessional.

IAGO.   Cassio, my lord! No, sure, I cannot think it,
That he would steal away so guilty-like,
Seeing your coming.
OTHELLO.   I do believe 'twas he.   40
DESDEMONA.   How now, my lord!
I have been talking with a suitor here,
A man that languishes in your displeasure.
OTHELLO.   Who is't you mean?
DESDEMONA.   Why, your lieutenant, Cassio. Good my
    lord,   45
If I have any grace or power to move you,
His present reconciliation take;
For if he be not one that truly loves you,
That errs in ignorance and not in cunning,
I have no judgement in an honest face.   50
I prithee, call him back.
OTHELLO.   Went he hence now?
DESDEMONA.   Yes, faith; so humbled
That he hath left part of his grief with me
To suffer with him. Good love, call him back.
OTHELLO.   Not now, sweet Desdemon; some other
    time.   55
DESDEMONA.   But shall't be shortly?
OTHELLO.   The sooner, sweet, for you.
DESDEMONA.   Shall't be to-night at supper?
OTHELLO.   No, not to-night.
DESDEMONA.   To-morrow dinner, then?
OTHELLO.   I shall not dine at home;
I meet the captains at the citadel.
DESDEMONA.   Why, then , to-morrow night; on Tues-
    day morn;   60
On Tuesday noon, or night; on Wednesday morn.
I prithee, name the time, but let it not
Exceed three days. In faith, he's penitent;
And yet his trespass, in our common reason—
Save that, they say, the wars must make example 65
Out of [their] best—is not almost a fault
T' incur a private check. When shall he come?
Tell me, Othello. I wonder in my soul
What you would ask me that I should deny,   69
Or stand so mamm'ring on. What! Michael Cassio,
That came a-wooing with you, and so many a time,

When I have spoke of you dispraisingly,
Hath ta'en your part,—to have so much to do
To bring him in! Trust me, I could do much.
OTHELLO.   Prithee, no more; let him come when he
    will,   75
I will deny thee nothing.
DESDEMONA.   Why, this is not a boon.
'Tis as I should entreat you wear your gloves,
Or feed on nourishing dishes, or keep you warm,
Or sue to you to do a peculiar profit
To your own person. Nay, when I have a suit   80
Wherein I mean to touch your love indeed,
It shall be full of poise and difficult weight
And fearful to be granted.
OTHELLO.   I will deny thee nothing.
Whereon, I do beseech thee, grant me this,
To leave me but a little to myself.   85
DESDEMONA.   Shall I deny you? No. Farewell, my lord.
OTHELLO.   Farewell, my Desdemona; I'll come to thee
    straight.
DESDEMONA.   Emilia, come.—Be as your fancies teach
    you;
Whate'er you be, I am obedient.

[*Exeunt* DESDEMONA *and* EMILIA.

OTHELLO.   Excellent wretch! Perdition catch my soul,
But I do love thee! and when I love thee not,   91
Chaos is come again.
IAGO.   My noble lord,—
OTHELLO.   What dost thou say, Iago?
IAGO.   Did Michael Cassio, when [you] woo'd my
    lady,
Know of your love?   95
OTHELLO.   He did, from first to last. Why dost thou
    ask?
IAGO.   But for a satisfaction of my thought;
No further harm.
OTHELLO.   Why of thy thought, Iago?
IAGO.   I did not think he had been acquainted with
    her.
OTHELLO.   O, yes; and went between us very oft. 100
IAGO.   Indeed!

---

66. [*their*]. *her* QF.   *not almost:* hardly.
70. *mamm'ring:* hesitating.

.74. *bring . . . in: i.e.,* into your favor.   82. *poise:* weight.
94. [*you*] Q. *he* F.

OTHELLO.   Indeed! ay, indeed. Discern'st thou aught
   in that?
   Is he not honest?
IAGO.   Honest, my lord?
OTHELLO.   Honest! ay, honest.
IAGO.   My lord, for aught I know.
OTHELLO.   What dost thou think?
IAGO.   Think, my lord?
OTHELLO.   Think, my lord!   105
   [By heaven, he echoes] me,
   As if there were some monster in [his] thought
   Too hideous to be shown.—Thou dost mean some-
      thing.
   I heard thee say even now, thou lik'st not that,
   When Cassio left my wife. What didst not like? 110
   And when I told thee he was of my counsel
   [In] my whole course of wooing, thou criedst, "In-
      deed!"
   And didst contract and purse thy brow together,
   As if thou then hadst shut up in thy brain
   Some horrible conceit. If thou dost love me,   115
   Show me thy thought.
IAGO.   My lord, you know I love you.
OTHELLO.   I think thou dost;
   And, for I know thou'rt full of love and honesty,
   And weigh'st thy words before thou giv'st them
      breath,
   Therefore these stops of thine fright me the more;
   For such things in a false disloyal knave   121
   Are tricks of custom; but in a man that's just
   They're close dilations, working from the heart
   That passion cannot rule.
IAGO.   For Michael Cassio,
   I dare be sworn I think that he is honest.   125
OTHELLO.   I think so too.
IAGO.   Men should be what they seem;
   Or those that be not, would they might seem none!
OTHELLO.   Certain, men should be what they seem.
IAGO.   Why, then, I think Cassio's an honest man.
OTHELLO.   Nay, yet there's more in this.   130
   I prithee, speak to me as to thy thinkings,

As thou dost ruminate, and give thy worst of
   thoughts
   The worst of words.
IAGO.   Good my lord, pardon me.
   Though I am bound to every act of duty,
   I am not bound to that all slaves are free to.   135
   Utter my thoughts? Why, say they are vile and false;
   As where's that palace whereinto foul things
   Sometimes intrude not? Who has that breast so pure
   [But some] uncleanly apprehensions
   Keep leets and law-days and in sessions sit   140
   With meditations lawful?
OTHELLO.   Thou dost conspire against thy friend, Iago,
   If thou but think'st him wrong'd and mak'st his ear
   A stranger to thy thoughts.
IAGO.   I do beseech you—
   Though I perchance am vicious in my guess,   145
   As, I confess, it is my nature's plague
   To spy into abuses, and [oft] my jealousy
   Shapes faults that are not—that your wisdom yet,
   From one that so imperfectly conceits,
   Would take no notice, nor build yourself a trouble
   Out of his scattering and unsure observance.   151
   It were not for your quiet nor your good,
   Nor for my manhood, honesty, and wisdom,
   To let you know my thoughts.
OTHELLO.   What dost thou mean?
IAGO.   Good name in man and woman, dear my
      lord,   155
   Is the immediate jewel of their souls.
   Who steals my purse steals trash; 'tis something,
      nothing;
   'Twas mine, 'tis his, and has been slave to thousands;
   But he that filches from me my good name
   Robs me of that which not enriches him,   160
   And makes me poor indeed.
OTHELLO.   [By heaven,] I'll know thy thoughts.
IAGO.   You cannot, if my heart were in your hand;
   Nor shall not, whilst 'tis in my custody.
OTHELLO.   Ha!
IAGO.   O, beware, my lord, of jealousy!   165
   It is the green-ey'd monster which doth mock
   The meat it feeds on. That cuckold lives in bliss

---

106. [By . . . echoes] Q. Alas, thou eccho'st F.   107. [his] Q.
thy F.   112. [In] Q. of F.   123. close dilations: secret (i.e.,
unconscious) expressions.

---

139. [But some] Q. Wherein F.   140. leets: court-days.
147. [oft] Q. of F. jealousy: suspicion.   151. scattering: random.

Who, certain of his fate, loves not his wronger;
But, O, what damned minutes tells he o'er
Who dotes, yet doubts, suspects, yet soundly loves!
OTHELLO.   O misery!   171
IAGO.   Poor and content is rich, and rich enough;
But riches fineless is as poor as winter
To him that ever fears he shall be poor.
Good heavens, the souls of all my tribe defend 175
From jealousy!
OTHELLO.   Why, why is this?
Think'st thou I'd make a life of jealousy,
To follow still the changes of the moon
With fresh suspicions? No! to be once in doubt
Is [once] to be resolv'd. Exchange me for a goat
                                                       180
When I shall turn the business of my soul
To such exsufflicate and [blown] surmises,
Matching thy inference. 'Tis not to make me jealous
To say my wife is fair, feeds well, loves company,
Is free of speech, sings, plays, and dances [well]; 185
Where virtue is, these are more virtuous.
Nor from mine own weak merits will I draw
The smallest fear or doubt of her revolt;
For she had eyes, and chose me. No, Iago;
I'll see before I doubt; when I doubt, prove;   190
And on the proof, there is no more but this,—
Away at once with love or jealousy!
IAGO.   I am glad of this, for now I shall have reason
To show the love and duty that I bear you
With franker spirit; therefore, as I am bound,   195
Receive if from me. I speak not yet of proof.
Look to your wife; observe her well with Cassio;
Wear your eyes thus, not jealous nor secure.
I would not have your free and noble nature,
Out of self-bounty, be abus'd; look to't.   200
I know our country disposition well;
In Venice they do let Heaven see the pranks
They dare not show their husbands. Their best con-
    science
Is not to leave 't undone, but keep 't unknown.
OTHELLO.   Dost thou say so?   205

IAGO.   She did deceive her father, marrying you;
And when she seem'd to shake and fear your looks,
She lov'd them most.
OTHELLO.   And so she did.
IAGO.   Why, go to then.
She that, so young, could give out such a seeming,
To seel her father's eyes up close as oak—   210
He thought 'twas witchcraft—but I am much to
    blame.
I humbly do beseech you of your pardon
For too much loving you.
OTHELLO.   I am bound to thee for ever.
IAGO.   I see this hath a little dash'd your spirits.
OTHELLO.   Not a jot, not a jot.
IAGO.   Trust me! I fear it has.   215
I hope you will consider what is spoke
Comes from [my] love. But I do see you're mov'd.
I am to pray you not to strain my speech
To grosser issues nor to larger reach
Than to suspicion.   220
OTHELLO.   I will not.
IAGO.   Should you do so, my lord,
My speech should fall into such vile success
Which my thoughts aim'd not at. Cassio's my worthy
    friend,—
My lord, I see you're mov'd.
OTHELLO.   No, not much mov'd.
I do not think but Desdemona's honest.   225
IAGO.   Long live she so! and long live you to think so!
OTHELLO.   And yet, how nature erring from itself,—
IAGO.   Ay, there's the point; as—to be bold with you—
Not to affect many proposed matches
Of her own clime, complexion, and degree,   230
Whereto we see in all things nature tends—
Foh! one may smell in such, a will most rank,
Foul disproportions, thoughts unnatural.
But pardon me; I do not in position
Distinctly speak of her; though I may fear   235
Her will, recoiling to her better judgement,
May fall to match you with her country forms,
And happily repent.

---

173. *fineless:* unlimited.   180. [*once*] Q. Om. F.   182. *exsuf-*
flicate: inflated. [*blown*] Q. *blowed* F.   185. [*well*] Q. Om. F.
198. *secure:* careless.   200. *self-bounty:* inherent generosity.

217. [*my*] Q. *your* F.   222. *success:* consequence.   225. *hon-*
est: chaste.   232, 236. *will:* desire, appetite.   232. *rank:* foul.
234. *position: i.e.,* conviction.

OTHELLO.   Farewell, farewell!
  If more thou dost perceive, let me know more;
  Set on thy wife to observe. Leave me, Iago.   240
IAGO [going].   My lord, I take my leave.
OTHELLO.   Why did I marry? This honest creature doubtless
  Sees and knows more, much more, than he unfolds.
IAGO. [returning].   My lord, I would I might entreat your honour
  To scan this thing no farther; leave it to time.   245
  Although 'tis fit that Cassio have his place,
  For, sure, he fills it up with great ability,
  Yet, if you please to [hold] him off a while,
  You shall by that perceive him and his means.
  Note if your lady strain his entertainment   250
  With any strong or vehement importunity;
  Much will be seen in that. In the mean time,
  Let me be thought too busy in my fears—
  As worthy cause I have to fear I am—
  And hold her free, I do beseech your honour.   255
OTHELLO.   Fear not my government.
IAGO.   I once more take my leave. [Exit.
OTHELLO.   This fellow's of exceeding honesty,
  And knows all [qualities], with a learn'd spirit,
  Of human dealings. If I do prove her haggard,   260
  Though that her jesses were my dear heartstrings,
  I'd whistle her off and let her down the wind
  To prey at fortune. Haply, for I am black
  And have not those soft parts of conversation
  That chamberers have, or for I am declin'd   265
  Into the vale of years,—yet that's not much—
  She's gone. I am abus'd: and my relief
  Must be to loathe her. O curse of marriage,
  That we can call these delicate creatures ours,
  And not their appetites! I had rather be a toad   270
  And live upon the vapour of a dungeon
  Than keep a corner in the thing I love
  For others' uses. Yet, 'tis the plague [of] great ones;
  Prerogativ'd are they less than the base.

'Tis destiny unshunnable, like death.   275
Even then this forked plague is fated to us
When we do quicken. Look where she comes:

Re-enter DESDEMONA *and* EMILIA.

If she be false, [O, then heaven mocks] itself!
I'll not believe 't.
DESDEMONA.   How now, my dear Othello!
  Your dinner, and the generous islanders   280
  By you invited, do attend your presence.
OTHELLO.   I am to blame.
DESDEMONA.   Why do you speak so faintly?
  Are you not well?
OTHELLO.   I have a pain upon my forehead here.
DESDEMONA.   Why, that's with watching; 'twill away again.   285
  Let me but bind it hard, within this hour
  It will be well.
OTHELLO.   Your napkin is too little [*he puts the handkerchief from him; and it drops*];
  Let it alone. Come, I'll go in with you.
DESDEMONA.   I am very sorry that you are not well.

  [*Exeunt* [OTHELLO *and* DESDEMONA].

EMILIA.   I am glad I have found this napkin;   290
  This was her first remembrance from the Moor.
  My wayward husband hath a hundred times
  Woo'd me to steal it; but she so loves the token,
  For he conjur'd her she should ever keep it,
  That she reserves it evermore about her   295
  To kiss and talk to. I'll have the work ta'en out
  And give 't Iago. What he will do with it
  Heaven knows, not I;
  I nothing but to please his fantasy.

Re-enter IAGO.

IAGO.   How now! what do you here alone?   300
EMILIA.   Do not you chide; I have a thing for you.
IAGO.   A thing for me? It is a common thing—
EMILIA.   Ha!

---

248. [hold] Q. Om. F.   250. *strain his entertainment:* press his reappointment.   255. *free:* guiltless.   256. *government:* management.   259. [qualities] Q. quantities F.   260. *haggard:* wild.   261. *jesses:* strings by which hawks were held.   264. *parts of conversation:* social graces.   265. *chamberers:* gallants.   273. [of] Q. to F.

276. *forked plague:* curse of cuckold's horns.   277. *quicken:* begin to live.   278. [O . . . mocks] Q.   Heaven mock'd F. 280. *generous:* noble.   287. *napkin:* handkerchief.   288. *it:* i.e., his forehead.   296. *work . . . out:* pattern copied.

IAGO.   To have a foolish wife.

EMILIA.   O, is that all? What will you give me now

For that same handkerchief?   306

IAGO.   What handkerchief?

EMILIA.   What handkerchief!

Why, that the Moor first gave to Desdemona;

That which so often you did bid me steal.

IAGO.   Hast stol'n it from her?   310

EMILIA.   No, [faith;] she let it drop by negligence,

And, to th' advantage, I, being here, took 't up.

Look, here it is.

IAGO.   A good wench; give it me.

EMILIA.   What will you do with 't, that you have been

so earnest

To have me filch it?

IAGO [*snatching it*].   Why, what is that to you?   315

EMILIA.   If it be not for some purpose of import,

Give 't me again. Poor lady, she'll run mad

When she shall lack it.

IAGO. Be not acknown on't; I have use for it.

Go, leave me.   320

[*Exit* EMILIA.

I will in Cassio's lodging lose this napkin,

And let him find it. Trifles light as air

Are to the jealous confirmations strong

As proofs of holy writ; this may do something.

The Moor already changes with my poison.   325

Dangerous conceits are, in their natures poisons,

Which at the first are scarce found to distaste,

But with a little act upon the blood

Burn like the mines of sulphur. I did say so.

Re-enter OTHELLO.

Look, where he comes! Not poppy, nor mandragora,

Nor all the drowsy syrups of the world   331

Shall ever medicine thee to that sweet sleep

Which though ow'dst yesterday.

OTHELLO.   Ha! ha! false to me?

IAGO.   Why, how now, General! no more of that.

OTHELLO.   Avaunt! be gone! thou hast set me on the

rack   335

I swear 'tis better to be much abus'd

Than but to know 't a little.

IAGO.   How now, my lord!

OTHELLO.   What sense had I [of] her stol'n hours of

lust?

I saw 't not, thought it not, it harm'd not me.

I slept the next night well, fed well, was free and

merry;   340

I found not Cassio's kisses on her lips.

He that is robb'd, not wanting what is stolen,

Let him not know 't, and he's not robb'd at all.

IAGO.   I am sorry to hear this.

OTHELLO.   I had been happy, if the general camp, 345

Pioners and all, had tasted her sweet body,

So I had nothing known. O, now, for ever

Farewell the tranquil mind! farewell content!

Farewell the plumed troops and the big wars

That make ambition virtue! O, farewell!   350

Farewell the neighing steed and the shrill trump,

The spirit-stirring drum, th' ear-piercing fife,

The royal banner, and all quality,

Pride, pomp, and circumstance of glorious war!

And, O you mortal engines, whose rude throats 355

Th' immortal Jove's dread clamours counterfeit,

Farewell! Othello's occupation 's gone!

IAGO.   Is 't possible, my lord?

OTHELLO.   Villain, be sure thou prove my love a

whore;

Be sure of it. Give me the ocular proof;   360

Or, by the worth of mine eternal soul,

Thou hadst been better have been born a dog

Than answer my wak'd wrath!

IAGO.   Is 't come to this?

OTHELLO.   Make me to see 't; or, at the least, so prove

it

That the probation bear no hinge nor loop   365

To hang a doubt on; or woe upon thy life!

IAGO.   My noble lord,—

OTHELLO.   If thou dost slander her and torture me,

Never pray more; abandon all remorse;

On horror's head horrors accumulate;   370

Do deeds to make heaven weep, all earth amaz'd;

For nothing canst thou to damnation add

Greater than that.

---

311. [*faith*] Q. but F.   312. *to th' advantage*: opportunely.
319. *acknown*: aware.   328. *act*: action.   330. *mandragora*: a
soporific.   333. *ow'dst*: hadst.

---

338. [*of*] Q. *in* F.   346. *Pioners*: the lowest rank of soldiers.

IAGO. O grace! O Heaven forgive me!
  Are you a man? Have you a soul or sense?
  God buy you; take mine office. O wretched fool,
  That lov'st to make thine honesty a vice! 376
  O monstrous world! Take note, take note, O world,
  To be direct and honest is not safe.
  I thank you for this profit; and from hence
  I'll love no friend, sith love breeds such offence. 380
OTHELLO. Nay, stay. Thou shouldst be honest.
IAGO. I should be wise, for honesty's a fool
  And loses that it works for.
OTHELLO. By the world,
  I think my wife be honest and think she is not; 384
  I think that thou are just and think thou art not.
  I'll have some proof. [Her] name, that was as fresh
  As Dian's visage, is now begrim'd and black
  As mine own face. If there be cords, or knives,
  Poison, or fire, or suffocating streams,
  I'll not endure it. Would I were satisfied! 390
IAGO. I see, [sir], you are eaten up with passion;
  I do repent me that I put it to you.
  You would be satisfied?
OTHELLO. Would! nay, I will.
IAGO. And may; but, how? How satisfied, my lord?
  Would you, the [supervisor], grossly gape on— 395
  Behold her topp'd?
OTHELLO. Death and damnation! O!
IAGO. It were a tedious difficulty, I think,
  To bring them to that prospect; [damn] them then,
  If ever mortal eyes do see them bolster
  More than their own! What then? How then? 400
  What shall I say? Where's satisfaction?
  It is impossible you should see this,
  Were they as prime as goats, as hot as monkeys,
  As salt as wolves in pride, and fools as gross
  As ignorance made drunk. But yet, I say, 405
  If imputation and strong circumstances
  Which lead directly to the door of truth
  Will give you satisfaction, you might have't.
OTHELLO. Give me a living reason she's disloyal.

IAGO. I do not like the office; 410
  But, sith I am ent'red in this cause so far,
  Prick'd to't by foolish honesty and love,
  I will go on. I lay with Cassio lately;
  And, being troubled with a raging tooth,
  I could not sleep. 415
  There are a kind of men so loose of soul,
  That in their sleeps will mutter their affairs;
  One of this kind is Cassio.
  In sleep I heard him say, "Sweet Desdemona,
  Let us be wary, let us hide our loves;" 420
  And then, sir, would he gripe and wring my hand,
  Cry, "O sweet creature!" then kiss me hard,
  As if he pluck'd up kisses by the roots
  That grew upon my lips; then lay his leg
  Over my thigh, and sigh, and kiss; and then 425
  Cry, "Cursed fate that gave thee to the Moor!"
OTHELLO. O monstrous! monstrous!
IAGO. Nay, this was but his dream.
OTHELLO. But this denoted a foregone conclusion.
  'Tis a shrewd doubt, though it be but a dream.
IAGO. And this may help to thicken other proofs 430
  That do demonstrate thinly.
OTHELLO. I'll tear her all to pieces.
IAGO. Nay, [but] be wise; yet we see nothing done.
  She may be honest yet. Tell me but this,
  Have you not sometimes seen a handkerchief
  Spotted with strawberries in your wife's hand? 435
OTHELLO. I gave her such a one; 'twas my first gift.
IAGO. I know not that; but such a handkerchief—
  I am sure it was your wife's—did I to-day
  See Cassio wipe his beard with.
OTHELLO. If it be that,—
IAGO. If it be that, or any [that] was hers, 440
  It speaks against her with the other proofs.
OTHELLO. O, that the slave had forty thousand lives!
  One is too poor, too weak for my revenge.
  Now do I see 'tis true. Look here, Iago;
  All my found love thus do I blow to heaven.
  'Tis gone.
  Arise, black vengeance, from the hollow hell!
  Yield up, O love, thy crown and hearted throne

375. buy: be with. 376. lov'st F. livest Q. 386. [Her] Q. My
F. 391. [sir] Q. Om. F. 393. nay Q. Nay, and F.
395. [supervisor] Q. supervision F. 398. [damn] Q. Om. F.
399. bolster: lie on a bolster (together). 403. prime: lecherous. 404. pride: heat.

428. foregone conclusion: earlier act. 429. shrewd doubt:
strong reason for suspicion. 432. [but] Q. yet F.
440. [that]. it QF.

To tyrannous hate! Swell, bosom, with thy fraught,
For 'tis of aspics' tongues!

IAGO.   Yet be content.   450

OTHELLO.   O, blood, blood, blood!

IAGO.   Patience, I say; your mind [perhaps] may
    change,

OTHELLO.   Never, Iago. Like to the Pontic Sea,
    Whose icy current and compulsive course
    Ne'er [feels] retiring ebb, but keeps due on   455
    To the Propontic and the Hellespont,
    Even so my bloody thoughts, with violent pace,
    Shall ne'er look back, ne'er ebb to humble love,
    Till that a capable and wide revenge
    Swallow them up. Now, by yond marble heaven,
    In the due reverence of a sacred vow [kneels]   461
    I here engage my words.

IAGO.   Do not rise yet.
    Witness, you ever-burning lights above,
    You elements that clip us round about, [kneels]
    Witness that here Iago doth give up   465
    The execution of his wit, hands, heart,
    To wrong'd Othello's service! Let him command,
    And to obey shall be in me remorse,
    What bloody business ever.

[They rise.]

OTHELLO.   I greet thy love,   470
    Not with vain thanks, but with acceptance boun-
      teous,
    And will upon the instant put thee to't:
    Within these three days let me hear thee say
    That Cassio's not alive.

IAGO.   My friend is dead; 'tis done at your request.
    But let her live.

OTHELLO.   Damn her, lewd minx! O, damn her! damn
    her!   475
    Come, go with me apart; I will withdraw
    To furnish me with some swift means of death
    For the fair devil. Now art thou my lieutenant.

IAGO.   I am your own for ever.

[Exeunt.

---

449. *fraught:* burden. 450. *aspics':* asps'. 452. [*perhaps*] Q. Om.
F. 453. *Pontic Sea:* Black Sea. 455. [*feels*] Q₂. *keeps* F. 459. *capable:* comprehensive. 464. *clip:* embrace. 466. *execution:*
action. 468. *remorse:* obligation.

SCENE 4.   [*Before the castle.*]

Enter DESDEMONA, EMILIA, *and* CLOWN.

DESDEMONA.   Do you know, sirrah, where Lieutenant
    Cassio lies?

CLOWN.   I dare not say he lies anywhere.

DESDEMONA.   Why, man?

CLOWN.   He's a soldier, and for me to say a soldier lies,
    'tis stabbing.

DESDEMONA.   Go to! Where lodges he?   5

CLOWN.   To tell you where he lodges, is to tell you
    where I lie.

DESDEMONA.   Can anything be made of this?

CLOWN.   I know not where he lodges, and for me to
    devise a lodging and say he lies here or he lies
    there, were to lie in mine own throat.

DESDEMONA.   Can you inquire him out, and be edified
    by report?   10

CLOWN.   I will catechize the world for him; that is,
    make questions, and by them answer.

DESDEMONA.   Seek him, bid him come hither. Tell
    him I have mov'd my lord on his behalf, and hope
    all will be well.

CLOWN.   To do this is within the compass of man's
    wit; and therefore I will attempt the doing it.
    [Exit.   16

DESDEMONA.   Where should I lose the handkerchief,
    Emilia?

EMILIA.   I know not, madam.

DESDEMONA.   Believe me, I had rather have lost my
    purse
    Full of crusadoes; and, but my noble Moor   20
    Is true of mind and made of no such baseness
    As jealous creatures are, it were enough
    To put him to ill thinking.

EMILIA.   Is he not jealous?

DESDEMONA.   Who, he? I think the sun where he was
    born
    Drew all such humours from him.

EMILIA.   Look, where he comes.   25

Enter OTHELLO.

Scene iv, 1. *lies:* lodges. 21. *crusadoes:* Portuguese coins stamped
with a cross.

DESDEMONA.   I will not leave him now till Cassio
  Be call'ed to him.—How is't with you, my lord?
OTHELLO.   Well, my good lady. [*Aside.*] O, hardness
    to dissemble!—
  How do you, Desdemona?
DESDEMONA.   Well, my good lord.
OTHELLO.   Give me your hand. This hand is moist, my
    lady.   30
DESDEMONA.   It [yet] hath felt no age nor known no
    sorrow.
OTHELLO.   This argues fruitfulness and liberal heart;
  Hot, hot, and moist. This hand of yours requires
  A sequester from liberty, fasting and prayer.
  Much castigation, exercise devout;   35
  For here's a young and sweating devil here
  That commonly rebels. 'Tis a good hand,
  A frank one.
DESDEMONA.   You may, indeed, say so;
  For 'twas that hand that gave away my heart.
OTHELLO.   A liberal hand. The hearts of old gave
    hands;   40
  But our new heraldry is hands, not hearts.
DESDEMONA.   I cannot speak of this. Come now, your
    promise.
OTHELLO.   What promise, chuck?
DESDEMONA.   I have sent to bid Cassio come speak
    with you.
OTHELLO.   I have a salt and sorry rheum offends me;
  Lend me thy handkerchief.   46
DESDEMONA.   Here, my lord.
OTHELLO.   That which I gave you.
DESDEMONA.   I have it not about me.
OTHELLO.   Not?
DESDEMONA.   No, indeed, my lord.
OTHELLO.   That's a fault. That handkerchief
  Did an Egyptian to my mother give;   50
  She was a charmer, and could almost read
  The thoughts of people. She told her, while she kept
    it
  'Twould make her amiable and subdue my father
  Entirely to her love, but if she lost it,
  Or made a gift of it, my father's eye   55

Should hold her loathed and his spirits should hunt
After new fancies. She, dying, gave it me
And bid me, when my fate would have me wiv'd,
To give it her. I did so; and take heed on't;
Make it a darling like your precious eye.   60
To lose't or give't away were such perdition
As nothing else could match.
DESDEMONA.   Is't possible?
OTHELLO.   'Tis true; there's magic in the web of it.
  A sibyl, that had numb'red in the world
  The sun to course two hundred compasses,   65
  In her prophetic fury sew'd the work;
  The worms were hallowed that did breed the silk;
  And it was dy'd in mummy which the skilful
  Conserv'd of maidens' hearts.
DESDEMONA.   Indeed! is't true?
OTHELLO.   Most veritable; therefore look to't well. 70
DESDEMONA.   Then would to [God] that I had never
    seen 't!
OTHELLO.   Ha! wherefore?
DESDEMONA.   Why do you speak so startingly and
    rash?
OTHELLO.   Is't lost? Is't gone? Speak, is't out o' th' way?
DESDEMONA.   [Heaven] bless us!   75
OTHELLO.   Say you?
DESDEMONA.   It is not lost; but what an if it were?
OTHELLO.   How?
DESDEMONA.   I say, it is not lost.
OTHELLO.   Fetch 't, let me see 't.
DESDEMONA.   Why, so I can, [sir,] but I will not now.
  This is a trick to put me from my suit.   81
  Pray you, let Cassio be receiv'd again.
OTHELLO.   Fetch me the handkerchief; my mind
    misgives.
DESDEMONA.   Come, come;
  You'll never meet a more sufficient man.   85
OTHELLO.   The handkerchief!
[DESDEMONA.   I pray, talk me of Cassio.
OTHELLO.   The handkerchief!]
DESDEMONA.   A man that all his time
  Hath founded his good fortunes on your love,
  Shar'd dangers with you,—

---

31. [*yet*] Q. Om. F. 34. *sequester:* separation. 41. *our new
heraldry.* Probably a topical allusion. 45. *sorry:* distressing.
50. *Egyptian:* gypsy. 51. *charmer:* sorcerer. 53. *amiable:* lovable.

---

68. *mummy:* embalming fluid. 69. *Conserv'd:* prepared.
80. [*sir*] Q. Om. F. 86–87. [DESDEMONA. *I . . . handkerchief*] Q.
Om. F.

OTHELLO.   The handkerchief!   90
DESDEMONA.   In sooth, you are to blame.
OTHELLO.   ['Zounds!] [*Exit.*
EMILIA.   Is not this man jealous?
DESDEMONA.   I ne'er saw this before.
Sure, there's some wonder in this handkerchief;   95
I am most unhappy in the loss of it.
EMILIA.   'Tis not a year or two shows us a man.
They are all but stomachs, and we all but food;
They eat us hungerly, and when they are full
They belch us.

Enter CASSIO *and* IAGO.

Look you, Cassio and my husband!   100
IAGO.   There is no other way, 'tis she must do't;
And, lo, the happiness! Go, and importune her.
DESDEMONA.   How now, good Cassio! What's the news
with you?
CASSIO.   Madam, my former suit. I do beseech you
That by your virtuous means I may again   105
Exist, and be a member of his love
Whom I with all the office of my heart
Entirely honour. I would not be delay'd.
If my offence be of such mortal kind
That nor my service past, nor present sorrows,   110
Nor purpos'd merit in futurity
Can ransom me into his love again,
But to know so must be my benefit;
So shall I clothe me in a forc'd content,
And shut myself up in some other course,   115
To fortune's alms.
DESDEMONA.   Alas, thrice-gentle Cassio!
My advocation is not now in tune.
My lord is not my lord; nor should I know him
Were he in favour as in humour alter'd.
So help me every spirit sanctified   120
As I have spoken for you all my best
And stood within the blank of his displeasure
For my free speech! You must a while be patient.
What I can do I will; and more I will
Than for myself I dare. Let that suffice you.   125
IAGO.   Is my lord angry?

EMILIA.   He went hence but now,
And certainly in strange unquietness.
IAGO.   Can he be angry? I have seen the cannon
When it hath blown his ranks into the air,
And, like the devil, from his very arm   130
Puff'd his own brother:—and is he angry?
Something of moment then. I will go meet him.
There's matter in't indeed, if he be angry. [*Exit* IAGO.
DESDEMONA.   I prithee, do so. Something, sure, of
state,
Either from Venice, or some unhatch'd practice 135
Made demonstrable here in Cyprus to him,
Hath puddled his clear spirit; and in such cases
Men's natures wrangle with inferior things,
Though great ones are their object. 'Tis even so;
For let our finger ache, and it indues   140
Our other, healthful members even to a sense
Of pain. Nay, we must think men are not gods,
Nor of them look for such observancy
As fits the bridal. Beshrew me much, Emilia,
I was, unhandsome warrior as I am,   145
Arraigning his unkindness with my soul;
But now I find I had suborn'd the witness,
And he's indicted falsely.
EMILIA.   Pray Heaven it be state-matters, as you think,
And no conception nor no jealous toy   150
Concerning you.
DESDEMONA.   Alas the day! I never gave him cause.
EMILIA.   But jealous souls will not be answer'd so;
They are not ever jealous for the cause,
But jealous for they're jealous. It is a monster
Begot upon itself, born on itself.   155
DESDEMONA.   Heaven keep the monster from Othello's
mind!
EMILIA.   Lady, amen.
DESDEMONA.   I will go seek him. Cassio, walk
hereabout;
If I do find him fit, I'll move your suit
And seek to effect it to my uttermost.   160
CASSIO.   I humbly thank your ladyship.

[*Exeunt* [DESDEMONA *and* EMILIA]. *Enter* BIANCA.

BIANCA.   Save you, friend Cassio!
CASSIO.   What make you from home?

---

92. ['Zounds] Q. *Away* F.   102. *happiness:* luck.   105. *virtuous:* effective.   119. *favour:* appearance.   122. *blank:* target; strictly, the white spot in the center.

---

135. *practice:* plot.

How it is with you, my most fair Bianca?
Indeed, sweet love, I was coming to your house.
BIANCA.   And I was going to your lodging, Cassio. 165
What, keep a week away? seven days and nights?
Eightscore eight hours? and lovers' absent hours,
More tedious than the dial eightscore times?
O weary reck'ning!
CASSIO.   Pardon me, Bianca.
I have this while with leaden thoughts been press'd;
But I shall, in a more continuate time,   171
Strike off this score of absence. Sweet Bianca [*giving
her* DESDEMONA's *handkerchief*],
Take me this work out.
BIANCA.   O Cassio, whence came this?
This is some token from a newer friend;
To the felt absence now I feel a cause,   175
Is't come to this? Well, well.
CASSIO.   Go to, woman!
Throw your vile guesses in the devils' teeth,
From whence you have them. You are jealous now
That this is from some mistress, some remembrance.
No, in good troth, Bianca.
BIANCA.   Why, whose is it?   180
CASSIO.   I know not, [*sweet*]; I found it in my cham-
ber.
I like the work well; ere it be demanded—
As like enough it will—I'd have it copied.
Take it, and do't; and leave me for this time.
BIANCA.   Leave you! Wherefore?   185
CASSIO.   I do attend here on the General;
And think it no addition, nor my wish,
To have him see me woman'd.
BIANCA.   Why, I pray you?
CASSIO.   Not that I love you not.
BIANCA.   But that you do not love me.
I pray you, bring me on the way a little,   190
And say if I shall see you soon at night.
CASSIO.   'Tis but a little way that I can bring you,
For I attend here; but I'll see you soon.
BIANCA.   'Tis very good; I must be circumstanc'd.

[*Exeunt.*

---

171. *continuate:* uninterrupted.   181. [*sweet*] Q. *neither* F.
187. *addition:* credit.   194. *circumstanc'd:* reconciled.

ACT FOUR

SCENE 1.   [*Cyprus. Before the castle.*]

Enter OTHELLO *and* IAGO.

IAGO.   Will you think so?
OTHELLO.   Think so, Iago!
IAGO.   What,
To kiss in private?
OTHELLO.   An unauthoriz'd kiss.
IAGO.   Or to be naked with her friend in bed
An hour or more, not meaning any harm?
OTHELLO.   Naked in bed, Iago, and not mean harm! 5
It is hypocrisy against the devil.
They that mean virtuously, and yet do so,
The devil their virtue tempts, and they tempt
heaven.
IAGO.   If they do nothing, 'tis a venial slip;
But if I give my wife a handkerchief,—   10
OTHELLO.   What then?
IAGO.   Why, then, 'tis hers, my lord; and, being hers,
She may, I think bestow 't on any man.
OTHELLO.   She is protectress of her honour too;
May she give that?   15
IAGO.   Her honour is an essence that's not seen;
They have it very oft that have it not:
But, for the handkerchief,—
OTHELLO.   By heaven, I would most gladly have forgot
it.
Thou said'st—O, it comes o'er my memory,   20
As doth the raven o'er the infectious house,
Boding to all—he had my handkerchief.
IAGO.   Ay, what of that?
OTHELLO.   That's not so good now.
IAGO.   What
If I had said I had seen him do you wrong?
Or heard him say,—as knaves be such abroad,   25
Who having, by their own importunate suit,
Or voluntary dotage of some mistress,
Convinced or suppli'd them, cannot choose
But they must blab—
OTHELLO.   Hath he said anything?
IAGO.   He hath, my lord; but be you well assur'd,   30
No more than he'll unswear.
OTHELLO.   What hath he said?
IAGO.   Why, that he did—I know not what he did.
OTHELLO.   What? what?

Plate XII Michelangelo, *The Creation of Adam*. Ceiling, Sistine Chapel, the Vatican, Rome. (Scala/Art Resource)

Plate XIII Raphael, *The School of Athens*. Stanza della Segnatura, the Vatican. (Vatican Museum, Rome)

Plate XIV Raphael, *Pope Leo X with Cardinals Giulio de' Medici and Luigi de' Rossi*. Panel Painting, c. 1517. Galleria degli Uffizi, Florence. (Scala/Art Resource)

Plate XV Gelede dancer, Meko. (Copyright F. Willett, Glasgow)

Plate XVI Gelede dance scene. (Howard Wildman)

IAGO. Lie—

OTHELLO. With her?

IAGO. With her, on her; what you will.   34

OTHELLO. Lie with her! lie on her! We say lie on her, when they belie her. Lie with her! ['Zounds,] that's fulsome!—Handkerchief— confessions— handkerchief!—To confess, and be hang'd for his labour;—first to be hang'd, and then to confess.—I tremble at it. Nature would not invest herself in such shadowing passion without some instruction. It is not words that shakes me thus. Pish! Noses, ears, and lips.—Is't possible?—Confess—handker- chief!—O devil! [*Falls in a trance.*   42

IAGO. Work on,
My medicine, work! Thus credulous fools are caught;
And many worthy and chaste dames even thus,   45
All guiltless, meet reproach.—What, ho! my lord!
My lord, I say! Othello!

Enter CASSIO.

How now, Cassio!

CASSIO. What's the matter?

IAGO. My lord is fall'n into an epilepsy.
This is his second fit; he had one yesterday.   50

CASSIO. Rub him about the temples.

IAGO. [No, forbear;]
The lethargy must have his quiet course;
If not, he foams at mouth and by and by
Breaks out to savage madness. Look, he stirs.
Do you withdraw yourself a little while;   55
He will recover straight. When he is gone,
I would on great occasion speak with you.

[*Exit* CASSIO

How is it, General? Have you not hurt your head?

OTHELLO. Dost thou mock me?

IAGO. I mock you not, by heaven.
Would you would bear your fortune like a man!   60

OTHELLO. A horned man's a monster and a beast.

IAGO. There's many a beast then in a populous city,

And many a civil monster.

OTHELLO. Did he confess it?

IAGO. Good sir, be a man;
Think every bearded fellow that's but yok'd   65
May draw with you. There's millions now alive
That nightly lie in those unproper beds
Which they dare swear peculiar; your case is better.
O, 'tis the spite of hell, the fiend's arch-mock,
To lip a wanton in a secure couch,   70
And to suppose her chaste! No, let me know;
And knowing what I am, I know what she shall be.

OTHELLO. O, thou art wise; 'tis certain.

IAGO. Stand you a while apart;
Confine yourself but in a patient list.
Whilst you were here o'erwhelmed with your grief—   75
A passion most [unsuiting] such a man—
Cassio came hither. I shifted him away,
And laid good 'scuse upon your ecstasy;
Bade him anon return and here speak with me,
The which he promis'd. Do but encave yourself,   80
And mark the fleers, the gibes, and notable scorns
That dwell in every region of his face;
For I will make him tell the tale anew,
Where, how, how oft, how long ago, and when
He hath, and is again to cope your wife.   85
I say, but mark his gesture. Marry, patience;
Or I shall say you're all in all in spleen,
And nothing of a man.

OTHELLO. Dost thou hear, Iago?
I will be found most cunning in my patience;
But—dost thou hear?—most bloody.

IAGO. That's not amiss;   90
But yet keep time in all. Will you withdraw?

[OTHELLO *retires.*]

Now will I question Cassio of Bianca,
A housewife that by selling her desires
Buys herself bread and clothes. It is a creature
That dotes on Cassio, as 'tis the strumpet's plague
To beguile many and be beguil'd by one.   96

Act IV, Scene i, 39–40. *invest . . . instruction:* i.e., create such imaginings unless to teach me.   51. [*No, forbear*] Q. Om. F. 53. *by and by:* straightway.

63. *civil:* civilized.   67. *unproper:* not exclusively their own. 68. *peculiar:* their own.   70. *secure:* supposed safe from others. 74. *a patient list:* the bounds of patience.   76. [*unsuiting*] Q. re- sulting F.   78. *ecstasy:* trance.   87. *spleen:* anger, passion.

He, when he hears of her, cannot [refrain]
From the excess of laughter. Here he comes.

Re-enter CASSIO.

As he shall smile, Othello shall go mad;
And his unbookish jealousy must [conster]   100
Poor Cassio's smiles, gestures, and light behaviors
Quite in the wrong. How do you, Lieutenant?

CASSIO.   The worser that you give me the addition
Whose want even kills me.

IAGO.   Ply Desdemona well, and you are sure on't.
[*Speaking lower.*] Now, if this suit lay in Bianca's
[power],   106
How quickly should you speed!

CASSIO.   Alas, poor caitiff!

OTHELLO.   Look how he laughs already!

IAGO.   I never knew woman love man so.

CASSIO.   Alas, poor rogue! I think, indeed, she loves
me.   110

OTHELLO.   Now he denies it faintly, and laughs it out.

IAGO.   Do you hear, Cassio?

OTHELLO.   Now he importunes him
To tell it o'er. Go to; well said, well said.

IAGO.   She gives it out that you shall marry her.   115
Do you intend it?

CASSIO.   Ha, ha, ha!

OTHELLO.   Do ye triumph, Roman? Do you triumph?

CASSIO.   I marry [her]!! What? a customer! Prithee,
bear some charity to my wit; do not think it so
unwholesome. Ha, ha, ha!   120

OTHELLO.   So, so so, so; they laugh that win.

IAGO.   Why, the cry goes that you [shall] marry her.

CASSIO.   Prithee, say true.

IAGO.   I am a very villain else.

OTHELLO.   Have you scor'd me? Well.   125

CASSIO.   This is the monkey's own giving out. She is
persuaded I will marry her, out of her own love and
flattery, not out of my promise.

OTHELLO.   Iago [beckons] me; now he begins the
story.

CASSIO.   She was here even now; she haunts me in
every place. I was the other day talking on the sea-

bank with certain Venetians; and thither comes
the bauble, and, falls me thus about my neck—

OTHELLO.   Crying, "O dear Cassio!" as it were; his gesture imports it.   132

CASSIO.   So hangs, and lolls, and weeps upon me; so
shakes and pulls me. Ha, ha, ha!

OTHELLO.   Now he tells how she pluck'd him to my
chamber. Oh, I see that nose of yours, but not that
dog I shall throw it to.   136

CASSIO.   Well, I must leave her company.

IAGO.   Before me! look, where she comes.

Enter BIANCA.

CASSIO.   'Tis such another fitchew! Marry, a perfum'd
one.—What do you mean by this haunting of
me?   140

BIANCA.   Let the devil and his dam haunt you! What
did you mean by that same handkerchief you gave
me even now? I was a fine fool to take it. I must
take out the work?—A likely piece of work, that
you should find it in your chamber, and know not
who left it there! This is some minx's token, and I
must take out the work? There; give it your hobby-
horse. Wheresoever you had it, I'll take out no
work on't.   146

CASSIO.   How now, my sweet Bianca! how now! how
now!

OTHELLO.   By heaven, that should be my handkerchief!

BIANCA.   If you'll come to supper to-night, you may; if
you will not, come when you are next prepar'd for.
[*Exit.*   150

IAGO.   After her, after her.

CASSIO.   [Faith,] I must; she'll rail in the streets else.

IAGO.   Will you sup there?

CASSIO.   Yes, I intend so.

IAGO.   Well, I may chance to see you; for I would very
fain speak with you.   156

CASSIO.   Prithee, come; will you?

IAGO.   Go to; say no more.

[*Exit* CASSIO.

OTHELLO [*advancing*].   How shall I murder him, Iago?

---

97. [*refrain*] Q. *restraine* F.   100. [*conster*] Q: construe. *conserve*
F.   106. [*power*] Q. *dowre* F.   119. [*her*] Q. Om. F. *customer:*
harlot.   122. [*shall*] Q. Om. F.   125. scor'd: branded.   128. [*beck-
ons*] Q. *becomes* F.

---

139. *fitchew:* polecat.

IAGO.   Did you perceive how he laugh'd at his vice?

OTHELLO.   O Iago!   161

IAGO.   And did you see the handkerchief?

OTHELLO.   Was that mine?

IAGO.   Yours, by this hand. And to see how he prizes the foolish woman your wife! She gave it him, and he hath given it his whore.   165

OTHELLO.   I would have him nine years a-killing. A fine woman! a fair woman! a sweet woman!

IAGO.   Nay, you must forget that.

OTHELLO.   Ay, let her rot, and perish, and be damn'd to-night; for she shall not live. No, my heart is turn'd to stone; I strike it, and it hurts my hand. O, the world hath not a sweeter creature! She might lie by an emperor's side and command him tasks.

IAGO.   Nay, that's not your way.   173

OTHELLO.   Hang her! I do but say what she is. So delicate with her needle! an admirable musician! O! she will sing the savageness out of a bear. Of so high and plenteous wit and invention!   176

IAGO.   She's the worse for all this.

OTHELLO.   O, a thousand thousand times. And then, of so gentle a condition!

IAGO.   Ay, too gentle.   180

OTHELLO.   Nay, that's certain. But yet the pity of it, Iago! O Iago, the pity of it, Iago!

IAGO.   If you are so fond over her iniquity, give her patent to offend; for if it touch not you, it comes near nobody.

OTHELLO.   I will chop her into messes. Cuckold me!

IAGO.   O, 'tis foul in her.   186

OTHELLO.   With mine officer!

IAGO.   That's fouler.

OTHELLO.   Get me some poison, Iago; this night. I'll not expostulate with her, lest her body and beauty unprovide my mind again. This night, Iago.   191

IAGO.   Do it not with poison; strangle her in her bed, even the bed she hath contaminated.

OTHELLO.   Good, good; the justice of it pleases; very good.

IAGO.   And for Cassio, let me be his undertaker. You shall hear more by midnight.   196

[*A trumpet. Enter* LODOVICO, DESDEMONA, *and* Attendants.

OTHELLO.   Excellent good. What trumpet is that same?

IAGO.   I warrant, something from Venice, 'Tis Lodovico, this, comes from the Duke. See, your wife's with him.

LODOVICO.   Save you, worthy General!

OTHELLO.   With all my heart, sir.   200

LODOVICO.   The Duke and Senators of Venice greet you. [*Gives him a letter.*]

OTHELLO.   I kiss the instrument of their pleasures. [*Opens the letter, and reads.*]

DESDEMONA.   And what's the news, good cousin Lodovico?

IAGO.   I am very glad to see you, signior; Welcome to Cyprus.

LODOVICO.   I thank you. How does Lieutenant Cassio?
                                                                                205

IAGO.   Lives, sir.

DESDEMONA.   Cousin, there's fall'n between him and my lord
An unkind breach; but you shall make all well.

OTHELLO.   Are you sure of that?

DESDEMONA.   My lord?   210

OTHELLO [*reads*].   "This fail you not to do, as you will."—

LODOVICO.   He did not call; he's busy in the paper. Is there division 'twixt my lord and Cassio?

DESDEMONA.   A most unhappy one. I would do much T' atone them, for the love I bear to Cassio.   215

OTHELLO.   Fire and brimstone!

DESDEMONA.   My lord?

OTHELLO.   Are you wise?

DESDEMONA.   What, is he angry?

LODOVICO.   May be the letter mov'd him;
For, as I think, they do command him home,
Deputing Cassio in his government.

DESDEMONA.   Trust me, I am glad on't.

OTHELLO.   Indeed!

DESDEMONA.   My lord?   220

OTHELLO.   I am glad to see you mad.

DESDEMONA.   Why, sweet Othello,—

OTHELLO [*striking her*].   Devil!

---

185. *messes:* portions of food.   195. *undertaker:* dispatcher.

215. *atone:* reconcile.   227. *teem:* breed.   230. [an] Q. Om. F.

DESDEMONA.   I have not deserv'd this.

LODOVICO.   My lord, this would not be believ'd in
    Venice
  Though I should swear I saw 't. 'Tis very much. 225
  Make her amends: she weeps.

OTHELLO.   O devil, devil!
  If that the earth could teem with woman's tears,
  Each drop she falls would prove a crocodile.
  Out of my sight!

DESDEMONA.   I will not stay to offend you. [Going.]

LODOVICO.   Truly, [an] obedient lady: 230
  I do beseech your lordship, call her back.

OTHELLO.   Mistress!

DESDEMONA.   My lord?

OTHELLO.   What would you with her, sir?

LODOVICO.   Who, I, my lord?

OTHELLO.   Ay; you did wish that I would make her
    turn.
  Sir, she can turn, and turn, and yet go on,   235
  And turn again; and she can weep, sir, weep;
  And she's obedient, as you say, obedient,
  Very obedient. Proceed you in your tears.
  Concerning this, sir,—O well-painted passion!—
  I am commanded home.—Get you away;   240
  I'll send for you anon.—Sir, I obey the mandate,
  And will return to Venice.—Hence, avaunt!—

[Exit DESDEMONA.]

  Cassio shall have my place. And, sir, to-night
  I do entreat that we may sup together.
  You are welcome, sir, to Cyprus.—Goats and mon-
    keys! [Exit.   245

LODOVICO.   Is this the noble Moor whom our full Sen-
    ate
  Call all in all sufficient? Is this the nature
  Whom passion could not shake? whose solid virtue
  The shot of accident nor dart of chance
  Could neither graze nor pierce?

IAGO.   He is much chang'd.   250

LODOVICO.   Are his wits safe? Is he not light of brain?

IAGO.   He's that he is; I may not breathe my censure
  What he might be. If what he might he is not,
  I would to heaven he were!

LODOVICO.   What, strike his wife!

IAGO.   Faith, that was not so well; yet would I knew
  That stroke would prove the worst!   256

LODOVICO.   Is it his use?
  Or did the letters work upon his blood
  And new-create [this] fault?

IAGO.   Alas, alas!
  It is not honesty in me to speak
  What I have seen and known. You shall observe
    him,   260
  And his own courses will denote him so
  That I may save my speech. Do but go after,
  And mark how he continues.

LODOVICO.   I am sorry that I am deceiv'd in him.

[Exeunt.

SCENE 2.   [A room in the castle.]

Enter OTHELLO and EMILIA.

OTHELLO.   You have seen nothing then?

EMILIA.   Nor ever heard, nor ever did suspect.

OTHELLO.   Yes, you have seen Cassio and she together.

EMILIA.   But then I saw no harm, and then I heard
  Each syllable that breath made up between them. 5

OTHELLO.   What, did they never whisper?

EMILIA.   Never, my lord.

OTHELLO.   Nor send you out o' th' way?

EMILIA.   Never.

OTHELLO.   To fetch her fan, her gloves, her mask, nor
    nothing?

EMILIA.   Never, my lord.   10

OTHELLO.   That's strange.

EMILIA.   I durst, my lord, to wager she is honest,
  Lay down my soul at stake. If you think other,
  Remove your thought; it doth abuse your bosom.
  If any wretch have put this in your head,   15
  Let Heaven requite it with the serpent's curse!
  For, if she be not honest, chaste, and true,
  There's no man happy; the purest of their wives
  Is foul as slander.

OTHELLO.   Bid her come hither; go.

[Exit EMILIA.

  She says enough; yet she's a simple bawd   20
  That cannot say as much. This is a subtle whore,

---

258. [this] Q. his F.

A closet lock and key of villanous secrets;
And yet she'll kneel and pray; I have seen her do't.

[*Enter* DESDEMONA *with* EMILIA.

DESDEMONA.   My lord, what is your will?
OTHELLO.   Pray, chuck, come hither.
DESDEMONA.   What is your pleasure?
OTHELLO.   Let me see your eyes;   25
    Look in my face.
DESDEMONA.   What horrible fancy's this?
OTHELLO [*to* EMILIA].   Some of your function, mis-
    tress;
    Leave procreants alone and shut the door;
    Cough, or cry "hem," if anybody come.
    Your mystery, your mystery; nay, dispatch.   30

[*Exit* EMILIA.

DESDEMONA.   Upon my knee, what doth your speech
    import?
    I understand a fury in your words,
    [But not the words.]
OTHELLO.   Why, what art thou?
DESDEMONA.   Your wife, my lord; your true
    And loyal wife.
OTHELLO.   Come, swear it, damn thyself,   35
    Lest, being like one of heaven, the devils themselves
    Should fear to seize thee; therefore be double
    damn'd,
    Swear thou art honest.
DESDEMONA.   Heaven doth truly know it.
OTHELLO.   Heaven truly knows that thou art false as
    hell.
DESDEMONA.   To whom, my lord? With whom? How
    am I false?   40
OTHELLO.   Ah, Desdemon! Away! away! away!
DESDEMONA.   Alas the heavy day! Why do you weep?
    Am I the motive of these tears, my lord?
    If haply you my father do suspect
    An instrument of this your calling back,   45
    Lay not your blame on me. If you have lost him,
    [Why,] I have lost him too.

OTHELLO.   Had it pleas'd Heaven
    To try me with affliction; had they rain'd
    All kind of sores and shames on my bare head,
    Steep'd me in poverty to the very lips,   50
    Given to captivity me and my utmost hopes,
    I should have found in some place of my soul
    A drop of patience; but, alas, to make me
    The fixed figure for the time of scorn
    To point his slow and moving finger at!   55
    Yet could I bear that too, well, very well;
    But there, where I have garner'd up my heart,
    Where either I must live or bear no life;
    The fountain from which my current runs
    Or else dries up; to be discarded thence!   60
    Or keep it as a cistern for foul toads
    To knot and gender in! Turn thy complexion there,
    Patience, thou young and rose-lipp'd cherubin,
    [Ay, there] look grim as hell!
DESDEMONA.   I hope my noble lord esteems me hon-
    est.   65
OTHELLO.   O, ay; as summer flies are in the shambles,
    That quicken even with blowing. O thou weed,
    Who art so lovely fair and smell'st so sweet
    That the sense aches at thee, would thou hadst ne'er
    been born!
DESDEMONA.   Alas, what ignorant sin have I commit-
    ted?   70
OTHELLO.   Was this fair paper, this most goodly book,
    Made to write "whore" upon? What committed!
    Committed! O thou public commoner!
    I should make very forges of my cheeks,
    That would to cinders burn up modesty,   75
    Did I but speak thy deeds. What committed!
    Heaven stops the nose at it, and the moon winks;
    The bawdy wind, that kisses all it meets,
    Is hush'd within the hollow mine of earth
    And will not hear it. What committed!   80
    [Impudent strumpet!]
DESDEMONA.   By heaven, you do me wrong.

---

54. *time of scorn:* scorn of the age. 55. *slow and moving:* slowly moving. Q reads *slow unmoving.* 62. *Turn thy complexion:* change thy color. 64. [*Ay, there*] *I here* Ff Qq. 67. *quicken . . . blowing:* come to life as soon as impregnated. 73. *commoner:* harlot. 77. *winks:* shuts her eyes. 81. [*Impudent strumpet*] Q. Om. F.

Scene ii, 24. *Pray* Q. *Pray you* F. 30. *mystery:* trade. 33. [*But . . . words*] Q. Om. F. 47. [*Why*] Q. Om. F.

OTHELLO.   Are not you a strumpet?

DESDEMONA.   No, as I am a Christian.
   If to preserve this vessel for my lord
   From any other foul unlawful touch
   Be not to be a strumpet, I am none.   85

OTHELLO.   What, not a whore?

DESDEMONA.   No, as I shall be sav'd.

OTHELLO.   Is't possible?

DESDEMONA.   O, Heaven forgive us!

OTHELLO.   I cry you mercy, then.
   I took you for that cunning whore of Venice
   That married with Othello. [*Raising his voice.*]—You,
   mistress,   90

Re-enter EMILIA.

   That have the office opposite to Saint Peter,
   And keeps the gate of hell! You, you, ay, you!
   We have done our course; there's money for your
      pains.
   I pray you, turn the key and keep our counsel. [*Exit.*

EMILIA.   Alas, what does this gentleman conceive?   95
   How do you, madam? How do you, my good lady?

DESDEMONA.   Faith, half asleep.

EMILIA.   Good madam, what's the matter with my
   lord?

DESDEMONA.   With who?

EMILIA.   Why, with my lord, madam.   100

DESDEMONA.   Who is thy lord?

EMILIA.   He that is yours, sweet lady.

DESDEMONA.   I have none. Do not talk to me, Emilia;
   I cannot weep, nor answers have I none
   But what should go by water. Prithee, tonight
   Lay on my bed my wedding sheets, remember;   105
   And call thy husband hither.

EMILIA.   Here's a change indeed! [*Exit.*

DESDEMONA.   'Tis meet I should be us'd so, very meet.
   How have I been behav'd, that he might stick
   The small'st opinion on my least misuse?

Re-enter EMILIA *with* IAGO.

IAGO.   What is your pleasure, madam? How is't with
   you?   110

DESDEMONA.   I cannot tell. Those that do teach young
   babes
   Do it with gentle means and easy tasks.
   He might have chid me so; for, in good faith,
   I am a child to chiding.

IAGO.   What's the matter, lady?   114

EMILIA.   Alas, Iago, my lord hath so bewhor'd her,
   Thrown such despite and heavy terms upon her,
   That true hearts cannot bear it.

DESDEMONA.   Am I that name, Iago?

IAGO.   What name, fair lady?

DESDEMONA.   Such as she said my lord did say I was.

EMILIA.   He call'd her whore. A beggar in his drink
   Could not have laid such terms upon his callet. 121

IAGO.   Why did he so?

DESDEMONA.   I do not know; I am sure I am none
   such.

IAGO.   Do not weep, do not weep. Alas the day!

EMILIA.   Hath she forsook so many noble matches,
   Her father and her country and her friends,   126
   To be call'd whore? Would it not make one weep?

DESDEMONA.   It is my wretched fortune.

IAGO.   Beshrew him for't!
   How comes this trick upon him?

DESDEMONA.   Nay, Heaven doth know.

EMILIA.   I will be hang'd if some eternal villain,   130
   Some busy and insinuating rogue,
   Some cogging, cozening slave, to get some office,
   Have not devis'd this slander. I'll be hang'd else.

IAGO.   Fie, there is no such man; it is impossible.

DESDEMONA.   If any such there be, Heaven pardon
   him.   135

EMILIA.   A halter pardon him! and hell gnaw his
   bones!
   Why should he call her whore? Who keeps her com-
   pany?
   What place? what time? what form? what likelihood?
   The Moor's abus'd by some most villanous knave,
   Some base notorious knave, some scurvy fellow. 140
   O heavens, that such companions thou'dst unfold,
   And put in every honest hand a whip
   To lash the rascals naked through the world
   Even from the east to th' west!

---

104. *go by water:* be rendered by tears.   109. *opinion:* censure.
misuse: misconduct.

121. *callet:* whore.   132. *cogging:* lying. *cozening:* cheating.
141. *unfold:* expose.

IAGO.   Speak within door.

EMILIA.   O, fie upon them! Some such squire he was
That turn'd your wit the seamy side without,   146
And made you to suspect me with the Moor.

IAGO.   You are a fool; go to.

DESDEMONA.   Alas, Iago,
What shall I do to win my lord again?
Good friend, go to him; for, by this light of heaven,
I know not how I lost him. Here I kneel: 151
If e'er my will did trespass 'gainst his love,
Either in discourse of thought or actual deed,
Or that mine eyes, mine ears, or any sense
Delighted them [in] any other form;   155
Or that I do not yet, and ever did,
And ever will—though he do shake me off
To beggarly divorcement—love him dearly,
Comfort forswear me! Unkindness may do much:
And his unkindness may defeat my life,   160
But never taint my love. I cannot say "whore."
It does abhor me now I speak the word;
To do the act that might the addition earn
Not the world's mass of vanity could make me.

IAGO.   I pray you, be content; 'tis but his humour.
The business of the state does him offence,   166
[And he does chide with you.]

DESDEMONA.   If 'twere no other,—

IAGO.   It is but so, I warrant.

[*Trumpets within.*]

Hark, how these instruments summon to supper!
The messengers of Venice stay the meat.   170
Go in, and weep not; all things shall be well.

[*Exeunt* DESDEMONA *and* EMILIA. *Enter* RODERIGO.

How now, Roderigo!

RODERIGO.   I do not find that thou deal'st justly with
me.

IAGO.   What in the contrary?   174

RODERIGO.   Every day thou daff'st me with some device, Iago; and rather, as it seems to me now,
keep'st from me all conveniency than suppliest me

with the least advantage of hope. I will indeed no
longer endure it, nor am I yet persuaded to put up
in peace what already I have foolishly suff'red.

IAGO.   Will you hear me, Roderigo?   180

RODERIGO.   I have heard too much, and your words
and performances are no kin together.

IAGO.   You charge me most unjustly.

RODERIGO.   With nought but truth. I have wasted
myself out of my means. The jewels you have had
from me to deliver Desdemona would half have
corrupted a votarist. You have told me she hath
receiv'd them and return'd me expectations and
comforts of sudden respect and acquaintance, but I
find none.

IAGO.   Well; go to; very well.   190

RODERIGO.   Very well! go to! I cannot go to, man; nor
'tis not very well. Nay, I think it is scurvy, and
begin to find myself fopp'd in it.

IAGO.   Very well.

RODERIGO.   I tell you 'tis not very well. I will make
myself known to Desdemona. If she will return me
my jewels, I will give over my suit and repent my
unlawful solicitation; if not, assure yourself I will
seek satisfaction of you.   197

IAGO.   You have said now.

RODERIGO.   Ay, and said nothing but what I protest
intendment of doing.

IAGO.   Why, now I see there's mettle in thee, and even
from this instant do build on thee a better opinion
than ever before. Give me thy hand, Roderigo.
Thou hast taken against me a most just exception;
but yet, I protest, I have dealt most directly in thy
affair.

RODERIGO.   It hath not appear'd.   205

IAGO.   I grant indeed it hath not appear'd, and your
suspicion is not without wit and judgement. But,
Roderigo, if thou hast that in thee indeed, which I
have greater reason to believe now than ever, I
mean purpose, courage, and valour, this night show
it. If thou the next night following enjoy not
Desdemona, take me from this world with treachery and devise engines for my life.   211

---

153. *discourse:* course. 155. *[in]* Q$_2$ or F. 160. *defeat:* destroy.
167. *[And . . . you]* Q. Om. F. 170. *stay the meat:* wait to
dine. 175. *daff'st me:* puttest me off.

---

186. *votarist:* nun. 187. *sudden respect:* speedy notice.
192. *fopp'd:* duped. 211. *engines:* plots.

RODERIGO.   Well, what is it? Is it within reason and
compass?

IAGO.   Sir, there is especial commission come from
Venice to depute Cassio in Othello's place.

RODERIGO.   Is that true? Why, then Othello and
Desdemona return again to Venice.   216

IAGO.   O, no; he goes into Mauritania and taketh away
with him the fair Desdemona, unless his abode be
ling'red here by some accident; wherein none can
be so determinate as the removing of Cassio.

RODERIGO.   How do you mean, removing him?

IAGO.   Why, by making him uncapable of Othello's
place; knocking out his brains.

RODERIGO.   And that you would have me to do? 223

IAGO.   Ay, if you dare do yourself a profit and a right.
He sups tonight with a harlotry, and thither will I
go to him; he knows not yet of his honourable fortune. If you will watch his going thence, which I
will fashion to fall out between twelve and one,
you may take him at your pleasure. I will be near to
second your attempt, and he shall fall between us.
Come, stand not amaz'd at it, but go along with
me; I will show you such a necessity in his death
that you shall think yourself bound to put it on
him. It is now high supper-time, and the night
grows to waste. About it.   232

RODERIGO.   I will hear further reason for this.

IAGO.   And you shall be satisfi'd.

[*Exeunt.*

SCENE 3.   [*Another room in the castle.*]

Enter OTHELLO, LODOVICO, DESDEMONA, EMILIA, *and*
Attendants.

LODOVICO.   I do beseech you, sir, trouble yourself no
further.

OTHELLO.   O, pardon me; 'twill do me good to walk.

LODOVICO.   Madam, good-night; I humbly thank your
ladyship.

DESDEMONA.   Your honour is most welcome.

OTHELLO.   Will you walk, sir?   5
O,—Desdemona,—

DESDEMONA.   My lord?

OTHELLO.   Get you to bed on th' instant; I will be
return'd forthwith.
Dismiss your attendant there. Look 't be done.

DESDEMONA.   I will, my lord.

[*Exeunt* [OTHELLO, LODOVICO, *and* Attendants.]

EMILIA.   How goes it now? He looks gentler than he
did.   10

DESDEMONA.   He says he will return incontinent;
And hath commanded me to go to bed,
And bid me to dismiss you.

EMILIA.   Dismiss me!

DESDEMONA.   It was his bidding; therefore, good
Emilia,
Give me my nightly wearing, and adieu.   15
We must not now displease him.

EMILIA.   I would you had never seen him!

DESDEMONA.   So would not I. My love doth so approve
him
That even his stubbornness, his checks, his frowns,—
Prithee, unpin me,—have grace and favour [in
them].   20

EMILIA.   I have laid those sheets you bade me on the
bed.

DESDEMONA.   All's one. Good [faith], how foolish are
our minds!
If I do die before, prithee, shroud me
In one of these same sheets.

EMILIA.   Come, come, you talk.

DESDEMONA.   My mother had a maid call'd Barbary;
She was in love, and he she lov'd prov'd mad   26
And did forsake her. She had a song of "Willow";
An old thing 'twas, but it express'd her fortune,
And she died singing it. That song to-night
Will not go from my mind; I have much to do   30
But to go hang my head all at one side
And sing it like poor Barbary. Prithee, dispatch.

EMILIA.   Shall I go fetch your night-gown?

DESDEMONA.   No, unpin me here.
This Lodovico is a proper man.

EMILIA.   A very handsome man.   35

DESDEMONA.   He speaks well.

EMILIA.   I know a lady in Venice would have walk'd
barefoot to
Palestine for a touch of his nether lip.

DESDEMONA [*singing*].

Scene iii, 19. *stubbornness:* roughness.   20. [*in them*] Q. Om.
F.   22. [*faith*] Q. *Father* F.

"The poor soul sat [sighing] by a sycamore tree,
  Sing all a green willow;   40
Her hand on her bosom, her head on her knee,
  Sing willow, willow, willow.
The fresh streams ran by her, and murmur'd her
    moans;
  Sing willow, willow, willow;
Her salt tears fell from her, and soft'ned the
    stones;   45
  Sing willow, willow, willow;"

  Lay by these;—

           [*Singing.*] "Willow, willow;"—

Prithee, hie thee; he'll come anon;—
[*Singing.*] "Sing all a green willow must be my
  garland.   50
Let nobody blame him, his scorn I approve,"—

  Nay, that's not next.—Hark! who is't that knocks?
EMILIA. It's the wind.
DESDEMONA [*Singing*].

"I call'd my love false love; but what said he then?
  Sing willow, willow, willow.   55
If I court moe women, you'll couch with moe men."—
  So, get thee gone; good-night. Mine eyes do itch;
  Doth that bode weeping?
EMILIA. 'Tis neither here nor there.
DESDEMONA. I have heard it said so. O, these men,
  these men!
  Dost thou in conscience think,—tell me, Emilia,—
  That there be women do abuse their husbands 61
  In such gross kind?
EMILIA. There be some such, no question.
DESDEMONA. Wouldst thou do such a deed for all the
  world?
EMILIA. Why, would not you?
DESDEMONA. No, by this heavenly light!
EMILIA. Nor I neither by this heavenly light;   65
  I might do't as well i' th' dark.
DESDEMONA. Wouldst thou do such a deed for all the
  world?
EMILIA. The world's a huge thing; it is a great price
  For a small vice.

DESDEMONA. In troth, I think thou wouldst not. 69
EMILIA. In troth, I think I should; and undo't when I
  had done. Marry, I would not do such a thing for a
  joint-ring, nor for measures of lawn, nor for gowns,
  petticoats, nor caps, nor any petty exhibition; but,
  for all the whole world,—['ud's pity], who would
  not make her husband a cuckold to make him a
  monarch? I should venture purgatory for't.
DESDEMONA. Beshrew me, if I would do such a wrong
  For the whole world.   76
EMILIA. Why, the wrong is but a wrong i' th' world;
  and having the world for your labour, 'tis a wrong
  in your own world, and you might quickly make it
  right.
DESDEMONA. I do not think there is any such
  woman.   80
EMILIA. Yes, a dozen; and as many to th' vantage as
  would store the world they play'd for.
  But I do think it is their husbands' faults
  If wives do fall. Say that they slack their duties
  And pour our treasures into foreign laps,   85
  Or else break out in peevish jealousies,
  Throwing restraint upon us; or say they strike us,
  Or scant our former having in despite;
  Why, we have galls, and though we have some grace,
  Yet have we some revenge. Let husbands know 90
  Their wives have sense like them; they see and smell
  And have their palates both for sweet and sour
  As husbands have. What is it that they do
  When they change us for others? Is it sport?
  I think it is. And doth affection breed it?   95
  I think it doth. Is't frailty that thus errs?
  It is so too. And have not we affections,
  Desires for sport, and frailty, as men have?
  Then let them use us well; else let them know,
  The ills we do, their ills instruct us so.   100
DESDEMONA. Good-night, good-night. Heaven me
  such uses send
  Not to pick bad from bad, but by bad mend.

  [*Exeunt.*

---

39. [*sighing*] Q₂ *singing* F.

71. *joint-ring*: ring made in separable halves. 72. *exhibition*: allowance. 73. [*'ud's pity*] Q: God's pity. *Why* F. 81. *to th' vantage*: more, to boot. 86. *peevish*: silly. 88. *having*: allowance.
89. *galls*: spirits to resent injury.

ACT FIVE

SCENE 1. [*Cyprus. A street.*]

Enter IAGO *and* RODERIGO.

IAGO.   Here, stand behind this [bulk]; straight will he
  come.
  Wear thy good rapier bare, and put it home.
  Quick, quick; fear nothing; I'll be at thy elbow.
  It makes us, or it mars us; think on that,
  And fix most firm thy resolution.   5
RODERIGO.   Be near at hand; I may miscarry in't.
IAGO.   Here, at thy hand; be bold, and take thy stand.
    [*Retires.*]
RODERIGO.   I have no great devotion to the deed,
  And yet he hath given me satisfying reasons.
  'Tis but a man gone. Forth, my sword: he dies. 10
IAGO.   I have rubb'd this young quat almost to the
  sense,
  And he grows angry. Now, whether he kill Cassio,
  Or Cassio him, or each do kill the other,
  Every way makes my gain. Live Roderigo,
  He calls me to a restitution large   15
  Of gold and jewels that I bobb'd from him
  As gifts to Desdemona;
  It must not be. If Cassio do remain,
  He hath a daily beauty in his life
  That makes me ugly; and, besides, the Moor   20
  May unfold me to him; there stand I in much peril.
  No, he must die. But so; I heard him coming.

Enter CASSIO.

RODERIGO.   I know his gait, 'tis he.—Villain, thou
  diest! [*Makes a pass at* CASSIO.]
CASSIO.   That thrust had been mine enemy indeed,
  But that my coat is better than thou know'st. 25
  I will make proof of thine. [*Draws, and wounds*
  RODERIGO.]
RODERIGO.   O, I am slain.

[IAGO *from behind wounds* CASSIO *in the leg, and exit.*]

Act V, Scene i, 1. [bulk] Q: jutting part of a building. *barke* F.
11. *quat:* pimple. *the sense:* the quick.   16. *bobb'd:* cheated,
swindled.   25. *coat: i.e.,* of mail (worn under outer clothing).

CASSIO.   I am maim'd for ever. Help, ho! murder!
  murder! [*Falls.*]

Enter OTHELLO.

OTHELLO.   The voice of Cassio! Iago keeps his word.
RODERIGO.   O, villain that I am!
OTHELLO.   It is even so.
CASSIO.   O, help, ho! light! a surgeon!   30
OTHELLO.   'Tis he!—O brave Iago, honest and just,
  That hast such noble sense of thy friend's wrong!
  Thou teachest me. Minion, your dear lies dead,
  And your unblest fate hies; strumpet, I come.
  [Forth] of my heart those charms, thine eyes, are
  blotted;   35
  Thy bed, lust-stain'd, shall with lust's blood be
  spotted. [*Exit.*

Enter LODOVICO *and* GRATIANO.

CASSIO.   What, ho! no watch? no passage? Murder!
  murder!
GRATIANO.   'Tis some mischance; the voice is very
  direful.
CASSIO.   O, help!
LODOVICO.   Hark!   40
RODERIGO.   O wretched villain!
LODOVICO.   Two or three groan. 'Tis heavy night,
  These may be counterfeits; let's think 't unsafe
  To come in to the cry without more help.
RODERIGO.   Nobody come? Then shall I bleed to
  death.   45

Re-enter IAGO, *with a light.*

LODOVICO.   Hark!
GRATIANO.   Here's one comes in his shirt, with light
  and weapons.
IAGO.   Who's there? Whose noise is this that cries on
  murder?
LODOVICO.   We do not know.
IAGO.   Do not you hear a cry?
CASSIO.   Here, here! for Heaven's sake, help me!
IAGO.   What's the matter?   50
GRATIANO.   This is Othello's ancient, as I take it.

---

33. *Minion:* hussy.   35. [Fourth] Q. *For* F.   37. *passage:*
passers-by.   42. *heavy:* dark.

LODOVICO.   The same indeed; a very valiant fellow.

IAGO.   What are you here that cry so grievously?

CASSIO.   Iago? O, I am spoil'd, undone by villains!
Give me some help.   55

IAGO.   O me, Lieutenant! what villains have done this?

CASSIO.   I think that one of them is hereabout
And cannot make away.

IAGO.   O treacherous villains!
What are you there?—Come in, and give some
help. [*To* LODOVICO *and* GRATIANO.]

RODERIGO.   O, help me there!

CASSIO.   That's one of them.

IAGO.   O murd'rous slave! O villain! [*Thrusts*
[RODERIGO] *in.*

RODERIGO.   O damn'd Iago! O inhuman dog!

IAGO.   Kill men i' th' dark!—Where be these bloody
thieves?—
How silent is this town!—Ho! murder! murder!—
What may you be? Are you of good or evil?   65

LODOVICO.   As you shall prove us, praise us.

IAGO.   Signior Lodovico?

LODOVICO.   He, sir.

IAGO.   I cry you mercy. Here's Cassio hurt by villains.

GRATIANO.   Cassio!   70

IAGO.   How is't, brother!

CASSIO.   My leg is cut in two.

IAGO.   Marry, heaven forbid!
Light, gentlemen! I'll bind it with my shirt.

Enter BIANCA.

BIANCA.   What is the matter, ho? Who is't that cried?

IAGO.   Who is't that cried!   75

BIANCA.   O my dear Cassio! my sweet Cassio!
O Cassio, Cassio, Cassio!

IAGO.   O notable strumpet! Cassio, may you suspect
Who they should be that have thus mangled you?

CASSIO.   No.   80

GRATIANO.   I am sorry to find you thus; I have been to
seek you.

IAGO.   Lend me a garter. So. O, for a chair,
To bear him easily hence!

BIANCA.   Alas, he faints! O Cassio, Cassio, Cassio!

IAGO.   Gentlemen all, I do suspect this trash   85
To be a party in this injury.

---
82. *chair:* sedan chair.

Patience a while, good Cassio. Come, come;
Lend me a light. Know we this face or no?
Alas, my friend and my dear countryman
Roderigo! No:—yes, sure:—yes, 'tis Roderigo.   90

GRATIANO.   What, of Venice?

IAGO.   Even he, sir; did you know him?

GRATIANO.   Know him! ay.

IAGO.   Signior Gratiano? I cry your gentle pardon;
These bloody accidents must excuse my manners
That so neglected you.

GRATIANO.   I am glad to see you.   95

IAGO.   How do you, Cassio? O, a chair, a chair!

GRATIANO.   Roderigo!

IAGO.   He, he, 'tis he.

[A chair brought in.]

O, that's well said; the chair.
Some good man bear him carefully from hence;
I'll fetch the General's surgeon. [*To* BIANCA.]   For
you, mistress,   100
Save you your labour. He that lies slain here, Cassio,
Was my dear friend. What malice was between you?

CASSIO.   None in the world; nor do I know the man.

IAGO [*to* BIANCA].   What, look you pale? O, bear him
out o' th' air.

[CASSIO and RODERIGO are borne off.]

Stay you, good gentlemen. Look you pale, mistress?
Do you perceive the gastness of her eye?   106
Nay, if you stare, we shall hear more anon.
Behold her well; I pray you, look upon her.
Do you see, gentlemen? Nay, guiltiness will speak.
Though tongues were out of use.   110

Enter EMILIA.

EMILIA.   Alas, what's the matter? What's the matter,
husband?

IAGO.   Cassio hath here been set on in the dark
By Roderigo and fellows that are scap'd.
He's almost slain, and Roderigo quite dead.

EMILIA.   Alas, good gentleman! alas, good Cassio! 115

IAGO.   This is the fruits of whoring. Prithee, Emilia,
Go know of Cassio where he supp'd to-night.

[*To* BIANCA.]   What, do you shake at that?

---
106. *gastness:* ghastliness.

BIANCA.   He supp'd at my house; but I therefore shake
   not.
IAGO.   O, did he so? I charge you, go with me.   120
EMILIA.   Oh, fie upon thee, strumpet!
BIANCA.   I am no strumpet, but of life as honest
   As you that thus abuse me.
EMILIA.   As I? Fie upon thee!
IAGO.   Kind gentlemen, let's go see poor Cassio dress'd.
   Come, mistress, you must tell's another tale.   125
   Emilia, run you to the citadel,
   And tell my lord and lady what hath happ'd.
   Will you go on afore? [Aside.]   This is the night
   That either makes me or fordoes me quite.

[Exeunt.

SCENE 2.   [A bedchamber in the castle.]

DESDEMONA in bed [asleep]. Enter OTHELLO with a light.

OTHELLO.   It is the cause, it is the cause, my soul,—
   Let me not name it to you, you chaste stars!—
   It is the cause. Yet I'll not shed her blood,
   Nor scar that whiter skin of hers than snow,
   And smooth as monumental alabaster.   5
   Yet she must die, else she'll betray more men.
   Put out the light, and then put out the light.
   If I quench thee, thou flaming minister,
   I can again thy former light restore,
   Should I repent me; but once put out thy light,   10
   Thou cunning'st pattern of excelling nature,
   I know not where is that Promethean heat
   That can thy light relume. When I have pluck'd the
     rose
   I cannot give it vital growth again,
   It needs must wither. I'll smell [it] on the
     tree. [Kisses her.   15
   Oh, balmy breath, that dost almost persuade
   Justice to break her sword! One more, one more.
   Be thus when thou art dead, and I will kill thee
   And love thee after. One more, and that's the last;
   So sweet was ne'er so fatal. I must weep,   20
   But they are cruel tears. This sorrow's heavenly;
   It strikes where it doth love. She wakes.

DESDEMONA.   Who's there? Othello?
OTHELLO.   Ay, Desdemona.
DESDEMONA.   Will you come to bed, my lord?
OTHELLO.   Have you pray'd to-night, Desdemon?
DESDEMONA.   Ay, my lord.   25
OTHELLO.   If you bethink yourself of any crime
   Unreconcil'd as yet to Heaven and grace,
   Solicit for it straight.
DESDEMONA.   Alack, my lord, what may you mean by
   that?
OTHELLO.   Well, do it, and be brief; I will walk by.   30
   I would not kill thy unprepared spirit;
   No; heavens forfend! I would not kill thy soul.
DESDEMONA.   Talk you of killing?
OTHELLO.   Ay, I do.
DESDEMONA.   Then Heaven
   Have mercy on me!
OTHELLO.   Amen, with all my heart!
DESDEMONA.   If you say [so], I hope you will not kill
   me.   35
OTHELLO.   Hum!
DESDEMONA.   And yet I fear you; for you're fatal then
   When your eyes roll so. Why I should fear I know
     not,
   Since guiltiness I know not; but yet I feel I fear.
OTHELLO.   Think on thy sins.
DESDEMONA.   They are loves I bear to you.   40
OTHELLO.   Ay, and for that thou diest.
DESDEMONA.   That death's unnatural that kills for lov-
   ing.
   Alas, why gnaw you so your nether lip?
   Some bloody passion shakes your very frame.
   These are portents; but yet I hope, I hope,   45
   They do not point on me.
OTHELLO.   Peace, and be still!
DESDEMONA.   I will so. What's the matter?
OTHELLO.   That handkerchief which I so lov'd and
   gave thee
   Thou gav'st to Cassio.
DESDEMONA.   No, by my life and soul!
   Send for the man, and ask him.
OTHELLO.   Sweet soul, take heed,   50
   Take heed of perjury; thou art on thy deathbed.
DESDEMONA.   Ay, but not yet to die.

---

129. fordoes: destroys.

Scene ii, 12. Promethean heat: divine fire.   15. [it] Q. thee F.

35. [so] Q. Om. F.

OTHELLO.   [Yes], presently:
 Therefore confess thee freely of thy sin;
 For to deny each article with oath
 Cannot remove nor choke the strong conception 55
 That I do groan withal. Thou art to die.
DESDEMONA.   O, Heaven, have mercy on me!
OTHELLO.   I say, amen.
DESDEMONA.   And have you mercy too! I never did
 Offend you in my life; never lov'd Cassio
 But with such general warranty of heaven 60
 As I might love; I never gave him token.
OTHELLO.   By heaven, I saw my handkerchief in 's
 hand.
 O perjur'd woman! thou dost stone my heart,
 And makes me call what I intend to do
 A murder, which I thought a sacrifice. 65
 I saw the handkerchief.
DESDEMONA.   He found it then;
 I never gave it him. Send for him hither;
 Let him confess a truth.
OTHELLO.   He hath confess'd.
DESDEMONA.   What, my lord?
OTHELLO.   That he hath us'd thee.
DESDEMONA.   How? unlawfully?
OTHELLO.   Ay. 70
DESDEMONA.   He will not say so.
OTHELLO.   No, his mouth is stopp'd;
 Honest Iago hath ta'en order for't.
DESDEMONA.   O! my fear interprets. What, is he dead?
OTHELLO.   Had all his hairs been lives, my great re-
 venge
 Had stomach for them all. 75
DESDEMONA.   Alas! he is betray'd and I undone.
OTHELLO.   Out, strumpet! weep'st thou for him to my
 face?
DESDEMONA.   O, banish me, my lord, but kill me not!
OTHELLO.   Down, strumpet!
DESDEMONA.   Kill me to-morrow; let me live to-night!
OTHELLO.   Nay, if you strive,— 81
DESDEMONA.   But half an hour!
OTHELLO.   Being done, there is no pause.
DESDEMONA.   But while I say one prayer!
OTHELLO.   It is too late. [He smothers her.
EMILIA. (at the door).   My lord, my lord!
 What, ho! my lord, my lord! 85

OTHELLO.   What noise is this? Not dead? not yet
 quite dead?
 I that am cruel am yet merciful;
 I would not have thee linger in thy pain.
 So, so.
EMILIA. (within).   What, ho! my lord, my lord!
OTHELLO.   Who's there?
EMILIA [within].   O, good my lord, I would speak a
 word with you! 90
OTHELLO.   Yes:—'tis Emilia.—By and by.—She's
 dead.
 'Tis like she comes to speak of Cassio's death.
 The noise was high. Ha! no more moving?
 Still as the grave. Shall she come in? Were't good?—
 I think she stirs again:—no. What's best to do? 95
 If she come in, she'll sure speak to my wife.
 My wife! my wife! what wife? I have no wife.
 O, insupportable! O heavy hour!
 Methinks it should be now a huge eclipse
 Of sun and moon, and that th' affrighted globe 100
 Did yawn at alteration.
EMILIA [within].   I do beseech you.
 That I may speak with you, O, good my lord!
OTHELLO.   I had forgot thee. O, come in, Emilia.
 Soft; by and by.—Let me the curtains draw.—
 Where art thou? [Unlocks the door.]

 Enter EMILIA.

What's the matter with thee now? 105
EMILIA.   O, my good lord, yonder's foul murders
 done!
OTHELLO.   What, now?
EMILIA.   But now, my lord.
OTHELLO.   It is the very error of the moon;
 She comes more nearer earth than she was wont,
 And makes men mad. 111
EMILIA.   Cassio, my lord, hath kill'd a young Vene-
 tian
 Call'd Roderigo.
OTHELLO.   Roderigo kill'd!
 And Cassio kill'd!
EMILIA.   No, Cassio is not kill'd.
OTHELLO.   Not Cassio kill'd! Then murder's out of
 tune, 115
 And sweet revenge grows harsh.

---

52. [Yes] Q. Om. F. 55. conception: purpose.

109. error: aberration.

DESDEMONA.   O, falsely, falsely murder'd!

EMILIA.   O Lord, what cry is that?

OTHELLO.   That! what?

EMILIA.   Out, and alas! that was my lady's voice.
Help! help, ho! help! O lady, speak again!   120
Sweet Desdemona! O sweet mistress, speak!

DESDEMONA.   A guiltless death I die.

EMILIA.   O, who hath done this deed?

DESDEMONA.   Nobody; I myself. Farewell!
Commend me to my kind lord. O, farewell! [Dies.

OTHELLO.   Why, how should she be murd'red?   126

EMILIA.   Alas, who knows?

OTHELLO.   You heard her say herself, it was not I.

EMILIA.   She said so; I must needs report the truth.

OTHELLO.   She's, like a liar, gone to burning hell.
'Twas I that kill'd her.

EMILIA.   O, the more angel she,   130
And you the blacker devil!

OTHELLO.   She turn'd to folly, and she was a whore.

EMILIA.   Thou dost belie her, and thou art a devil.

OTHELLO.   She was false as water.

EMILIA.   Thou art rash as fire to say
That she was false: O, she was heavenly true!   135

OTHELLO.   Cassio did top her; ask thy husband else.
O, I were damn'd beneath all depth in hell
But that I did proceed upon just grounds
To this extremity. Thy husband knew it all.

EMILIA.   My husband!   140

OTHELLO.   Thy husband.

EMILIA.   That she was false to wedlock?

OTHELLO.   Ay, with Cassio. Had she been true,
If Heaven would make me such another world
Of one entire and perfect chrysolite,   145
I'd not have sold her for it.

EMILIA.   My husband!

OTHELLO.   Ay, 'twas he that told me on her first.
An honest man he is, and hates the slime
That sticks on filthy deeds.

EMILIA.   My husband!

OTHELLO.   What needs this iterance, woman? I say
thy husband.   150

EMILIA.   O mistress, villainy hath made mocks with
love!
My husband say [that] she was false!

---

145. *chrysolite:* a precious stone.   150. *iterance:* repetition.
152. [*that*] Q₂. Om. F.

OTHELLO.   He, woman;
I say thy husband; dost understand the word?
My friend, thy husband, honest, honest Iago.

EMILIA.   If he say so, may his pernicious soul   155
Rot half a grain a day! He lies to the heart.
She was too fond of her most filthy bargain.

OTHELLO.   Ha!

EMILIA.   Do thy worst!
This deed of thine is no more worthy heaven   160
Than thou wast worthy her.

OTHELLO.   Peace, you were best.

EMILIA.   Thou hast not half that power to do me
harm
As I have to be hurt. O gull! O dolt!
As ignorant as dirt! Thou hast done a deed—
I care not for thy sword; I'll make thee known 165
Though I lost twenty lives.—Help! help, ho! help!
The Moor hath kill'd my mistress! Murder! murder!

Enter MONTANO, GRATIANO, IAGO, *and others.*

MONTANO.   What is the matter? How now, general!

EMILIA.   O, are you come, Iago? You have done well,
That men must lay their murders on your neck.

GRATIANO.   What is the matter?   171

EMILIA.   Disprove this villain, if thou be'st a man.
He says thou told'st him that his wife was false.
I know thou didst not, thou'rt not such a villain.
Speak, for my heart is full.   175

IAGO.   I told him what I thought, and told no more
Than what he found himself was apt and true.

EMILIA.   But did you ever tell him she was false?

IAGO.   I did.

EMILIA.   You told a lie, an odious, damned lie;   180
Upon my soul, a lie, a wicked lie.
She false with Cassio!—did you say with Cassio?

IAGO.   With Cassio, mistress. Go to, charm your
tongue.

EMILIA.   I will not charm my tongue; I am bound to
speak.
My mistress here lies murdered in her bed,—   185

ALL.   O heavens forfend!

EMILIA.   And your reports have set the murderer on.

OTHELLO.   Nay, stare not, masters; it is true, indeed.

GRATIANO.   'Tis a strange truth.

MONTANO.   O monstrous act!

EMILIA.   Villany, villany, villany!   190

I think upon't,—I think I smell't,— O villany!
I thought so then,—I'll kill myself for grief—
O villany, villany!
IAGO.   What, are you mad? I charge you, get you home.
EMILIA.   Good gentlemen, let me have leave to speak;
'Tis proper I obey him, but not now.   196
Perchance, Iago, I will ne'er go home.
OTHELLO.   O! O! O! [*He falls on the bed.*
EMILIA.   Nay, lay thee down and roar;
For thou hast kill'd the sweetest innocent
That e'er did lift up eye.
OTHELLO [*rising*].   O, she was foul!   200
I scarce did know you, uncle; there lies your niece,
Whose breath, indeed, these hands have newly
stopp'd.
I know this act shows horrible and grim.
GRATIANO.   Poor Desdemon! I am glad thy father's
dead.
Thy match was mortal to him, and pure grief 205
Shore his old thread in twain. Did he live now,
His sight would make him do a desperate turn,
Yea, curse his better angel from his side,
And fall to reprobance.
OTHELLO.   'Tis pitiful; but yet Iago knows   210
That she with Cassio hath the act of shame
A thousand times committed. Cassio confess'd it;
And she did gratify his amorous works
With that recognizance and pledge of love
Which I first gave her. I saw it in his hand;   215
It was a handkerchief, an antique token
My father gave my mother.
EMILIA.   O [God]! O heavenly [God]!
IAGO.   ['Zounds,] hold your peace.
EMILIA.   'Twill out, 'twill out! I peace!
No, I will speak as liberal as the north,   220
Let Heaven and men and devils, let them all,
All, all, cry shame against me, yet I'll speak.
IAGO.   Be wise, and get you home.
EMILIA.   I will not.

   [*Iago offers to stab* EMILIA.]

GRATIANO.   Fie!
Your sword upon a woman?
EMILIA.   O thou dull Moor! that handkerchief thou
speak'st of   225
I found by fortune and did give my husband;
For often, with a solemn earnestness,
More than indeed belong'd to such a trifle,
He begg'd of me to steal't.
IAGO.   Villanous whore!
EMILIA.   She give it Cassio! No, alas! I found it, 230
And I did give't my husband.
IAGO.   Filth, thou liest!
EMILIA.   By heaven, I do not, I do not, gentlemen.
O murd'rous coxcomb! what should such a fool
Do with so good a wife?
OTHELLO.   Are there no stones in heaven   234
But what serves for the thunder?—Precious villain!

[*He runs at* IAGO: IAGO KILLS EMILIA.]

GRATIANO.   The woman falls; sure, he hath kill'd his
wife.
EMILIA.   Ay, ay! O, lay me by my mistress' side.

   [*Exit* IAGO.

GRATIANO.   He's gone, but his wife's kill'd.
MONTANO.   'Tis a notorious villain. Take you this
weapon
Which I have [here] recover'd from the Moor. 240
Come, guard the door without; let him not pass,
But kill him rather. I'll after that same villain,
For 'tis a damned slave.

   [*Exeunt* MONTANO *and* GRATIANO.

OTHELLO.   I am not valiant neither,
But every puny whipster gets my sword.
But why should honour outlive honesty?   245
Let it go all.
EMILIA.   What did thy song bode, lady?
Hark, canst thou hear me? I will play the swan,
And die in music. [*Singing*] "Willow, willow, wil-
low!"—
Moor, she was chaste; she lov'd thee, cruel Moor;

---

192. *I . . . then.* See IV.ii.130–133.   209. *reprobance:* damnation.   218. [*God*] . . . [*God*] Q. *Heaven . . . Powers* F.
219. [*'Zounds*] Q. *Come* F.   220. *liberal:* freely.

234. *stones:* bolts.   240. [*here*] Q. Om. F.   244. *whipster:*
term of contempt.

So come my soul to bliss, as I speak true;   250
So speaking as I think, alas, I die. [*Dies.*

OTHELLO.   I have another weapon in this chamber;
It was a sword of Spain, the ice-brook's temper,—
O, here it is. Uncle, I must come forth.

GRATIANO (*within*).   If thou attempt it, it will cost thee
dear: 255
Thou hast no weapon, and perforce must suffer.

OTHELLO.   Look in upon me then and speak with me,
Or, naked as I am, I will assault thee.

[*Re-enter* GRATIANO.]

GRATIANO.   What is the matter?

OTHELLO.   Behold, I have a weapon;
A better never did itself sustain   260
Upon a soldier's thigh. I have seen the day
That, with this little arm and this good sword,
I have made my way through more impediments
Than twenty times your stop. But, O vain boast!
Who can control his fate? 'tis not so now.   265
Be not afraid though you do see me weapon'd;
Here is my journey's end, here is my butt
And very sea-mark of my utmost sail.
Do you go back dismay'd? 'Tis a lost fear;
Man but a rush against Othello's breast   270
And he retires. Where should Othello go?
Now, how dost thou look now? O ill-starr'd wench!
Pale as thy smock! when we shall meet at compt,
This look of thine will hurl my soul from heaven,
And fiends will snatch at it. Cold, cold, my girl!   275
Even like thy chastity. O cursèd, cursèd slave!
Whip me, ye devils,
From the possession of this heavenly sight!
Blow me about in winds! roast me in sulphur!
Wash me in steep-down gulfs of liquid fire!   280
O Desdemon! dead, Desdemon! dead!
Oh! Oh!

Enter LODOVICO, MONTANO, CASSIO *carried in a chair,
and* Officers, *with* IAGO [*prisoner*].

LODOVICO.   Where is this rash and most unfortunate
man?

OTHELLO.   That's he that was Othello; here I am.

LODOVICO.   Where is that viper? Bring the villain
forth.   285

OTHELLO.   I look down towards his feet; but that's a
fable.
If that thou be'st a devil, I cannot kill thee. [*Wounds*
IAGO.]

LODOVICO.   Wrench his sword from him.

IAGO.   I bleed, sir; but not kill'd.

OTHELLO.   I am not sorry neither. I'd have thee live;
For, in my sense, 'tis happiness to die.   290

LODOVICO.   O thou Othello, that [wast] once so good,
Fall'n in the practice of a cursed slave,
What shall be said to thee?

OTHELLO.   Why, anything.
An honourable murderer, if you will;
For nought I did in hate, but all in honour.   295

LODOVICO.   This wretch hath part confess'd his villainy.
Did you and he consent in Cassio's death?

OTHELLO.   Ay.

CASSIO.   Dear General, I never gave you cause.

OTHELLO.   I do believe it, and I ask your pardon. 300
Will you, I pray, demand that demi-devil
Why he hath thus ensnar'd my soul and body?

IAGO.   Demand me nothing; what you know, you
know.
From this time forth I never will speak word.

LODOVICO.   What, not to pray?

GRATIANO.   Torments will ope your lips.   305

OTHELLO.   Well, thou dost best.

LODOVICO.   Sir, you shall understand what hath
befall'n,
Which, as I think, you know not. Here is a letter
Found in the pocket of the slain Roderigo,
And here another. The one of them imports   310
The death of Cassio to be undertook
By Roderigo.

OTHELLO.   O villain!

CASSIO.   Most heathenish and most gross!

LODOVICO.   Now here's another discontented paper,

---

253. *ice-brook's temper:* its steel tempered in icy water.
258. *naked:* unarmed.   264. *stop:* power to stop.   267. *butt:*
goal.   273. *compt:* accounting, *i.e.,* Judgment Day.

286. *I . . . feet: i.e.,* to see if they are cloven.   291. [*wast*] *was*
F. *wert* Q.   292. *practice:* plot.

Found in his pocket too; and this, it seems,   315
Roderigo meant t' have sent this damned villain;
But that, belike, Iago in the interim
Came in and satisfi'd him.
OTHELLO.   O thou pernicious caitiff!—
How came you, Cassio, by that handkerchief
That was my wife's?
CASSIO.   I found it in my chamber,   320
And he himself confess'd but even now
That there he dropp'd it for a special purpose
Which wrought to his desire.
OTHELLO.   O fool! fool! fool!
CASSIO.   There is besides in Roderigo's letter,
How he upbraids Iago, that he made him   325
Brave me upon the watch, whereon it came
That I was cast; and even but now he spake,
After long seeming dead, Iago hurt him,
Iago set him on.
LODOVICO.   You must forsake this room and go with
us.   330
Your power and your command is taken off,
And Cassio rules in Cyprus. For this slave,
If there be any cunning cruelty
That can torment him much and hold him long,
It shall be his. You shall close prisoner rest,   335
Till that the nature of your fault be known
To the Venetian state. Come, bring away.
OTHELLO.   Soft you; a word or two before you go.
I have done the state some service, and they know't.
No more of that. I pray you, in your letters,   340
When you shall these unlucky deeds relate,
Speak of me as I am; nothing extenuate,
Nor set down aught in malice. Then must you speak
Of one that lov'd not wisely but too well;
Of one not easily jealous, but, being wrought,   345
Perplex'd in the extreme; of one whose hand,

Like the base [Indian], threw a pearl away
Richer than all his tribe; of one whose subdu'd eyes,
Albeit unused to the melting mood,
Drops tears as fast as the Arabian trees   350
Their medicinal gum. Set you down this;
And say besides, that in Aleppo once,
Where a malignant and a turban'd Turk
Beat a Venetian and traduc'd the state,
I took by th' throat the circumcised dog,   355
And smote him—thus. [Stabs himself.
LODOVICO.   O bloody period!
GRATIANO.   All that's spoke is marr'd.
OTHELLO.   I kiss'd thee ere I kill'd thee: no way but
this,
Killing myself, to die upon a kiss. [Falls on the bed,
and] dies.
CASSIO.   This did I fear, but thought he had no
weapon;   360
For he was great of heart.
LODOVICO [to IAGO].   O Spartan dog,
More fell than anguish, hunger, or the sea!
Look on the tragic loading of this bed;
This is thy work. The object poisons sight;
Let it be hid. Gratiano, keep the house,   365
And seize upon the fortunes of the Moor,
For they succeed on you. To you, Lord Governor,
Remains the censure of this hellish villain;
The time, the place, the torture. O, enforce it!
Myself will straight aboard; and to the state   370
This heavy act with heavy heart relate.

[Exeunt.

Curtain

---

321. *but* Q. *it but* F.   346. *Perplex'd:* distraught.

347. *[Indian]* Q. *Indean* F. The allusion has not been identified.   356. *period:* end.   361. *Spartan dog:* bloodhound.
366. *seize upon:* take legal possession of.   368. *censure:* sentenc-
ing.

Music in *Othello*

Music in Shakespeare's drama had many uses: military fanfare and pageantry, accompaniment to dance, an enhancement to a social setting, a part of an intimate lyrical mood. In *Othello*, the instrumental music is associated with the world of action; the vocal music (folk ballads rather than art songs) with the inner world of character. Two examples of the latter appear on pages 380 and 381: Iago's drinking song, "And let me the cannakin clinke" (Act II, scene iii); and Desdemona's ballad, "The Willow Song" (Act IV, scene iii). Iago's song, like most of what he says, seems to be something that it is not and serves his purpose. Creating an atmosphere of drunken gaiety, the song is really intended to inebriate Cassio. Desdemona's ballad, once sung by a maid called Barbary (the name recalls Africa) who loved a man who went mad, allows her to express her subconscious forebodings of imminent death. The song's sad rhythms tell more vividly than Desdemona would in her speech of a deep love that somehow went wrong. It creates in the spectator a moment of agonized suspense over what will come next.

COMMENTS AND QUESTIONS ON *OTHELLO*

1. For what different purposes does Shakespeare use blank verse, prose, rhymed verse, and music?
2. In what ways do the dramatic purposes of the music for *Othello* differ from those of *The Play of Daniel*?
3. What effect do the songs have on you? Would you include them in a modern production of the play?
4. How do you interpret the character of Iago? The English Romantic writer and critic Coleridge described the evil in Iago as a "motiveless malignancy." Others have called him a kind of devil, a totally evil figure. Some argue that he has (in his own mind) real motives for hating Othello. What are these motives, and which are believable?
5. How does Iago manipulate Roderigo? Cassio? Othello?
6. What is the role and the significance of the handkerchief?
7. To what extent does racial prejudice influence Iago and the other characters?
8. Describe the character of Othello. What qualifies him as a tragic hero? What is Othello's social position as a black man in a white society? Does this contribute to his insecurity and to his jealousy?
9. Does Othello at any point apply racial stereotypes to himself? Is this Iago's doing?
10. Do you think that Othello's final assessment of himself, in the speech just before his suicide, is accurate? How do you think this scene should be acted?
11. What is Desdemona's role and character? Do you have the impression that she and Othello know each other well? To what extent is the love between her and Othello endangered by their society, and to what extent is its destruction a result of Iago's manipulation?
12. Language, particularly images, plays an important part in *Othello*. We have mentioned images of black and white, animal images, and images related to poison. What effects do these have in the play? What other types can you find?
13. Compare Oedipus and Othello as tragic figures.
14. Do you find that *Othello* is a "depressing" tragedy, as some readers do, or that it ends on a note of redemption, as does *Oedipus Rex*?
15. To what extent does Shakespeare's tragedy exemplify the humanist belief in the dignity of man, and to what extent does it show late Renaissance skepticism?
16. What does the play tell you about European perceptions of Africa and Africans?
17. In what ways does *Othello* seem relevant to our own time?

Iago's Drinking Song

And let me the can-na-kin clinke - - - - - clinke And let me the

can-na-kin clinke - - - clinke A sol-dier's a man, oh man's life's but a

span Why - then let a sol - dier - - - drinke - - - - drinke.

The Willow Song

RENAISSANCE AND REFORMATION: ROOTS AND CONTINUITIES

In the section on the Italian Renaissance, we focused on its beginnings in Florence rather than on its "high" (early sixteenth-century) phase in Rome. It is in fifteenth-century Florence that we can best witness the radical departures from medieval mentality; the innovations in art, life, and thought; and the new fusion of Christian and classical traditions that laid the basis for much of our modern art, thought, and institutions. The roots of the humanities as we know them are certainly there. We have seen how Florentine humanism spread to northern Europe, influencing the development of a literature at least equal to its own, and how its original self-confidence underwent a crisis that is still with us.

Individualism   "The discovery of the individual was made in early fifteenth-century Florence," proclaims Kenneth Clark in his *Civilization* series, "Nothing can alter that fact." Certainly, when one looks at the portraits of Renaissance Florentines (the art of the portrait had been lost in Europe since Roman times!), or when one reads about their lives or views the different styles of each artist, one senses an individuality that was not present in the more collective and symbolic arts of the Middle Ages. The development of a more naturalistic way of portraying individual characters and their natural surroundings is part of this trend—we see its beginnings in the fourteenth century with Giotto.

Civic Sense   If fifteenth-century Florentines were highly conscious of themselves as individuals, they were also very much aware of being part of a community. Florence in many ways resembled a Greek city-state; and, like the ancient Athenians, the Florentines believed that participation in the affairs of state was essential for the realization of one's full humanity. But the men of the Renaissance needed to justify this classical value in Christian terms. Whereas medieval people believed that the contemplative life, or the life devoted to God, was of highest value, the fifteenth-century Florentines believed that Christian ideals could be served just as well in a secular, active life. Their political ideal of republicanism, rule by a body of citizens, has served as a basis for modern political theory. Although the modern state developed out of the medieval monarchies, since the nineteenth century these states have been on the whole republican.

By the last half of the fifteenth century, Florence came under the more autocratic rule of the Medici family. An ardent republican, Machiavelli nevertheless saw that by this time the ideal form of government was no longer practical for Florence. Yet through the early sixteenth century the spirit of republicanism, as seen in Michelangelo's *David*, with his proud, youthful defiance of tyranny, and his *Brutus*, the defender of Roman liberty, remained identified with the city. Republicanism was a part of the civic humanism of which Florentines were proud. The Florentines with their urban-centered lifestyle created a city whose physical aspect expressed their values. The architecture and sculpture, which even today give Florence its distinctive character, reflect a sense of beauty and proportion keyed to the measure of man. City planning as we know it today was born in Florence with the treatises of Leon Battista Alberti.

Visual and Verbal Eloquence   Beautiful architecture was for the practitioner Brunelleschi and the theoretician Alberti what beautiful speech was for the Florentine humanists. Visual and verbal eloquence were means of using newly rediscovered classical values in the service of Christian truth. Brunelleschi and (after him) Michelangelo observed closely the remains of Roman buildings and statues; Petrarch, Salutati, and Bruni edited and studied Latin, and eventually Greek, texts. The use of language was for the humanists the art that made man most truly human; consequently, the studies that they called the humanities focused on literature.

Historical and Visual Perspective In their study of ancient rhetoric, the humanists observed a truth that the medieval mind seemed not to realize: language and other human customs, institutions, and ideas change; they have a history. The notion of seeing oneself and one's culture in historical perspective, as part of a continuum of time, has become a habit with us; it has its origins in the humanists' new way of thought.

Intimately connected with this sense of historical perspective was the humanists' awareness that man constructed his own history. This led them to view the past, particularly the ancient pagan and early Christian past, as providing cultural alternatives to their contemporary world. This helps to explain the humanist concern for introducing moral, political, and religious reforms into their society. Their efforts were predicated on the belief that it was possible to bring society back to better and purer times. This same commitment to the idea that human beings can shape the future has come to characterize the modern world. Now, however, the models we utilize are rarely drawn from societies that have actually existed but rather from those we envision in our mind's eye.

The ability to see with the perspective of time has its artistic parallel in the ability to see, and to draw, with the perspective of space. There is no doubt that the technical development permitting artists to give the illusion of three dimensions on the flat surface of a canvas was a major step in the history of art. Renaissance painters established a formal visual language for their art that remained until recently the official standard of all Western art academies. Yet *perspective*, it must be remembered, was a means, not an end in itself. It permitted artists to represent what they observed, rather than to create symbols of the unseen. The sources of their observation were primarily two: nature (inanimate, animate, and human) and antiquity. From these they derived an art centered on the human being and the here-and-now; yet, like the humanists, they wished to put these new modes of expression to the service of Christian values. Leonardo, who stressed the scientific nature of painting and its worthiness to be

placed among the liberal arts, created one of the most mystical Virgins ever painted.

Practicality Leonardo was also a creator of tools and devices by which man could control his natural surroundings. In this he reflects the tendency in the Renaissance for the theoretical to become increasingly united with the practical. The great scientific advances of the seventeenth century would have been impossible without the creation of better instrumentation with which to measure, view, and manipulate the material world. Incidentally, as we will explain in the discussion of the Scientific Revolution, the development of Neoplatonism in the fifteenth century led to a new concern with mathematics, which also made a fundamental contribution to new approaches in natural science.

Developments in Music In music, too, nature and antiquity were sources that helped new forms to flourish. Renaissance composers were not acquainted with the actual musical works of the Greeks and Romans, but they read their musical theory and were interested in the ways in which music could be wedded to words. We have seen how this was done in the Isaac composition; we have also seen how nature (such as the flowing fountain) and human emotion are "tone painted" in this piece. Today's composer would write different sounds to depict a fountain or to express grief and anguish, but the concept of musical sound affecting human emotions stretches continuously back through history to classical Greece. Much of Renaissance music was religious, but secular music gained prominence at this time. Isaac's death lament for Lorenzo and Poliziano's poem lament the passing of this life but do not refer to the next one, and the only god mentioned in the piece is Phoebus Apollo!

Non-Christian Subject Matter The use of pagan, classical subjects in painting, sculpture, music, and literature represents a radical break with medieval culture. Much of this "pagan" art developed under the influence of Lorenzo de' Medici and the circle of Neoplatonic scholars around him. The lyrical Venuses and nymphs of Botticelli represent joy in this world but also an underlying melancholy. One senses in them a spiritual world beyond the visible forms. Similarly, Lorenzo's carnival song and the music accompanying it use a subject from classical mythology to urge people to enjoy life in the present—before it slips away. The medieval focus on the salvation of the immortal soul has shifted.

The Dignity of Man One of Lorenzo's Neoplatonic acquaintances, Pico della Mirandola, made what is considered by many to be the classical Renaissance statement on the dignity and grandeur of man. Pico's success at fusing the Judeo-Christian and Greco-Roman ways of thinking is problematic: although he recognized Christianity as the truest of all religions, he nonetheless endowed man with creative powers exceeding those of celestial beings, thus sounding a note that had not been heard since antiquity. Yet, when this brilliant, handsome prince of Mirandola died in Florence of fever at the age of thirty-one, he met death wrapped in the robes of a Dominican friar.

Northern Humanism When Italian humanism spread to northern Europe, its Christian aspect was emphasized more than its pagan one. Humanists such as Erasmus read and delighted in the classical authors but turned their attention more toward the study and editing of Greek and Latin Christian texts. Erasmus believed strongly in the value of reading and study: through knowledge and the development of inner piety, individual Christians could help to reform the ignorance and emphasis on externals that pervaded the Church, especially its monasteries.

Northern Europe made its greatest contribution to our culture through the printed word. Ever since the development of printing we have relied on communications media for the circulation of news and ideas. Radio and television have, of course, speeded up the process enormously, and film has come to fuse visual with literary statements; but we still rely heavily on books for the dissemination of intellectual developments and for knowledge of the past. Books, such as those published by Erasmus, enabled more people to form intelligent opinions and thus to question authority. Humanistic educators still share Erasmus' faith in the printed word's capacity to aid in the process of creating well-informed, soundly reasoning, independently thinking human individuals.

Reformation Martin Luther pushed Erasmus' emphasis on the study of texts and rejection of authority to what Erasmus considered a radical extreme. Trained in humanistic methods, Luther used his extensive knowledge of Hebrew, Greek, and Latin to study the Bible directly, without the official interpretations of the Church, and to translate it into German, thus making it available to his countrymen. Luther's studies led him to believe that the original message of Christ had been distorted over the centuries. Given this insight, he felt compelled to reject "on conscience" certain doctrines and practices of the Church and, with many other contributing factors, launched the Reformation. Although Luther became as doctrinaire as the authorities he had rejected, the impetus he gave to thinking independently of authority has had far-reaching influences on the culture of the modern world. There is a direct line from Luther to the twentieth-century individual's sense of isolation, lack of direction, and need, in a tangle of conflicting values, to find himself.

Cultural Relativism Religious wars between Catholics and Protestants raged throughout Europe in the sixteenth century. Paradoxically, this period of religious troubles coincided with a tremendous economic boom, fueled in part by the importation of gold and silver from the New World. Swift economic change, population increase, and rapidly rising prices, however, probably added to the unsettling atmosphere created by religious controversy. At the intellectual level individuals like Montaigne reflect a new and very modern feeling that truth and belief are, after all, relative matters.

Cultural relativism became during the sixteenth century a corollary to relativism in matters of opinion. In this era of travel and exploration, Europeans discovered in America, Africa, and Asia people who lived with customs and institutions very different from theirs. Just as Mediterranean peoples had once viewed Europeans as barbaric, many Europeans now thought the newly discovered cultures uncivilized, vastly inferior to their own. Intelligent observers such as Montaigne used the different cultural values to reflect what was corrupt and unjust in European society. Cultural relativism has served self-criticism and social satire ever since.

European Contact with Africa   The travels of Europeans in Africa led whites to reflect on the strange phenomenon of the existence of black people and blacks, as we will see in Part IV, to reflect on the strange phenomenon of the existence of white people. Prejudice was reinforced by a black/white symbolism already built into European languages, with black generally representing evil and white good. We have seen how Shakespeare used this symbolism in English for his original purposes and how he created the first black hero of the European stage.

William Shakespeare embodies nearly all of the currents that we have witnessed in the Renaissance-Reformation period. Like Leonardo, Michelangelo, and Luther, he was a giant in an age of geniuses—one who discovered and mastered new worlds of thought and expression. His characters demonstrate a range of feeling from the early humanists' confidence in man's abilities and powers to late Renaissance skepticism and relativism and the Reformation's doubt that man can accomplish much of anything on his own. Shakespeare combined the medieval and the classical traditions to lay the basis for the modern theater. His Othello, conqueror and noble warrior, yet prey to unconscious passions, black in a white society, is both a hero of the late Renaissance and a representative modern man.

PART FOUR

The African
Cultural Root

AFRICA TODAY

14

African
Backgrounds

The cultures of Western Europe and those of Africa begin to mingle and to affect each other during the European age of exploration and expansion in the Renaissance. Since that time, and particularly with the beginning of the trans-Atlantic slave trade in the fifteenth century, European, American, and African civilizations have been inextricably intertwined. Our introduction of Africa into the humanities at this point indicates the time period during which the cultures of West Africa, in particular, became one of the cultural roots of Americans.

Africa has influenced the West economically, as well as in the social and cultural realms. Profits from trade with Africa contributed to the development of northern Europe leading to the Industrial Revolution. Subsequently, the pursuit of markets for the goods produced by this revolution was an important economic motivation for the partition of Africa and the onset of colonial rule in the late nineteenth century. Patterns of economic relationships stimulated by colonialism, wherein Africa continued to provide raw materials or primary agricultural products to the industrialized West, remained little changed by the fact of independence for most of the African states in the 1960s and 1970s.

Images of Africa in the West   As Europe and America passed through the Enlightenment and into the age of democracy and nationalism, Africa remained a persistent symbol of "the other," of a civilization founded on principles of thought and religious behavior that were perceived to be fundamentally different from those of the West. The "noble savage" of the eighteenth century became the "primitive savage" at the bottom of the evolutionary ladder in the annals of Darwinian thought. Social and religious movements springing from the latter spurred intense efforts to Christianize and to "civilize" Africans in the twentieth century. In America it underlay missionary appeals and the Tarzan image of Africa, shaken but still powerful in our day. Europeans and Americans involved in the effort to "tame" Africans, to make them more like themselves, often succumbed to the "heart of darkness" as it appears in the novel by Joseph Conrad and in the works of others like Graham Greene. This image, a creation of the European mind, was rarely informed by substantive knowledge or the capacity to accept the legitimacy of different civilizations. Nevertheless, the idea of Africa and the African exercised a significant cultural influence on Western art and thought and will appear as a theme in Volume II of this book.

Africa and America   Perhaps more relevant to our purposes here is the direct role that Africa has played in the formation of American culture. Between the sixteenth and nineteenth centuries, more Africans came to the Americas than did people of other lands. Although the African slaves were put under great pressure to forget all aspects of their own, very diverse cultures, an amazing number of their customs were able to survive. We will look closely at the African "survivals" in Afro-American culture (and their impact on the whole of American culture) at the end of Part Four and again in the chapter on Afro-American culture in Vol-

ume II. Let us turn now to the study of Africa itself, both before and after the crucial contact with the West.

The continent of Africa is so large—and so diverse in its geographical, racial, linguistic, and cultural aspects—that it is almost impossible to speak of it generally, as a whole. Although we will need to make some remarks about the entire continent, we will concentrate primarily on the area that was the homeland of most Africans sent to the New World: the western coast ranging from 20° north to 20° south of the equator and extending up to one thousand miles inland— roughly the areas comprising the coastline and the drainage basins of the two great rivers, the Niger and Congo (see map). We will look briefly at some important points in the history of this area, particularly the great empires that flourished around the time of the Renaissance in Europe. Our focus will then be on traditional arts, values, and systems of thought in the cultures of a few West African peoples. "Traditional" refers to non-Westernized, nonindustrialized Africa, as opposed to modern Africa, whose societies have been significantly transformed by the colonial experience. It is important to bear in mind that the concept of time in traditional African cultures is different from that in the West. Western art and thought, beginning with the Greeks, has been characterized by rapid change and a sense of evolution through time. African religions tend to emphasize the circularity, rather than the linearity, of time, and African artists put more value on community and tradition than on individuality and change. Thus, when we talk about a Yoruba style, we will not be particularly concerned with whether the work dates from the eighteenth or the twentieth century. In the case of oral poetry and tales, the dates of origin are usually not known. In the case of early African history, however, we will be interested in attempting to establish the times when the great civilizations flourished.

Stages in African History: The Great Empires

The systematic exploration of Africa by Europeans began in the fifteenth century. Europe had been in contact for hundreds of years with the north coast of Africa and in the fourteenth century had undertaken colonization of the Canary Islands off the mainland. But

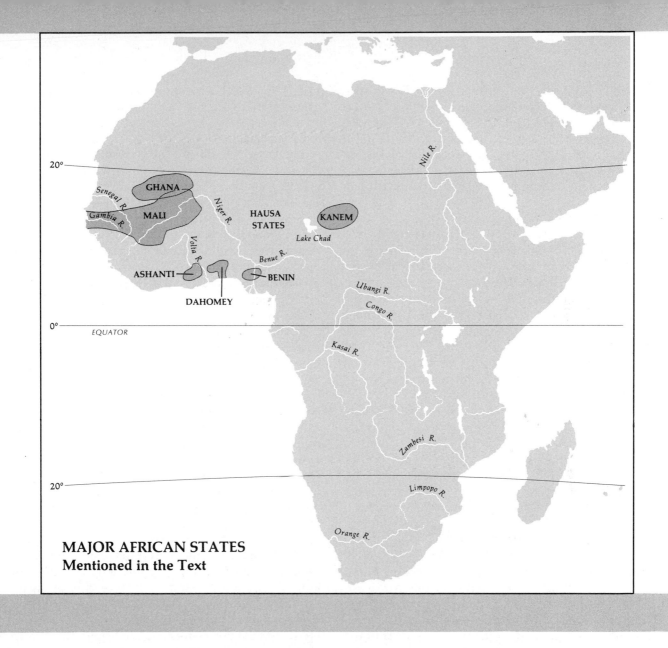

MAJOR AFRICAN STATES
Mentioned in the Text

in the middle decades of the fifteenth century, under the sponsorship of Prince Henry the Navigator (1394–1460), son of John I of Portugal, a succession of ambitious expeditions were undertaken. By the time of the prince's death, Europe's knowledge of Africa extended far down the Guinea coast. By 1497 Vasco da Gama had successfully rounded the Cape of Good Hope, traveled up the east African coast, and made his way to Calicut on the west coast of India. His safe return to Lisbon in September 1499 marked the establishment of a sea route to the East, ushering in a major era in the history of Europe's relationship with Africa and Asia. Because of the significance of the European contact, the history of Africa for our purposes is divided into two periods with the fifteenth century as the point of demarcation.

Early Africa The sources of knowledge of African history before the late fifteenth century are various. Most written evidence comes from travelers' accounts

—primarily by Arabs who regularly traded with sub-Saharan peoples in West Africa and along the eastern coast of the continent. Few African peoples used writing, but a good deal is known from oral traditions transferred from generation to generation by specialists entrusted with preserving the history of their people. Studies of these traditions have shown that they may contain biases and time distortions because of the social and political function they have in a society at a given time. But they are also likely to contain factual details, from the recent and sometimes from the remote past, that have been retained because of their importance. Recently, scholars have developed techniques for analyzing oral traditions more sophisticated than those available in the past. Coupled with the conclusions of modern research in archaeology, anthropology, botany, and linguistics, these written and oral accounts have enabled historians in recent years to establish the outlines of Africa's history before the fifteenth century.

For most archaeologists Africa is the cradle of mankind, although the relationship between the early forms of man discovered in the Olduvai Gorge in Kenya and the peopling of the continents remains an unsolved question. On the African continent itself human society in the course of its development evolved an incredible array of cultures characterized by divergent languages and beliefs; a wide range of technological levels; and many political and social organizations.

The varying development of Africa's people is closely related to the vast diversity of ecological setting found on the continent. The major areas include North Africa, dominated by the Sahara Desert in the west; the Nile valley; the Savannah grasslands of eastern, central, and southern Africa; and the tropical rain forest of the West African coast and Congo River valley regions. The challenges of these different environments—their climates, soils, flora and fauna—have influenced the population growth, and the choices of economic, social, and political organization of Africa's peoples.

Stone Age groupings, characterized by hunting and gathering economies and small-scale bands as the principle of social organization, were the earliest form of society in evolutionary terms. The next major stage in human development led to the systematic cultivation of grains and root crops and the domestication of animals, known as the Neolithic Revolution. The significance of the Neolithic was that it created stable and sometimes surplus food supplies, enabling the expansion of population.

The lower Nile valley, where seasonal flooding inundated the nearby plains, was the first Neolithic site in Africa. Developing between the third and fourth millennia B.C., it nurtured the flowering of ancient Egypt. Spontaneous domestication of grains occurred in West Africa around the same time. The cultivation of crops like the yam and the banana, introduced through ancient contacts between Malaysian peoples and those of the southeastern coast of Africa, spread to the rain forest areas of central and western Africa by the beginning of the Christian era.

In northern and western Africa pastoralism, often accompanied by nomadic forms of social organization, emerged in ancient times in the grasslands and the steppe areas where agriculture was marginally successful because of precarious rainfall. Agriculturalist and pastoralist groups tended to be distinct, and relationships between sedentary farming and fishing communities and the pastoralists was a major factor in historical developments over the centuries for this area of Africa. Down the eastern half of the continent, however, techniques of agriculture and herding spread side by side within the same groups, and patterns of mixed farming evolved.

These stages in the development of African society can be dated only in the most general terms for most of the continent. With the introduction of metals, however, a more precise chronology of events is possible. The manufacture of metals meant more effective instruments for cultivating the field and better weapons. Greater production of food entailed population growth, and the military superiority of an army equipped with metal arms led to conquest and the creation of larger political organizations. Cities arose as political, religious, and economic centers; they were embellished with important buildings and a wealth of art objects.

The history of North Africa and Egypt in particular can be chronicled from the fourth millennium with the advent of first the Bronze Age and then the Copper Age.

Sub-Saharan Africa never produced either bronze or copper, but moved directly from the Stone Age into the

Age of Iron. By the seventh or sixth century B.C., iron was being manufactured at Meroe, far up the Nile valley in modern-day Sudan. By the second century B.C., the trade routes served as the medium for diffusing the techniques of metal making as far as western Nigeria. Recent discoveries in the area north of the juncture of the Niger and the Benue rivers indicate that between 200 B.C. and A.D. 200 a rich civilization, referred to as the Nok, dominated an area three hundred miles long in this river valley. Clay heads of animals and human beings, some of them going back as far as the ninth century B.C., testify to the artistic originality of the Nok peoples (Fig. 14-1).

Together with the neolithic advances in the forest area the production of iron triggered what is now referred to as the Bantu expansion. In the area of the Cameroons and western Nigeria agricultural, fishing, and iron-working peoples expanding in population and equipped with superior weapons worked out from their homeland toward the south and east, conquering or expelling the resident hunting and gathering peoples. Although the process endured for more than a thousand years, modern linguistic studies of peoples speaking Bantu languages show that gradually the Bantu speakers gained domination in the whole of central and southern Africa. While each of the African peoples that we are going to study has its own language, they are all descended from Africans whose languages (like those of the Bantu speakers) ultimately derived from a common ancestral stock.

The secret of iron manufacture was only one of the items involved in African trade before the first century B.C. Trade between non-African peoples—Indians, Persians, and Arabs—and Africans along the eastern coast of the continent flourished in this period. At the same time Phoenician trading colonies in North Africa, centuries before the Roman conquest of this region, were active in exploring the Saharan oases and initiating

14–1 Far left. Nok terra-cotta head. (Jos Museum, Nigeria; photograph by Eliot Elisofon, Museum of African Art, Eliot Elisofon Archives) Center. Ife bronze head. (Ife Museum, Nigeria; photograph by Eliot Elisofon, Museum of African Art, Eliot Elisofon Archives) Below. Benin bronze head. (The Metropolitan Museum of Art. The Michael C. Rockefeller Memorial Collection of Primitive Art.)

commercial links with them. After the rapid spread of Islam across North Africa in the seventh century A.D., Arabs and Berber-speaking North Africans were the principal merchants engaging in trade with sub-Saharan Africa. Along the West African coast, Niger Delta peoples also traded in seagoing vessels with others as far west as modern-day Ghana. In the interior, cycles of regional markets extended the frontiers of contact, permitting the exchange of agricultural, craft, and some exotic products. Barter techniques—the exchange of one item for another—were widespread, but so were currencies. Some of the latter included cowrie shells, iron bars, salt, cloth, and gold. Such patterns of long-distance trade suggest the existence of other kinds of highly developed crafts in leather goods, iron implements, and cloth products.

Increasing complexity of social and political organization accompanied economic specialization. Complementarity of roles evolved between men and women as well as between whole subgroups within a given society. In contrast to the patterns of most Western societies, African women dominated agricultural production of subsistence economies. Men sometimes assisted in the preparation of fields for cultivation, but their main responsibilities lay in hunting and in the defense of their communities. Both men and women engaged in trade, although men tended to specialize in long-distance trade, including that with the Europeans when it began. These separate and complementary economic activities were buttressed by patterns of social organization sharply delineating men's and women's roles. For some societies descent was matrilineal; that is, inheritance of goods, access to land, and group leadership passed to the children through the family of the mother. In these societies women themselves, while still under the daily dominance of men, had greater control over their own lives than did those in patrilineal societies.

Other kinds of social distinctions existed in addition to that between men and women. A few societies already had slavery, but the onset of the trans-Atlantic slave trade would expand its institutionalization in African societies of the west coast. Some groups, often those with specialist knowledge of iron-working or traditional medicines, operated as distinct castes: they married only within their own group and were set apart by special rules of dress, residence, and religious taboos that regulated their relationships with others. Such groups were not pariahs, however, and often occupied critical political and religious roles within the larger society.

Diversity in forms of political organization also characterized African societies. Two poles of political organization have traditionally been identified: "stateless societies" and state systems. Any one society, however, might lie at a point somewhere along the continuum between these two poles. "Stateless societies" were characterized by the predominance of kinship—family, lineage, and clan—as the basis of political organization. The units within which peoples interacted tended to be relatively small. There was little concentration of authority in the hands of any one person or group, spontaneous leadership emerging as the need arose. Residence patterns in "stateless societies" ranged from dispersed family homesteads to compact villages, but an important feature of such units was the equivalence of power between them; no one group could enforce its rules on another. There were some social institutions in "stateless societies" that extended across village boundaries. Age-group, religious, and initiation societies frequently were shared by others speaking the same language and sometimes by outsiders as well. The art and ideologies of ritual surrounding such organizations provided the potential for cultural unity of widely divergent groups despite the restricted range of political authority.

At the other extreme from the stateless societies lay the states characterized by a high degree of centralization of large territories; elaborate palace and government offices functioning in a wide range of economic and political tasks; court systems with constitutional and religious authorization to enforce their decisions; complex military organization; and close association between ritual and political authority most often focused on the king.

The Great Medieval Kingdoms

Ghana   The ancient empire of Ghana (700–1230) owed its rise to its control of the gold supply so vital to Muslim merchants engaged in the trans-Saharan trade between Morocco and the far western Sudan. Though its kings and citizenry in the early days of the empire were not Muslim themselves, the kings worked closely with the Arab merchant community. They came to adopt techniques of trade and administration, facilitated by literacy in Arabic learned through contacts with the Muslim strangers. Trans-Saharan trade and Islam spurred the emergence of other West African states like Kanem, the Hausa states, and the greatest of the successor states to Ghana, Mali. We will discuss the Mali empire in connection with the epic *Sundiata* in the next chapter.

Benin   One of the first African states to engage in trade with the Europeans was Benin, centered in the forest area just north of the Niger Delta, beyond the influence of the trans-Saharan trade and Islam. Historians believe that sometime between 900 and 1000 people from the kingdom of Ife to the northwest merged with those of the forest area. Ife itself reached the height of its power in the following centuries. Benin traditions claim that the founder of the major dynasty of Benin kings was Oranmiyan, the son of Oduduwa, ruler of the Ife.

After a time of troubles, the peoples of Benin had sent messages to Oduduwa requesting that he send a wise prince to rule them. After some time Oranmiyan, accompanied by courtiers and a medical specialist, settled in a palace at a place called Usama. He married a beautiful woman named Erinwinde, who gave birth to a son. Oranmiyan, as the traditions state, did not remain in Benin long; having established proper government, he resigned, saying that only a son of the land could rule such a troublesome people, and returned to Ife. His son by Erinwinde, named Eweka, was chosen by Oranmiyan to succeed him; and, at the time of Eweka's coronation, royal regalia and other symbols of office were sent by his father from Ife. Ruling many years, Eweka I strengthened the kingdom and probably began to extend Benin's influence over other peoples by settling colonies of his relatives and officers among them. Although Benin was probably never subject to Ife's political authority, the ancient city's spiritual authority is clear: the kings of Benin adopted the title of *Oba* from Ife. They also adopted Ife's technique of brass and bronze casting.

Art in Benin   The Benin bronzes, illustrated in Figures 14-1 through 14-6 are among the masterpieces of African art. The masks, heads, and plaques, reflecting prominent royal figures and scenes of the court, were closely associated with kingship and its rituals. For example, in Figure 14-6 can be seen the elaborate details of royal costume and paraphernalia, as well as the supreme power of the king in comparison to his subjects and servants (reflected in their relative degrees

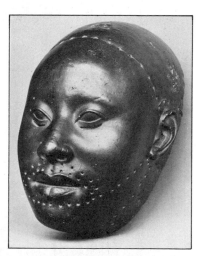

14–2   Mask from Wunmonijie, "Obalufon," bronze. (Reproduced by Courtesy of the Trustees of the British Museum)

14–3   Queen Mother of Benin, bronze. (Reproduced by Courtesy of the Trustees of the British Museum)

14–4   European soldier with crossbow and ammunition, Benin bronze plaque. (Reproduced by Courtesy of the Trustees of the British Museum)

14–6   The Oba and his Assistants, bronze plaque. (Reproduced by Courtesy of the Trustees of the British Museum)

14–5   Master Merchant, Benin bronze plaque. (Reproduced by Courtesy of the Trustees of the British Museum)

of prominence and position in the composition). Scenes of court life, including foreign visitors, were also portrayed, as illustrated by the figures of the merchant and the European soldier. The naturalism of Benin art derived from its Ife heritage, and its representation of historical scenes sets it apart from other examples of traditional art to be studied later.

Creation of the bronzes was the sole preserve of craftsmen appointed by the king. They were made by a technique called the *cire perdu* or "lost wax" method. Over a solid clay core a fine layer of wax was pressed and then carved in intricate detail. The wax layer was then encased in another clay mold provided with core holes for the wax to drain out when the entire piece was heated. Molten metal was poured into the open space between the inner core and outer layer of the mold. Finally, after cooling, the clay molds would be broken away, revealing the bronze object ready for fine sanding and polishing. The delicate details and regal simplicity of earlier Benin bronzes gave way in the late seventeenth and eighteenth centuries to heavier, more elaborate, but still naturalistic objects. Some scholars believe that this apparent coarsening of the Benin style can be attributed to the surplus of casting metals acquired in greater abundance through the European trade.

At the apogee of its power and influence in the sixteenth and seventeenth centuries, Benin held authority over land and peoples in a triangle whose borders went deep into the delta in the east and as far as modern-day Benin (Dahomey) in the west (see map).

Culture of Benin   The traditions of the people of Benin and accounts by early European visitors, to which we now turn, illuminate the culture of a major African state as the worlds of Africa and Europe came together. The first three selections come from *A Short History of Benin*, containing the most famous collection of Benin oral traditions. The book was compiled in 1934 by Chief Jacob V. Egharevba, a member of a distinguished family in Benin and founder of the Benin Museum. Chief Egharevba's work itself is a synthesis of traditions from many groups within Benin: among others the *obas* themselves; *ihogbe*, historians of deceased kings; *ogbelaka*, Royal Bards; and *iguneronmwo*, the Royal Brass Smith. While most dates for the ancient pe-

riod of Benin must remain relative, Chief Egharevba's work has been shown to be remarkably accurate when it can be compared to eyewitness accounts by travelers; it remains an indispensable source for the history of this African state. The fourth selection is a traditional poem extolling the oba and his office. It is taken from *African Poetry*, compiled and edited by Ulli Beier.

THE INTRODUCTION OF BRASS-CASTING FROM IFE

Oba Oguola wished to introduce brass-casting into Benin similar to various works of art sent him from Uhe Ife. He therefore sent to the Oghene of Uhe for a brass-smith and Igue-igha was sent to him. Igue-igha was very clever and left many designs to his successors and was in consequence deified and is worshiped to this day by brass-smiths. The practice of making brass-castings for the preservation of the records of events was originated during the reign of Oguola. He lived to a very old age.

EWUARE THE GREAT

After the murder of Uwaifiokun, Ogus was crowned the Oba of Benin with the title Ewuare (Oworuare) meaning "It is cool" or "The trouble has ceased." (His reign traditionally began in about A.D. 1440.) Prior to his accession he caused a great conflagration in the city which lasted two days and nights as a revenge for his banishment.

Ewuare was a great magician, physician, traveler and warrior. He was also powerful, courageous and sagacious. He fought against and captured 201 towns and villages in Ekiti, Ikare, Kukuruku, Eka and the Ibo country on this side of the river Niger. He took their petty rulers captive and caused the people to pay tribute to him.

He made good roads in Benin City and especially the streets known as Akpakpaya and Utantan. In fact the town rose to importance and gained the name "City" during his reign. It was he who had the innermost and greatest of the walls and ditches made around the City and he made powerful charms and had them buried at each of the nine gateways to the city, to nullify any evil charms which might be brought by people of other countries to injure his subjects.

Ewuare was the first Oba of Benin to come into contact with Europeans, for Ruy de Sigueira visited the Benin area in 1472 although it is not known whether he actually reached the city.

THE COMING OF THE PORTUGUESE TO BENIN

Guns and Coconuts

A Portuguese explorer named John Affonso d'Aveiro visited Benin City for the first time in 1485–1486. He introduced guns and coconuts into this country.

Missionaries

It is said that John Affonso d'Aveiro came to Benin City for the second time during this reign (of Oba Esigie, which began in 1504). He advised the Oba to become a Christian, and said that Christianity would make his country better. Esigie therefore sent Ohenokun, the Olokun priest at Ughoton, with him, as an Ambassador to the King of Portugal, asking him to send priests who would teach him and his people the faith. In reply the King of Portugal sent Roman Catholic missionaries and many rich presents, such as a copper stool (*erhe*), coral beads and a big umbrella, with an entreaty that Esigie should embrace the faith. At the same time he also gave presents to the Ambassador and his wife. The King of Portugal also sent some Portuguese traders who established trading factories at Ughoton, the old port of Benin. They traded in ivory, Benin cloths, pepper and other commodities in the King of Portugal's interest. Owing to the unhealthy state of the country their commerce soon ceased.

But John Affonso d'Aveiro with the other missionaries remained in Benin to carry on the mission work, and churches were built at Ogbelaka, Idumwerie and Akpakpava (Ikpoba Road), the last named being the "Holy Cross Cathedral." . . . The work of the Mission made progress and thousands of people were baptized before the death of the great explorer John Affonso d'Aveiro, who was buried with great lamentations by the Oba and the Christians of Benin City.

The missionaries went with Esigie to the Idah war which took place in 1515–1516.

QUESTIONS

1. Discuss the significance of metal working and the origins of political power.
2. Note the characteristics of King Ewuare described in these selections: what values do they reflect?
3. What was the impression made by the early Portuguese visitors on their hosts?
4. How did Benin react to Christianity?

THE OBA OF BENIN

He who knows not the Oba
let me show him.
He has piled a throne upon a throne.
Plentiful as grains of sand on the earth
are those in front of him.
Plentiful as grains of sand on the earth
are those behind him.
There are two thousand people
to fan him.
He who owns you
is among you here.
He who owns you
has piled a throne upon a throne.
He has lived to do it this year;
even so he will live to do it again.

QUESTIONS

1. What is the effect of *hyperbole* (figures of exaggeration) in this poem?
2. Compare the portrait of the Oba in this poem with that of Ewuare the Great in the preceding texts.
3. Compare the portrayal of the Oba's power in this poem with the suggestions of his power in Figure 14-6.

European Accounts of Benin   The final selections in this chapter are European accounts of Benin. Although the first European visitor was probably Ruy de Sigueira (who came, as noted in "Ewuare the Great," in 1472), John Affonso d'Aveiro was the first to engage Benin in sustained relationships with the Portuguese ruler and his subjects. Trading contact was initiated at Benin's port city of Gwato. The Portuguese description of the early period of contact is told in an excerpt from Ruy de Pina's *Chronicle of John II* (1792), translated by J. W. Blake. Compare this version with Egharevba's: what are the differences and similarities between them?

RUY DE PINA

Chronicle of John II

THE DISCOVERY OF THE KINGDOM
OF BENIN

In this year [1486], the land of Beny beyond Myna to the Rios dos Escravos was first discovered by Joham Affom da Aveiro, who died there; whence there came to these kingdoms the first pepper from Guinee, whereof a great quantity was produced in that land; and presently samples of it were sent to Framdes [Flanders] and to other parts, and soon it fetched a great price and was held in high esteem. The king of Beny sent as ambassador to the king a negro, one of his captains, from a harbouring place by the sea, which is called Ugato [Gwato], because he desired to learn more about these lands, the arrival of people from them in his country being regarded as an unusual novelty. This ambassador was a man of good speech and natural wisdom. Great feasts were held in his honour, and he was shown many of the good things of these kingdoms. He returned to his land in a ship of the king's, who at his departure made him a gift of rich clothes for himself and his wife: and through him he also sent a rich present to the king of such things as he understood he would greatly prize. Moreover, he sent holy and most catholic advisers with praiseworthy admonitions for the faith to administer a stern rebuke about the heresies and great idolatries and fetishes, which the negroes practise in that land. Then also there went with him new factors of the king, who were to remain in that country and to traffic for the said pepper and for other things, which pertained to the trades of the king. But owing to the fact that the land was afterwards found to be very dangerous from sickness and not so profitable as had been hoped, the trade was abandoned.

The next selection describes some facets of Benin culture in the seventeenth century near the apogee of

the kingdom's power, but at a time when rivals elsewhere, notably Oyo, were posing a challenge. The account is a letter written to Willem Bosman by David Van Nyendael and published in Bosman's *New and Accurate Description of the Coast of Guinea* (1705). Bosman was an employee of the Dutch West India Company; during his fourteen years in West Africa he served for a time as the chief factor at Axim in the Gold Coast.

WILLEM BOSMAN

New and Accurate Description of the Coast of Guinea

BENIN IN 1700

The Inhabitants of this Country, if possessed of any Riches, eat and drink very well; that is to say, of the best. The common Diet of the Rich is Beef, Mutton or Chickens, and Jammes (yams) for their Bread; which, after they have boiled, they beat very fine, in order to make Cakes of it: they frequently treat one another, and impart a Portion of their Superfluity to the Necessitous.

The meaner Sort content themselves with smoak'd or dry'd Fish, which, if salted, is very like what we in *Europe* call Raf or Reekel; their Bread is also Jammes, Bananas, and Beans; their Drink Water and *Pardon*-Wine, which is none of the best. The richer Sort Drink Water and Brandy when they can get it. The King, the Great Lords, and every Governor, who is but indifferently rich, subsist several Poor at their Place of Residence on their Charity, employing those who are fit for any Work, in order to help them to a Maintenance, and the rest they keep for God's sake, and to obtain the Character of being charitable; so that here are no Beggars: And this necessary Care succeeds so well, that we do not see many remarkably poor amongst them....

The King hath a very rich Income; for his Territories are very large, and full of Governors, and each knows how many Bags of Boesies (the Money of this Country) (cowries) he must annually raise to the King, which amounts to a vast Sum, which 'tis impossible to make any Calculation of. Others, of a meaner Rank than the former, instead of Money, deliver to the King Bulls,

Cows, Sheep, Chickens, Jammes, and Cloaths; in short, whatever he wants for his Housekeeping; so that he is not oblig'd to one Farthing Expense on that account, and consequently he lays up his whole pecuniary Revenue untouch'd.

Duties or Tolls on imported and exported Wares are not paid here; but everyone pays a certain Sum annually to the Governor of the Place where he lives, for the Liberty of Trading; the Viceroy sends part of it to the King; so that his Revenue being determin'd and settled, he can easily compute what he hath to expect annually.

QUESTIONS AND COMMENTS

1. Compare Ruy de Pina's *Chronicle of John II* with Egharevba's account. What are the differences and similarities between them?
2. Look at Figure 14-4 for an African image of the European soldier. Compare this to the figure of the master merchant or to that of the Oba (Figures 14-5, 14-6). What strikes you about the images portrayed?
3. What is the evidence of social and political stratification in the letter to Bosman? Was the Benin monarchy an oppressive one in the seventeenth century? What qualities in Benin society appealed to its Dutch observers?

The Decline of Benin   Other Europeans besides the Portuguese and the Dutch visited Benin, notably the English. William Hawkins first came to Benin in 1530. Thomas Windham in 1553 found that the king, "a Blacke moore," could easily converse in Portuguese. However, since the trading nations found more profitable sources of slaves elsewhere in Africa, Benin's direct contact with the Europeans diminished. The principal causes for the kingdom's decline remain unclear. It seems certain, however, that the trans-Atlantic slave trade engendered economic, political, and military rivals in Dahomey and Oyo in the seventeenth and eighteenth centuries. The monarchy at Benin nevertheless remained intact until the beginning of the colonial era.

Africa Since Contact with Europe   African history since the initial era of European contact in the fifteenth century has been one of uneven change and growth. The slave trade, followed by the shift to trade in natural products in the nineteenth century, affected those African peoples involved in it in many different ways. Kingdoms rose and fell, imported consumer goods replaced those of traditional manufacture, and the moral and social fabric was transformed by the loss of millions of individuals during their most productive years.

When powerful economic and political forces moved European countries to partition Africa in the late nineteenth century and to impose colonial rule, even those African peoples previously unaffected by Europe were now brought face to face with the West. Subjugated to the goals and needs of the colonial powers, African societies experienced much more intensive alteration of their political, economic, and social systems than in previous centuries. The science and technology of an industrialized Europe and a Christianity laden with Western interpretation and institutions were symbols of the Europeans' power over Africa. Some individuals and whole cultures adopted many Western forms in the hope of participating in that power; others resisted the new way. Both responses led to change in the ways that Africans perceived their world and acted in it. For the most part now independent, African countries that emerged in the twentieth century are attempting to overcome the colonial legacy of dependence and to combine material and technological progress with a nurturing of Africa's rich cultural heritage. It is to aspects of this traditional culture that we now turn.

15

West African Literature: The Oral Tradition

African Languages   The literary traditions of Africa are even more diverse than the literatures of Europe are. For one thing, the languages in which they are composed are more varied. Whereas nearly all European languages can be traced back to a common "proto" language (Indo-European) and thus belong to the same language family, Africa's languages are not only more than one thousand in number but also represent four major language families. These are: (1) Afro-Asiatic, including among others Arabic, Berber, Hausa, and Cushitic; (2) Nilo-Saharan; (3) Khoisan, the languages of the hunting and gathering peoples of southern Africa; and (4) Congo-Kordofanian. Most of the languages in our area of concentration spring from the latter family.

Written Literature in Africa Apart from Arabic, which has a rich tradition of written literature including some works by black Africans, only a few African languages were written before the nineteenth or twentieth centuries. These include Ge'ez, the liturgical tongue of the Ethiopian Christian church, and Amharic, for which the oldest documents date from the fourteenth century. Works in Swahili and Hausa dating from the eighteenth and nineteenth centuries respectively can be found written in Arabic script. Modern African writers write either in their own language in Arabic or Roman script or, in order to reach a wider audience, in French, English, or Portuguese.

Oral Literature The rich body of oral literature, however, permits us to understand the primary tradition of West Africa. A century ago the expression "oral literature" seemed a contradiction in terms. "Literature," to those educated in the Western humanistic tradition, meant something written down, a book in a library. Recent studies, however, have shown that European literature included many works composed orally, most notably, as we have seen, the epics of Homer. This fact has perhaps enabled Westerners to appreciate the fact that poetry and prose of great beauty and complexity can be composed and passed down through the generations without being in written form.

The existence of an oral tradition implies a mentality very different from that of a society relying on documents. For one thing, the faculties of memory must be much more highly developed in an oral society. If the kingdom of Benin was able to rule a wide area without written documents, this was partly because it was able to rely on the extensive memories of its administrators. Most African societies have been able to preserve their histories through the *griot*, an official poet-historian whose job it is to tell and transmit the history of his people. These histories may take the form of an epic poem, as we shall see in the excerpts from *Sundiata*.

In addition to history and the epic, oral literature in Africa includes *myths*, *tales*, *riddles*, *proverbs*, and *lyric* poetry. The most widespread type of poetry is the praise poem. Found nearly everywhere in Africa, praise poems extol kings, courtiers, and prominent personalities in the society as well as the gods. Popular poetry is composed and recited, often spontaneously, for the entertainment of the public. All of these *genres* are represented in the examples that follow.

It must be kept in mind that the texts in this book are not only translations from languages very different from English, they are also written transcriptions of an oral event. In the recitation of tale or poem in Africa, the performer and the act of performance are as integral to the work as the arrangement of the words. Poetry, as with the ancient Greeks, is sung; and some types of poems are distinguished entirely by the style, pitch, and quality of voice associated with particular groups of singers. The merit of a poem is often judged not only by the skill of the artist-performer but also by the successful integration of words, music, and dance. Poetry and the epic histories are often the domain of specialists, but folk tales, riddles, and proverbs were and are available to all. Even with these forms, though, the skill of the teller is an important factor.

Appreciation of the written materials here will thus require some creative imagination on the part of the reader; yet, even divorced from performance and in translation, these works can be appreciated both for their literary qualities and for what they convey about African perceptions of the cosmos, creation, human dilemmas, and cultural priorities. We have included a few poems by modern African writers, written in English but drawing on the oral tradition. While several western and central African cultures are represented, three major and distinct civilizations, from which we have taken several examples, deserve further introduction. These are the Mande complex (with specific reference to the Mandinka peoples), the Hausa, and the Yoruba (see map on page 431).

Mande Mande is the name of a cultural complex and group of languages in western Sudan. Mande peoples were among the earliest to develop agriculture in sub-Saharan Africa. Mandinka (also called Mandingo or Malinke) is one of about twelve subgroups that make up the Mande group and that formed the core population of the Mali empire. Around the year 1200 several of them were joined together in revolt against the declining empire of Ghana. The remarkable leader of this revolt was a Mandinka man named Sundiata, the hero of the epic that follows. As a result of his mili-

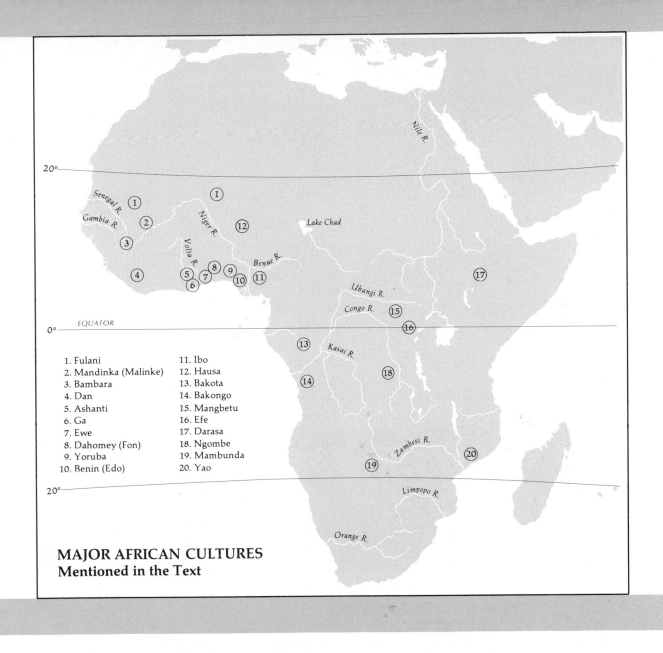

1. Fulani
2. Mandinka (Malinke)
3. Bambara
4. Dan
5. Ashanti
6. Ga
7. Ewe
8. Dahomey (Fon)
9. Yoruba
10. Benin (Edo)
11. Ibo
12. Hausa
13. Bakota
14. Bakongo
15. Mangbetu
16. Efe
17. Darasa
18. Ngombe
19. Mambunda
20. Yao

MAJOR AFRICAN CULTURES
Mentioned in the Text

tary victories, Mali flourished. With its economy based on the rich agricultural lands of the upper Niger and on secure control of the gold mines of Bambuk and Bure, Mali expanded to become the largest of the medieval African empires. Included within its boundaries were peoples and lands in parts of modern Guinea, Mali, Sierra Leone, Liberia, Ivory Coast, Senegal, northern Ghana, and Upper Volta.

The fabulous wealth and high culture of Mali became known to the outside world through the pilgrim-age of Mansa Musa in 1324 (Fig. 15-1). He and succeeding mansas, or kings, attracted scholars from North Africa and the Middle East to Timbuktu, Mali's principal port city of the trans-Saharan trade. These scholars, together with the local people, created a great center of Islamic learning around the famous mosque of Sankore. Muslim traders of various Mande groups spread Islam far beyond the core areas around Niani, the capital, and Timbuktu, some reaching as far east as Hausaland. Succession disputes and aggressive neighbors

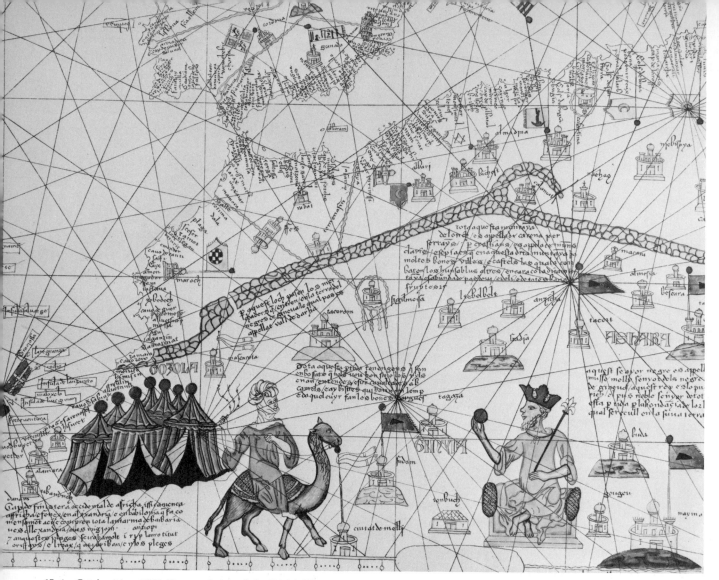

15–1 Catalan Map, 1375. (By permission of the British Library. *BL Maps Ref. A.6.(3)*)

nurtured internal tensions in the empire, which, nevertheless, survived until the seventeenth century.

Hausa Hausa is a linguistic term describing the several million peoples in West Africa who speak Hausa as their first language. Though their homeland is northern Nigeria and southern Niger, the Hausa have been engaged in long-distance trade for centuries; there are substantial Hausa-speaking communities in northern Ghana and in every major city in West Africa. Politically, the Hausa were long ago grouped into separate walled city-states to which the surrounding rural folk owed allegiance. From about the fourteenth century (perhaps stimulated by contact with Mande traders), Islam was the religion of the courts. In the early nineteenth century a holy war, or *jihad*, sparked a revolution that replaced the Hausa rulers with those from another group, the Fulani, and united them into a centralized state known as the Fulani empire. The Fulani empire included many non-Muslim groups from the lands north of the Benue and Niger rivers within its borders. By creating an area of unprecedented size within which trade, agriculture, travel, and communi-

432

cation could develop in relative peace, the empire imposed use of Hausa language and Islamic values on many more peoples than before.

Yoruba The Yoruba are an agricultural and trading people numbering several million who reside in southwestern Nigeria and the republic of Benin. Throughout most of the period of contact between Africa and Europe, the Yoruba were subjects of the Benin and Oyo empires. The latter was a kingdom of far-flung boundaries that disintegrated in the early nineteenth century. Oyo and the successor kingdoms were constitutional monarchies in which the power of the king was balanced by a council of state and an institutionalized priesthood. The richness of the Yoruba aesthetic is better known to outsiders than, perhaps, that of any other African people. The traditions of poetry, sculpture, and dance are founded on an elaborate system of religious beliefs and practices. The hierarchy and ritual among the Yoruba gods mirrors that of traditional Yoruba political structure. Yoruba religious beliefs have been remarkably successful in retaining their dynamism through accommodation with both Christian and Islamic practice. Perhaps one of the key reasons for this dynamism is the vitality of the poetry, myths, and proverbs (seen in the examples that follow) and their continued integration into social, political, and religious festivals of contemporary society.

The Epic

The original purpose of epic poetry, as we saw in the section on Homer in Chapter 1, was to "sing the famous deeds of men": to teach people in a pleasurable way about great heroes and historical events important to their culture. The epic hero, who exists or has existed in nearly all of the world's cultures, is a human being with certain superhuman qualities, someone who overcomes great obstacles and accomplishes both physical and spiritual triumphs for his people. Such a hero is Sundiata, whose legendary dimensions have informed the cultural identity of the Mande peoples down to the present time. The oral epic *Sundiata* was told by the griot Mamadou Kouyaté to Djibril Tamsir Niane, who transcribed it and translated it into French in 1960. What follows are excerpts from Niane's version, translated into English by G. D. Pickett.

From *Sundiata*

THE WORDS OF THE GRIOT MAMADOU KOUYATÉ

I am a griot. It is I, Djeli Mamadou Kouyaté, son of Bintou Kouyaté and Djeli Kedian Kouyaté, master in the art of eloquence. Since time immemorial the Kouyatés have been in the service of the Keita princes of Mali; we are vessels of speech, we are the repositories which harbour secrets many centuries old. The art of eloquence has no secrets for us; without us the names of kings would vanish into oblivion, we are the memory of mankind; by the spoken word we bring to life the deeds and exploits of kings for younger generations.

I derive my knowledge from my father Djeli Kedian, who also got it from his father; history holds no mystery for us; we teach to the vulgar just as much as we want to teach them, for it is we who keep the keys to the twelve doors of Mali.

I know the list of all the sovereigns who succeeded to the throne of Mali. I know how the black people divided into tribes, for my father bequeathed to me all his learning; I know why such and such is called Kamara, another Keita, and yet another Sibibé or Traoré; every name has a meaning, a secret import.

I teach kings the history of their ancestors so that the lives of the ancients might serve them as an example, for the world is old, but the future springs from the past.

My word is pure and free of all untruth; it is the word of my father; it is the word of my father's father. I will give you my father's words just as I received them; royal griots do not know what lying is. When a quarrel breaks out between tribes it is we who settle the difference, for we are the depositaries of oaths which the ancestors swore.

Listen to my word, you who want to know; by my mouth you will learn the history of Mali.

By my mouth you will get to know the story of the ancestor of great Mali, the story of him who, by his exploits, surpassed even Alexander the Great; he who, from the East, shed his rays upon all the countries of the West.

Listen to the story of the son of the Buffalo, the son of the Lion. I am going to tell you of Maghan Sundiata, of Mari-Djata, of Sogolon Djata, of Naré Maghan Djata; the man of many names against whom sorcery could avail nothing.

THE FIRST KINGS OF MALI

Listen then, sons of Mali, children of the black people, listen to my word, for I am going to tell you of Sundiata, the father of the Bright Country, of the savanna land, the ancestor of those who draw the bow, the master of a hundred vanquished kings.

I am going to talk of Sundiata, Manding Diara, Lion of Mali, Sogolon Djata, son of Sogolon, Naré Maghan Djata, son of Naré Maghan, Sogo Sogo Simbon Salaba, hero of many names.

I am going to tell you of Sundiata, he whose exploits will astonish men for a long time yet. He was great among kings, he was peerless among men; he was beloved of God because he was the last of the great conquerors.

Right at the beginning then, Mali was a province of the Bambara kings; those who are today called Mandingo, inhabitants of Mali, are not indigenous; they come from the East. Bilali Bounama, ancestor of the Keitas, was the faithful servant of the Prophet Muhammad (may the peace of God be upon him). Bilali Bounama had seven sons of whom the eldest, Lawalo, left the Holy City and came to settle in Mali; Lawalo had Latal Kalabi for a son, Latal Kalabi had Damul Kalabi who then had Lahilatoul Kalabi.

Lahilatoul Kalabi was the first black prince to make the Pilgrimage to Mecca. On his return he was robbed by brigands in the desert; his men were scattered and some died of thirst, but God saved Lahilatoul Kalabi, for he was a righteous man. He called upon the Almighty and jinn appeared and recognized him as king. After seven years' absence Lahilatoul was able to return, by the grace of Allah the Almighty, to Mali where none expected to see him any more.

Lahilatoul Kalabi had two sons, the elder being called Kalabi Bomba and the younger Kalabi Dauman; the elder chose royal power and reigned, while the younger preferred fortune and wealth and became the ancestor of those who go from country to country seeking their fortune.

Kalabi Bomba had Mamadi Kani for a son. Mamadi Kani was a hunter king like the first kings of Mali. It was he who invented the hunter's whistle; he communicated with the jinn of the forest and bush. These spirits had no secrets from him and he was loved by Kondolon Ni Sané. His followers were so numerous that he formed them into an army which became formidable; he often gathered them together in the bush and taught them the art of hunting. It was he who revealed to hunters the medicinal leaves which heal wounds and cure diseases. Thanks to the strength of his followers, he became king of a vast country; with them Mamadi Kani conquered all the lands which stretch from the Sankarani to the Bouré. Mamadi Kani had four sons—Kani Simbon, Kamignogo Simbon, Kabala Simbon and Simbon Tagnogokelin. They were all initiated into the art of hunting and deserved the title of Simbon. It was the lineage of Bamari Tagnogokelin which held on to the power; his son was M'Bali Nènè whose son was Bello. Bello's son was called Bello Bakon and he had a son called Maghan Kon Fatta, also called Frako Maghan Keigu, Maghan the handsome.

Maghan Kon Fatta was the father of the great Sundiata and had three wives and six children—three boys and three girls. His first wife was called Sassouma Bérété, daughter of a great divine; she was the mother of King Dankaran Touman and Princess Nana Triban. The second wife, Sogolon Kedjou, was the mother of Sundiata and the two princesses Sogolon Kolonkan and Sogolon Djamarou. The third wife was one of the Kamaras and was called Namandjé; she was the mother of Manding Bory (or Manding Bakary), who was the best friend of his half-brother Sundiata.

THE BUFFALO WOMAN

Maghan Kon Fatta, the father of Sundiata, was renowned for his beauty in every land; but he was also a good king loved by all the people. In his capital of Nianiba he loved to sit often at the foot of the great silk-cotton tree which dominated his palace of Canco. Maghan Kon Fatta had been reigning a long time and his eldest son Dankaran Touman was already eight years old and often came to sit on the ox-hide beside his father.

Well now, one day when the king had taken up his usual position under the silk-cotton tree surrounded by his kinsmen he saw a man dressed like a hunter coming towards him; he wore the tight-fitting trousers of the favourites of Kondolon Ni Sané, and his blouse oversewn with cowries showed that he was a master of the hunting art. All present turned towards the unknown man whose bow, polished with frequent usage, shone in the sun. The man walked up in front of the king, whom he recognized in the midst of his courtiers. He bowed and said, "I salute you, king of Mali, greetings all you of Mali. I am a hunter chasing game and come from Sangaran; a fearless doe has guided me to the walls of Nianiba. By the grace of my master the great Simbon[1] my arrows have hit her and now she lies not far from your walls. As is fitting, oh king, I have come to bring you your portion." He took a leg from his leather sack whereupon the king's griot, Gnankouman Doua, seized upon the leg and said, "Stranger, whoever you may be you will be the king's guest because you respect custom; come and take your place on the mat beside us. The king is pleased because he loves righteous men." The king nodded his approval and all the courtiers agreed. The griot continued in a more familiar tone, "Oh you who come from the Sangaran, land of the favourites of Kondolon Ni Sané, you who have doubtless had an expert master, will you open your pouch of knowledge for us and instruct us with your conversation, for you have no doubt visited several lands."

The king, still silent, gave a nod of approval and a courtier added, "The hunters of Sangaran are the best soothsayers; if the stranger wishes we could learn a lot from him."

The hunter came and sat down near Gnankouman Doua who vacated one end of the mat for him. Then he said, "Griot of the king, I am not one of these hunters whose tongues are more dexterous than their arms; I am no spinner of adventure yarns, nor do I like playing upon the credulity of worthy folk; but, thanks to the lore which my master has imparted to me, I can boast of being a seer among seers."

He took out of his hunter's bag twelve cowries which he threw on the mat. The king and all his entourage now turned towards the stranger who was jumbling up the twelve shiny shells with his bare hand. Gnankouman Doua discreetly brought to the king's notice that the soothsayer was left-handed. The left hand is the hand of evil, but in the divining art it is said that left-handed people are the best. The hunter muttered some incomprehensible words in a low voice while he shuffled and jumbled the twelve cowries into different positions which he mused on at length. All of a sudden he looked up at the king and said, "Oh king, the world is full of mystery, all is hidden and we know nothing but what we can see. The silk-cotton tree springs from a tiny seed—that which defies the tempest weighs in its germ no more than a grain of rice. Kingdoms are like trees; some will be silk-cotton trees, others will remain dwarf palms and the powerful silk-cotton tree will cover them with its shade. Oh, who can recognize in the little child the great king to come? The great comes from the small; truth and falsehood have both suckled at the same breast. Nothing is certain, but, sire, I can see two strangers over there coming towards your city."

He fell silent and looked in the direction of the city gates for a short while. All present silently turned towards the gates. The soothsayer returned to his cowries. He shook them in his palm with a skilled hand and then threw them out.

"King of Mali, destiny marches with great strides, Mali is about to emerge from the night. Nianiba is lighting up, but what is this light that comes from the east?"

"Hunter," said Gnankouman Doua, "your words are obscure. Make your speech comprehensible to us, speak in the clear language of your savanna.[2]"

"I am coming to that now, griot. Listen to my message. Listen, sire. You have ruled over the kingdom which your ancestors bequeathed to you and you have no other ambition but to pass on this realm, intact if not increased, to your descendants; but, fine king, your successor is not yet born. I see two hunters coming to your city; they have come from afar and a woman accompanies them. Oh, that woman! She is ugly, she is hideous, she bears on her back a disfiguring hump. Her monstrous eyes seem to have been merely laid on her face, but, mystery of mysteries, this is the woman you must marry, sire, for she will be the mother of him who will make the name of Mali immortal for ever. The child will be the seventh star, the seventh con-

---

[1] Honorific term for a great hunter; later applied to Sundiata.

[2] The language of those who live in the savannah grasslands is, like their environment, clear and bright.

queror of the earth. He will be more mighty than Alexander. But, oh king, for destiny to lead this woman to you a sacrifice is necessary; you must offer up a red bull, for the bull is powerful. When its blood soaks into the ground nothing more will hinder the arrival of your wife. There, I have said what I had to say, but everything is in the hands of the Almighty."

The hunter picked up his cowries and put them away in his bag.

"I am only passing through, king of Mali, and now I return to Sangaran. Farewell."

The hunter disappeared but neither the king, Naré Maghan, nor his griot, Gnankouman Doua, forgot his prophetic words; soothsayers see far ahead, their words are not always for the immediate present; man is in a hurry but time is tardy and everything has its season. . . .

Summary   After some time the old man's prophecy came to pass. One day two hunters came from the land of Do to present to the king a young girl who, though she was shrouded in traveling clothes, was apparently a hunchback. They related to the king and his court how the king of Do Mansa-Gnemo Dearra had promised to reward anyone who killed an astounding buffalo that had been destroying the fields in the area. Having set out themselves to find the buffalo, the two hunters had befriended an old woman who confessed that she was the Buffalo of Do. She told them how to capture and kill it on the promise that when offered the reward of a beautiful young maiden, they choose an ugly girl who would be seated in the crowd.

Events transpired as the old woman had predicted, and the hunters were laughed out of town when they chose the ugly girl, Sogolon Kedjou. Unable to possess her, the hunters only later thought to present her to the king of Mali. Recognizing the fulfillment of what the old man had foretold, Naré Maghan married Sogolon.

THE LION CHILD

A wife quickly grows accustomed to her state. Sogolon now walked freely in the king's great enclosure and people also got used to her ugliness. But the first wife of the king, Sassouma Bérété, turned out to be unbearable. She was restless, and smarted to see the ugly Sogolon proudly flaunting her pregnancy about the palace.

What would become of her, Sassouma Bérété, if her son, already eight years old, was disinherited in favour of the child that Sogolon was going to bring into the world? All the king's attentions went to the mother-to-be. On returning from the wars he would bring her the best portion of the booty—fine loin-cloths and rare jewels. Soon, dark schemes took form in the mind of Sassouma Bérété; she determined to kill Sogolon. In great secrecy she had the foremost sorcerers of Mali come to her, but they all declared themselves incapable of tackling Sogolon. In fact, from twilight onwards, three owls came and perched on the roof of her house and watched over her. For the sake of peace and quiet Sassouma said to herself, "Very well then, let him be born, this child, and then we'll see."

Sogolon's time came. The king commanded the nine greatest midwives of Mali to come to Niani, and they were now constantly in attendance on the damsel of Do. The king was in the midst of his courtiers one day when someone came to announce to him that Sogolon's labours were beginning. He sent all his courtiers away and only Gnankouman Doua stayed by his side. One would have thought that this was the first time that he had become a father, he was so worried and agitated. The whole palace kept complete silence. Doua tried to distract the sovereign with his one-stringed guitar but in vain. He even had to stop this music as it jarred on the king. Suddenly the sky darkened and great clouds coming from the east hid the sun, although it was still the dry season. Thunder began to rumble and swift lightning rent the clouds; a few large drops of rain began to fall while a strong wind blew up. A flash of lightning accompanied by a dull rattle of thunder burst out of the east and lit up the whole sky as far as the west. Then the rain stopped and the sun appeared and it was at this very moment that a midwife came out of Sogolon's house, ran to the antechamber and announced to Naré Maghan that he was the father of a boy.

The king showed no reaction at all. He was as though in a daze. Then Doua, realizing the king's emotion, got up and signalled to two slaves who were already standing near the royal "tabala."[3] The hasty beats of the

---

[3] Ceremonial drum.

royal drum announced to Mali the birth of a son; the village tam-tams took it up and thus all Mali got the good news the same day. Shouts of joy, tam-tams and "balaſons"[4] took the place of the recent silence and all the musicians of Niani made their way to the palace. His initial emotion being over, the king had got up and on leaving the antechamber he was greeted by the warm voice of Gnankouman Doua singing:

"I salute you, father; I salute you, king Naré Maghan; I salute you, Maghan Kon Fatta, Frako Maghan Keigu. The child is born whom the world awaited. Maghan, oh happy father, I salute you. The lion child, the buffalo child is born, and to announce him the Almighty has made the thunder peal, the whole sky has lit up and the earth has trembled. All hail, father, hail king Naré Maghan!"

All the griots were there and had already composed a song in praise of the royal infant. The generosity of kings makes griots eloquent, and Maghan Kon Fatta distributed on this day alone six granaries of rice among the populace. Sassouma Bérété distinguished herself by her largesses, but that deceived nobody. She was suffering in her heart but did not want to betray anything.

The name was given the eighth day after his birth. It was a great feast day and people came from all the villages of Mali while each neighbouring people brought gifts to the king. First thing in the morning a great circle had formed in front of the palace. In the middle, serving women were pounding rice which was to serve as bread, and sacrificed oxen lay at the foot of the great silk-cotton tree.

In Sogolon's house the king's aunt cut off the baby's first crop of hair while the poetesses, equipped with large fans, cooled the mother who was nonchalantly stretched out on soft cushions.

The king was in his antechamber but he came out followed by Doua. The crowd fell silent and Doua cried, "The child of Sogolon will be called Maghan after his father, and Mari Djata, a name which no Mandingo prince has ever borne. Sogolon's son will be the first of this name."

Straight away the griots shouted the name of the infant and the tam-tams sounded anew. The king's aunt,

who had come out to hear the name of the child, went back into the house, and whispered the double name of Maghan and Mari Djata in the ear of the newly-born so that he would remember it.

The festivity ended with the distribution of meat to the heads of families and everyone dispersed joyfully. The near relatives one by one went to admire the newly-born.

CHILDHOOD

God has his mysteries which none can fathom. You, perhaps, will be a king. You can do nothing about it. You, on the other hand, will be unlucky, but you can do nothing about that either. Each man finds his way already marked out for him and he can change nothing of it.

Sogolon's son had a slow and difficult childhood. At the age of three he still crawled along on all fours while children of the same age were already walking. He had nothing of the great beauty of his father Naré Maghan. He had a head so big that he seemed unable to support it; he also had large eyes which would open wide whenever anyone entered his mother's house. He was taciturn and used to spend the whole day just sitting in the middle of the house. Whenever his mother went out he would crawl on all fours to rummage about in the calabashes in search of food, for he was very greedy.

Malicious tongues began to blab. What three-year-old has not yet taken his first steps? What three-year-old is not the despair of his parents through his whims and shifts of mood? What three-year-old is not the joy of his circle through his backwardness in talking? Sogolon Djata (for it was thus that they called him, prefixing his mother's name to his), Sogolon Djata, then, was very different from others of his own age. He spoke little and his severe face never relaxed into a smile. You would have thought that he was already thinking, and what amused children of his age bored him. Often Sogolon would make some of them come to him to keep him company. These children were already walking and she hoped that Djata, seeing his companions walking, would be tempted to do likewise. But nothing came of it. Besides, Sogolon Djata would brain the poor little things with his already strong arms and none of them would come near him any more.

The king's first wife was the first to rejoice at Sogolon

---

[4] A type of xylophone in which the wooden keys are often mounted upon gourds.

Djata's infirmity. Her own son, Dankaran Touman, was already eleven. He was a fine and lively boy, who spent the day running about the village with those of his own age. He had even begun his initiation in the bush. The king had had a bow made for him and he used to go behind the town to practise archery with his companions. Sassouma was quite happy and snapped her fingers at Sogolon, whose child was still crawling on the ground. Whenever the latter happened to pass by her house, she would say, "Come, my son, walk, jump, leap about. The jinn[5] didn't promise you anything out of the ordinary, but I prefer a son who walks on his two legs to a lion that crawls on the ground." She spoke thus whenever Sogolon went by her door. The innuendo would go straight home and then she would burst into laughter, that diabolical laughter which a jealous woman knows how to use so well.

Her son's infirmity weighed heavily upon Sogolon Kedjou; she had resorted to all her talent as a sorceress to give strength to her son's legs, but the rarest herbs had been useless. The king himself lost hope.

How impatient man is! Naré Maghan became imperceptibly estranged but Gnankouman Doua never ceased reminding him of the hunter's words. Sogolon became pregnant again. The king hoped for a son, but it was a daughter called Kolonkan. She resembled her mother and had nothing of her father's beauty. The disheartened king debarred Sogolon from his house and she lived in semi-disgrace for a while. Naré Maghan married the daughter of one of his allies, the king of the Kamaras. She was called Namandjé and her beauty was legendary. A year later she brought a boy into the world. When the king consulted soothsayers on the destiny of this son he received the reply that Namandjé's child would be the right hand of some mighty king. The king gave the newly-born the name of Boukari. He was to be called Manding Boukari or Manding Bory later on.

Naré Maghan was very perplexed. Could it be that the stiff-jointed son of Sogolon was the one the hunter soothsayer had foretold?

"The Almighty has his mysteries," Gnankouman Doua would say and, taking up the hunter's words, added, "The silk-cotton tree emerges from a tiny seed."

---

[5] A Muslim term for invisible spirits, supernatural agencies.

One day Naré Maghan came along to the house of Nounfaïri, the blacksmith seer of Niani. He was an old, blind man. He received the king in the anteroom which served as his workshop. To the king's question he replied, "When the seed germinates growth is not always easy; great trees grow slowly but they plunge their roots deep into the ground."

"But has the seed really germinated?" said the king.

"Of course," replied the blind seer. "Only the growth is not as quick as you would like it; how impatient man is."

This interview and Doua's confidence gave the king some assurance. To the great displeasure of Sassouma Bérété the king restored Sogolon to favour and soon another daughter was born to her. She was given the name of Djamarou.

However, all Niani talked of nothing else but the stiff-legged son of Sogolon. He was now seven and he still crawled to get about. In spite of all the king's affection, Sogolon was in despair. Naré Maghan aged and he felt his time coming to an end. Dankaran Touman, the son of Sassouma Bérété, was now a fine youth.

One day Naré Maghan made Mari Djata come to him and he spoke to the child as one speaks to an adult. "Mari Djata, I am growing old and soon I shall be no more among you, but before death takes me off I am going to give you the present each king gives his successor. In Mali every prince has his own griot. Doua's father was my father's griot, Doua is mine and the son of Doua, Balla Fasséké here, will be your griot. Be inseparable friends from this day forward. From his mouth you will hear the history of your ancestors, you will learn the art of governing Mali according to the principles which our ancestors have bequeathed to us. I have served my term and done my duty too. I have done everything which a king of Mali ought to do. I am handing an enlarged kingdom over to you and I leave you sure allies. May your destiny be accomplished, but never forget that Niani is your capital and Mali the cradle of your ancestors."

The child, as if he had understood the whole meaning of the king's words, beckoned Balla Fasséké to approach. He made room for him on the hide he was sitting on and then said, "Balla, you will be my griot."

"Yes, son of Sogolon, if it pleases God," replied Balla Fasséké.

The king and Doua exchanged glances that radiated confidence.

THE LION'S AWAKENING

A short while after this interview between Naré Maghan and his son the king died. Sogolon's son was no more than seven years old. The council of elders met in the king's palace. It was no use Doua's defending the king's will which reserved the throne for Mari Djata, for the council took no account of Naré Maghan's wish. With the help of Sassouma Bérété's intrigues, Dankaran Touman was proclaimed king and a regency council was formed in which the queen mother was all-powerful. A short time after, Doua died.

As men have short memories, Sogolon's son was spoken of with nothing but irony and scorn. People had seen one-eyed kings, one-armed kings, and lame kings, but a stiff-legged king had never been heard tell of. No matter how great the destiny promised for Mari Djata might be, the throne could not be given to someone who had no power in his legs; if the jinn loved him, let them begin by giving him the use of his legs. Such were the remarks that Sogolon heard every day. The queen mother, Sassouma Bérété, was the source of all this gossip.

Having become all-powerful, Sassouma Bérété persecuted Sogolon because the late Naré Maghan had preferred her. She banished Sogolon and her son to a back yard of the palace. Mari Djata's mother now occupied an old hut which had served as a lumber-room of Sassouma's.

The wicked queen mother allowed free passage to all those inquisitive people who wanted to see the child that still crawled at the age of seven. Nearly all the inhabitants of Niani filed into the palace and the poor Sogolon wept to see herself thus given over to public ridicule. Mari Djata took on a ferocious look in front of the crowd of sightseers. Sogolon found a little consolation only in the love of her eldest daughter, Kolonkan. She was four and she could walk. She seemed to understand all her mother's miseries and already she helped her with the housework. Sometimes, when Sogolon was attending to the chores, it was she who stayed beside her sister Djamarou, quite small as yet.

Sogolon Kedjou and her children lived on the queen mother's left-overs, but she kept a little garden in the open ground behind the village. It was there that she passed her brightest moments looking after her onions and gnougous. One day she happened to be short of condiments and went to the queen mother to beg a little baobab leaf.

"Look you," said the malicious Sassouma, "I have a calabash full. Help yourself, you poor woman. As for me, my son knew how to walk at seven and it was he who went and picked these baobab leaves. Take them then, since your son is unequal to mine." Then she laughed derisively with that fierce laughter which cuts through your flesh and penetrates right to the bone.

Sogolon Kedjou was dumbfounded. She had never imagined that hate could be so strong in a human being. With a lump in her throat she left Sassouma's. Outside her hut Mari Djata, sitting on his useless legs, was blandly eating out of a calabash. Unable to contain herself any longer, Sogolon burst into sobs and seizing a piece of wood, hit her son.

"Oh son of misfortune, will you never walk? Through your fault I have just suffered the greatest affront of my life! What have I done, God, for you to punish me in this way?"

Mari Djata seized the piece of wood and, looking at his mother, said, "Mother, what's the matter?"

"Shut up, nothing can ever wash me clean of this insult."

"But what then?"

"Sassouma has just humiliated me over a matter of a baobab leaf. At your age her own son could walk and used to bring his mother baobab leaves."

"Cheer up, Mother, cheer up."

"No. It's too much. I can't."

"Very well then, I am going to walk today," said Mari Djata. "Go and tell my father's smiths to make me the heaviest possible iron rod. Mother, do you want just the leaves of the baobab or would you rather I brought you the whole tree?"

"Ah, my son, to wipe out this insult I want the tree and its roots at my feet outside my hut."

Balla Fasséké, who was present, ran to the master smith, Farakourou, to order an iron rod.

Sogolon had sat down in front of her hut. She was weeping softly and holding her head between her two hands. Mari Djata went calmly back to his calabash of rice and began eating again as if nothing had happened.

From time to time he looked up discreetly at his mother who was murmuring in a low voice, "I want the whole tree, in front of my hut, the whole tree."

All of a sudden a voice burst into laughter behind the hut. It was the wicked Sassouma telling one of her serving women about the scene of humiliation and she was laughing loudly so that Sogolon could hear. Sogolon fled into the hut and hid her face under the blankets so as not to have before her eyes this heedless boy, who was more preoccupied with eating than with anything else. With her head buried in the bed-clothes Sogolon wept and her body shook violently. Her daughter, Sogolon Djamarou, had come and sat down beside her and she said, "Mother, Mother, don't cry. Why are you crying?"

Mari Djata had finished eating and, dragging himself along on his legs, he came and sat under the wall of the hut for the sun was scorching. What was he thinking about? He alone knew.

The royal forges were situated outside the walls and over a hundred smiths worked there. The bows, spears, arrows and shields of Niani's warriors came from there. When Balla Fasséké came to order the iron rod, Farakourou said to him, "The great day has arrived then?"

"Yes. Today is a day like any other, but it will see what no other day has seen."

The master of the forges, Farakourou, was the son of the old Nounfaïri, and he was a soothsayer like his father. In his workshops there was an enormous iron bar wrought by his father Nounfaïri. Everybody wondered what this bar was destined to be used for. Farakourou called six of his apprentices and told them to carry the iron bar to Sogolon's house.

When the smiths put the gigantic iron bar down in front of the hut the noise was so frightening that Sogolon, who was lying down, jumped up with a start. Then Balla Fasséké, son of Gnankouman Doua, spoke.

"Here is the great day, Mari Djata. I am speaking to you, Maghan, son of Sogolon. The waters of the Niger can efface the stain from the body, but they cannot wipe out an insult. Arise, young lion, roar, and may the bush know that from henceforth it has a master."

The apprentice smiths were still there, Sogolon had come out and everyone was watching Mari Djata. He crept on all fours and came to the iron bar. Supporting himself on his knees and one hand, with the other hand he picked up the iron bar without any effort and stood it up vertically. Now he was resting on nothing but his knees and held the bar with both his hands. A deathly silence had gripped all those present. Sogolon Djata closed his eyes, held tight, the muscles in his arms tensed. With a violent jerk he threw his weight on to it and his knees left the ground. Sogolon Kedjou was all eyes and watched her son's legs which were trembling as though from an electric shock. Djata was sweating and the sweat ran from his brow. In a great effort he straightened up and was on his feet at one go—but the great bar of iron was twisted and had taken the form of a bow!

Then Balla Fasséké sang out the "Hymn to the Bow," striking up with his powerful voice:

"Take your bow, Simbon,
Take your bow and let us go.
Take your bow, Sogolon Djata."

When Sogolon saw her son standing she stood dumb for a moment, then suddenly she sang these words of thanks to God who had given her son the use of his legs:

"Oh day, what a beautiful day,
Oh day, day of joy;
Allah Almighty, you never created a finer day.
So my son is going to walk!"

Standing in the position of a soldier at ease, Sogolon Djata, supported by his enormous rod, was sweating great beads of sweat. Balla Fasséké's song had alerted the whole palace and people came running from all over to see what had happened, and each stood bewildered before Sogolon's son. The queen mother had rushed there and when she saw Mari Djata standing up she trembled from head to foot. After recovering his breath Sogolon's son dropped the bar and the crowd stood to one side. His first steps were those of a giant. Balla Fasséké fell into step and pointing his finger at Djata, he cried:

"Room, room, make room!
The lion has walked;
Hide antelopes,
Get out of his way."

Behind Niani there was a young baobab tree and it was there that the children of the town came to pick leaves for their mothers. With all his might the son of Sogolon tore up the tree and put it on his shoulders and went back to his mother. He threw the tree in front of the hut and said, "Mother, here are some baobab leaves for you. From henceforth it will be outside your hut that the women of Niani will come to stock up."

Sogolon Djata walked. From that day forward the queen mother had no more peace of mind. But what can one do against destiny? Nothing. Man, under the influence of certain illusions, thinks he can alter the course which God has mapped out, but everything he does falls into a higher order which he barely understands. That is why Sassouma's efforts were vain against Sogolon's son, everything she did lay in the child's destiny. Scorned the day before and the object of public ridicule, now Sogolon's son was as popular as he had been despised. The multitude loves and fears strength. All Niani talked of nothing but Djata; the mothers urged their sons to become hunting companions of Djata and to share his games, as if they wanted their offspring to profit from the nascent glory of the buffalo-woman's son. The words of Doua on the name-giving day came back to men's minds and Sogolon was now surrounded with much respect; in conversation people were fond of contrasting Sogolon's modesty with the pride and malice of Sassouma Bérété. It was because the former had been an exemplary wife and mother that God had granted strength to her son's legs for, it was said, the more a wife loves and respects her husband and the more she suffers for her child, the more valorous will the child be one day. Each is the child of his mother; the child is worth no more than the mother is worth. It was not astonishing that the king Dankaran Touman was so colourless, for his mother had never shown the slightest respect to her husband and never, in the presence of the late king, did she show that humility which every wife should show before her husband. People recalled her scenes of jealousy and the spiteful remarks she circulated about her co-wife and her child. And people would conclude gravely, "Nobody knows God's mystery. The snake has no legs yet it is as swift as any other animal that has four."

Sogolon Djata's popularity grew from day to day and he was surrounded by a gang of children of the same age as himself. These were Fran Kamara, son of the king of Tabon; Kamandjan, son of the king of Sibi; and other princes whose fathers had sent them to the court of Niani. The son of Namandjé, Manding Bory, was already joining in their games. Balla Fasséké followed Sogolon Djata all the time. He was past twenty and it was he who gave the child education and instruction according to Mandingo rules of conduct. Whether in town or at the hunt, he missed no opportunity of instructing his pupil. Many young boys of Niani came to join in the games of the royal child.

He liked hunting best of all. Farakourou, master of the forges, had made Djata a fine bow, and he proved himself to be a good shot with the bow. He made frequent hunting trips with his troops, and in the evening all Niani would be in the square to be present at the entry of the young hunters. The crowd would sing the "Hymn to the Bow" which Balla Fasséké had composed, and Sogolon Djata was quite young when he received the title of Simbon, or master hunter, which is only conferred on great hunters who have proved themselves.

Every evening Sogolon Kedjou would gather Djata and his companions outside her hut. She would tell them stories about the beasts of the bush, the dumb brothers of man. Sogolon Djata learnt to distinguish between the animals; he knew why the buffalo was his mother's wraith[6] and also why the lion was the protector of his father's family. He also listened to the history of the kings which Balla Fasséké told him; enraptured by the story of Alexander the Great, the mighty king of gold and silver, whose sun shone over quite half the world. Sogolon initiated her son into certain secrets and revealed to him the names of the medicinal plants which every hunter should know. Thus, between his mother and his griot, the child got to know all that needed to be known.

Sogolon's son was now ten. The name Sogolon Djata in the rapid Mandingo language became Sundiata or Sondjata. He was a lad full of strength; his arms had the strength of ten and his biceps inspired fear in his companions. He had already that authoritative way of

---

[6] In Mandingo religion, the double of a spirit. The spirit may leave the body and reincarnate itself in other persons or animals. In this case the mother's spirit became reincarnate in the buffalo.

speaking which belongs to those who are destined to command. His brother, Manding Bory, became his best friend, and whenever Djata was seen, Manding Bory appeared too. They were like a man and his shadow. Fran Kamara and Kamandjan were the closest friends of the young princes, while Balla Fasséké followed them all like a guardian angel.

But Sundiata's popularity was so great that the queen mother became apprehensive for her son's throne. Dankaran Touman was the most retiring of men. At the age of eighteen he was still under the influence of his mother and a handful of old schemers. It was Sassouma Bérété who really reigned in his name. The queen mother wanted to put an end to this popularity by killing Sundiata and it was thus that one night she received the nine great witches of Mali. They were all old women. The eldest, and the most dangerous too, was called Soumosso Konkomba. When the nine old hags had seated themselves in a semi-circle around her bed the queen mother said:

"You who rule supreme at night, nocturnal powers, oh you who hold the secret of life, you who can put an end to one life, can you help me?"

"The night is potent," said Soumosso Konkomba, "Oh queen, tell us what is to be done, on whom must we turn the fatal blade?"

"I want to kill Sundiata," said Sassouma. "His destiny runs counter to my son's and he must be killed while there is still time. If you succeed, I promise you the finest rewards. First of all I bestow on each of you a cow and her calf and from tomorrow go to the royal granaries and each of you will receive a hundred measures of rice and a hundred measures of hay on my authority."

"Mother of the king," rejoined Soumosso Konkomba, "life hangs by nothing but a very fine thread, but all is interwoven here below. Life has a cause, and death as well. The one comes from the other. Your hate has a cause and your action must have a cause. Mother of the king, everything holds together, our action will have no effect unless we are ourselves implicated, but Mari Djata has done us no wrong. It is, then, difficult for us to compass his death."

"But you are also concerned," replied the queen mother, "for the son of Sogolon will be a scourge to us all."

"The snake seldom bites the foot that does not walk," said one of the witches.

"Yes, but there are snakes that attack everybody. Allow Sundiata to grow up and we will all repent of it. Tomorrow go to Sogolon's vegetable patch and make a show of picking a few gnougou leaves. Mari Djata stands guard there and you will see how vicious the boy is. He won't have any respect for your age, he'll give you a good thrashing."

"That's a clever idea," said one of the old hags.

"But the cause of our discomfiture will be ourselves, for having touched something which did not belong to us."

"We could repeat the offence," said another, "and then if he beats us again we would be able to reproach him with being unkind, heartless. In that case we would be concerned, I think."

"The idea is ingenious," said Soumosso Konkomba. "Tomorrow we shall go to Sogolon's vegetable patch."

"Now there's a happy thought," concluded the queen mother, laughing for joy. "Go to the vegetable patch tomorrow and you will see that Sogolon's son is mean. Beforehand, present yourselves at the royal granaries where you will receive the grain I promised you; the cows and calves are already yours."

The old hags bowed and disappeared into the black night. The queen mother was now alone and gloated over her anticipated victory. But her daughter, Nana Triban, woke up.

"Mother, who were you talking to? I thought I heard voices."

"Sleep, my daughter, it is nothing. You didn't hear anything."

In the morning, as usual, Sundiata got his companions together in front of his mother's hut and said, "What animal are we going to hunt today?"

Kamandjan said, "I wouldn't mind if we attacked some elephants right now."

"Yes, I am of this opinion too," said Fran Kamara. "That will allow us to go far into the bush."

And the young band left after Sogolon had filled the hunting bags with eatables. Sundiata and his companions came back late to the village, but first Djata wanted to take a look at his mother's vegetable patch as was his custom. It was dusk. There he found the nine witches stealing gnougou leaves. They made a show of running away like thieves caught red-handed.

"Stop, stop, poor old women," said Sundiata, "what is the matter with you to run away like this. This garden belongs to all."

Straight away his companions and he filled the gourds of the old hags with leaves, aubergines and onions.

"Each time that you run short of condiments come to stock up here without fear."

"You disarm us," said one of the old crones, and another added, "And you confound us with your bounty."

"Listen, Djata," said Soumosso Konkomba, "we had come here to test you. We have no need of condiments but your generosity disarms us. We were sent here by the queen mother to provoke you and draw the anger of the nocturnal powers upon you. But nothing can be done against a heart full of kindness. And to think that we have already drawn a hundred measures of rice and a hundred measures of millet—and the queen promises us each a cow and her calf in addition. Forgive us, son of Sogolon."

"I bear you no ill-will," said Djata. "Here, I am returning from the hunt with my companions and we have killed ten elephants, so I will give you an elephant each and there you have some meat!"

"Thank you, son of Sogolon."

"Thank you, child of Justice."

"Henceforth," concluded Soumosso Konkomba, "we will watch over you." And the nine witches disappeared into the night. Sundiata and his companions continued on their way to Niani and got back after dark.

"You were really frightened; those nine witches really scared you, eh?" said Sogolon Kolonkan, Djata's young sister.

"How do you know," retorted Sundiata, astonished.

"I saw them at night hatching their scheme, but I knew there was no danger for you." Kolonkan was well versed in the art of witchcraft and watched over her brother without his suspecting it.

Summary Sogolon, knowing the danger that awaited her children in the court ruled by the jealous Sassouma, decided to leave until such time that Djata could return in safety to reign over Mali. In a parting act of malice Dankaran Touman sent Djata's griot, Balla Fasséké, on an embassy to the king of Sosso, Soumaoro Kanté, thereby depriving Djata of his friend and teacher. There Balla Fasséké remained along with Nana Triban until the eve of Soumaoro's major battle with Sundiata.

Vowing to return, Sogolon's son and his family began their seven years of exile during which Sundiata would grow to manhood. After brief stops in Djedeba and Tabon, they remained for a time at the court of the Cisse's at Wagadou. There Sundiata learned much from the merchants and officials engaged in the trans-Saharan trade. After a time the Cisse king sent them on to the king of Mema, his cousin. The king of Mema's hospitality was generous, and Sundiata quickly became a favorite at the court. His first military campaigns were fought on behalf of the king of Mema, and so valorous were his exploits that he soon was named viceroy.

SOUMAORO KANTÉ, THE SORCERER KING

While Sogolon's son was fighting his first campaign far from his native land, Mali had fallen under the domination of a new master, Soumaoro Kanté, king of Sosso.

When the embassy sent by Dankaran Touman arrived at Sosso, Soumaoro demanded that Mali should acknowledge itself tributary to Sosso. Balla Fasséké found delegates from several other kingdoms at Soumaoro's court. With his powerful army of smiths the king of Sosso had quickly imposed his power on everybody. After the defeat of Ghana and Diaghan no one dared oppose him any more. Soumaoro was descended from the line of smiths called Diarisso who first harnessed fire and taught men how to work iron, but for a long time Sosso had remained a little village of no significance. The powerful king of Ghana was the master of the country. Little by little the kingdom of Sosso had grown at the expense of Ghana and now the Kantés dominated their old masters. Like all masters of fire, Soumaoro Kanté was a great sorcerer. His fetishes had a terrible power and it was because of them that all kings trembled before him, for he could deal a swift death to whoever he pleased. He had fortified Sosso with a triple curtain wall and in the middle of the town loomed his palace, towering over the thatched huts of the villages.

He had had an immense seven-storey tower built for himself and he lived on the seventh floor in the midst of his fetishes. This is why he was called "The Untouchable King."

Soumaoro let the rest of the Mandingo embassy return but he kept Balla Fasséké back and threatened to destroy Niani if Dankaran Touman did not make his submission. Frightened, the son of Sassouma immediately made his submission, and he even sent his sister, Nana Triban, to the king of Sosso.

One day when the king was away, Balla Fasséké managed to get right into the most secret chamber of the palace where Soumaoro safeguarded his fetishes. When he had pushed the door open he was transfixed with amazement at what he saw. The walls of the chamber were tapestried with human skins and there was one in the middle of the room on which the king sat; around an earthenware jar nine heads formed a circle; when Balla had opened the door the water had become disturbed and a monstrous snake had raised its head. Balla Fasséké, who was also well versed in sorcery, recited some formulas and everything in the room fell quiet, so he continued his inspection. He saw on a perch above the bed three owls which seemed to be asleep; on the far wall hung strangely-shaped weapons, curved swords and knives with three cutting edges. He looked at the skulls attentively and recognized the nine kings killed by Soumaoro. To the right of the door he discovered a great balafon, bigger than he had ever seen in Mali. Instinctively he pounced upon it and sat down to play. The griot always has a weakness for music, for music is the griot's soul.

He began to play. He had never heard such a melodious balafon. Though scarcely touched by the hammer, the resonant wood gave out sounds of an infinite sweetness, notes clear and as pure as gold dust; under the skilful hand of Balla the instrument had found its master. He played with all his soul and the whole room was filled with wonderment. The drowsy owls, eyes half closed, began to move their heads as though with satisfaction. Everything seemed to come to life upon the strains of this magic music. The nine skulls resumed their earthly forms and blinked at hearing the solemn "Vulture Tune"; with its head resting on the rim, the snake seemed to listen from the jar. Balla Fasséké was pleased at the effect his music had had on the strange inhabitants of this ghoulish chamber, but he quite un-

derstood that this balafon was not at all like any other. It was that of a great sorcerer. Soumaoro was the only one to play this instrument. After each victory he would come and sing his own praises. No griot had ever touched it. Not all ears were made to hear that music. Soumaoro was constantly in touch with this xylophone and no matter how far away he was, one only had to touch it for him to know that someone had got into his secret chamber.

The king was not far from the town and he rushed back to his palace and climbed up to the seventh storey. Balla Fasséké heard hurried steps in the corridor and Soumaoro bounded into the room, sword in hand.

"Who is there?" he roared. "It is you, Balla Fasséké!"

The king was foaming with anger and his eyes burnt fiercely like hot embers. Yet without losing his composure the son of Doua changed key and improvised a song in honour of the king:

There he is, Soumaoro Kanté.
All hail, you who sit on the skins of kings.
All hail, Simbon of the deadly arrow.
I salute you, you who wear clothes of human skin.

This improvised tune greatly pleased Soumaoro and he had never heard such fine words. Kings are only men, and whatever iron cannot achieve against them, words can. Kings, too, are susceptible to flattery, so Soumaoro's anger abated, his heart filled with joy as he listened attentively to this sweet music:

All hail, you who wear clothes of human skin.
I salute you, you who sit on the skins of kings.

Balla sang and his voice, which was beautiful, delighted the king of Sosso.

"How sweet it is to hear one's praises sung by someone else; Balla Fasséké, you will nevermore return to Mali for from today you are my griot."

Thus Balla Fasséké, whom king Naré Maghan had given to his son Sundiata, was stolen from the latter by Dankaran Touman; now it was the king of Sosso, Soumaoro Kanté, who, in turn, stole the precious griot from the son of Sassouma Bérété. In this way war between Sundiata and Soumaoro became inevitable.

Summary The second half of the epic relates Sundiata's leave-taking of Mema in response to the pleas for rescue of a search party sent to find him, and tells of his triumphal series of battles against the terrible Soumaoro.

Allied with the armies of his childhood friends and with those who had offered him sanctuary during his exile, Sundiata led a massive force that included the cavalry of Mema and Wagadou; blacksmiths and the mountain Djallonkes; and groups under Fran Kamara of Tabon Wana. A victory at the valley of Tabon was followed by the first clash with Soumaoro's magic at Negueboria. The fame of Sundiata spread until all the sons of Mali were under his banner. But even a warrior like Sundiata was challenged to the limits by Soumaoro's sorcery. He was saved by the clever escape from Sosso of Balla Fasséké and Nana Triban; on the eve of the battle of Krina it was they who revealed Soumaoro's secret taboo. Reunited with his master, the griot Balla Fasséké sang the praises and history of Mali and challenged the assembled armies to prove themselves worthy of their heritage. At Krina, Soumaoro's power and magic were dissolved by Sundiata's mighty army and his destruction of Soumaoro's protective fetish. Despite hard-driven pursuit by Sundiata and Soumaoro's nephew Fakoli, Soumaoro avoided capture and ultimately disappeared into a mountain cave, never to be seen again. The city of Sosso was destroyed, and the rest of Soumaoro's allies now in disarray were vanquished.

The final sections relate the triumphal festival, the Kouroukan Fougan or the Division of the World, and the rebuilding of Sundiata's capital at Niani.

KOUROUKAN FOUGAN OR THE DIVISION OF THE WORLD

Leaving Do, the land of ten thousand guns, Sundiata wended his way to Ka-ba, keeping to the river valley. All his armies converged on Ka-ba and Fakoli and Tabon Wana entered it laden with booty. Sibi Kamandjan had gone ahead of Sundiata to prepare the great assembly which was to gather at Ka-ba, a town situated on the territory belonging to the country of Sibi. . . .

To the north of the town stretches a spacious clearing and it is there that the great assembly was to foregather. King Kamandjan had the whole clearing cleaned up and a great dais was got ready. Even before Djata's arrival the delegations from all the conquered peoples had made their way to Ka-ba. Huts were hastily built to house all these people. When all the armies had reunited, camps had to be set up in the big plain lying between the river and the town. On the appointed day the troops were drawn up on the vast square that had been prepared. As at Sibi, each people was gathered round its king's pennant. Sundiata had put on robes such as are worn by a great Muslim king. Balla Fasséké, the high master of ceremonies, set the allies around Djata's great throne. Everything was in position. The sofas,[7] forming a vast semicircle bristling with spears, stood motionless. The delegations of the various peoples had been planted at the foot of the dais. A complete silence reigned. On Sundiata's right, Balla Fasséké, holding his mighty spear, addressed the throng in this manner:

"Peace reigns today in the whole country; may it always be thus. . . ."

"Amen," replied the crowd, then the herald continued:

"I speak to you, assembled peoples. To those of Mali I convey Maghan Sundiata's greeting; greetings to those of Do, greetings to those of Ghana, to those from Mema greetings, and to those of Fakoli's tribe. Greetings to the Bobo warriors and, finally, greetings to those of Sibi and Ka-ba. To all the peoples assembled, Djata gives greetings.

"May I be humbly forgiven if I have made any omission. I am nervous before so many people gathered together.

"Peoples, here we are, after years of hard trials, gathered around our saviour, the restorer of peace and order. From the east to the west, from the north to the south, everywhere his victorious arms have established peace. I convey to you the greetings of Soumaoro's vanquisher, Maghan Sundiata, king of Mali.

"But in order to respect tradition, I must first of all address myself to the host of us all, Kamandjan, king of Sibi; Djata greets you and gives you the floor."

Kamandjan, who was sitting close by Sundiata, stood up and stepped down from the dais. He mounted his horse and brandished his sword, crying "I salute you all, warriors of Mali, of Do, of Tabon, of Mema, of Wagadou, of Bobo, of Fakoli . . . ; warriors, peace has returned to our homes, may God long preserve it."

"Amen," replied the warriors and the crowd. The king of Sibi continued.

---

7 Army troops, often of slave origin.

"In the world man suffers for a season, but never eternally. Here we are at the end of our trials. We are at peace. May God be praised. But we owe this peace to one man who, by his courage and his valiance, was able to lead our troops to victory.

"Which one of us, alone, would have dared face Soumaoro? Ay, we were all cowards. How many times did we pay him tribute? The insolent rogue thought that everything was permitted him. What family was not dishonoured by Soumaoro? He took our daughters and wives from us and we were more craven than women. He carried his insolence to the point of stealing the wife of his nephew Fakoli! We were prostrated and humiliated in front of our children. But it was in the midst of so many calamities that our destiny suddenly changed. A new sun arose in the east. After the battle of Tabon we felt ourselves to be men, we realized that Soumaoro was a human being and not an incarnation of the devil, for he was no longer invincible. A man came to us. He had heard our groans and came to our aid, like a father when he sees his son in tears. Here is that man. Maghan Sundiata, the man with two names foretold by the soothsayers.

"It is to you that I now address myself, son of Sogolon, you, the nephew of the valorous warriors of Do. Henceforth it is from you that I derive my kingdom for I acknowledge you my sovereign. My tribe and I place ourselves in your hands. I salute you, supreme chief, I salute you, Fama of Famas.[8] I salute you, Mansa!"[9]

The huzza that greeted these words was so loud that you could hear the echo repeat the tremendous clamour twelve times over. With a strong hand Kamandjan struck his spear in the ground in front of the dais and said, "Sundiata, here is my spear, it is yours."

Then he climbed up to sit in his place. Thereafter, one by one, the twelve kings of the bright savanna country got up and proclaimed Sundiata "Mansa" in their turn. Twelve royal spears were stuck in the ground in front of the dais. Sundiata had become emperor. The old tabala of Niani announced to the world that the lands of the savanna had provided themselves with one single king. When the imperial tabala had stopped reverberating, Balla Fasséké, the grand master

of ceremonies, took the floor again following the crowd's ovation.

"Sundiata, Maghan Sundiata, king of Mali, in the name of the twelve kings of the "Bright Country," I salute you as 'Mansa.' "

The crowd shouted "Wassa, Wassa. . . . Ayé."

It was amid such joy that Balla Fasséké composed the great hymn "Niama" which the griots still sing:

Niama, Niama, Niama,
You, you serve as a shelter for all,
All come to seek refuge under you.
And as for you, Niama,
Nothing serves you for shelter,
God alone protects you.

The festival began. The musicians of all the countries were there. Each people in turn came forward to the dais under Sundiata's impassive gaze. Then the war dances began. The sofas of all the countries had lined themselves up in six ranks amid a great clatter of bows and spears knocking together. The war chiefs were on horseback. The warriors faced the enormous dais and at a signal from Balla Fasséké, the musicians, massed on the right of the dais, struck up. The heavy war drums thundered, the bolons gave off muted notes while the griot's voice gave the throng the pitch for the "Hymn to the Bow." The spearmen, advancing like hyenas in the night, held their spears above their heads; the archers of Wagadou and Tabon, walking with a noiseless tread, seemed to be lying in ambush behind bushes. They rose suddenly to their feet and let fly their arrows at imaginary enemies. In front of the great dais the Kéké-Tigui, or war chiefs, made their horses perform dance steps under the eyes of the Mansa. The horses whinnied and reared, then, overmastered by the spurs, knelt, got up and cut little capers, or else scraped the ground with their hooves.

The rapturous people shouted the "Hymn to the Bow" and clapped their hands. The sweating bodies of the warriors glistened in the sun while the exhausting rhythm of the tam-tams wrenched from them shrill cries. But presently they made way for the cavalry, beloved by Djata. The horsemen of Mema threw their swords in the air and caught them in flight, uttering mighty shouts. A smile of contentment took shape on Sundiata's lips, for he was happy to see his cavalry manoeuvre with so much skill.

---

[8] King of Kings.
[9] Emperor.

In the afternoon the festivity took on a new aspect. It began with the procession of prisoners and booty. Their hands tied behind their backs and in triple file, the Sosso prisoners made their entry into the giant circle. All their heads had been shaved. Inside the circle they turned and passed by the foot of the dais. Their eyes lowered, the poor prisoners walked in silence, abuse heaped upon them by the frenzied crowd. Behind came the kings who had remained faithful to Soumaoro and who had not intended to make their submission. They also had their heads shorn, but they were on horseback so that everyone could see them. At last, right at the back, came Sosso Balla, who had been placed in the midst of his father's fetishes. The fetishes had been loaded onto donkeys. The crowd gave loud cries of horror on seeing the inmates of Soumaoro's grisly chamber. People pointed with terror at the snake's pitcher, the magic balafon, and the king of Sosso's owls. Soumaoro's son Balla, his hands bound, was on a horse but did not dare look up at this throne, which formerly used to tremble with fear at mere talk of his father. In the crowd could be heard:

"Each in his turn, Sosso Balla; lift up your head a bit, impudent little creature!" Or else: "Did you have any idea that one day you would be a slave, you vile fellow!"

"Look at your useless fetishes. Call on them then, son of a sorcerer!"

When Sosso Balla was in front of the dais, Djata made a gesture. He had just remembered the mysterious disappearance of Soumaoro inside the mountain. He became morose, but his griot Balla Fasséké noticed it and so he spoke thus:

"The son will pay for the father, Soumaoro can thank God that he is already dead."

When the procession had finished Balla Fasséké silenced everyone. The sofas got into line and the tam-tams stopped.

Sundiata got up and a graveyard silence settled on the whole place. The Mansa moved forward to the edge of the dais. Then Sundiata spoke as Mansa. Only Balla Fasséké could hear him, for a Mansa does not speak like a town-crier.

"I greet all the peoples gathered here." And Djata mentioned them all. Pulling the spear of Kamandjan, king of Sibi, out of the ground, he said:

"I give you back your kingdom, king of Sibi, for you have deserved it by your bravery; I have known you since childhood and your speech is as frank as your heart is straightforward.

"Today I ratify for ever the alliance between the Kamaras of Sibi and the Keitas of Mali. May these two people be brothers henceforth. In future, the land of the Keitas shall be the land of the Kamaras, and the property of the Kamaras shall be henceforth the property of the Keitas.

"May there nevermore be falsehood between a Kamara and a Keita, and may the Kamaras feel at home in the whole extent of my empire."

He returned the spear to Kamandjan and the king of Sibi prostrated himself before Djata, as is done when honoured by a Fama.

Sundiata took Tabon Wana's spear and said, "Fran Kamara, my friend, I return your kingdom to you. May the Djallonkés and Mandingoes be forever allies. You received me in your own domain, so may the Djallonkés be received as friends throughout Mali. I leave you the lands you have conquered, and henceforth your children and your children's children will grow up at the court of Niani where they will be treated like the princes of Mali."

One by one all the kings received their kingdoms from the very hands of Sundiata, and each one bowed before him as one bows before a Mansa.

Sundiata pronounced all the prohibitions which still obtain in relations between the tribes. To each he assigned its land, he established the rights of each people and ratified their friendships. The Kondés of the land of Do became henceforth the uncles of the imperial family of Keita, for the latter, in memory of the fruitful marriage between Naré Maghan and Sogolon, had to take a wife in Do. The Tounkaras and the Cissés became "banter-brothers" of the Keitas. While the Cissés, Bérétés and Tourés were proclaimed great divines of the empire. No kin group was forgotten at Kouroukan Fougan; each had its share in the division. To Fakoli Koroma, Sundiata gave the kingdom of Sosso, the majority of whose inhabitants were enslaved. Fakoli's tribe, the Koromas, which others call Doumbouya or Sissoko, had the monopoly of the forge, that is, of iron working. Fakoli also received from Sundiata part of the lands situated between the Bafing and Bagbé rivers. Wagadou and Mema kept their kings who continued to bear the title of Mansa, but these two kingdoms acknowledged the suzerainty of the supreme Mansa. The Konaté of Toron became the cadets of the Keitas so that on reaching maturity a Konaté could call himself Keita.

When Sogolon's son had finished distributing lands and power he turned to Balla Fasséké, his griot, and said: "As for you, Balla Fasséké, my griot, I make you grand master of ceremonies. Henceforth the Keitas will choose their griot from your tribe, from among the Kouyatés. I give the Kouyatés the right to make jokes about all the tribes, and in particular about the royal tribe of Keita."

Thus spoke the son of Sogolon at Kouroukan Fougan. Since that time his respected word has become law, the rule of conduct for all the peoples who were represented at Ka-ba.

So, Sundiata had divided the world at Kouroukan Fougan. He kept for his tribe the blessed country of Kita, but the Kamaras inhabiting the region remained masters of the soil.

If you go to Ka-ba, go and see the glade of Kouroukan Fougan and you will see a linké tree planted there, perpetuating the memory of the great gathering which witnessed the division of the world.

. . .

With Sundiata peace and happiness entered Niani. Lovingly Sogolon's son had his native city rebuilt. He restored in the ancient style his father's old enclosure where he had grown up. People came from all the villages of Mali to settle in Niani. The walls had to be destroyed to enlarge the town, and new quarters were built for each kin group in the enormous army.

Sundiata had left his brother Manding Bory at Bagadou-Djeliba on the river. He was Sundiata's Kankoro Sigui, that is to say, viceroy. Manding Bory had looked after all the conquered countries. When reconstruction of the capital was finished he went to wage war in the south in order to frighten the forest peoples. He received an embassy from the country of Sangaran where a few Kondé clans had settled, and although these latter had not been represented at Kouroukan Fougan, Sun-

diata granted his alliance and they were placed on the same footing as the Kondés of the land of Do.

After a year Sundiata held a new assembly at Niani, but this one was the assembly of dignitaries and kings of the empire. The kings and notables of all the tribes came to Niani. The kings spoke of their administration and the dignitaries talked of their kings. Fakoli, the nephew of Soumaoro, having proved himself too independent, had to flee to evade the Mansa's anger. His lands were confiscated and the taxes of Sosso were payed directly into the granaries of Niani. In this way, every year, Sundiata gathered about him all the kings and notables; so justice prevailed everywhere, for the kings were afraid of being denounced at Niani.

Djata's justice spared nobody. He followed the very word of God. He protected the weak against the strong and people would make journeys lasting several days to come and demand justice of him. Under his sun the upright man was rewarded and the wicked one punished.

In their new-found peace the villages knew prosperity again, for with Sundiata happiness had come into everyone's home. Vast fields of millet, rice, cotton, indigo and fonio surrounded the villages. Whoever worked always had something to live on. Each year long caravans carried the taxes in kind to Niani. You could go from village to village without fearing brigands. A thief would have his right hand chopped off and if he stole again he would be put to the sword.

New villages and new towns sprang up in Mali and elsewhere. "Dyulas," or traders, became numerous and during the reign of Sundiata the world knew happiness.

There are some kings who are powerful through their military strength. Everybody trembles before them, but when they die nothing but ill is spoken of them. Others do neither good nor ill and when they die they are forgotten. Others are feared because they have power, but they know how to use it and they are loved because they love justice. Sundiata belonged to this group. He was feared, but loved as well. He was the father of Mali and gave the world peace. After him the world has not seen a greater conqueror, for he was the seventh and last conqueror. He had made the capital of an empire out of his father's village, and Niani became the navel of the earth.

COMMENTS AND QUESTIONS

1. What is the griot Djeli Mamadou Kouyaté's conception of his role of historian? How would he define history? Does his definition differ from ours?
2. What is the Malinke view of fate or destiny as expressed here?
3. In the section "Soumaoro Kanté, the Sorcerer King," you read, "His fetishes had a terrible power...." *Fetish* means here an object believed to contain a supernatural power that may be used to protect the owner of the fetish or may be directed to harm another person. In this case Soumaoro used his fetishes to protect himself and to confuse his enemies. How does it appear that Soumaoro's power vanished when their secret was discovered?
4. What are the attributes of the hero as expressed in this Malian epic? How does it correspond with views expressed in the Greek epics?
5. What are the ideals of government and of good leadership?
6. Seek out some *proverbs* from the text. How do they inform us in a capsulized way of Malinke values?

Myths

Myths, as we saw in the section on Greek mythology (Chapter 1), are intimately allied with the religious beliefs and the values of a particular culture. Unlike legends or epics, they are not based on historical events but attempt rather to explain or clarify the primal mysteries of nature, creation, and man's relationship with the gods. African myths are primarily oral; they are told and sung. They are often used in religious rituals; but, because there are a great many African religions, there is also a tremendous variety in African mythology. It is possible, nevertheless, to identify certain common features in the religions of the West African peoples under consideration here and to trace fundamental themes in their mythology. Since religion is such an important and unifying element of African culture, an understanding of some of the basic African beliefs will be useful in studying all aspects of that culture.

African Religions: Some Generalizations   All West African religions postulate the existence of a su-preme God (whose name varies with the culture), associated with the creation of the universe. One of the great questions that the African myths ask is, Why is this God now so distant from the human world? The answer (as in the Judeo-Christian doctrine of the Fall) seems to lie in the fact of man's imperfection. African myths show in a variety of ways how the supreme deity, exasperated with human perversity or troublesomeness, simply withdrew from his creation, leaving the administration of it to lesser gods, natural spirits, or ancestors of living humans. Unlike the Judeo-Christian God, the African supreme being did not return to intervene in human affairs. People in Africa rarely worship the high God by direct means; rather they seek understanding and redress through lesser deities and spirits, each of whom represents an aspect of God. Communication between men and these highly charged spiritual forces is achieved through rituals in honor of them and through sacrifice.

Another important feature of African religion is the belief in the spiritual vitality of the natural world or, as it is called in the West, animism. According to this belief, supernatural spirits or "souls" (Latin, *anima*) may inhabit the bodies of animals or even inanimate parts of nature such as trees, rocks, forests, mountains, and rivers. These spirits are often guardian spirits who must be acknowledged and appeased, for some of them are capable of causing or controlling events in the natural world. The blessings of resident spirits must be sought, for example, when a new settlement is built.

The spirits inhabiting the natural world are nonhuman in origin and therefore close to the realm of the gods. Nearer to the world of men are the spirits of ancestors, the dead, whose souls are very much present in the everyday world and who may, for example, come to inhabit the body of a new baby. While the ancestral souls do not have "power" like the spirits, they do have "awareness" and can be communicated with. They may act as mediators between the living and the spirits.

All of the spirits are believed to be inherently neither good nor evil—they can affect human lives in either positive or negative ways. The beautiful and beneficent natural world can also be malevolent and destructive. To live in it, one must acknowledge those powerful forces that are outside of, but intrinsically part of, the cycles of one's life. Because of this complex relationship of people to the phenomena of the world, there is a profound duality that pervades every aspect of African life. For example, one may believe in sky spirits and earth spirits, and they may contradict each other. Some spirits, such as the "tricksters," may embody contradictory traits. It is up to human wit and ingenuity to learn to appease the spirits and to determine what course to take.

The myths that follow address themselves, in the context of African religion, to three basic questions: (1) How did the world begin? (creation); (2) What caused God to withdraw from the world of men? and (3) Why do people have to die? The two creation myths are Yoruba; they require a word of explanation on Yoruba religion, which will be discussed more fully in the poetry section. The highest God, named Oludumare or Olorun, has many aspects, which are represented by lesser deities called *orisha*. One of these is Obatala, god of creation.

Two Yoruba Myths of Creation

THE CREATION OF LAND

At the beginning everything was water. Then Oludumare the supreme god sent Obatala (or Orishanla) down from heaven to create the dry land. Obatala descended on a chain and he carried with him: a snail shell filled with earth, some pieces of crow and a cock. When he arrived he placed the crow on the water, spread the earth over it and placed the cock on top. The cock immediately started to scratch and thus the land spread far and wide.

When the land had been created, the other Orisha descended from heaven in order to live on the land with Obatala.

THE CREATION OF MAN

Obatala made man out of earth. After shaping men and women he gave them to Oludumare to blow in the breath of life.

One day Obatala drank palm wine. Then he started to make hunchbacks and cripples, albinos and blind men.

From that day onwards hunchbacks and albinos and all deformed persons are sacred to Obatala. But his worshipers are forbidden to drink palm wine.

Obatala is still the one who gives shape to the new babe in the mother's womb.

QUESTIONS

1. How is the role of the supreme God, Oludumare, distinguished from that of the orisha Obatala?
2. What similarities and differences do you find in these creation myths and the story of creation in Genesis?

Myths on the Separation of Man from God

[This myth comes from the Yao, one of a cluster of peoples speaking Bantu languages who live in northern Mozambique and adjacent lands in Tanzania. The translator of this myth, and those following, is Susan Feldmann.]

MULUNGU AND THE BEASTS

In the beginning man was not, only Mulungu and his people, the beasts. They lived happily on earth.

One day a chameleon found a human pair in his fish trap. He had never seen such creatures before and he was surprised. The chameleon reported his discovery to Mulungu. Mulungu said, "Let us wait and see what the creatures will do."

The men started making fires. They set fire to the bush so that the beasts fled into the forest. Then the men set traps and killed Mulungu's people. At last Mulungu was compelled to leave the earth. Since he could not climb a tree he called for the spider.

The spider spun a thread up to the sky and down again. When he returned he said, "I have gone on high nicely, now you Mulungu go on high." And Mulungu ascended to the sky on the spider's thread to escape from the wickedness of men.

[The following myth comes from the Ngombe, one of the many Mongo groups who live in the heart of the equatorial rain forest of Zaire. Their language and culture form part of the larger Bantu-speaking peoples of central and southern Africa.]

WITHDRAWAL OF GOD

Akongo was not always as he is now. In the beginning the creator lived among men; but men were quarrelsome. One day they had a big quarrel and Akongo left them to themselves. He went and hid in the forest and nobody has seen him since. People today can't tell what he is like.

[The next two are from the Ashanti peoples of modern Ghana. They are one of the populous Akan cultural complex, one of whose characteristics is matrilineal descent. The Ashanti state, founded around 1680, became a principal political power on the Gold Coast during the eighteenth and nineteenth centuries. Its greatness lay in part because of the European trade and in part because it integrated under its king (the *asantehene*) and ruling council many more of the Akan peoples into one state than had been achieved before. The Ashanti were also splendid craftsmen whose court art, textiles, and gold weights are among the highest achievements of West African art.]

THE TOWER TO HEAVEN

Long, long ago Onyankopon lived on earth, or at least was very near to us. Now there was a certain old woman who used to pound her mashed yams and the pestle kept knocking up against Onyankopon, who was not then high in the sky. So Onyankopon said to the old woman: "Why do you keep doing this to me? Because of what you are doing I am going to take myself away up in the sky." And of a truth he did so.

Now the people could no longer approach Onyankopon. But the old woman thought of a way to reach him and bring him back. She instructed her children to go and search for all the mortars they could find and bring them to her. Then she told them to pile one mortar on top of another til they reached to where Onyankopon was. And her children did so, they piled up many mortars, one on top of another, til they needed only one more mortar to reach Onyankopon.

Now, since they could not find another mortar anywhere, their grandmother the old woman said to them: "Take one out from the bottom and put it on top to make them reach." So her children removed a mortar from the bottom and all the mortars rolled and fell to the ground, causing the death of many people.

QUESTIONS ON MYTHS ON THE SEPARATION OF MAN FROM GOD

1. What generalization can you make from these myths about the basic cause of man's fall from his idyllic relationship with God?
2. What is the difference between the relationship between God and man and that between God and the animals in "Mulungu and the Beasts"?
3. What does "The Tower to Heaven" say about human ingenuity in relation to God? Compare the biblical story of the tower of Babel.

Myths on the Origin of Death

THE PERVERTED MESSAGE

In primeval times, God had familiar intercourse with men and gave them all they needed. This state, however, came to an end when some women who were grinding their food became embarrassed by God's presence and told him to go away, and beat him with their pestles. God then withdrew from the world, and left its government to the spirits.

Afterward God sent a goat from heaven to the seven human beings on earth with the following message: "There is something called death. One day it will kill some of you. Even if you die, however, you will not be altogether lost. You will come to live with me in the sky."

On the way, the goat lingered at a bush in order to eat, and when God discovered this he sent a sheep with the same message. But the sheep changed the message to the effect that men should die, and that as far as they were concerned this would be the end of all things. When the goat then arrived with her true message, men would not believe it. They had already accepted the message delivered by the sheep. Shortly afterward the first case of death took place, and God taught men to bury their dead. He also told them that as a foil to death they should be given the capacity to multiply.

According to another version, God sent the sheep with eternal life as a gift to men. But the he-goat ran on ahead and gave them death as a gift from God. They eagerly accepted this gift, as they did not know what death was. The sheep arrived after a while, but it was too late.

[The Efe are a small branch of the Mbuti hunting and gathering peoples who live in the Ituri forest of Zaire. They are seminomadic and often live in symbiotic relationships with nearby black African groups. This myth is from the Efe.]

FORBIDDEN FRUIT

God created the first human being Ba-atsi with the help of the moon. He kneaded the body into shape, covered it with a skin, and poured in blood. When the man had thus been given life, God whispered in his ear that he, Ba-atsi, should beget children, and upon them he should impress the following prohibition: "Of all the trees of the forest you may eat, but of the Tahu tree you may not eat." Ba-atsi had many children, impressed upon them the prohibition, and then retired to heaven. At first men respected the commandment they had been given, and lived happily. But one day a pregnant woman was seized with an irresistible desire to eat of the forbidden fruit. She tried to persuade her husband to give her some of it. At first he refused, but after a time he gave way. He stole into the wood, picked a Tahu fruit, peeled it, and hid the peel among the leaves. But the moon had seen his action and reported it to God. God was so enraged over man's disobedience that as punishment he sent death among them.

[The following myth comes from the Darasa, one of a cluster of ancient Cushitic peoples who practice intensive agriculture by irrigation and terracing of mountain slopes in southern Ethiopia.]

MAN CHOOSES DEATH IN EXCHANGE
FOR FIRE

Formerly men had no fire but ate all their food raw. At that time they did not need to die for when they became old, God made them young again. One day they decided to beg God for fire. They sent a messenger to God to convey their request. God replied to the messenger that he would give him fire if he was prepared to die. The man took the fire from God, but ever since then all men must die.

[Madagascar, the source of this next myth, lies in the Indian Ocean off the southeastern coast of Africa. Its peoples include descendants of both mainland Africans and Malayo-Polynesians who probably followed the seasonal trade winds from southeast Asia to settle on the island around the beginning of the Christian era.]

MAN CHOOSES DEATH IN EXCHANGE
FOR CHILDREN

One day God asked the first human couple who then lived in heaven what kind of death they wanted, that of the moon or that of the banana. Because the couple wondered in dismay about the implications of the two modes of death, God explained to them: the banana puts forth shoots which take its place and the moon itself comes back to life. The couple considered for a long time before they made their choice. If they elected to be childless they would avoid death, but they would also be very lonely, would themselves be forced to carry out all the work, and would not have anybody to work and strive for. Therefore they prayed to God for children, well aware of the consequences of their choice. And their prayer was granted. Since that time man's sojourn is short on this earth.

QUESTIONS ON MYTHS ON THE
ORIGIN OF DEATH

1. Notice the closeness of animals to God in comparison to men. How do you interpret the significance of the "perverted message"?
2. Compare "Forbidden Fruit" with the similar story in Genesis. Is the religious message of the two stories the same?
3. What is the cultural significance of fire? Why would man choose it over immortality? Look up the Greek myth of Prometheus to compare it with this.
4. How are the importance of children and continuity of the community over time expressed? Notice the expression of this value in other aspects of African culture.

Tales (Hausa)

Myths have to do with gods, spirits, and religious questions; but *tales*, the second type of oral prose literature, are more concerned with the social world of human beings. All African oral literatures contain a large body of tales, divided into distinct types according to their purpose, the context in which they are told, and the status of the teller.

Taken from the oral literature of the Hausa, the following tales exemplify the two main types told by these people. *Tatsuniyoyi* are entertaining stories about animals and people, generally told by the older women to young children around the fire at night. They cloak lessons in social etiquette, morality, and personal values in amusing, memorable stories. The other type, *labarai*, are told by old men to each other and to young male adults. Their subject matter is most often cultural, family, and group history. While not to be taken literally, the labarai contain factual occurrences and represent for any given period of time the Hausa's view of their own past.

The labarai example below, "The Origin of All Kings"—sometimes called the Daura legend—relates the origin of the Hausa city-state political system. The legend probably developed in the eighteenth century at a time when Bornu, a kingdom to the east, exercised subtle political influence over the Hausa states. The attribution of Eastern origin (in this case Baghdad) is common among Islamic states in West Africa. The translator of this selection, and of the following tatsuniyoyi tales (with the exception of "The Kano Man," originally compiled by Frank Edgar) is Roberta Ann Dunbar.

Labarai Tale

THE ORIGIN OF ALL KINGS

This is the story of the first Kings of Daura, Kano, Katsina Gobir, Zazzau (Zaria) and Nuru (Rano), who descended from a man named Bayajibda, son of Abdullahi, King of Baghdad. Now the reason Bayajibda left Baghdad was that a heathen named Zidawa made war against them—a devastating war—and their land was divided into 40 parts.

Bayajibda went with twenty towards Bornu. Together with his soldiers they were a greater and more powerful force than the men of the King of Bornu. The Bornu king came from Syria. When Bayajibda's men realized they were more powerful than those of the King of Bornu they said to him, "Let's kill the King of Bornu so that you may succeed him."

But the King of Bornu hearing this was wary and could not be killed. The King of Bornu asked, "What is our plan for these intruders, my countrymen? The only plan I can see is to marry him off." So Bayajibda was given a daughter of the King named Magira to marry.

Peace and trust developed between them. When he went out on campaigns, Bayajibda would say to the King of Bornu, "Give me some of your men. I will take them to some villages and together we will conquer them." Sometimes he was given two thousand men; at others three thousand. But when he returned from war, he would not return with them. Rather, he set them up in towns in Bornu's territory.

After a time there were only two of Bayajibda's fellow countrymen left. He said to them, "Brothers, I want to look for a place for each of you to live." He set out with one of them and went to Kanem. He is King of Kanem. He set out with the other and went to Bagirmi. He is King of Bagirmi. Then Bayajibda, now alone, left, accompanied by his wife, the daughter of the King of Bornu, and his horse.

When the Bornu people saw that Bayajibda was alone, they kept trying to seek him out to kill him. Because of this he fled at great pace with his wife Magira who was pregnant. In this way they arrived at a certain town called Gabas. Bayajibda left his wife there as she was unable to travel further, and continued on his way. After his departure, she bore a son who was named Biram. He became King of Gabas, or as it was called Gabas of Biram.

When Bayajibda reached Daura, a queen was ruling there. Among the women who had ruled in Daura before, the first was Kufunu. After her the next was Gufunu, then Yakunu, Yakunya, Waizam, Waiwaina, Gidirgidir, Anagari, and Daura. It was she whom Bayajibda found ruling when he came.

When he arrived he alighted at the house of an old woman named Awaina and asked her to give him water. But she said to him, "Alas, my son, one can get water in this town only on Friday when people are gathered together." He replied, "I will draw water. Give me a bucket." She brought a bucket and gave him. It was nighttime when they spoke together about this.

When he had taken the bucket, he went to the well and dropped the bucket down inside. Now in the well lived a female snake. When the snake heard someone drop the bucket, she raised her head from the well and tried to kill Bayajibda. The name of the snake was Sarki. But he took out his sword, cut off her head and took the head and hid it. He drew water, drank and gave some to his horse. He took the rest to the old woman Awaina. He went into the house and lay down to rest.

At daybreak, people saw what this Arab from Syria had done. They were surprised at the size of what remained of the snake at the well. In a while the news reached Daura and she came with her warriors to the well site.

When the queen saw that the snake's head had been cut off and what remained behind, she was filled with wonder because this thing had so harassed the people. She said, "If I discover whoever has killed this snake, I will divide the kingdom in two and give him half." One man said, "I killed it." She asked, "Where is its head? If he doesn't show the head he is lying." So that man left. Another man came and exclaimed, "It was I who killed it." This one too was lying. Many men came forward, but each one was proclaiming himself falsely.

Then the old woman appeared and said, "Last night a stranger stopped at my house. He came with an animal, though whether it was an ox or a horse, I don't know. He took the bucket, drew water from the well, drank and gave some to his animal, bringing me the rest of it. Perhaps he is the one who killed the snake. We should find him and ask." So Bayajibda was summoned and Daura asked him, "Are you the one who killed the snake?" "It was I," he replied. She said, "Where is its head?" "Here it is," he said. Then the queen said, "I promised that for whoever did this thing, I would divide my town in two and give him half." He said, "Do not divide your town. As for me, I request your hand in marriage." So she married him and he lived in her house. She gave him a slave girl whom he took as a concubine. When people came to Daura's house they didn't say her name. Rather they said, "We are going to the house of Makas-Sarki, 'the killer of Sarki'." Thus it happened that she assumed the name Sarki [the Hausa word for chief].

After some time, the concubine became pregnant although Daura did not. The concubine gave birth to a son. Bayajibda sought Daura's permission and she gave it to name him Makarabgari (Receiver of the town). After this Daura became pregnant and when she gave birth to a son, she sought her husband's permission to name him. They agreed and the child was called Bawugari. He was the first of the kings.

When Makas-Sarki, his father, died, Bawugari inherited his father's dwelling place and bore six children. The first named Gazaura, was King of Daura. Another of the same mother named Bagauda became King of Kano. Another son named Gunguma became King of Zazzau and another by the same mother named Dami became King of Gobir. The last two, also of the same mother, were Kumayau who became King of Katsina and Zamgugu who was King of Rano.

Thus ends the story of the kings.

COMMENTS AND QUESTIONS

1. The marriage between an indigenous queen and a newcomer is not an uncommon motif in legends of origin and may reflect the transition from an earlier matrilineal or matriarchal stage to a patrilineal and patriarchal stage in society. This kind of marriage is also a frequent way of explaining accommodation between foreign invaders and local people over whom they had established hegemony. Compare the story of Oedipus.
2. Political power was recognized not only because of military conquest, but also because of technological expertise. Bayajibda killed the snake that had restricted Daura's water supply; he also came with an animal, the horse, unfamiliar to the old woman who gave him shelter. Does this suggest anything to you about levels of technology or modes of warfare in pre-Bayajibda Hausa society?
3. Compare this tale with the epic *Sundiata*. Is Bayajibda a hero in the same sense that Sundiata is? What is the difference in the way in which an epic and a tale present a hero?

Tatsuniyoyi Tales

DOG, HYENA, AND LIZARD

Dog got up from his sickbed and was hungry. He saw Lizard stealing some beans, grabbed him, and headed for home. On the way he ran into Hyena. Dog dropped Lizard and took to his heels. Hyena said, "Let me take this thing in hand home first before I come back to take that thing in the bush." So she picked up Lizard and carried him to her hole. Then she came back looking for Dog, but couldn't find him. She went home and Lizard was gone. Poor Hyena said,

"Alas, whatever you manage to get hold of in this world, if it is not your fate to have it, having gotten it is useless—you'll lose it anyway."

TWO FROGS

One day two frogs fell into a calabash of milk and couldn't get out. They swam around for a while, then one of them tired out and said,

"Today my days are finished."

So he gave up and sank to the bottom and died.

But the other frog kept on swimming and swimming. He churned the milk so hard with all of his swimming, that it turned into butter. The frog climbed on top of the ball of butter and jumped out of the calabash.

God said, "Rise so that I may help you."

SQUIRREL AND HEDGEHOG

One day it was raining. Hedgehog was wandering around when she came to the door of Squirrel's hole. She greeted him and said,

"I'm really cold. Is there any room there for me to take shelter?"

Squirrel said,

"There's a little space here, come on in."

They sat down together. After a while Squirrel said,

"Hey Hedgehog, our being together like this isn't very pleasant. Your body is all prickly. Why don't you go find another spot?"

Hedgehog said,

"Gee, this place is fine for me. Whoever doesn't find this place suitable, *he* should be the one to move!"

THE BLIND MAN WITH THE LAMP

A young man was strolling along one night when he caught sight of a man with a lamp. When he drew near he realized that the man was blind. The boy said,

"Hey blind man, have you lost your senses? What brings you to wandering around with a lamp? Aren't day and night all the same to you?"

The blind man said,

"Of course they are, stupid. Even at night I see better than you do. I don't carry this lamp for myself, but so that you silly people without eyes don't bump into me."

LIFE IS BETTER THAN WEALTH

Once there was a man who was so poor he didn't know what to do. So he went to the king and said,

"I don't have anything to eat for today, or for tomorrow either. I don't have anything at all in the world save this loincloth. I'm tired of living. I want you to kill me."

The king said,

"All right."

He called some soldiers and told them to kill the man so that he could find rest. The soldiers were about to dispatch him when another came by and said,

"If you kill him, please give me his loincloth."

When the poor man heard that he said,

"Stop! Take me back to the king. I have something to say."

So they took him back and the king asked them what happened. The poor man fell on his knees and said,

"Your highness, let me go. Today I have seen someone poorer than I am. Truly, life is great."

The king said,

"Be off with you and thank God that he has given you life and health."

HASARA AND RIBA

Hasara and Riba were sisters—same mother same father. Hasara was an extremely beautiful girl but poor Riba was ugly. Tinau and Sule sought their hands in marriage. Tinau was richer and better looking than Sule and he courted Hasara. So Sule proceeded to court Riba. The couples were married at the same time and each girl went to the home of her husband.

Now Hasara was proud and haughty. She liked elegant food, jewelry, and very expensive clothes. Riba, however, worked together with her husband. She helped him take goods to market and when they earned a profit, they put aside half of it, using the rest for their trading. Before a year was out Sule was a rich man. Tinau by that time was flat broke. To make a long story short, Tinau left Hasara with all her beauty. She married another and the same thing happened. Before the second year was past, Hasara had been married four times. But Riba is still there with her husband Sule. They are very prosperous and even have many cattle with shepherds to look after them. Whoever follows his heart's desire surely he will be wed to loss.

THE RIVALS

There were two boys who were courting the same girl. She couldn't decide which to accept, so she told them she would marry whichever one was the braver.

One day, the boys went to her place for a chat. When they got ready to go home, she accompanied them to the edge of the "bush." Suddenly, a leopard came upon them. The first boy hurled his spear at the leopard but missed it. The other did the same. They continued until all their spears were gone. Meanwhile the girl hid behind a tree. Then, one boy said to the other,

"Hurry home to my mother's house. There are some spears there near the bed. Gather them up and bring them back."

When the other boy departed, the one left behind fell on the leopard and wrestled with it. He got the leopard down and killed it. Then, he propped the leopard up, called to the girl, and told her to lie down in front of it. He then hid himself.

The other boy returned without any spears since they had already been borrowed by someone else. He came upon the leopard where he had left it and saw the girl lying on the ground in front of it. The boy said,

"Oh no, is that the way he is? He gets rid of me so that he can run off and lets the leopard kill the poor girl?"

Then he attacked the leopard with full force and grabbed it around the neck. The leopard's body fell over in a heap. The boy who had been hiding came out laughing.

So now, which one of them will the girl marry?

THE KANO MAN

This is the sharp fellow, the city slicker.

His character: A Kano man puts on a dark-blue gown, and a white Nupe one, and a black-and-white one; then he wears Kano-style trousers, either white or black-and-white; puts on a length of muslin for a turban; hangs a book over his shoulder and off he goes to school to recite the Koran; he takes a staff, a little gourd water-bottle, and away he goes. When he has fin-

ished at school, he returns home. When it is time for market he goes to market. Returning from there, when it is night, he puts on a leather loincloth, picks up a rope-ladder, and off he goes to steal. Sometimes he gets shot or wounded with a sword, and sometimes dies, and sometimes gets better.

The Kano character is also, if a rich visitor arrives, to receive him joyfully, and give him a gown, or a turban or a length of cloth. Then they get together with one of the household where he is staying and start bringing shoddy stuff to sell him. When the householder sees it, he praises its quality. They abuse his trust in them and trick him. But if the visitor is shrewd, he rejects all the stuff they bring him, saying, "I'm not buying it," and waits till he gets to the market and buys what he wants.

Trickery and fraud are Kano characteristics. Whoever you are, a Kano man will trick you—unless he thinks it can't be done. For there is no one so cowardly.

COMMENTS AND QUESTIONS

1. A major characteristic of African tales evident in the Hausa tatsuniyoyi is their realism and recognition of the flaws in human nature and in society. Some tales exhort people to good behavior; others express stereotypes about people from different places or walks of life as seen here in "The Kano Man." Kano was and is a major commercial center. Its markets attracted merchants from all over West and North Africa. How does this tale's image of the Kano man—the quintessential merchant—compare with our own image of the "city slicker"?

2. *Hasara* and *Riba* are not usual Hausa names as suggested in that story. Rather they are respectively the Hausa words for "loss" and "profit." What does this tale tell you about values of work and discipline?

3. What other Hausa values are expressed in these tales?

4. What shows you that these tales are well grounded in the socioeconomic realities of the Hausa people?

5. What model is suggested in the tales "Hasara and Riba" and "The Rivals" for a proper relationship between husband and wife?

6. Do the morals to these tales appear to be "tacked on," or are they woven into the fabric of the story? Give examples.

Riddles

Riddles, like folk tales, are most often told at night around the fire. They, too, form the early associations in the mind of the young person with the wisdom and style of his elders. Frequently uttered as a statement rather than as a question, the essence of the idea and metaphors drawn instruct the young in the indirect but pithy aphorisms of life. In addition to allusions to the natural world that approach the poetic, riddles, like some poetry, allow explicit sexual references. The cleverness and wit of the stock phrases create the entertainment and memorability of the occasion. These riddles are reprinted from *Black Orpheus,* and the *Journal of American Folklore.*

Yoruba Riddles

A round calabash in the spear grass.
Ans.: Moon and stars.

We cut its head, we cut its tail. It still insists on performing the ritual of its ancestors.
Ans.: A piece of cassava. However small a piece you cut—it will still grow.

We tie a horse in the house, but its mane flies above the roof.
Ans.: Fire and smoke.

We invited him to warm himself in the sun—he came. We asked him to take his bath. He said: death has come.
Ans.: Salt.

One cooked yam all over the world.
Ans.: The moon.

They cut off his head; they cut off his waist; his stump says he will inherit the title of his father's house.
Ans.: Yam.

Children walking; mother crawling.
Ans.: Gourd.

It bears fruit, we cannot pick it; the fruit falls, we cannot gather it.
Ans.: Dew.

Fat wife inside many thorns.
Ans.: Tongue and teeth.

Ancient will of my father, ancient will of my father; if a child gets into it, it reaches his neck; if an elder gets into it, it reaches his neck.
Ans.: A shirt or gown.

We seize hold of it; the child in its womb walks away.
Ans.: Gun.

Who is it that goes down the street past the king's house without greeting the king?
Ans.: Rainwater.

My father complained that I was late coming back from the farm. I said the road divided into three and I had to travel on three paths simultaneously.
Ans.: Putting on trousers.

People run away from her when she is pregnant. But they rejoice when she has delivered.
Ans.: A gun.

Proverbs

Proverbs have a special place in oral literature. Rather than being told for entertainment like riddles and tales, they are most often used within conversation and, more formally, in the litigation of disputes within a community. The fluency with which a speaker can use proverbs is widely accepted as a measure of one's literary skill. Social relationships, philosophical observations, and ultimate moral values are illuminated in proverbs.

The Yoruba proverbs included below are keys to the values of the Yoruba people. They sometimes express a surprising candor about political relationships, hospitality, and attitudes toward the elderly—areas where candor outside of proverbial speech would be impolitic and rude. The translators are Bakare Gbadamosi and Ulli Beier.

Yoruba Proverbs

The egg eater does not think of the pain it cost the hen.

The dignified crawl of the earthworm arouses the envy of the cock.

A man has been beaten six times and is advised to be patient. What else is there for him to do?

When death is not ready to receive a man, it sends an expert physician at the right time.

A bachelor who asks for food too often will soon hear the price of vegetables.

The small hand of the child cannot reach the high shelf. The large hand of the adult cannot enter the neck of the calabash.

Only the man whom his child buries has really got a child.

It is the honour of the father that allows the son to walk about proudly.

We are talking about pumpkins. A woman asks what are we talking about. We say: this is a man's talk. But when we gather the fruit, who will break them and cook them?

Anger does not help. Patience is the father of character.

The river carries away an elderly person who does not know his own weight.

The thinking of a wolf is enough to tail a sheep.

What only stops a hawk from laughing will make the hen faint on her eggs.

The eagle makes the owner of the fowl go crazy.

The wisdom of others prevents a chief from being called a fool.

The god who favors a lazy man does not exist. It is one's hands that bring prosperity.

Everybody who comes to this world must become something. Only we don't know what.

The effort of forcing another man to be like oneself makes one an unpleasant person.

What causes a dog to bark is not sufficient to make a sheep gaze.

Having become king you prepare charms. Do you want to become a god?

One who takes another to court does not think that the other man has his own statement to make.

After the man has been cured, he beats the doctor.

The proud pond stands alone from the river, forgetting that water is common to both.

Mean people are common like trees in the forest.

An elderly man who cannot keep his mouth shut when he sees something strange, must use his mouth in court.

Do not be seen counting the toes of the man who has only nine.

QUESTIONS

1. What Yoruba social values and philosophical beliefs can you discern in the riddles? In the proverbs?
2. Attempt to define "riddle" as a literary genre. Which riddles here show evidence of a sophisticated wit?
3. Can you compare any of the proverbs here with those in the Bible?

Poetry

Most of the poems that follow have been taken from the rich oral tradition of the Yoruba language. They represent not only a wide variety of forms and subjects but also the intimate relationship that exists between poetry and everyday life in Africa. Two non-Yoruba poems illustrating this relationship are a Fulani love poem and the naming poem from the Ga people in Ghana. In addition, we have included three modern poems written in European languages but making use of traditional themes.

The ritual character of the first four Yoruba poems calls for a further explanation of Yoruba religion and traditional forms of Yoruba poetry. We saw in the mythology section that in Yoruba belief the first, high God, Olorun, is represented on earth by lesser deities called orisha. Orisha may also symbolize ancestor figures, ancient kings, and founders of cities. Each orisha is associated with some form of nature, or with a particular color or metal. Each of the four poems is a praise poem dedicated to one of the orisha. The first is about Obatala, god of creation (recall the Yoruba myths of creation); the second on Eshu, the unpredictable god of fate and the agent for change, good and bad. The subject of the third is Oshun, the mother goddess, protector of the town of Oshogbo and source of healing and fertility; and that of the fourth, Ogun, whose association with iron and war is linked to survival, innovation, and technology. These poems are classified as *oriki* by the Yoruba—meaning poems based on names given to gods, places, rulers, and important persons. The oriki poetry is performed by professional singers or, in the case of poems about deities such as these, by the priests of the particular deity whose oriki is being sung.

Yoruba poetry is classified by the style of specific groups of performers more than by subject matter or poetic form. Whereas the oriki are sung by priests, *ijala* are sung by hunters, and the *iwi*, represented by "Children," are poems sung by the *egungun*, the masqueraders. These have a specific religious function: they mediate between the community of the living and that of the recently dead. Masqueraders embody the spirit and imitate the voice of the person involved; during the ceremonial, dances are sacred. Reflecting the high degree of integration of religious beliefs with other aspects of social life, masqueraders may also entertain, sometimes offering social satires and commentaries.

In addition to being concerned with man's relationship to god and the spirits, all African poetry marks important experiences or transitions in the lives of people as seen in the funeral, love, and naming poems. In the Ga naming poem, as in the Yoruba iwi on children, the fragility of life, the desirability of children, and their symbolic importance as links between the living and dead appear as critical elements of belief.

The final three poems—written by Birago Diop, a Senegalese who writes in French, and Chinua Achebe and Wole Soyinka, two Nigerians who write in English—illustrate the fact that modern African writers continue to draw inspiration from traditional beliefs and from the themes and styles of oral literature. The Yoruba poetry is translated by Bakare Gbadamosi and Ulli Beier; the Ga poem by Neils Augustine Hesse.

Oriki—Yoruba Praise Poems

ORIKI OBATALA

He is patient, he is not angry.
He sits in silence to pass judgement.
He sees you even when he is not looking.
He stays in a far place—but his eyes are on the town.

The granary of heaven can never be full.
The old man full of life force.

He kills the novice.
And wakens him to let him hear his words.
We leave the world to the owner of the world.
Death acts playfully till he carries away the child.
He rides on the hunchback.
He stretches out his right hand.
He stretches out his left hand.

He stands by his children and lets them succeed.
He causes them to laugh—and they laugh.
Ohoho—the father of laughter.
His eye is full of joy,
He rests in the sky like a swarm of bees.

We dance to your sixteen drums that sound jingin,
    jingin,
To eight of the drums we dance bending down,

To eight of the drums we dance erect.
We shake our shoulders, we shake our hips,
Munusi, munusi, munusi,
We dance to your sixteen drums.

Those who are rich owe their property to him.
Those who are poor, owe their property to him.
He takes from the rich and gives to the poor.
Whenever you take from the rich—come and give it to
    me!

Obatala—who turns blood into children.
I have only one cloth to dye with blue indigo.
I have only one headtie to dye with red camwood.
But I know that you keep twenty or thirty children for
    me
Whom I shall bear.

ORIKI ESHU

When he is angry he hits a stone until it bleeds.
When he is angry he sits on the skin of an ant.
When he is angry he weeps tears of blood.

Eshu, confuser of men.
The owner of twenty slaves is sacrificing,
So that Eshu may not confuse him.
The owner of thirty "iwofa" is sacrificing,
So that Eshu may not confuse him.
Eshu confused the newly married wife.
When she stole the cowries from the sacred shrine of
    Oya
She said she had not realized
That taking two hundred cowries was stealing.
Eshu confused the head of the queen—
And she started to go naked.
Then Eshu beat her to make her cry.
Eshu, do not confuse me!
Eshu, do not confuse the load on my head.

Eshu, lover of dogs.
If a goat gets lost in Ogbe,—don't ask me.
Do you think I am a thief of goats?
If a huge sheep is missing from Ogbe—don't ask me.
Do you think I am a thief of sheep?
If any fowl get lost in Ogbe—don't ask me.
Do you think I am a thief of birds?

But if a black dog is missing from Ogbe—ask me!
You will find me eating Eshu's sacrifice in a wooden
    bowl.

Eshu slept in the house.—
But the house was too small for him.
Eshu slept on the verandah—
But the verandah was too small for him.
Eshu slept in a nut—
At last he could stretch himself.

Eshu walked through the groundnut farm.
The tuft of his hair was just visible.
If it had not been for his huge size,
He would not have been visible at all.

Having thrown a stone yesterday—he kills a bird today.
Lying down, his head hits the roof.
Standing up he cannot look into the cooking pot.
Eshu turns right into wrong, wrong into right.

ORIKI OSHUN

We call her and she replies with wisdom.
She can cure those whom the doctor has failed.
She cures the sick with cold water.
When she cures the child, she does not charge the
    father.
We can remain in the world without fear.
Iyalode who cures children—help me to have my own
    child.
Her medicines are free—she feeds honey to the
    children.
She is rich and her words are sweet.
Large forest with plenty of food.
Let a child embrace my body.
The touch of a child's hand is sweet.

Owner of brass. Owner of parrots' feathers.
Owner of money.

My mother, you are beautiful, very beautiful.
Your eyes sparkle like brass.
Your skin is soft and smooth.
You are black like velvet.

Everybody greets you when you descend on the world.
Everybody sings your praises.

ORIKI OGUN

Ogun kills on the right and destroys on the right.
Ogun kills on the left and destroys on the left.
Ogun kills suddenly in the house and suddenly in the
    field.
Ogun kills the child with the iron with which it plays.
Ogun kills in silence.
Ogun kills the thief and the owner of the stolen goods.
Ogun kills the owner of the slave—and the slave runs
    away.
Ogun kills the owner of thirty "iwofa"—and his
    money, wealth and children disappear.
Ogun kills the owner of the house and paints the
    hearth with his blood.
Ogun is the death who pursues a child until it runs
    into the bush.
Ogun is the needle that pricks at both ends.
Ogun has water but he washes in blood.

Ogun, do not fight me. I belong only to you.
The wife of Ogun is like a tim tim.
She does not like two people to rest on her.

Ogun has many gowns. He gives them all to the
    beggars.
He gives one to the woodcock—the woodcock dyes it
    indigo.
He gives one to the coucal—the coucal dyes it in
    camwood.
He gives one to the cattle egret—the cattle egret leaves
    it white.

Ogun is not like pounded yam:
Do you think you can knead him in your hand
And eat of him until you are satisfied?
Ogun is not like maize gruel:
Do you think you can knead him in your hand
And eat of him until you are satisfied?
Ogun is not like some thing you can throw into your
    cap:
Do you think you can put on your cap and walk away
    with him?

Ogun scatters his enemies.
When the butterflies arrive at the place where the
    cheetah excretes,
They scatter in all directions.

The light shining on Ogun's face is not easy to behold.
Ogun, let me not see the red of your eye.

Ogun sacrifices an elephant to his head.
Master of iron, head of warriors,
Ogun, great chief of robbers.
Ogun wears a bloody cap.
Ogun has four hundred wives and one thousand four
    hundred children.
Ogun, the fire that sweeps the forest.
Ogun's laughter is no joke.
Ogun eats two hundred earthworms and does not
    vomit.

Ogun is a crazy orisha who still asks questions after 780
    years!
Whether I can reply, or whether I cannot reply.
Ogun please don't ask me anything.

The lion never allows anybody to play with his cub.
Ogun will never allow his child to be punished.
Ogun do not reject me!
Does the woman who spins ever reject a spindle?
Does the woman who dyes ever reject a cloth?
Does the eye that sees ever reject a sight?
Ogun, do not reject me!

COMMENTS AND QUESTIONS

1. In "Oriki Obatala" note the dualistic nature of Obatala. He is the creator, a kindly deity, who can also
   kill (as in line 7). Refer to the myth of Obatala earlier in this chapter. What characteristics are portrayed in both the myth and this poem?
2. Eshu, as the poem "Oriki Eshu" states, is the "confuser of men." In Yoruba cosmology he symbolizes
   disorder, the unexpected. And yet this quality permits him to turn "wrong into right." How does the
   poem express the contradictions of his character?
3. Is the *tone* of the poem on the feminine deity,
   Oshun, different from those on the masculine deities? How so?
4. How does the poetic principle of *anaphora*, the successive repetition of words or phrases, operate in all
   of the oriki and especially in "Oriki Ogun"? What
   would be the effect and usefulness of this device in
   oral poetry?

Ijala—The Poetry of Yoruba Hunters

ADIYE (FOWL)

One who sees corn and is glad.
The chicken wears its shin at the back.
We eat it with pounded yam.
Every fool will be buried in the cheek.
The foolish chicken has many relations:
Oil is its relative on the father's side.
Pepper and onion are its relatives on the mother's side.
If it does not see its friend salt even for a day
It will not sleep peacefully.

ETU-DUIKER (ANTELOPE)

Beautiful antelope with the slender neck.
Your thighs are worth twenty slaves.
Your arms are more precious than thirty servants.
Your neck is exquisite like a sacred carving.
You step out like a nobleman
Shaking the grass like bells.
Your facial marks are beautiful and bold
Even like those of the king of Ogbomosho.
You wash your body with white.
God has honoured you with white.
The hunter is happy when the owner of white appears.
I cannot be happy when I kill you,
Until I have found your body in the bush.
The pregnant woman demands your skin.
Lying on your skin she will bear a beautiful child.

NEW YAM

New yam causes the wife of yesterday to lose her
    manners,
New yam causes the head of the household to reject
    food.
It makes a rich person speak out.
Yam will pay its own debt.
"Lay me on a fine bed
And I will lay you on a fine lady."

COMMENTS AND QUESTIONS

1. What is the difference in tone between the poem on
   the chicken and the poem on the antelope? How do
   the poems render what the poets see as the essence
   of these two animals?

2. How is the antelope in "Etu-Duiker" personified?
   What dimension do *similes* give to the poem?

3. Yam, a root vegetable, is the staple food of many African peoples along the Guinea coast. While yam is
   relatively easy to grow, it may be ravaged by drought
   or, to the contrary, rotted by untimely rains. The annual harvest of the new yams, often following a time
   of hardship and meager food supply, is the occasion
   for celebration. It is often signaled by religious rituals of thanks and communal solidarity.

4. Explain the relation of the last two lines of "New
   Yam" to the first part of the poem.

Iwi—The Poetry of Yoruba Masqueraders

CHILDREN

A child is like a rare bird.
A child is precious like coral.
A child is precious like brass.
You cannot buy a child on the market.
Not for all the money in the world.
The child you can buy for money is a slave.
We may have twenty slaves,
We may have thirty labourers,
Only a child brings us joy,
One's child is one's child.
The buttocks of our child are not so flat
That we should tie the beads on another child's hips.
One's child is one's child.
It may have a watery head or a square head,
One's child is one's child.
It is better to leave behind a child,
Than let the slaves inherit one's house.
A child is the beginning and end of happiness.
One must not rejoice too soon over a child.
Only the one who is buried by his child,
Is the one who has truly born a child.
On the day of our death, our hand cannot hold a single
    cowrie.
We need a child to inherit our belongings.

COMMENTS AND QUESTIONS

1. Describe the style of this poem. What is the effect of
   the very short sentences?

2. What does this poem tell you about the importance of children in African society?

FUNERAL POEM I

Come nearer home,
Mother of Aina.
You knew how to produce children,
but never learned to chide them.
Come and receive the sacrifice
from your children.
You people of the road,
where did you meet her?
The mother of Kujusola
the mother of Alawede.
They met her on the road to Ede.
I thank the trees that did not fall on her.
I thank the river
that did not carry her away.
No one can bar her way
for she travels an underground path.
Like a new bride
She covers her head with a cloth.

FUNERAL POEM II

The hunter dies
and leaves his poverty to his gun.
The blacksmith dies
and leaves his poverty to his anvil.
The farmer dies
and leaves his poverty to his hoe.
The bird dies
and leaves its poverty to its nest.
You have died
and left me abandoned in the dark.
Where are you now?
Are you the goat
eating grass around the house?
Are you the motionless lizard
on the hot mud wall?
If I tell you not to eat earthworms
it's like asking you to go hungry.
But whatever they may eat in heaven
Partake with them.
A dead body cannot receive double punishment:
If there is not cloth to cover it—
There will always be earth to cover it.

COMMENTS AND QUESTIONS

1. What different emotions on the mourners' part are conveyed in these two poems, and how does the imagery express them?
2. How do the Yoruba beliefs that the dead live on as spirits or else are reincarnated appear in these poems?

Fulani Poetry
AMADOU HAMPATÉ BA

THE BELOVED

Diko,
of light skin, of smooth hair and long;
her smells sweet and gentle
she never stinks of fish
she never breathes sweat
like gatherers of dry wood.
She has no bald patch on her head
like those who carry heavy loads.
Her teeth are white
her eyes are like
those of a new born fawn
that delights in the milk
that flows for the first time
from the antelope's udder.
Neither her heel nor her palm
are rough; but sweet to touch
like liver; or better still
the fluffy down of kopok.

COMMENTS AND QUESTIONS

1. The Fulani, cattle-herding nomads, stem from the grasslands of the upper Senegal river, but have migrated over the centuries as far east as the Cameroons. How does the poet reflect here an intimate familiarity with nature and especially with the "bush" land?
2. The romantic idea of love does not play an important social role in African society. Husbands and wives may, of course, love each other; but the existence of love is not a prerequisite for marriage. Love is not a major theme in African poetry although

beautiful love lyrics, like the above, do exist. Fulani women have a reputation for being especially beautiful and exciting. What image of Diko, the beloved, do you have from this poem?

3. Compare the way in which the poet here uses imagery to describe his beloved and his feelings about her to similar techniques in the poems of Sappho (Chapter 1) and in the Song of Songs (Chapter 6).

Ga Poetry

NAMING POEM

May good fortune come
May our stools be clean
May our brooms be clean
In a circle of unity
    have we met
When we dig a well
May we find water
When of this water we drink
May our shoulders find peace
The stranger who has come
On his mother's head be life
On his father's head be life
Behind his back may
    darkness be
Before his face may
    all be bright
May his head the world respect
And his brethren may he know
May we have forgiveness
    to forgive him
May he work and eat
When he sees he has
    not seen
When he hears he has
    not heard
In black he has come
In white may he return
May good fortune come

COMMENTS AND QUESTIONS

1. In many African societies the naming of a child is surrounded with ceremony; it is the public recogni-

tion of the personhood of the newborn and the acknowledgment of his or her full membership in the community. The "naming" or "outdooring" does not occur usually until one or two weeks following birth, when it seems certain that the child will survive his entry into the world. On the chosen day, significant members of the youngster's family may whisper the name into the child's ear before announcing it publicly. Special blessings and prayers follow, and the day is filled with gift-giving and celebration by the many relatives and guests invited to share in the occasion.

2. The Ga are a southern Ghanaian people of the Ewe linguistic subgroup of Twi speakers (just as the Ashanti, discussed earlier, are members of the Akan subgroup of Twi languages). For many Ghanaian peoples there is a close link between the individual and his stool (line 2); for some, a person's soul is said to reside in his stool. (See the discussion of art objects in Chapter 16.) Many rites of passage in the individual's life are carried out in connection with his or her stool, so it is appropriate that "stools" appear in connection with the naming.

3. How does the invocation of this poem illustrate by a shift in focus the link between the child and the community?

4. What are the values that the community wishes for the child?

5. What do "darkness," "bright," "black," and "white" seem to signify?

BIRAGO DIOP

Forefathers

Listen more often to things rather than beings.
Hear the fire's voice,
Hear the voice of water.
In the wind hear the sobbing of the trees,
It is our forefathers breathing.

The dead are not gone forever.
They are in the paling shadows
And in the darkening shadows.

The dead are not beneath the ground,
They are in the rustling tree,
In the murmuring wood,
In the still water,
In the flowing water,
In the lonely place, in the crowd;
The dead are not dead.

Listen more often to things rather than beings.
Hear the fire's voice.
Hear the voice of water.
In the wind hear the sobbing of the trees.
It is the breathing of our forefathers
Who are not gone, not beneath the ground,
Not dead.

The dead are not gone forever.
They are in a woman's breast,
A child's crying, a glowing ember.
The dead are not beneath the earth,
They are in the flickering fire,
In the weeping plant, the groaning rock,
The wooded place, the home.
The dead are not dead.

Listen more often to things rather than beings.
Hear the fire's voice,
Hear the voice of water.
In the wind hear the sobbing of the trees.
It is the breath of our forefathers.

CHINUA ACHEBE

Generation Gap

A son's arrival
is the crescent moon
too new too soon to lodge
the man's returning.
His feast of re-incarnation
must await the moon's
reopening at the naming
ceremony of his
grandson.

COMMENTS AND QUESTIONS

1. Many African religions view human existence as a cyclical phenomenon wherein spirits may proceed through various phases of what we know as birth, life, and death in human, but sometimes animal form. This view, articulated in both traditional and modern poetry, reinforces man's sensitivity to, and awareness of, the natural world. Compare the metaphor of nature in "Forefathers" with that in the Yoruba funeral poems.
2. How is the cyclical nature of man's existence conveyed in "Forefathers," Achebe's "Generation Gap," and the iwi on children?

WOLE SOYINKA

Death in the Dawn

Traveller, you must set out
At dawn. And wipe your feet upon
The dog-nose wetness of the earth.

Let sunrise quench your lamps. And watch
Faint brush pricklings in the sky light
Cottoned feet to break the early earthworm
On the hoe. Now shadows stretch with sap
Not twilight's death and sad prostration.
This soft kindling, soft receding breeds
Racing joys and apprehensions for
A naked day. Burdened hulks retract,
Stoop to the mist in faceless throng
To wake the silent markets—swift, mute
Processions on grey byways. . . . On this
Counterpane, it was—
Sudden winter at the death
Of dawn's lone trumpeter. Cascades
Of white feather-flakes . . . but it proved
A futile rite. Propitiation sped
Grimly on, before.
The right foot for joy, the left, dread
And the mother prayed, Child
May you never walk
When the roads waits, famished.

Traveller, you must set forth
At dawn.
I promise marvels of the holy hour
Presages as the white cock's flapped
Perverse impalement—as who would dare
The wrathful wings of man's Progression. . . .

But such another wraith! Brother,
Silenced in the startled hug of
Your invention—is this mocked grimace
This closed contortion—I?

COMMENTS AND QUESTIONS

1. Wole Soyinka has consistently addressed human issues through the voice of Yoruba belief and expression. Although his works are masterpieces in English, and can be understood within the English reading of them, their power and subtlety are magnified for the reader who understands something of Yoruba culture. Ogun, the god of war and destruction, of the rains, of harvest, of disintegration and death, is a favorite though not always explicit subject of Soyinka. In modern Nigeria, Ogun is god of the road, a claimant of countless lives on overcrowded highways; taxi and truck drivers are among those who worship him. He is the real subject of "Death in the Dawn." When the poet writes "May you never walk/When the road waits, famished," it is Ogun that one fears may be famished. "Death in the Dawn" is not an oriki, but go back and reread "Oriki Ogun" after you have read Soyinka's poem. What traditional images of Ogun do you find in Soyinka's poem?

16

Visual and
Musical Arts
of West Africa

Just as each African language has its own literary tradition, each African society has its own artistic and musical styles. We cannot hope to give even a bird's-eye view of the range and variety of African art and music in the present space. Rather, we will concentrate on the close observation of a few works in order to understand something of the African aesthetic. Since both African art and music have had a profound impact on their modern Western counterparts (see Chapter 36 in Volume II), we are already used to certain conventions, such as *abstraction* in art and the *pentatonic* ("jazz") *scale* in music, which shocked and puzzled earlier Western observers. We are not likely to view these arts, as did the European colonists, as awkward, tribal, or primitive. Nevertheless, there are characteristics of African art and music that make them significantly different from Western forms and that require our attention if we are to appreciate them. In spite of the great diversity of traditions and styles, even within West Africa alone, African art shares some common premises that we will examine first in the visual realm.

Visual Arts

Art and Communal Life   One of the basic differences between Western art and African art lies in the simple fact of classification. The art of the West is usually divided into "fine" and "applied" arts. In the first category are painting, sculpture, and architecture—the arts usually studied in the humanities. The second category includes more utilitarian objects such as furniture, ceramics, textiles, and clothing. This dichotomy does not exist in African art. For the African artist, the objects of everyday life may express beauty, harmony, and philosophical concepts as much or more than something to hang on a wall. The museum or the gallery does not exist in traditional Africa. While some Western and African arts are "useful" in the same way—palaces for kings, temples, objects for religious ceremonies—it must be kept in mind that *all* African art is in some way integrated into life in the community. At the same time, even the most humble object may manifest a complex relationship between people and society and their experiences and understanding of the world.

Understanding the world and interpreting one's experiences in it are the basis for art everywhere. The world of the traditional West African is one of close adherence to nature in all its manifestations; in the unchanging cycles of birth and death, planting and harvest, night and day, and the seasons. Yet circumstances may alter the seemingly permanent aspects of these events, and one is forced to assure their timely appearance. The seasonal migration of the herds that provide food and other staples of life, the natural cycles of fertility in animals, the beginning of the rainy seasons, the success of the planting and subsequent harvest, the normal, healthy birth of a child, are all subject to the vicissitudes of nature. This extraordinary awareness of inevitability and change in the face of natural phenomena is closely related to the *animism*, or belief in natural spirits, that characterizes African religions (see the "Myths" section of Chapter 15). The necessity to appease various spirits has been a motivating force for one type of African art. Objects, usually small statues, are created to invite a particular spirit, either "natural" or ancestor, to inhabit it. Great care is taken to make the object beautiful enough to entice the spirit to rest in it.

One might define the constant in African art and life as a tension between order and disorder, permanence and change. African societies place a great value on tradition; and ritual objects such as masks, costumes, and figurines pass on the values, laws, and beliefs of a people from one generation to another, as do the myths and tales of the oral tradition. This assures the permanence and the continuity of the community. On the other hand, the inevitability of change and the need to cope with it are reflected by the importance of *initiation* societies and the arts and rites associated with them. The process of the initiation is the passage of a boy or girl from childhood to adulthood, and the ritual takes place at the time of puberty. Women, in the case of girls, and men, in the case of boys, initiate the child by teaching certain practices, laws, and pieces of wisdom. The process recognizes the fact that the young adults will be agents of change within the community but assures that change will come about within the framework of tradition.

Much African art is religious in its orientation, not because it is all designed for cults or temples but because religion is so woven into the fabric of everyday African life. African plastic art contains multiple layers of meaning, and any one piece may contain elements in addition to religious ones that evoke commemoration of a ruler (as do the Benin bronzes seen in Chapter 14); regalia of office, such as pendants or staffs; or allusions to favorite mythical or tale characters, which may suggest ribaldry or even laughter. Although sculptural forms and symbolic elements often refer to the past, to beliefs or practices that are traditional, they may also incorporate the innovative and modern. Just as the objects of African art are intimately related to African life, so they are also related to one another. The many rituals and festivals in Africa, one of which we will study in the next chapter, use masks, costume, music, poetry, and dance in the creation of a complete ensemble. The stylistic principles in a mask, for example, are closely related to those in the other arts. We will examine some of these aesthetic relationships when we look at the art of the festival.

We began this section on the visual arts by discussing the differences in classification between Western and African art and by pointing out that the West's distinction between "fine" and "applied" art does not exist. But how, then, has African art been classified? Africans designate their sculptures, masks, textile patterns, and dances with names appropriate to their function or style within a given culture. On the other hand, Westerners have been interested in a much broader scope—African art as a whole—and have therefore analyzed the relationship of art works across the continent, using ethnic-group or formal stylistic criteria as the basis of their categorization. One of the most interesting systems of classification is that developed some years ago by Arnold Rubin[1]; it employs a combination of geographical, artistic, and cultural criteria to identify three major zones of African sculpture: the Sudanic, the Guinea Coast, and the Equatorial. Each zone is divided into style regions and in some instances, sub-regions. The sculptural art of each of these regions or sub-regions has particular characteristics that distinguish it from the art forms of other regions. These characteristics may include, for example, a preference for certain types of masks, figures, or utilitarian objects over others; for emphasis on two-dimensional lines rather than on volume; for shared choice of color or medium in relation to sculpture; for the presence or absence of surface decoration; or for the degree of naturalism, as opposed to *abstractionism* or *expressionism*, in the sculpture. Art from the frontier areas of these regions is likely to show the influences of the adjacent region. The advantage of this system enables the observer to escape from rigid ethnic or formal classification to an understanding of African art that encompasses the aesthetic and the cultural; it also permits him to visualize relationships on a broader scale, not only between art forms but also between art and other cultural features. Thus, it is interesting to note that the major sculpture-producing regions in Africa coincide with the area in which the Congo-Kordofanian languages, mentioned at the beginning of Chapter 15, are spoken.

---

[1] Arnold Rubin, *The Sculptor's Eye* (Washington, D.C.: Museum of African Art, 1976).

Although we have chosen a simpler organization than Rubin's for the discussion of individual examples of African objects that follows (physical type and social function), the reader should bear in mind some of the ways, suggested earlier, in which sculptural forms may differ from region to region, in order to better appreciate the richness of the African plastic art tradition.

Masks and Headpiecess   Masks and headpieces are usually worn by men in the context of the social and religious rituals of associations, sometimes referred to as secret societies. These societies function as the community's agents for social control, education (through initiation), and communication with the spirits of the ancestors. They are particularly important and powerful in ethnic groups that do not have centralized chieftaincies or kingships. Secret societies may be very specialized in their function, although some also operate in a variety of situations. Usually the associations consist of several grades or ranks through which individuals of skill and prestige may rise to positions of great influence. They are "secret" because their specialist knowledge is reserved to initiates of the societies and because the members are anonymous to the public when performing the masked rituals or acting on behalf of the association. When an individual dons the mask, he becomes the receptacle for the spiritual force of whatever essence is portrayed and is identified as that essence by those who behold him.

The Chi Wara headpieces are found among the Bambara, who live near the upper Niger in Senegal, Guinea, and Mali (Fig. 16-1). Chi Wara (sometimes also spelled Tyiwara) is a legendary figure who taught the Bambara to cultivate with digging sticks. It is also the name of one of a series of graded associations for Bambara men. In preparation for clearing the fields, two members of the association wear these headpieces in imitation of the male and female antelope—the antelope having become identified with the Chi Wara figure. They engage in ritual play to please the spirits of the earth and to ensure the earth's fertility.

These beautiful wooden forms display one of the major characteristics of much African sculpture. The artist has exaggerated those features of the animals that are most important for recognition by those who use or observe the ritual and that call attention to each ani-

mal's particular important aspect. The female antelope's body is reduced to a simple flattened oval form,
while the enlarged neck, head, and ears, which fit into
tight curves, convey an impression of energy and
strength. On her back rides a tiny young antelope
whose form echoes that of his mother. The male antelope has a similar body; but his neck is formed of two
curves with spiky extensions, his ears tilt backward,
and his horns, stylized into a powerful upward thrust,
tilt forward. The combination of curves with the antelope's spiky mane and the sharply contrasting direction
of the ears and horns create a powerful sense of forward motion while the female's representation seems
to recoil slightly from his onslaught. The distinguishing features of heads, body color, and texture are reduced or ignored. It is the power of procreation that is
emphasized.

Another characteristic frequently evident in African
sculpture that is also present in the Chi Wara headpieces is the sense of reduction of a single piece of
wood—the trunk of a tree perhaps—from which the
objects were carved. This is part of the explanation for
the polar, columnar aspects of these figures.

A mask that seems to represent qualities in opposition to the forceful flowing motion of the Chi Wara,
however, is the *kponiugo*, fire-spitting helmet (Fig. 16-
2) of the Senufo. It is used by the Lo association, a
group responsible for initiation schools among the Senufo of the Ivory Coast, Upper Volta, and Mali regions.
Its fearsome, expressionistic visage is comprised of the
important features of equally important animals. The
teeth are those of the crocodile; the tusks represent the
wart hog; the horns are those of the water buffalo or the
antelope; and the chameleon, which perches on the
head between the horns, is a symbol for the continua-
tion of life. Sometimes these masks are also painted
with leopard spots. Each of these animals represents a
powerful spirit; and, combined in a powerful symmetry, they are said to represent the chaos of primordial
times. As the wearer stalks through the night, tinder is
struck under the chin to create the fire-spitting image.
This wooden mask, probably cut from green wood for
lightness, was blackened. Its wearer could both invoke
and provoke powerful spirits.

Another initiation mask is this one used by the
Mambunda of Zambia, a people who share many common institutions, like the *Mukanda* schools (Fig. 16-3).

16–1   Above. Chi Wara
headpiece, male antelope.
Right. Chi Wara headpiece,
female antelope. (Erle & Clyta
Loran collection)

16–2 Above. Senufo. Kponiugo, fire-spitting mask. (Lowie Museum of Anthropology, University of California, Berkeley)

16–3 Right. Mambunda initiation mask. (© Livingstone Museum, Zambia)

During the instructional period of two to nine months, young boys between the ages of seven and fifteen are secluded. Among the dances performed and/or taught is one danced by the older men wearing these kinds of masks, which are used to evoke ancestral spirits and to drive away women and younger boys. It is a powerful mask that emphasizes the potential of facial curves for exaggeration. The pure symmetry of the form and the protruding mouth form sharp contrasts. The great expanse of forehead and the attached feathers across the scalp are another juxtaposition of opposites—smoothness with the ruffled feathers.

The white-faced masks, which may symbolize ancestor spirits or a young maiden, are worn by men of the Mmwo society of the Northern Ibo peoples near Onitsha and Awka (Fig. 16-4). Those representing male ancestral spirits are used at funerals, festivals, and initia-

tion rites to cause fear and awe among nonmembers of the society. These kinds of masks remind us again of the importance of the benign presence of the ancestors of the tribe. One of the important stylistic features of these, as of other, masks is the reduction of features and their orderly composition into a symmetrical whole. Since a spirit, not a person, is being evoked, naturalism of form, texture, and color are not prerequisites. We have here the principle of *abstraction* used for the representation of a being not of the natural world.

This Dan mask (Fig. 16-5) seems almost realistic when compared to the white-faced mask that we have just considered. The scale of the features and their realization seem much more human. But a brief consideration of the reduction of eyebrows to a single plane, the nose to perfect symmetry, the cheeks and chin to

16-4   Ibo. Mmwo mask. (Reproduced by permission of The University Museum, University of Pennsylvania)

mains of the dead. The "head" of the figure is exaggerated to enormous size in proportion to what Picasso, concentrating on the object as a figure in space, interprets as a body. Actually, the "body" is the base, intended to hold a basket containing a skull or bones and thus to protect the remains of an ancestor. Compare this rendition of the head with that of the Mambunda mask. Notice particularly the use of incising, the way in which facial features are stylized, and the way in which one seems volumetric and the other two-dimensional.

Another way in which ancestral forces could be evoked or released is shown in this Bakongo charm figure (Fig. 16-7). Cavities in the head or stomach were the receptacles for magical substances. These *fetishes*— or objects embodying supernatural power—could be used for benevolent or malevolent effects. The pose

smooth planes, and the whole to this elegant oval shape contradicts the apparent naturalism. Like the masks of the Mmwo society and those of the Mambunda, masks of this type represent ancestral powers. They were often carried in miniature form by men as guardians and were also used to hide young boys in seclusion from the view of women.

Figurines   The possible artistic range of the transformation of the human visage is only hinted at by the masks that we have considered, but they do suggest how terribly exciting such forms must have been to Western artists when they first saw them. Pablo Picasso, one of the first European artists to be inspired by African art, used this Bakota reliquary figure (Fig. 16-6) for a series of studies. How little he understood of its real importance is emphasized by the use to which it was actually put, that is, to drive away evil from the re-

16-5   Dan mask. (Copyright F. Willett, Glasgow)

16-6 Bakota reliquary figure. (Lowie Museum of Anthropology, University of California, Berkeley)

Following initial discussion and ritual cleansing, the petitioner who has come to the priest is seated opposite him. Between them lies the divination tray, which has a light layer of sand on the surface. The priest takes a number of palm nut kernels, tosses them into the air, and marks on the tray the number of those that he catches. At the end of a series of tosses he uses the number and arrangement of marks on the tray to select those odu poems to be interpreted. The interpretations reflect the ordered intentions of the deities and the ancestors. But there is always the element of chance and disorder. The face of Eshu, the god of unpredictable fate and change, is inevitably present on the border of the tray. Placed opposite the priest during the divina-

16-7 Nail fetish figure, "Konde." Wood, nails, other material, 32½". Kongo tribe, lower Congo, central Africa. (University Museum, University of Pennsylvania)

sometimes reflected the purpose. A stiffened pose, upraised arm, and grimacing face were used to make the forms more menacing, while nails or sharp iron studs were driven into the body to release malevolent forces. The fetishes used in voodoo have their origins in this kind of object.

Divination Tray   Objects not representing the human figure and designed for specific, utilitarian purposes may also reflect religious principles. This Yoruba tray (Fig. 16-8) is used in the process of *divination*, foretelling the future or discovering secret knowledge. One of the features of Yoruba religion is the oracle of *Ifa*, a secret body of wisdom that may be made available to a believer through the intervention of a *babalawo*, or priest. The priest then interprets the secret body of poems, called *odu*, in various combinations, using the Ifa divination tray.

16–9   Above. Ashanti. Wooden stool for a queen mother. (Reproduced by Courtesy of the Trustees of the British Museum)

16–8   Left. Yoruba. Ifa tray. (Copyright F. Willett, Glasgow)

tion process, the face reminds both priest and petitioner of the potential in man's destiny for good or evil.

Stools   The manifestation of African spiritual and political principles in utilitarian objects is perhaps best exemplified by the Ashanti stools (Fig. 16-9). The Ashanti, like other Akan peoples of Ghana and the Ivory Coast, believe that a person's spirit resides in his stool. When not in use, a stool is turned on its side so that no spirit other than the owner's will "sit" on the stool. Special stools are carved for an individual at important stages in his or her life such as at puberty or marriage.

This personal metaphor was extended to that of the state at the time of the founding of the Ashanti Confederacy by the king (*asantehene*) Osei Tutu in 1701. On a particular day when the king, subchiefs, and the Ashanti people were gathered together, Osei Tutu's chief priest summoned from the heavens a Golden Stool to enshrine and protect the soul of the new nation. The Golden Stool remains the single most important item of Ashanti court regalia: it stands for leadership and union. In this way stools also became symbols of political office for those with political authority delegated by the asantehene. The high status of

members of the court, like the queen mother, is reflected in this ceremonial stool adorned with fine sculpture and a silver sheath overlay. The intricate surface designs frequently recall proverbs that the officeholder uses to convey a message or motto of his rule. Ceremonial stools like this one are reserved for state occasions; others are specially carved for domestic and personal use. At the death of an Ashanti ruler his ceremonial stool is blackened with soot and becomes the object of propitiation in the state ancestor cult.

Kente Cloth   A further example of artistic accomplishment and political authority manifest in utilitarian objects is the *kente* cloth of the Ashanti and Ewe peoples of Ghana. Kente is a large cloth, draped for ceremonial dress, made out of narrow strips sewn together that have been woven from cotton, silk, or wool threads. While strip weaving is common in Africa, that which distinguishes kente is the elaboration of silk weft inlay designs that are geometric in character. There is a hierarchy of kente weavers and designs. At the pinnacle are the royal *asasia* cloths woven exclusively for the asantehene and his family, and for individuals granted a cloth as a symbol of loyalty or in return for services to the king. Pattern and color of the royal cloths carry special meanings appropriate to their owners. As do all kente, each asasia cloth has its name. The example shown here (Fig. 16-10) is called Everyone-Depends-on-Somebody. Its colors are gold, red, and

16–10 Left. Ashanti. Kente cloth (detail). (Reprinted from *African Art in Motion* by Robert Farris Thompson. Katherine Coryton White collection, UCLA Art Council, University of California, Los Angeles)

16–11 Above. Mangbetu pots. (Reproduced by Courtesy of the Trustees of the British Museum)

16–12 Below. Mangbetu woman. (Barbara W. Merriam)

blue. The gold and red are references to kingship and governmental power; blue refers to playfulness and humor. The equal intensity of the overall colors is coupled with the striking alternation of rectangles dominated by blue with those dominated by gold and red. The arrangement suggests the worth of both qualities in balance in the ideal society; power and authority must be matched by humor and simplicity.

Sculpture in Everyday Objects While items of court regalia symbolize the authority of a ruler, other carved objects may commemorate a single person or group of persons, common and familiar. The Mangbetu of northeastern Zaire apply their excellent figurative sculpture to everyday objects rather than to statuary. Knife handles, harps, pipe bowls, and other containers are decorated with human heads and figures. Among them, the most famous of Mangbetu motifs are the pots carved to commemorate the bound heads and elaborate hairstyles of Mangbetu women (Figs. 16-11, 16-12). The coiffure itself is reminiscent of a woven basket. It consists of a fiber structure through which the hair is pulled, elongated with the addition of false hair, and then woven back through the fiber. The delicate woven lines of the coiffure are replicated in fine detail on the heads that sit atop the clay pots. The lower body of the pot reinforces the cylindrical shape of the head by curvilinear lines covering its surface.

QUESTIONS AND COMMENTS

1. How is exaggeration of natural features of human and animal form used to stress spiritual or social principles? Give examples.
2. As has been stated above, masks may have varied purposes: some are intended to invoke powers of natural or supernatural forces. They represent mystery and the potential for good or evil. These often rely upon images of the forest or bush to convey their meaning. Others symbolize civilization: man's imposition of pattern and order on the natural world or idealized human values. Review the objects presented in this section and identify ones that seem to you to bear out each of these two purposes.
3. The nature–civilization contrast may be seen in statues and other sculpted objects as well. Compare the reliance upon natural substance versus the reliance upon human reference in the images of the Bakongo figure and the Ashanti stool. Identify the different images.
4. How does the form and placement during use of the Ifa divination tray suggest general principles of Yoruba cosmology?
5. There are many elements to consider in analyzing a work of sculpture: proportion; volume and dimension; compactness versus open space; surface texture (rough versus smooth, painted or unpainted). Of those objects that incorporate aspects of naturalism and stylized interpretation of the human form, which elements contribute to the effect of naturalism? Which to the effect of stylization?

African visual art may be utilitarian, decorative, symbolic, spiritual, or all of these at once. Masks and sculptures emphasize communication of spiritual forces and the interpretation of cosmic order to the human community; other objects symbolize or reinforce social relationships. There is, as we have seen, no dichotomy between "fine" and "applied" arts. Similarly, there is no division in African music between "concert" and "folk" music. Just as there are no museums in traditional Africa, there are no concert halls; music, like visual art objects, is intended to be used as part of the rituals and celebrations of everyday life.

African Music

The first observation that a careful observer of African music will surely make is some conclusion about the tremendous variety and complexity of the sounds emanating from this gigantic continent. The languages and cultures of the people of North Africa are closely related to those of the Arab world and the Middle East, traditions which differ—for geographic, economic, and political reasons—from those of South, Central, and West Africa. The music of this region, so oriental in its *modal*, *melodic*, and *improvisational* characteristics, although African for perhaps centuries, must be excluded from our consideration of indigenous African music, the music of black Africans. Likewise, one finds alongside the music of sub-Saharan Africa a tradition of Western music brought by the colonists from Europe, a practice that has its own traditions and has helped generate a new black African urban music called "high life," a chic modern music of the cities. Even when we dampen all the sounds that can be identified as "non-native" to the original peoples of Africa, we are still engulfed in an endless variety of musics and languages and peoples. The culture and the music of the Pygmies, Bushmen, and Saharan peoples are not the same as those of the Yoruba, Ashanti, and Susu ethnic groups. Here, as in the literature and art sections, we will concentrate on the music of West African societies. After discussing some general characteristics shared by the music of these societies, we will move on to a more detailed study of one specific example: music from the Festival of the Tohossuo, legendary princes of the royal family from the ancient kingdom of Dahomey.

Characteristics of West African Music: Similarities with Jazz　Most music performed by Africans is part of a social activity. Of course, individual music-making takes place in response to personal or ritual needs, but most musical performance accompanies the group activities of games, religious rites, feasts, festivals, and work. Music provides an opportunity for sharing in a communal creative experience. With the transferral of Africans to the New World, this West African music deeply influenced the development of jazz, with which, as we will see, it shares many characteristics. Because of a number of factors, black slaves in America were able to maintain much of their African musical heritage, all the while joining to it certain elements of the Euro-American musical tradition. The resulting hybrid had a markedly African base. The important points to keep in mind are these: the rich West African musical tradition; the comparative cultural isolation in which many black American slaves lived; the tolerance of musical activities among the slave communities accorded by white American masters; the compatibility of the important elements of West African music with the current tradition of Euro-American music. As West African music is communal in its basic approach, jazz, too, is a shared creative experience: those in the normal small group of musicians, the combo, respond improvisationally to one other's musical signals and the social signals of the audience or dance crowd in a way different from the performance practice of a Western string quartet or a chamber orchestra. African musicians, when composing collectively, are part of a social interaction that often communicates a group sentiment or message, an extramusical consideration that is found only rarely in music of the West.

Depending on the event and local customs, the performing groups may be made up of young or old, male or female, or mixed. However, there is usually a hierarchical differentiation among the players—leading roles are played by professional musicians or specialists; secondary roles are performed by the others in both choruses and instrumental ensembles. As the *Sundiata* epic indicated, in Africa the griot, or praise singer, is a highly respected musician-poet, usually a professional, in many of these societies. The leading blues singers and jazz musicians of black America are often seen to be held in the same esteem by the regular members of the black community.

Elements in African Music   Little, if any, traditional African music takes any interest in *harmony* as we know it in the West, but most African sounds are compatible with European harmonies. The leading elements of African music are *melody*, *rhythm*, *timbre* (the distinctive sound of the instruments and voices), and text. Although verbal art is intertwined with African musical art, some societies are able to convey specific messages by instrumental sounds alone. That is, *pitch* and rhythm can be explicitly equated to textual messages, for speech in some languages is musical in the sense that pitch variations affect word meanings. But "talking drums" and "talking winds" are not characteristic of the music of most of the peoples who were brought to America from Africa as slaves. Even though there may be a tendency to overemphasize this particular feature of African music because it is so unique and fascinating, we might be well advised to consider that most music is communicative in a general way once we have learned the conventions. For example, we are all familiar with the sounds of military music, love songs, sad songs, happy dance music, and so on. We know that words for one variety cannot be properly set to sounds of another, or, if they are, then a joke is intended, a mistake has been made, or something is out of kilter. In other words, the sound of the music without the words conveys a somewhat specific message anyway. In like manner, it is accurate to say that most African music communicates messages and feelings, ideas that are extramusical. But to the degree that particular sounds are wedded to specific social functions, it is probably true that African music is more communicative than most Western music.

Rhythm   The complex rhythms of most African drumming depend on the use of a recurring rhythmic pattern within the totality of the ensemble. This time-line in African music is what the jazz drummer refers to as "time," that unwavering sense of beat that must prevail regardless of what else is happening in solo or in ensemble. In its simplest form, the time-line can be projected by a "beat" or metronomic pulse that sounds audibly and continuously. But it can also function as an unsounded, but understood, quantity of the time-line part, which the musicians perceive as an *ostinato* or regularly recurring rhythm pattern. Another obvious conclusion at which the impartial observer of African music will arrive is the distinct bias toward percussion that is a part of the aesthetics of African music. As in jazz, there is a tendency to include a rhythm section in every instrumental ensemble, and surely the close association of African music and jazz with dance—both as part of the dance and as accompaniment for the dance—explains, or at least accounts for, the importance of rhythm as a chief feature of both musics. In fact, African drummers often perform on the move as part of the dance. Even when stationary, African drummers—and jazz drummers—have bodies in motion, with elbows flying, shoulders leaning, fingers tapping or pressing, and heads and mouths going.

Vocal Music: Call and Response Although drumming and rhythm are probably preeminent in West African music, great stress is laid on vocal music. An exceptional variety may be found among the themes treated, such as war songs, hunting songs, play and work songs, religious and festival songs, and social commentary, a type not unlike the artifices of the American bluesman. Eileen Southern, renowned historian of the music of black Americans, cites the following as the earliest example of an African song text written down in a European language (1800):

> The winds roared, and the rains fell;
> The poor white man, faint and weary,
> Came and sat under our tree.
> He has no mother to bring him milk,
> No wife to grind his corn.
>
> *Chorus:*
> Let us pity the white man.
> No mother has he to bring him milk,
> No wife to grind his corn.

The leader-and-chorus format of much African vocal music often displays a call-and-response mode of performance; this, too, is another characteristic eagerly seized by jazz historians seeking stylistic parallels between jazz and native African music. The typical jazz performance of the vocal and instrumental blues has a singer or lead instrument perform the first half of each phrase, only to be answered by another instrumentalist or the ensemble itself. The tie between the jazz blues and the African responsorial performance may be

16–13   First Day of the Yam Custom in Dahomey, 1818. From Edward Thomas Bowdich, *Mission from Cape Coast Castle to Ashantee,* 3rd ed. London: F. Cass & Co., Ltd. 1960. (Reproduced by permission of Frank Cass & Co., London; photo courtesy of the Trustees of the Boston Public Library)

tenuous, but the leader-chorus performance among African vocal ensembles is, in fact, the norm and a characteristic to be savored. Much is lost if the words are not understood, of course; but the virtuosity of the leader, in contrast to the solidity and enthusiastic response of the remaining performers, is a distinctive sound of the black African tradition. As we read more about the cultural traditions of black Africa, we would also do well to keep in mind these observations:

> From the first African captives, through the years of slavery, and into the present century black Americans kept alive important strands of African consciousness and verbal art in their humor, songs, dance, speech, tales, games, folk beliefs, and aphorisms. . . . Cultural diffusion between whites and blacks was by no means a one-way street with blacks the invariable beneficiaries. . . . Black

relationship to the larger culture was complex and multi-dimensional.[1]

Music from the Festival of the Tohossou The princes of Dahomey are called the Tohossou, descendants of a legendary king; their worship is the object of a cult whose ceremonies are performed in the twenty temples of the city of Abomey, capital of the ancient kingdom of Dahomey (Fig. 16-13). The music for portions of these ceremonies has been recorded.[2] We should prepare ourselves to hear, in addition to the sounds of human voices, the music of three oblong

drums, which are beaten by sticks on one side and the naked hand on the other; three iron bells struck with a short wooden stick; pairs of rattles contained in wicker baskets; and a small bell shaken by a priest. The festivities for one Tohossou last four days, and the recorded excerpts sample music from morning to nightfall of one festival day. Five groups of people, the entire community, participate: the priests, the princes (descendants of the royal line), men, women, and musicians. Even children have a part to play, and this day's ceremony will have dancing, singing, and sacrifice. As the day progresses, the bull will be bound, its throat will be slit, and a lamb will later be sacrificed to appease the spirit of the bull. The mysteries of all these ceremonies and ritual acts are not all known and entirely understood; but, since the Tohossou represent proud de-

[1] Lawrence J. Levine, *Black Culture & Black Consciousness.* (London: Oxford University Press, 1977).
[2] *Anthology of the Music of Black Africa* (Everest 3254-3), Record 3 Sides A and B.

scendants of a warrior race, there are various songs, dances, and ritual acts dealing with the enemy, fallen brothers-in-arms, vengeance, and sacred deities. The first excerpt, "Song of Zomadonou," is sung by a young man portraying Zomadonou, a reincarnated prince, his words telling of the feats that made him famous. He is accompanied by one bell, struck in two places to obtain contrasting pitches, and the song of the bell creates the time-line ostinato: High (slow) High (slow) High (quick) Low (quick). Over and over again the pattern repeats as the prince sings his song to a *pentatonic* (five-note) *scale*. As Zomadonou sings, he is answered by the chorus, their response picking up the principal melodic figure of his solo song.

The second excerpt captures the voices of a male chorus grouped around the drums. It is basically a choral song meant to accompany a serpentine dance by the women as they snake their way three times around the sacred tree and sacrificial bull. The sound of the drums is not continuous, but the rattles keep a steady beat for the dance. Occasionally a solo voice will interject a brief exclamation, but the pattern of the music is choral song, not call and response. The music of this example is similar to the first in that the melody employs an abbreviated scale, ostinato patterns prevail, and tone production by the vocalists is full voiced, lusty, and somewhat strained.

Adomoussi, a priest devoted to the worship of the third Tohossou, performs the third excerpt himself. Striking a bell in two places, he follows with a short declamatory phrase—"O thou, when thou raise the saber it is to kill . . . Thou panther which avenges itself . . . Thou shark in the water . . . An enemy . . ." The pattern is simple—bell, statement, bell, statement—and one can see the parallel in the country bluesman who strums a chord to arrange his thoughts and follows with the simply sung phrase. The priest has something to tell his people; his bell and method of delivery catch their attention.

The choir for the next recorded example, "The Way Is Free," is entirely composed of women. Using a piercing chest tone, the leader sings short phrases to be answered by the remaining choir members. The percussion accompaniment, which is not heavy, seems to be but loosely attached to the singing of the women. Since no dance is employed at this point in the ceremony, the drums seem to act more as background than accompaniment. Not so for the Nifossousso dance that follows. The regular beat is stately and dignified; it accompanies a procession of women who have shed their brightly colored costumes for white loincloths in a slow procession to the temple. Following this, the men call Botro, a woman, to come and perform her dance. In the seventh example the woman advances to dance and to sing a warlike and frightening ritual with a stick that she finally plunges into the earth.

Throughout the performance of each of these snippets of music and ceremony it is obvious that certain musical sounds relate to general feelings in the same way that certain musical sounds of the Western tradition do. The priest who shouted his exclamations to the accompaniment of a bell could not have been describing a quiet forest glade; the slow processional of the noble line of women moving to the temple would have been inappropriate to accompany the active dance of Botro. The sounds of African music, although different from those we are most accustomed to hear, open up to meaningful interpretation upon careful listening and a little reflection. Then, as the similarities to our own music begin to surface, we see the heritage that has blended with Euro-American music to form that American music called jazz. Only recently have American jazz musicians begun to take a new look at African roots in a search for further inspiration and replenishment, and we will see in Chapter 18 and in Volume II how another transformation in American music has taken place as our sense of history draws us to new ideas from our past.

17

African Arts in Festival: The Efe/Gelede of the Western Yoruba

The unity of the arts with one another and with the values and lifestyle of a particular culture is nowhere so evident as in the ways in which people celebrate together. We have seen how the festival of Dionysus in ancient Greece brought together wine drinking, love making, song, dance, mask, drama, and the architecture of the theater. The Romans honored Saturn, the god of agriculture, with a general feasting and unleashing of social restraints at the end of the year. Seeing that they could not do away with the Saturnalia, the Christians declared that Christmas would be celebrated at the end of December and retained certain pagan customs such as the yule log and the Christmas tree. Christian festivals also combined drama, music, visual effects, and dance, as we saw with *The Play of Daniel*, part of a Christmas celebration in the cathedral. The Christian holiday for ''letting go'' became carnival, the pre-Lent season, which in Renaissance Florence produced splendid festivals of poetry, song, dance, costumes, and painted floats.

Western peoples continued to put on festivals and celebrations in the early modern period, and in some instances (witness Mardi Gras in New Orleans) they continue today; but modern industrialism and individualism have tended to wipe out what once seemed a communal necessity. Many of us are forced to "celebrate" our holidays by turning on the TV. In traditional African societies, however, and in countries (like Brazil) where African influence is strong, festivals continue to be both a vital part of living and an important means of aesthetic expression. Even those Africans who are Christians or Muslim continue to participate in the festivals that have their roots in traditional religion.

The Yoruba culture, many aspects of which we have already studied, provides excellent examples of the synthesis of myth, poetry, dance, music, and visual arts in traditional festivals. One of these is the Efe/Gelede, celebrated by certain Yoruba subgroups in western Nigeria and the republic of Benin. The festival occurs annually before the beginning of the spring rains (between March and May) that will initiate the agricultural activities of the coming year. One of its purposes is thus to ensure the fertility of the earth. Women have always been symbols of fertility.

Significance of the Festival   In a patriarchal society where most ritual ceremonies reinforce the dominance of men over women, Efe/Gelede highlights the importance of women and serves as an occasion to recognize their spiritual powers. The specific context of Efe/Gelede derives from the importance of *Iyanla*, the Earth Mother or Great Mother, feminine counterpart of the supreme god Olorun or Oludumare.

Three Yoruba myths, all of which celebrate the mystical power and fertility of Iyanla, explain the background of the Efe/Gelede festival. The first tells that at the beginning of time when Oludumare sent Obatala, Ogun, and Iyanla, the first three orisha to earth, Iyanla complained that she, unlike the other two, had been given no special power. So Oludumare gave her the title "Mother of All," and presented her with a calabash containing a bird. The Great Mother promised to use her power by inflicting punishment on her enemies,

but to those who appeased her she promised to grant wealth and children. In the second myth, the Great Mother, who had previously been blessed with many children, found that she could not bear any after her marriage to a man from Ketu (a Yoruba town in Benin). Upon consulting the oracle of Ifa, she was told to make sacrifices of corn and clay dishes and to dance with wooden figures on her head and metal anklets on her feet. She did so and promptly bore two children: a boy named Efe ("the Joker"), and a girl named Gelede. Her children found that when they grew up it was necessary for them, too, to dance with wooden images and iron anklets before they could have children. This dancing is reenacted in the festival.

The third myth recounts that another orisha, Orunmila, was told to sacrifice a wooden image, a waistcloth, and metal anklets before he undertook a visit to the haven of the witches. He performed the sacrifice, made his journey, and returned safely, proclaiming that he had made friends with Sickness and Death and that he would die no more. The Yoruba believe that the destructive power of Iyanla is manifested through the witches, symbolized by the bird in the calabash. Elements of the Gelede costume recall this myth.

By honoring the great mother Iyanla and her children Efe and Gelede, the celebrants hope that the mystical powers granted to women by Iyanla may be channeled into constructive behavior of use to the community rather than into activity destructive of it. The festival thus in a sense honors and celebrates all women, especially mothers. It is generally performed over a two-day period. The first, the day of Efe, is devoted primarily to poetry, the songs of Efe. The second, the day of Gelede, places more emphasis on costumes and dancing.

First Day: Efe

The Efe ceremony takes place in the market area, a setting of social, religious, and economic activity primarily involving women. At one end of the arena a small enclosure with double arches of palms is constructed. It serves as the entrance for the principal performer, *Oro Efe*, literally the word of Efe. As the audience gathers, masqueraders and dancers perform in anticipation of the Oro Efe, whose songs will last throughout the night.

17–1   Far left. Oro Efe. Dressing of dancer. Layers of embroidered and appliqued cloth panels (gberi) are tied over a horizontally suspended bamboo hoop (agboja). (Henry John Drewal)

17–3   Left. Oro Efe in full dress. (Henry John Drewal)

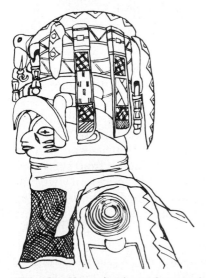

17–2   Oro Efe mask. After a photograph of Oro Efe in performance at Ketu, April 24, 1971. (Henry John Drewal)

Costume and Performance   The Oro Efe's elaborate costume, abounding in symbolism, includes leggings, iron gongs, and multicolored, appliqued cloth over a bamboo hoop (Figs. 17-1, 17-3). The headdress consists of a veil and a frontal view of the human face in mask. It is topped by an elaborate superstructure containing symbolic animal figures, colors, and suspended knives. The lions, leopards, and snakes connote strength and royalty, while the knives are associated with Soponnon, god of smallpox, and Ogun, god of iron. The goddess of the rainbow, Osumare, is connected with the python. The crowning symbol on the headdress is the bird of the mothers, alluding to the belief that mothers, like witches, can transform themselves into birds at night to fly about their business (Figs. 17-2, 17-3).

The Oro Efe is veiled to enhance his spiritual remove from the audience, but the cult head who summons him by striking the sacred bells calls him by name. A flute player also summons the Oro Efe, and the crowd awaits him in silence. The Oro Efe appears, swaying and sounding his leg rattles, swinging the whisks in his hand. His first words honor deities, ancestors, mothers, and elders. The angle of his body and slow pace express recognition and reverence to the spiritual powers. In the second stage of the ceremony, a chorus and, gradually, the audience join in the Oro Efe's songs. The public's participation symbolizes agreement with the Oro Efe's words; it strengthens the spiritual and social communality of the occasion. The performance continues throughout the night with occasional interludes offered by the drummers, who present praise poems, proverbs, jokes, and riddles. The Oro Efe departs near dawn while the audience is distracted by a stilted dancer in hyena masquerade, and the night's activities are over.

Efe Poetry   The poetry recited by the Oro Efe and in choral repetition is based on the belief that *ase*—power, authority, potential energy—can be embodied in words as well as in deities, living men and women, and the ancestors. Women are perceived to have a special ase that can be used for the good or the ill of the community. The voicing of poetry also contains ase and may be used to help direct that of the women toward potential good.

The types of poetry recited include invocation, social comment or satire, history, and funeral commemoration. Several of each type may be sung throughout the night; examples of some of these follow.

Invocation   One segment of the invocation requests blessing for the community as a whole. The songs invariably mention smallpox and cholera, scourges on the population. They plea for agricultural success, which means wealth, and for progeny. Since the mothers are associated with both procreativity and fertility of the earth, these are not surprising themes. In this example the singer prays for the end of unexpected deaths caused by farming accidents. He protests in the first line that he (the community) has offered *orijio*—medicinal leaves—to placate the mothers. Shango, god of thunder, would never strike one of his shrines; why should the progenitors *ose* and *aje* strike down their own offspring? Agbojo and Onidofoi, the ancestral spir-

its of the town, have been duly honored. Making his points, the singer displays his respect for the mothers and acknowledges their power by summoning the support of onlookers to join in his prayers.

Efe Poetry

INVOCATION

Orijio leaves charmed you to forgive my misdeeds.
Never have we suffered deaths from hoes, never from
    knives.
Have I lied?
Have I lied?
Never have we seen a thunderbolt strike a young *ose*
    tree.
Oso in the house were you not the one who gave birth
    to me?
Why do you not know us any longer?
Aje in the house, were you not the one who gave us
    birth?
Why do you not know us any longer?
Never have we seen a dog devour its child.
Never have we seen a dog devour its child.
Our mother, *opake*, forgive us our misdeed.
Our mother, do not allow me to falter
If a cult member has offended, expose him.
You joined our offering of thanksgiving to Agbojo,
Onidofoi was the one who saved us from death.
Young, old, households, and visitors, pray for my
    success.

Social Comment   In social comment songs the Oro Efe uses praises, cajolery, and condemnation to highlight events that have occurred in the community. The tone is ribald, the poetry often sarcastic, the images satirical, posing the opposite to their traditional meaning. Even though the Efe ceremony is to appease the mothers, male dominance is lauded; women who have shown too great an independence from their husbands are ridiculed. The second poem bewails two outrages: not only did the man decried commit adultery against Ogunsola, but Ogunsola was in addition his elder. In the third poem the Oro Efe also stresses the theme of respect for elders by admonishing youth to remember that age, not wealth or Western education, brings wisdom.

Efe Poetry

SOCIAL COMMENT I

For a husband to grind pepper and grate cassava.
For a husband to grind pepper and grate cassava.
For a husband to cook *eba* and wash pots.
For a husband to cook *eba* and wash pots.
The wife you married, Sango, is wonderful.
She threatened her husband with a cutlass at the
    market.
She threatened her husband with a cutlass at the
    market.
I heard him shout to all around "help me!"
She threatened her husband with a cutlass at the
    market.

SOCIAL COMMENT II

The conceited man with all his money is teasing his
    elder.
The conceited man with all his money is teasing his
    elder.
Did Ogunsola marry his wife for you?
Did Ogunsola marry his wife for you?
Wretched person who pulls on the snake's tail.
Wretched person who pulls on the snake's tail.
If the snake bites you should I be concerned?
Wretched person who pulls on the snake's tail.

SOCIAL COMMENT III

Ah, truly young children are very wise.
However I say they are not as wise as their elders.
We called you to get the soup, but you went to add
    water to it.
But you are not as wise as the one who cooked it.
A goat is different from a horse, a white man is
    different from a Hausa.
You are not as wise as the one who did the cooking.

Funerary Commemoration This final type of
song delivered by the Oro Efe is a memorial for someone recently deceased, a person who in this case was
probably a singer and member of the cult. He challenges the chorus (*akijele*) to sing long and well. The
good character and positive influence of the deceased
is recalled by equating him with animals—the elephant
and hippopotamus who also, despite their greatness,
succumb to death. In the last line the permanence of
lineage is stressed with the allusion that the whisk—its
emblem—has been left behind for the deceased's
successors.

Efe Poetry

FUNERARY COMMEMORATION

I am looking at you to see how you do the ceremony.
You *akijele* have not sung enough.
Elephant died in the farm and the pot ate it up.
Hippopotamus died in the farm and the pot ate it up.
You sang well during Bello's performance.
All Oro Efe who are in the market,
We must all use mournful voice in singing.
We are calling upon you to come, come, father
    Adebayo, sleep no longer away from home.
We are calling upon you to come, come Akewe Bello,
    sleep no longer away from home.
He could no longer rise up, could no longer sing.
Father Labode, death caused the whisk to fall from the
    hand of the cult member.

The Efe poems again exemplify the close relationship
between word and performance in African literary art.
The dramatic convergence of the Oro Efe's costume,
voice, and gestures serves to heighten the spiritual and
emotional exhilaration of the ceremony, while the
poet's words command social discipline of the audience and remind them of the qualities that have enabled the community to survive. Together, they summon the ase of the community and lead the people in a
telling reaffirmation of faith.

The Gelede Celebration

The Gelede is performed on the afternoon following
the Efe festivities. Its purpose is to embody an approach
to the mothers that appeals to their positive attributes.
The priests and elders summon from the spectators attitudes necessary for the worship of the mothers: patience, indulgence, and composure. By upholding tradition and ridiculing those who offend it, the visual
symbols, along with the music and dance of Gelede, attempt to please and honor the mothers.

The main performers for Gelede are masqueraders.

While they are all men, they traditionally appear in pairs portraying males or females. The pairing probably alludes to the spiritual duality assigned to the mothers, and the males and females to the two children Efe and Gelede. The costumes, which consist essentially of mask, headwrap, and leg rattles (Fig. 17-4), exaggerate the sex characteristics of the male or female. Hoops and layers of cloth accentuate the chest of the male; a breastplate with elaborate carved breasts and wooden structures behind emphasize the female's physical attributes.

Masks consist of a head fitting over the upper portion of the masquerader's head and a superstructure above. The two components reflect different aesthetic

17–4   Female Gelede dancer with breastplate carved in the form of ibeji statues. Joga-Orile/Imasai, Northern Egbado, April, 1965. Regional Style Egbado. (Henry John Drewal)

values. The head is frontal, symmetrical, composed, and static, reflecting an ideal of patience, while the elaborate superstructure with its extended parts and asymmetrical design creates an effect of surprise. Colors in both parts are symbolic and frequently associated with the gods (Color Plate XV).

The elaborate art of the Gelede masks touches on all aspects of Yoruba life. Some of the motifs frequently occurring in them are animals, deities, social roles, historical personalities, fashion, and foreign elements. More than one motif may appear in a given mask. The principal animals of Gelede are the snake, bird, mongoose, tortoise, and lizard. Animal compositions may embody qualities of personality and behavior, as in Figure 17-5, where the snake symbolizes patience and "coolness" but is attacked by the "hot" or vengeful quadruped, a mongoose.

Goddesses, such as Oya, goddess of the Niger River (Fig. 17-6) are frequently represented in the Gelede part of the festival. Certain masks proclaim the hierarchical ordering in Yoruba social roles and religion. The mask represented in Figure 17-7 has a superstructure dominated by Yemoja, another name for Iyanla. Before the priestess is a figure prostrate in traditional greeting and at her side a small boy seeking her protection and support. This reiterates Yemoja's praises, which proclaim her the protector of children. The relative proportion suggests the religious hierarchical ordering, while the balance creates the notion of stability.

Foreigners—particularly Europeans with products of their culture such as cameras, sewing machines, cars, and trucks—often appear on the masks (Fig. 17-8). These elements of Western technology are used both for sheer entertainment and for satire, but they also imply a deeper spiritual message. Technological inventions are held by Yoruba commentators to be the result of the Europeans' spiritual power. Their appearance in Gelede masks may reflect a plea to the mothers to use their own spiritual powers in a positive way.

Dance   The visual imagery of the Gelede masks and costumes is enhanced by that of the dance, which is given great importance (Color Plate XVI). Dance patterns in Africa, as elsewhere, evolve from habitual movements, posture, and gestures of work and play. Here the movements imitate qualities appropriate to

17–5   Top left. Gelede mask: quadruped and snake. (Reproduced by Courtesy of the Trustees of the British Museum)

17–6   Above. Male Gelede mask. Oya. (Courtesy of Roger de la Burde)

17–7   Left. Female Gelede mask. Yemoja. (Reproduced by Courtesy of the Trustees of the British Museum)

17–8   Gelede mask. "The Lorry." (Federal Department of Antiquities, National Museum, Lagos, Nigeria)

the male or female sex, depending on the costume of the dancer. Like the words and performance of Efe and the dual composition of the masks, the dance heightens the tension inherent in this festival between male and female and between the perceived duality of the mothers. An example is the dance of the female masks performed by the young male dancer dressed as Tetede, wife of Efe. Tetede's costume with its pointed breasts emphasizes the male aggressive aspect of the feminine personality. The dance combines sequential deep knee bends, suggestive of a graceful curtsey, with a beating of shoulders and swaying of hips emphasizing female aggressivity. The dancer disguised as Efe also represents a male-female tension with both costume and mask. The heavy, layered costume suggests the ample figures of pregnant or mature women. Yet the Efe's dance, accompanied by the explosion of ceremonial guns, vigorously approaches abandon as the tempo increases and the dance reaches its culmination. This abandon, while masculine in tone, implies caricature and exaggeration

of movement and gesture associated with older women.

Through festival, as seen in both the Tohossou cult ceremony of the Dahomean kings and the Efe/Gelede of the western Yoruba, we have witnessed the interplay of many facets of African aesthetic expression. Poetry, music, song, sculptured mask, costume, and dance create together an experience of high drama for participants and observers, enhancing the social, spiritual, and moral concerns of the community. Entertaining and at times ribald, the performers nevertheless establish the priority of the spiritual powers that energize life on earth. They reinforce old values and symbols and acknowledge new realities. Audience and performers in communion celebrate the continuity of the community over time and affirm its vitality. While specific to certain groups of western Nigeria and Benin, these festivals evoke an essentially African mode of perception—the integration and wholeness of life.

COMMENTS AND QUESTIONS

1. African festivals—combining as they do music, costume, plastic art, and dance—confront all the senses with images and symbols of beliefs about human society and about spiritual forces. In reviewing this section, identify some of these in the case of Yoruba society by answering the following:
   (a) What elements of the masks are symbols of the Yoruba deities?
   (b) How is color used symbolically in mask and costume?
   (c) How does the organization of both Efe and Gelede segments of this festival illustrate the tension in Yoruba society between the roles of men and those of women? Who are the dancers? How do their costumes and dance styles convey the tension?
2. Think of other festivals that you have studied or know about from Western traditions. Can you identify similar components and purposes in them?
3. How does Gelede incorporate new experiences of cross-cultural contact of the Yoruba and integrate them into traditional Yoruba belief systems?

18

African Roots
and Continuities

General Characteristics of the
African Humanities

While a great diversity characterizes the many cultures on the continent of Africa and even within the area of West Africa studied here, there are certain modes of perception and cultural forms that may be characterized as African. These include, in the social realm, the veneration of elders, ancestors, and kinship ties generally, as well as the importance given to secret societies and initiation rites. We have seen that traditional religion, sometimes even among Muslim or Christian Africans, acts as a binding communal force. The close relationship with nature and the belief in a spirit world influencing it are primary motivating forces in the African arts and in the multifaceted art of the festival. African oral literature is devoted not only to religious ritual but also to moral instruction of the young and to the perpetuation of the history and traditions of a people. The griot, or oral historian-poet, plays a vital role in the latter aspect.

The traditional character of African art and culture makes the stylistic periodization that we have used in the study of Western culture somewhat irrelevant in terms of Africa. Aside from the sculptures of the Nok culture, and the arts of Ife and Benin, which can be dated, our examples of literature, art, and music have been drawn from several centuries of African experience including the present one. The festivals performed in the 1970s include modern elements while they derive from ancient forms and ideas. Similarly the poems of Diop, Achebe, and Soyinka express this continuity between ancient and modern.

Certain fundamental ideas and beliefs are shared across traditional African cultures. These include the commitment to a holistic view of life; the definition of community as the living, the dead, and the unborn; and a sensibility to the delicate balance between human society and natural forces in the universe—sometimes visible, sometimes invisible. If man must recognize the importance of natural and supernatural forces, his intelligence nevertheless is responsible for affecting his destiny. African ideas share with Western humanism a respect for the dignity of human beings and an acceptance of the foibles of human nature.

The African humanities exhibit perhaps even more than those of classical Greece a profound aesthetic and philosophical unity. Robert Farris Thompson, in his study *African Art in Motion*, has attempted to describe some of the basic principles that unite African arts and thought, particularly around the central art of dance. His conclusions, presented in brief form below, are well worth our consideration.

(1) Age and wisdom are venerated in African society. African art nonetheless shows a particular dynamic of age that would not in the West be associated with advanced years, for the elder is supposed to retain a certain youthful vitality. Even the terra cotta mask from the ancient Nok culture (see Fig. 14-1), while representing a high official who would necessarily be someone of advanced years, does not show the face of an aged man. The elder dancer who executes his performance with disciplined vitality is highly regarded.

(2) In dance, plastic art, and music, great attention is given to proportion and balance. Silence, or the "suspended beat" in music, and open space in art are not passive qualities but active components of the rhythmic flow. Balance is vitalized in perceiving the individual qualities and motions of body parts integrated into a whole. The ability to imagine and perform multiple rhythms in dance is an extension of this principle.

(3) Sharpness of line and a crisp beginning and ending characterize both dance and sculpture. The Ibo *Mmwo* mask (Fig. 16-4) demonstrates the clear boundaries of pattern that the carver's knife establishes.

(4) African arts portray an ideal of *resemblance* rather than *identity*. Sculptors, in particular, seek to represent a moral or spiritual force rather than to make an individual portrait. Although African art runs a gamut from the rather naturalistic Benin bronzes to abstract masks, it is never totally realistic or totally nonfigurative, but rather seeks a balance somewhere between the two poles.

(5) *Ancestorism*, which Thompson defines as "the belief that the closest harmony with the ancient way is the highest of experiences, the force that enables a man to rise to his destiny," is a powerful motivation in the African arts. The sculpture of the mask, mythology, music, and dance are used in rites to establish links between living sons and daughters and the community of ancestors.

(6) A final principle of "coolness," a word that has equivalents in many African languages, unites all the preceding ones. Aspects of "coolness" are visibility and openness, luminosity, and smoothness coupled with clarity. A dance, for example, may be characterized by extreme vitality but also by extreme control and by facial composure, the "mask of the cool." The belief in rebirth and reincarnation, which unites living vitality with orientation toward the ancestral, is an important component in "coolness." This unison of energy and balance, of "hot" movement and "cool" composure in African art, music, and dance is perhaps the most unique feature of African aesthetics.

African Survivals in Afro-American Culture

We have introduced Africa in this textbook between the European Renaissance and early modern period not only because this time saw the flourishing of the great West African empires, but especially because of the fact that it was at this point that the destinies of America and Europe became intertwined with that of Africa.

The fact that almost one million Africans, originating primarily in the western regions that we have studied, were imported to North America as a result of the slave trade has had profound effects on American culture. These effects have been transmitted to American culture as a whole by means of the continuities of African culture in Afro-American culture, and it is to these continuities or "survivals," as they are called, that we now turn.

African Survivals   The term "African survival" is used by scholars to denote a specific form or function of an institution, ritual, belief, language, or art that is clearly identifiable with an African origin, although adapted to the New World situation. Such survivals have always been noticeable among black populations in South America and the Caribbean. North Americans of the white majority culture, however, along with many blacks, tended until recently to deny that there was anything African about Afro-American culture. For them, the American Negro had no past; his or her culture was purely a product of the slaves' adaptation to white America. In the early twentieth century, the black scholars W. E. B. DuBois and Carter Woodson were among the first to point out African survivals in the religious, social, and aesthetic life of Afro-Americans. An anthropologist, Melville H. Herskovits, continued the investigation of this question in his work *The Myth of the Negro Past*, published in 1941. Herskovits challenged the popularly held assumption that Afro-Americans had no cultural past. Outlining principal features of a "cultural complex" based on common patterns of behavior of the African cultures in the regions of slave origin, he identified certain features of Afro-American culture in the Americas and the Caribbean that evolved from African cultural institutions. Aspects of Afro-American culture that differed from comparable institutions of the white society would thus be explained by the different cultural heritage of black Americans rather than by their failure to imitate white behavior properly.

Other scholars, such as E. Franklin Frazier, argued that conditions of oppression were the real cause of the distinctive features of black culture, especially in regard to family structure. For example, the sale of family members to different masters during slavery and the need for black men to seek work away from home after emancipation resulted in an apparent predominance of single-parent and matriarchal households.

Numerous recent studies of both the African and the Afro-American past have defined more precisely both the types of African survivals to be found in Afro-American culture and the means by which they may have survived. The formation of Afro-American culture was a complex process indeed; but certain features of its social institutions, religious organizations, and beliefs, as well as its arts and letters, can now be identified as having distinctly African origins.

The Extended Family   Identification with the extended (as opposed to the nuclear) family, the great importance of children to the sense of a community's continuity over time, and the special roles played by men and women in family life are African features that have persisted in Afro-American social life. Coupled with the latter is the acceptability of the economic independence of women. African women, unlike their European counterparts, could have rights in land and property. In certain circumstances, children born outside marriage were welcome additions to the woman's family. In many African societies children are often raised by people other than their own parents: sometimes grandparents, sometimes friends of their parents' generation. While preferences of these types may have been reinforced by the conditions of slavery and the plight of freed slaves, they provided adaptable models for a "normal" Afro-American family life, if different from those of the majority culture.

Groups and Associations   Types of bonding and grouping characteristic of traditional African societies reappear in various ways in Afro-America. At the time of initiation, African boys and girls form close bonds with their agemates that continue, in the form of a society, throughout their lives. Age or initiation mates treat each other as brothers and sisters, granting reciprocal rights and obligations. Such groups are often the focus of festival, entertainment, and mutual support activities. Related to these groups are "titled" societies in which individuals can display their wealth and enhance their status by the purchase of a succession of "titles" bringing them recognition and respect. Titled societies also encourage cooperation in economic activities through the use of fees for insurance, burial, or investment purposes. Aspects of both the age-grade and titled societies may be seen in the structure and vitality of men's and women's groups, brotherhoods, and so on, among Afro-Americans. Even the organization of black American churches and their auxiliary societies reflects these African patterns of association.

Importance of Oral Eloquence   The Afro-American church, where permitted to develop independently, incorporated other social norms and roles of African society. Among these were leadership by elders and/or by individuals who were gifted speakers. In those African societies where leadership was informal or officially vested in a group of elders, individual influence and leadership were exercised through one's knowledge of custom and traditions as well as through sound judgment and rhetorical skill. Since the New World experience rarely permitted free and open public expression to black people, especially to men, these highly valued skills were developed in the single largest institution that the blacks had to themselves, the churches. Preachers in Afro-American churches have traditionally been political leaders in a society within a society. It is significant that many of the civil rights' leaders were first of all ministers in black churches. Martin Luther King, Jr., for example, was a gifted politician noted as well for his eloquence and his sense of history. As such, his leadership role in Afro-American society is reminiscent of that of the griot. In highly centralized states, the griots were important officials of the court. They exhorted troops to battle and counseled the ruler by recalling past heroes and events of their people's history. Their fate, as we have seen in the epic *Sundiata*, was closely bound to that of the king, who symbolized his people.

Oral Literature   The importance of the oral tradition in African life appears, as we have seen, not only in political and historical rhetoric but also in the tales used to transmit the wisdom of elders to the young. Some of the animal and human characters in African tales—notably Hare, Tortoise, and Spider—found their way to the New World in the tales told by African nursemaids to their children and to those of their masters. The transfer of animal characters was not the only African pattern to appear in this setting. The performance of the "uncle" and "auntie" figures who recited the tales was important. These stories utilized the theme of the trickster hare, common in African folklore, who outwitted those of superior physical strength (or social position) by his swiftness and cunning. The language of the tales was often replete with proverbs, riddles, and double meaning. They also sustained the pedagogical purpose of African tales: to impart a moral lesson or model of behavior.

Other kinds of Afro-American tales also reflect an African origin. For instance, there is a predominance of tales concerned with questions about the origin of the cosmos or, more generally, about how things came to be as they are. Religious tales containing plots about conjuring, voodoo, and natural phenomena reflect African religious practices that have been adapted to the New World setting. "Preacher" tales—ones by and about ministers—may combine elements of the trickster character with the primacy of the performance element. In the folk genre of the "black sermon" it is the preacher's skill in heightening the spiritual experience of his congregation through poetic use of the popular language that, more than the substance of the words, creates the popularity of the teller. Spirituals, Christian religious songs created in the context of slavery, often included actual hidden messages or codes. The importance of rhythm and verse is characteristic of Afro-American field hollers, riddles, and proverbs, as well as of some of the tales.

Written Literature   Many of the themes and stylistic devices of Afro-American folk literature mentioned above—trickster, animal, preacher subjects; moralistic purpose; the use of exaggeration, double meaning, hidden messages, rhythm, and verse—have been utilized by black American writers in their short stories, poetry, and novels. One of the earliest examples is Charles Waddell Chesnutt's *The Conjure Woman*, published in 1899, and widely read by white as well as black Americans. In this work a series of short stories develops around an elderly former slave named Uncle Julius. Uncle Julius, the epitome of deference and helpfulness toward his employer, frequently "explains things" to him through stories strongly reminiscent of the folk tale. The strange ways of nature, conjure, and animals are common subjects. Irony and satire provide the tales with various levels of meaning that belie Uncle Julius' innocence and simplicity. James Weldon Johnson's *God's Trombones: Seven Negro Sermons in Verse* is an excellent early example of the use of the black folk sermon in literature. The themes and literary techniques explored by Jean Toomer in *Cane*, Ralph Ellison in *Invisible Man*, and Richard Wright in *Native Son* are more recent examples of literature reflecting a great sensitivity to their African and Afro-American folk heritage by black American writers.

Language   African languages themselves have left their mark on the speech of Afro-American communities. Lorenzo Turner was the first to point out specific words from a variety of African languages in the speech of the Gullah communities off the South Carolina coast. More subtle—and, because of that, more persistent—linguistic influences were patterns of sentence construction. The speech of black Americans, long thought to be merely bad English, has been shown in recent years to be black English, the result of an English vocabulary superimposed on grammatical and syntactical patterns common to related African languages. It is strikingly similar to contemporary African dialects derived from contact with European languages. Other African linguistic influences are even more widespread.

Beliefs   African beliefs about the nature of the universe, about mankind's relationship to the world of nature, and about man's relationship to man have also survived in Afro-American cultures of the New World. Embodying what could be called aspects of religion, these survivals appear both within and without established black churches. Blacks in Latin America and the West Indies (and some influenced by them in the United States) worship and venerate numerous African deities, particularly those of the Yoruba. Often their names have been joined with those of the Christian saints whose personalities are perceived to be similar. In some instances the body of worshipers follow African patterns of cult organization, leadership, and ritual, although most have been altered by Christian forms.

We have seen how the spiritual vitality of the natural world and the belief in resident spirits influence all aspects of traditional African life. Acknowledgment of the spiritual power of water remains a recognizably African feature of Afro-American religion. It is not without reason that the Baptist church, which baptizes by immersion in water, is the most populous black American church. The spiritual potential of plants or of objects controlled by powerful spirits appears in the New World practices of "working roots" and of voodoo. Here a human agent, using herbs or objects as an intermediary, may direct powerful spirits to hinder or assist another person, often at the request of a third party. Inveighed against as superstitions or regarded more positively as folk medicine, such skills involve closely guarded secret knowledge and have rarely been studied in a systematic way. Credible witnesses testifying to the psychic power of such skills or forces at work have in recent years led modern scientists in the fields of pharmacology and psychiatry to study these phenomena in both Africa and the New World.

Music   African music and dance are the most well known African influences upon Afro-American and American culture in general. In Africa, the two arts are not easily distinguished from poetry and song, and none of these from the pervasive quality of ritual. Above all is the predominant role in African and Afro-American music of rhythm. It is varied and multiple in composition, often emphasizing the unexpected by the coincidence of otherwise differing rhythms upon a normally unaccented beat, called *syncopation*. Jazz music was founded upon this predominance of rhythm. In addition to rhythm, jazz musicians preferred harmonic scales, intervals of thirds, and the call-and-response pattern of solo instrument or voice with a chorus, all features widely used in Africa. Generally speaking, the African and Afro-American singing style uses the voice like an instrument, placing greater emphasis on its percussive role and on particular *timbres* of voice than European music does. The call-and-response pattern of leader and chorus was a distinctive feature of Afro-American spirituals, of course, before it was extended to the secular realm by jazz musicians.

Dance   While less studied than music, Afro-American dance can be seen to bear African characteristics of form, composition, and body stance. Preferences for group dancing in lines or in circles, with movement running counterclockwise in the latter, are typical in African dance continent-wide. A frontal pose of the face and the vigorous use of separate parts of the body to accent different rhythms of the dance were readily remarked by early European visitors to Africa. The survival of these features is generally, if not always precisely, noted by observers of Afro-American dance.

Interrelation of Arts   In traditional Africa poetry, song, music, and dance are always integrated into patterns of work and ritual as well as into those of sheer entertainment. Nothing is too sacred or too profane to be celebrated in art. Moreover, the participation in celebration, as we saw with the Efe/Gelede festival, serves to unite the community, to restore balance, and to reaffirm values. It seems likely that Afro-American artistic values and expression drew upon African content, form, occasion, and style; moreover, they also served to develop and sustain the slaves' self-conscious sense of community. Their extension and elaboration since slavery have created a distinctive Afro-American aesthetic and have greatly enriched American culture as well as Western culture as a whole.

Influence of Africa on Western Humanism Generally   The most direct impact of the African humanities on those of the West beyond Afro-America has been in the fields of music and art. Artists like Picasso who "discovered" African sculpture in the early part of this century brought a vibrant, shocking, and refreshing set of aesthetic norms to Western art. Similarly, the African rhythms that Afro-Americans developed in jazz revitalized a tradition of Western music. Other aspects of Afro-American culture—dance, language and poetry, religion—that have their roots in Africa have been adopted or imitated by others in the West. More indirectly, Africa has influenced the humanities in Europe and America as a symbol, or an object of meditation. Black people appear in Western literature and art as evil, mysterious, savage, passionate, or as inherently noble, like Othello. Europe's contact with Africa was a source of the important theme of cultural relativity that began in the sixteenth century. The enormous burden of guilt which slavery left to the Western mind had its impact on the humanities. In Volume II we will see some examples of poets and philosophers in the eighteenth and nineteenth centuries who spoke out against the slave trade in various ways. The inhumaneness of such an institution called into question the very foundations of the humanities, and humanists were among the first to decry it. It is nonetheless true that the great flourishing of European culture, which dominated the world in the seventeenth century, was made possible in part by the exploitation of Africa.

Glossary

Italics are used within the definitions to indicate terms that are themselves defined elsewhere in the glossary and, in a few cases, to distinguish titles of works or foreign words.

ABA Form MUSIC: A particular organization of parts used in a musical *composition* in which there are three units, the first and third of which are the same. See *Da capo aria.*

Abbey Religious body governed by an abbot or abbess, or the collection of buildings themselves, also called a monastery.

Abstract VISUAL ARTS: Not representational or *illusionistic.* Describes painting or sculpture which simplifies or distills figures from the material world into *forms*, lines, *colors.*

African Survival A specific form or function of an institution, ritual, belief, language, or art that is clearly identifiable with an African origin, although adapted to the situation of African descendants in the New World.

Allegory LITERATURE, VISUAL ARTS: The technique of making concrete things, animals, or persons represent abstract ideas or morals. A literary allegory usually takes the form of a *narrative* which may be read on at least two levels; for example, Dante's *Divine Comedy.* Medieval sculptures often have allegorical significance.

Altarpiece VISUAL ARTS: A painted or sculptured decoration on canvas or panels placed behind or above an altar.

Ambulatory ARCHITECTURE: A covered passageway for walking. In a church, the semicircular passage around the main altar.

Anaphora (ah-na'fo-rah) LITERATURE: A rhetorical figure which uses the repetition of the same word or phrase to introduce two or more clauses or lines of verse.

Animism The belief that parts of nature, such as water, trees, etc., have souls and can influence human events. The term is used by Westerners to describe African religions.

Antiphon MUSIC: In Gregorian chant, a short text from the Scriptures or elsewhere set to music in a simple *style*, and sung before and after a Psalm or a canticle.

Antiphonal MUSIC: See *Antiphony.*

Antiphony (an-ti'fo-ny) MUSIC: The sound produced by *choirs* or instruments "answering" one another. For instance, one choir will sing, and then it is "answered" by another choir.

Apse (aap'ss) ARCHITECTURE: A large semicircular or polygonal *niche*, *domed* or *vaulted.* In a Roman *basilica* the apse was placed at one or both ends or sides of the building. In a Christian church it is usually placed at the east end of the *nave* beyond the *choir.*

Arcade ARCHITECTURE: A covered walk made of *arches* on *piers* or *columns*, rather than *lintels.*

Arch ARCHITECTURE: 1. Commonly, any curved structural member that is used to span an opening. 2. Specifically, restricted to the spanning members of a curved opening that are constructed of wedge-shaped stones called *voussoirs.* Arches may be of many shapes, basically round or pointed. See Roman Architecture (Ch. 5) and Gothic Architecture (Ch. 7).

Archaic 1. Obsolete. 2. In its formative or early stages.

Architrave (ahr'kuh-trave) ARCHITECTURE: A *beam* that rests directly on the *columns*; the lowest part of the *entablature.*

Aria (ah'ree-ah) MUSIC: An elaborate *composition* for solo voice with instrumental accompaniment.

Aristocracy Form of government from Greek word meaning "rule by the few for the common good."

Asantehene (a-sahn'tee-hee-nee) The Akan term for the King of the Ashanti state.

Ase (ah-say') Yoruba word meaning power, authority, potential energy.

Atmospheric Perspective See *Perspective.*

Aulos (ow'los) MUSIC: The most important wind instrument of the ancient Greeks. It is not a flute (as is often stated), but a shrill-sounding oboe. It originated in the Orient and was associated with the orgiastic rites of the god Dionysus.

Axis VISUAL ARTS: The imaginary line that can be passed through a building or a figure, around which the principal parts revolve. See *Balance*.

Balance VISUAL ARTS: The creation of an apparent equilibrium or *harmony* between all the parts of a *composition*, be it a building, painting, or sculpture.

Ballad A narrative poem or song in short stanzas, usually with a refrain, often handed down orally.

Balustrade ARCHITECTURE: A rail or handrail along the top edge of a roof or balcony, made up of a top horizontal rail, a bottom rail, and short *columns* between.

Baptistry ARCHITECTURE: The building or room for performing the rite of baptism. Contains a basin or pool.

Barrel Vault See *Vault*.

Base ARCHITECTURE: 1. The lowest visible part of a building. 2. The slab on which some *column* shafts rest. See *Orders*.

Basilica (bah-sil′i-cah) ARCHITECTURE: A large, rectangular hall with a central space surrounded by aisles on the sides and an *apse* at one or each end or side. The basilica was used as a court of justice by the Romans and adopted by the early Christians as a church.

Bay ARCHITECTURE: One of a series of regularly repeated spaces of a building marked off by vertical elements.

Beam ARCHITECTURE: A large piece of squared timber, long in proportion to its breadth and thickness, used for spanning spaces. A *lintel* is a specific kind of beam.

Blank Verse LITERATURE: Unrhymed lines in *iambic pentameter*. A common form for dramatic verse in English. See Shakespeare (Ch. 13).

Boss ARCHITECTURE: The circular *keystone* at the crossing of diagonal *ribs*. May be richly carved and decorated.

Buttress ARCHITECTURE: The vertical exterior mass of masonry built at right angles into the *wall* to strengthen it and to counteract the lateral *thrust* of a *vault* or *arch*. Architecture of the Gothic period developed this *form* into the flying buttress, which is a combination of the regular or *pier*-like buttress and the arched buttress. See *Chartres* (Ch. 7).

Capital ARCHITECTURE: The uppermost or crowning member of a *column*, *pilaster*, or *pier* that forms the visual transition from the post to the *lintel* above. See *Orders*.

Caryatid (kahr′-ee-ah-tid) ARCHITECTURE: The name given a *column* when it is disguised as a female figure.

Casting SCULPTURE: A method of reproducing sculpture through the use of a mold that is the receptacle for a liquid which hardens when cooled. The method may be used to produce solid or hollow cast *forms*.

Cathedral Principal church of a diocese, literally the location of the bishop's throne, or cathedra.

Cella ARCHITECTURE: The principal chamber of a Greek or Roman temple, housing the cult image.

Centering ARCHITECTURE: The temporary wooden *structure* that supports an *arch* or dome while it is being erected.

Chapel ARCHITECTURE: 1. A small church. 2. A separate compartment in a large church that has its own altar.

Choir ARCHITECTURE: The part of the church reserved for clergy and singers, usually the space between the crossing and the *apse*. MUSIC: A group of singers in a church.

Chord MUSIC: The simultaneous sounding of three or more usually harmonious *tones*.

Chromatic MUSIC: Describes a scale progressing by half-tones instead of the normal degress of the scale; e.g., in C major: c-c♯-d-d♯-e instead of c-d-e. VISUAL ARTS: Refers to the visual spectrum of hues. See *Color*.

Cire Perdu (seer pehr-doo′) SCULPTURE: French expression meaning "lost wax." Technique for making bronze sculpture that involves molding wax over a clay mold, encasing it with another clay mold, heating the mold, then allowing the wax to drain out and replacing it with molten bronze.

Classic, Classical ALL ARTS: Recognized generally to be excellent, time-tested. LITERATURE AND VISUAL ARTS: 1. From ancient Greece or Rome. 2. From "classical" (fifth century B.C.) Greece or having properties such as *harmony*, *balance*, moderation and magnitude characteristic of art of that period. MUSIC: The musical *style* of the late 18th century. Leading composers in the classical style are Haydn, Mozart, and the early Beethoven.

Clerestory (clear′story) ARCHITECTURE: An upper story in a building that carries windows or openings for the transmission of light to the space beneath.

Coffer, Coffering ARCHITECTURE: Originally a casket or box, later, a recessed ceiling panel. Coffering is a technique for making a ceiling of recessed panels.

Colonnade ARCHITECTURE: A series of regularly spaced *columns* supporting a *lintel* or *entablature*.

Color VISUAL ARTS: A quality perceived in objects by the human eye that derives from the length of the light waves reflected by individual surfaces. The visible spectrum is divided into six basic hues: red, orange, yellow, green, blue, and violet. Red, yellow and blue are called the *primary colors*; the others, which result from mixing adjacent primary colors, are called *secondary colors*. White, black, and grays result from mixing these six hues and are not *chromatic*: they cannot be distinguished by hue, only by value. Value is the property of a color that distinguishes it as light or dark. Colors that are "high" in value are light colors; those that are "low" in value are dark colors. Adding white to a color will raise its value to make a *tint*; adding black to a color will lower its value to make a *shade*. Saturation is the property of a color by which its vividness or purity is distinguished. See also *Complementary Colors*, *Cool Colors, Warm Colors*.

Column   ARCHITECTURE: A cylindrical, upright post or pillar. It may contain three parts: *base*, shaft, and *capital*.

Comedy   LITERATURE: A drama that ends happily, intended to provoke laughter from its audience. Comedy often includes *satire* on types of characters or societies.

Complementary Colors   Hues that form a neutral grey when mixed but, when juxtaposed, form a sharp contrast. The complementary of any *primary color* (red, yellow, or blue) is made by mixing the other two primaries. Example: The complementary of red is green, obtained by mixing yellow with blue.

Composition   VISUAL ARTS: The arrangements of elements within the work in order to create a certain effect based on a variety of principles and conventions: e.g., *balance, color, contour, focal point*, proportion, scale, *symmetry, volume*. MUSIC: The putting together of elements such as *melody, harmony, rhythm*, and orchestration into a musical *form*. The term may be used similarly to denote a putting together of elements in a dance or film. LITERATURE: The act of composing an oral or written work.

Compound Pier   ARCHITECTURE: A *pier* or post made up of attached *columns*. See *Chartres* (Ch 7).

Content   ALL ARTS: What the *form* contains and means. Content may include subject matter and theme. The quality of a work of art is often judged by the appropriateness, or apparent inseparability, of form and content.

Contour   PAINTING, DRAWING: The visible edge or outline of an object, *form* or shape, used especially to suggest *volume* or mass by means of the distinctness, thickness, or color of the edge or line.

Contrapuntal   (con-tra-pun'tal)   MUSIC: In a *style* that employs *counterpoint*.

Cool Colors   VISUAL ARTS: Blues, greens, and associated hues. Cool colors will appear to recede from the viewer in a picture, while *warm colors* will tend to project.

Cornice   ARCHITECTURE: 1. The horizontal projection that finishes the top of a *wall*. 2. In classical architecture, the third or uppermost horizontal section of an *entablature*. See *Orders*.

Counterpoint   MUSIC: Music consisting of two or more *melodies* played simultaneously. The term is practically synonymous with *polyphony*.

Couplet   LITERATURE: Two lines of poetry together, of the same meter and rhyme.

Crossing   In a church, the intersection of the *nave* and *transept* in front of the *apse*.

Da Capo Aria   (dah cah'poh ahr'ee-ah)   MUSIC: A particular type of *aria* that developed in the baroque period (17th and 18th centuries). It consists of two sections, the first of which is repeated after the second. The result is the *ABA form*. See *Aria, ABA Form*.

Democracy   From the Greek word meaning "rule by the people." A form of government in which the electorate is coincident with the adult population (sometimes only the adult males) of the community.

Despotism   Government by a ruler with unlimited powers.

Dialectic   PHILOSOPHY: 1. Platonic—A method of logical examination of beliefs, proceeding by question and answer. 2. Hegelian and Marxian—A logical method that proceeds by the contradiction of opposites (thesis, antithesis) to their resolution in a synthesis.

Dome   ARCHITECTURE: A curved or hemispherical roof structure spanning a space and resting on a curved, circular, or polygonal *base*. Theoretically, a dome is an *arch* rotated 360 degrees around a central *axis*. See *Pantheon* (Ch. 5).

Drapery   SCULPTURE: The clothing of a figure or *form* in a usually nonspecific but *tactile* and responsive material.

Drum   ARCHITECTURE: The cylindrical or polygonal *structure* that rises above the body of a building to support a *dome*.

Duration   MUSIC: The time-value assigned to a musical note; that is, how long it is to be played or sung.

Dynamics   MUSIC: Words or signs that indicate the varying degrees of loudness in the music. For instance, *forte* (loud), *piano* (soft, quiet), *diminuendo* (decrease *volume* gradually).

Egungun   (eh-goon-goon)   Yoruba masqueraders concerned with mediating between the community of the living and that of the recently dead.

Elevation   ARCHITECTURE: 1. Generally, a term that refers to one of the sides of a building. 2. Specifically, a drawing or graphic representation showing one face or side of a building. It can be of the interior or exterior.

Entablature   ARCHITECTURE: The upper section of a classical *order* resting on the *capitals* of the *columns* and including *architrave, frieze, cornice*, and *pediment*.

Epic   LITERATURE: A long *narrative* poem that recounts an event of importance in a culture's history and presents a hero of that culture. See section on Homer (Ch. 1).

Episode   LITERATURE: In Greek tragedy, a section of action between two choruses. In drama and fiction generally, a group of events having unity in itself. A story is created from a series of related episodes. A fiction is said to be episodic if the episodes fall into no logical relationship.

Epithet   LITERATURE: A short phrase used to modify a noun by pointing out a salient characteristic. Epithets (e.g., Homer's "swift-footed Achilles") are often used in epic poetry.

Eros In Greek mythology, son of Aphrodite and god of sexual love, called "Cupid" by the Romans.

Ethics PHILOSOPHY: The branch of philosophy dealing with problems of good and bad, right and wrong, in human conduct.

Façade (fa-sahd') ARCHITECTURE: A face of a building.

Fetish Statue or other object believed to embody supernatural power.

Fluting ARCHITECTURE: The grooves or channels, usually parallel, that decorate the shafts of *columns*. Fluting may run up and down a shaft or around the shaft in various directions.

Focal Point VISUAL ARTS: The place of major or dominant interest on which the eyes repeatedly focus in a painting, drawing, or architectural arrangement.

Foreshortening PAINTING: The method of representing objects or parts of objects as if seen from an angle so that the object seems to recede into space instead of being seen in a frontal or profile view. The technique is based on the principle of continuous diminution in size along the length of the object or figure. See *Perspective* and *Vanishing Point*.

Form ALL ARTS: The arrangement or organization of the elements of a work of art in space (visual arts) or time (literary, musical, performing arts). A form may be conventional or imposed by tradition (the Greek temple, the sonnet, the sonata, the five-act play) or original with the artist. In the latter case, form is said to follow from, or adapt itself to, *content.*

Fresco PAINTING: The technique of making a painting on new, wet plaster. Fresco painting was particularly favored in Italy from Roman times until the eighteenth century. See Ch. 10.

Frieze ARCHITECTURE: 1. Middle horizontal element of the classical *entablature*. See *Orders*. 2. A decorative band near the top of an interior wall that is below the *cornice* molding.

Gable ARCHITECTURE: The triangular space at the end of a building formed by the slopes of a pitched roof, extending from the *cornice* or eaves to the *ridge*. In classical architecture the gable is called a *pediment.*

Gallery ARCHITECTURE: A long, covered area, usually elevated, that acts as a passageway on the inside or exterior of a building.

Genre (john'ruh) LITERATURE: A literary type or form. Genres include *tragedy, comedy, epic, lyric,* novel, short story, essay.

Greco-Roman Belonging to the cultures of ancient Greece and Rome.

Griot (gree-oh') African oral poet, musician, and historian.

Groin Vault See *Vault.*

Groundplan ARCHITECTURE: A drawing of a horizontal *section* of a building that shows the arrangement of the *walls*, windows, supports and other elements. A groundplan is used to produce blueprints.

Ground Plane PAINTING: In a picture, the surface, apparently receding into the distance, on which the figures seem to stand. It is sometimes thought of as comparable to a kind of stage space.

Harmony MUSIC: The chordal structure of music familiar to most Western listeners in popular music accompanied by guitars, in Romantic orchestral music, etc.

Hebraic Belonging to the Hebrews, Jews, or Israelites. Refers primarily to the culture of the ancient Hebrews of Biblical times.

Hebraism Hebrew culture, thought, institutions.

Hellenic Greek. Usually refers to the "classical" period of Greek culture; i.e., the fifth and fourth centuries B.C.

Hellenism The culture of ancient Greece.

Hellenistic Literally, "Greek-like." Refers to Greek history and artistic style from the third century B.C.

Homophonic (hawm-o-fon'ic) Characteristic of *homophony.*

Homophony (hoh-maw'foh-nee) MUSIC: A single *melody* line supported by its accompanying *chords* and/or voice parts. See *Monophony, Polyphony, Chord,* and *Texture.*

Hubris (hyoo'bris) A Greek word meaning arrogance or excessive pride.

Hue See *Color.*

Hyperbole (high-purr'boh-lee) LITERATURE: A figure of speech that uses obvious exaggeration.

Iamb (eye'amb) LITERATURE: A metrical "foot" consisting of one short (or unaccented) syllable and one long (or accented) syllable. Example: hĕllō.

Iambic Pentameter (eye-am'bic pen-tam'eh-ter) LITERATURE: The most common metrical line in English verse, consisting of five *iambs*. Example, from Shakespeare: "Shăll Ī cŏmpāre thĕe tō ă sūmmĕr's dāy?"

Ifa (ee'fah) A Yoruba system of divination in which a priest advises his clients of proper courses of behavior based upon the casting of palm kernels and the interpretation of poems chosen for their numerical links to the patterns of thrown kernels.

Illusionism VISUAL ARTS: The attempt by artists to create the illusion of reality in their work. Illusionism may also be called realism. It is important to remember that illusionism is not the motivating intention of all works of art.

Image ALL ARTS: The representation of sense impressions to the imagination. Images are a fundamental part of the language of art. They differ from the abstract terminology of science and philosophy in that they are a means whereby complex emotional experience is communicated. Images may be tactile, auditory, olfactory, etc., but the word is ordinarily used for visual impressions.

Imagery LITERATURE: Patterns of images in a specific work or in the entire works of an author. May refer to a specific type (animal imagery, garden imagery). VISUAL ARTS: The objects, *forms* or shapes depicted by the artist in a particular work.

Improvisation MUSIC: The art of performing music spontaneously rather than the practice of recreating written music.

Induction PHILOSOPHY: Reasoning from particular facts or cases to a general conclusion.

Initiation Ceremonies or rites by which a young person is brought into manhood or womanhood, or an older person is made a member of a secret society, brotherhood, etc.

Irony LITERATURE: A manner of speaking by which the author says the opposite of what he means, characteristically using words of praise to imply scorn. Dramatic or tragic irony means that the audience is aware of truths which the character speaking does not understand.

Iwi (ee'wee) Yoruba poems sung by Egungun masqueraders.

Jamb ARCHITECTURE: A vertical member at either side of a door frame or window frame. When sculpture is attached to this member it is called a jamb sculpture or jamb figure. See *Chartres* (Ch. 7).

Kente (ken'teh) Large ceremonial cloth from Ghana made of narrow strips sewn together and distinguished by elaborate, multicolored geometric designs of silk.

Keystone ARCHITECTURE: The central wedge-shaped stone of an *arch* that locks together the others.

Komos Greek word for a revel. Root of the word *comedy*.

Kouros (koo'rohs), **Kore** (koh'ray) SCULPTURE: Greek for a male nude votive figure, female votive figure.

Labarai (lah-bah-rye') Hausa tales told by old men, involving cultural, family, and group history.

Linear Perspective See *Perspective*.

Lintel ARCHITECTURE: The horizontal member or *beam* that spans an opening between two upright members, or posts, over a window, door, or similar opening.

Lyric LITERATURE: A short poem or song characterized by personal feeling and intense emotional expression. Originally, in Greece, lyrics were accompanied by the music of a lyre.

Matrilineal System of descent in which inheritance of goods, access to land, and group leadership pass to the children through the family of the mother.

Medium (pl. media) ALL ARTS: 1. The material or materials with which the artist works. Examples from VISUAL ARTS: paint, stone, wood, bronze, plaster, concrete. MUSIC:

sound. LITERATURE: language. CINEMA: film. DANCE human body. DRAMA: language, costume, lighting, actors, sound, etc. 2. Modern means of communication (television, radio, newspapers). PAINTING: A substance such as oil, egg, or water with which *pigment* is mixed.

Melody MUSIC: A succession of musical *tones*. Often the melody is known as the "tune," and is not to be confused with the other accompanying parts of a song. See *Homophony*.

Metaphor LITERATURE: A figure of speech that states or implies an analogy between two objects or between an object and a mental or emotional state. Example: "My days are in the yellow leaf;/The flowers and fruits of love are gone" (Byron) makes an analogy between the poet's life and the seasonal changes of a tree.

Meter POETRY: A regularly recurring rhythmic pattern. Meter in English is most commonly measured by accents, or stresses, and syllables. MUSIC: A pattern of fixed temporal units. For example, $3/4$ meter means one beat to a quarter note and three beats to a measure. In a musical *composition* meter is the basic grouping of notes in time.

Metope (meh'toh-pay) ARCHITECTURE: The blank space of block between the *triglyphs* in the Doric *frieze*, sometimes sculpted in low *relief*. See *Orders*.

Modal MUSIC: Describes a type of music conforming to the scale patterns of the medieval Church *modes*. See *Modes*.

Modeling VISUAL ARTS: 1. The creation of a three-dimensional *form* in clay or other responsive material, such as wax, soap, soft bone, ivory, etc. 2. By analogy, in painting and drawing, the process of suggesting a three-dimensional *form* by the creation of *shade* and shadow.

Modes MUSIC: Melodic scales used for church music of the Middle Ages. The modes are organized according to *pitches* similar to our modern major and minor scales, yet different enough to set them apart from the modern scales.

Molding ARCHITECTURE: A member used in construction or decoration that produces a variety in edges or contours by virtue of its curved surface.

Monastery The dwelling place of a community of monks. See *Abbey*.

Monasticism A way of life assumed by those who voluntarily separate themselves from the world to contemplate divine nature. See *Monastery*.

Monophonic (mo-no-fohn'ic) Characteristic of *monophony*.

Monophony (mo-nof'o-nee) MUSIC: A simple *melody* without additional parts or accompaniment, such as the music of a flute playing alone or of a woman singing by herself. See *Homophony, Polyphony, Texture*.

Mosaic VISUAL ARTS: A *form* of surface decoration made by inlaying small pieces of glass, tile, enamel, or varicolored stones in a cement or plaster matrix or ground.

Motet (moh-tette') MUSIC: Usually an unaccompanied choral composition based on a Latin sacred text. The motet was one of the most important forms of *polyphonic* composition from the thirteenth through the seventeenth centuries.

Motif (moh-teef'), **Motive** (moh-teev') LITERATURE: A basic element that recurs, and may serve as a kind of foundation, in a long poem, fiction, or drama. A young woman awakened by love is the motif of many tales, such as *Sleeping Beauty*. VISUAL ARTS: An element of design repeated and developed in a painting, sculpture, or building. MUSIC: A recurring melodic phrase, sometimes used as a basis for variation.

Myth Stories developed anonymously within a culture that attempt to explain natural events from a supernatural or religious point of view.

Mythology The body of myths from a particular cultural group.

Naos (nah'ohs) ARCHITECTURE: Greek word for the *cella* or main body of a Greek temple.

Narrative LITERATURE: 1. (noun) Any *form* that tells a story or recounts a sequence of events (novel, *tale*, essay, article, film). 2. (adj.) In story form, recounting.

Narthex ARCHITECTURE: The entrance hall or porch that stands before the *nave* of a church.

Naturalism LITERATURE, VISUAL ARTS: Faithful adherence to the appearance of nature or outer reality.

Nave ARCHITECTURE: In Roman architecture, the central space of a *basilica;* in Christian architecture, the central longitudinal or circular space in the church, bounded by aisles.

Nave Arcade ARCHITECTURE: The open passageway or screen between the central space and the *side aisles* in a church.

Nemesis (neh'ma-sis) Greek goddess of Fate. Word means retribution, punishment.

Neolithic The stage in the evolution of human societies when peoples began systematic cultivation and the domestication of animals.

Niche (nish) ARCHITECTURE: A semicircular or similarly shaped recess in a wall designed to contain sculpture, an urn, or other object. It is usually covered by a half-*dome*.

Oba Name for the chief ruler of Benin.

Oculus (ock'you-luhs) ARCHITECTURE: Circular opening at the crown of a *dome*. See *Pantheon* (Ch. 5).

Odu (oh'doo) A secret body of poetry used in the Yoruba *Ifa* divination process.

Oil Painting The practice of painting by using *pigments* suspended in oil (walnut, linseed, etc.).

Oligarchy (oh'lih-gar-key) Greek word meaning "rule by the few." Rule by the few where the state is primarily utilized to serve the interest of the governors. Traditionally contrasted with *aristocracy*, rule by the few for the common good.

Olorun (oh-low'roon), **Oludumare** (oh-loo-doo-mah'ray) The Yoruba term for the supreme high deity.

Open Fifths MUSIC: *Chords*, normally made of three sounds, with the middle *pitch* absent.

Orders ARCHITECTURE: Types of *columns* with *entablatures* developed in classical Greece. The orders are basically three: Doric, Ionic, and Corinthian. They determine not only the scale and therefore dimensions of a temple but also the experience generated by the building, or its *style*. See section on Greek Architecture and diagram of the orders (Ch. 2).

Oriki (ohr-ee'key) Yoruba term meaning praise poems based on names given to gods, places, rulers, and important persons.

Orisha (ohr-ee'sha) In Yoruba religion, lesser gods (below the chief god) and sometimes ancestor figures, ancient kings, and founders of cities who have been deified.

Ostinato (aw-stee-nah'toe) MUSIC: Italian for obstinate or stubborn; the persistent repetition of a clearly defined *melody*, usually in the same voice. This device is often used in a bass part to organize a *composition* for successive variations.

Oxymoron (ock-see-mohr'on) LITERATURE: A figure of speech that brings together two contradictory terms, such as "sweet sorrow."

Palazzo (pa-laht'so) ARCHITECTURE: Italian for palace, or large, impressive building.

Panel Painting A painting made on a ground or panel of wood, as distinguished from a *fresco* or a painting on canvas.

Parapet ARCHITECTURE: In an exterior *wall*, the part entirely above the roof. The term may also describe a low wall that acts as a guard at a sudden edge or drop, as on the edge of a roof, battlement, or wall.

Parody LITERATURE: A work that exaggerates or burlesques another, serious one. Often a parody pokes fun at an author and his style. The parody may be compared to a visual caricature or cartoon.

Pathos (pay'thaws) ALL ARTS: A quality that sets off deep feeling or compassion in the spectator or reader.

Patrilineal System of descent in which inheritance of goods, access to land, and group leadership passes to the children through the family of the father.

Pediment ARCHITECTURE: In classical architecture the triangular space at the end of a roof formed by the sloping ridges of the roof. The pediment was often filled with decoration which could be painted or sculpted or both.

Pentatonic Scale MUSIC: Five-note scale that occurs in the music of nearly all ancient cultures. It is common in West African music and is found in jazz.

Perspective VISUAL ARTS: Generally, the representation of three-dimensional objects in space on a two-dimensional surface. There are a variety of means to achieve this. The most familiar is that of "linear perspective" developed in the fifteenth century and codified by Brunelleschi, in which all parallel lines and edges of surfaces recede at the same angle and are drawn, on the picture plane, to converge at a single *vanishing point*. The process of diminution in size of objects with respect to location is very regular and precise. Other techniques, often used in combination with linear perspective, include: (a) vertical perspective—objects further from the observer are shown higher up on the picture, (b) diagonal perspective—objects are not only higher but aligned along an oblique *axis* producing the sensation of continuous recession, (c) overlapping, (d) *foreshortening*, (e) *modeling*, (f) *shadows*, and (g) atmospheric perspective, the use of conventions such as blurring of outlines, alternation of hue toward blue, and decrease of *color* saturation.

Phrase MUSIC: A natural division of the *melody*; in a manner of speaking, a musical "sentence."

Picture Plane PAINTING: The surface on which the picture is painted.

Picture Space PAINTING: The space that extends behind or beyond the picture plane; created by devices such as *linear perspective*. Picture space is usually described by foreground, middleground, and background.

Pier ARCHITECTURE: A *column*, post, or similar member designed to carry a great load; may also refer to a thickened vertical mass within the *wall* designed to provide additional support.

Pigment PAINTING: The grains or powder that give a *medium* its *color*. Can be derived from a variety of sources: clays, stones, metals, shells, animal and vegetable matter.

Pilaster (pih'lass-ter) ARCHITECTURE: A flattened engaged *column* or *pier* that may have a *capital* and base. It may be purely decorative or it may reinforce a *wall*.

Pitch MUSIC: A technical term identifying a single musical sound, taking into consideration the frequency of its fundamental vibrations. Some songs, or instruments, are pitched high and others are pitched low.

Plan See *Groundplan*.

Plane A flat surface.

Plasticity VISUAL ARTS: The quality of roundness, palpability, solidity, or three-dimensionality of a *form*.

Plinth A block or slab on which a statue, pedestal, or column is placed, and, by extension, the base on which a building rests or appears to rest.

Podium ARCHITECTURE: The high platform or *base* of a Roman temple, or any elevated platform.

Polis (poh'liss) The ancient Greek city-state.

Polyphonic (paul-ee-fon'ick) Characteristic of *polyphony*.

Polyphony (paul-if'o-nee) MUSIC: Describes *composition* or *improvisations* in which more than one *melody* sounds simultaneously—that is, two or more tunes at the same time. Polyphony is characterized by the combining of a number of individual melodies into a harmonizing and agreeable whole. See *Homophony*, *Monophony*, and *Texture*.

Portico ARCHITECTURE: Porch or covered walk consisting of a roof supported by *columns*.

Post-and-Lintel ARCHITECTURE: an essential system of building characterized by the use of uprights—posts—which support horizontal *beams*—lintels—in order to span spaces. Used as supports for a window or door, the posts are the *jambs* and the *lintel* is the window head.

Primary Colors Red, Yellow, Blue—the three primary hues of the spectrum. See *Color*.

Pronaos (pro'nah-ohs) ARCHITECTURE: In classical architecture, the inner *portico* or room in front of the *naos* or *cella*.

Prose LITERATURE: Generally, may mean any kind of discourse, written or spoken, which cannot be classified as poetry. More specifically, prose refers to written expression characterized by logical, grammatical order, *style*, and even *rhythm* (but not *meter*).

Proverb A saying that succinctly and effectively expresses a truth recognized by a community or a wise observation about life. Proverbs are most often transmitted orally.

Relief Sculpture Sculpture that is not freestanding but projects from a surface of which it is a part. A slight projection is called low relief (bas-relief); a more pronounced projection, high relief.

Republic A form of government in which ultimate power resides in the hands of a fairly large number of people but not necessarily the entire community. This power is exercised through representatives. The word derives from Latin meaning "public thing."

Response MUSIC: A solo-chorus relationship in which the soloist alternates performance with the chorus. The response is a particularly noteworthy device in traditional African music as well as in Gregorian chant.

Responsorial MUSIC: Describing the performance of a

chant in alternation between a soloist and a chorus. (It is unlike *antiphonal* music, where alternating choruses sing.)

Rhythm ALL ARTS: An overall sense of systematic movement. In music, poetry, and dance this movement may be literally felt; in the visual arts it refers to the regular repetition of a *form*, conveying a sense of movement by the contrast between a form and its interval.

Rib ARCHITECTURE: Generally a curved structural member that supports any curved shape or panel.

Ribbed Vault ARCHITECTURE: A *vault* whose sections seem to be supported or are supported by slender, curved structural members that also define the sections of the vault. The ribs may run either transversely, that is from side to side, or diagonally, from corner to corner of the vault.

Riddle A form of popular, usually oral, literature that asks an answer to a veiled question. Riddles often make use of striking *images* and *metaphors*.

Ridge ARCHITECTURE: The line defined by the meeting of the two sides of a sloping roof.

Romance LITERATURE: A long narrative in a *Romance language*, presenting chivalrous ideals, heroes involved in adventures, and love affairs from medieval legends.

Romance Language One of the languages that developed from popular Latin speech during the Middle Ages, and that exist now as French, Italian, Spanish, Portuguese, Catalan, Provençal, Romanic, and Rumanian.

Romanesque An artistic movement of the eleventh and twelfth centuries, primarily in architecture. The name comes from similarities with Roman architecture.

Rose Window ARCHITECTURE: The round ornamental window frequently found over the entrances of Gothic cathedrals.

Sarcophagus (sahr-cough'a-gus) A large stone coffin. It may be elaborately carved and decorated.

Satire A mode of expression that criticizes social institutions or human foibles humorously. The Roman invented the verse satire, but satire may appear in any literary *genre*, in visual art, in film, mime, and dance.

Satyr (say'ter) **Play** LITERATURE: A light, burlesque play given along with *tragedies* and *comedies* at the festival of Dionysus in ancient Athens.

Scholasticism PHILOSOPHY: A way of thought that attempted to reconcile Christian truth with truth established by natural reason. Originating in the early Middle Ages, it reached its height in the thirteenth century in response to the recovery of Aristotle's scientific and philosophical writings.

Secondary Colors See *Color*.

Section ARCHITECTURE: The drawing that represents a vertical slice through the interior or exterior of a building, showing the relation of floor to floor.

Shade PAINTING: A *color* mixed with black. Mixing a color with white produces a *tint*.

Shading VISUAL ARTS: The process of indicating by means of graphics or paint the change in *color* of an object when light falls on its surface revealing its three-dimensional qualities. Shading can be produced not only by a change of color, but also by the addition of black, brown, or gray, or by drawing techniques.

Shadow VISUAL ARTS: The *form* cast by an object in response to the direction of light.

Shed Roof ARCHITECTURE: A roof shape with only one sloping *plane*, such as the roof of a lean-to, or that over the *side aisle* in a Gothic or Romanesque church.

Side Aisle ARCHITECTURE: The aisles on either side of, and therefore parallel to, the *nave* in a Christian church or Roman *basilica*.

Simile (sim'eh-lee) LITERATURE: A type of *metaphor* which makes an explicit comparison. Example: "My love is like a red, red rose."

Sonnet LITERATURE: A fourteen-line poem, usually in iambic pentameter. The most popular form is the Italian, which traditionally divides the poem into two quatrains, or the octave (eight lines), and two tercets, or the sestet (six lines).

Span ARCHITECTURE: The interval between two posts, *arches*, *walls*, or other supports.

Stained Glass ARCHITECTURE: Glass to which a *color* is added during its molten state, or glass which is given a hue by firing or otherwise causing color to adhere to the glass.

Stele (stee'lee) ARCHITECTURE: In classical Greece a stone upright or slab used commemoratively; it may mark a grave or record an offering or important event.

Structure ALL ARTS: The relationship of the parts to the whole in a work of art. A structure may be mechanical (division of a play into acts, a symphony into movements) or may be more concealed and based on such things as the inter-relationships of *images*, *themes*, *motifs*, *colors*, shapes. In a *narrative* the structure usually refers to the arrangement of the sequence of events. In architecture structure may refer either to the actual system of building or to the relationships between the elements of the system of building.

Style ALL ARTS: Characteristics of *form* and technique that enable us to identify a particular work with a certain historical period, place, group, or individual. Painters in Florence in the 15th and 16th centuries used *perspective*, *color*, etc., in ways that allow us to identify a Renaissance style, but within that group we may distinguish the individual style of Leonardo from that of Raphael. Literary style is determined by choices of words, sentence *structure* and syntax *rhythm*, figurative language, rhetorical devices, etc. One may speak of an ornate, simple, formal, or colloquial style; of a period style, or of an individual's style. Style is sometimes contrasted with *content*.

Subject ALL ARTS: What the work is about. The subject of a statue of Apollo is the god Apollo; the subject of *Sundiata* is that hero's life. MUSIC: The *melody* used as the basis of a *contrapuntal composition* (e.g., the subject of a fugue).

Symbol VISUAL ARTS, LITERATURE: An *image* that suggests an idea, a spiritual or religious concept, or an emotion beyond itself. It differs from *metaphor* in that the term of comparison is not explicitly stated. Symbols may be conventional; i.e., have a culturally defined meaning such as the Christian cross or the Jewish star of David. Since the nineteenth century, symbols have tended to denote a variety or an ambiguity of meanings.

Symbolism The use of symbol in any art.

Symmetry VISUAL ARTS: The balance of proportions achieved by the repetition of parts on either side of a central *axis*. The two sides may be identical, in which case we can speak of bilateral symmetry.

Syncopation MUSIC: A rhythmic device characterized as a deliberate disturbance of a regularly recurring pulse. Accented off beats or irregular *meter* changes are two means of achieving syncopation.

Tactile VISUAL ARTS, LITERATURE: Refers to the sense of touch. In the visual arts, tactile *values* are created by techniques and conventions that specifically stimulate the sense of touch in order to enhance suggestions of weight, *volume* (roundness), visual approximation, and therefore three-dimensionality. Writers may also create tactile effects, as in the description of cloth or skin.

Tale LITERATURE: A simple *narrative*, whose subject matter may be real or imaginary, and whose purpose is primarily to entertain. Tales may also make use of "morals" to instruct.

Tatsuniyoyi (taht-soon-yoh'yee) Hausa tales about animals and people told by old women to entertain and instruct young children.

Tempera (tehm'per-ah) PAINTING: Technique in which the *pigment* is suspended in egg, glue, or a similar soluble *medium*, like water. Tempera paint dries very quickly and does not blend easily, producing a matte (flat, nonreflective) surface, because, unlike *oil paint*, it is essentially an opaque medium.

Texture VISUAL ARTS: Surface quality (rough, smooth, grainy, etc.) LITERATURE: elements such as *imagery*, sound patterns, etc., apart from the *subject* and *structure* of the work. MUSIC: The working relationship between the *melody* line and the other accompanying parts, or the characteristic "weaving" of a musical *composition*. There are three basic musical textures: *Monophonic* (a single line), *Homophonic* (a melody supported by *chords*), and *Polyphonic* (multiple meolodic lines).

Theme VISUAL ARTS: A *color* or pattern taken as a subject for repetition and modification. Example: A piece of sculpture may have a cubical theme. MUSIC: A *melody* that constitutes the basis of variation and development. LITERATURE AND PERFORMING ARTS: An emotion or idea that receives major attention in the work. A novel or film may contain several themes, such as love, war, death. A dance may be composed on the theme of struggle, joy, etc. Theme is sometimes used in this sense for visual arts and music as well.

Threnody (threh'no-dee) MUSIC: A song of lamentation, a very mournful song.

Through-Composed MUSIC: Describes a type of song in which new music is provided for each stanza. A through-composed song is thus unlike most modern hymns, folk, and popular songs, which use the same tune for each stanza.

Thrust ARCHITECTURE: The downward and outward pressure exerted by a *vault* or *dome* on the *walls* supporting it.

Timbre (taam'bruh) MUSIC: The quality of "color" of a particular musical *tone* produced by the various instruments. For instance, the very "nasal" sound of the oboe is markedly different from the very "pure" sound of the flute.

Tint VISUAL ARTS: The *color* achieved by adding white to a hue to raise its *value*, in contrast to a *shade*, which is a hue mixed with black to lower its value.

Tone ALL ARTS: The creation of a mood or an emotional state. In painting, tone may refer specifically to the prevailing effect of a *color*. Thus, a painting may be said to have a silvery, bluish, light, or dark tone as well as a wistful, melancholy, or joyful tone. The term may also refer to *value* or *shade* (see *Color*). In literature, tone usually describes the prevailing attitude of an author toward his material, audience, or both. Thus a tone may be cynical, sentimental, satirical, etc. In music, "tone color" may be used as a synonym for *timbre*. Tone in music also means a sound of definite *pitch* and duration (as distinct from noise), the true building material of music. The notes on a written page of music are merely symbols that represent the tones that actually make the music.

Tornada (tore-nah'dah) MUSIC: In troubadour songs, a short stanza added at the end as a "send-off."

Tracery ARCHITECTURE: The curvilinear or rectilinear pattern of open stonework or wood that supports the glass or other transparent or translucent material in a window or similar opening. May also be used generally to refer to decorative patterns carved similarly on wood or stone.

Tragedy LITERATURE: A serious drama that recounts the events in the life of a great person which bring him or her from fortune to misfortune. Tragedies usually meditate on the relation between human beings and their destiny. Tragedies first developed in ancient Greece; other great periods of tragedy include Elizabethan England and France under Louis XIV. The word is sometimes used to describe a novel or story.

Transept ARCHITECTURE: The transverse portion of a church that crosses the central *axis* of the *nave* at right angles between the nave and *apse* to form a cross-shaped (cruciform) planned building.

Triglyph (try'glif) ARCHITECTURE: The block carved with three channels or grooves that alternates with the *metopes* is a classical Doric *frieze*. See *Orders*.

Triumphal Arch ARCHITECTURE: The monumental urban gateway, invented by the Romans, set up along a major street to commemorate important military successes. It may have one or three arched openings and is usually decorated with inscriptions, *reliefs*, and freestanding sculpture on the top.

Trope MUSIC: Lengthened musical passage or elaboration on the Mass used during the Middle Ages. LITERATURE: 1. Verbal amplification of the text of the Mass. 2. A figure of speech.

Troubadour A lyric poet and singer, including wandering minstrels, originating in Provence in the eleventh century and flourishing throughout southern France, northern Italy, and Eastern Spain during the twelfth and thirteenth centuries.

Truss ARCHITECTURE: Originally a wooden structural member composed of smaller, lighter pieces of wood joined to form rigid triangles and capable of spanning spaces by acting as a *beam*.

Tympanum (tihm'pah-nuhm) ARCHITECTURE: The triangular or similarly shaped space enclosed by an *arch* or *pediment*.

Tyranny In ancient Greece, meant "rule of the strong man." Historically, came to mean arbitrary rule of one, but generally taken to mean arbitrary political rule of any kind.

Value See *Color*.

Vanishing Point PAINTING: The point or points of convergence for all lines forming an angle to the *picture plane* in pictures constructed according to the principles of linear *perspective*.

Vault ARCHITECTURE: The covering or spanning of a space employing the principle of the *arch* and using masonry, brick, plaster, or similar malleable materials. The extension of an arch infinitely in one plane creates a barrel or tunnel vault. The intersection of two barrel vaults at right angles to each other produces a cross or groin vault. *Ribs* are sometimes placed along the intersections of a groin vault to produce a *ribbed vault*.

Veneer VISUAL ARTS: A thin layer of precious or valuable material glued or otherwise attached to the surface of another, less expensive, or less beautiful material. The Romans, for example, applied thin layers of marble to the concrete and rubble fill surfaces of their buildings to produce a more splendid effect. In this century, valuable woods like walnut or mahogany are applied as veneers to the surfaces of plywood.

Vernacular The common daily speech of the people; nonliterary language. During the Middle Ages, any language that was not Latin.

Viewpoint The position or place from which the viewer looks at an object or the visual field.

Volume ARCHITECTURE: Refers to the void or solid three-dimensional quality of a space or *form* whether completely enclosed or created by the presence of forms which act as boundaries. Compare the "volume" of the *Parthenon* with the "volume" of the *Pantheon*.

Volute A spiral or scroll-like ornamental form, which may be used either as a purely decorative or as a supporting member in an architectural ensemble. The curvilinear portion of an Ionic capital is a volute, and by extension a portion of such a shape is a volute.

Voussoir (voo-swahr') ARCHITECTURE: The wedge-shaped stone or masonry unit of an *arch*, wider at the top and tapering toward the bottom.

Wall ARCHITECTURE: A broad, substantial upright slab that acts as an enclosing *form* capable of supporting its own weight and the weight of *beams* or *arches* to span and enclose space.

Warm Colors VISUAL ARTS: The hues commonly associated with warmth—yellow, red, and orange. In *compositions* the warm colors tend to advance, in contrast to the *cool colors*, which tend to recede from the viewer.

Index